# FUNDAMENTAL
# ACCOUNTING
# PRINCIPLES

EIGHTH CANADIAN EDITION
VOLUME I

# FUNDAMENTAL
# ACCOUNTING
# PRINCIPLES

## EIGHTH CANADIAN EDITION
## VOLUME I

KERMIT D. LARSON
University of Texas—Austin

MORTON NELSON
Wilfrid Laurier University

MICHAEL ZIN
Professor Emeritus
University of Windsor

RAY F. CARROLL
Dalhousie University

Represented in Canada by:

 **McGraw-Hill
Ryerson Limited**

Toronto • Chicago • Bogotá • Boston • Buenos Aires
Caracas • London • Madrid • Mexico City • Sydney

## McGraw-Hill
## Ryerson Limited

*A Subsidiary of The* **McGraw·Hill** *Companies*

*Photo Credits*

Prologue: *Logos courtesy of Certified Accountants' Association of Canada, Chartered Accountants of Canada, and the Society of Management Accountants of Canada;* Chapter 1: *Bernard Mendoza/Tony Stone Images;* Chapter 2: *Sharon Hoogstraten;* Chapter 3: *Courtesy of Imperial Oil;* Chapter 4: *Sharon Hoogstraten;* Chapter 5: *Michael Poselli;* Chapter 6: *Sharon Hoogstraten;* Chapter 7: *Sharon Hoogstraten;* Chapter 8: *Sharon Hoostraten;* Chapter 9: *George Kavanagh/Tony Stone Images;* Chapter 10: *Sharon Hoogstraten.*

**Irwin Book Team**

| | |
|---|---|
| Publisher: | *Roderick T. Banister* |
| Developmental editor: | *Sabira Hussain* |
| Marketing manager: | *Murray Moman* |
| Project editor: | *Waivah Clement* |
| Production supervisor: | *Bob Lange* |
| Assistant manager, graphics: | *Charlene R. Perez* |
| Senior designer: | *Heidi J. Baughman* |
| Coordinator, Graphic and Desktop Services: | *Keri Johnson* |
| Photo researcher: | *Randall Nicholas/ Nicholas Communications, Inc.* |
| Compositor: | *York Graphic Services, Inc.* |
| Typeface: | *10½ /12½ Times Roman* |
| Printer: | *Von Hoffmann Press, Inc.* |

ISBN 0-256-17506-3
Library of Congress Catalog No. 95–80682

*Printed in the United States of America*
5 6 7 8 9 0 VH 3 2 1 0 9 8

# Preface

The tradition of *Fundamental Accounting Principles* includes clear explanations of accounting concepts and practices with closely related assignment material. Recent editions also reflect an educational philosophy we call *action learning*. We are firmly convinced that students learn most effectively when their study activities are designed to emphasize active behaviour. The eighth Canadian edition continues this focus on the effective use of student study time.

By providing a wide variety of action-oriented items in the text and in support of the text, we hope to encourage student involvement within the classroom as well as during study outside of class. Newly developed and thoroughly revised assignment materials provide an extensive basis for varied assignments that stimulate interest, promote a sense of accomplishment, show the real-world relevance of the subject matter, and sharpen the analytical and communications abilities of each student. In addition, the study guide and the computerized tutorial give students a number of action-learning opportunities.

The eighth Canadian edition has changed *Fundamental Accounting Principles* in many important ways. Extensive input obtained through surveys, focus groups, reviewers, and personal correspondence has driven the revision plan. Instructors confirm several trends that are affecting the world of accounting. The trends most prevalent in accounting education today include the visual orientation of students, the need for flexibility and innovation in the classroom, new pedagogy, and the impact of technology. The many changes that have been integrated throughout this revision are in response to these trends.

## Chapter Opening Scenarios

**NEW FEATURES**

A scenario at the beginning of each chapter raises questions related to the material covered in the chapter. Later in the chapter, one or more references show how the ideas being explained at that point apply to the company described in the chapter opening. Even before students read a chapter, they realize from the opening scenarios that what they will be learning is useful in solving real problems.

## Use of Colour

Conscious, deliberate thought and effort have gone into the use of colour to add more interest and appeal to the book. More importantly, colour is used as a code to aid in learning. Blue indicates financial statements and reports that provide accounting information to be used in decision making. The primary documents that accountants generate for themselves as they develop informative statements and reports are green. Finally, documents that serve as sources of the data that go into accounting reports are yellow.

## Progress Checks with Answers

A new feature in this edition is a series of Progress Checks integrated in each chapter. These review questions follow the discussion related to a learning objective. The goal is to have students stop momentarily and reflect on whether they should spend more time studying a given section of the text before moving on. Answers to the Progress Check questions are provided at the end of each chapter.

## Excerpts and Assignments from Annual Reports

The financial statements of Imperial Oil Limited and other companies are used throughout as a basis for discussing the different aspects of the financial statements. In this way, the relevance of the discussion to actual decision situations is emphasized. Most chapters also contain one or more assignments relating to the annual report of Geac Computer Corporation Limited.

## Using the Information

A new section at the end of each financial chapter reinforces real-world business applications. Most of these sections use real-world examples and many of them relate directly to the company vignettes that open the chapters. A few examples of Using the Information topics are:

>   Debt ratio—Chapter 2
>   Business segment information—Chapter 6
>   Return on total assets—Chapter 12
>   Price-earnings ratio—Chapter 16
>   Cash flow analyses—Chapter 18

## Enhanced Emphasis on Critical Thinking, Analysis, and Communication Skills

The assignment material in the book has been extensively revised. Many assignments have been reoriented to increase the emphasis on critical thinking and communication skills. For example, the requirements for selected problems in each chapter now include a *preparation component* and a separate *analysis component.*

The analysis component generally requires students to think about the financial statement consequences of alternative situations. Students learn to consider the consequences of alternatives and the resulting effects on their interpretation of the results. This complements the more usual preparation component of the end-of-chapter assignments.

## Quick Study (Five-Minute Exercises)

Instructors indicate an increasing reliance on shorter problem material for use as in-class illustrations and as homework assignments. Undoubtedly the prospect of solving problems in a short time and the rapid feedback of having done so successfully are motivating factors that lead students to extend their study efforts. Accordingly, this edition contains a new category of very short exercises that are identified as Quick Study. At least one exercise is provided for each learning objective.

## Additional Problems

In response to requests for more and varied problem material, we have replaced the alternate problems which previously mirrored the main problems with new, different problems. The traditional alternate problems are available in a separate booklet.

## Concept Testers

To encourage additional study of important glossary terms, all chapters conclude the assignment material with a *concept tester* in the form of a short crossword puzzle.

**FEATURES RETAINED**

Features about which our adopters have expressed enthusiasm have been retained. These include integrated learning objectives, illustrative diagrams, acetate overlays, "As a Matter of Ethics" cases, "As a Matter of Opinion" interviews, the comprehensive accounting cycle illustration, the summary in terms of learning objectives, chapter glossaries, demonstration problems with solutions and the various forms of problem material including Questions, Exercises, Problems, Provocative Problems, Analytical and Review Problems, the Serial Problem and Comprehensive Review Problems (after Chapters 4, 6, 13, and 22).

**CONTENT-SPECIFIC CHANGES**

## Expanded Prologue

An important change in this edition is an expanded Prologue that describes the accounting function in the context of other organizational functions such as finance, human resources, research and development, production, marketing, and executive management. The Prologue also explains the work accountants do—including their certifications and the fields within which they work—and the pervasive importance of ethics in accounting. As a separate learning unit, the Prologue emphasizes the overall importance of these topics to the understanding of the role accounting plays in providing information to a variety of decision makers.

## Financial Statement Orientation of Chapter 1

As a result of the Prologue revision, Chapter 1 is now a much shorter and more manageable learning unit with a clear focus on financial statements. This includes the information contained in the statements, the basic concepts that guide the development and use of accounting information, and the relationship of the statements to the transactions and events in the life of a business. Appendix A following Chapter 1 describes the process by which generally accepted accounting principles are established.

## Deletions in Chapters 4 and 5

Reviewers and adopters have overwhelmingly encouraged limiting the early examples in the book to proprietorships. As a result, the discussion of partnerships and corporations has been moved from the body of Chapter 4 to Appendix D following Chapter 4. Corporations are considered in the early chapters only as necessary to support student interaction with the financial statements at the back of the book and to recognize the existence of alternative forms of business organization.

Work sheets are now presented as an *optional* step in the accounting cycle. However, we also describe several reasons why an understanding of work sheets is useful. In addition, a more concise discussion of the adjusting entry method of accounting for inventories has reduced the size of the appendix at the end of Chapter 5.

## Discounting Notes Receivable

The revision of Chapter 8 recognizes the fact that an increasing number of companies routinely convert their receivables into cash without waiting to receive customer payments. In dealing with this modern business practice, the discussion of discounting notes receivable has been supplemented with a more general examination of the various ways receivables may be converted into cash.

## Topics Related to Inventories

The discussion in Chapter 9 of lower of cost or market has been simplified to avoid the details of considering ceiling and floor limits on market value. The treatment of markups and markdowns has been eliminated from the discussion of the retail inventory method. Reviewers agree that all of these topics are better left to intermediate level courses.

## Topics Related to Capital Assets

To help students appreciate the differences between financial accounting and tax accounting, we continue to discuss accelerated amortization. However, the discussion has been condensed to exclude the calculations that underlie the apportioning of accelerated amortization between accounting periods. We also eliminated the discussions of capital asset subsidiary records.

## Consolidated Financial Statements

Adopters indicate that the consolidated statements chapter in prior editions was the one they most frequently omitted. Nevertheless, long-term investments are an important financial consideration in evaluating many companies. The answer was to eliminate the consolidated statements chapter and to develop a more balanced set of asset chapters. As a result, Chapter 12 completes the asset coverage by discussing natural resources, intangible assets, and long-term investments. The long-term investments portion naturally concludes with a discussion of investments in international operations. The appendix on investments in equity securities from the seventh Canadian edition has been eliminated.

## Leases and Accounting for Corporate Income Taxes

In Chapter 13, the discussion of leases has been significantly shortened. Students learn the differences between capital and operating leases without having to journalize the entries related to capital leases. However, Appendix H, "Accounting for Corporate Income taxes," has been retained.

## Streamlined Coverage of Partnerships and Corporations

Reviewers suggested that we compress the coverage of partnerships and corporations and eliminate seldom used procedures and material that are best left for more advanced textbooks. In response, we streamlined discussion of material in these chapters and eliminated coverage of obsolete or nonessential material such as participating preferred, par value shares and the appendix on treasury stock.

## Segmental Reporting

The illustration and discussion of segmental reporting have been eliminated from Chapter 19. However, a short section at the close of Chapter 6 recognizes that operating in several business segments complicates the design of the accounting system. Then, the use of business segment information by decision makers is briefly discussed.

## Expanded Coverage of Activity-Based Costing

The practice of managerial accounting in Canadian industry continues to undergo a wide range of significant changes. Among these, the increasing implementation of activity-based costing systems is particularly noticeable. Accordingly, the introductory coverage of activity-based costing in Chapter 23 has been expanded in this new edition.

**APPENDIXES AND END-OF-TEXT ITEMS**

To provide instructors flexibility in planning course content, the eighth Canadian edition includes several appendixes. Those that clearly relate to a single chapter are placed at the end of that chapter. Appendixes F, G, H, and I appear at the end of the book.

## Comprehensive List of Accounts Used in Exercises and Problems

This list provides students with the large variety of accounts that companies use and that are needed to solve the exercises and problems provided in the text. This list is located at the end of this text.

**SUPPLEMENTS**

## For the Instructor

The support package for *Fundamental Accounting Principles* includes many items to assist the instructor. They include the following:

- *Solutions Manuals,* Volumes I, II, and III, which have more extensive supporting calculations in this edition.

- *Solutions Transparencies,* Volumes I, II, and III, which include all exercises, problems, and comprehensive problems. These transparencies are now printed in boldface in a new, exceptionally large typeface so that visibility from a distance is strikingly improved.

- *Teaching Transparencies,* many of which are now in colour.

- *Powerpoint Slides,* developed by Bruce MacLean of Dalhousie University, which are designed to support teaching the course using a computer, data display, and an overhead projector.

- *Video tapes,* available upon adoption, which reinforce important topics and procedures. They may be used in the classroom or media lab.

- *Instructor's Resource Manual,* prepared by Ray Carroll of Dalhousie University, which includes sample course syllabi, suggested homework assignments, a series of lecture outlines, demonstration problems, suggested points for emphasis, and background material for discussing ethics in accounting.

- *Testbank,* which contains a wide variety of test questions, including true-false, multiple-choice, quantitative, matching, and essay questions of varying levels of difficulty.

- *Computest,* a computerized version of the manual testbank for more efficient use, which is available in Macintosh, Windows, or DOS versions. The extensive features of this test-generator program include random question selection based on the user's specification of learning objectives, type of question, and level of difficulty.

- *Teletest.* By calling a toll-free number, users can specify the content of exams and have laser-printed copies of the exams mailed or faxed to them.

- *SPATS (Spreadsheet Applications Template Software),* prepared by Jack Terry and Christopher L. Polselli, C.A., which includes Lotus 1-2-3 (or the equivalent) templates for selected problems and exercises from the text. The templates gradually become more complex, requiring students to build a variety of formulas. What-if questions are added to show the power of spreadsheets and a simple tutorial is included. Instructors may request a free master template for students to use or copy, or students can buy shrinkwrapped versions at a nominal fee. Both DOS and Windows versions are available.

- *Tutorial Software,* prepared by Leland Mansuetti, Keith Weidkamp, and J. Russell Curtis of the British Columbia Institute of Technology. Multiple-choice, true-false, journal entry review and glossary review questions are randomly accessed by students. Explanations of right and wrong answers are provided and scores are tallied. Instructors may request a free master template for students to use or copy, or students can buy shrinkwrapped versions for a nominal fee. Both DOS and Windows versions are available.

- *Solutions Manual to accompany the practice sets* will include detailed solutions to all of the practice sets accompanying the text.

## For the Student

In addition to the text, the package of support items for the student includes the following:

- *Working Papers,* Volumes I, II, and III, which include working papers for the exercises, problems, serial problem, and comprehensive problems.
- The *Study Guide,* Volumes I, II, and III, which provides a basis for independent study and review and has been expanded to include multiple-choice and true/false questions as well as several additional problems with solutions for each chapter and appendix.
- *Check Figures* for the problems.
- *Barns Bluff Camping Equipment,* by Barrie Yackness of the British Columbia Institute of Technology and Terrie Kroshus. A manual, single proprietorship practice set with business papers that may be assigned after Chapter 7. This practice set is also available in an Alternate Edition prepared by Tilly Jensen of the Northern Alberta Institute of Technology.
- *Student's Name Book Centre,* by Harvey C. Freedman of Humber College of Applied Arts and Technology. A manual, single proprietorship practice set covering a one-month accounting cycle. The set includes business papers and can be assigned after Chapter 7. This practice set is also available in an Alternate Edition.
- *K.J.C. Manufacturing Company,* by Barrie Yackness and Sylvia Ong. A manual practice set with a narrative of transactions for a manufacturing corporation. This may be assigned after Chapter 20.

**ACKNOWLEDGMENTS**

We are grateful for the encouragement, suggestions, reviews, and counsel provided by students, colleagues, and instructors from across the country. A tremendous amount of useful information was gathered from over 300 responses to an Introductory Accounting Survey organized by the publisher. Although the identities of the respondents were anonymous to the authors, we learned a great deal from you and appreciate the detail you provided.

Many of the improvements in the Eighth Canadian Edition were based on the input from the reviewers of the seventh edition and the manuscript for the eighth edition. We want to thank this important group of people for their contributions to this edition. They include:

Peter McNeil, C.A.
Camosun College

Donna P. Grace
Sheridan College

Terry Fegarty
Seneca College of Applied
Arts and Technology

Barrie Yackness
British Columbia Institute of
Technology

Paul Molgat
Red Deer College

Tilly Jensen
Northern Alberta Institute of
Technology

Gregg Tranter
Southern Alberta Institute of
Technology

Sheila Simpson
Humber College of Applied Arts
and Technology

We also want to recognize the contribution of Robert Nichols of the British Columbia Institute of Technology who prepared the update of the payroll liabilities chapter and solutions for this edition.

Last but not least, we gratefully acknowledge the contribution from students, faculty members, and secretarial staff at the University of Windsor, Wilfrid Laurier University, and Dalhousie University. Special thanks go to Sharon Roth and Sandra J. Berlasty at the University of Windsor, Allan Russell at Wilfrid Laurier University, and Helen Cruickshanks and Carmen Tam at Dalhousie University.

**Kermit D. Larson**
**Morton Nelson**
**Michael Zin**
**Ray F. Carroll**

# To the Student

*Fundamental Accounting Principles* is designed to get you actively involved in the learning process so you will learn quickly and more thoroughly. The more time you spend expressing what you are learning, the more effectively you will learn. In accounting, you do this primarily by answering questions and solving problems. But this is not the only way to learn. You also can express your ideas by using the book's wide margins for taking notes, summarizing a phrase, or writing down a question that remains unanswered in your mind. Ideas that pop into your head can lead to fruitful exploration. These notes will assist in your later review of the material, and the simple process of writing them will help you learn.

To guide your study, *learning objectives* are listed near the beginning of each chapter. Read these objectives to form some expectations about what you will learn from studying the chapter. Think of them as your goals while you study. Each learning objective is repeated in the margin at the point the chapter begins to provide material related to that objective. You will find each objective repeated at the end of each chapter in the summary. The exercises and problem assignments following each chapter also are coded to these objectives.

As you progress in your study of each chapter, you will periodically encounter Progress Check questions relating to the material you have just studied. Answer the questions and compare your answers with the correct answers at the end of each chapter. If you are not able to answer the questions correctly, review the preceding section of the chapter before going on.

Several features of the text emphasize the real-world usefulness of the material in the book. For example, the *opening paragraphs* of each chapter raise questions about a real business. As you progress through the chapter, keep a sharp eye out for points in the discussion that apply to the scenario in the opening paragraphs. You will find brief inserts entitled *"As a Matter of Opinion"* in which business and community leaders tell how they use accounting in making decisions.

The use of colour in the book has been carefully planned to facilitate your learning. For example, the financial statements and reports that accounting provides as information to be used in decision making are blue. The primary documents that accountants generate for their own use as they develop informative statements and reports are green. Documents that serve as sources of the data that go into an accounting system are yellow.

As you read the text, you will learn many important new terms. These key terms are printed in black boldface the first time they appear, and they are listed again in a *glossary* after each chapter. In addition, you can find these key terms in the index at the end of the book. As a reinforcement to learning, but also as a light break from regular study, all chapters close with a *crossword puzzle* that involves some of the glossary terms.

Computer technology is changing the way businesses operate and will continue to be a driving force in the twenty-first century. To reflect this change and to give you practice with software, some of the assignments in the book are preloaded on a set of computer templates called *SPATS*. These assignments are identified with the following logo:

Ask your instructor or check your school's bookstore for information about other supplemental items that are available to assist your study. The *tutorial software* contains multiple-choice, true-false, journal entry review, and glossary review questions to help you prepare for exams. The *study guide* reviews learning objectives and provides practice problems for each chapter. *Working papers* provide familiarity with the actual framework used in creating accounting information.

Accounting can be an informative, relevant, and engaging field of inquiry. *Fundamental Accounting Principles* offers many tools to lead you into an understanding of the importance of accounting. Read, discuss, and enjoy! What you learn in this course will be useful in your personal and professional affairs for the rest of your life.

# Contents in Brief

# Contents

## 4    The Work Sheet and the Closing Process    183

## 5    Accounting for Merchandising Activities    237

# Your Introduction to Business, Accounting, and Ethics

*Accountancy is the fastest growing of the professions. These are the accounting bodies that provide education and professional training in Canada.*

aren White and Mark Smith are currently undergraduates in a business program. They have been assigned a case in one of their business courses. In the case, Jarrett and Wilson have decided to start a new business which would seek contracts with companies in the Hamilton area to provide a shuttle service for their employees to and from Pearson airport. They began operations under the name of JW Shuttle.

Jarrett and Wilson agreed that since Jarrett had the original idea and had done a substantial amount of the work to get started, Jarrett should receive 75% and Wilson 25% of any income the business earned during its first year of operations.

Karen and Mark understand that the amount of income reported in the first year depends on the methods used to measure the income. More precisely, the total income for the first two years will include $30,000 that will either be recognized in the first year or the second year, depending on the accounting method used. Based on projections through the end of the second year, the following table shows the results of the two alternatives:

|  | First Year | Second Year | Total |
|---|---|---|---|
| Using Method A: |  |  |  |
| Reported income ............. | $40,000 | $40,000 | $80,000 |
| Allocation to Jarrett and Wilson: ... |  |  |  |
| Jarrett (75% and 50%) ........ | 30,000 | 20,000 | 50,000 |
| Wilson (25% and 50%) ........ | 10,000 | 20,000 | 30,000 |
| Using Method B: |  |  |  |
| Reported income ............. | $10,000 | $70,000 | $80,000 |
| Allocation to Jarrett and Wilson: ... |  |  |  |
| Jarrett (75% and 50%) ........ | 7,500 | 35,000 | 42,500 |
| Wilson (25% and 50%) ........ | 2,500 | 35,000 | 37,500 |

## LEARNING OBJECTIVES

**After studying the Prologue, you should be able to:**

1. **Describe the main purpose of accounting and its role in organizations.**
2. **Describe the external role of accounting for organizations.**
3. **List the main fields of accounting and the activities carried on in each field.**
4. **State several reasons for the importance of ethics in accounting.**
5. **Define or explain the words and phrases listed in the prologue glossary.**

What goes on in business and other organizations? How are their activities carried out? Who is responsible for them? And, what part does accounting play? This prologue answers these questions and explains why your study of accounting is important even if you are not planning to be an accountant. You also learn about different kinds of accountants and the work they do. Finally, we consider the great importance of ethics in business and accounting.

## ACCOUNTING AND ITS ROLE IN ORGANIZATIONS

**LO 1**

Describe the main purpose of accounting and its role in organizations.

The main purpose of **accounting** is to provide useful information to people who make rational investment, credit, and similar decisions.[1] Because accountants serve decision makers by providing them with financial information that helps them make better decisions, accounting is often described as a service activity. Decision makers who use accounting information include present and potential investors, lenders, managers, suppliers, and customers.

Accounting provides information about all profit-oriented businesses. Accountants also supply information about nonprofit organizations such as churches, hospitals, museums, schools, and various government agencies. The people who use accounting information about nonprofit organizations include their managers and people who donate to or pay taxes to them, use their services, or otherwise work with them. Whether you are planning to be an accountant, an employee, a manager within an organization, or an external user of the information, your knowledge of accounting will help you achieve more success in your career.

## WHAT GOES ON IN ORGANIZATIONS?

Illustration PR–1 shows the major activities of businesses that manufacture and sell products. Businesses such as airlines and express delivery companies that sell services have similar activities. So do governmental and nonprofit organizations. The following paragraphs describe these functions in more detail.

**Finance.** Every organization needs money to operate and grow. Organizations use money to acquire equipment, buildings, vehicles, and financial holdings. The finance function has the task of planning how to obtain money from sources such as payments from customers, loans from banks, and new investments from owners. Government organizations acquire cash by collecting taxes and fees, while nonprofit organizations acquire most of their cash from contributions by donors. In preparing plans, the finance department identifies and evaluates alternative

---

[1]*CICA Handbook,* "Financial Statement Concepts," par. 1000.12.

**Illustration PR-1** Activities within an Organization

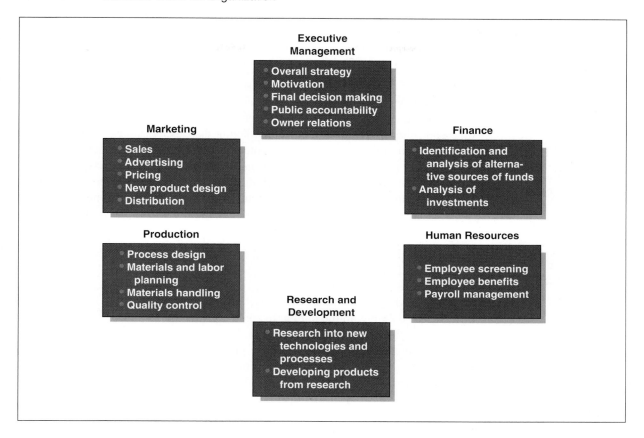

sources of funds. In addition, finance analyzes alternative investment opportunities to identify which to take and which to reject.

**Human Resources.** All organizations require efforts from people. As a result, employees must be located, screened, hired, trained, compensated, promoted, and counseled. And, they may be released from employment by being retired or laid off. The human resources function is responsible for handling these tasks. In large companies, literally hundreds of employees may be engaged in looking after the other employees.

**Research and Development.** All organizations need to find new ways to meet the needs of their customers and others. Thus, research into new technologies and products or services is essential. This may be as simple as testing a new recipe for pizza or as complex as creating a more powerful computer. Once research is completed, the development process uses the new knowledge to design or modify specific products or services. If organizations are to survive, this function is essential.

**Production.** Many companies produce and then sell goods to their customers. Producing these goods requires planning and coordinating many specific activities. These activities include designing the production process, acquiring materials used in production, and selecting the workers' skills to be applied. In addition, materials handling systems must be in place to ensure that raw materials and finished goods are delivered on time. Production management also requires paying a great deal of attention to the quality of the goods. Similar activities in retail and service organizations ensure that quality merchandise and services are delivered to consumers.

**Marketing.**  Companies can sell goods and services only if customers are willing to buy them. Marketing provides customers with information about goods and services and encourages them to make purchases. This includes sales efforts that involve contacting customers directly. Marketing also includes advertising that provides information to large numbers of potential customers. Another activity is to set prices that are low enough to encourage sales and high enough to earn profits. Marketing also involves identifying new products that might meet customers' needs. It includes developing systems that distribute products to customers when and where they need them. These activities are sometimes summed up as the four P's of marketing—product, promotion, price, and place.

**Executive Management.**  All organizations must have leadership, vision, and coordination. Long-term strategies need to be established, and employees must be motivated to do their best. In addition, major decisions have to be made. These tasks are the duty of the company's executive managers, who also represent the company in dealing with the public. In some companies, the owner or owners carry out the executive management functions. In others, key employees take on these responsibilities. They may be called the president, the chief executive officer, or the chair of the board of directors. In nonprofit organizations, the top managers often are called executive directors.

## USING ACCOUNTING TO SERVE INTERNAL NEEDS

The internal role of accounting is to serve the organization's various functions by providing information that helps them complete their tasks. By providing this information, accounting helps the organization reach its overall goals. Illustration PR–2 shows some of the information accounting provides within an organization.

The finance function uses information about actual cash flows as a basis for projecting future cash flows and evaluating past decisions. Human resources can carry out its work more effectively if it has information about the company's employees, including payroll costs. Research and development managers need information about the costs they already have incurred so they can decide whether to continue their projects. Marketing managers also use accounting information, especially reports about the company's sales and its marketing costs.

The production division of a company depends heavily on accounting information to determine whether its operating costs are occurring as expected. In carrying out its work, the production department operates within a set of *internal controls* designed by the accounting department. To promote efficiency and prevent unauthorized use of the company's resources, these controls specify procedures that must be followed before certain actions can take place. For example, internal controls may require a manager's approval before any materials are moved to the production line. Internal controls also dictate procedures that are necessary to ensure that accounting reports about production activities are dependable and useful. You will learn more about internal control procedures in Chapter 7.

**Illustration PR-2**  The Internal Role of Accounting

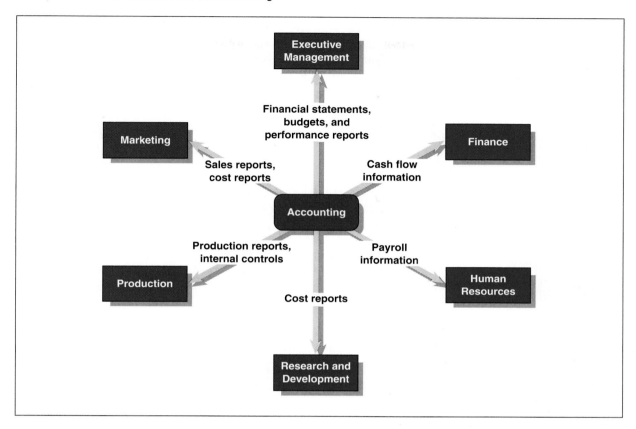

Because executive management has overall responsibility for the organization, it depends heavily on accounting information to understand what is happening. One important set of reports includes the *financial statements.* We explain the contents, usefulness, and limits of these statements throughout this book. (Chapter 1 introduces you to the four primary financial statements.) Executive management also receives and uses budget reports that describe future plans. After events have unfolded, accounting provides performance reports that help the managers to understand what was done well and to identify where improvements might be made.

Perhaps the most important point to learn at this stage is that accounting activities are not important by themselves. They are important only because they provide information that is useful to other parts of the organization.

---

**Progress Check**
*(Answers to Progress Checks are provided at the end of the Prologue.)*

PR-1    **The primary function of accounting is to provide financial information:  *(a)* To an organization's managers;  *(b)* To an organization's creditors;  *(c)* That is useful in making rational investment, credit, and similar decisions.**

PR-2    **Identify six different categories of activities carried on within most organizations.**

## USING ACCOUNTING TO SERVE EXTERNAL NEEDS

**LO 2**

Describe the external role of accounting for organizations

**External Decision Makers**

**Financial reports (including the statements)**

**Executive Management**

**Financial statements**

**Accounting**

In addition to using accounting information to meet internal needs, organizations use it for reporting to various external groups. These external decision makers include owners not actively involved in managing the business. For example, owners can use information about the company's performance and financial strength to help them determine whether to hold their investments.

In making decisions about an organization, internal and external decision makers generally begin by asking questions. The answers are often based on accounting information. For example, owners and managers use accounting information to help them answer questions like these:

- What resources does the organization own?
- What debts does it owe?
- How much income is it earning?
- Are the expenses appropriate for the amount of sales?
- Are customers' accounts being collected promptly?

Other decision makers include people who loan money to the organization. These lenders, also called *creditors*, need information to decide whether the company has enough financial strength and profits to pay its debts. For example, they look for answers to questions like these:

- Has the organization promptly paid its debts in the past?
- Does it have the ability to pay its current debts?
- Does it have good prospects for future earnings?
- Should it be granted additional credit now?

Accounting information is used by voters, legislators, and officials who are concerned about a government agency's receipts and expenditures. Contributors to a nonprofit organization also use accounting information to understand what happens to their donations.

A company's employees have a special interest in knowing whether an organization represents a stable source of employment. They can use accounting information to help them understand their employer's financial health and performance.

Some government agencies are charged with regulating business activities. They often need financial information to carry out that responsibility. Other government agencies are responsible for collecting income taxes. As you know from personal experience, taxpayers use accounting information to determine how much income they have and how much tax they owe.

We explained earlier that executive management is responsible for an organization's relationships with external decision makers. As the diagram on page 5 shows, accounting provides most of the financial information that executive management presents to external decision makers. An objective of this book is to explain the contents and usefulness of the financial statements created for these reporting activities.

Some accounting information is designed to satisfy the needs of a particular external party. For example, information provided to the government for tax calculations may differ significantly from the information in the financial statements. We describe the work of tax accountants later in the Prologue.

Because accounting and bookkeeping both are concerned with financial information and records, some people mistakenly think that they are the same thing. In fact, accounting involves much more than bookkeeping. Although bookkeeping is critical to developing useful accounting information, it is only the clerical part of accounting. That is, **bookkeeping** is the part of accounting that records transactions and other events, either manually or with computers. In contrast, accounting involves analyzing transactions and events, deciding how to report them in financial statements, and interpreting the results. Accounting also involves designing and implementing systems to produce useful reports and to control the operations of an organization. Accounting involves more professional expertise and judgment than bookkeeping because accountants must analyze complex and unusual events.

Whether you want to be an accountant, plan to hold some other position in an organization, or expect to be an investor or creditor, you will benefit by understanding how accounting information is developed. To gain this understanding, initially you will study some basic bookkeeping practices. Later in the book, you will use this knowledge to learn how accountants present financial data in meaningful reports. Eventually, you will be able to use the reports more effectively because you will understand how the information has been processed.

## THE DIFFERENCE BETWEEN ACCOUNTING AND BOOKKEEPING

Since computers first became available in the 1950s, they have spread throughout our everyday lives and the business world. Computers are widely used in accounting because they efficiently store, process, and summarize large quantities of financial data. Furthermore, computers perform these functions quickly with limited operator involvement. Thus, computers reduce the time, effort, and cost of processing data while improving clerical accuracy. As a result of these advantages, most accounting systems are now computerized. Even so, manual accounting systems are still used by a surprisingly large number of small businesses.

To prepare, analyze, and use accounting information in today's world, you need to understand the important role computers play in most accounting systems. In essence, computers are tools that help accountants provide useful information for decision makers. The huge growth in the number and power of computers has greatly changed how accountants and other people work. However, computers have not eliminated the need for people to learn about accounting. A strong demand exists for people who can design accounting systems, supervise their operation, analyze complex transactions, and interpret reports. A strong demand also exists for people who can make good decisions because they clearly understand how accounting information relates to business activities. While computers have taken over many routine tasks, they are not substitutes for qualified people with abilities to generate and apply accounting information.

## ACCOUNTING AND COMPUTERS

---

**Progress Check**

PR–3   **Accounting's external function is to provide:**  *(a)* **assurance that management has complied with all laws;**  *(b)* **information to users who are not involved in the organization's daily activities;**  *(c)* **information that managers use to control business operations.**

PR–4   **What is the relationship between accounting and bookkeeping?**

---

## WHY STUDY ACCOUNTING?

Because of the wide range of questions that are answered with accounting information, you will almost certainly use accounting in your future career. (In fact, you probably already use some accounting information as a result of having a credit card or chequing account.) To use accounting effectively, you need to understand the unique accounting words and terms widely used in business.

You should also understand the concepts and procedures that are followed in generating accounting information. One important benefit of this understanding is that it will make you aware of the limitations of accounting information. For example, much of it is based on estimates rather than precise measurements. By understanding how these estimates are made, you will be able to avoid misinterpreting the information.

Another very good reason for studying accounting is to make it the basis for an interesting and rewarding career. The next section of this prologue describes what accountants do.

## THE TYPES OF ACCOUNTANTS

**LO 3**

List the main fields of accounting and the activities carried on in each field.

One way to classify accountants is to identify the kinds of work they perform. In general, accountants work in these three broad fields:

- Financial accounting
- Managerial accounting
- Tax accounting

These fields provide a variety of information to different users. We describe the activities of accountants in these fields later in this prologue.

Another way to classify accountants is to identify the kinds of organizations in which they work. Most accountants are **private accountants.** A private accountant works for a single employer, which is often a business. A large business might employ a hundred or more private accountants, but most companies have fewer.

Many other accountants are **public accountants.** Public accountants provide their services to many different clients. They are called *public accountants* because their services are available to the public. Some public accountants are self-employed. Many others work for public accounting firms that may have thousands of employees or only a few. Canada's leading public accounting firms as of 1995 are:

| Firm | Revenue (000's) |
|---|---|
| KPMG Peat Marwick Thorne . . . . . . . | $475,100 |
| Deloitte & Touche . . . . . . . . . . . . . . | 406,000 |
| Ernst & Young  . . . . . . . . . . . . . . . . | 366,000 |
| Coopers & Lybrand . . . . . . . . . . . . . | 284,927 |
| Arthur Andersen . . . . . . . . . . . . . . . | 280,573 |
| Price Waterhouse . . . . . . . . . . . . . . . | 240,000 |
| Doane Raymond Grant Thornton  . . . . | 204,400 |
| BDO Dunwoody Ward Mallette  . . . . . | 119,103 |

Source: *The Bottom Line,* April 1995, p. 9.

**Government accountants** work for local, provincial, and federal government agencies. Some government accountants perform accounting services for their own agencies. Other government accountants are involved with business regulation. Still others investigate violations of laws.

Accounting is a profession like law and medicine because accountants have special abilities and responsibilities. The professional status of an accountant is often indicated by one or more certificates.

## Professional Certification

In Canada, there are a number of accounting organizations providing education and professional training. These include the provincial **Institutes of Chartered Accountants,** the **Certified General Accountants' Associations**, and the **Societies of Management Accountants**. Successful completion of the prescribed courses of instruction and practical experience lead to the following designations:

> **Chartered Accountant (CA)**
> **Certified General Accountant (CGA)**
> **Certified Management Accountant (CMA)**

Activities of the three accounting organizations that have shaped accounting thought have been their education and the publication programs. Each has an extensive educational program and has maintained the publication of journals which enjoy wide readership.

In the past decade reliance on postsecondary accounting education has become a significant part of the educational process and complements the extensive correspondence, university distance study, and lecture programs of the **Certified General Accountants' Association of Canada (CGAAC).** The provincial bodies of the **Canadian Institute of Chartered Accountants (CICA)** require a university degree with specified courses. A university degree is required also by some of the provincial bodies of the **Society of Management Accountants of Canada (SMAC).**[2]

Accountancy is the fastest growing of the professions. This growth is in response to the expansion and complexity of the economy, the increasing involvement of the accountant in the process of management decision making, and a growing number of financial reporting activities.

**THE FIELDS OF ACCOUNTING**

Accountants practice in three fields—financial, managerial, and tax accounting. The actual work done by an accountant depends on both the field and the type (private, public, or government) of accounting in which the person is employed. Illustration PR–3 identifies the specific activities of the three types of accountants within these fields.

## Financial Accounting

Financial accounting provides information to decision makers who are not involved in the day-to-day operations of an organization. As we described earlier, these external decision makers include investors, creditors, and others. The information is distributed primarily through general purpose financial statements. Financial

---

[2] As of January 1995, the provincial Societies of Management Accountants of Ontario and east require a university degree; the four provincial societies in the west do not require university degrees. The Associations of Certified General Accountants do not require university degrees.

**Illustration PR-3**   Activities of Accountants

| Types of Accountants | Fields of Accounting | | |
|---|---|---|---|
| | Financial Accounting | Managerial Accounting | Tax Accounting |
| **Private accountants** | Preparing financial statements | General accounting<br>Cost accounting<br>Budgeting<br>Internal auditing | Preparing tax returns<br>Planning |
| **Public accountants** | Auditing financial statements | Providing management advisory services | Preparing tax returns<br>Planning |
| **Government accountants** | Preparing financial statements<br>Reviewing financial reports<br>Writing regulations<br>Assisting companies<br>Investigating violations | General accounting<br>Cost accounting<br>Budgeting<br>Internal auditing | Reviewing tax returns<br>Assisting taxpayers<br>Writing regulations<br>Investigating violations |

statements describe the condition of the organization and the events that happened during the year. Chapter 1 explains the form and contents of financial statements.

The Financial Accounting column of Illustration PR–3 shows that financial statements are prepared by a company's private accountants. However, many companies issue their financial statements only after an **audit.** An audit is an independent review and test of an organization's accounting systems and records; it is performed to add credibility to the financial statements.[3] For example, banks require audits of the financial statements of companies applying for large loans. Also, federal and provincial laws require companies to have audits before their securities (shares and bonds) can be sold to the public. Thereafter, their financial statements must be audited as long as the securities are traded.

To perform an audit, auditors examine the financial statements and the accounting system. Their objective is to decide whether the statements reflect the company's financial position and operating results in agreement with **generally accepted accounting principles (GAAP).** These principles are rules adopted by the accounting profession as guides for measuring and reporting the financial condition and activities of a business. You will learn more about GAAP in Chapter 1 and in many of the following chapters.

When an audit is completed, the auditors prepare a report that expresses their professional opinion about the financial statements. The auditors' report must accompany the statements when they are distributed.

As the first column of Illustration PR–3 shows, some government accountants prepare financial statements. These statements describe the financial status of gov-

---

[3]To achieve this result, audits are performed by independent professionals who are public accountants. Little or no credibility would be added to the statements if they were audited by a company's own employees.

ernment agencies and results of events occurring during the year. The financial statements of governmental bodies are usually audited by the auditor general (federal), provincial auditors, and/or independent accountants.

Other government accountants are involved with regulating financial accounting practices used by businesses. For example, some accountants work for the provincial **Securities Commissions** which regulate securities markets, including the flow of information from companies to the public. Securities Commission accountants review companies' financial reports that are distributed to the public to be sure that the reports comply with the appropriate regulations.

As we mentioned briefly, some government accountants investigate possible violations of laws and regulations. For example, accountants who work for the provincial Securities Commissions (e.g., the Ontario Securities Commission) investigate crimes related to securities. Other accountants investigate financial frauds and white-collar crimes in their capacity as officers of the RCMP and provincial police forces.

## Managerial Accounting

The field of managerial accounting involves providing information to an organization's managers. Managerial accounting reports often include much of the same information used in financial accounting. However, managerial accounting reports also include a great deal of information that is not reported outside the company.

Look at the upper and lower sections of the Managerial Accounting column in Illustration PR–3. Notice that private and government accountants have the same four major activities. The middle section of the column shows that public accountants also perform activities related to managerial accounting. These activities are described next.

**General Accounting.** The task of recording transactions, processing the recorded data, and preparing reports for managers is called **general accounting.** General accounting also includes preparing the financial statements that executive management presents to external users. An organization's own accountants usually design the accounting information system, often with help from public accountants. The general accounting staff is supervised by a chief accounting officer, who is often called the **controller.** (See the organization chart on page 12.) This title stems from the fact that accounting information is used to control the organization's operations.

**Cost Accounting.** To plan and control operations, managers need information about the nature of costs incurred. **Cost accounting** is a process of accumulating the information managers need about operating costs. It helps managers identify, measure, and control these costs. Cost accounting may involve accounting for the costs of products, services, or specific activities. Cost accounting information is also useful for evaluating each manager's performance. Large companies usually employ many cost accountants because cost accounting information is so important.

**Budgeting. Budgeting** is the process of developing formal plans for an organization's future activities. A primary goal of budgeting is to give managers from different areas in the organization a clear understanding of how their activities affect the entire organization. After the budget has been put into effect, it provides a basis for evaluating actual performance.

Organization Chart of Controller's Department

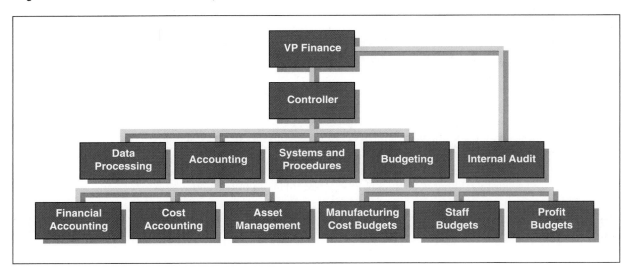

**Internal Auditing.** Just as independent auditing adds credibility to financial statements, **internal auditing** adds credibility to reports produced and used within an organization. Internal auditors not only examine record-keeping processes but also assess whether managers are following established operating procedures. In addition, internal auditors evaluate the efficiency of operating procedures. Almost all large companies and government agencies employ internal auditors.

**Management Advisory Services.** Public accountants participate in managerial accounting by providing **management advisory services** to their clients. Independent auditors gain an intimate knowledge of a client's accounting and operating procedures when they conduct their examinations. As a result, auditors are in an excellent position to offer suggestions for improving the company's procedures. Most clients expect these suggestions as a useful by-product of the audit. For example, public accountants often help companies design and install new accounting and internal control systems. This effort includes offering advice on selecting new computer systems. Other advice might relate to budgeting procedures or employee benefit plans.

## Tax Accounting

Income taxes raised by federal and provincial governments are based on the income earned by taxpayers. These taxpayers include both individuals and corporate businesses. The amount of taxes is based on what the laws define to be income. Tax accountants help taxpayers comply with these laws by preparing their tax returns. Another **tax accounting** activity involves planning future transactions to minimize the amount of tax to be paid. The Tax Accounting column of Illustration PR–3 identifies the activities of accountants in this field.

Large companies usually have their own private accountants who are responsible for preparing tax returns and doing tax planning. However, large companies may consult with public accountants when they need special tax expertise. Most small companies rely on public accountants for their tax work.

Many accountants are employed on the government side of the tax process. For example, Revenue Canada employs numerous tax accountants. **Revenue Canada** has the duty of collecting federal taxes and otherwise enforcing tax laws. Most Revenue Canada accountants review tax returns filed by taxpayers, while others offer assistance to taxpayers and help write regulations. Still others investigate possible violations of tax laws.

## Summary

The preceding discussion shows how important accounting is for most organizations. Regardless of your career goals, you will surely use accounting information and work with accountants. The discussion also shows the variety of opportunities available if you find accounting to be enjoyable and challenging. Next we consider the important role of ethics in business and accounting.

---

**Progress Check**

PR-5    The services performed by public accountants generally include: *(a)* income tax services, management advisory services, and independent auditing; *(b)* general accounting, independent auditing, and budgeting; *(c)* government accounting, private accounting, and independent auditing.

PR-6    What are the three broad fields of accounting?

PR-7    What is the purpose of an audit? Describe what public accountants do when they perform an audit.

---

## THE IMPORTANCE OF ETHICS IN ACCOUNTING

**LO 4**
State several reasons for the importance of ethics in accounting.

As a student, you realize that ethics and ethical behaviour are important features of any society. Disappointing stories in the media often remind us how much ethics affect our society. These stories tell us about attempts to defraud the elderly and other vulnerable people, missed child support payments, harassment, misconduct by public figures, bribery of government officials, and the use of insider information for personal gain in the stock market. Events like these make it difficult for people to trust each other. If trust is lacking, our commercial and personal lives are much more complicated, inefficient, and unpleasant.

In this section of the Prologue, we introduce the meaning of ethics in general and describe how ethics affect business and accounting in particular. Because the purpose of accounting is to provide useful information that can be trusted, it is essential that accountants be ethical. How could the users of accounting information rely on it if they could not trust accountants? The need to avoid this difficult situation has prompted the development of special ethics for accountants.

## The Meaning of Ethics

**Ethics** are the "principles that determine the rightness or wrongness of particular acts or activities." Ethics are also "accepted standards of good behaviour . . . in a profession or trade."[4] Ethics and laws often coincide, with the result that many unethical actions (such as theft and physical violence) are also illegal. Other actions

---

[4]*The New Lexicon Webster's Dictionary of the English Language* (New York: Lexington Publications, 1989), p. 324.

may not be against the law but are generally recognized as unethical. For example, the crime of perjury (not telling the truth) occurs only if the liar has been put under an oath. However, not telling the truth is nearly always unethical.[5] Because of differences between laws and ethics, we cannot count on laws to keep people ethical.

In some cases, a person may face difficulty in deciding whether an action is right or wrong. In these situations, the most ethical choice may be to take a course of action that avoids any doubt about the ethical correctness of the action. For example, financial statement readers would not trust an auditor's report on the statements if the auditor's financial success depended on the success of the reporting company.

Should this prevent an auditor from investing in a client if the investment is only a small part of the auditor's personal wealth? To avoid the question of how much would be too much, ethics rules for auditors simply forbid any direct investment in their clients' securities, regardless of the amount.[6] Also, auditors cannot accept contingent fees that depend on amounts reported in a client's financial statements.[7] These rules are designed to prevent conflicts of interest or even the possibility that the auditor might appear to lack independence.

Many controversial issues that we face in school, the workplace, or elsewhere have ethical implications. These ethical issues are an unavoidable part of life. However, a commitment to being ethical requires us to think carefully before we act to be certain that we are making ethical choices. Our success in making those choices affects how we feel about ourselves and how others feel about us. In fact, our combined individual choices greatly affect the quality of our entire society and the individual experience that each of us enjoys.

Beyond these general ideas, how do ethics relate to business, and more specifically, how do they relate to accounting?

## Ethics in Business

We discuss ethics at the beginning of this book because business activity is so central to everyone's life and because useful accounting information is so important for business. Recent history shows that many people have been concerned about what they see as low ethical standards in business. For example, a survey of more than 1,100 executives, deans of business schools, and members of the U.S. Congress showed that 94% of the respondents agreed with the statement that "the business community is troubled by ethical problems."[8] However, we can be encouraged because the survey also showed that the vast majority of the respondents believed high ethical standards are followed by companies that are successful over the long run. This second finding confirms an old saying: "Good ethics is good business." Ethical business practices build trust, which in turn promotes loyalty and productive relationships with customers, suppliers, and employees. As a result, good ethics contribute to a company's reputation and eventually its success.

Because of the important public interest in business ethics, many companies have adopted their own codes of ethics. These codes establish standards for inter-

---

[5]The usual exceptions to this rule involve protecting another person against harm.

[6]Institute of Chartered Accountants of Ontario, *Member's Handbook*.

[7]Ibid.

[8]Touche Ross & Co., *Ethics in American Business* (New York, 1988), pp. 1-2.

## As a Matter of Opinion

*Mr. Wray received his BA from McMaster University and his LLB from Osgoode Hall Law School. He is a Fellow of the Institute of Chartered Accountants of Ontario and a member of the Ontario Bar. He is the chair of the Interprovincial Committee to Harmonize the Rules of Professional Conduct which govern the ethics of Chartered Accountants across Canada. He has been a partner in Price Waterhouse since 1977, specializing in taxation and forensic accounting.*

**The accounting profession has earned high regard because of its ethical standards. Our standards require ethical behaviour in our relationships with our clients and our employers. They also require ethical behaviour in our dealings with the public and its interests. And, our standards require us to render high-quality professional services. By adhering to the concepts of objectivity, integrity, and independence, and by continued striving for quality, the profession has won a respected place in the entire business community and among the other professions.**

**As a student of accounting, be aware of the ethical implications of all that you study. As a member of the accounting profession, or any other profession, practice ethics in all that you do. By doing so, you will bring honour to yourself and your profession.**

Donald G. Wray, FCA

nal activities and for relationships with customers, suppliers, regulators, the public, and even competitors. Companies often use their codes as public statements of their commitment to ethical business practices. More importantly, they serve as guides for employees to follow.

## Ethics in Accounting

As we mentioned earlier, ethics are important in accounting because accountants are expected to provide useful information for decision makers. These decisions can have a profound effect on many individuals, businesses, and other institutions. As a result, accountants often face ethical issues as they consider what information should be provided to decision makers. Accountants' choices can affect such things as the amount of money a company pays in taxes or distributes to its shareholders. The information can affect the price that a buyer pays for a business or the amount of compensation paid to a company's managers. Internal information can affect judgments about the success of a company's specific products or divisions. If inadequate accounting information would cause a successful division to be closed, its employees, customers, and suppliers would be significantly harmed. Accountants need to consider all these effects in deciding what information will be most useful for these important decisions.

In response to the need for guidance for accountants, ethics codes have been adopted and enforced by professional accounting organizations. These include the provincial Institutes of Chartered Accountants, Associations of Certified General Accountants, and Societies of Management Accountants. To keep their codes up to date, these organizations continually monitor their effectiveness and applicability to new ways of operating. The As a Matter of Opinion box presents the views of Donald G. Wray, FCA, the 1994–95 president of the Public Accountants Council of Ontario, on the importance of ethical behaviour for accountants and others.

As an example of an ethical accounting issue, recall the JW Shuttle business described at the beginning of the Prologue. This case shows how accounting can affect the allocation of wealth between people. Wilson receives $7,500 more and Jarrett receives $7,500 less if Method B is used instead of Method A.

More information is needed in this case to help Jarrett and Wilson decide which method should be used. However, in explaining the appropriate uses of Method A and Method B, the accountant has an ethical responsibility to be fair to both parties. Knowing that Method B is more favourable to Wilson, the accountant must be careful to avoid giving a biased argument in favor of Method B.

Accountants and managers often face situations that are similar to the JW Shuttle case. For example, many companies pay their managers bonuses based on the amount of income reported. Generally, the managers benefit from the use of accounting alternatives that accelerate the reporting of income. However, those alternatives reduce the money available to invest for the benefit of the owners.

Another ethics issue in accounting involves the confidential nature of the information that accountants deal with in their work. For example, auditors have access to salary records and plans for the future. Their clients could be damaged if the auditors released this information to others. To prevent this, auditors' ethics require them to keep information confidential. In addition, internal accountants are not supposed to use confidential information for personal advantage.

These examples show why accountants, their clients, and the public need ethical guidance and commitment. Guidance provides a basis for knowing which actions to take and commitment provides the courage to do what needs to be done. Guidance also tells clients what they can rightfully expect from their accountants and gives the public a basis for having confidence in financial statements. In fact, the performance of the entire economy depends to a considerable extent on having financial information that is trustworthy.

## The Ethical Challenge

As you proceed in your study of accounting, you will encounter many other situations in which ethical issues are raised. We encourage you to explore these issues. We also urge you to remember that accounting must be done ethically if it is to be an effective tool in the service of society. Of all the principles of accounting that you learn from this book, the need for ethics is certainly the most fundamental.

In your own approach to life, you are in control of your ethical standards and the ethical decisions that you make. Each of us is individually free to shape our personal morals. To paraphrase former U.S. Supreme Court Chief Justice Earl Warren, it can be said that civilized society "floats on a sea of ethics." It is your choice how you elect to navigate this sea. Do not be misled into thinking that your choice does not matter. Eventually, your choice affects everyone, and that is the ethical challenge each of us faces.

---

**Progress Check**

PR-8    **All of the provincial accounting bodies have adopted codes of ethics. Is this true or false?**

PR-9    **Ethical rules prevent auditors from accepting certain kinds of contingent fees. Is this true of false?**

---

**LO 1. Describe the main purpose of accounting and its role in organizations.** The main purpose of accounting is to provide useful information to people who make rational investment, credit, and similar decisions. These decision makers include present and potential investors, lenders, and other users. The other users include managers of organizations, suppliers who sell to them, and customers who buy from them. Internally, accounting provides information that managers use in the following areas of activity: finance, human resources, research and development, production, marketing, and executive management.

**LO 2. Describe the external role of accounting for organizations.** In addition to using accounting information to meet internal needs, organizations also report accounting information to various external parties. These external decision makers include people who invest in the organizations and people who loan money to them. Lenders need information to assess whether the company has enough financial strength and profitability to pay its debts.

**LO 3. List the main fields of accounting and the activities carried on in each field.** Accountants work in private, public, and government accounting. All three have members who work in financial, managerial, and tax accounting. Financial accountants prepare or audit financial statements that are distributed to people who are not involved in day-to-day management. Managerial accountants provide information to people who are involved in day-to-day management. Managerial accounting activities include general accounting, cost accounting, budgeting, internal auditing, and management advisory services. Tax accounting includes preparing tax returns and tax planning.

**LO 4. State several reasons for the importance of ethics in accounting.** Ethics are principles that determine the rightness or wrongness of particular acts or activities. Ethics are also principles of conduct that govern an individual or a profession. The foundation for trust in business activities is the expectation that people are trustworthy. Ethics are especially important for accounting because users of the information have to trust that it has not been manipulated. Without ethics, accounting information could not be trusted, and economic activity would be much more difficult to accomplish.

**SUMMARY OF THE PROLOGUE IN TERMS OF LEARNING OBJECTIVES**

## GLOSSARY

**Accounting**  a service activity that provides useful information to people who make rational investment, credit, and similar decisions to help them make better decisions. p. 2

**Audit**  a thorough check of an organization's accounting systems and records that adds credibility to financial statements; the specific goal is to determine whether the statements reflect the company's financial position and operating results in agreement with generally accepted accounting principles. p. 10

**Bookkeeping**  the part of accounting that records transactions and other events, either manually or with computers. p. 7

**Budgeting**  the process of developing formal plans for future activities, which then serve as a basis for evaluating actual performance. p. 11

**CA**  Chartered Accountant, p. 9.

**CGA**  Certified General Accountant, p. 9.

**CGAAC**  Certified General Accountants' Association of Canada, the national professional organization of Certified General Accountants, p. 9.

**CICA**  Canadian Institute of Chartered Accountants, the national professional organization of Chartered Accountants, p. 9.

**CMA**  Certified Management accountant, p. 9

**Controller** the chief accounting officer of an organization. p. 11

**Cost accounting** a managerial accounting activity designed to help managers identify, measure, and control operating costs. p. 11

**Ethics** principles that determine the rightness or wrongness of particular acts or activities; also accepted standards of good behavior in a profession or trade. p. 13

**GAAP** the abbreviation for *generally accepted accounting principles.* p. 10

**General accounting** the task of recording transactions, processing the recorded data, and preparing reports for managers; also includes preparing the financial statements that executive management presents to external users. p. 11

**Generally accepted accounting principles (GAAP)** rules adopted by the accounting profession as guides for measuring and reporting the financial condition and activities of a business. p. 10

**Government accountants** accountants employed by local, provincial, and federal government agencies. p. 8

**Internal auditing** an activity that adds credibility to reports produced and used within an organization; internal auditors not only examine record-keeping processes but also assess whether managers are following established operating procedures; internal auditors also evaluate the efficiency of operating procedures. p. 12

**Management advisory services** the public accounting activity in which suggestions are offered for improving a company's procedures; the suggestions may concern new accounting and internal control systems, new computer systems, budgeting, and employee benefit plans. p. 12

**Private accountants** accountants who work for a single employer, which is often a business. p. 8

**Public accountants** accountants who provide their services to many different clients. p. 8

**Revenue Canada** the federal agency that has the duty of collecting federal taxes and otherwise enforcing tax laws. p. 12

**Securities Commissions** the agencies that regulate securities markets, including the flow of information from companies to the public. p. 11

**SMAC** Society of Management Accountants of Canada, the national professional organization of Certified Management Accountants, p. 9.

**Tax accounting** the field of accounting that includes preparing tax returns and planning future transactions to minimize the amount of tax; involves private, public, and government accountants. p. 12

---

# QUESTIONS

1. What is the main purpose of accounting?
2. Describe the internal role of accounting for organizations.
3. What are three or four questions that business owners might try to answer by looking to accounting information?
4. Why should people study accounting since computers are used to process accounting data?
5. Why do provinces license public accountants?
6. Identify the three types of services typically offered by public accountants.
7. What title is frequently used for an organization's chief accounting officer? Why?
8. Identify four managerial accounting activities performed by private and government accountants.
9. Identify two management advisory services typically provided by public accountants.
10. Identify several examples of the types of work performed by government accountants.
11. What do tax accountants do in addition to preparing tax returns?
12. Identify the auditing firm that audited the financial statements of Geac Computer Corporation Ltd., in Appendix I at the end of this book.

# CONCEPT TESTER

Test your understanding of the concepts introduced in this chapter by completing the following crossword puzzle.

**Across Clues**

2. Accountants who provide their services to many different clients.
4. The chief accounting officer of an organization.
5. The national accounting body that provides extensive correspondence, distance study and lecture programs.
7. The process of developing formal plans for future activities.

**Down Clues**

1. Rules adopted as guides for reporting the financial condition and activities of a business.
3. The part of accounting that records transactions and other events.
5. A certification of professional competence in management accounting.
6. The national organization of CAs.

# ANSWERS TO PROGRESS CHECKS

**PR–1**  *c*

**PR–2**  The activities are finance, human resources, research and development, production, marketing, and executive management.

**PR–3**  *b*

**PR–4**  Bookkeeping is the part of accounting that records transactions and other events, either manually or with computers. Accounting activities are concerned with identifying how transactions and events should be described in financial statements. Accounting activities also involve designing and implementing systems that make it possible to produce useful reports and to control the operations of an organization. Accounting involves more professional expertise and judgment than bookkeeping because accountants must analyze complex and unusual events. Also, accountants must be able to interpret and explain the information in the financial reports.

**PR–5**  *a*

**PR–6**  The three broad fields of accounting are financial, managerial, and tax accounting.

**PR–7**  The purpose of an audit is to add credibility to financial statements. When performing an audit, auditors examine financial statements and the accounting records used to prepare them. During the audit, they decide whether the statements reflect the company's financial position and operating results in agreement with generally accepted accounting principles.

**PR–8**  True

**PR–9**  True

# CHAPTER 1

# Financial Statements and Accounting Principles

*Many organizations provide accounting information to managers and other decision makers in the form of financial statements. The statements help to describe the organization's financial health and performance using a condensed and highly informative format.*

*H*aving solved the Jarrett and Wilson case, Karen White and Mark Smith are ready for their next challenge! One of their assignments is to examine financial statements to determine if an investment in a company would be useful as part of a long-term savings program. One investment possibility that has been suggested to them is Imperial Oil Limited. Karen and Mark know that the company's major businesses include natural resources, petroleum products, and chemicals.

Karen and Mark are trying to understand the financial information contained in Imperial's annual report.

| Imperial Oil Limited SELECTED FINANCIAL DATA (in millions) | Year Ended December 31 | |
|---|---|---|
| | 1994 | 1993 |
| **For the year:** | | |
| Total revenues . . . . . . . . | $8,911 | $8,795 |
| Net earnings . . . . . . . . . | 359 | 279 |
| **At year end:** | | |
| Total assets . . . . . . . . . . | $11,928 | $12,861 |
| Shareholders' equity . . . . | 5,995 | 6,566 |

## LEARNING OBJECTIVES

**After studying Chapter 1, you should be able to:**

1. **Describe the information presented in financial statements, be able to prepare simple financial statements, and analyze a business's performance with the return on equity ratio.**

2. **Explain the accounting principles introduced in the chapter.**

3. **Describe single proprietorships, partnerships, and corporations, including any differences in the owners' responsibilities for the debts of the organizations.**

4. **Analyze business transactions to determine their effects on the accounting equation.**

5. **Define or explain the words and phrases listed in the chapter glossary.**

**After studying Appendix A at the end of the chapter, you should be able to:**

6. **Describe the process by which generally accepted accounting principles are established.**

In this chapter, you start to learn about the information accountants provide to decision makers in financial statements. Next, you study some general principles that guide accountants in developing these statements. The discussion in Appendix A also describes some of the organizations that regulate and influence financial accounting. To continue your introduction to business, this chapter explains several ways a business can be organized. The chapter also shows you how accountants analyze business transactions to generate useful information. This is important for understanding why financial statements are useful. Finally, the chapter explains the return on equity ratio, which you can use in evaluating a company's operating success during a reporting period.

## FINANCIAL STATEMENTS

**LO 1**

Describe the information presented in financial statements, be able to prepare simple financial statements, and analyze a business's performance with the return on equity ratio.

Accounting exists for the purpose of providing useful information to people who make rational investment, credit, and similar decisions.[1] These decision makers include investors, lenders, managers, suppliers, customers, and other interested people. Be sure to read the As a Matter of Opinion box to learn how one decision maker uses accounting information to help him fulfill his responsibilities as a manager in a regional municipality.

Many organizations provide accounting information to managers and other decision makers in the form of financial statements. The statements are useful because they help to describe the organization's financial health and performance in a condensed and highly informative format. Because they give an overall view of the entire organization, financial statements are a good place to start your study of accounting. We begin by looking at the income statement and the balance sheet.

### The Income Statement

Look at the **income statement** in Illustration 1–1 (page 24). The income statement shows whether the business earned a profit (also called *net income*.) A company

---

[1] *CICA Handbook,* "Financial Statement Concepts," par. 1000.12.

## As a Matter of Opinion

*Mr. Parent received his BBA from Wilfrid Laurier University and his MBA from the University of Toronto. He has been a certified member of the Society of Management Accountants of Ontario since 1991. He is presently the Manager of Financial Services in the Regional Municipality of Waterloo's Finance Department. He works with the Community Health and Social Services Departments with a combined annual operating budget in excess of $170 million.*

I find the practice of accounting in the public sector to be challenging and rewarding. Today, all levels of government are being challenged to rethink how services will be provided to the public. My accounting education allows me to examine the intricacies of the many different programs the Municipality offers. This enables me to advise senior management and Council of the financial impacts of proposed initiatives. Often the impact of proposed changes will have differing implications for various stakeholders. Accountants in these situations must take a broad view of the issues when making their recommendations.

Wm. Lee Parent, MBA, CMA

earns a **net income** if its revenues exceed its expenses. A company incurs a **net loss** if its expenses exceed its revenues. In Illustration 1–1, observe that the income statement does not simply report the amount of net income or net loss. Instead, it lists the types and amounts of the revenues and expenses. As another example, **Canadian Pacific Limited** classifies the revenues and expenses on its income statement into the following categories: energy, forest products, real estate and hotels, and telecommunications and manufacturing. This detailed information is more useful for decision making than just a simple net income or loss number.

**Revenues** are inflows of cash or other assets received in exchange for providing goods or services to customers. Revenues also may occur from decreases in liabilities, for example, providing goods and services for which payment was received in advance.[2] For now, think of assets as economic resources owned by a business and liabilities as the debts owed by a business. Later, we define these terms more completely.

The income statement in Illustration 1–1 shows that the business of Clear Copy earned revenues of $3,900 by providing copy services to customers during the month of December. Examples of revenues for other businesses include sales of products, rent, commissions, and interest.

**Expenses** are costs incurred by a firm in the process of earning revenue and are measured by the cost of goods and services consumed in the operation of the business.[3] The income statement in Illustration 1–1 shows that Clear Copy used an employee's services. This cost is reported as salaries expense of $700. The business also used services in the form of office space rented to the business by the owner of the building. This cost is reported in Illustration 1–1 as rent expense of $1,000.

Notice that the heading in Illustration 1–1 names the business, states that the report is an income statement, and shows the time period covered by the statement. Information about the time period is important for evaluating the company's

---

[2]*CICA Handbook,* "Financial Statement Concepts," par. 1000.37.

[3]Ibid., par. 1000.38.

Illustration 1-1
Income Statement for
Clear Copy

**CLEAR COPY**
**Income Statement**
**For Month Ended December 31, 1996**

Revenues:
Copy services revenue . . . . . .          $3,900

Operating expenses:
Rent expense . . . . . . . . . . . .    $1,000
Salaries expense  . . . . . . . . .        700

Total operating expenses  . . . .          1,700

Net income . . . . . . . . . . . . . . .    $2,200

performance. For example, you need to know that Clear Copy earned the $2,200 net income during a one-month period to judge whether that amount is satisfactory.

## The Balance Sheet

The purpose of the **balance sheet** is to provide information that helps users understand a company's financial status as of a given date. As a result, the balance sheet often is called the **statement of financial position.** The balance sheet describes financial position by listing the types and dollar amounts of assets, liabilities, and equity of the business. (Equity is the difference between a company's assets and its liabilities.)

Illustration 1–2 presents the balance sheet for Clear Copy as of December 31, 1996. Unlike the income statement that refers to a period of time, the balance sheet describes conditions that exist at a point in time. Thus, the heading shows the specific date on which the assets and liabilities are identified and measured. The amounts in the balance sheet are stated as of the close of business on that date.

The balance sheet in Illustration 1–2 reports that the company owned three different assets at the close of business on December 31, 1996. The assets were cash, store supplies, and copy equipment. The total dollar amount for these assets was $38,000. The balance sheet also shows that there were liabilities of $6,200. Owner's equity was $31,800. This amount is the difference between the assets and the liabilities.

Notice that the total amounts on the two sides of the balance sheet are equal. This equality is why the statement is called a *balance sheet*. The name also reflects the fact that the statement reports the balances of the assets, liabilities, and equity on a given date.

## ASSETS, LIABILITIES, AND EQUITY

In general, the **assets** of a business are the items (economic resources) owned by the business and expected to benefit future operations.[4] One familiar asset is cash. Another asset consists of amounts owed to the business by its customers for goods and services sold to them on credit. This asset is called **accounts receivable.** In general, individuals who owe amounts to the business are called its **debtors.** Other

---

[4]Ibid., par. 1000.29.

Illustration 1–2
Balance Sheet for
Clear Copy

**CLEAR COPY**
**Balance Sheet**
**December 31, 1996**

| Assets | | Liabilities | |
|---|---|---|---|
| Cash . . . . . . . . . . . . . . | $ 8,400 | Accounts payable . . . . . | $ 6,200 |
| Store supplies . . . . . . . | 3,600 | **Owner's Equity** | |
| Copy equipment . . . . . . | 26,000 | Terry Dow, capital . . . . | 31,800 |
| | | Total liabilities and | |
| Total assets . . . . . . . . . | $38,000 | owner's equity . . . . . | $38,000 |

assets owned by businesses include merchandise held for sale, supplies, equipment, buildings, and land. Assets also can be intangible rights, such as those granted by a patent or copyright.

The **liabilities** of a business are its debts. These debts normally require future payment in assets or the rendering of services, or both.[5] One common liability consists of amounts owed for goods and services bought on credit. This liability is called **accounts payable.** Other liabilities are salaries and wages owed to employees, taxes payable, notes payable, and interest payable.

A liability represents a claim against a business. In general, those who have the right to receive payments from a company are called its **creditors.** From the creditor's viewpoint, a liability is the right to be paid by a business. (In effect, one company's payable is another company's receivable.) If a business fails to pay its debts, the law gives creditors the right to force the sale of its assets to obtain the money to meet their claims. When the assets are sold under these conditions, the creditors are paid first, up to the full amount of their claims, with the remainder (the residual) going to the owner of the business.

Creditors often use a balance sheet to help them decide whether to loan money to a business. They can use the balance sheet to compare the amounts of existing liabilities and assets. A loan is less risky if the liabilities are small in comparison to the assets. There is less risk because there is a larger cushion if the assets are sold for less than the amounts shown on the balance sheet. On the other hand, a loan is more risky if the liabilities are large compared to the assets. The risk is greater because it is more likely that the assets cannot be sold for enough cash to pay all the debts.

**Equity** is defined as "the residual interest in the assets of an entity that remains after deducting its liabilities."[6] Equity is also called **net assets.** If a business is organized as a corporation (which we describe later), the owners of the business are called shareholders or stockholders and the equity is called *shareholders' (stockholders') equity*. Because Clear Copy is owned by one person and is not a corporation, the equity section in Illustration 1–2 is simply called *owner's equity*.

Earlier we defined net income as the difference between revenue and expense for a time period. Net income is also the change in owner's equity that occurred during the period as a result of the company's major or central operations. By

[5]Ibid., par. 1000.32.
[6]Ibid., par. 1000.35.

describing this change, the income statement links the company's balance sheets as of the beginning and end of the reporting period. The following diagram represents the relationship between these two statements.

We use this background on the balance sheet and income statement to explain more about financial accounting. The next sections of the chapter describe the principles that guide the practice of financial accounting.

---

**Progress Check**
*(Answers to Progress Checks are provided at the end of the chapter.)*

1-1    **Which set of information is reported on an income statement?** *(a)* **Assets, liabilities, and owner's equity;** *(b)* **Revenues, expenses, and owner's equity;** *(c)* **Assets, liabilities, and net income;** *(d)* **Revenues, expenses, and net income.**

1-2    **What do accountants mean by the term** *expense?*

---

## GENERALLY ACCEPTED ACCOUNTING PRINCIPLES (GAAP)

**LO 2**
Explain the accounting principles introduced in the chapter.

In the Prologue, we explained that financial accounting practice is governed by a set of rules called *generally accepted accounting principles,* or *GAAP.* To use and interpret financial statements effectively, you need to have a basic understanding of these principles.

A primary purpose of GAAP is to make the information in financial reports relevant, reliable, and comparable. Information that is relevant has the capacity to affect the decisions made by financial statement users. Reliable information is necessary if decision makers are to depend on it. In addition, the information should allow statement users to compare companies. These comparisons are more likely to be useful if all companies use similar practices. GAAP impose limits on the variety of accounting practices that companies can use, thereby making the financial statements more useful.

### The Development of GAAP

Prior to the 1930s, GAAP developed through common usage. In effect, a practice was considered suitable if it was acceptable to most accountants. This history is still reflected in the phrase *generally accepted.* However, as the accounting profession grew and the world of business became more complex, many people were not satisfied with the profession's progress in providing useful information.

The desire for improvement caused many accountants, managers, and government regulators to want more uniformity in practice. Thus, in the 1930s, they began to give authority for defining accepted principles to small groups of experienced professional accountants. Since then, a series of committees or boards have had authority to establish GAAP. In general, the authority of these groups has increased over time. We describe the present arrangement for establishing GAAP in Appendix A at the end of this chapter.

## Broad and Specific Accounting Principles

GAAP include both broad and specific principles. The broad principles describe the basic assumptions and general guidelines that accountants follow in preparing financial statements. The specific principles provide more detailed rules that accountants follow in reporting the results of various business activities. The broad principles stem from observing long-used accounting practices. In contrast, the specific principles are established more often by the rulings of authoritative bodies.

As a user of financial statements, an understanding of both broad and specific principles will give you insight as to what the information means. It will also help you know what the information does not mean and thereby avoid using it incorrectly. Because the broad principles are especially helpful for learning about accounting, we emphasize them in the early chapters of the book. The broad principles include the following:[7]

|  | First Introduced | |
|---|:---:|:---:|
|  | Chapter | Page |
| Business entity principle . . . . . . . | 1 | 28 |
| Objectivity principle . . . . . . . . . . | 1 | 28 |
| Cost principle  . . . . . . . . . . . . . . | 1 | 28 |
| Going-concern principle . . . . . . . . | 1 | 29 |
| Revenue recognition principle . . . . | 1 | 35 |
| Time period principle . . . . . . . . . | 3 | 128 |
| Matching principle . . . . . . . . . . . | 3 | 130 |
| Conservatism principle . . . . . . . . . | 8 | 410 |
| Materiality principle . . . . . . . . . . | 8 | 417 |
| Full-disclosure principle . . . . . . . . | 8 | 425 |
| Consistency principle . . . . . . . . . | 9 | 456 |

Specific principles are especially important for understanding individual items in the financial statements. They are described throughout the book as we come to them.

At the beginning of this chapter, we said that the purpose of accounting is to provide useful information to people who make rational investment, credit, and similar decisions. In fact, this description of the purpose of accounting comes from "Financial Statement Concepts," section 1000, in the *CICA Handbook*. This section defines several accounting concepts that should be understood by financial statement users as well as accountants. For example, we relied on these concepts in preceding discussions when we defined revenues, expenses, assets, liabilities, and equity.

Another purpose of the concepts is to describe the characteristics that make accounting information useful for decisions. Earlier, we referred to the section's commonsense ideas that information is useful only if it has both *relevance* and *reliability.*

**UNDERSTANDING GENERALLY ACCEPTED ACCOUNTING PRINCIPLES**

---

[7]In describing these accounting principles, some writers have used different words to mean the same thing. For example, broad principles also have been called *concepts, theories, assumptions,* and *postulates.* We call them *principles,* but don't be confused if you see them called by other names in other books.

We will begin our discussion of accounting principles by describing some of the broad principles (listed on page 27) that will help you understand financial statements and the procedures used to prepare them.

## Business Entity Principle

The **business entity principle** requires every business to be accounted for separately and distinctly from its owner or owners. This principle also requires separate accounting for other entities that might be controlled by the same owners. The reason behind this principle is that separate information for each business is relevant to decisions that the users of the information make.

To illustrate, suppose that the owner of a business wants to see how well it is doing. To be useful, the financial statements for the business should not mix the owner's personal transactions with the business's transactions. For example, the owner's personal expenses should not be subtracted from the company's revenues on its income statement because they do not contribute to the company's success. Thus, the income statement should not report such things as the owner's personal entertainment and transportation expenses. Otherwise, the company's reported net income would be understated and the business would appear less profitable than it really is.

In summary, a company's reports should not include its owner's personal transactions, assets, and liabilities or the transactions, assets, and liabilities of another business. If this principle is not carefully followed, the reported information about the company's financial position and net income is not useful for rational investment and credit decisions.

## Objectivity Principle

The **objectivity principle** requires financial statement information to be supported by evidence other than someone's opinion or imagination. Information would not be reliable if it were based only on what the statement preparer thinks might be true. The preparer might be too optimistic or too pessimistic. In the worst case, an unethical preparer might try to mislead financial statement users by deliberately misrepresenting the truth. The objectivity principle is intended to make financial statements useful by ensuring that they present reliable information.

## Cost Principle

The **cost principle** requires financial statement information to be based on costs incurred in business transactions. Sales and purchases are examples of **business transactions.** Business transactions are exchanges of economic consideration between two parties. The consideration may include such things as goods, services, money, or rights to collect money. In applying the cost principle, cost is measured on a cash or cash equivalent basis. If cash is given for an asset or service, the cost of the asset or service is measured as the entire amount of cash paid. If something other than cash is exchanged (such as an old vehicle traded in for a new one), cost is measured as the cash equivalent value of what was given up or of the item received, whichever is more clearly evident.[8]

---

[8]*CICA Handbook,* "Non-monetary Transactions," par. 3830.05.

The *cost principle* is accepted because it puts relevant information in the financial statements. Cost is the amount initially sacrificed to purchase an asset or service. Cost also approximates the market value of the asset or service when it was acquired. Information about the amount sacrificed and the initial market value of what was received is generally thought to be relevant to decisions. Complying with the cost principle provides this information.

In addition, the cost principle is consistent with the *objectivity principle.* Most accountants believe that information based on actual costs is more likely to be objective than information based on estimates of values. For example, reporting purchases of assets and services at cost is more objective than reporting the manager's estimate of their value. Thus, financial statements based on costs are believed to be more reliable because the information is more objective.

To illustrate, suppose that a business pays $50,000 for land used in its operations. The cost principle tells us to record the purchase at $50,000. It would make no difference if the buyer thinks that the land is worth at least $60,000. The cost principle requires the purchase to be recorded at the cost of $50,000. However, you learn in later chapters that to provide more useful information, objective estimates of value are sometimes reported instead of costs.

## Going-Concern Principle

The **going-concern principle** (also called the **continuing-concern principle**) requires financial statements to reflect the assumption that the business will continue operating instead of being closed or sold. Thus, a company's balance sheet does not report the liquidation values of operating assets that are being held for long-term use. Instead, these assets are reported at amounts based on their cost. Many accountants have argued that the going-concern principle leads to reporting relevant information because many decisions about a business are made with the expectation that it will continue to exist in the future.

As a result of applying the cost and going-concern principles, a company's balance sheet seldom describes what the company is worth. Thus, if a company is to be bought or sold, the buyer and seller are well advised to obtain additional information from other sources such as a professional appraiser.[9]

The going-concern principle must be ignored if the company is expected to fail or be liquidated. In these cases, the going-concern principle and the cost principle do not apply. Instead, estimated market values are relevant and costs are not relevant.

---

**Progress Check**

**1-3   Name and describe two qualities of useful information identified by the "Financial Statement Concepts."**

**1-4   Why are the personal activities of a business owner excluded from the financial statements of the owner's business?**

---

[9]GAAP require supplemental disclosures (in the notes to the financial statements) of the current market values of many assets and liabilities.

1-5     If a company finds a bargain on some equipment worth $40,000 to the company and is able to buy the equipment for $25,000, what amount should be reported for the equipment on the company's balance sheet prepared immediately after the purchase? Which principle governs your answer?

## LEGAL FORMS OF BUSINESS ORGANIZATIONS

**LO 3**

Describe single proprietorships, partnerships, and corporations, including any differences in the owners' responsibilities for the debts of the organizations.

This section of the chapter describes three legal forms for business organizations. The forms are *single proprietorships, partnerships,* and *corporations.* The particular form chosen for a company creates some differences in its financial statements.

### Single Proprietorships and Partnerships

A **single proprietorship** (or **sole proprietorship**) is owned by one person and is not organized under federal or provincial laws as a corporation. Small retail stores and service enterprises are often operated as single proprietorships. No special legal requirements must be met to start this kind of business. As a result, single proprietorships are the most numerous of all types of businesses.

A **partnership** is owned by two or more people, called partners, and is not organized as a corporation. Like a single proprietorship, no special legal requirements must be met in starting a partnership. All that is required is an agreement between the partners to operate a business together. The agreement can be either oral or written. However, a written partnership agreement may help the partners avoid or resolve later disputes.

In a strict legal sense, single proprietorships and partnerships are not separate from their owners. Thus, for example, a court can order an owner to sell personal assets to pay the debts of a proprietorship or partnership. In fact, an owner's personal assets may have to be sold to satisfy *all* the debts of a proprietorship or a partnership, even if this amount exceeds the owner's equity in the company. This unlimited liability feature of proprietorships and partnerships is an important disadvantage.

Despite the lack of separate legal existence from their owners, the *business entity principle* applies to the financial statements of single proprietorships and partnerships. That is, relevant information for ordinary investment and credit decisions is more likely to be reported in the financial statements if each business is treated as being separate from its owner or owners.

### Corporations

A **corporation** is a separate legal entity chartered (or *incorporated*) under federal or provincial laws. Unlike proprietorships or partnerships, corporations are legally separate and distinct from their owners.

A corporation's equity is divided into units called **shares** or *stocks* and its owners are called **shareholders** or *stockholders.* For example, **Pier 1 Imports, Inc.,** is a corporation that had issued 37,617,000 shares at the close of its 1994 business year. In other words, Pier 1's equity was divided into 37,617,000 units. A shareholder who owned 376,617 shares would own 1% of the company.

When a corporation issues only one class of shares, it is called **common shares,** *common stock,* or *capital stock.* We discuss other classes of shares in Chapter 15 (Volume II).

A very important characteristic of a corporation is its status as a separate legal entity. This characteristic means that the corporation is responsible for its own acts and its own debts. As a result, the corporation's shareholders are not personally liable for these acts and debts. This limited liability feature is a major advantage of corporations over proprietorships and partnerships.

The separate legal status of a corporation also means that it can enter into its own contracts. For example, a corporation can buy, own, and sell property in its own name. It also can sue and be sued in its own name. In short, the separate legal status enables a corporation to conduct its business affairs with all the rights, duties, and responsibilities of a person. Of course, a corporation lacks a physical body and must act through its managers, who are its legal agents.

In addition, the separate legal status of a corporation means that its life is not limited by its owners' lives or by a need for them to remain owners. Thus, a shareholder can sell or transfer shares to another person without affecting the operations of the corporation.

There are fewer corporations in Canada than proprietorships and partnerships. However, the corporate form of business offers advantages for accumulating and managing capital resources. As a result, corporations control the most economic wealth.

## Differences in Financial Statements

Despite the major legal differences among the three forms of businesses, there are only a few differences in their financial statements.

One difference is in the equity section of the balance sheet. A proprietorship's balance sheet lists the capital balance beside the single owner's name. Partnership balance sheets use the same approach, unless there are too many owners for their names to fit in the available space. The names of a corporation's shareholders are not listed in the balance sheet. Instead, the total shareholders' equity is divided into **contributed capital** (also called **paid-in capital**) and **retained earnings.** Contributed capital is created by the shareholders' investments. Retained earnings are created by the corporation's income earning activities.

Another difference exists in the term used to describe payments by a company to its owners. When an owner of a proprietorship or a partnership receives cash from the company, the payments are called **withdrawals.** When owners of a corporation receive cash from the company, the payments are called **dividends.** Withdrawals and dividends are not reported on a company's income statement because they are not expenses incurred to generate revenues but represent reductions in equity.

Another difference involves reporting of payments to a company's managers when the managers are also owners. Because a corporation is a separate legal entity, salaries paid to its managers are reported as expenses on its income statement. In contrast, if the owner of a single proprietorship is also its manager, no salary expense is reported on the income statement for these services. The same is true for a partnership. This different treatment requires special consideration when analyzing the income statement. Our discussion at the end of this chapter describes this analysis in more detail.

To keep things simple while you are beginning to learn accounting, the examples in the first portion of this book are all based on single proprietorships. Chapters 14, 15, and 16 (Volume II) provide additional information about the financial statements of partnerships and corporations.

---

**Progress Check**

1-6    A single proprietorship: *(a)* divides its equity into shares;   *(b)* is a separate legal entity;   *(c)* is owned by one person who is personally responsible for all its debts.

1-7    Why are a proprietor's withdrawals not reported on the company's income statement?

---

## USING THE BALANCE SHEET EQUATION TO PROVIDE USEFUL INFORMATION

**LO 4**

Analyze business transactions to determine their effects on the accounting equation.

Up to this stage, you have learned that financial statements describe the financial activities of a business. You also know that many of these activities (for example, purchases and sales) involve business transactions.  To clearly understand the information in the statements, you need to see how an accounting system captures relevant data from the transactions, classifies and saves it, and then organizes it on the financial statements. We begin to explain this in the next section of the chapter. Our explanation continues through Chapter 4. We start with a simple example.

The beginning point for accounting systems is the definition of *owner's equity* as the difference between an organization's assets and liabilities. This definition can be stated as the following equation for a single proprietorship:

$$\text{Assets} - \text{Liabilities} = \text{Owner's Equity}$$

Creditors and owners provide the resources for acquiring the assets. Like any equation, this one can be modified by rearranging the terms. The following modified form of the equation is called the **balance sheet equation:**

$$\text{Assets} = \text{Liabilities} + \text{Owner's Equity}$$

Because it serves as the basis for financial accounting information, the balance sheet equation also is called the **accounting equation.** The next section shows you how to use this equation to keep track of changes in a company's assets, liabilities, and owner's equity in a way that provides useful information.

## THE EFFECTS OF TRANSACTIONS ON THE ACCOUNTING EQUATION

A transaction is an exchange between two parties of such things as goods, services, money, or rights to collect money. Because the two parties exchange assets and liabilities, transactions affect the components of the accounting equation. Importantly, each and every transaction always leaves the equation in balance. That is, the total assets always equal the sum of the liabilities and the equity regardless of what happens in a transaction. We show how this equality is preserved by looking at the transactions of a new small business called Clear Copy.

**Transaction 1.**  On December 1, 1996, Terry Dow formed a new photocopying store that was organized as a single proprietorship. Dow planned to be the manager of the store as well as its owner. The marketing plan for the store is to focus primarily on serving business customers who place relatively large orders. Dow

| | | Assets | | | | Owner's Equity | |
|---|---|---|---|---|---|---|---|
| | Cash | + | Store Supplies | + | Copy Equipment | = | Terry Dow, Capital | Explanation of Change |
| (1) | $30,000 | | | | | | $30,000 | Investment |
| (2) | − 2,500 | | +$2,500 | | | | | |
| Bal. | $27,500 | | $2,500 | | | | $30,000 | |
| (3) | −20,000 | | | | +$20,000 | | | |
| Bal. | $ 7,500 | + | $2,500 | + | $20,000 | = | $30,000 | |

**Illustration 1-3**
Changes in the
Balance
Sheet Equation
Caused
by Asset Purchases for
Cash

invested $30,000 cash in the new company and deposited it in a bank account opened under the name of Clear Copy. After this event, the cash (an asset) and the owner's equity each equal $30,000; as you can see, the accounting equation is in balance:

$$\text{Assets} \quad = \quad \text{Owner's Equity}$$
$$\overline{\text{Cash, \$30,000}} \quad \overline{\text{Terry Dow, Capital, \$30,000}}$$

The equation shows that the business has one asset, cash, equal to $30,000. It has no liabilities, and the owner's equity is $30,000.

**Transactions 2 and 3.** In its second business transaction, Clear Copy used $2,500 of its cash to purchase store supplies. In a third transaction, Clear Copy spent $20,000 to buy photocopying equipment. These events, which we call transactions 2 and 3, were both exchanges of cash for other assets. Neither transaction produced an expense because no value was lost to the company. The purchases merely changed the form of the assets from cash to supplies and equipment.

The effects of these transactions are shown in colour in the equations in Illustration 1–3. Observe that the decreases in cash are exactly equal to the increases in the store supplies and the copy equipment. As a result, the equation remains in balance after each transaction.

**Transaction 4.** Next, Dow decided that the business needed more store supplies and additional copy equipment. The items to be purchased would have a total cost of $7,100. However, as shown on the last line of the first column in Illustration 1–3, the business had only $7,500 in cash after transaction 3. Because these purchases would use almost all of Clear Copy's cash, Dow arranged to purchase them on credit from Handy Supply Company. That is, Clear Copy took delivery of the items in exchange for a promise to pay for them later. The supplies cost $1,100, the copy equipment cost $6,000, and the total liability to Handy Supply is $7,100.

The effects of this purchase are shown in Illustration 1–4 as transaction 4. Notice that the purchase increased total assets by $7,100 while the company's liabilities (called *accounts payable*) increased by the same amount. The transaction did not create an expense, so the amount of equity remained unchanged from the original $30,000 balance.

**Illustration 1-4**  Changes in the Balance Sheet Equation Caused by Asset Purchases on Credit, Revenues Received in Cash, and Expenses Paid in Cash

|  | \multicolumn{5}{c}{Assets} | Liabilities | \multicolumn{2}{c}{Owner's Equity} |
|---|---|---|---|---|---|---|---|
|  | Cash | + | Store Supplies | + | Copy Equipment | = | Accounts Payable | + | Terry Dow, Capital | Explanation of Change |

| | Cash | Store Supplies | Copy Equipment | Accounts Payable | Terry Dow, Capital | Explanation of Change |
|---|---|---|---|---|---|---|
| Bal. | $7,500 | $2,500 | $20,000 | | $30,000 | |
| (4) | | +1,100 | + 6,000 | +$7,100 | | |
| Bal. | $7,500 | $3,600 | $26,000 | $7,100 | $30,000 | |
| (5) | +2,200 | | | | + 2,200 | Revenue |
| Bal. | $9,700 | $3,600 | $26,000 | $7,100 | $32,200 | |
| (6) | −1,000 | | | | − 1,000 | Expense |
| Bal. | $8,700 | $3,600 | $26,000 | $7,100 | $31,200 | |
| (7) | − 700 | | | | −700 | Expense |
| Bal. | $8,000 | + $3,600 | + $26,000 | = $7,100 | + $30,500 | |

**Transaction 5.** A primary objective of a business is to increase its owner's wealth. This goal is met when the business produces a profit (also called *net income*). A net income is reflected in the accounting equation as a net increase in owner's equity. Clear Copy's method of generating revenues is to sell photocopying services to its customers. The business produces a net income only if its revenues are greater than the expenses incurred in earning them. As you should expect, the process of earning copy services revenues and incurring expenses creates changes in the accounting equation.

We can see how the accounting equation is affected by earning revenues in transaction 5. In this transaction, Clear Copy provided copying services to a customer on December 10 and immediately collected $2,200 cash. Illustration 1–4 shows that this event increased cash by $2,200 and increased owner's equity by $2,200. This increase in equity is identified in the last column as a revenue because it was earned by providing services. This information can be used later to prepare the income statement.

**Transactions 6 and 7.** Also on December 10, Clear Copy paid $1,000 rent to the owner of the building in which its store is located. Paying this amount allowed Clear Copy to occupy the space for the entire month of December. The effects of this event are shown in Illustration 1–4 as transaction 6. On December 12, Clear Copy paid the $700 salary of the company's only employee. This event is reflected in Illustration 1–4 as transaction 7.

Both transactions 6 and 7 produced expenses for the business. That is, they used up cash for the purpose of providing services to customers. Unlike the asset purchases in transactions 2 and 3, the cash payments in transactions 6 and 7 acquired services. The benefits of these services do not last beyond the end of the month. The equations in Illustration 1–4 show that both transactions reduced cash and Terry Dow's equity. Thus, the accounting equation remains in balance after each event. The last column in Illustration 1–4 shows that these decreases were expenses. This information is useful when the income statement is prepared.

**Summary.** We said before that a business produces a net income when its revenues exceed its expenses. Net income increases owner's equity. If the expenses exceed the revenues, a net loss occurs and equity is decreased. Remember that the amount of net income or loss is not affected by transactions completed between a business and its owner. Thus, Terry Dow's initial investment of $30,000 is not income to the business, even though it increased the equity.

To keep things simple and to emphasize the fact that revenues and expenses produce changes in equity, the illustrations in this first chapter add the revenues directly to owner's equity and subtract the expenses directly from owner's equity. In actual practice, however, information about the revenues and expenses is accumulated separately and the amounts are added to or subtracted from owner's equity. We describe more details about this process in Chapters 2, 3, and 4.

Because of the importance of earning revenues for a company's success, we briefly interrupt the description of Clear Copy's transactions to describe the *revenue recognition principle*. This principle guides us in knowing when to record a company's revenue so that it can be usefully reported in the income statement.

Managers need guidance in deciding when to recognize revenue. (*Recognize* means to record an event for the purpose of reporting its effects in the financial statements.) For example, if revenue is recognized too early, the income statement reports net income sooner than it should and the business looks more profitable than it really is. On the other hand, if the revenue is not recognized on time, the income statement shows lower amounts of revenue and net income than it should and the business looks less profitable than it really is. In either case, the income statement does not provide decision makers with useful information about the company's success.

The question of when revenue should be recognized on the income statement is addressed by the **revenue recognition principle** (also called the **realization principle**). This principle includes three important guidelines:

1. *Revenue should be recognized at the time it is earned.* The whole process of getting ready to provide services, finding customers, convincing them to buy, and providing a service contributes to the earning of revenue. However, the amount of revenue earned at any point in the process usually cannot be determined reliably until the entire process is complete. This does not occur until the business acquires the right to collect the selling price. Therefore, in most cases, revenue should not be recognized on the income statement until the earnings process is essentially complete. For most businesses, the earnings process is completed only when services are rendered or when the seller transfers ownership of goods sold to the buyer. For example, suppose that a customer pays in advance of taking delivery of a good or service. Because the earnings process is not completed, the seller should not recognize any revenue. Instead, the seller must actually complete the earnings process before recognizing the revenue.[10] This practice is known as the *sales basis of* revenue recognition.

## REVENUE RECOGNITION PRINCIPLE

LO 2

Explain the accounting principles introduced in the chapter.

---

[10]*CICA Handbook,* "Revenue," par. 3400.06–.09.

**Illustration 1-5** Changes in the Balance Sheet Equation Caused by Noncash Revenues, the Later Receipt of Cash, the Payment of Payables, and Withdrawals by the Owner

| | Assets | | | | Liabilities | Owner's Equity | |
|---|---|---|---|---|---|---|---|
| | **Cash** + | **Accounts Receivable** + | **Store Supplies** + | **Copy Equipment** = | **Accounts Payable** + | **Terry Dow, Capital** | **Explanation of Change** |
| Bal. | $8,000 | | $3,600 | $26,000 | $7,100 | $30,500 | |
| (8) | | +$1,700 | | | | + 1,700 | Revenue |
| Bal. | $8,000 | $1,700 | $3,600 | $26,000 | $7,100 | $32,200 | |
| (9) | +1,700 | −1,700 | | | | | |
| Bal. | $9,700 | $ 0 | $3,600 | $26,000 | $7,100 | $32,200 | |
| (10) | − 900 | | | | − 900 | | |
| Bal. | $8,800 | $ 0 | $3,600 | $26,000 | $6,200 | $32,200 | |
| (11) | − 400 | | | | | − 400 | Withdrawal |
| Bal. | $8,400 + | $ 0 + | $3,600 + | $26,000 = | $6,200 + | $31,800 | |

2. *The inflow of assets associated with revenue does not have to be in the form of cash.* The most common noncash asset acquired by the seller in a revenue transaction is an account receivable from a customer. These transactions, called *credit sales,* occur because it is convenient for the customer to get the goods or services now and pay for them later. (Remember that Clear Copy took advantage of this convenience in transaction 4 when it bought supplies and equipment on credit.) If objective evidence shows that the seller has the right to collect the account receivable, the seller should recognize the revenue. When the cash is collected later, no additional revenue is recognized. Instead, collecting the cash simply changes the form of the asset from a receivable to cash.

3. *The amount of recognized revenue should be measured as the cash received plus the cash equivalent value (fair market value) of any other asset or assets received.* For example, if the transaction creates an account receivable, the seller should recognize revenue equal to the value of the receivable, which is usually equivalent to the amount of cash to be collected.

The notes to a company's financial statements should include an explanation of the specific approach to revenue recognition used by the company. For example, **Magna International, Inc.** states in its 1994 annual report that "Revenue from sales of manufactured products is recognized upon shipment to customers."

## THE EFFECTS OF ADDITIONAL TRANSACTIONS ON THE ACCOUNTING EQUATION

To show how the revenue recognition principle works, we return to the example of Clear Copy.

**Transactions 8 and 9.** Assume that Clear Copy provided copy services for a customer and billed that customer $1,700. This event is identified as transaction 8 in Illustration 1–5. Ten days later, the customer paid Clear Copy the full $1,700, shown in transaction 9.

Illustration 1–5 shows that transaction 8 created a new asset, the account receivable from the customer. The $1,700 increase in assets produces an equal increase in owner's equity. Notice that this increase in equity is identified as a revenue in the last column of Illustration 1–5.

Transaction 9 occurred when the customer in transaction 8 paid the account receivable. This event merely converted the receivable to cash. Because transaction 9 did not increase total assets and did not affect liabilities, equity did not change. Thus, this transaction did not create any new revenue. The revenue was generated when Clear Copy rendered the services, not when the cash was collected. This emphasis on the earning process instead of cash flows reflects the goal of providing useful information in the income statement by applying the *revenue recognition principle.*

**Transaction 10.** In transaction 10, Clear Copy paid $900 to Handy Supply Company on December 24. The $900 payment relates to the earlier purchase of equipment from Handy. (The amount due Handy for the supplies purchase remains unpaid.) Illustration 1–6 shows that this transaction decreased Clear Copy's cash by $900 and decreased its liability to Handy Supply by the same amount. As a result, there was no reduction in owner's equity. This event did not create an expense, even though cash flowed out of the company.

**Transaction 11.** Another type of event, the payment of cash to the company's owner, is identified in Illustration 1–5 as transaction 11. In this case, Clear Copy paid $400 to Terry Dow to use for personal living expenses. Traditionally, a company's payments of cash (or other assets) to its owner are called *withdrawals.* Notice that this decrease in owner's equity is not called an expense in Illustration 1–5. Withdrawals are not expenses because they do not create revenues for the company. And because withdrawals are not expenses, they are not used to calculate net income.

**Summary.** Illustration 1–6 presents the effects of the entire series of 11 transactions for Clear Copy. Take time now to see that the equation remains in balance after each transaction. This is because the effects of each transaction are always in balance. In transactions 1, 5, and 8, total assets and equity increased by equal amounts. In transactions 2, 3, and 9, one asset increased while another decreased by an equal amount. Transaction 4 increased total assets and a liability by equal amounts. In transactions 6, 7, and 11, assets and equity decreased by equal amounts. Finally, transaction 10 decreased an asset and a liability by the same amount. The equality of these effects is central to the working of double entry accounting. You learn more about double entry accounting in the next chapter.

---

**Progress Check**

1–8    A new business has the following transactions: (1) the owner invested $3,600 cash; (2) supplies were purchased for $2,600 cash; (3) services were provided to a customer for $2,300 cash; (4) a salary of $1,000 was paid to an employee; and (5) $3,000 cash was borrowed from the bank. After these transactions, total assets, total liabilities, and total owner's equity are: *(a)* $7,900, $5,300, $2,600; *(b)* $7,900, $3,000, $4,900; *(c)* $7,900, $3,000, $3,600.

1–9    Is it possible for a transaction to increase a liability without affecting any other asset, liability, or owner's equity? Explain.

---

**Illustration 1-6**   Changes in the Balance Sheet Equation Caused by Noncash Revenues, the Later Receipt of Cash, the Payment of Payables, and Withdrawals by the Owner

| | Cash | + Accounts Receivable | + Store Supplies | + Copy Equipment | = Accounts Payable | + Terry Dow, Capital | Explanation of Change |
|---|---|---|---|---|---|---|---|
| | | | Assets | | Liabilities | Owner's Equity | |
| (1) | $30,000 | | | | | $30,000 | Investment |
| (2) | − 2,500 | | +$2,500 | | | | |
| Bal. | $27,500 | | $2,500 | | | $30,000 | |
| (3) | −20,000 | | | +$20,000 | | | |
| Bal. | $ 7,500 | | $2,500 | $20,000 | | $30,000 | |
| (4) | | | +1,100 | + 6,000 | +$7,100 | | |
| Bal. | $7,500 | | $3,600 | $26,000 | $7,100 | $30,000 | |
| (5) | +2,200 | | | | | +2,200 | Revenue |
| Bal. | $9,700 | | $3,600 | $26,000 | $7,100 | $32,200 | |
| (6) | −1,000 | | | | | −1,000 | Expense |
| Bal. | $8,700 | | $3,600 | $26,000 | $7,100 | $31,200 | |
| (7) | − 700 | | | | | − 700 | Expense |
| Bal. | $8,000 | | $3,600 | $26,000 | $7,100 | $30,500 | |
| (8) | | +$1,700 | | | | +1,700 | Revenue |
| Bal. | $8,000 | $1,700 | $3,600 | $26,000 | $7,100 | $32,200 | |
| (9) | +1,700 | −1,700 | | | | | |
| Bal. | $9,700 | $ 0 | $3,600 | $26,000 | $7,100 | $32,200 | |
| (10) | − 900 | | | | − 900 | | |
| Bal. | $8,800 | $ 0 | $3,600 | $26,000 | $6,200 | $32,200 | |
| (11) | − 400 | | | | | − 400 | Withdrawal |
| Bal. | $8,400 + | $ 0 + | $3,600 + | $26,000 = | $6,200 + | $31,800 | |

## UNDERSTANDING MORE ABOUT THE FINANCIAL STATEMENTS

LO 1

Describe the information presented in financial statements, be able to prepare simple financial statements, and analyze a company's performance with the return on equity ratio.

Up to this point, you have learned about only two financial statements: the income statement and the balance sheet. GAAP also require companies to include two other statements in their reports. They are the statement of changes in owner's equity and the statement of changes in financial position.

The following diagram shows how all four financial statements are linked:

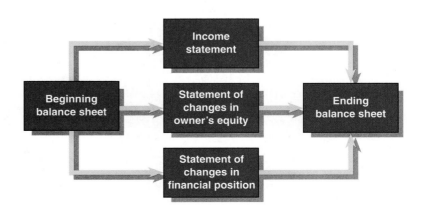

The income statement describes how owner's equity changed during the period through the company's income earning activities. The statement of changes in owner's equity describes all changes in equity, including net income, new investments by the owner, and withdrawals by the owner. The statement of changes in financial position describes how the amount of cash changed between the beginning and ending balance sheets. The statement of changes in financial position also describes many of the changes in the company's other assets and liabilities. Thus, most of the company's activities are described by the three statements in the middle, while the balance sheets describe the company's financial position before and after those activities occurred.

## The Income Statement

The top section of Illustration 1–7 shows Clear Copy's income statement as it appeared in Illustration 1–1. Now you can see that it is based on the information about revenues and expenses recorded in the owner's equity column in Illustration 1–6.

In the income statement, the copy services revenue of $3,900 resulted from transactions 5 and 8. If the business had earned other kinds of revenues, they would have been listed separately to help users understand more about the company's activities. The income statement then lists the rent and salaries expenses incurred in transactions 6 and 7. The types of expenses are identified to help users form a more complete picture of the events of the time period. Finally, the income statement presents the amount of net income earned during the month.

## The Statement of Changes in Owner's Equity

The **statement of changes in owner's equity** presents information about everything that happened to equity during the reporting period. The statement shows the beginning equity, the events that increased it (new investments by the owner and net income), and the events that decreased it (withdrawals and a net loss instead of net income).

The middle section of Illustration 1–7 shows the statement of changes in owner's equity for Clear Copy. The heading refers to December 1996 because the statement describes events that happened during that month. The beginning balance of equity is stated as of the beginning of business on December 1. It is zero because the business did not exist before then. An existing business would report the balance as of the end of the prior reporting period. The Clear Copy statement shows that $30,000 of equity was created by Dow's initial investment. It also shows the $2,200 net income earned during the month. This item links the income statement to the statement of changes in owner's equity. The statement also reports Dow's $400 withdrawal and the $31,800 equity balance at the end of the month.

## The Balance Sheet

The lower section of Illustration 1–7 presents Clear Copy's balance sheet (the same statement appeared in Illustration 1–2). The heading shows that the statement describes the company's financial condition at the close of business on December 31, 1996.

The left side of the balance sheet lists the company's assets: cash, store supplies, and copy equipment. The right side of the balance sheet shows that the

**Illustration 1-7**   Financial Statements for Clear Copy

**CLEAR COPY**
**Income Statement**
**For Month Ended December 31, 1996**

| | | |
|---|---:|---:|
| Revenues: | | |
| Copy services revenue . . . . . . . . . . . . . | | $3,900 |
| Operating expenses: | | |
| Rent expense . . . . . . . . . . . . . . . . . . . | $1,000 | |
| Salaries expense . . . . . . . . . . . . . . . . | 700 | |
| Total operating expenses . . . . . . . . . . . . | | 1,700 |
| Net income . . . . . . . . . . . . . . . . . . . . . | | $2,200 |

**CLEAR COPY**
**Statement of Changes in Owner's Equity**
**For Month Ended December 31, 1996**

| | | |
|---|---:|---:|
| Terry Dow, capital, December 1, 1996 . . . . . | | $ –0– |
| Plus: Investments by owner . . . . . . . . . . . . | $30,000 | |
| Net income . . . . . . . . . . . . . . . . . . . . | 2,200 | 32,200 |
| Total . . . . . . . . . . . . . . . . . . . . . . . . . . | | $32,200 |
| Less withdrawals by owner . . . . . . . . . . . . | | 400 |
| Terry Dow, capital, December 31, 1996 . . . . . | | $31,800 |

**CLEAR COPY**
**Balance Sheet**
**December 31, 1996**

| Assets | | Liabilities | |
|---|---:|---|---:|
| Cash . . . . . . . . . . | $ 8,400 | Accounts payable . . . | $ 6,200 |
| Store supplies . . . . | 3,600 | **Owner's Equity** | |
| Copy equipment . . | 26,000 | Terry Dow, capital . . . | 31,800 |
| | | Total liabilities and | |
| Total assets . . . . . | $38,000 | owner's equity . . . . | $38,000 |

company owes $6,200 on accounts payable. If any other liabilities had existed (such as bank loans), they would have been listed in this section. The equity section shows an ending balance of $31,800. Note the link between the statement of changes in owner's equity and the balance sheet.

## The Statement of Changes in Financial Position

The fourth financial statement is the **statement of changes in financial position,** which describes where cash came from and where it went during the period. The statement also shows how much cash was on hand at the beginning of the period and how much was left at the end. This information is important because good cash management is essential if a business is to prosper or even survive.

The statement of changes in financial position, covered in Chapter 18, has complexities that you do not have the background to grasp at this stage of your course. You should, however, be able to prepare a schedule of cash changes during the pe-

Illustration 1-8
A Schedule of Cash
Changes for Clear
Copy

**CLEAR COPY**
**Schedule of Cash Changes**
**For Month Ended December 31, 1996**

| Cash inflows: | | |
|---|---|---|
| Investment by owner . . . . . . . . . . | $30,000 | |
| Receipts from customers . . . . . . . . | 3,900 | |
| Total cash inflows . . . . . . . . . . . . | | $33,900 |
| Cash outflows: | | |
| Payment to employee . . . . . . . . . . | $   700 | |
| Payment of rent . . . . . . . . . . . . . . | 1,000 | |
| Payment for store supplies . . . . . . . | 2,500 | |
| Payment for copy equipment . . . . . . | 20,000 | |
| Payment on account payable . . . . . . | 900 | |
| Withdrawal by owner . . . . . . . . . . . | 400 | |
| Total cash outflows . . . . . . . . . . . . | | 25,500 |
| Increase in cash . . . . . . . . . . . . . . . | | $ 8,400 |
| Cash balance, December 1, 1996 . . . . . | | –0– |
| Cash balance, December 31, 1996 . . . . | | $ 8,400 |

riod. Illustration 1–8 shows the schedule of cash changes for Terry Dow's business. The information reported in the schedule was taken from the first column (labeled Cash) of Illustration 1–6. The heading identifies December as the time period covered by the statement.

An important reason for recording and reporting information about a company's assets, liabilities, equity, and net income is to help the owner judge the business venture's relative success compared to other activities or investments. One way to describe this success is to calculate the **return on equity ratio,** which equals the amount of income achieved in a period divided by the amount of owner's equity. The formula for this ratio is as follows:

$$\text{Return on equity} = \frac{\text{Net income}}{\text{Beginning owner's equity}}$$

Recall from the beginning of this chapter the story of Karen White and Mark Smith, who are considering the investment in **Imperial Oil.** In starting to analyze that company, they could use the financial information presented on page 21 to calculate Imperial Oil's 1994 return on equity, as follows:

$$\frac{\text{Net earnings}}{\text{Beginning shareholders' equity}} = \frac{\$359}{\$6,566} = 5.5\%$$

Interpreting the rate of return achieved by a company requires an understanding of several factors. For example, the rate should be compared with the rates that could be earned on other kinds of investments.

In the example of Clear Copy, the financial statements show that Terry Dow earned a return on equity at the rate of 7.3% for the month of December. To find this rate, we divide $2,200 of net income by the $30,000 beginning balance of owner's equity.

## USING THE INFORMATION— RETURN ON EQUITY

**LO 1**

Describe the information presented in financial statements, be able to prepare simple financial statements, and analyze a company's performance with the return on equity ratio.

Dow's rate for December is high compared to most investments and may appear very appealing. Recall, however, that the income reported for a single proprietorship does not reflect any expense for the effort exerted by the owner in managing its operations.

Dow should compare this rate with other investment alternatives to determine whether Clear Copy is producing an adequate return on equity. Because 7.3% for the month appears very high it is likely that Dow will be encouraged to stay in the business. However, we have not completely measured the income for the month. Chapters 2 and 3 introduce additional revenues and expenses, the net effect of which will be to reduce the net income amount shown here.

---

**Progress Check**

**1-10**   What financial statement item appears on both the income statement and the statement of changes in owner's equity?

**1-11**   What financial statement item appears on both the statement of changes in owner's equity and the balance sheet?

**1-12**   Why might a business owner calculate the return on equity ratio?

---

## SUMMARY OF THE CHAPTER IN TERMS OF LEARNING OBJECTIVES

**LO 1.  Describe the information presented in financial statements, be able to prepare simple financial statements, and analyze a company's performance with the return on equity ratio.** The income statement shows a company's revenues, expenses, and net income or loss. The balance sheet lists a company's assets, liabilities, and owner's equity. The statement of changes in owner's equity shows the effects on owner's equity from investments by the owner, withdrawals, and net income or net loss. The statement of changes in financial position shows the changes in cash that resulted from operating, investing, and financing activities. The financial statements are prepared with information about the effects of each transaction on the accounting equation. The company's performance can be analyzed by comparing the company's return on equity with rates on other investments available to the owner.

**LO 2.  Explain the accounting principles introduced in the chapter.** Accounting principles help accountants produce relevant and reliable information. Among others, broad accounting principles include the business entity principle, the objectivity principle, the cost principle, the going-concern principle, and the revenue recognition principle.

**LO 3.  Describe single proprietorships, partnerships, and corporations, including any differences in the owners' responsibilities for the debts of the organizations.** A single (or sole) proprietorship is an unincorporated business owned by one individual. A partnership differs from a single proprietorship in that it has more than one owner. Proprietors and partners are personally responsible for the debts of their businesses. A corporation is a separate legal entity. As such, its owners are not personally responsible for its debts.

**LO 4.  Analyze business transactions to determine their effects on the accounting equation.** The accounting equation states that Assets = Liabilities +

Owner's Equity. Business transactions always have at least two effects on the elements in the accounting equation. The equation is always in balance when business transactions are properly recorded.

After several months of planning, Barbara Schmidt started a haircutting business called The Cutlery. The following events occurred during its first month:

a. On August 1, Schmidt put $3,000 cash into a chequing account in the name of The Cutlery. She also invested $15,000 of equipment that she already owned.

b. On August 2, $600 cash was paid for furniture for the shop.

c. On August 3, $500 cash was paid to rent space in a strip mall for August.

d. On August 4, the shop was furnished by installing the old equipment and some new equipment that was bought on credit for $1,200. This amount is to be repaid in three equal payments at the end of August, September, and October.

e. On August 5, The Cutlery opened for business. Receipts from cash sales in the first week and a half of business (ended August 15) were $825.

f. On August 17, $125 was paid to an assistant for working during the grand opening.

g. Cash receipts from sales during the second half of August were $930.

h. On August 31, an installment was paid on the account payable.

i. On August 31, Schmidt withdrew $900 cash for her personal use.

## DEMONSTRATION PROBLEM

### Required

1. Arrange the following asset, liability, and owner's equity titles in a table similar to the one in Illustration 1–6: Cash, Furniture, Store Equipment, Accounts Payable, and Barbara Schmidt, Capital. Show the effects of each transaction on the equation. Explain each of the changes in owner's equity.

2. Prepare an income statement for August.

3. Prepare a statement of changes in owner's equity for August.

4. Prepare a balance sheet as of August 31.

5. Prepare a schedule of cash changes for the month of August.

6. Determine the return on equity ratio for August.

## Planning the Solution

- Set up a table with the appropriate columns, including a final column for describing the events that affect owner's equity.

- Analyze each transaction and show its effects as increases or decreases in the appropriate columns. Be sure that the accounting equation remains in balance after each event.

- To prepare the income statement, find the revenues and expenses in the last column. List those items on the statement, calculate the difference, and label the result as *net income* or *net loss*.

- Use the information in the Explanation of Change column to prepare the statement of changes in owner's equity.

- Use the information on the last row of the table to prepare the balance sheet.

- To prepare the schedule of cash changes follow the example in Illustration 1–8.

- Calculate the return on equity by dividing net income by the beginning equity.

*Solution to Demonstration Problem*

1.

| | Assets | | | = Liabilities + | Owner's Equity | |
|---|---|---|---|---|---|---|
| | Cash | + Furniture + | Store Equipment | = Accounts Payable | + Barbara Schmidt, Capital | Explanation of Change |
| a. | $3,000 | | | $15,000 | $18,000 | Investment |
| b. | − 600 | $600 | | | | |
| Bal. | $2,400 | $600 | $15,000 | | $18,000 | |
| c. | − 500 | | | | − 500 | Expense |
| Bal. | $1,900 | $600 | $15,000 | | $17,500 | |
| d. | | | +1,200 | +$1,200 | | |
| Bal. | $1,900 | $600 | $16,200 | $1,200 | $17,500 | |
| e. | + 825 | | | | + 825 | Revenue |
| Bal. | $2,725 | $600 | $16,200 | $1,200 | $18,325 | |
| f. | − 125 | | | | − 125 | Expense |
| Bal. | $2,600 | $600 | $16,200 | $1,200 | $18,200 | |
| g. | + 930 | | | | + 930 | Revenue |
| Bal. | $3,530 | $600 | $16,200 | $1,200 | $19,130 | |
| h. | − 400 | | | − 400 | | |
| Bal. | $3,130 | $600 | $16,200 | $ 800 | $19,130 | |
| i. | − 900 | | | | − 900 | Withdrawal |
| Bal. | $2,230 + | $600 + | $16,200 = | $ 800 + | $18,230 | |

2.

**THE CUTLERY**
**Income Statement**
**For Month Ended August 31**

| | | |
|---|---|---|
| Revenues: | | |
| Sales .......................... | | $1,755 |
| Operating expenses: | | |
| Rent expense .................... | $500 | |
| Salaries expense .................. | 125 | |
| Total operating expenses ............. | | 625 |
| Net income ....................... | | $1,130 |

3.

**THE CUTLERY**
**Statement of Changes in Owner's Equity**
**For Month Ended August 31**

| | | |
|---|---|---|
| Barbara Schmidt, capital, August 1 ..... | | $ 0 |
| Plus: Investments by owner ......... | $18,000 | |
| Net income ............... | 1,130 | 19,130 |
| Total ......................... | | $19,130 |
| Less withdrawals by owner .......... | | (900) |
| Barbara Schmidt, capital, August 31 .... | | $18,230 |

4.

**THE CUTLERY**
**Balance Sheet**
**August 31**

| Assets | | Liabilities | |
|---|---|---|---|
| Cash. . . . . . . . . . . . . . . . . | $ 2,230 | Accounts payable . . . . . . . . | $   800 |
| Furniture. . . . . . . . . . . . . . | 600 | **Owner's Equity** | |
| Store equipment . . . . . . . . | 16,200 | Barbara Schmidt, capital . . . | 18,230 |
| | | Total liabilities and | |
| Total assets . . . . . . . . . . . . | $19,030 | owner's equity . . . . . . . . | $19,030 |

5.

**THE CUTLERY**
**Schedule of Cash Changes**
**For Month Ended August 31**

| | | |
|---|---|---|
| Cash inflows: | | |
| Investment by owner . . . . . . . . . . | $3,000 | |
| Receipts from customers . . . . . . . | 1,755 | |
| Total cash inflows . . . . . . . . . . . | | $4,755 |
| Cash outflows: | | |
| Payment to employee . . . . . . . . . | $   125 | |
| Payment of rent . . . . . . . . . . . . | 500 | |
| Payment for furniture . . . . . . . . | 600 | |
| Payment on account payable . . . . | 400 | |
| Withdrawal by owner . . . . . . . . | 900 | |
| Total cash outflows . . . . . . . . . . | | 2,525 |
| Increase in cash . . . . . . . . . . . . . . | | $2,230 |
| Cash balance, August 1, 1996 . . . . . | | 0 |
| Cash balance, August 31, 1996 . . . . | | $2,230 |

6. $$\text{Return on equity} = \frac{\text{Net income}}{\text{Beginning owner's equity}} = \frac{\$1,130}{\$18,000} = 6.3\%$$

# Developing Accounting Standards

## ACCOUNTING PRINCIPLES, AUDITING STANDARDS, AND FINANCIAL ACCOUNTING

**LO 6**
Describe the process by which generally accepted accounting principles are established.

Generally accepted accounting principles are not natural laws like the laws of physics or other sciences. Instead, GAAP are identified in response to the needs of users and others affected by accounting. Thus, GAAP are subject to change as needs change.

Three groups of people are most directly affected by financial reporting: preparers, auditors, and users. The following diagram shows the relationship between the financial statements and these groups.

Private accountants prepare the financial statements. To give users more confidence in the statements, independent auditors usually examine the financial statements and develop an audit report. The statements and the audit report are then distributed to the users.

Illustration A–1 expands this diagram to show how accounting principles and auditing standards relate to the financial reporting process. First, in Illustration A–1, we show that GAAP are applied in preparing the financial statements. Preparers use GAAP to decide what procedures to follow as they account for business transactions and put the statements together.

Second, in Illustration A–1, we show that audits are performed in accordance with **generally accepted auditing standards (GAAS)** which are developed by the CICA's **Auditing Standards Board (ASB).** GAAS are the rules adopted by the accounting profession as guides for conducting audits of financial statements. GAAS tell auditors what they must do in their audits to determine whether the financial statements comply with GAAP.

Applying both GAAP and GAAS assures users that financial statements include relevant, reliable, and comparable information. The audit does not, however, ensure that they can safely invest in or loan to the company. The audit does not reduce the risk that the company's products and services will not be successfully marketed or that other factors, such as the loss of a key executive, could cause it to fail.

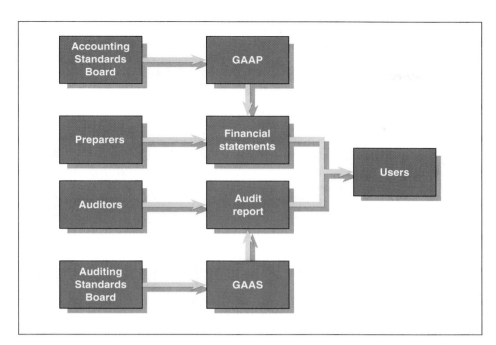

**Illustration A-1**
Generally Accepted
Accounting Principles
(GAAP), Generally
Accepted Auditing
Standards (GAAS),
and the Groups that
Participate in Financial
Accounting

In Illustration A–1, we also identify the two organizations that are the primary authoritative sources of GAAP and GAAS. The primary authoritative source of GAAP is the **Accounting Standards Board (AcSB).** The board members, supported by a research staff, use their collective knowledge to identify problems in financial accounting and to find ways to solve them. The board also seeks advice from groups and individuals affected by GAAP. The advice comes via comments on the board's "exposure drafts" on specific issues. The finalized recommendations are published as part of the *CICA Handbook.*

The Accounting Standards Board gains its authority from both law and the members of the Canadian Institute of Chartered Accountants. Under the regulations of the Canada Business Corporations Act, the accounting standards for external reporting set out in the *CICA Handbook* have the force of law. Also, in 1969 the CICA adopted paragraph 1500.06, which states:

> Where the accounting treatment or statement presentation does not follow the
> recommendations of this *Handbook,* the practice used should be explained
> in notes to the financial statements with an indication of the reason why the
> recommendation concerned was not followed.

A number of other professional organizations support the Accounting Standards Board's process by providing input. In summary, the Accounting Standards Board's job is to improve financial reporting while balancing the interests of the affected groups.

In today's world, people in different countries engage in business with each other more easily than in the past. A company in Canada might sell its products all over the world. Another company in Singapore might raise cash by selling shares to Canadian and Japanese investors. At the same time, it might borrow from creditors in Saudi Arabia and Germany.

## HOW ACCOUNTING PRINCIPLES ARE ESTABLISHED

## INTERNATIONAL ACCOUNTING STANDARDS

An increasing number of companies have international operations. For example, **Four Seasons Hotels, Inc.,** is a Canadian company with operations in lodging and contract services. Most of the company's operations are in the United States. However, the company also managed properties in the West Indies, New Zealand, Thailand, Hong Kong, Malaysia, England, Australia, Fiji, Singapore, and Taiwan. It also has properties under construction or development in Germany, Hawaii, and the Czech Republic.

Despite this trend toward global business, a major problem exists because each country has its own unique set of acceptable accounting practices. Consider, for example, the Singapore company we described earlier. Should it prepare financial statements that comply with Singapore accounting standards, or with the standards used in Canada, Japan, Saudi Arabia, or Germany? Should it have to prepare five different sets of reports to gain access to financial markets in all five countries?

Accounting organizations from around the world responded to this problem by creating the International Accounting Standards Committee **(IASC)** in 1973. With headquarters in London, the IASC issues *International Accounting Standards* that identify preferred accounting practices and then encourages their worldwide acceptance. By narrowing the range of alternative practices, the IASC hopes to create more harmony among the accounting practices of different countries. If standards could be harmonized, a single set of financial statements could be used by one company in all financial markets.

In many countries, the bodies that set accounting standards have encouraged the IASC to reduce the differences. The CICA's Accounting Standards Committee has provided this encouragement and technical assistance. However, the IASC does not have the authority to impose its standards on companies. Although progress has been slow, interest is growing in moving Canadian GAAP toward the IASC's preferred practices.

---

**Progress Check**

A–1   Which body currently establishes generally accepted accounting principles in Canada?   *(a)* The Ontario Securities Commission; *(b)* Parliament; *(c)* The AcSB; *(d)* The IASC.

A–2   What is the difference between GAAP and GAAS?

A–3   Is it true that Canadian companies with operations in foreign countries are required to prepare their financial statements according to the rules established by the IASC?

---

## SUMMARY OF APPENDIX A IN TERMS OF LEARNING OBJECTIVES

**LO 6. Describe the process by which generally accepted accounting principles are established.** Specific accounting principles for financial accounting are established in Canada by the Accounting Standards Board (AcSB), with input from various interested parties. Auditing standards are established by the Auditing Standards Board (ASB), another committee of the Canadian Institute of Chartered Accountants (CICA). The International Accounting Standards Committee (IASC) identifies preferred practices and encourages their adoption throughout the world.

# GLOSSARY

**Accounting equation** a description of the relationship between a company's assets, liabilities, and equity; expressed as Assets = Liabilities + Owner's Equity; also called the *balance sheet equation.* p. 32

**Accounts payable** liabilities created by buying goods and services on credit. p. 25

**Accounts receivable** assets created by selling goods and services on credit. p. 24

**AcSB** the Accounting Standards Board; the authoritative committee of the CICA that identifies generally accepted accounting principles. p. 47

**ASB** the Auditing Standards Board; the authoritative committee of the CICA that identifies generally accepted auditing standards. p. 46

**Assets** items (economic resources) owned by the business and expected to benefit future operations. p. 24

**Balance sheet** a financial statement providing information that helps users understand a company's financial status; lists the types and dollar amounts of assets, liabilities, and equity as of a specific date; also called the *statement of financial position.* p. 24

**Balance sheet equation** another name for the *accounting equation.* p. 32

**Business entity principle** the principle that requires every business to be accounted for separately and distinctly from its owner or owners; based on the goal of providing relevant information about the business. p. 28

**Business transaction** an exchange between two parties of economic consideration, such as goods, services, money, or rights to collect money. p. 28

**CICA Handbook** the publication of the CICA that establishes generally accepted accounting principles in Canada p. 47

**Common shares** the name given to a corporation's shares when it issues only one kind or class of shares, also known as *common stock.* p. 31

**Continuing-concern principle** another name for the *going-concern principle.* p. 29

**Contributed capital** the category of shareholders' equity created by the shareholders' investments, also called *paid-in capital.* p. 31

**Corporation** a business chartered, or incorporated, as a separate legal entity under federal or provincial laws. p. 30

**Cost principle** the accounting principle that requires financial statement information to be based on costs in-

curred in business transactions; it requires assets and services to be recorded initially at the cash or cash-equivalent amount given in exchange. p. 28

**Creditors** individuals or organizations entitled to receive payments from a company. p. 25

**Debtors** individuals or organizations that owe amounts to a business. p. 24

**Dividends** payments of cash by a corporation to its shareholders. p. 31

**Equity** the difference between a company's assets and its liabilities; more precisely, the residual interest in the assets of an entity that remains after deducting its liabilities; also called *net assets.* p. 25

**Expenses** costs incurred by a firm in the process of earning revenue; measured by the cost of goods and services consumed in the operation of the business. p. 23

**GAAS** the abbreviation for *generally accepted auditing standards.* p. 46

**Generally accepted auditing standards** rules adopted by the accounting profession as guides for conducting audits of financial statements. p. 46

**Going-concern principle** the rule that requires financial statements to reflect the assumption that the business will continue operating instead of being closed or sold, unless evidence shows that it will not continue; also called *continuing-concern* principle: p. 29

**IASC** International Accounting Standards Committee; a committee that attempts to create more harmony among the accounting practices of different countries by identifying preferred practices and encouraging their worldwide acceptance. p. 48

**Income statement** the financial statement that shows whether the business earned a profit or suffered a loss; it lists the types and amounts of the revenues and expenses. p. 22

**Liabilities** debts owed by a business or organization; normally require future payments in assets or the rendering of services, or both p. 25

**Net assets** assets minus liabilities; another name for *equity.* p. 25

**Net income** the excess of revenues over expenses for a period. p. 23

**Net loss** the excess of expenses over revenues for a period. p. 23`

**Objectivity principle** the accounting guideline that requires financial statement information to be supported by evidence other than someone's opinion or imagination;

objectivity adds to the reliability and usefulness of accounting information. p. 28

**Paid-in capital**  another name for *contributed capital*. p. 31

**Partnership**  a business that is owned by two or more people and that is not organized as a corporation. p. 30

**Realization principle**  another name for the *revenue recognition principle*. p. 35

**Retained earnings**  the category of shareholders' equity created by a corporation's profitable activities. p. 31

**Return on equity ratio**  the ratio of net income to beginning owner's equity; used to judge a business's success compared to other activities or investments; may be modified for proprietorships or partnerships by subtracting the value of the owner's efforts in managing the business from the reported income. p. 41

**Revenue recognition principle**  the rule that (1) requires revenue to be recognized at the time it is earned, (2) allows the inflow of assets associated with revenue to be in a form other than cash, and (3) measures the amount of revenue as the cash plus the cash equivalent value of any noncash assets received from customers in exchange for goods or services. p. 35

**Revenues**  inflows of cash or other assets received in exchange for providing goods or services to customers; may also occur as decreases in liabilities. p. 23

**Shareholders**  the owners of a corporation; also called *stockholders*. p. 30

**Shares**  units of ownership in a corporation; also called *stock*. p. 30

**Single proprietorship**  a business owned by one individual that is not organized as a corporation. p. 30

**Sole proprietorship**  another name for a *single proprietorship*. p. 30

**Statement of changes in financial position**  a financial statement that describes where a company's cash came from and where it went during the period. p. 40

**Statement of changes in owner's equity**  a financial statement that shows the beginning balance of owner's equity, the changes in equity that resulted from new investments by the owner, net income (or net loss), and withdrawals, and the ending balance. p. 39

**Statement of financial position**  another name for the *balance sheet*. p. 24

**Withdrawal**  a payment from a proprietorship or partnership to its owner or owners. p. 31

## SYNONYMOUS TERMS

**Accounting equation**  balance sheet equation.

**Balance sheet**  statement of financial position; position statement.

**Economic resources**  assets.

**Equity**  net assets; owner's equity.

**Going-concern principle**  continuing-concern principle.

**Revenue recognition principle**  realization principle.

**Shareholders**  stockholders.

**Single proprietorship**  sole proprietorship.

## QUESTIONS

1.  What information is presented in an income statement?

2.  What do accountants mean by the term *revenue?*

3.  Why does the user of an income statement need to know the time period that it covers?

4.  What information is presented in a balance sheet?

5.  Define (a) assets, (b) liabilities, (c) equity, and (d) net assets.

6.  Identify two categories of generally accepted accounting principles.

7.  What AcSB recommendations identify generally accepted accounting principles?

8.  What does the objectivity principle require for information presented in financial statements? Why?

9.  A business shows office stationery on the balance sheet at its $430 cost, although it cannot be sold for more than $10 as scrap paper. Which accounting principles require this treatment?

10.  Why is the revenue recognition principle needed? What does it require?

11.  What events or activities change owner's equity?

12.  Identify four financial statements that a business presents to its owners and other users.

13. What should a company's return on equity ratio be compared with to determine whether the owner has made a good investment?

14. Find the financial statements of Geac Computer Corporation Limited in Appendix I. To what level of significance are the dollar amounts rounded? What time period does the income statement cover?

Geac

15. Review the financial statements of Geac Computer Corporation Limited in Appendix I. What is the amount of total assets reported at April 30, 1994? How much net cash was provided by operating activities during the 1994 year?

---

## QUICK STUDY (Five-Minute Exercises)

Name the financial statement on which each of the following items appears:

**QS 1–1
(LO 1)**

| | | | |
|---|---|---|---|
| a. | Rent expense. | e. | Service fees earned. |
| b. | Store equipment. | f. | Accounts payable. |
| c. | Cash received from customers. | g. | Repayment of bank loan. |
| d. | Owner, withdrawals. | h. | Supplies. |

Identify which broad accounting principle describes most directly each of the following practices:

**QS 1–2
(LO 2)**

a. If $15,000 cash is paid to buy land, the land should be reported on the purchaser's balance sheet at $15,000.

b. Jan Jacobson owns Freeland Bakery and also owns Westside Supplies, both of which are sole proprietorships. In having financial statements prepared for the bakery, Jacobson should be sure that the expense transactions of Westside Supplies are excluded from the statements.

c. In December, 1995, Bartel Great Outdoors received a customer's order to provide two experienced guides for a June 1996 fishing trip in the Yukon. Bartel should record the revenue for the service in June 1996, not in December 1995.

For each of the following situations, determine whether the business is a sole proprietorship, partnership, or corporation.

**QS 1–3
(LO 3)**

a. The equity of Foster Company is divided into 10,000 common shares.

b. Metal Roofing Company is owned by Chris Fisher, who is personally liable for the debts of the business.

c. Jerry Forrentes and Susan Montgomery own Money Services, a company that cashes payroll cheques for individuals and provides a variety of personal services. Neither Forrentes nor Montgomery has personal responsibility for the debts of Money Services.

d. Nancy Kerr and Frank Maples own Downtown Runners, a courier service. Both Kerr and Maples are personally liable for any debts of the business.

**QS 1–4**
**(LO 4)**

Determine the missing amount for each of the following equations:

|  | Assets = | Liabilities + | Owner's Equity |
|---|---|---|---|
| a. | $ 25,000 | $13,500 | ? |
| b. | $100,000 | ? | $28,500 |
| c. | ? | $62,500 | $31,800 |

**QS 1–5**
**(LO 4)**

Use the accounting equation to determine:

a.  The owner's equity in a business that has $249,800 of assets and $168,300 of liabilities.

b.  The liabilities of a business having $100,600 of assets and $84,000 of owner's equity.

c.  The assets of a business having $25,100 of liabilities and $75,000 of owner's equity.

**QS 1–6**
**(LO 1)**

In its 1993 financial statements, the Boeing Company, which is the largest aerospace company in North America, reported the following:

| | |
|---|---|
| Sales and other operating revenues . . . . . . . . . | $25,438 million |
| Net earnings (net income) . . . . . . . . . . . . . . | 1,244 million |
| Total assets . . . . . . . . . . . . . . . . . . . . . . . . . | 20,450 million |
| Total beginning-of-year shareholders' equity . . | 8,056 million |
| Total end-of-year shareholders' equity . . . . . . . | 8,983 million |

Calculate the return on beginning equity.

# EXERCISES

**Exercise 1–1**
Effects of transactions on the accounting equation
**(LO 4)**

The following equation shows the effects of five transactions on the assets, liabilities, and owner's equity of Dr. Kirby's dental practice. Write short descriptions of the probable nature of each transaction.

| | | Assets | | | | Liabil-ities | | Owner's Equity |
|---|---|---|---|---|---|---|---|---|
| | Cash | + Accounts Receivable | + Office Supplies | + Land = | Accounts Payable | + M. Kirby, Capital |
| | $15,000 | | $5,000 | $29,000 | | $49,000 |
| a. | − 6,000 | | | + 6,000 | | |
| | $ 9,000 | | $5,000 | $35,000 | | $49,000 |
| b. | | | + 800 | | $ 800 | |
| | $ 9,000 | | $5,800 | $35,000 | $ 800 | $49,000 |
| c. | | $2,100 | | | | + 2,100 |
| | $ 9,000 | $2,100 | $5,800 | $35,000 | $ 800 | $51,100 |
| d. | − 800 | | | | − 800 | |
| | $ 8,200 | $2,100 | $5,800 | $35,000 | $ 0 | $51,100 |
| e. | + 2,100 | −2,100 | | | | |
| | $10,300 + | $ 0 + | $5,800 + | $35,000 = | $ 0 + | $51,100 |

**Exercise 1–2**
Analyzing the accounting equation
**(LO 4)**

Chris Bevit began operating a new consulting firm on January 15. The accounting equation showed the following balances after each of the company's first five transactions. Analyze the equations and describe each of the five transactions with their amounts.

| After Transaction | Cash | + Accounts Receivable | + Office Supplies | + Office Furniture | = Accounts Payable | + C. Bevit, Capital |
|---|---|---|---|---|---|---|
| a. ........ | $60,000 | $ 0 | $ 0 | $ 0 | $ 0 | $60,000 |
| b. ........ | 58,000 | 0 | 3,500 | 0 | 1,500 | 60,000 |
| c. ........ | 42,000 | 0 | 3,500 | 16,000 | 1,500 | 60,000 |
| d. ........ | 42,000 | 4,000 | 3,500 | 16,000 | 1,500 | 64,000 |
| e. ........ | 35,000 | 4,000 | 3,500 | 16,000 | 1,500 | 57,000 |

A business had the following amounts of assets and liabilities at the beginning and end of a recent year:

Exercise 1–3
Determining net income
(LO 1, 4)

| | Assets | Liabilities |
|---|---|---|
| Beginning of the year . . . . | $150,000 | $60,000 |
| End of the year . . . . . . . | 240,000 | 92,000 |

Determine the net income earned or net loss incurred by the business during the year under each of the following unrelated assumptions:

a.  The owner made no additional investments in the business and withdrew no assets during the year.

b.  The owner made no additional investments in the business during the year but withdrew $3,500 per month to pay personal living expenses.

c.  The owner withdrew no assets during the year but invested an additional $65,000 cash in the business.

d.  The owner withdrew $4,500 per month to pay personal living expenses and invested an additional $20,000 cash in the business at the end of the year.

Cathy Egan began a professional practice on July 1 and plans to prepare financial statements at the end of each month. During July, Egan completed these transactions:

Exercise 1–4
The effects of
transactions on the
accounting equation
(LO 1, 4)

a.  Invested $25,000 cash and equipment that had a $5,000 fair market (cash equivalent) value.

b.  Paid $800 rent for office space for the month.

c.  Purchased $6,000 of additional equipment on credit.

d.  Completed work for a client and immediately collected $1,000 cash.

e.  Completed work for a client and sent a bill for $3,500 to be paid within 30 days.

f.  Purchased $4,000 of additional equipment for cash.

g.  Paid an assistant $1,200 as wages for the month.

h.  Collected $2,500 of the amount owed by the client described in transaction e.

i.  Paid for the equipment purchased in transaction c.

**Required**

Create a table like the one in Illustration 1–6, using the following headings for the columns: Cash; Accounts Receivable; Equipment; Accounts Payable; and Cathy Egan, Capital. Then, use additions and subtractions to show the effects of the transactions on the elements of the equation. Show new totals after each transaction. Once you have completed the table, determine Egan's income for July. Determine the return on Egan's initial investment for the month of July.

**Exercise 1–5**
The effects of
transactions on the
accounting equation
**(LO 4)**

Following are seven pairs of changes in elements of the accounting equation. Provide an example of a transaction that creates the described effects:

a.  Decreases an asset and decreases equity.

b.  Decreases an asset and decreases a liability.

c.  Decreases a liability and increases a liability.

d.  Increases an asset and decreases an asset.

e.  Increases an asset and increases a liability.

f.  Increases an asset and increases equity.

g.  Increases a liability and decreases equity.

**Exercise 1–6**
Income statement
**(LO 1)**

On July 1, Maia Mears began the practice of tax accounting under the name of Maia Mears, Accountant. On July 31, the company's records showed the following items. Use this information to prepare a July income statement for the business.

| | | | |
|---|---|---|---|
| Cash . . . . . . . . . . . . . . . | $ 4,000 | Owner's withdrawals . . . . . . | $1,500 |
| Accounts receivable . . . . | 5,000 | Tax fees earned . . . . . . . . . . | 5,000 |
| Office supplies . . . . . . . | 750 | Miscellaneous expenses . . . . | 180 |
| Tax library . . . . . . . . . . | 12,000 | Rent expense . . . . . . . . . . . | 850 |
| Office equipment . . . . . . | 9,000 | Salaries expense . . . . . . . . . | 2,000 |
| Accounts payable . . . . . . | 2,500 | Telephone expense . . . . . . . | 220 |
| Owner's investments . . . | 28,000 | | |

**Exercise 1–7**
Statement of changes in
owner's equity
**(LO 1)**

Use the facts in Exercise 1–6 to prepare a July statement of changes in owner's equity for the business of Maia Mears, Accountant.

**Exercise 1–8**
Balance sheet
**(LO 1)**

Use the facts in Exercise 1–6 to prepare a July 31 balance sheet for the business of Maia Mears, Accountant.

**Exercise 1–9**
Information in financial
statements
**(LO 1)**

Match each of these numbered items with the financial statement or statements on which it should be presented. Indicate your answer by writing the letter or letters for the correct statement in the blank space next to each item.

A. Income statement          C. Balance sheet
B. Statement of changes      D. Statement of changes in financial position
   in owner's equity

____ 1. Cash received from customers.          ____ 5. Accounts payable.

____ 2. Office supplies.                        ____ 6. Investments of cash by owner.

____ 3. Rent expense paid in cash.             ____ 7. Accounts receivable.

____ 4. Consulting fees earned and received as cash. ____ 8. Cash withdrawals by owner.

**Exercise 1–10**
Missing information
**(LO 4)**

Calculate the amount of the missing item in each of the following independent cases:

| | a | b | c | d |
|---|---|---|---|---|
| Owner's equity, January 1 . . . . . . . . . . . | $    0 | $    0 | $    0 | $    0 |
| Owner's investments during the year . . . . | 80,000 | ? | 42,000 | 50,000 |
| Owner's withdrawals during the year . . . . | ? | (36,000) | (20,000) | (21,000) |
| Net income (loss) for the year . . . . . . . . | 21,000 | 54,000 | (6,000) | ? |
| Owner's equity, December 31 . . . . . . . . | 68,000 | 66,000 | ? | 57,000 |

Match each of these numbered descriptions with the term it best describes. Indicate your answer by writing the letter for the correct principle in the blank space next to each description.

A. Broad principle
B. Cost principle
C. Business entity principle
D. Revenue recognition principle
E. Specific principle
F. Objectivity principle
G. Going-concern principle

___1. Requires every business to be accounted for separately from its owner or owners.

___2. Requires financial statement information to be supported by evidence other than someone's opinion or imagination.

___3. Usually created by a pronouncement from an authoritative body.

___4. Requires financial statement information to be based on costs incurred in transactions.

___5. Derived from long-used accounting practices.

___6. Requires financial statements to reflect the assumption that the business will continue operating instead of being closed or sold.

___7. Requires revenue to be recorded only when the earnings process is complete.

Use the information for each of the following independent cases to calculate the company's return on equity:

|  | a | b | c | d |
|---|---|---|---|---|
| Beginning equity . . . . | $25,000 | $400,000 | $150,000 | $286,400 |
| Net income . . . . . . . . | 5,400 | 108,000 | 45,750 | 88,965 |

# PROBLEMS

Ranca Carr secured her license and opened an architect's office. During its first year, the following transactions affected Carr's business:

Problem 1–1
Analyzing the effects of
transactions on the
accounting equation
(LO 4)

a. Carr sold a personal investment in Royal Bank for $44,000, and deposited $30,000 of the proceeds in a bank account opened in the name of the business.

b. Carr invested $15,000 of her own personal office equipment in the business.

c. The business paid $150,000 for a small building to be used as an office. It paid $25,000 in cash and signed a note payable promising to pay the balance over several years.

d. Purchased $2,000 of office supplies for cash.

e. Purchased $18,000 of office equipment on credit.

f. Completed a project design on credit and billed the client $2,000 for the work.

g. Paid a local newspaper $500 for an announcement that the office had opened.

h. Designed a house for a client and collected a $9,000 cash commission on completion of the construction.

i. Made a $1,000 payment on the equipment purchased in transaction e.

j. Received $1,500 from the client described in transaction f.

*k.* Paid $1,250 cash for the office secretary's wages.

*l.* Carr withdrew $4,000 from the company bank account to pay personal living expenses.

**Required**

*Preparation component:*

1. Create a table like the one in Illustration 1–6, using the following headings for the columns: Cash; Accounts Receivable; Office Supplies; Office Equipment; Building; Accounts Payable; Notes Payable; and Ranca Carr, Capital. Leave space for an Explanation column to the right of the Capital column.

2. Use additions and subtractions to show the transactions' effects on the elements of the equation. Show new totals after each transaction. Also, indicate next to each change in the owner's equity whether it was caused by an investment, a revenue, an expense, or a withdrawal.

3. Once you have completed the table, determine the company's net income.

4. Determine the return on the beginning-of-period equity, which consisted of the two amounts invested by Carr in transactions *a* and *b*.

*Analysis component:*

5. State whether you think the practice is a good use of Carr's money, if an investment in low-risk bonds would have returned 6% for the same period.

**Problem 1–2**
Balance sheet and income statement
**(LO 1, 3)**

Benny Gates graduated from college in May with a degree in photographic arts. On June 1, Gates invested $30,000 in a new business under the name Benny Gates, Photographer. Gates plans on preparing financial statements for the business at the end of each month. The following transactions occurred during the first month:

| June | 1 | Rented the furnished office and darkroom equipment of a photographer who was retiring. Gates paid $1,600 cash for the rent. |
| | 2 | Purchased photography supplies for $840 cash. |
| | 4 | Paid $400 cash for the month's cleaning services. |
| | 7 | Completed work for a client and immediately collected $300 cash. |
| | 13 | Completed work for Carl Simone on credit, $1,500. |
| | 15 | Paid $425 cash for an assistant's salary for the first half of the month. |
| | 20 | Received payment in full for the work completed for Carl Simone on June 13. |
| | 20 | Completed work for Wendy Nation on credit, $1,400 |
| | 21 | Purchased additional photography supplies on credit, $500. |
| | 25 | Completed work for Billie Carr on credit, $950. |
| | 26 | Picked up brochures to be used right away to advertise the studio. Gates purchased them from a printer at a cost of $180, which he is to pay within 30 days. |
| | 28 | Received full payment from Wendy Nation for the work completed on June 20. |

| June | 29 | Paid for the photography supplies purchased on June 21. |
|------|----|---------------------------------------------------------|
|      | 30 | Paid $100 cash for the month's telephone bill. |
|      | 30 | Paid $240 cash for the month's utilities. |
|      | 30 | Paid $425 cash for an assistant's salary for the second half of the month. |
|      | 30 | Purchased insurance protection for the next 12 months (beginning July 1) by paying a $1,500 premium. Because none of this insurance protection had been used up, it was considered to be an asset called Prepaid Insurance. |
|      | 30 | Gates withdrew $560 from the business for personal use. |

**Required**

1. Arrange the following asset, liability, and owner's equity titles in an equation like Illustration 1–6: Cash; Accounts Receivable; Prepaid Insurance; Photography Supplies; Accounts Payable; and Benny Gates, Capital. Include an Explanation column for changes in owner's equity.

2. Show the effects of the transactions on the elements of the equation by recording increases and decreases in the appropriate columns. Indicate an increase with a + and a decrease with a − before the amount. Do not determine new totals for the items of the equation after each transaction. Next to each change in Benny Gates, Capital, state whether it was caused by an investment, a revenue, an expense, or a withdrawal. Determine the final total for each item and verify that the equation is in balance.

3. Prepare an income statement for June, a statement of changes in owner's equity for June, and a June 30 balance sheet.

The accounting records of Carmen King's dental practice show the following assets and liabilities as of the end of 1996 and 1997:

**Problem 1–3**
Calculating and interpreting net income and preparing a balance sheet
**(LO 1, 3)**

|  | December 31 | |
|--|:--:|:--:|
|  | **1996** | **1997** |
| Cash | $35,000 | $ 12,500 |
| Accounts receivable | 19,000 | 14,900 |
| Dental supplies | 3,000 | 2,200 |
| Dental equipment | 92,000 | 98,000 |
| Office equipment | 36,000 | 36,000 |
| Land | | 30,000 |
| Building | | 120,000 |
| Accounts payable | 5,000 | 25,000 |
| Note payable | | 70,000 |

Late in December 1997 (just before the amounts in the second column were calculated), King purchased a small office building in the name of the practice, Carmen King, D.D.S., and moved the practice from rented quarters to the new building. The building and the land it occupies cost $150,000. The practice paid $80,000 in cash and a note payable was signed for the balance. King had to invest an additional $35,000 cash in the practice to enable it to pay the $80,000. The practice earned a satisfactory net income during 1997, which enabled King to withdraw $3,000 per month from the practice for personal living expenses.

**Required**

*Preparation component:*

1.  Prepare balance sheets for the business as of the end of 1996 and the end of 1997. (Remember that owner's equity equals the difference between the assets and the liabilities.)

2.  By comparing the owner's equity amounts from the balance sheets and using the additional information presented in the problem, prepare a calculation to show how much net income was earned by the business during 1997.

3.  Calculate the return on equity for the dental practice, using the beginning balance of owner's equity for the year.

*Analysis component:*

4.  Consider the possibility that King might have organized the business as a corporation which would have paid King a salary of $25,000. Would organizing the business as a corporation instead of as a proprietorship affect your evaluation of return on equity? Explain why.

**Problem 1–4**
Analyzing transactions
and preparing financial
statements
**(LO 1, 3)**

Thom Stone began a new financial planning practice and completed these transactions during April:

| April | 1 | Transferred $28,000 from a personal savings account to a checking account opened in the name of the business, Thom Stone, C.F.P. |
|---|---|---|
| | 1 | Rented the furnished office of a planner who was retiring, and paid cash for the month's rent of $400. |
| | 2 | Purchased the retiring person's professional library for $7,000 by paying $1,600 in cash and agreeing to pay the balance in six months. |
| | 4 | Purchased office supplies by paying $450 cash. |
| | 6 | Completed planning work for Karl Hubbell and immediately collected $500 for doing the work. |
| | 9 | Purchased $1,900 of office equipment on credit. |
| | 15 | Completed planning work for Carol Banks on credit in the amount of $2,000. |
| | 19 | Purchased $250 of office supplies on credit. |
| | 21 | Paid for the office equipment purchased on April 9. |
| | 25 | Billed Sy Young $300 for planning work; the balance is due in 30 days. |
| | 29 | Received $2,000 from Carol Banks for the work completed on April 15. |
| | 30 | Paid the office assistant's salary of $1,600. |
| | 30 | Paid the monthly utility bills of $220. |
| | 30 | Withdrew $500 from the business for personal living expenses. |

**Required**

*Preparation component:*

1.  Arrange the following asset, liability, and owner's equity titles in an equation like Illustration 1–6: Cash; Accounts Receivable; Office Supplies; Professional Library; Office Equipment; Accounts Payable; and Thom Stone, Capital. Leave space for an Explanation column to the right of Thom Stone, Capital.

2. Use additions and subtractions to show the effects of each transaction on the items in the equation. Show new totals after each transaction. Next to each change in owner's equity, state whether the change was caused by an investment, a revenue, an expense, or a withdrawal.

3. Use the increases and decreases in the last column of the equation to prepare an income statement and a statement of changes in owner's equity for the month. Also prepare a balance sheet as of the end of the month.

4. Calculate the return on equity for the month, using the initial investment as the beginning balance of equity.

*Analysis component:*

5. Assume that the investment transaction on April 1 had been for $20,000 instead of $28,000 and the $8,000 difference had been borrowed from a bank. Explain the effect of this change on total assets, total liabilities, owner's equity, and return on equity.

The following financial statement information is known about five unrelated companies:

**Problem 1–5**
Missing information
**(LO 1)**

| | Company A | Company B | Company C | Company D | Company E |
|---|---|---|---|---|---|
| **December 31, 1996:** | | | | | |
| Assets .......... | $90,000 | $70,000 | $58,000 | $40,000 | $82,000 |
| Liabilities ........ | 47,000 | 45,000 | 28,000 | 19,000 | ? |
| **December 31, 1997:** | | | | | |
| Assets .......... | 96,000 | 82,000 | ? | 62,500 | 75,000 |
| Liabilities ....... | ? | 55,000 | 38,000 | 32,000 | 50,000 |
| **During 1997:** | | | | | |
| Owner investments .. | 10,000 | 3,000 | 15,500 | ? | 3,000 |
| Net income ....... | 15,000 | ? | 9,000 | 6,000 | 12,000 |
| Owner withdrawals .. | 5,000 | 7,000 | 6,500 | 0 | 6,000 |

**Required**

1. Answer the following questions about Company A:

   *a.* What was the owner's equity on December 31, 1996?

   *b.* What was the owner's equity on December 31, 1997?

   *c.* What was the amount of liabilities owed on December 31, 1997?

2. Answer the following questions about Company B:

   *a.* What was the owner's equity on December 31, 1996?

   *b.* What was the owner's equity on December 31, 1997?

   *c.* What was the net income for 1997?

3. Calculate the amount of assets owned by Company C on December 31, 1997.

4. Calculate the amount of owner investments in Company D made during 1997.

5. Calculate the amount of liabilities owed by Company E on December 31, 1996.

Identify how each of the following transactions affects the company's financial statements. For the balance sheet, identify how each transaction affects total assets, total liabilities, and owner's equity. For the income statement, identify how each transaction affects Net Income. For the statement of changes in financial position, identify how each transaction affects cash flows from operating activities, cash flows from financing activities, and cash flows from investing activities. If there is an increase, place a + in the column or columns. If

**Problem 1–6**
Identifying the effects of transactions on the financial statements
**(LO 1, 3)**

there is a decrease, place a − in the column or columns. If there is both an increase and a decrease, place +/− in the column or columns. The line for the first transaction is completed as an example.

| Transaction | Balance Sheet | | | Income Statement | Statement of Changes in Financial Position | | |
| | Total Assets | Total Liabilities | Equity | Net Income | Operating | Financing | Investing |
|---|---|---|---|---|---|---|---|
| 1  Owner invests cash | + | | + | | | + | |
| 2  Sell services for cash | | | | | | | |
| 3  Acquire services on credit | | | | | | | |
| 4  Pay wages with cash | | | | | | | |
| 5  Owner withdraws cash | | | | | | | |
| 6  Borrow cash with note payable | | | | | | | |
| 7  Sell services on credit | | | | | | | |
| 8  Buy office equipment for cash | | | | | | | |
| 9  Collect receivable from (7) | | | | | | | |
| 10  Buy asset with note payable | | | | | | | |

**Problem 1–7**
Analytical essay
**(LO 4)**

Review the facts presented in Problem 1–2. Now assume that all of the company's revenue transactions generated cash (that is, none had been made on credit). Also assume that all of the expense and purchase transactions used cash and none were on credit. Describe the differences, if any, these alternate assumptions would create for the income statement, the statement of changes in owner's equity, and the balance sheet. Construct your answer in general terms without stating the actual dollar amounts of each difference. Be certain to explain why each statement would or would not be affected by the changes in the assumptions.

Review the facts presented in Problem 1–1 for transactions *f* and *j*. Identify the transaction that creates a revenue and explain your answer. Then explain why the other transaction did not create a revenue. Next, review the facts for transactions *d* and *k*. Identify the transaction that creates an expense for the current reporting period and explain your answer. Finally, explain why the other transaction did not create an expense.

**Problem 1–8**
Analytical essay
**(LO 2, 4)**

Carol Olds secured her broker's license and opened a real estate office. During a short period, she completed these transactions:

**Problem 1–9**
Effects of transactions on the accounting equation
**(LO 4)**

*a.* Sold for $62,500 a personal investment in General Electric shares, which she had inherited, and deposited $60,000 of the proceeds in a bank account opened in the name of the business, Carol Olds, Realtor.

*b.* Purchased for $150,000 a small building to be used as an office. She paid $45,000 in cash and signed a note payable promising to pay the balance over a period of years.

*c.* Purchased office equipment for cash, $11,600.

*d.* Took from home for use in the business office equipment having a $700 fair value.

*e.* Purchased on credit office supplies, $100, and office equipment, $5,000.

*f.* Paid the local paper $165 for advertising.

*g.* Completed a real estate appraisal for a client on credit and billed the client $250 for the work done.

*h.* Sold a house and collected a $10,000 cash commission on completion of the sale.

*i.* Carol Olds withdrew $2,000 from the business to pay personal expenses.

*j.* The client paid for the appraisal of transaction *g*.

*k.* Made a $2,500 installment payment on the amount owed from transaction *e*.

*l.* Paid the office secretary's wages, $950.

**Required**

1. Arrange the following asset, liability, and owner's equity titles in an equation like Illustration 1–6: Cash; Accounts Receivable; Office Supplies; Office Equipment; Building; Accounts Payable; Notes Payable; and Carol Olds, Capital. Leave space for an Explanation column to the right of Carol Olds, Capital.

2. Show by additions and subtractions the effects of each transaction on the elements of the equation. Show new totals after each transaction. Next to each change in Carol Olds, Capital, state whether the change was caused by an investment, a revenue, an expense, or a withdrawal.

Gary Meyer graduated from law school in May 1996, and on June 1 began a law practice by investing $5,000 in cash in the practice. He also transferred to the business office equipment having a cash value of $8,500. Then, he completed these additional transactions during June:

**Problem 1–10**
Analyzing transactions and preparing financial statements
**(LO 1, 3)**

June   1   Rented the office of a lawyer who was retiring and paid the rent for June, $800.

    1   Moved from home to the law office law books acquired at university. (In other words, invested the books in the practice.) The books had a $600 fair value.

June    2    Purchased office supplies for cash, $120.

         4    Purchased additional law books costing $1,500. Paid $500 in cash and promised to pay the balance within 90 days.

         5    Completed legal work for a client and immediately collected $500 for the work done.

      10    Completed legal work for Village Bank on credit, $1,500.

      15    Purchased additional office supplies on credit, $50.

      20    Received $1,500 from Village Bank for the work completed on June 10.

      25    Completed legal work for Astor Realty on credit, $1,300.

      30    Made a $300 installment payment on the law books purchased on June 4.

      30    Paid the June telephone bill, $70.

      30    Paid the office secretary's wages, $1,200.

      30    Gary Meyer took $1,400 out of the business for his personal use.

**Required**

1. Arrange the following asset, liability, and owner's equity titles in an equation like Illustration 1–6: Cash; Accounts Receivable; Office Supplies; Law Library; Office Equipment; Accounts Payable; and Gary Meyer, Capital. Leave space for an Explanation column to the right of Gary Meyer, Capital.

2. Show by additions and subtractions the effects of each transaction on the elements of the equation. Show new totals after each transaction. Next to each change in Gary Meyer, Capital, state whether the change was caused by an investment, a revenue, an expense, or a withdrawal.

3. Analyze the items in the last column of the equation and prepare a June income statement for the practice.

4. Prepare a June statement of changes in owner's equity.

5. Prepare a June 30 balance sheet.

**Problem 1–11**
Preparation of balance sheet; calculation of net income
(LO 1, 3)

The accounting records of Viola Nunez's medical practice show the following assets and liabilities as of the end of 1995 and 1996:

|  | December 31 | |
|---|---|---|
|  | 1995 | 1996 |
| Cash .............. | $ 9,600 | $ 1,600 |
| Accounts receivable .... | 5,700 | 7,000 |
| Office supplies ........ | 1,000 | 800 |
| Automobile .......... | 4,800 | 4,800 |
| Office equipment ...... | 18,500 | 23,200 |
| Land .............. |  | 70,000 |
| Building ............ |  | 125,000 |
| Accounts payable ...... | 1,400 | 1,600 |
| Notes payable ........ |  | 145,000 |

During the last week of December 1996 (just before the amounts above were calculated), Dr. Nunez purchased a small office building in the name of the medical practice, Viola Nunez, M.D., and moved her practice from rented quarters to the new building. The building and the land it occupies cost $195,000; the practice paid $50,000 in cash and signed a note payable for the balance. Dr. Nunez had to invest an additional $40,000 in the practice to enable it to pay the $50,000. The practice earned a satisfactory net income during 1995, which enabled Dr. Nunez to withdraw $3,200 per month from the practice to pay her personal living expenses.

**Required**

1.  Prepare two balance sheets for the business, as of the end of 1995 and the end of 1996. (Remember that the owner's equity equals assets less liabilities.)
2.  Using the information presented above and by comparing the owner's equity in the balance sheets, prepare a calculation to show the net income earned by the business during 1996.

An analysis of cash and accounts receivable transactions of Townsend Office Services for the month of October 1996 indicates the following:

**Problem 1–12**
Analyzing transactions
and preparing financial
statements
**(LO 1, 4)**

Cash account:

| | |
|---|---:|
| Beginning balance | $ 900 |
| Sandy Townsend, additional investment | 9,000 |
| Collection of accounts receivable | 4,500 |
| Payment of office rent for 3 months (Oct.–Dec.) | 1,800 |
| Rental payment for office equipment (for October) | 450 |
| Payment of wages including Townsend of $2,250 | 5,250 |
| Payment of utilities, telephone, and advertising | 900 |
| Partial payment for office supplies (cost $1,500) | 750 |

Accounts receivable:

| | |
|---|---:|
| Beginning balance | 1,800 |
| Billings during the month | 6,750 |
| Collection of accounts receivable | 4,500 |

**Additional information**

$1,400 of office supplies were on hand on October 31.

**Required**

1.  Prepare the October income statement.
2.  Prepare the October 31 balance sheet.
3.  Determine the October 1, 1996, balance in Sandra Townsend's capital account.

Megan Brinks ran out of money at the end of the first semester of her sophomore year in college. She had to go to work, but she could not find a satisfactory job. However, since she had an automobile, she decided to go into business for herself. Consequently, she began Megan's Delivery Service with no assets other than the automobile, which had a fair market value of $8,400. She kept no accounting records; and now, at the year-end, she has engaged you to determine the net income earned by the service during its first year. You find that the service has a $700 year-end bank balance plus $50 of undeposited cash. Local stores owe the service $125 for delivering packages during the past month. In the last week of the year, Megan sold the automobile for $7,500, and used the cash proceeds to help buy a new delivery truck that cost $16,800. The service still owes a finance company $7,000 as a result of the truck's purchase. Also, when the truck was purchased, Megan borrowed $1,500 from her father to help make the down payment. The loan was made to the delivery service, was interest free, and has not been repaid. Finally, since the service has been profitable from the beginning, Megan has withdrawn $300 of its earnings each week for the 52 weeks of its existence to pay personal living expenses.

Determine and present a calculation to prove the net income earned by the business during the first year of its operations.

**Problem 1–13**
Analytical essay
**(LO 4)**

**Problem 1–14**
Identifying the effects of transactions on the financial statements
**(LO 1, 3)**

Identify how each of the following transactions affects the company's financial statements. For the balance sheet, identify how each transaction affects total assets, total liabilities, and owner's equity. For the income statement, identify how each transaction affects Net Income. For the statement of changes in financial position, identify how each transaction affects cash flows from operating activities, cash flows from financing activities, and cash flows from investing activities. If there is an increase, place a "+" in the column or columns. If there is a decrease, place "−" in the column or columns. If there is both an increase and a decrease, place "+/−" in the column or columns. The line for the first transaction is completed as an example.

| Transaction | Balance Sheet | | | Income Statement | Statement of Changes in Financial Position | | |
| --- | --- | --- | --- | --- | --- | --- | --- |
| | Total Assets | Total Liabilities | Equity | Net Income | Operating | Financing | Investing |
| 1  Owner invests cash | + | | + | | | + | |
| 2  Buy store equipment for cash | | | | | | | |
| 3  Buy asset with note payable | | | | | | | |
| 4  Sell services for cash | | | | | | | |
| 5  Acquire services on account | | | | | | | |
| 6  Sell services on credit | | | | | | | |
| 7  Borrow cash from bank | | | | | | | |
| 8  Collect receivable from (6) | | | | | | | |
| 9  Owner withdraws cash | | | | | | | |
| 10  Pay wages with cash | | | | | | | |

**Problem 1–15**
Analytical essay
**(LO 4)**

Review the facts presented in Problem 1–10. Now assume that all of the company's revenue transactions generated cash (that is, none had been made on credit). Also assume that all of the expense and purchase transactions used cash and none were on credit. Describe the differences, if any, these alternate assumptions would create for the income statement, the statement of changes in owner's equity, and the balance sheet. Construct your answer in general terms without stating the actual dollar amounts of each difference. Be certain to explain why each statement would or would not be affected by the changes in the assumptions.

Review the facts presented in Problem 1–9 for transactions *g* and *j*. Identify the transactions that creates a revenue and explain your answer. Then explain why the other transaction did not create a revenue. Next, review the facts for transactions *e* and *l*. Identify the transaction that creates an expense for the current reporting period and explain your answer. Finally, explain why the other transaction did not create an expense.

**Problem 1–16**
Analytical essay
**(LO 2, 4)**

---

# PROVOCATIVE PROBLEMS

On Friday, September 3, Ann Walker invested $1,000 cash in a small enterprise to participate in a local flea market set up in her neighbourhood for the Labour Day weekend. In the name of her business, Ann's Bangles and Baubles, she paid $250 rent for space in the market to sell various kinds of costume jewellery. She also paid $50 cash for plastic jewellery boxes and paid her teenage children $130 to build a booth just for the market. Because she didn't plan to do this again until the next year, she planned to abandon the booth after the market closed. Walker purchased her jewellery from a local wholesaler at a total cost of $900 but because she had only $570 in cash, could not pay the full price in cash. However, the wholesaler knew that Walker's credit was good and agreed to accept $500 in cash and the promise that she would pay the $400 balance the day after the market closed. Over the weekend, she sold most of the jewellery for $2,000 cash and paid an assistant $90 cash for helping her. When the market closed, Walker estimated that her unsold goods could be returned to the wholesaler for their original cost of $60. Because of the large number of sales, none of the jewellery boxes was left.

Walker cannot decide whether this venture might be a good thing to repeat in the future. She needs to know whether she earned a satisfactory profit for the time and money that she put into it. Use the methods described in the chapter to develop the information. Prepare an income statement and a statement of changes in owner's equity for the four-day period ending on Monday, September 6. Also prepare a balance sheet as of the close of business on September 6. Then, evaluate whether you think her effort was suitably rewarded by the results, assuming that she could have earned $540 in wages on another job.

**Provocative Problem
1–1**
Weekend market
**(LO 1, 3)**

Geac Computer Corporation Limited, is in the business of manufacturing and marketing computer systems as well as software and other related products and services. The financial statements and other information from Geac's 1994 annual report are included in Appendix I at the end of the book. Use information from that report to answer the following questions:

**Provocative Problem
1–2**
Financial statement
analysis case
**(LO 1)**

1. Examine Geac's consolidated balance sheet. To what level of significance are the dollar amounts rounded?
2. What is the closing date of Geac's most recent annual reporting period?
3. What amount of net income did Geac have during the 1994 year?
4. How much cash (and cash equivalents) did the company hold at the end of the 1994 reporting period?
5. What was the net amount of cash provided by the company's operating activities during the 1994 year?
6. Did the company's investing activities for 1993 create a net cash inflow or outflow? What was the amount of the net flow?
7. Compare 1994's results to 1993's results to determine whether the company's total revenues increased or decreased. If so, what was the amount of the increase or decrease?

8. What was the change in the company's net income between 1994 and 1993?
9. What amount was reported as total assets at the end of the 1994 reporting period?
10. Calculate the return on beginning shareholders' equity that Geac achieved in 1994.

**Provocative Problem 1–3
Dofasco Inc.
(LO 3)**

Dofasco Inc. is one of Canada's leading steel producers. In a recent annual report, the notes to the financial statements included the following comments:

14. RELATED PARTY TRANSACTIONS

Mr J.D. Leitch, a director and chairman of the Corporation [Dofasco], is a director of Upper Lakes Group Inc., which controls ULS Corporation. During 1993, the Corporation was required by contract to offer ULS Corporation its entire requirements for water transport of the Corporation's bulk raw materials to Hamilton, and ULS Corporation was required to provide such transport. Freight rates are negotiated annually. Shipping charges totalled $28.5 million in 1993 (1992–$34.6 million).

The Corporation purchases iron ore pellets under contract from the Quebec Cartier Mining Company at market prices and on normal trade terms. [Authors' note: Dofasco owns 50% of QCM.] Total pellet purchases from QCM amounted to $96.1 million in 1993 (1992–$90.9 million). At December 31, 1993 the Corporation owed QCM $10.1 million (1992–$7.3 million).

**Required**

Explain why Dofasco might have included these comments in its report. What accounting principle might be compromised by related-party transactions like the ones described?

---

# ANALYTICAL AND REVIEW PROBLEMS

**A & R Problem 1–1**

Allan Russell began his Auto Repair Shop the first part of this month. The balance sheet, prepared by an inexperienced part-time bookkeeper is shown below:

**RUSSELL AUTO REPAIR SHOP**
**Balance Sheet**
**November 30, 1996**

| Assets | | Liabilities and Owner's Equity | |
|---|---|---|---|
| Cash | $ 4,500 | Parts and supplies | $ 7,875 |
| Accounts payable | 24,750 | Accounts receivable | 33,750 |
| Equipment | 15,750 | Prepaid rent | 2,250 |
| Allan Russell, capital | 19,125 | Mortgage payable | 20,250 |
| Total assets | $64,125 | Total equities | $64,125 |

**Required**

1. Prepare a correct balance sheet.
2. Explain why the incorrect balance sheet can be in balance.

**A & R Problem 1–2**

Gitanjli Datt began the practice of law the first day of October with an initial investment of $7,500 in cash. After completing the first month of practice, the financial statements were being prepared by Jim Graham, the secretary/bookkeeper Ms. Datt had hired. The statements were completed, and Ms. Datt almost burst out laughing when she saw them. She had completed a course in legal accounting in law school and knew the statements prepared by Mr. Graham left much to be desired. Consequently, she asks you to revise the statements. The Graham version is presented below:

**GITANJLI DATT, LAWYER**
**Balance Sheet**
**October 31, 1996**

| Assets | | Owner's Equity | |
|---|---|---|---|
| Cash ............ | $2,700 | G. Datt, capital ... | $5,250 |
| Prepaid rent ....... | 1,500 | | |
| Supplies expense ..... | 300 | | |
| Accounts payable .... | 750 | | $5,250 |
| | $5,250 | | |

**GITANJLI DATT, LAWYER**
**Income Statement**
**For the Month Ended October 31, 1996**

| | | |
|---|---|---|
| Revenues: | | |
| Legal fees .......... | $8,250 | |
| Accounts receivable .... | 1,500 | $ 9,750 |
| Expenses: | | |
| Salaries expense ....... | $2,100 | |
| Telephone expense ..... | 150 | |
| Rent expense ......... | 1,500 | |
| Supplies ............ | 750 | |
| Law library ......... | 6,000 | 10,500 |
| Loss ................ | | $ 750 |

**Required**

Prepare the corrected financial statements for Gitanjli Datt.

# CONCEPT TESTER

Test your understanding of the concepts introduced in this chapter by completing the following crossword puzzle.

**Across Clues**

1. Equity of a corporation divided into units.
4. Generally accepted accounting principles.
6. The owners of a corporation.
8. Inflows of assets received in exchange for goods and services provided to customers.
9. The difference between a company's assets and liabilities.
10. Payments of cash by a corporation to its shareholders.

**Down Clues**

2. Generally accepted auditing standards.
3. Debts owed by a business organization.
5. Property or economic resources owned by a business.
7. Outflows or the using up of assets as a result of the major operations of a business.

## ANSWERS TO PROGRESS CHECKS

1–1  *d*

1–2  An expense is a cost incurred by a firm in the process of earning revenue.

1–3  "Financial Statement Concepts" identifies relevance and reliability as two qualities of useful information.

1–4  A company's financial statements present its activities separately from its owner's activities because separate information is necessary for evaluating the company.

1–5  The equipment should be reported at its $25,000 cost, according to the cost principle.

1–6  *c*

1–7  A proprietor's withdrawals are not reported on the company's income statement because they are not expenses incurred to generate revenues.

1–8  *b*

1–9  No. If a liability increases, one or more of three other things must happen: an asset increases, or equity decreases, or another liability decreases.

1–10  Net income appears on both the income statement and the statement of changes in owner's equity.

1–11  The owner's capital account balance at the end of the period appears on both the statement of changes in owner's equity and the balance sheet.

1–12  Owners use the return on equity ratio to describe the success of the business in a way that can be compared to other investment opportunities.

A–1  *c*

A–2  GAAP are the principles that govern the reporting of information in the financial statements. GAAS, on the other hand, are the standards that guide auditors in performing an audit.

A–3  No. The IASC does not have the authority to impose standards. The Canadian company must comply with the GAAP established by the CICA's AcSB.

# CHAPTER 2

# Recording Transactions

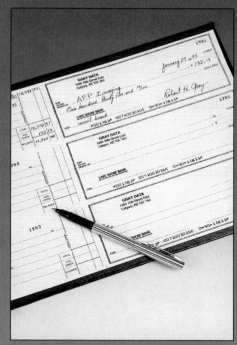

*Whether an organization is small or large, an important key to gathering useful information is a system that records the effects of transactions as soon as they occur. Double-entry accounting serves this purpose very well.*

In their continuing examination of Imperial's 1994 financial statements, Karen White and Mark Smith decided to read the narrative part of the report. As is true for most companies, Imperial includes a letter from the executive officers in their annual report. Karen and Mark found this "Letter to Shareholders from the Chairman and President" interesting and informative. They were particularly interested in the statement: "First, there is our financial position, one of the strongest in the industry. This gives us flexibility and allows us to manage through periods of uncertainty and volatility, such as we have recently experienced in crude-oil pricing." As Karen and Mark only started their first course in accounting, they wondered how "strength of financial position" is measured.

**IMPERIAL OIL LIMITED**
Selected financial data
(in millions)

| December 31 | Total Assets | Total Liabilities* | Total Shareholders' Equity |
|---|---|---|---|
| 1994 . . . . . . | $11,928 | $5,933 | $5,995 |
| 1993 . . . . . . | 12,861 | 6,295 | 6,566 |
| 1992 . . . . . . | 13,135 | 6,499 | 6,636 |
| 1991 . . . . . . | 13,491 | 6,701 | 6,790 |
| 1990 . . . . . . | 14,458 | 7,593 | 6,865 |

*Including deferred income taxes.

## LEARNING OBJECTIVES

**After studying Chapter 2, you should be able to:**

1. **Describe the events recorded in accounting systems and the importance of source documents and business papers in those systems.**

2. **Describe how accounts are used to record information about the effects of transactions, how code numbers are used to identify each account, and the meaning of the words *debit* and *credit*.**

3. **Describe how debits and credits are used to analyze transactions and record their effects in the accounts.**

4. **Record transactions in a General Journal, describe balance column accounts, and post entries from the journal to the ledger.**

5. **Prepare a trial balance and explain its usefulness. Calculate a company's debt ratio.**

6. **Define or explain the words and phrases listed in the chapter glossary.**

In Chapter 1, you learned how the accounting equation (Assets = Liabilities + Owner's Equity) is affected by business transactions. In this chapter, you learn how the effects of transactions are recorded in accounts. All accounting systems, small or large, manual or computerized, use procedures similar to those described in this chapter. No matter how unusual or complicated a business may be, these procedures are the first steps in a process that leads to financial statements.

We begin by describing how source documents provide useful information about transactions. Then, we describe accounts and explain how they are used. Next, we explain debits and credits and use them to show how transactions affect the accounts. With this background in place, we describe the process of recording events in the journal and ledger. The chapter concludes by describing how to use a company's debt ratio to assess risk.

## THE ACCOUNTING PROCESS

**LO 1**

Describe the events recorded in accounting systems and the importance of source documents and business papers in those systems.

Chapter 1 explains that accounting provides useful financial information to decision makers. To generate this information, a company uses an accounting process that analyzes economic events, records the results, and classifies and summarizes the information in reports and financial statements. These reports and statements are provided to individuals who find the information to be useful for making investment, credit, and other decisions about the entity. You can see the overall steps in this process in the flowchart in Illustration 2–1.

### Business Transactions and Other Events

Notice that the economic events in Illustration 2–1 consist of business transactions and other events. Recall from Chapter 1 that business transactions are exchanges of economic consideration between two parties. Also, remember that a company's accounting equation is affected by transactions. The accounting process begins by analyzing transactions to determine how they affect the equation. Then, those effects are recorded in accounting records, informally referred to as *the books*. Additional processing steps summarize and classify the effects of all transactions. The process is not complete until it provides useful information to decision makers in financial statements or other reports.

**Illustration 2-1**   The Accounting Process

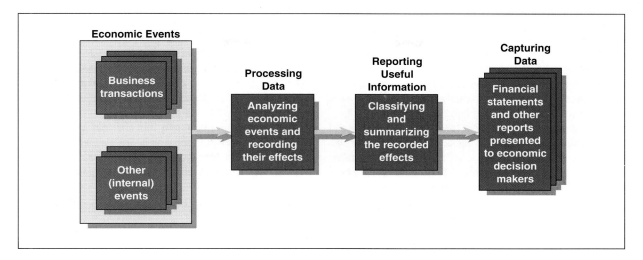

Because business transactions are exchanges between the entity and some other person or organization, they are sometimes called **external transactions.** Other economic events, called **internal transactions,** can affect the accounting equation. These events are not transactions with outside parties. For example, suppose that a company uses a machine in its operations. As the machine is used, its total remaining usefulness decreases. This using up of the machine's economic benefit is an economic event that decreases assets and decreases owner's equity.

Other events that can affect a company's accounting equation include natural events such as floods that destroy assets and create losses. In a few circumstances, changes in the market values of certain assets are also recorded. Economic events like these are not transactions between the company and other parties. We explain the analysis and recording of these economic events in Chapter 3.

Companies use various documents and other papers when they conduct business. These **business papers** include sales tickets, cheques, purchase orders, bills to customers, bills from suppliers, employee earnings records, and bank statements. Business papers are also called **source documents** because they are the source of the information recorded with accounting entries. Source documents may be printed on paper or they may exist only in computer records.

For example, when you buy a pocket calculator on credit, the store prepares at least two copies of a sales ticket. One copy is given to you. Another is sent to the store's accounting department and triggers an entry in the system to record the sale. (In many systems, this copy is sent electronically without a physical document.) Or, if you pay cash for the calculator, the sale is rung up on a cash register that records and stores the amount of each sale.

Some cash registers print the amount of each sale on a paper tape locked inside the register. Most newer registers store the data electronically. In either case, the proper keyboard commands at the end of the day cause the cash register to determine the total cash sales for that day. This total is then used to record the day's sales in the accounting records. These systems are designed to ensure that the

## SOURCE DOCUMENTS AND BUSINESS PAPERS

While taking classes toward her business degree, Kim Li accepted a part-time job at a busy fast food restaurant in a large downtown mall. As a new employee, she received training from the restaurant's assistant manager, including instructions on operating the cash register. The assistant manager explained that the formal policy is to ring up each sale when an order is placed and the cash is received.

The assistant manager also told Li that the pressure of the noon-hour rush makes it easier to just accept the customers' cash and make change without ringing up the sales. The assistant manager explained that the formal policy is ignored because it is more important to serve the cus-

tomers promptly to keep them from going to any of the other restaurants in the mall. Then, after two o'clock, the assistant manager adds up the cash in the drawer and rings up sufficient sales to equal the collected amount. This way, the record in the register always comes out right and there are no problems to explain when the manager arrives at four o'clock to handle the dinner traffic.

Li sees the advantages in this shortcut but wonders whether something is wrong with it. She also wonders what will happen if the manager comes in early some day and finds out that she isn't following the formal policy.

accounting records include all transactions. They also help prevent mistakes and theft. The As a Matter of Ethics case above describes a challenge created by an instruction to overlook these accounting procedures. Read the case and think about what you would do if you were Kim Li.

Both buyers and sellers use sales tickets (also called *invoices*) as source documents. For example, if the new calculator is going to be used in your business, your copy of the invoice is a source document. It provides information to record the purchase in accounting records for your business.

To summarize, business papers are the starting point in the accounting process. These source documents, especially if they are created outside the business, provide objective evidence about transactions and the amounts to be recorded for them. As you learned in Chapter 1, this type of evidence is important because it makes the reported information more reliable and useful.

Years ago, most accounting systems required pen and ink to manually record and process data about transactions. Today, only very small companies use manual systems. Now, large and small companies use computers to record and process the data. However, you will find it easier to understand the steps in the accounting process by learning to prepare accounting data manually. Despite the differences, the general concepts you learn by studying manual methods apply equally well to computerized accounting systems. More importantly, these concepts help you use financial statements because you understand the source of their information.

**Progress Check**
*(Answers to Progress Checks are provided at the end of the chapter.)*

2-1     Which of the following are examples of accounting source documents? *(a)* Journals and ledgers; *(b)* Income statements and balance sheets; *(c)* External transactions and internal transactions; *(d)* Bank statements and sales tickets; *(e)* All of the above.

2-2     What kinds of economic events affect a company's accounting equation?

2-3     Why are business papers called source documents?

An **account** is a place or location within an accounting system in which the increases and decreases in a specific asset, liability, owner's equity, revenue, or expense are recorded and stored. The diagram in Illustration 2–2 shows how the information about the company's events flows into the accounts and from the accounts into the financial statements.

When financial statements (or other reports) are needed, the information is taken from the accounts, summarized, and presented in helpful formats. To display information about a specific item in the statements, a separate account must be maintained for that item. Thus, a company's accounting system includes a separate account for each revenue and expense on the income statement. The system also includes a separate account for each asset, liability, and owner's equity item on the balance sheet. In addition, important changes such as withdrawals by the owner are captured in separate accounts. Because each company is different from all others, each has its own unique set of accounts. However, most companies use many accounts that are similar. The following paragraphs describe some commonly used accounts.

## Asset Accounts

Because most companies own the following kinds of assets, their accounting systems include accounts for them.

**Cash.** Increases and decreases in the amount of cash are recorded in a *Cash* account. A company's cash consists of money, balances in chequing accounts, or any document that a bank accepts for deposit. Thus, cash includes coins, currency, cheques, money orders, and credit card bills.

**Accounts Receivable.** Goods and services are often sold to customers in return for promises to pay in the future. These transactions are called *credit sales* or *sales on account.* The promises from the buyers are called the seller's *accounts receivable.* Accounts receivable are increased by new credit sales and are decreased by customer payments. Because a company sends bills to its credit customers, it needs to know the amount currently due from each of them. Therefore, it creates a separate record of each customer's purchases and payments. We describe the system for maintaining these separate records in Chapter 6. For now, however, we can use the simpler practice of recording all increases and decreases in receivables in a single account called *Accounts Receivable.*

**Notes Receivable.** A **promissory note** is an unconditional written promise to pay a definite sum of money on demand or on a defined future date (or dates). If a company holds one of these notes signed by another party, it owns a valuable asset. These assets called notes receivable are recorded in a *Notes Receivable* account.

**Prepaid Insurance.** Insurance contracts provide protection against losses caused by fire, thefts, accidents, or other events. Normally, an insurance policy requires the fee (called a *premium*) to be paid in advance, and the protection usually lasts for a year or even as long as three years. As a result, the unused portion of the coverage may be an asset for a substantial time after the premium is paid.

When an insurance premium is paid in advance, the cost is typically recorded in an asset account called *Prepaid Insurance*. When financial statements are prepared later, the expired portion of the insurance cost is removed from the asset account

## RECORDING INFORMATION IN THE ACCOUNTS

**LO 2**

Describe how accounts are used to record information about the effects of transactions, how code numbers are used to identify each account, and the meaning of the words *debit* and *credit.*

**Illustration 2-2**   The Flow of Information through the Accounts into the Financial Statements

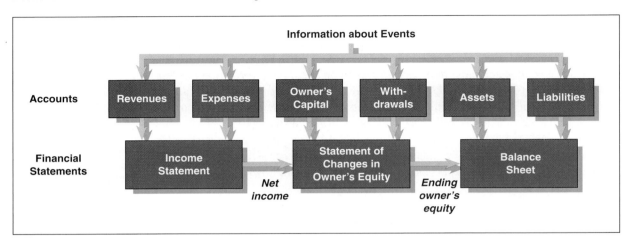

and reported as an expense on the income statement. The unexpired portion remains in the Prepaid Insurance account and is reported on the balance sheet as an asset.

**Office Supplies.**   All companies use office supplies such as computer diskettes, printer ribbons and cartridges, stationery, paper, and pens. These supplies are assets until they are used. When they are consumed, their cost becomes an expense. Increases and decreases in the cost of the assets are recorded in an *Office Supplies* account.

**Store Supplies.**   Many stores keep plastic and paper bags, gift boxes, cartons, and similar items on hand to use in wrapping purchases for their customers. Increases and decreases in the cost of the assets are recorded in a *Store Supplies* account.

**Other Prepaid Expenses.**   When payments are made for assets that are not used until later, the assets are often called **prepaid expenses.** Then, as the economic benefits of the assets are used up, the costs of the assets become expenses. As a practical matter, an asset's cost can be initially recorded as an expense if its benefits will be consumed before the next set of financial statements are prepared. If the asset's benefits will not be used up before the end of the current reporting period, the prepayments are recorded in asset accounts.

Office supplies and store supplies are usually described as prepaid expenses. Other examples of prepaid expenses include prepaid insurance, prepaid rent, and legal or accounting fees paid in advance of receiving the services. To provide useful information, each prepaid expense is typically accounted for in a separate asset account.

**Equipment.**   Virtually all companies own computers, printers, typewriters, desks, chairs, and other equipment that they use in their business. The costs incurred to buy the equipment are recorded in an *Office Equipment* account. The costs of assets used in a store, such as counters, showcases, and cash registers, are recorded in a separate *Store Equipment* account.

**Buildings.**  A building owned by a business provides space for a store, an office, a warehouse, or a factory. Because they produce future benefits, buildings are assets, and their costs are recorded in a *Buildings* account. If several buildings are owned, separate accounts may record the cost incurred in buying each of them.

**Land.**  A *Land* account is used to record the cost of land owned by a business. The cost of land is separated from the cost of buildings located on the land to provide more useful information in the financial statements. Although the land and the buildings may appear to be inseparable and a single asset, the buildings wear out and their costs become expenses. Land does not wear out, and thus its cost does not become an expense. Therefore, the costs of the land and the buildings are recorded in separate accounts to simplify accounting for amoritzation of costs.

## Liability Accounts

Chapter 1 explained that liabilities are present obligations to transfer assets or provide services to other entities in the future. A business may have several different types of liabilities. Therefore, each type is represented by a separate account. The following liability accounts are widely used.

**Accounts Payable.**  When purchases of merchandise, supplies, equipment, or services are made by an oral or implied promise to pay later, the resulting debts are called *accounts payable*. Because it is useful to know the amount owed to each creditor, accounting systems keep separate records about purchases from and the payments to each of them. We describe these individual records in Chapter 6. For now, however, we can use the simpler practice of recording all increases and decreases in payables in a single account called *Accounts Payable.*

**Notes Payable.**  When an entity's promise to pay is formally recognized by having the entity sign a promissory note, the resulting liability is called a *note payable.* Depending on how soon the liability must be repaid, its amount may be recorded in a *Short-Term Notes Payable* account or a *Long-Term Notes Payable* account.

**Unearned Revenues.**  As you learned in Chapter 1, the *revenue recognition principle* requires accountants to report revenues on the income statement only after they are earned. This principle demands careful treatment of transactions in which customers pay in advance for products or services. Because the cash from these transactions is received before the revenues are earned, the seller considers them to be **unearned revenues.** An unearned revenue is a liability that is satisfied by delivering the product or service in the future. Unearned revenues include subscriptions collected in advance by a magazine publisher. Other unearned revenues include rent collected in advance by a building owner and professional or other service fees collected in advance.

When cash is received in advance, the seller records the amount in a liability account such as *Unearned Subscriptions, Unearned Rent,* or *Unearned Professional Fees.* When the products or services are delivered, the earned revenues are transferred to revenue accounts such as *Subscription Fees Earned, Rent Earned,* or *Professional Fees Earned.*

**Other Short-Term Liabilities.**  Other short-term liabilities include wages payable, taxes payable, and interest payable. Each of these debts is normally recorded in a separate liability account. However, if they are not large in amount, one or more of them may be added together and reported as a single amount on the balance sheet.

## Owner's Equity, Withdrawals, Revenue, and Expense Accounts

In Chapter 1, we described four types of transactions that affected the owner's equity of a proprietorship. They are (1) investments by the owner, (2) withdrawals of assets by the owner, (3) revenues, and (4) expenses. Recall that in Chapter 1 we entered all equity transactions in a single column under the owner's name. We did this to help you understand how transactions affect the accounting equation. However, this simple approach caused a problem later when we needed to prepare an income statement and the statement of changes in owner's equity. The problem was that we had to analyze the items in the single column to see which ones belonged on which statement.

A better approach is to use separate accounts for the owner's capital, the owner's withdrawals, each revenue, and each expense. This allows us to record the effects of each kind of change in owner's equity in its own account. Then, the information in these accounts can be taken directly to the financial statements without further analysis. The following paragraphs describe these equity accounts.

**Capital Account.** When a person invests in a proprietorship, the invested amount is recorded in an account identified by the owner's name and the word **Capital.** For example, an account called *Terry Dow, Capital* can be used to record Dow's original investment in Clear Copy. If the owner makes additional investments, they also are recorded in the owner's capital account.

**Withdrawals Account.** When a business earns income, the owner's equity increases. The owner may choose to leave this equity intact or may withdraw assets from the business as needed. Whenever the owner withdraws assets, perhaps to pay personal living expenses, the withdrawal reduces the company's assets and the owner's equity.

In many situations, owners of unincorporated businesses plan to withdraw regular weekly or monthly amounts of cash. The owners may even think of these withdrawals as salaries. However, the owners of unincorporated businesses cannot receive salaries because they are not legally separate from their companies. As a result, they cannot enter into salary (or any other) contracts with themselves. Therefore, withdrawals are neither income to the owners nor expenses of the businesses. They are simply the opposite of investments by the owners.

To record the owner's withdrawals, most accounting systems use an account that has the name of the owner and the word *Withdrawals.* For example, an account called *Terry Dow, Withdrawals* would be used to record Dow's withdrawals from Clear Copy. The owner's **withdrawals account** also may be called the owner's *personal* account or *drawing* account.

**Revenue and Expense Accounts.** Decision makers often want information about the amounts of revenue earned and expenses incurred during the reporting period. A business uses a variety of revenue and expense accounts to provide this information on its income statement. As you might expect, various companies have different kinds of revenues and expenses. Examples of possible revenue accounts are *Sales, Commissions Earned, Professional Fees Earned, Rent Earned,* and *Interest Earned.* Examples of expense accounts are *Advertising Expense, Store Supplies Expense, Office Salaries Expense, Office Supplies Expense, Rent Expense, Utilities Expense,* and *Insurance Expense.*

You can get an idea of the variety of accounts that a company might use by looking at the list of accounts at the end of this text. It lists the accounts you need to solve the exercises and problems in this book.[1]

Accounts may have different physical forms, depending on the system. In computerized systems, accounts are stored in files on floppy or hard disks. In manual systems, each account may be a separate page in a loose-leaf book or a separate card in a tray of cards. Regardless of their physical form, the collection of all accounts is called the **ledger.** If the accounts are in files on a hard disk, those files are the ledger. If the accounts are pages in a book or cards in a file, the book or file is the ledger. In other words, a ledger is simply a group of accounts.

A company's size affects the number of accounts needed in its accounting system. A small company may get by with as few as 20 or 30 accounts, while a large company may use several thousand. The **chart of accounts** is a list of all accounts used by a company. The chart also includes an identification number assigned to each account. To be efficient, companies assign their account identification numbers in a systematic manner. For example, a small business might use this numbering system for its accounts:

101–199    Asset accounts
201–299    Liability accounts
301–399    Owner's equity accounts
401–499    Revenue accounts
501–699    Operating expense accounts

Although this system provides for 99 asset accounts, a company may not use all of them. The numbers create a three-digit code that conveys information to the company's accountants and bookkeepers. For example, the first digit of the code numbers assigned to the asset accounts is a 1, while the first digit assigned to the liability accounts is a 2, and so on. In each case, the first digit of an account's number reveals whether the account appears on the balance sheet or the income statement. The second and third digits may also relate to the accounts' categories. We describe account numbering systems more completely in the next chapter.

In its simplest form, an account looks like the letter T:

**THE LEDGER AND THE CHART OF ACCOUNTS**

**USING T-ACCOUNTS**

|  **(Name)** ||
| --- | --- |
| (Left side) | (Right side) |

---

[1] Remember that different companies may use account titles that are different from the titles in the list. For example, a company might use Interest Revenue instead of Interest Earned or Rental Expense instead of Rent Expense. All that is required is that an account title describe the item it represents.

Because of its shape, this simple form is called a **T-account.** Notice that the T format gives the account a left side, a right side, and a convenient place for its name.

The shape of a T-account provides one side for recording increases in the item and the other side for recording decreases. For example, the following T-account represents Clear Copy's cash account after the transactions in Chapter 1:

|  | **Cash** |  |
|---|---|---|
| Investment by owner | 30,000 | Purchase of store supplies |
| Copy services revenue earned | 2,200 | Purchase of copy equipment |
| Collection of account receivable | 1,700 | Payment of rent |
|  |  | Payment of salary |
|  |  | Payment of account payable |
|  |  | Withdrawal by owner |

| | | 2,500 |
| | | 20,000 |
| | | 1,000 |
| | | 700 |
| | | 900 |
| | | 400 |

## Calculating the Balance of an Account

An **account balance** is simply the difference between the increases and decreases recorded in the account. Thus, for example, the balance of an asset account is the amount of that asset on the date the balance is calculated. The balance of a liability account is the amount owed on the date of the balance. Putting the increases on one side of the account and the decreases on the other makes it easy to find an account's balance. To determine the balance, simply find the total increases shown on one side (including the beginning balance), find the total decreases shown on the other side, and then subtract the sum of the decreases from the sum of the increases.

For example, the total increases in Clear Copy's Cash account were $33,900, the total decreases were $25,500, and the account balance is $8,400. This T-account shows how to calculate the $8,400 balance:

|  | **Cash** |  |  |
|---|---|---|---|
| Investment by owner | 30,000 | Purchase of store supplies | 2,500 |
| Copy services revenue earned | 2,200 | Purchase of copy equipment | 20,000 |
| Collection of account receivable | 1,700 | Payment of rent | 1,000 |
|  |  | Payment of salary | 700 |
|  |  | Payment of account payable | 900 |
|  |  | Withdrawal by owner | 400 |
| Total increases | **33,900** | Total decreases | **25,500** |
| Less decreases | **−25,500** |  |  |
| Balance | **8,400** |  |  |

## Debits and Credits

In accounting terms, the left side of a T-account is called the **debit** side, often abbreviated Dr. The right side is called the **credit** side, abbreviated Cr.[2] To enter

---

[2]These abbreviations are remnants of 18th-century English bookkeeping practices that used the terms *Debitor* and *Creditor* instead of *debit* and *credit*. These abbreviations use the first and last letters from the words, just as we still do for *Saint* (St.) and *Doctor* (Dr.).

amounts on the left side of an account is to *debit* the account. To enter amounts on the right side is to *credit* the account. The difference between the total debits and the total credits in an account is the account balance. When the sum of the debits exceeds the sum of the credits, the account has a debit balance. It has a credit balance when the sum of the credits exceeds the sum of the debits.

From looking at the Cash account, you might think that the terms *debit* and *credit* mean *increase* and *decrease*. That is not correct. Whether a debit is an increase or decrease depends on the type of account. Similarly, whether a credit increases or decreases an account depends on the type of account. In any account, however, a debit and a credit have opposite effects. That is, in an account where a debit is an increase, a credit is a decrease. And, if a debit is a decrease in a particular account, a credit is an increase.

When we work with T-accounts, a debit simply means an entry on the left side and a credit simply means an entry on the right side. For example, notice how Terry Dow's initial investment in Clear Copy is recorded in the Cash and capital accounts:

| Cash | | Terry Dow, Capital | |
|---|---|---|---|
| Investment 30,000 | | | Investment 30,000 |

Notice that the cash increase is recorded on the left side of the Cash account with a $30,000 debit entry; the corresponding increase in owner's equity is recorded on the right side of the capital account with a $30,000 credit entry. This method of recording the transaction is an essential feature of *double-entry accounting,* which we explain in the next section.

Debits and credits are neither favourable nor unfavourable. The actual effect depends on what is debited and credited. For example, a debit to an asset might be considered favourable, while a debit to an expense might be considered unfavourable. On the other hand, a credit to a liability might be considered unfavourable while a credit to a revenue would be favourable. These practices will become more clear after studying the transactions later in this chapter.

---

**Progress Check**

2-4 Which of the following answers properly classifies these commonly used accounts? (1) Prepaid Rent, (2) Unearned Fees, (3) Buildings, (4) Owner's Capital, (5) Wages Payable, (6) Office Supplies.

| | Assets | Liabilities | Owner's Equity |
|---|---|---|---|
| a. | 1,6 | 2,5 | 3,4 |
| b. | 1,3,6 | 2,5 | 4 |
| c. | 1,3,6 | 5 | 2,4 |

2-5 What are accounts? What is a ledger?

2-6 What determines the quantity and types of accounts used by a company?

2-7 Does debit always mean increase and credit always mean decrease?

---

## USING DEBITS AND CREDITS IN DOUBLE-ENTRY ACCOUNTING

**LO 3**

Describe how debits and credits are used to analyze transactions and record their effects in the accounts.

In **double-entry accounting,** every transaction affects and is recorded in at least two accounts. When recording each transaction, *the total amount debited must equal the total amount credited.* Because each transaction is recorded with total debits equal to total credits, the sum of the debits for all entries must equal the sum of the credits for all entries. Furthermore, the sum of the debit account balances in the ledger must equal the sum of the credit account balances. The only reason the sum of the debit balances would not equal the sum of the credit balances would be that an error has occurred. Thus, an important result of double-entry accounting is that many errors are avoided by being sure that the debits and credits for each transaction are equal.

According to traditional double-entry accounting, increases in assets are recorded on the debit side of asset accounts.[3] Why are asset accounts given debit balances? There is no specific reason. The choice is simply a convention that makes it easier for accountants by having all accounting systems work the same way. Then, because asset accounts have debit balances, increases in those balances are recorded with debits and decreases are recorded with credits.

Because asset accounts have debit balances and because debits must equal credits, liability accounts and owner's equity accounts must have credit balances. This follows from the logic of the accounting equation (Assets = Liabilities + Owner's Equity). Therefore, increases in liability and owner's equity accounts are recorded with credit entries. In other words, if asset increases are recorded with debit entries, equal debits and credits for a transaction are possible only if increases in liabilities and owner's equity are recorded as credits. To summarize, double-entry accounting systems record increases and decreases in balance sheet accounts as follows:

| Assets | | | Liabilities | | | Owner's Equity | |
|---|---|---|---|---|---|---|---|
| Debit for increases | Credit for decreases | = | Debit for decreases | Credit for increases | + | Debit for decreases | Credit for increases |

The practices shown in these T-accounts can be expressed as the following rules for recording transactions in a double-entry accounting system:

1.  Increases in assets are debited to asset accounts; therefore, decreases in assets are recorded with credit entries to asset accounts.
2.  Increases in liabilities are credited to liability accounts; therefore, decreases in liabilities are recorded with debit entries to liability accounts.
3.  Increases in owner's equity are credited to owner's equity accounts; therefore, decreases in owner's equity are recorded with debit entries to owner's equity accounts.

Debits and credits may be confusing because of previous exposure to the terms. When you make a deposit to your chequing account, the bank credits your account's balance. To understand this practice, decide whether your chequing account is an asset or a liability to the bank. How does your deposit affect the bank's assets and liabilities?

---

[3]These double-entry practices originated in 15th-century Italy and have stood the test of more than 500 years of change and progress in business.

Chapter 1 taught you that owner's equity is increased by owner's investments and by revenues. You also learned that owner's equity is decreased by expenses and by withdrawals. Therefore, the following rules also apply:

4. The owner's investments are credited to the owner's capital account because they increase equity.
5. The owner's withdrawals of assets are debited to the owner's withdrawals account because they decrease equity.
6. Revenues are credited to revenue accounts because they increase equity. The system should include a separate account for each type of revenue.
7. Expenses are debited to expense accounts because they decrease equity. The system should include a separate account for each type of expense.

At this stage, you may find it helpful to memorize these rules. You will use them over and over in the course of your study. Before long, the rules will become second nature to you.

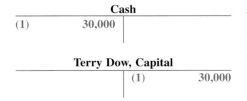

## EXAMPLES OF DEBITS AND CREDITS

The following transactions for Clear Copy will help you learn how to apply these debit and credit rules. Study each transaction carefully to be sure that you understand it before you go on to the next one.

Each transaction is numbered so you can identify the transaction's effects on the accounts. You should recognize the first 11 transactions because they were used in Chapter 1 to show how transactions affect the accounting equation. In this chapter, we add five more transactions (numbers 12 through 16) to illustrate different kinds of events.

Before recording a transaction, the bookkeeper first analyzes it to determine what was increased or decreased. Then, the debit and credit rules are applied to decide how to record the increases or decreases. The bookkeeper's analysis for each of the example transactions appears next to the T-accounts. Study each analysis carefully to be sure that you understand the process.

1. On December 1, Terry Dow invested $30,000 in Clear Copy.

| Cash | |
|---|---|
| (1)          30,000 | |

| Terry Dow, Capital | |
|---|---|
| | (1)          30,000 |

*Analysis of the transaction:* The transaction increased the company's cash. At the same time, it increased Dow's equity. Increases in assets are debited and increases in owner's equity are credited. Therefore, record the transaction with a debit to Cash and a credit to Terry Dow, Capital, for $30,000.

2. Purchased store supplies by paying $2,500 cash.

| Store Supplies | |
|---|---|
| (2)          2,500 | |

| Cash | |
|---|---|
| (1)          30,000 | (2)          2,500 |

*Analysis of the transaction:* The cost of the store supplies is increased by the purchase and cash is decreased. Increases in assets are debited and decreases are credited. Therefore, record the transaction with a debit to Store Supplies and a credit to Cash for $2,500.

3. Purchased copying equipment by paying $20,000 cash.

**Copy Equipment**

| (3) | 20,000 | |
|---|---|---|

**Cash**

| (1) | 30,000 | (2) | 2,500 |
|---|---|---|---|
| | | (3) | 20,000 |

*Analysis of the transaction:* The cost of the copying equipment is increased and cash is decreased. Increases in assets are debited and decreases are credited. Debit Copy Equipment and credit Cash for $20,000.

4. Purchased $1,100 of store supplies and $6,000 of copying equipment on credit from Handy Supply Company.

**Store Supplies**

| (2) | 2,500 | |
|---|---|---|
| (4) | 1,100 | |

**Copy Equipment**

| (3) | 20,000 | |
|---|---|---|
| (4) | 6,000 | |

**Accounts Payable**

| | (4) | 7,100 |
|---|---|---|

*Analysis of the transaction:* This transaction increased two assets, store supplies and copy equipment. It also created a new liability. Increases in assets are debits and increases in liabilities are credits. Therefore, debit Store Supplies for $1,100, debit Copy Equipment for $6,000, and credit Accounts Payable for $7,100.

5. Provided copying services to a customer and immediately collected $2,200 cash.

**Cash**

| (1) | 30,000 | (2) | 2,500 |
|---|---|---|---|
| (5) | 2,200 | (3) | 20,000 |

**Copy Services Revenue**

| | (5) | 2,200 |
|---|---|---|

*Analysis of the transaction:* This revenue transaction increased both assets and owner's equity. Increases in assets are debits and increases in owner's equity are credits. Revenue accounts are increased with credits because revenues increase owner's equity. Therefore, debit Cash $2,200 to record the increase in assets. Credit Copy Services Revenue $2,200 to increase owner's equity and to accumulate information for the income statement.

6. Paid $1,000 cash for rent for December.

**Rent Expense**

| (6) | 1,000 | |
|---|---|---|

**Cash**

| (1) | 30,000 | (2) | 2,500 |
|---|---|---|---|
| (5) | 2,200 | (3) | 20,000 |
| | | (6) | 1,000 |

*Analysis of the transaction:* The cost of renting the store during December is an expense, which decreases owner's equity. Because decreases in owner's equity are debits, expenses are recorded as debits. Therefore, debit Rent Expense $1,000 to decrease owner's equity and to accumulate information for the income statement. Also, credit Cash $1,000 to record the decrease in assets.

7. Paid $700 cash for the employee's salary for the pay period ended on December 12.

**Salaries Expense**

| | | | |
|---|---|---|---|
| (7) | 700 | | |

*Analysis of the transaction:* The employee's salary is an expense that decreased owner's equity. Debit Salaries Expense $700 to decrease owner's equity and to accumulate information for the income statement. Also, credit Cash $700 to record the decrease in assets.

**Cash**

| | | | |
|---|---|---|---|
| (1) | 30,000 | (2) | 2,500 |
| (5) | 2,200 | (3) | 20,000 |
| | | (6) | 1,000 |
| | | (7) | 700 |

8. Completed copying work on credit and billed the customer $1,700 for the services.

**Accounts Receivable**

| | | | |
|---|---|---|---|
| (8) | 1,700 | | |

*Analysis of the transaction:* This revenue transaction gave Clear Copy the right to collect $1,700 from the customer. Thus, it increased both assets and owner's equity. Therefore, debit Accounts Receivable $1,700 for the increase in assets and credit Copy Services Revenue $1,700 to increase owner's equity and to accumulate information for the income statement.

**Copy Services Revenue**

| | | | |
|---|---|---|---|
| | | (5) | 2,200 |
| | | (8) | 1,700 |

9. The customer paid the $1,700 account receivable created in transaction 8.

**Cash**

| | | | |
|---|---|---|---|
| (1) | 30,000 | (2) | 2,500 |
| (5) | 2,200 | (3) | 20,000 |
| (9) | 1,700 | (6) | 1,000 |
| | | (7) | 700 |

*Analysis of the transaction:* One asset was increased and another decreased. Debit Cash $1,700 to record the increase in cash, and credit Accounts Receivable $1,700 to record the decrease in the account receivable.

**Accounts Receivable**

| | | | |
|---|---|---|---|
| (8) | 1,700 | (9) | 1,700 |

10. Paid Handy Supply Company $900 cash on the $7,100 owed for the supplies and equipment purchased on credit in transaction 4.

**Accounts Payable**

| | | | |
|---|---|---|---|
| (10) | 900 | (4) | 7,100 |

*Analysis of the transaction:* A payment to a creditor decreases an asset and a liability by the same amount. Decreases in liabilities are debited, and decreases in assets are credited. Debit Accounts Payable $900 and credit Cash $900.

**Cash**

| | | | |
|---|---|---|---|
| (1) | 30,000 | (2) | 2,500 |
| (5) | 2,200 | (3) | 20,000 |
| (9) | 1,700 | (6) | 1,000 |
| | | (7) | 700 |
| | | (10) | 900 |

11. Terry Dow withdrew $400 from Clear Copy for personal living expenses.

**Terry Dow, Withdrawals**

| | | | |
|---|---|---|---|
| (11) | 400 | | |

*Analysis of the transaction:* This event reduced owner's equity and assets by the same amount. The Terry Dow, Withdrawals account is debited $400 to decrease owner's equity and to accumulate information for the statement of changes in owner's equity. Cash is credited $400 to record the asset reduction.

**Cash**

| | | | |
|---|---|---|---|
| (1) | 30,000 | (2) | 2,500 |
| (5) | 2,200 | (3) | 20,000 |
| (9) | 1,700 | (6) | 1,000 |
| | | (7) | 700 |
| | | (10) | 900 |
| | | (11) | 400 |

12. Signed a contract with a customer and accepted $3,000 cash in advance of providing any services.

**Cash**

| | | | |
|---|---|---|---|
| (1) | 30,000 | (2) | 2,500 |
| (5) | 2,200 | (3) | 20,000 |
| (9) | 1,700 | (6) | 1,000 |
| (12) | 3,000 | (7) | 700 |
| | | (10) | 900 |
| | | (11) | 400 |

*Analysis of the transaction:* The $3,000 inflow of cash increased assets but a revenue was not earned. Instead, the transaction creates a liability that will be satisfied by doing the client's copying work in the future. Record the asset increase by debiting Cash for $3,000 and record the liability increase by crediting Unearned Copy Services Revenue for $3,000.

**Unearned Copy Services Revenue**

| | | | |
|---|---|---|---|
| | | (12) | 3,000 |

13. Paid $2,400 cash for the premium on a two-year insurance policy.

**Prepaid Insurance**

| | | | |
|---|---|---|---|
| (13) | 2,400 | | |

*Analysis of the transaction:* The advance payment of the insurance premium creates an asset (a prepaid expense) by decreasing another asset. The new asset is recorded with a $2,400 debit to Prepaid Insurance and the payment is recorded with a $2,400 credit to Cash.

**Cash**

| | | | |
|---|---|---|---|
| (1) | 30,000 | (2) | 2,500 |
| (5) | 2,200 | (3) | 20,000 |
| (9) | 1,700 | (6) | 1,000 |
| (12) | 3,000 | (7) | 700 |
| | | (10) | 900 |
| | | (11) | 400 |
| | | (13) | 2,400 |

14. Paid $120 cash for additional store supplies.
15. Paid $230 cash for the December utilities bill.
16. Paid $700 cash for the employee's salary for two weeks ended December 26.

**Store Supplies**

| | | | |
|---|---|---|---|
| (2) | 2,500 | | |
| (4) | 1,100 | | |
| (14) | 120 | | |

*Analysis of the transactions:* These transactions are similar because each of them decreased cash. They are different from each other because the store supplies are assets while the utilities and employee's salary are expenses. The $120 cost of the supplies should be debited to the Store Supplies asset account, while the $230 for utilities and the $700 salary should be debited to separate expense accounts. Each transaction requires its own credit to Cash.

**Utilities Expense**

| | |
|---|---|
| (15) | 230 |

**Salaries Expense**

| | |
|---|---|
| (7) | 700 |
| (16) | 700 |

**Cash**

| (1) | 30,000 | (2) | 2,500 |
|---|---|---|---|
| (5) | 2,200 | (3) | 20,000 |
| (9) | 1,700 | (6) | 1,000 |
| (12) | 3,000 | (7) | 700 |
| | | (10) | 900 |
| | | (11) | 400 |
| | | (13) | 2,400 |
| | | (14) | 120 |
| | | (15) | 230 |
| | | (16) | 700 |

Illustration 2–3 shows the accounts of Clear Copy after the 16 transactions have been recorded and the balances computed. The three columns in the illustration relate the accounts to the assets, liabilities, and owner's equity elements of the accounting equation. When we take the totals of the balance in each of the three columns, we find that total assets are $40,070 ($7,950 + $0 + $2,400 + $3,720 + $26,000). The total liabilities are $9,200 ($6,200 + $3,000), and the total of the equity accounts is $30,870 ($30,000 − $400 + $3,900 − $1,000 − $1,400 − $230). Thus, the total assets of $40,070 equals the $40,070 sum of the liabilities and the owner's equity ($9,200 + $30,870). The withdrawals, revenue, and expense accounts in the box record the events that change equity; their balances are reported as events on the income statement and statement of changes in owner's equity. Their balances are eventually combined with the balance of the capital account to produce the amount of equity reported on the balance sheet. Chapter 4 describes the bookkeeping (closing) process for combining these balances.

## ACCOUNTS AND THE ACCOUNTING EQUATION

---

**Progress Check**

**2-8** Double-entry accounting requires that:
a. All transactions that create debits to asset accounts must create credits to liability or owner's equity accounts.
b. A transaction that requires a debit to a liability account must require a credit to an asset account.
c. Every transaction must be recorded with total debits equal to total credits.

**2-9** What kinds of transactions increase owner's equity? What kinds decrease owner's equity?

**2-10** Why are most accounting systems called double-entry?

**Illustration 2-3**  The Ledger for Clear Copy

| Assets | | | | = | Liabilities | | | + | Owner's Equity | |
|---|---|---|---|---|---|---|---|---|---|---|

**Cash**

| (1) | 30,000 | (2) | 2,500 |
|---|---|---|---|
| (5) | 2,200 | (3) | 20,000 |
| (9) | 1,700 | (6) | 1,000 |
| (12) | 3,000 | (7) | 700 |
| | | (10) | 900 |
| | | (11) | 400 |
| | | (13) | 2,400 |
| | | (14) | 120 |
| | | (15) | 230 |
| | | (16) | 700 |
| Total | 36,900 | Total | 28,950 |
| | −28,950 | | |
| Balance | 7,950 | | |

**Accounts Payable**

| (10) | 900 | (4) | 7,100 |
|---|---|---|---|
| Total | 900 | Total | 7,100 |
| | | | −900 |
| | | Balance | 6,200 |

**Terry Dow, Capital**

| | | (1) | 30,000 |
|---|---|---|---|

**Unearned Copy Services Revenue**

| | | (12) | 3,000 |
|---|---|---|---|

**Terry Dow, Withdrawals**

| (11) | 1,500 | |
|---|---|---|

**Copy Services Revenue**

| | | (5) | 2,200 |
|---|---|---|---|
| | | (8) | 1,700 |
| | | Balance | 3,900 |

**Accounts Receivable**

| (8) | 1,700 | (9) | 1,700 |
|---|---|---|---|

**Prepaid Insurance**

| (13) | 2,400 | |
|---|---|---|

**Store Supplies**

| (2) | 2,500 | |
|---|---|---|
| (4) | 1,100 | |
| (14) | 120 | |
| Balance | 3,720 | |

**Copy Equipment**

| (3) | 20,000 | |
|---|---|---|
| (4) | 6,000 | |
| Balance | 26,000 | |

**Rent Expense**

| (6) | 1,000 | |
|---|---|---|

**Salaries Expense**

| (7) | 700 | |
|---|---|---|
| (16) | 700 | |
| Balance | 1,400 | |

**Utilities Expense**

| (15) | 230 | |
|---|---|---|

The accounts in this box record increases and decreases in owner's equity. Their balances are reported on the income statement or the statement of changes in owner's equity.

| $40,070 | = | $9,200 | + | $30,870 |
|---|---|---|---|---|

# TRANSACTIONS ARE FIRST RECORDED IN THE JOURNAL

In the preceding pages, we used debits and credits to show how transactions affect accounts. This process of analyzing transactions and recording their effects directly in the accounts is helpful as a learning exercise. However, real accounting systems do not record transactions directly in the accounts. If the bookkeeper recorded the effects directly in the accounts, errors would be easily made and difficult to track down and correct.

To help avoid errors, accounting systems record transactions in a **journal** before recording them in the accounts. This practice provides a complete record of each transaction in one place and links the debits and credits for each transaction. After the debits and credits for each transaction are entered in the journal, they are transferred to the ledger accounts. This two-step process produces useful records for the auditor about a company's transactions. At the same time, the process helps the bookkeeper avoid errors. And, if errors are made, the process makes it easier to find and correct them.

The process of recording transactions in a journal is called *journalizing.* The process of transferring journal entry information to the ledger is called **posting.** This sequence of steps is represented in Illustration 2–4. Various source documents provide the evidence that transactions have occurred. Next, these transactions are recorded in the journal. Finally, the journal entries are posted to the ledger. This sequence causes the journal to be called the **book of original entry** while the ledger is sometimes called the **book of final entry.**

LO 4

Record transactions in a General Journal, describe balance column accounts, and post entries from the journal to the ledger.

## The General Journal

The most flexible type of journal is the **General Journal.** The General Journal can be used to record any kind of transaction. A journal entry records this information about each transaction:

1.  The transaction's date.
2.  The names of the affected accounts.
3.  The amount of each debit and credit.
4.  An explanation of the transaction.
5.  The identifying numbers of the accounts.

Illustration 2–5 shows how the first four transactions for Clear Copy would be recorded in a typical General Journal in a manual system. The General Journals used in computerized systems may look like the manual journal page, or they may differ. Regardless of their form or appearance, journals serve the same purpose in every system.

Notice that the fourth entry in Illustration 2–5 uses three accounts to record the credit purchase of store supplies and additional copying equipment. A transaction that affects at least three accounts is recorded in the General Journal with a **compound journal entry.**

## Recording Transactions in a General Journal

A bookkeeper follows routine procedures when recording entries in the General Journal. The following steps were used to record the entries in Illustration 2–5. As you read these steps, compare them to the illustration to see how they produced the journal entries:

1.  Enter the year at the top of the first column of the first line on the page.
2.  Enter the month on the first line of the journal entry in the first column. (Successive entries in the same month on the same page of the journal would not show the month again.)
3.  Enter the day's date for the transaction in the second column on the first line of each entry.

**Illustration 2-4**   The Sequence of Steps in Recording Transactions

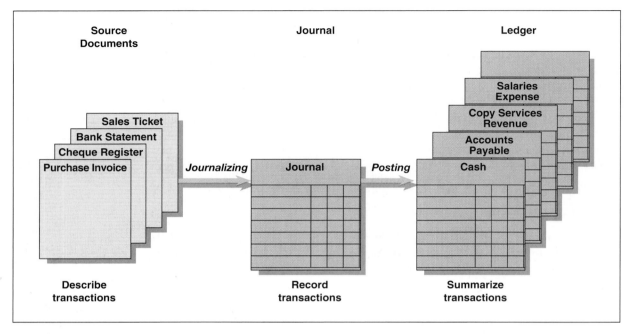

4.  Enter the names of the accounts to be debited. The account titles are taken from the chart of accounts and are aligned with the left margin of the Account Titles and Explanation column.

5.  Enter the amount debited to each account in the Debit column of the journal on the same line as the account title.

6.  Enter the names of the accounts to be credited. The account titles are taken from the chart of accounts and are indented far enough from the left margin of the column to distinguish them from the debited accounts (perhaps as much as an inch).

7.  Enter the amount credited to each account in the Credit column of the journal on the same line as the account title.

8.  Provide a brief explanation of the transaction to help an auditor or other person understand what happened. The explanation is indented about half as far as the credited account titles to avoid confusing the explanation with either a debit or credit entry. (For clarity, this book italicizes the explanations.)

9.  Skip a single line between each journal entry to keep them separate.

Once the journalizing process is completed, the journal entry provides a complete and useful description of the event's effects on the organization.

In a manual system, nothing is entered in the **Posting Reference (PR) column** when a transaction is initially recorded in the journal. As a control over the

**Illustration 2-5** A General Journal Showing Transactions for Clear Copy

| | GENERAL JOURNAL | | | Page 1 | |
|---|---|---|---|---|---|
| Date | Account Titles and Explanation | PR | Debit | Credit | |
| 1996 Dec. 1 | Cash | | 30,000 00 | | |
| | Terry Dow, Capital | | | 30,000 00 | |
| | *Investment by owner.* | | | | |
| | | | | | |
| 2 | Store Supplies | | 2,500 00 | | |
| | Cash | | | 2,500 00 | |
| | *Purchased supplies for cash.* | | | | |
| | | | | | |
| 3 | Copy Equipment | | 20,000 00 | | |
| | Cash | | | 20,000 00 | |
| | *Purchased copy equipment for cash.* | | | | |
| | | | | | |
| 6 | Store Supplies | | 1,100 00 | | |
| | Copy Equipment | | 6,000 00 | | |
| | Accounts Payable | | | 7,100 00 | |
| | *Purchased supplies and equipment on credit.* | | | | |

posting process, the account numbers are not entered until the entries are posted to the ledger. (Because the old word for page was *folio,* and because each account used to be a separate page in a book, the Posting Reference column in the journal is occasionally called the *folio column.*)

**Computerized Journals.** Journals in computerized accounting systems serve the same purpose of providing a complete record of each transaction. In some systems, they even look like the manual journal page in Illustration 2–5. In addition, they may include error-checking routines that ensure the debits in the entry equal the credits. They often provide shortcuts that allow the computer operator to enter account numbers instead of names, or to enter the account names and numbers with pull-down menus or other easy-to-use techniques.

**BALANCE COLUMN ACCOUNTS**

T-accounts are used in textbooks and accounting classes to show how accounts work. T-accounts are helpful because they allow you to disregard some details and concentrate on the main ideas. Actual accounting systems, however, use **balance column accounts** like the one in Illustration 2–6.

The balance column account format is similar to a T-account because it has columns for entering each debit and credit. It is different because it provides space for the entry's date and any explanation that might be needed. It also has a third column for showing the balance of the account after each entry is posted. As a result, the amount on the last line in this column is the account's current balance. For example, Clear Copy's Cash account in Illustration 2–6 was debited on December 1 for the $30,000 investment by Terry Dow. As a result, the account had a $30,000 debit balance. The account was then credited on December 2 for $2,500, and its new $27,500 balance was entered in the third column. On December 3, it was credited again, this time for $20,000, and its balance was reduced to $7,500. Finally, the Cash account was debited for $2,200 on December 10, and its balance was increased to $9,700.

When the balance column format is used, the heading of the Balance column does not indicate whether the account has a debit or credit balance. However, this omission should not create any problems because every account has a *normal balance*. The normal balance of each type of account (asset, liability, owner's equity, revenue, or expense) is the same as the debit or credit entry used to record an increase in the account. The table below shows the normal balances for accounts.

| Type of Account | Increases Are Recorded as | Normal Balance |
|---|---|---|
| Asset . . . . . . . . . . | Debits | Debit |
| Liability . . . . . . . . | Credits | Credit |
| Owner's equity: | | |
|    Capital . . . . . . . . | Credits | Credit |
|    Withdrawals . . . . | Debits | Debit |
|    Revenue . . . . . . . | Credits | Credit |
|    Expense . . . . . . . | Debits | Debit |

**Abnormal Balances.** Some unusual events may cause an account to have an abnormal balance. For example, a credit customer might accidentally pay its balance twice, which would give the account receivable a credit balance instead of a zero balance. If an abnormal balance is created, the bookkeeper can identify it by circling the amount or by entering the balance in red or some other nonstandard colour. Many computerized systems automatically provide a code beside the balance, such as *dr* or *cr* to identify the kind of balance.

**Zero Balances.** If an account has a zero balance, it is customary to indicate that fact by writing zeros or a dash in the Balance column. This practice avoids confusion between a zero balance and an accidentally omitted balance.

## POSTING JOURNAL ENTRIES

Illustration 2–4 on page 90 shows that journal entries are posted to the accounts in the ledger. To ensure that the ledger is up to date, journal entries are posted as promptly as possible, which may be daily, weekly, or as time permits. All entries need to be posted before the end of the reporting period to provide the accounts with updated balances when the financial statements are prepared.

Illustration 2-6   The Cash Account for Clear Copy in the Balance Column Format

| Date | | Explanation | PR | Debit | Credit | Balance |
|---|---|---|---|---|---|---|
| 1996 Dec. | 1 | | G1 | 30,000 00 | | 30,000 00 |
| | 2 | | G1 | | 2,500 00 | 27,500 00 |
| | 3 | | G1 | | 20,000 00 | 7,500 00 |
| | 10 | | G1 | 2,200 00 | | 9,700 00 |

Cash — Account No. 101

When posting the entries to the ledger, the bookkeeper copies the debits in the journal entries into the accounts as debits, and copies the journal entries' credits into the accounts as credits. The diagram in Illustration 2–7 identifies the six steps used in a manual system to post each debit and credit from the journal entry. Use the diagram to see how these six steps are completed:

For the debit:

1. Find the account that was debited in the journal entry.
2. Enter the date of the journal entry in the account on the next available line for the debit.
3. Write the amount debited in the journal entry in the debit column of the account.
4. To show where the debit came from, enter the letter G and the journal page number in the Posting Reference (PR) column for the account. (The letter G shows that the posted entry came from the General Journal. Other journals are identified by their own letters. We discuss other journals in Chapter 6.
5. Calculate and enter the account's new balance in the third column.
6. To show that the posting process is complete, enter the account number in the Posting Reference column on the entry's line in the journal. (If posting is interrupted, the bookkeeper can use the journal's Posting Reference column to take up the process where it was stopped.)

For the credit:

Repeat the six steps. However, the credit amount is entered in the Credit column and has a credit effect on the account balance.

Notice that step 6 in the posting procedure for either the debit or the credit of an entry inserts the account number in the journal's Posting Reference column. This creates a link between the ledger and the journal entry. This link provides a cross-reference that helps the bookkeeper and the auditor trace an amount from one record to the other.

**Illustration 2-7**   Six Steps for Posting a General Journal Entry to the Ledger

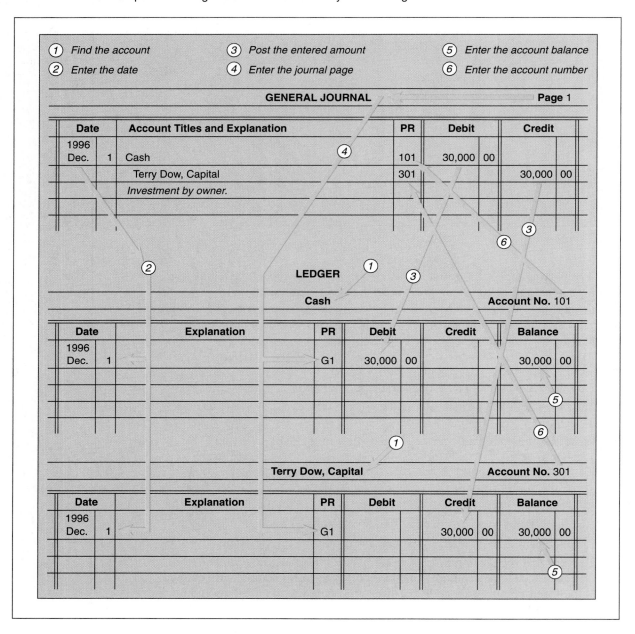

**Posting in Computerized Systems.** Computerized accounting systems do not require any additional effort by the operator to post the journal entries to the ledger. The programs in the systems are designed to automatically transfer the debit and credit entries from the journal into the database. In effect, the journal entries are posted directly into the accounts in the ledger without any additional steps.

Many systems include error-detection routines that test the reasonableness of the journal entry and the account balance when the new entry is recorded. Computerized data processing is discussed in Chapter 6.

---

**Progress Check**

2-11 The owner of Davis Company invested $15,000 cash and land with a fair market value of $23,000 in the business. The company also assumed responsibility for an $18,000 note payable originally issued to finance the purchase of the land. The journal entry to record this investment consists of: *(a)* One debit and one credit; *(b)* Two debits and one credit; *(c)* Two debits and two credits; or *(d)* Debits that total $38,000 and credits that total $33,000.

2-12 What is a compound journal entry?

2-13 Why are posting reference numbers entered in the journal when entries are posted to the accounts?

---

## PREPARING AND USING THE TRIAL BALANCE

LO 5

Prepare a trial balance, explain its usefulness, and calculate a company's debt ratio.

Recall that a double-entry accounting system records every transaction with equal debits and credits. As a result, the bookkeeper can tell that an error has occurred if the sum of the debit entries in the ledger does not equal the sum of the credit entries. The bookkeeper also knows that an error has occurred if the sum of the debit account balances does not equal the sum of the credit balances.

One purpose for preparing a **trial balance** is to find out if the debit and credit account balances are equal. A trial balance is a summary of the ledger that is a list of the accounts and their balances. The account balances are placed in either the debit or credit column of the trial balance. Illustration 2–8 presents the trial balance for Clear Copy after the 16 entries described earlier in the chapter have been posted to the ledger (shown in Illustration 2–3).

The trial balance also serves as a helpful internal document for preparing the financial statements. The task of preparing the statements is simplified if the accountant can take the account balances from the trial balance instead of looking them up in the ledger. (Chapter 3 describes the statement preparation process in more detail.)

The bookkeeper uses these five steps to prepare a trial balance:

1. Find the balance of each account in the ledger.
2. List each account and place its balance beside it. Debit balances are entered in the Debit column and credit balances are entered in the Credit column. (If an account has a zero balance, it may be included in the trial balance with a zero in the column for its normal balance.)
3. Compute the total of the debit balances.
4. Compute the total of the credit balances.
5. Verify that the sum of the debit balances equals the sum of the credit balances.

The trial balance for Clear Copy in Illustration 2–8 is presented in a typical format. Notice that the total of the debit balances equals the total of the credit balances. If

Illustration 2-8　Trial
Balance Drawn from
the Ledger of Clear
Copy

| CLEAR COPY Trial Balance December 31, 1996 | | |
|---|---|---|
| | Debit | Credit |
| Cash . . . . . . . . . . . . . . . . . . . . . . . | $ 7,950 | |
| Accounts receivable . . . . . . . . . . . . | 0 | |
| Prepaid insurance . . . . . . . . . . . . . | 2,400 | |
| Store supplies . . . . . . . . . . . . . . . | 3,720 | |
| Copy equipment . . . . . . . . . . . . . . | 26,000 | |
| Accounts payable . . . . . . . . . . . . . | | $ 6,200 |
| Unearned copy services revenue . . . . | | 3,000 |
| Terry Dow, capital . . . . . . . . . . . . . | | 30,000 |
| Terry Dow, withdrawals . . . . . . . . . | 400 | |
| Copy services revenue . . . . . . . . . . | | 3,900 |
| Rent expense . . . . . . . . . . . . . . . . | 1,000 | |
| Salaries expense . . . . . . . . . . . . . . | 1,400 | |
| Utilities expense . . . . . . . . . . . . . . | 230 | |
| Total . . . . . . . . . . . . . . . . . . . . . | $43,100 | $43,100 |

the two totals were not equal, we would know that at least one error had occurred. However, the fact that the two totals are equal does not prove that all errors were avoided.

## The Information Provided by a Trial Balance

When a trial balance does not balance (that is, the columns are not equal), we know that at least one error has occurred. The error (or errors) may have occurred during these steps in the accounting process: (1) preparing journal entries, (2) posting journal entries to the ledger, (3) calculating account balances, (4) copying account balances to the trial balance, or (5) totaling the trial balance columns.

If the trial balance does balance, the accounts are likely to be free from errors that create unequal debits and credits. However, bookkeeping accuracy is not assured if the column totals are equal because some errors do not create unequal debits and credits. For example, the bookkeeper may debit a correct amount to the wrong account in preparing the journal entry or in posting a journal entry to the ledger. This error would cause two accounts to have incorrect balances but the trial balance would not be out of balance. Another error would be to record an equal debit and credit of an incorrect amount. This error would give the two accounts incorrect balances but would not create unequal debits and credits. As a result, the fact that the trial balance column totals are equal does not prove that all journal entries have been recorded and posted correctly. However, equal totals do suggest that several types of errors probably have not occurred.

## Searching for and Correcting Errors

If the trial balance does not balance, at least one error has occurred. The error (or errors) needs to be found and corrected before going on to prepare the financial statements. The search for the error is more efficient if the bookkeeper checks the journalizing, posting, and trial balance preparation steps in reverse order.

First, the bookkeeper should verify that the trial balance columns were correctly added. Second, if that step does not find the error, the bookkeeper should verify that account balances were accurately copied from the ledger. Third, the bookkeeper should check to see if a debit or credit balance was mistakenly listed in the trial balance as a credit or debit. (A clue to this kind of error would be that the difference between the total debits and total credits in the trial balance would equal twice the amount of the incorrectly listed account balance.)

If the error remains undiscovered, the bookkeeper's fourth step is to recalculate each account balance. Then, if the error is not found, it is necessary to verify that each journal entry was properly posted to the accounts. Finally, the only remaining (and least likely) source of the error would be an original journal entry that did not have equal debits and credits.

One frequent error is called a *transposition*. This error occurs when two digits are switched or transposed within a number. For example, a $691 debit in a journal entry may be posted to the ledger as $619. If this happens and it is the only error, the difference between the two trial balance columns is evenly divisible by nine. For example, suppose that a posting error places a $619 debit in an account instead of the journal's correct amount of $691. As a result, the total credits in the trial balance would be larger than the total debits by $72 ($691 − $619). This number is evenly divisible by 9 ($72/9 = 8). Furthermore, the quotient (8) equals the difference between the two transposed numbers. The number of digits in the quotient also signals the location of the transposition. In this example, the fact that the quotient (8) has only one digit tells us that the transposition occurred in the first digit of the transposed numbers, starting from the right.[4]

## Correcting Errors

If errors are discovered in either the journal or the ledger, they need to be corrected to ensure that the financial statements provide useful information. The approach to correcting the records depends on the nature of the errors and when they are discovered.

If an error in a journal entry is discovered before the error is posted, it can be corrected in a manual system by drawing a line through the incorrect information. Then, the correct information can be written above it to create a record of the change for the auditor. (Most computerized systems allow the operator to simply replace the incorrect information.) If a correct amount in the journal was posted incorrectly in the ledger, the bookkeeper can correct it the same way.

If an error in a journal entry is not discovered before it is posted, the correction may have to be done differently. For example, suppose that a journal entry incorrectly debited (or credited) the wrong account. If the journal entry has already been posted to that incorrect account, the bookkeeper generally does not strike through both erroneous entries in the journal and ledger. Instead, the usual practice is to correct the error in the original journal entry by creating another journal entry. This *correcting entry* removes the amount from the wrong account and moves it to the

---

[4]If the transposition error had posted $961 instead of the correct $691, the difference would have been $270, and the quotient would have been $30 ($270/9). The fact that the quotient has two digits tells us to carefully examine the second digits from the right for a transposition of two numbers with a difference of 3.

right account. For example, suppose that the bookkeeper recorded a purchase of office supplies with this incorrect debit in the journal entry to the Office Equipment account and then posted it to the accounts in the ledger:

| Oct. | 14 | Office Equipment ......................... | 1,600.00 | |
|------|----|-------|----------|----------|
| | | Cash ................................ | | 1,600.00 |
| | | *To record the purchase of office supplies.* | | |

As a result of posting this incorrect entry, the Office Supplies account balance is too small (understated) by $1,600 and the Office Equipment account balance is too large (overstated) by the same amount. Three days later, the error is discovered and the following entry is made to correct both account balances:

| Oct. | 17 | Office Supplies ........................... | 1,600.00 | |
|------|----|-------|----------|----------|
| | | Office Equipment ....................... | | 1,600.00 |
| | | *To correct the entry of October 14 that incorrectly* | | |
| | | *debited Office Equipment instead of Office Supplies.* | | |

The credit in the correcting entry cancels the error from the first entry, and the debit correctly records the supplies. The explanation in the correcting entry allows the auditor to know exactly what happened. There are no specific guidelines for writing journal entry explanations. As mentioned earlier in the chapter, the explanation should be short but provide enough information to describe why the entry was made.

Similar correcting entries may be needed in computerized accounting systems. The exact procedure depends on the particular program being used.

## OTHER FORMATTING CONVENTIONS

When amounts are entered manually on ruled accounting paper in a journal, ledger, or trial balance, commas are not needed to indicate thousands and decimal points are not needed to separate dollars and cents. However, commas and decimal points are used in financial statements and other reports.

As a matter of convenience, dollar signs are not used in journals and ledgers. However, they do appear in financial statements and other reports, including trial balances. This book follows the practice of putting a dollar sign beside the first amount in each column of numbers and the first amount appearing after a ruled line indicating that an addition or subtraction has been performed. The financial statements in Illustrations 1–7 and 1–8 on pages 40 and 41 demonstrate how dollar signs are used in this book. Different companies use various conventions for dollar signs. For example, some companies use dollar signs beside only the first and last numbers in the columns in the financial statements.

If an amount entered manually in a ledger or a journal consists of even dollars without cents, a convenient shortcut uses a dash in the cents column instead of two zeros. To simplify the illustrations, this book usually shows exact dollar amounts.

Even small companies seldom show decimal points or cents in their financial statements. Normally, the amounts are rounded, perhaps to the nearest dollar but often to a higher level. **Imperial Oil Limited** is typical of many very large companies in that it rounds its financial statement amounts to the nearest million dollars.

With so much emphasis in this chapter on bookkeeping activities, it might be easy to temporarily overlook the fact that accounting records are created for the purpose of providing useful information in financial statements. This chapter closes by describing a ratio that users apply to assess a company's risk of inability to pay its debts as they become due.

Almost all companies finance some portion of their assets with liabilities and the remaining portion with owner's equity. A company that finances a relatively large portion of its assets with liabilities is said to have a high degree of financial leverage.

You learn more about financial leverage in later chapters. However, you should understand that financial leverage involves risk. Because liabilities must be repaid and also require a company to pay interest, the risk of liabilities is that the company may not be able to make the required payments. In general, the risk is higher if a company is highly leveraged.

One way to evaluate the risk associated with a company's use of liabilities to finance its assets is to calculate and evaluate the **debt ratio.** This ratio describes the relationship between the amounts of the company's liabilities and assets, as follows:

$$\text{Debt ratio} = \frac{\text{Total liabilities}}{\text{Total assets}}$$

To see how the debt ratio is applied, consider the example of **Imperial Oil Limited** discussed at the beginning of the chapter. Using the data that was presented on page 71, the company's debt ratios at the end of each year from 1990 through 1994 are as follows:

|   |   | 1994 | 1993 | 1992 | 1991 | 1990 |
|---|---|---|---|---|---|---|
| a. | Total liabilities* ...... | $ 5,933 | $ 6,295 | $ 6,499 | $ 6,701 | $ 7,593 |
| b. | Total assets* ........ | 11,928 | 12,861 | 13,135 | 13,491 | 14,458 |
| c. | Debt ratio (a ÷ b) .... | .497 | .489 | .495 | .497 | .525 |

Evaluating a company's debt ratio depends on several factors such as the nature of its operations, its ability to generate cash flows, the economic conditions at the time, and the industry in which it operates. Thus, it is not possible to say that a specific debt ratio is good for all companies. However, notice that Imperial's debt ratio was rather constant (range of .489 to .525) over the five-year period. Recall that according to the company's management, Imperial's financial position is one of the strongest in the industry and gives it the flexibility to manage through periods of uncertainty.

---

**Progress Check**

2-14 **Which of the following terms describes a list of all of a company's accounts and their identifying numbers?** *(a)* **A journal;** *(b)* **A ledger;** *(c)* **A trial balance;** *(d)* **A source document; or** *(e)* **A chart of accounts.**

**2-15    When are dollar signs used in accounting reports?**

**2-16    A $4,000 debit to Store Equipment in a journal entry was incorrectly posted to the ledger as a $4,000 credit, and the account had a resulting debit balance of $20,000. What is the effect of the error on the trial balance column totals?**

**2-17    Which debt ratio implies more risk, ignoring other factors?** *(a)* **6.6;** *(b)* **5.0.**

## SUMMARY OF THE CHAPTER IN TERMS OF LEARNING OBJECTIVES

**LO 1.    Describe the events recorded in accounting systems and the importance of source documents and business papers in those systems.** Accounting systems record transactions and other events that affect a company's assets, liabilities, and equity. The other events include internal transactions that use up assets or external events that cause the company's assets or liabilities to change. Source documents describe information that is recorded with accounting entries.

**LO 2.    Describe how accounts are used to record information about the effects of transactions, how code numbers are used to identify each account, and the meaning of the words *debit* and *credit*.** Accounts are the basic building blocks of accounting systems. In one sense, accounts are symbols of the company's assets, liabilities, owner's equity, revenues, and expenses. In another sense, accounts are special records used to store information about transactions. The ledger is the collection of accounts used by an organization. Each account is assigned an identification number based on a code that indicates what kind of account it is. Debits record increases in assets, withdrawals, and expenses. Credits record decreases in these same accounts. Credits also record increases in liabilities, the owner's capital account, and revenues, while debits record decreases in these accounts.

**LO 3.    Describe how debits and credits are used to analyze transactions and record their effects in the accounts.** To understand how a transaction affects a business, determine what accounts were increased or decreased. Every transaction affects at least two accounts, and the sum of the debits for each transaction equals the sum of the credits. As a result, the effects of business transactions never create an imbalance in the accounting equation (Assets = Liabilities + Owner's Equity).

**LO 4.    Record transactions in a General Journal, describe balance column accounts, and post entries from the journal to the ledger.** Transactions are first recorded in a journal that provides a record of all their effects in one location. Second, each entry in the journal is posted to the accounts in the ledger. This process places information in the accounts that is used to produce the company's financial statements. Balance column accounts are widely used in accounting systems. These accounts include columns for debit entries, credit entries, and the balance after each entry.

**LO 5.    Prepare a trial balance, explain its usefulness, and calculate a company's debt ratio.** A trial balance is a list of the accounts in the ledger that shows their debit and credit balances in separate columns. The trial balance is a convenient summary of the ledger's contents. It also reveals the existence of some kinds of errors if the sum of the debit account balances does not equal the sum of the credit account balances. A company's debt ratio is the ratio between its total liabilities and total assets. It provides information about the risk a company faces by using liabilities to finance its assets.

This demonstration problem is based on the same facts as the demonstration problem at the end of Chapter 1. The following events occurred during the first month of Barbara Schmidt's new haircutting business called The Cutlery:

*a.* On August 1, Schmidt put $3,000 cash into a chequing account in the name of The Cutlery. She also invested $15,000 of equipment that she already owned.

*b.* On August 2, she paid $600 cash for furniture for the shop.

*c.* On August 3, she paid $500 cash to rent space in a strip mall for August.

*d.* On August 4, she furnished the shop by installing the old equipment and some new equipment that she bought on credit for $1,200. This amount is to be repaid in three equal payments at the end of August, September, and October.

*e.* On August 5, The Cutlery opened for business. Receipts from cash sales in the first week and a half of business (ended August 15) were $825.

*f.* On August 17, Schmidt paid $125 to an assistant for working during the grand opening.

*g.* Cash receipts from sales during the second half of August were $930.

*h.* On August 31, Schmidt paid an installment on the accounts payable.

*i.* On August 31, she withdrew $900 cash for her personal use.

**Required**

1. Prepare general journal entries for the preceding transactions.
2. Open the following accounts: Cash, 101; Furniture, 161; Store Equipment, 165; Accounts Payable, 201; Barbara Schmidt, Capital, 301; Barbara Schmidt, Withdrawals, 302; Haircutting Services Revenue, 403; Wages Expense, 623; and Rent Expense, 640.
3. Post the journal entries to the ledger accounts.
4. Prepare a trial balance as of August 31.

- Analyze each transaction to identify the accounts affected by the transaction and the amount of each effect.
- Use the debit and credit rules to prepare a journal entry for each transaction.
- Post each debit and each credit in the journal entries to the appropriate ledger accounts and cross-reference each amount in the Posting Reference columns in the journal and account.
- Calculate each account balance and list the accounts with their balances on a trial balance.
- Verify that the total debits in the trial balance equal total credits.

*Solution to
Demonstration
Problem*

1.   General journal entries:

| Date | | Account Titles and Explanations | PR | Debit | Credit |
|---|---|---|---|---|---|
| Aug. | 1 | Cash . . . . . . . . . . . . . . . . . . . . . . . . . . . . . . . . . . | 101 | 3,000.00 | |
| | | Store Equipment . . . . . . . . . . . . . . . . . . . . . . | 165 | 15,000.00 | |
| | |    Barbara Schmidt, Capital | 301 | | 18,000.00 |
| | |    *Owner's initial investment.* | | | |
| | 2 | Furniture . . . . . . . . . . . . . . . . . . . . . . . . . . . . | 161 | 600.00 | |
| | |    Cash . . . . . . . . . . . . . . . . . . . . . . . . . . | 101 | | 600.00 |
| | |    *Purchased furniture for cash.* | | | |
| | 3 | Rent Expense . . . . . . . . . . . . . . . . . . . . . . . . . | 640 | 500.00 | |
| | |    Cash . . . . . . . . . . . . . . . . . . . . . . . . . . | 101 | | 500.00 |
| | |    *Paid rent for August.* | | | |
| | 4 | Store Equipment . . . . . . . . . . . . . . . . . . . . . . | 165 | 1,200.00 | |
| | |    Accounts Payable . . . . . . . . . . . . . . . . . . . | 201 | | 1,200.00 |
| | |    *Purchased additional equipment on credit.* | | | |
| | 15 | Cash . . . . . . . . . . . . . . . . . . . . . . . . . . . . . . . . | 101 | 825.00 | |
| | |    Haircutting Services Revenue . . . . . . . . . . . . | 403 | | 825.00 |
| | |    *Cash receipts from ten days of operations.* | | | |
| | 17 | Wages Expense . . . . . . . . . . . . . . . . . . . . . . . . | 623 | 125.00 | |
| | |    Cash . . . . . . . . . . . . . . . . . . . . . . . . . . | 101 | | 125.00 |
| | |    *Paid wages to assistant.* | | | |
| | 31 | Cash . . . . . . . . . . . . . . . . . . . . . . . . . . . . . . . . | 101 | 930.00 | |
| | |    Haircutting Services Revenue . . . . . . . . . . . . | 403 | | 930.00 |
| | |    *Cash receipts from second half of August.* | | | |
| | 31 | Accounts Payable . . . . . . . . . . . . . . . . . . . . . . | 201 | 400.00 | |
| | |    Cash . . . . . . . . . . . . . . . . . . . . . . . . . . | 101 | | 400.00 |
| | |    *Paid an installment on accounts payable.* | | | |
| | 31 | Barbara Schmidt, Withdrawals . . . . . . . . . . . . . . | 302 | 900.00 | |
| | |    Cash . . . . . . . . . . . . . . . . . . . . . . . . . . | 101 | | 900.00 |
| | |    *Owner withdrew cash from the business.* | | | |

2. 3.   Accounts in the ledger:

| | | Cash | | | Account No. 101 | |
|---|---|---|---|---|---|---|
| Date | | Explanation | PR | Debit | Credit | Balance |
| Aug. | 1 | | G1 | 3,000.00 | | 3,000.00 |
| | 2 | | G1 | | 600.00 | 2,400.00 |
| | 3 | | G1 | | 500.00 | 1,900.00 |
| | 15 | | G1 | 825.00 | | 2,725.00 |
| | 17 | | G1 | | 125.00 | 2,600.00 |
| | 31 | | G1 | 930.00 | | 3,530.00 |
| | 31 | | G1 | | 400.00 | 3,130.00 |
| | 31 | | G1 | | 900.00 | 2,230.00 |

### Furniture

Account No. 161

| Date | | Explanation | PR | Debit | Credit | Balance |
|------|---|-------------|-----|-------|--------|---------|
| Aug. | 2 | | G1 | 600.00 | | 600.00 |

### Store Equipment

Account No. 165

| Date | | Explanation | PR | Debit | Credit | Balance |
|------|---|-------------|-----|-------|--------|---------|
| Aug. | 1 | | G1 | 15,000.00 | | 15,000.00 |
| | 4 | | G1 | 1,200.00 | | 16,200.00 |

### Accounts Payable

Account No. 201

| Date | | Explanation | PR | Debit | Credit | Balance |
|------|---|-------------|-----|-------|--------|---------|
| Aug. | 4 | | G1 | | 1,200.00 | 1,200.00 |
| | 31 | | G1 | 400.00 | | 800.00 |

### Barbara Schmidt, Capital

Account No. 301

| Date | | Explanation | PR | Debit | Credit | Balance |
|------|---|-------------|-----|-------|--------|---------|
| Aug. | 1 | | G1 | | 18,000.00 | 18,000.00 |

### Barbara Schmidt, Withdrawals

Account No. 302

| Date | | Explanation | PR | Debit | Credit | Balance |
|------|---|-------------|-----|-------|--------|---------|
| Aug. | 31 | | G1 | 900.00 | | 900.00 |

### Haircutting Services Revenue

Account No. 403

| Date | | Explanation | PR | Debit | Credit | Balance |
|------|---|-------------|-----|-------|--------|---------|
| Aug. | 15 | | G1 | | 825.00 | 825.00 |
| | 31 | | G1 | | 930.00 | 1,755.00 |

### Wages Expense

Account No. 623

| Date | | Explanation | PR | Debit | Credit | Balance |
|------|---|-------------|-----|-------|--------|---------|
| Aug. | 17 | | G1 | 125.00 | | 125.00 |

### Rent Expense

Account No. 640

| Date | | Explanation | PR | Debit | Credit | Balance |
|------|---|-------------|-----|-------|--------|---------|
| Aug. | 3 | | G1 | 500.00 | | 500.00 |

4.

**THE CUTLERY**
**Trial Balance**
**August 31, 1996**

| | Debit | Credit |
|---|---|---|
| Cash . . . . . . . . . . . . . . . . . . . . . . | $ 2,230 | |
| Furniture . . . . . . . . . . . . . . . . . | 600 | |
| Store equipment . . . . . . . . . . . . . | 16,200 | |
| Accounts payable . . . . . . . . . . . . | | $ 800 |
| Barbara Schmidt, capital . . . . . . . . | | 18,000 |
| Barbara Schmidt, withdrawals . . . . | 900 | |
| Haircutting services revenue . . . . . | | 1,755 |
| Wages expense . . . . . . . . . . . . . . | 125 | |
| Rent expense . . . . . . . . . . . . . . . | 500 | |
| Totals . . . . . . . . . . . . . . . . . . . . | $20,555 | $20,555 |

# GLOSSARY

**Account** a place or location within an accounting system in which the increases and decreases in a specific asset, liability, owner's equity, revenue, or expense are recorded and stored. p. 75

**Account balance** the difference between the increases (including the beginning balance) and decreases recorded in an account. p. 80

**Balance column account** an account with debit and credit columns for recording entries and a third column for showing the balance of the account after each entry is posted. p. 91

**Book of final entry** another name for a ledger. p. 89

**Book of original entry** another name for a journal. p. 89

**Business papers** various kinds of documents and other papers that companies use when they conduct their business; sometimes called *source documents*. p. 73

**Capital account** an account used to record the owner's investments in the business plus any more or less permanent changes in the owner's equity. p. 78

**Chart of accounts** a list of all accounts used by a company; includes the identification number assigned to each account. p. 79

**Compound journal entry** a journal entry that affects at least three accounts. p. 89

**Credit** an entry that decreases asset and expense accounts, or increases liability, owner's equity, and revenue accounts; recorded on the right side of a T-account. p. 80

**Debit** an entry that increases asset and expense accounts, or decreases liability, owner's equity, and revenue accounts; recorded on the left side of a T-account. p. 80

**Debt ratio** the ratio between a company's liabilities and assets; used to describe the risk associated with the company's debts. p. 99

**Double-entry accounting** an accounting system that records the effects of transactions and other events in at least two accounts with equal debits and credits. p. 82

**External transactions** exchanges between the entity and some other person or organization. p. 73

**General Journal** the most flexible type of journal; can be used to record any kind of transaction. p. 89

**Internal transactions** a term occasionally used to describe economic events that affect an entity's accounting equation but that are not transactions between two parties. p. 73

**Journal** a record in which the effects of transactions are first recorded; amounts are posted from the journal to the ledger; also called the *book of original entry*. p. 88

**Ledger** the collection of all accounts used by a business. p. 79

**Posting** the process of copying journal entry information to the ledger. p. 89

**Posting Reference (PR) column** a column in journals and accounts used to cross-reference journal and ledger entries. p. 90

**Prepaid expenses** assets created by payments for economic benefits that are not used until later; as the benefits are used up, the cost of the assets becomes an expense. p. 76

**Promissory note** an unconditional written promise to pay a definite sum of money on demand or on a defined future date (or dates). p. 75

**Source documents** another name for *business papers*; these documents are the source of information recorded with accounting entries. p. 73

**T-account** a simple account form widely used in accounting education to illustrate how debits and credits work. p. 80

**Trial balance** a summary of the ledger that lists the accounts and their balances; the total debit balances should equal the total credit balances. p. 95

**Unearned revenues** liabilities created by advance cash payments from customers for products or services; satisfied by delivering the products or services in the future. p. 77

**Withdrawals account** the account used to record the transfers of assets from a business to its owner; also known as *personal account* or *drawing account*. p. 78

## SYNONYMOUS TERMS

**Business papers** source documents.
**Journal** book of original entry.
**Ledger** book of final entry.

**Posting Reference column** folio column.
**Withdrawals account** drawing account; personal account.

## QUESTIONS

1. What are the three fundamental steps in the accounting process?

2. What is the difference between a note receivable and an account receivable?

3. If assets are valuable resources and asset accounts have debit balances, why do expense accounts have debit balances?

4. Why does the bookkeeper prepare a trial balance?

5. Should a transaction be recorded first in a journal or the ledger? Why?

6. Are debits or credits listed first in general journal entries? Are the debits or the credits indented?

7. What kinds of transactions can be recorded in a General Journal?

8. If a wrong amount was journalized and posted to the accounts, how should the error be corrected?

9. Why is the evidence provided by business papers important to accounting?

10. If a transaction has the effect of decreasing an asset, is the decrease recorded as a debit or as a credit? If the transaction has the effect of decreasing a liability, is the decrease recorded as a debit or as a credit?

11. Why are some accounting systems called *double-entry* accounting systems?

12. What entry (debit or credit) would you make to (a) increase a revenue, (b) decrease an expense, (c) record an owner's withdrawals, and (d) record an owner's investment?

13. Why are the rules of debit and credit the same for both liability and owner's equity accounts?

14. What kinds of errors would cause the column totals of a trial balance to be unequal? What are some examples of errors that would not be revealed by a trial balance?

15. What is the purpose of posting reference numbers that are entered in the journal at the time entries are posted to the accounts?

# QUICK STUDY  (Five-Minute Exercises)

**QS 2–1**
**(LO 1)**

Select the items from the following list that are likely to serve as source documents:

- *a.* Sales ticket.
- *b.* Trial balance.
- *c.* Bank statement.
- *d.* Income statement.
- *e.* Invoice from supplier.
- *f.* Balance sheet.
- *g.* Utility bill.
- *h.* Owner's withdrawals account.

**QS 2–2**
**(LO 2)**

Indicate the financial statement on which each of the following accounts appears, using IS for income statement, SCOE for the statement of changes in owner's equity, and BS for balance sheet:

- *a.* Accounts Receivable.
- *b.* Consulting Services Revenue.
- *c.* Owner, Withdrawals.
- *d.* Land.
- *e.* Unearned Rent.
- *f.* Salaries Expense.
- *g.* Owner, Capital.
- *h.* Interest Payable.
- *i.* Office Supplies.
- *j.* Interest Earned.

**QS 2–3**
**(LO 3)**

Indicate whether a debit or credit is necessary to decrease the normal balance of each of the following accounts:

- *a.* Accounts Receivable.
- *b.* Consulting Services Revenue.
- *c.* Owner, Withdrawals.
- *d.* Land.
- *e.* Unearned Rent.
- *f.* Salaries Expense.
- *g.* Owner, Capital.
- *h.* Interest Payable.
- *i.* Office Supplies.
- *j.* Interest Earned.

**QS 2–4**
**(LO 2, 3)**

Identify whether a debit or credit entry would be made to record the indicated change in each of the following accounts:

- *a.* To increase Rent Earned.
- *b.* To increase Owner, Withdrawals.
- *c.* To decrease Owner, Capital.
- *d.* To decrease Cash.
- *e.* To decrease Prepaid Insurance.
- *f.* To decrease Unearned Fees.
- *g.* To increase Rent Expense.
- *h.* To increase Accounts Payable.
- *i.* To increase Office Equipment.
- *j.* To decrease Accounts Receivable.

**QS 2–5**
**(LO 4)**

Prepare journal entries for the following transactions:

- *a.* On January 3, Jan Davis opened a new consulting business by investing $5,000 cash.
- *b.* On January 5, Davis purchased office supplies on credit for $250.
- *c.* On January 14, Davis received $1,600 in return for providing consulting services to a customer.

**QS 2-6**
**(LO 5)**

A trial balance has total debits of $14,000 and total credits of $17,000. Which one of the following errors would create this imbalance? Explain.

- *a.* A $1,500 debit to Wages Expense in a journal entry was incorrectly posted to the ledger as a $1,500 credit, leaving the Wages Expense account with a $2,000 debit balance.
- *b.* A $3,000 debit to Wages Expense in a journal entry was incorrectly posted to the ledger as a $3,000 credit, leaving the Wages Expense account with a $500 debit balance.
- *c.* A $1,500 credit to Fees Earned in a journal entry was incorrectly posted to the ledger as a $1,500 debit, leaving the Fees Earned account with a $4,200 credit balance.

# EXERCISES

Complete the following table by (1) identifying the type of account listed on each line, (2) entering debit or credit in the blank spaces to identify the kind of entry that would increase or decrease the account balance, and (3) identifying the normal balance of the account.

Exercise 2–1
Increases, decreases, and normal balances of accounts
(LO 2, 3)

|     | Account | Type of Account | Increase | Decrease | Normal Balance |
| --- | --- | --- | --- | --- | --- |
| a. | Accounts payable | | | | |
| b. | Accounts receivable | | | | |
| c. | B. Baxter, capital | | | | |
| d. | B. Baxter, withdrawals | | | | |
| e. | Cash | | | | |
| f. | Equipment | | | | |
| g. | Fees earned | | | | |
| h. | Land | | | | |
| i. | Postage expense | | | | |
| j. | Prepaid insurance | | | | |
| k. | Rent expense | | | | |
| l. | Unearned revenue | | | | |

Franklin Consulting Company recently notified a client that it would have to pay a $32,000 fee for consulting services. Unfortunately, the client did not have enough cash to pay the entire bill. Fran Franklin, the owner of the company, agreed to accept the following items in full payment: $5,000 cash and computer equipment worth $50,000. Franklin also had to assume responsibility for a $23,000 note payable related to the equipment. Which of the following effects would be recorded by Franklin for this transaction? (Your answer may include more than one of the listed effects. Some of the effects of the transaction may not be listed.)

Exercise 2–2
Analyzing the effects of a transaction on the accounts
(LO 3)

a.   $23,000 increase in a liability account.

b.   $5,000 increase in the cash account.

c.   $5,000 increase in a revenue account.

d.   $32,000 increase in the F. Franklin, Capital account.

e.   $32,000 increase in a revenue account.

Open the following T-accounts: Cash; Accounts Receivable; Office Supplies; Office Equipment; Accounts Payable; R. J. Wainwright, Capital; Services Revenue; and Utilities Expense. Next, record these transactions of the Wainwright Company by recording the debit and credit entries directly in the T-accounts. Use the letters beside each transaction to identify the entries. Finally, determine the balance of each account.

Exercise 2–3
Recording the effects of transactions directly in T-accounts
(LO 3)

a.   R. J. Wainwright invested $8,500 cash in the business.

b.   Purchased $250 of office supplies for cash.

c.   Purchased $4,700 of office equipment on credit.

d.   Received $1,000 cash as fees for services provided to a customer.

e.   Paid for the office equipment purchased in transaction c.

f.   Billed a customer $1,800 as fees for services.

g.   Paid the monthly utility bills with $350 cash.

h.   Collected $750 of the account receivable created in transaction f.

**Exercise 2–4**
Preparing a trial balance
**(LO 5)**

After recording the transactions of Exercise 2–3 in T-accounts and calculating the balance of each account, prepare the trial balance for the ledger. Use November 30, 1996, as the date.

**Exercise 2–5**
Effects of posting errors
on the trial balance
**(LO 5)**

Complete the following table by filling in the blanks. For each of the listed posting errors, enter in column (1) the amount of the difference that the error would create between the two trial balance columns (show a zero if the columns would balance). If there would be a difference between the two columns, identify in column (2) the trial balance column that would be larger. The answer for the first error is provided as an example.

| | Description | (1) Difference between Debit and Credit Columns | (2) Column with the Larger Total |
|---|---|---|---|
| a. | A $1,600 debit to Utilities Expense was posted as a $1,060 debit. | $540 | credit |
| b. | A $28,000 debit to Automobiles was posted as a debit to Accounts Payable. | | |
| c. | A $3,300 credit to Fees Earned was posted as a $330 credit. | | |
| d. | A $960 debit to Office Supplies was not posted at all. | | |
| e. | A $1,500 debit to Prepaid Rent was posted as a debit to Rent Expense. | | |
| f. | A $2,700 credit to Cash was posted twice as two credits to the Cash account. | | |
| g. | A $6,600 debit to the owner's withdrawals account was debited to the owner's capital account. | | |

**Exercise 2–6**
Analyzing a trial balance
error
**(LO 5)**

As the bookkeeper for a company, you are disappointed to learn that the column totals in your new trial balance are not equal. After going through a careful analysis, you have discovered only one error. Specifically, the balance of the Office Equipment account has a debit balance of $15,600 on the trial balance. However, you have figured out that a correctly recorded credit purchase of a computer for $3,500 was posted from the journal to the ledger with a $3,500 debit to Office Equipment and another $3,500 debit to Accounts Payable. Answer each of the following questions and present the dollar amount of any misstatement.

a.   Is the balance of the Office Equipment account overstated, understated, or correctly stated in the trial balance?

b.   Is the balance of the Accounts Payable account overstated, understated, or correctly stated in the trial balance?

c.   Is the debit column total of the trial balance overstated, understated, or correctly stated?

d.   Is the credit column total of the trial balance overstated, understated, or correctly stated?

*e.*   If the debit column total of the trial balance is $240,000 before correcting the error, what is the total of the credit column?

On January 1, Rob Gregory created a new business called RG Public Relations Consulting. Near the end of the year, he hired a new bookkeeper without making a careful reference check. As a result, a number of mistakes have been made in preparing the following trial balance:

**Exercise 2–7**
Preparing a corrected trial balance
**(LO 5)**

**RG PUBLIC RELATIONS CONSULTING**
**Trial Balance**
**December 31**

| | Debit | Credit |
|---|---|---|
| Cash . . . . . . . . . . . . . . . . . | $ 11,000 | |
| Accounts receivable . . . . . . | | $ 15,800 |
| Office supplies . . . . . . . . . | 5,300 | |
| Office equipment . . . . . . . . | 41,000 | |
| Accounts payable . . . . . . . . | | 18,930 |
| R. Gregory, capital . . . . . . . | 51,490 | |
| R. Gregory, withdrawals . . . . | 18,000 | |
| Services revenue . . . . . . . . | | 45,600 |
| Wages expense . . . . . . . . . | | 12,000 |
| Rent expense . . . . . . . . . . . | | 9,600 |
| Advertising expense . . . . . . . | | 2,500 |
| Totals . . . . . . . . . . . . . . . . | $126,790 | $104,680 |

Gregory's analysis of the situation has uncovered these errors:

*a.*   The sum of the debits in the Cash account is $74,350 and the sum of the credits is $61,080.

*b.*   A $550 payment from a credit customer was posted to Cash but was not posted to Accounts Receivable.

*c.*   A credit purchase of office supplies for $800 was completely unrecorded.

*d.*   A transposition error occurred in copying the balance of the Services Revenue account to the trial balance. The correct amount was $46,500.

Other errors were made in placing account balances in the trial balance columns and in taking the totals of the columns. Use all this information to prepare a correct trial balance.

Use the information in each of the following situations to calculate the unknown amount:

**Exercise 2–8**
Analyzing account entries and balances
**(LO 2, 3)**

1.   During June, Sunnyside Company had $65,000 of cash receipts and $67,500 of cash disbursements. The June 30 Cash balance was $11,200. Determine how much cash the company had on hand at the close of business on May 31.

2.   On May 31, Sunnyside Company had a $65,000 balance in Accounts Receivable. During June, the company collected $59,300 from its credit customers. The June 30 balance in Accounts Receivable was $67,000. Determine the amount of sales on account that occurred in June.

3.   Sunnyside Company had $98,000 of accounts payable on May 31 and $91,000 on June 30. Total purchases on account during June were $180,000. Determine how much cash was paid on accounts payable during June.

Seven transactions were posted to these T-accounts. Provide a short description of each transaction. Include the amounts in your descriptions.

**Exercise 2–9**
Analyzing transactions from T-accounts
**(LO 2, 3)**

| Cash | | | |
|---|---|---|---|
| (a) | 3,500 | (b) | 1,800 |
| (e) | 1,250 | (c) | 300 |
| | | (f) | 1,200 |
| | | (g) | 350 |

| Truck | |
|---|---|
| (a) | 5,500 |

| Accounts Payable | | | |
|---|---|---|---|
| (f) | 1,200 | (d) | 4,800 |

| Plumbing Supplies | |
|---|---|
| (c) | 300 |
| (d) | 100 |

| Vinnie Doran, Capital | | | |
|---|---|---|---|
| | | (a) | 11,800 |

| Prepaid Insurance | |
|---|---|
| (b) | 1,800 |

| Plumbing Fees Earned | | | |
|---|---|---|---|
| | | (e) | 1,250 |

| Plumbing Equipment | |
|---|---|
| (a) | 2,800 |
| (d) | 4,700 |

| Gas and Oil Expense | |
|---|---|
| (g) | 350 |

**Exercise 2–10**
General journal entries
**(LO 4)**

Use the information in the T-accounts in Exercise 2–9 to prepare general journal entries for the seven transactions. (Omit the account numbers.)

**Exercise 2–11**
General journal entries
**(LO 4)**

Prepare general journal entries to record the following transactions of Wayne's Water-Taxi Service.

May 1    Wayne Oldham invested $15,000 cash and a boat with a $65,000 fair value in a new company that will operate a water-taxi service in the harbour.

1    Rented space in a marina by paying $6,000 for the next three months in advance.

2    Purchased a two-way radio for the boat for $2,800 cash.

15    Collected $5,300 in fares over the preceding two weeks.

31    Paid $1,750 cash for gas and oil used by the boat during May.

**Exercise 2–12**
T-accounts and the trial balance
**(LO 3, 5)**

Use the information provided in Exercise 2–11 to prepare a May 31 trial balance for Wayne's Water-Taxi Service. First, open these T-accounts: Cash; Prepaid Rent; Boat; Equipment; Wayne Oldham, Capital; Fares Earned; and Gas and Oil Expense. Then post the general journal entries to the T-accounts. Finally, prepare the trial balance.

**Exercise 2–13**
Analyzing and journalizing revenue transactions
**(LO 4)**

Examine the following transactions and identify those that created revenues for the business. Prepare general journal entries to record those transactions and explain why the other transactions did not create revenues.

a.    Received $25,500 cash from Dr. J. Runner, the owner of the medical practice.

b.    Provided $900 of medical services to a patient on credit.

c.    Received $1,050 cash for medical services provided to patient.

d.    Received $6,100 from a patient in payment for medical services to be provided next year.

e.    Received $3,000 from a patient in partial payment of an account receivable.

f.    Borrowed $100,000 from the bank by signing a promissory note.

Examine the following transactions and identify those that created expenses for the business. Prepare general journal entries to record those transactions and explain why the other transactions did not create expenses.

*a.* Paid $9,400 cash for medical supplies purchased 30 days previously.

*b.* Paid the $750 salary of the doctor's assistant.

*c.* Paid $30,000 cash for medical equipment.

*d.* Paid utility bill with $620 cash.

*e.* Paid $700 to the owner of the medical practice as a withdrawal.

**Exercise 2–14**
Analyzing and journalizing expense transactions
**(LO 4)**

Calculate the debt ratio for each of the following cases:

**Exercise 2–15**
Calculating the debt ratio
**(LO 5)**

| Case | Assets | Liabilities | Owner's Equity |
|---|---|---|---|
| 1 | $290,000 | $110,000 | $180,000 |
| 2 | 61,000 | 51,000 | 10,000 |
| 3 | 205,000 | 101,000 | 104,000 |
| 4 | 177,000 | 22,000 | 155,000 |
| 5 | 124,000 | 92,000 | 32,000 |
| 6 | 180,000 | 60,000 | 120,000 |

# PROBLEMS

Bobbie Benson opened a consulting firm and completed these transactions during June.

**Problem 2–1**
Recording transactions in T-accounts; preparing a trial balance
**(LO 2, 3, 5)**

*a.* Invested $40,000 cash and office equipment with a $15,000 fair value in a business called Benson Consulting.

*b.* Purchased land and a small office building. The land was worth $15,000, and the building was worth $85,000. The purchase price was paid with $20,000 cash and a long-term note payable for $80,000.

*c.* Purchased $1,200 of office supplies on credit.

*d.* Bobbie Benson transferred title of an automobile to the business. The car was worth $9,000.

*e.* Purchased $3,000 of additional office equipment on credit.

*f.* Paid $750 salary to an assistant.

*g.* Provided services to a client and collected $3,000 cash.

*h.* Paid $400 for the month's utilities.

*i.* Paid account payable created in transaction *c.*

*j.* Purchased $10,000 of new office equipment by paying $9,300 cash and trading in old equipment with a recorded cost of $700.

*k.* Completed $2,600 of services for a client. This amount is to be paid within 30 days.

*l.* Paid $750 salary to an assistant.

*m.* Received $1,900 payment on the receivable created in transaction *k.*

*n.* The owner withdrew $2,000 cash from the business.

**Required**

1. Open the following T-accounts: Cash; Accounts Receivable; Office Supplies; Automobiles; Office Equipment; Building; Land; Accounts Payable; Long-Term Notes Payable; Bobbie Benson, Capital; Bobbie Benson, Withdrawals; Fees Earned; Salaries Expense; and Utilities Expense.

2.  Record the effects of the listed transactions by entering debits and credits directly in the T-accounts. Use the transaction letters to identify each debit and credit entry.

3.  Determine the balance of each account and prepare a trial balance as of June 30.

**Problem 2–2**
Recording transactions in T-accounts; preparing a trial balance
**(LO 2, 3, 5)**

At the beginning of March, Avery Wilson created a custom computer programming company called Softouch. The following transactions occurred during the month:

a.  Created the business by investing $35,000 cash, office equipment with a value of $2,000, and $15,000 of computer equipment.

b.  Purchased land for an office. The land was worth $18,000, which was paid with $1,800 cash and a long-term note payable for $16,200.

c.  Purchased a portable building with $25,000 cash and moved it onto the land.

d.  Paid $2,000 cash for the premiums on two one-year insurance policies.

e.  Provided services to a client and collected $1,900 cash.

f.  Purchased additional computer equipment for $7,500. Paid $3,500 cash and signed a long-term note payable for the $4,000 balance.

g.  Completed $4,000 of services for a client. This amount is to be paid within 30 days.

h.  Purchased $750 of additional office equipment on credit.

i.  Completed another software job for $6,000 on credit.

j.  Received a bill for rent on a computer that was used on the completed job. The $400 rent must be paid within 30 days.

k.  Collected $2,400 from the client described in transaction g.

l.  Paid $500 wages to an assistant.

m.  Paid the account payable created in transaction h.

n.  Paid $225 cash for some repairs to an item of computer equipment.

o.  The owner wrote a $3,200 cheque on the company's bank account to pay some personal expenses.

p.  Paid $500 wages to an assistant.

q.  Paid $1,000 cash to advertise in the local newspaper.

**Required**

1.  Open the following T-accounts: Cash; Accounts Receivable; Prepaid Insurance; Office Equipment; Computer Equipment; Building; Land; Accounts Payable; Long-Term Notes Payable; Avery Wilson, Capital; Avery Wilson, Withdrawals; Fees Earned; Wages Expense; Computer Rental Expense; Advertising Expense; and Repairs Expense.

2.  Record the transactions by entering debits and credits directly in the accounts. Use the transaction letters to identify each debit and credit. Prepare a trial balance as of March 31.

3.  Calculate the company's debt ratio. Use $78,675 as the ending total assets.

**Problem 2–3**
Recording transactions in T-accounts; preparing a trial balance
**(LO 4, 5)**

Wayne Seale completed these transactions during a short period:

a.  Began business as an excavating contractor by investing cash. $37,500; office equipment, $2,200; and excavating machinery, $67,500.

b.  Purchased for $37,500 land to be used as an office site and for parking equipment. Paid $15,000 in cash and signed a promissory note payable for the balance.

c. Purchased additional excavating machinery costing $32,650. Paid $10,150 in cash and signed a promissory note payable for the balance.

d. Paid $6,700 cash for a used prefabricated building and moved it on the land for use as an office.

e. Completed an excavating job and immediately collected $1,275 in cash for the work.

f. Prepaid the premium on an insurance policy giving one year's protection, $960.

g. Completed an $1,875 excavating job for City-Wide Contractors on credit.

h. Paid the wages of the equipment operator, $1,200.

i. Paid $250 cash for repairs to excavating machinery.

j. Received $1,875 from City-Wide Contractors for the work of transaction (g).

k. Completed a $1,200 excavating job for SMK Contractors on credit.

l. Received and recorded as an account payable a $165 bill for the rent of a special machine used on the SMK Contractors job.

m. Purchased additional office equipment on credit, $790.

n. Wayne Seale withdrew $750 from the business for personal use.

o. Paid the wages of the equipment operator, $1,350.

p. Paid the $165 account payable resulting from renting the machine of transaction (l).

q. Paid for gas and oil consumed by the excavating machinery, $335.

**Required**

1. Open the following T-accounts; Cash; Accounts Receivable; Prepaid Insurance; Office Equipment; Machinery; Building; Land; Accounts Payable; Notes Payable; Wayne Seale, Capital; Wayne Seale, Withdrawals; Excavating Revenue; Machinery Repairs Expense; Wages Expense; Machinery Rentals Expense; and Gas and Oil Expense.

2. Record the transactions by entering debits and credits directly in the accounts. Use the transaction letters to identify each debit and credit.

3. Prepare a trial balance using the current date and headed Wayne Seale, Contractor.

Carrie Ford opened a new accounting practice called Carrie Ford, Public Accountant, and completed these transactions during March:

**Problem 2–4**
Preparing and posting general journal entries; preparing a trial balance
**(LO 4, 5)**

Mar. 1 Invested $25,000 in cash and office equipment that had a fair value of $6,000.

1 Prepaid $1,800 cash for three months' rent for an office.

3 Made credit purchases of office equipment for $3,000 and office supplies for $600.

5 Completed work for a client and immediately received $500 cash.

9 Completed a $2,000 project for a client, who will pay within 30 days.

11 Paid the account payable created on March 3.

15 Paid $1,500 cash as the annual premium on an insurance policy.

20 Received $1,600 as partial payment for the work completed on March 9.

23 Completed work for another client for $660 on credit.

27 Carrie Ford withdrew $1,800 cash from the business to pay some personal expenses.

Mar. 30    Purchased $200 of additional office supplies on credit.

  31    Paid $175 for the month's utility bill.

**Required**

1.  Prepare general journal entries to record the transactions.

2.  Open the following accounts (use the balance column format): Cash (101); Accounts Receivable (106); Office Supplies (124); Prepaid Insurance (128); Prepaid Rent (131); Office Equipment (163); Accounts Payable (201); Carrie Ford, Capital (301); Carrie Ford, Withdrawals (302); Accounting Fees Earned (401); and Utilities Expense (690).

3.  Post the entries to the accounts and enter the balance after each posting.

4.  Prepare a trial balance as of the end of the month.

**Problem 2–5**
Interpreting journals, posting, and analyzing trial balance errors
**(LO 4, 5)**

Ada Evans started a business called The Pine Bough on August 1 and completed several transactions during the month. Her accounting and bookkeeping skills are not well-polished, and she needs some help gathering information at the end of the month. She recorded the following journal entries during the month:

| | | | | |
|---|---|---|---|---|
| Aug. | 1 | Cash ..................................... | 15,000.00 | |
| | | Automobiles ............................... | 11,000.00 | |
| | |  Ada Evans, Capital ......................... | | 26,000.00 |
| | 3 | Store Supplies ............................. | 323.00 | |
| | |  Cash ................................... | | 323.00 |
| | 7 | Cash ..................................... | 500.00 | |
| | | Accounts Receivable ....................... | 2,500.00 | |
| | |  Fees Earned ............................. | | 3,000.00 |
| | 8 | Store Equipment .......................... | 3,200.00 | |
| | |  Accounts Payable ......................... | | 3,200.00 |
| | 15 | Cash ..................................... | 400.00 | |
| | |  Fees Earned ............................. | | 400.00 |
| | 17 | Prepaid Insurance ......................... | 625.00 | |
| | |  Cash ................................... | | 625.00 |
| | 23 | Cash ..................................... | 2,500.00 | |
| | |  Accounts Receivable ....................... | | 2,500.00 |
| | 25 | Accounts Payable .......................... | 3,200.00 | |
| | |  Cash ................................... | | 3,200.00 |
| | 27 | Office Equipment ......................... | 4,700.00 | |
| | |  Ada Evans, Capital ....................... | | 4,700.00 |
| | 28 | Ada Evans, Withdrawals ....................... | 1,230.00 | |
| | |  Cash ................................... | | 1,230.00 |
| | 29 | Store Supplies ............................. | 727.00 | |
| | |  Accounts Payable ......................... | | 727.00 |
| | 31 | Salaries Expense ........................... | 1,570.00 | |
| | |  Cash ................................... | | 1,570.00 |

Based on these entries, Evans prepared the following trial balance:

**THE PINE BOUGH**
**Trial Balance**
**August 31**

| | | |
|---|---:|---:|
| Cash . . . . . . . . . . . . . . . . . . | $11,452 | |
| Accounts receivable . . . . . . . . | 0 | |
| Store supplies . . . . . . . . . . . | 1,500 | |
| Prepaid insurance . . . . . . . . | 625 | |
| Automobiles . . . . . . . . . . . . | 11,000 | |
| Office equipment . . . . . . . . | 7,400 | |
| Store equipment . . . . . . . . . | | $ 3,200 |
| Accounts payable . . . . . . . . | | 7,270 |
| Ada Evans, capital . . . . . . . . | | 30,700 |
| Ada Evans, withdrawals . . . . . | 123 | |
| Fees earned . . . . . . . . . . . . | | 3,400 |
| Salaries expense . . . . . . . . . | 1,750 | |
| Totals . . . . . . . . . . . . . . . . | $33,850 | $44,570 |

**Required**

*Preparation component:*

Evans remembers something about trial balances and realizes that the preceding one has at least one error. To help her find the mistakes, set up the following balance column accounts and post the entries to them: Cash (101); Accounts Receivable (106); Store Supplies (125); Prepaid Insurance (128); Automobiles (151); Office Equipment (163); Store Equipment (165); Accounts Payable (201); Ada Evans, Capital (301); Ada Evans, Withdrawals (302); Fees Earned (401); and Salaries Expense (622).

*Analysis component:*

Although Evans's journal entries are correct, she forgot to provide explanations of the events. Analyze each entry and present a reasonable explanation of what happened. Then, prepare a correct trial balance and describe the errors that Evans made.

Jan Dell started a new business, Dimple Dell Day Care, and completed these transactions during October of the current year:

**Problem 2–6**
Journalizing, posting, and preparing financial statements
**(LO 4, 5)**

Oct. 1  Invested $35,000 in cash, $2,500 in teaching supplies, and school equipment worth $9,000.

2  Paid $750 cash for one month's rent for suitable space in a shopping centre.

3  Paid a liability insurance policy premium of $1,400 for the first month.

4  Purchased a van for picking up the kids by paying $14,000 cash.

10  Purchased $800 of additional teaching supplies on credit.

21  Paid $4,000 cash for helpers' salaries.

23  Paid one-half of the account payable created on October 10.

28  Collected $9,000 cash from customers.

29  Paid $1,150 for the month's utility bills.

31  Withdrew $1,200 cash from the business to pay some personal expenses.

**Required**

1. Open the following accounts: Cash (101); Teaching Supplies (126); Automobiles (151); School Equipment (167); Accounts Payable (201); Jan Dell, Capital (301); Jan Dell, Withdrawals (302); Day Care Fees Earned (401); Salaries Expense (622); Insurance Expense (637); Rent Expense (640); and Utilities Expense (690).

2. Prepare general journal entries to record the transactions, post them to the accounts, and prepare a trial balance as of October 31.

3. Prepare an income statement for the month ended October 31.

4. Prepare a statement of changes in owner's equity for the month ended October 31.

5. Prepare a balance sheet dated October 31.

**Problem 2–7**
Journalizing, posting, and preparing financial statements
**(LO 4, 5)**

Amy Tuck graduated from law school with a law degree in June of the current year, and during July she completed these transactions:

July 1    Began the practice of law by investing $3,000 in cash and law books acquired in school and having a $1,200 fair value.

1    Rented the furnished office of a lawyer who was retiring and paid the rent (expense) for July, $725.

2    Purchased law books costing $1,125 under an agreement calling for a $150 down payment and the balance in monthly installments. Paid the down payment and recorded the remaining $975 as an account payable.

5    Purchased office supplies on credit, $70.

6    Took out a liability insurance policy giving one year's protection and paid the premium (expense) for the month of July, $50.

8    Completed legal work for a client and immediately collected $450 for the work done.

12    Paid for the office supplies purchased on credit on July 5.

16    Completed legal work for York Bank on credit, $1,275.

22    Amy Tuck wrote a $30 cheque on the bank account of the legal practice to pay her home telephone bill.

24    Received $1,275 from York Bank for the work completed July 16.

26    Completed legal work for Royal Realty on credit, $900.

30    Paid the telephone bill of the legal practice, $40.

31    Paid the salary of the office secretary, $1,350.

31    Prepaid the rent on the office for August and September, $1,450.

31    Prepaid the liability insurance premium for the next 11 months, $550.

**Required**

1. Open the following accounts: Cash; Accounts Receivable; Prepaid Rent; Prepaid Insurance; Office Supplies; Law Library; Accounts Payable; Amy Tuck, Capital; Amy Tuck, Withdrawals; Legal Fees Earned; Rent Expense; Salaries Expense; Telephone Expense; and Insurance Expense.

2. Prepare general journal entries to record the transactions, post to the accounts, and prepare a trial balance titled Amy Tuck, Lawyer.

3. Prepare an income statement for the month ended July 31.

4. Prepare a statement of changes in owner's equity for the month ended July 31.

5. Prepare a balance sheet dated July 31.

Joan Conrod opened a real estate business and during a short period as an agent completed these business transactions:

Problem 2–8
Recording transactions in
T-accounts; preparing a
trial balance
(LO 3, 4, 5)

a. Invested $42,000 in cash and office equipment with a $6,000 fair value in a real estate agency she called Conrod Realty.

b. Purchased land valued at $30,000 cash and a small office building valued at $105,000, paying $35,000 cash and signing a note payable to pay the balance over a period of years.

c. Purchased office supplies on credit, $60.

d. Joan Conrod contributed her personal automobile, which had a $7,200 fair value, for exclusive use in the business.

e. Purchased additional office equipment on credit, $720.

f. Paid the office secretary's salary, $600.

g. Sold a house and collected an $8,500 cash commission on the sale.

h. Paid $150 for newspaper advertising that had appeared.

i. Paid for the supplies purchased on credit in transaction (c).

j. Purchased a new typewriter for the business, paying $840 cash plus an old typewriter carried in the accounting records at $140.

k. Completed a real estate appraisal on credit and billed the client $210 for the appraisal.

l. Paid the secretary's salary, $600.

m. Received payment in full for the appraisal of transaction (k).

n. Joan Conrod withdrew $1,500 from the business to pay personal expenses.

**Required**

1. Open the following T-accounts: Cash; Accounts Receivable; Office Supplies; Office Equipment; Automobile; Land; Building; Accounts Payable; Notes Payable; Joan Conrod, Capital; Joan Conrod, Withdrawals; Commissions Earned; Appraisal Fees Earned; Office Salaries Expense; and Advertising Expense.

2. Record the transactions by entering debits and credits directly in the accounts. Use the transaction letters to identify each debit and credit amount.

3. Determine the balance of each account in the ledger and prepare a trial balance using the current date and the title Conrod Realty.

Adam Uppe, Public Accountant, completed these transactions during September of the current year:

Problem 2–9
Posting from general
journal entries; preparing
a trial balance
(LO 3, 4, 5)

Sept. 1  Began a public accounting practice by investing $4,200 in cash and office equipment having a $4,800 fair value.

1  Prepaid two months' rent in advance on suitable office space, $1,800.

2  Purchased on credit office equipment, $420, and office supplies, $75.

4  Completed accounting work for a client and immediately received payment of $180 cash.

8  Completed accounting work on credit for Frontier Bank, $700.

Sept. 10   Paid for the items purchased on credit on September 2.

14   Paid the annual $750 premium on an insurance policy.

18   Received payment in full from Frontier Bank for the work completed on September 8.

24   Completed accounting work on credit for Travis Realty, $500.

28   Adam Uppe withdrew $300 cash from the practice to pay personal expenses.

29   Purchased additional office supplies on credit, $45.

30   Paid the September utility bills, $165.

**Required**

1.  Open the following accounts: Cash; Accounts Receivable; Office Supplies; Prepaid Insurance; Prepaid Rent; Office Equipment; Accounts Payable; Adam Uppe, Capital; Adam Uppe, Withdrawals; Accounting Fees Earned; and Utilities Expense.

2.  Prepare general journal entries to record the transactions.

3.  Post to the accounts.

4.  Prepare a trial balance. Title the trial balance Adam Uppe, Public Accountant.

**Problem 2–10**
Analytical essay
**(LO 3)**

Consider the facts in Problem 2–2 and focus on transactions *h* and *o*. Explain how transaction *h* affects the balance sheet, income statement, and statement of changes in owner's equity differently from transaction *o*. Describe how the effects of transaction *o* would differ if the company's owner had written the cheque to pay the company's property taxes instead of the described purpose.

**Problem 2–11**
Analytical essay
**(LO 3, 5)**

Consider the facts in Problem 2–4 and assume that the following mistakes were made in journalizing and posting the transactions. Explain how each mistake would affect the account balances and the column totals in the trial balance.

*a.*   The March 1 investment by Ford was recorded correctly in the journal but the debit to Cash was incorrectly posted to the Cash account as $52,000.

*b.*   The March 5 transaction was incorrectly recorded in the journal as a collection of an account receivable.

*c.*   In recording the March 15 transaction in the journal, the account that should have been debited was credited and the account that should have been credited was debited.

*d.*   The March 30 transaction was recorded correctly in the journal, and the debit was correctly posted, but the credit was not posted at all.

*e.*   The $175 payment on March 31 was recorded incorrectly in both accounts in the journal as a $715 payment.

**Problem 2–12**
Analytical essay
**(LO 3, 5)**

A trial balance may be in balance, yet there may be errors in specific accounts. Explain how the following may occur as a result of errors:

*a.*   Understated liability and understated asset.

*b.*   Overstated asset and overstated owner's equity.

*c.*   Understated asset and understated owner's equity.

*d.*   One asset understated and another asset overstated.

*e.*   One liability understated and another liability overstated.

# SERIAL PROBLEM

*This comprehensive problem starts in this chapter and continues in Chapters 3, 4, and 5. Because of its length, this problem is most easily solved if you use the Working Papers that accompany this text.)*

**Emerald Computer Services**

On October 1, 1996, Tracy Green created a single proprietorship called Emerald Computer Services. Emerald will provide consulting services, including computer system installations and custom program development. Green has adopted the calendar year for reporting and expects to prepare the company's first set of financial statements as of December 31, 1996. The initial chart of accounts for the accounting system includes these items:

| Account | No. | Account | No. |
|---|---|---|---|
| Cash | 101 | Tracy Green, Capital | 301 |
| Accounts Receivable | 106 | Tracy Green, Withdrawals | 302 |
| Computer Supplies | 126 | Computer Services Revenue | 403 |
| Prepaid Insurance | 128 | Wages Expense | 623 |
| Prepaid Rent | 131 | Advertising Expense | 655 |
| Office Equipment | 163 | Mileage Expense | 676 |
| Computer Equipment | 167 | Miscellaneous Expenses | 677 |
| Accounts Payable | 201 | Repairs Expense, Computer | 684 |

**Required**

1. Prepare journal entries to record each of the following transactions for Emerald Computer Services.

2. Open balance column accounts for the company and post the journal entries to them.

Transactions:

Oct. 1  Tracy Green invested $30,000 cash in the business, along with a $12,000 computer system and $6,000 of office equipment.

2  Rented office space for $750 per month and paid the first four months' rent in advance.

3  Purchased computer supplies on credit for $880 from AAA Supply Co.

4  Paid $1,440 cash for one year's premium on a property and liability insurance policy.

5  Billed Bravo Productions $2,200 for installing a new computer.

7  Paid for the computer supplies purchased from AAA Supply Co.

9  Hired Fran Sims as a part-time assistant for $125 per day, as needed. These wages will be paid once each month.

11  Billed Bravo Productions another $800 for services.

14  Received $2,200 from Bravo Productions on their account.

16  Paid $470 to repair computer equipment damaged when moving into the new office.

18  Paid $1,240 for an advertisement in the local newspaper.

21  Received $800 from Bravo Productions on their account.

24  Paid Fran Sims for seven days' work.

27  Billed Charles Company $2,150 for services.

31  Paid $2,000 to Tracy Green for personal use.

Nov. 1  Reimbursed Tracy Green for business usage of her automobile, 700 kilometres at $0.25 per km.

4  Received $3,100 cash from Delta Fixtures, Inc., for computer services.

6  Purchased $640 of computer supplies from AAA Supply Co.

7  Billed Fox Run Estates $2,900 for services.

10  Notified by Alpha Printing Co. that Emerald's bid of $2,500 for an upcoming project was accepted.

17  Paid $150 for Tracy Green's home utilities bill.

19  Received $1,250 from Charles Company against the bill dated October 27.

21  Donated $500 to the United Way in the company's name.

24  Completed work for Alpha Printing Co. and sent them a bill for $2,500.

26  Sent another bill to Charles Company for the past due amount of $900.

27  Paid $2,000 to Tracy Green as a withdrawal.

28  Reimbursed Tracy Green for business usage of her automobile, 800 kilometres at $0.25 per km.

30  Paid Fran Sims for 14 days' work.

# PROVOCATIVE PROBLEMS

**Provocative Problem 2–1**

Ella Fant, interior decorator

**(LO 2)**

Ella Fant operates an interior decorating business. For the first few months of the company's life (through May), the accounting records were maintained by an outside book-keeping service. According to those records, Fant's capital balance was $10,000 as of May 31. To save on expenses, Fant decided to keep the records herself. She managed to record June's transactions properly, but was a bit rusty when the time came to prepare the financial statements. Her first versions of the balance sheet and income statement follow; Fant is bothered that the company operated at a loss during the month, even though she had been very busy. Use the account balances included in the original financial statements to prepare revised statements (except for the capital account), including a statement of changes in owner's equity for the month.

**ELLA FANT INTERIORS**
**Income Statement**
**June 30**

| | | |
|---|---:|---:|
| Revenue: | | |
| Investments by owner | | $   725 |
| Unearned professional fees | | 10,575 |
| Total | | $11,300 |
| Operating expenses: | | |
| Prepaid insurance | $ 750 | |
| Rent expense | 450 | |
| Telephone expense | 300 | |
| Professional library | 8,000 | |
| Travel and entertainment expense | 3,100 | |
| Utilities expense | 400 | |
| Withdrawals by owner | 325 | |
| Total operating expenses | | 13,325 |
| Net income (loss) | | $(2,025) |

**ELLA FANT INTERIORS**
**Balance Sheet**
**For Month Ended June 30**

| Assets | | Liabilities | |
|---|---|---|---|
| Cash | $13,000 | Accounts payable | $ 2,725 |
| Accounts receivable | 2,900 | Professional fees earned | 8,400 |
| Insurance expense | 250 | Total liabilities | $11,125 |
| Prepaid rent | 900 | | |
| Office supplies | 250 | **Owner's Equity** | |
| Land | 12,000 | Ella Fant, capital | 34,975 |
| Salaries expense | 3,300 | | |
| Short-term notes payable | 13,500 | Total liabilities and | |
| Total assets | $46,100 | owner's equity | $46,100 |

At the end of the summer, Pat Hand closed down a small business that operated in Paradise Park. The business rented out two-passenger bicycles and sold shirts, sunglasses, and hats. Hand started the summer with $9,000 in cash and an agreement to rent a small building in the park for up to five years. The $2,400 annual rent must be paid every year, even though the business is open from only June 1 through August 31. At the beginning of the summer, Hand paid cash for the first year's rent and nine bicycles at the price of $250 each.

Over the summer, Hand also purchased shirts, sunglasses, and hats on credit for the total cost of $6,000. By August 31, all but $125 of the payables were paid. Over the summer, cash had been paid for $650 of utility bills and $3,000 of wages to several part-time workers. The owner had also withdrawn $250 cash from the business each week for 13 weeks.

The summer's revenues included $7,500 in bicycle rentals and $13,500 for shirts, sunglasses, and hats. All revenue was collected in cash, except for $80 owed by a local day care centre for some shirts.

Upon closing on August 31, Hand returned the unsold inventory of sunglasses to the distributor for a full cash refund of their $50 original cost. The owner took home the unsold inventory of shirts and hats as gifts for friends and family. Their original cost was $135. Finally, each of the nine used bicycles was sold for $110 cash.

Use the information to prepare an income statement describing the summer's business activities for the three months ended August 31. Also prepare a statement of changes in owner's equity for the same three months and a balance sheet as of August 31. The company's name is Paradise Pedals. As a first step in gathering the data, develop a list of brief explanations of the transactions. Next, post the amounts directly to T-accounts without using a general journal. Then use the T-account balances to prepare the statements. (Record the shirts, hats, and sunglasses in an account called Cost of Goods Sold and then reduce the balance for the unsold merchandise. Also record the difference between the original cost and the selling price of the bicycles in an account called Amortization Expense.)

**Provocative Problem 2–2**
Pat Hand, seasonal business operator
**(LO 4, 5)**

Refer to the financial statements and related information for Geac Computer, Corporation Limited in Appendix I. Find the answers to the following questions by analyzing the information in the report:

1. What four broad categories of expenses are reported on Geac's income statement (Consolidated Statements of Operations)?

2. What five current assets are reported on Geac's balance sheet?

**Provocative Problem 2–3**
Financial statement analysis case
**(LO 2)**

Geac

3.  What three current liabilities are reported on Geac's balance sheet?

4.  What dollar amounts of provisions for income taxes are reported by Geac on its income statements for the annual reporting periods ending in 1994 and 1993?

5.  Using the sum of the company's total liabilities, what is Geac's debt ratio at the end of the 1994 year? How does this compare to the ratio at the end of the 1993 year?

**Provocative Problem 2–4**
Ethical issues essay

Review the As a Matter of Ethics case on page 74. Discuss the nature of the dilemma faced by Kim Li and evaluate the alternative courses of action that she should consider.

---

# ANALYTICAL AND REVIEW PROBLEMS

**A & R Problem 2–1**

Lester Fenwick started a real estate agency and completed seven transactions, including Fenwick's initial investment of $8,500 cash. After these transactions, the ledger included the following accounts with their normal balances:

| | |
|---|---:|
| Cash ..................... | $11,300 |
| Office supplies ............. | 330 |
| Prepaid insurance ........... | 1,600 |
| Office equipment ........... | 8,250 |
| Accounts payable ........... | 8,250 |
| Lester Fenwick, capital ........ | 8,500 |
| Lester Fenwick, withdrawals .... | 3,900 |
| Commissions earned ......... | 12,000 |
| Advertising expense ......... | 3,370 |

**Required**

*Preparation component:*

Prepare a trial balance for the business.

*Analysis component:*

Analyze the accounts and balances and prepare a list that describes each of the seven transactions and its amount. Also, present a schedule that shows how the transactions resulted in the $11,300 Cash balance.

**A & R Problem 2–2**

Sabira Hussain began a computer consulting business called Aribas Computer Services. She invested $25,000 and her automobile which had a market value of $18,000. The business was an instant success; however, she could not say the same about her bookkeeper who prepared the following trial balance:

**ARIBAS COMPUTER SERVICES**
**Trial Balance**
**September 30, 1996**

| | | |
|---|---:|---:|
| Cash ................ | $26,200 | |
| Accounts receivable ....... | 4,000 | |
| Supplies .............. | 4,800 | |
| Automobile ............ | 21,000 | |
| Accounts payable ........ | | $     0 |
| Sabira Hussain, Capital .... | | 56,000 |
| Total ................ | $56,000 | $56,000 |

Upon seeing the trial balance, Hussain dismissed the bookkeeper and asked you to help her until she found a replacement. With Hussain's help you were able to determine the following:

a.  Consulting fees earned and billed during September amounted to $16,000 of which $9,000 was collected.

b.  Office equipment purchased but not as yet paid for, $3,000.

c.  Supplies purchased for cash, $1,800.

d.  Paid $1,800 for two months' office rent.

e.  Wages paid for September, $2,200.

f.  Hussain withdrew $3,000 for living expenses.

**Required**

1.  List the errors the bookkeeper made.

2.  Prepare a corrected trial balance.

3.  Explain why the original trial balance balanced.

# CONCEPT TESTER

Test your understanding of the concepts introduced in this chapter by completing the following crossword puzzle.

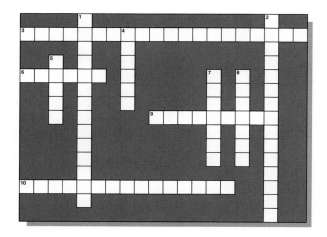

**Across Clues**

3. Exchanges between the entity and some other person or organization (2 words).

6. An entry that decreases assets and expenses but increases other financial statement items.

9. Total liabilities divided by total assets (2 words).

10. A list of the accounts used by a company, with identifying numbers (3 words).

**Down Clues**

1. An unconditional written promise to pay a definite sum on demand or a given future date (2 words).

2. Documents that are the source of information recorded with accounting entries (2 words).

4. The collection of all accounts used by a business.

5. An entry that increases assets and expenses or decreases other financial statement items.

7. A record in which the effects of transactions are first recorded.

8. The process of copying journal entry information to the ledger.

# ANSWERS TO PROGRESS CHECKS

2–1 *d*

2–2 External and internal transactions.

2–3 Business papers are called source documents because they provide information about an entity's transactions that is used as a basis for recording the transactions in the accounting records.

2–4 *b*

2–5 Business papers are important because of the objectivity principle, which requires that accounting be based on verifiable evidence whenever possible.

2–6 A company's size affects the number of accounts it uses.

2–7 No. For example, a debit increases an expense account and decreases a revenue account.

2–8 *c*

2–9 Owner's equity is increased by revenues and by owner's investments in the business. Owner's equity is decreased by expenses and owner's withdrawals.

2–10 The name *double-entry* is used because all transactions are recorded in at least two accounts, a debit in one account and a credit in another.

2–11 *c*

2–12 A journal entry with more than one debit or credit items.

2–13 To indicate that the item has been posted to the account in the ledger.

2–14 *e*

2–15 The use of the dollar sign may vary from company to company. However, most use dollar signs beside only the first and last numbers in the columns in the financial statements.

2–16 The debit column is understated by $4,000 and the credit column is overstated by $4,000, a difference of $8,000.

2–17 *a*

# CHAPTER 3

*Although most economic events that affect an organization occur as external transactions, other kinds of events also change its assets, liabilities, and net income. The adjusting process records these events so that the financial statements present more useful information.*

# Adjusting the Accounts and Preparing the Statements

Since their first encounter in the school library with Imperial Oil Limited, Karen White and Mark Smith have continued to study the company's 1994 Annual Report. Although their familiarity with financial statements is very limited, they did note just how large a company Imperial is. Its assets approached $13 billion and annual sales $9 billion in 1994.

Examining the balance sheet, Karen and Mark observed that a variety of assets were identified as "current assets." Likewise, several liabilities were identified as "current liabilities." White and Smith wondered why these items were segregated from the other items on the statement and described as current. Perhaps they are related to each other in some important way.

**IMPERIAL OIL LIMITED**
**(in millions)**

|  | Year Ended December 31 | |
|  | 1994 | 1993 |
| --- | --- | --- |
| Total current assets ..... | $2,797 | $2,899 |
| Total current liabilities .... | 1,581 | 1,593 |

## LEARNING OBJECTIVES

**After studying Chapter 3, you should be able to:**

1. **Explain why financial statements are prepared at the end of regular accounting periods, why the accounts must be adjusted at the end of each period, and why the accrual basis of accounting produces more useful income statements and balance sheets than the cash basis.**

2. **Prepare adjusting entries for prepaid expenses, amortization, unearned revenues, accrued expenses, and accrued revenues.**

3. **Prepare a schedule that includes the unadjusted trial balance, the adjustments, and the adjusted trial balance; use the adjusted trial balance to prepare financial statements; and prepare entries to record cash receipts and cash disbursements related to accrued assets and liabilities.**

4. **Define each asset and liability category for the balance sheet, prepare a classified balance sheet, and calculate the current ratio.**

5. **Define or explain the words and phrases listed in the chapter glossary.**

**After studying Appendix B at the end of Chapter 3, you should be able to:**

6. **Explain why some companies record prepaid and unearned items in income statement accounts and prepare adjusting entries when this procedure is used.**

In business for a century, Imperial Oil Limited, realizes the importance of communicating its position through its annual reports. For example, the company used its 1993 annual report to point out that it was selling less productive assets and changing its sales mix to emphasize more profitable products. In 1994 the company pointed out the resulting success. To accurately present this financial picture, a company must have an effective accounting system in place.

You learned in Chapter 2 that companies use accounting systems to collect information about transactions and other economic events. That chapter showed you how journals and ledgers are used to capture information about external transactions. This chapter explains how the accounting system gathers information about economic events that are not transactions with outside parties. The process involves adjusting the account balances at the end of the reporting period to reflect the economic events that are sometimes called internal transactions. As a result, the adjusted accounts contain the amounts to be reported on the financial statements according to generally accepted accounting principles. The chapter ends with a description of the current ratio, which is used by decision makers to assess the company's ability to pay its liabilities in the near future.

## ACCOUNTING PERIODS AND FISCAL YEARS

To be useful, information must reach decision makers frequently and promptly. To provide this timely information, accounting systems are designed to produce periodic reports at regular intervals. As a result, the accounting process is based on the **time period principle.** According to this principle, an organization's activities are identified with specific time periods, such as a month, a three-month quarter, or a year. Then, financial statements are prepared for each reporting period. The time periods covered by the reports are called **accounting periods.** Most organizations use one year as their primary accounting period. As a result, they prepare annual financial statements. However, nearly all organizations also prepare **interim financial reports** that cover one or three months of activity.

The annual reporting period is not always the same as the calendar year ending December 31. In fact, an organization can adopt a **fiscal year** consisting of any 12 consecutive months. For example, most banks use October 31 as the end of the fiscal period. An acceptable variation of this is to adopt an annual reporting period of 52 weeks.[1]

Companies that do not experience much seasonal variation in sales volume within the year often choose the calendar year as their fiscal year. On the other hand, companies that experience major seasonal variations in sales often choose a fiscal year that corresponds to their **natural business year.** The natural business year ends when sales activities are at their lowest point during the year. For example, the natural business year for retail stores ends around January 31, after the Christmas and January selling seasons. As a result, they often start their annual accounting periods on February 1.

During an accounting period, the normal process is to record the economic events that occur in the form of external transactions (with outside parties). After all external transactions are recorded, several accounts in the ledger need to be updated before their balances appear in the financial statements. This need arises from the fact that some economic events remain unrecorded because they did not occur as external transactions.

For example, the costs of some assets expire as time passes. Notice that the third item in the trial balance of Clear Copy in Illustration 3–1 is Prepaid insurance and that it has a balance of $2,400. This amount is the original cost of the premium for two years of insurance protection beginning on December 1, 1996. By December 31, 1996, one month's coverage has been used up, and $2,400 is no longer the cost of the remaining prepaid insurance. Because the coverage costs an average of $100 per month ($2,400/24 months), the Prepaid Insurance account balance should be reduced by that amount. In addition, the income statement should report $100 as insurance expense.

Similarly, the $3,720 balance in the Store Supplies account includes the cost of some supplies that were consumed during December. The cost of these supplies should be reported as an expense of the month. Because of these unrecorded events, the balances of the Prepaid Insurance and Store Supplies accounts should be *adjusted* before they are presented on the December 31 balance sheet.

Another adjustment is necessary because one month of the copy equipment's useful life has expired. In addition, the balances of the Unearned Copy Services Revenue, Copy Services Revenue, and Salaries Expense accounts should be adjusted before they appear on the December income statement.

The next section of the chapter explains how the adjusting process is accomplished. As you study the material, remember that our goal is to provide useful information in the financial statements.

**LO 1**

Explain why financial statements are prepared at the end of regular accounting periods, why the accounts must be adjusted at the end of each period, and why the accrual basis of accounting produces more useful income statements and balance sheets than the cash basis.

## WHY ARE THE ACCOUNTS ADJUSTED AT THE END OF AN ACCOUNTING PERIOD?

---

[1]Some companies actually choose a 52-week fiscal year, with the result that their annual reports end on a different date each year. The Oshawa Group uses a 52- or 53-week fiscal period with the end of the fiscal year falling on the last day of the last full week in January.

Illustration 3-1

**CLEAR COPY**
**Trial Balance**
**December 31, 1996**

|  | Debit | Credit |
|---|---|---|
| Cash | $ 7,950 | |
| Accounts receivable | 0 | |
| Prepaid insurance | 2,400 | |
| Store supplies | 3,720 | |
| Copy equipment | 26,000 | |
| Accounts payable | | $ 6,200 |
| Unearned copy services revenue | | 3,000 |
| Terry Dow, capital | | 30,000 |
| Terry Dow, withdrawals | 400 | |
| Copy services revenue | | 3,900 |
| Rent expense | 1,000 | |
| Salaries expense | 1,400 | |
| Utilities expense | 230 | |
| Total | $43,100 | $43,100 |

# THE ADJUSTING PROCESS

The adjusting process is consistent with two accounting principles, the *revenue recognition principle* and the *matching principle.* Chapter 1 explained that the *revenue recognition principle* requires revenue to be reported on the income statement only when it is earned, not before and not after. For most firms, revenue is earned when a service or a product is delivered to the customer. For example, if Clear Copy provides copy services to a customer during December, the revenue is earned during December. As a result, it should be reported on the December income statement, even if the customer paid for the services in November or will pay for them in January. One major goal for the adjusting process is to ensure that revenue is reported, or recognized, in the time period when it is earned.

The goal of the **matching principle** is to report expenses on the income statement in the same accounting period as the revenues that were earned as a result of the expenses. For example, assume that a business earns revenues during December while it operates out of rented store space. According to the *revenue recognition principle,* the business should report its revenues on the December income statement. In earning those revenues, the business incurs rent expense. The *matching principle* tells us that the rent should be reported on the income statement for December, even if the rent was paid in November or will be paid in January. As a result, the rent expense for December is matched with December's revenues. This matching of expenses with revenues is a major goal of the adjusting process.

Matching expenses with revenues often requires a company to predict future events. To use financial statements wisely, you need to understand that they are based on predictions and therefore include measurements that are not precise. For example, **The Walt Disney Company's** 1993 annual report explains that the company allocates film production costs among years based on a ratio of actual revenues to date from the film divided by its predicted total gross revenues.

When the adjusting process assigns revenues to the periods in which they are earned and matches expenses with the revenues, the company is using **accrual basis accounting.** The objective of the accrual basis is to report the economic effects of revenues and expenses when they are earned or incurred, not when cash is received or paid.

The alternative to accrual accounting is **cash basis accounting.** Under the cash basis, revenues are recognized when cash is received and expenses are reported when cash is paid. For example, if revenue is earned in December but cash is not received from the customer until January, the cash basis reports the revenue in January. Because revenues are reported when cash is received and expenses are deducted when cash is paid, cash basis net income for a period is the difference between revenues received in cash (called *receipts*) and expenses paid with cash (called *expenditures* or *disbursements*).

The conclusion of "Financial Statement Concepts" is: "Items recognized in financial statements are accounted for in accordance with the accrual basis of accounting. The accrual basis of accounting recognizes the effect of transactions and events in the period in which the transactions and events occur, regardless of whether there has been a receipt or payment of cash or its equivalent."[2] Some concerns use a cash basis, but it is acceptable only if the amount of prepaid, unearned, and accrued items is unimportant. One important benefit of accrual accounting is that it makes the information on accounting statements comparable from period to period.

For example, Clear Copy paid $2,400 for two years of insurance coverage beginning on December 1. Under accrual accounting, $100 of insurance expense is reported on the December 1996 income statement. During 1997, $1,200 of expense will be reported (the average monthly cost is $100). During 1998, $1,100 expense will be reported for the first 11 months of the year. This allocation of the insurance cost among the three fiscal years is represented graphically in Illustration 3–2.

In contrast, a cash basis income statement for December 1996 would report insurance expense of $2,400. The income statements for 1997 and 1998 would not report any insurance expense from this policy. To provide useful information about the company's activities and assets, the accrual basis shows that each of the 24 months had $100 of insurance expense. The balance sheet also reports the remaining unexpired premium as the cost of the prepaid insurance asset. However, the cash basis would never report an asset. In summary, the cash basis information would be less useful for decisions because the reported income for 1996, 1997, and 1998 would not reflect comparable measures of the cost of having insurance in those years.

The accrual basis is generally accepted for external reporting because it produces more useful information. The cash basis is not acceptable for a balance sheet or income statement because it provides incomplete information about assets, liabilities, revenues, and expenses.

**ACCRUAL BASIS COMPARED WITH CASH BASIS ACCOUNTING**

[2] *CICA Handbook,* par. 1000.41.

**Illustration 3-2** Allocating the $2,400 Cost of Insurance Protection for 24 Months Beginning December 1, 1996

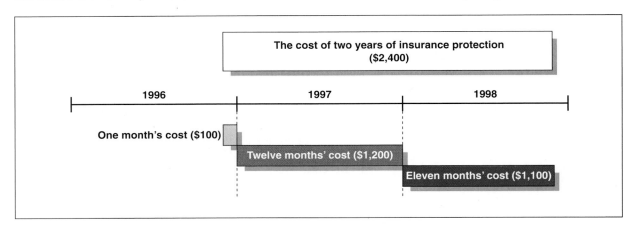

---

**Progress Check**
*(Answers to Progress Checks are provided at the end of the chapter.)*

3-1   **A company's annual reporting period:** *(a)* **Is called the fiscal year;** *(b)* **Always ends at the close of the natural business year;** *(c)* **Always ends at the close of the calendar business year;** *(d)* **Cannot be divided into shorter interim periods.**

3-2   **Why do companies prepare interim financial statements?**

3-3   **Which accounting principles lead most directly to the adjustment process?**

3-4   **Is the cash basis of accounting consistent with the matching principle?**

3-5   **On April 1, 1996, Collins Company paid a $4,800 premium for two years of insurance coverage. Under the cash basis, how much insurance expense will be reported in 1997?**

---

## ADJUSTING SPECIFIC ACCOUNTS

**LO 2**

Prepare adjusting entries for prepaid expenses, depreciation, unearned revenues, accrued expenses, and accrued revenues.

The process of adjusting the accounts is similar to the process used to analyze and record transactions. Each account balance and the economic events that affect it are analyzed to determine whether an adjustment is needed. If an adjustment is needed, an **adjusting entry** is recorded to bring the asset or liability account balance up to date. The adjustment also updates the related expense or revenue account. Like other journal entries, adjusting entries are posted to the accounts. The following paragraphs explain why adjusting entries are needed to provide useful information.

Adjusting entries for prepaid expenses, amortization, and unearned revenues involve previously recorded assets and liabilities. These entries are made to record the effects of economic events (including the passing of time) that have changed these assets and liabilities. On the other hand, adjusting entries for accrued expenses and accrued revenues involve liabilities and assets that have not yet been recorded. Adjusting entries record the effects of economic events that created these liabilities and assets as well as the related expenses and revenues.

# Prepaid Expenses

A prepaid expense is an economic benefit paid for in advance of its use. When it is paid for, the company acquires an asset that will expire or be used up. As the asset is used, its cost becomes an expense.

**Prepaid Insurance.** For example, recall that Clear Copy paid $2,400 for two years of insurance protection that went into effect on December 1, 1996. (The allocation of this cost to 1996, 1997, and 1998 is described in Illustration 3–2.) As each day of December went by, some of the benefit of the insurance protection expired, and a portion of the asset's cost became an expense. By December 31, one month's insurance coverage had expired. This expense is measured as $100, which is 1/24 of $2,400. The following adjusting entry records the expense with a debit, and reduces the cost of the asset with a credit to the asset account:

| | | Adjustment a | | |
|---|---|---|---|---|
| Dec. | 31 | Insurance Expense .......................... | 100.00 | |
| | | Prepaid Insurance ...................... | | 100.00 |
| | | *To record the expense created by expired insurance.* | | |

Posting the adjusting entry has the following effect on the accounts:

| **Prepaid Insurance** | | | | **Insurance Expense** | | |
|---|---|---|---|---|---|---|
| Dec. 26 | 2,400 | Dec. 31 | 100 | Dec. 31 | 100 | |
| | − 100 | | | | | |
| Balance | 2,300 | | | | | |

After the entry is posted, the $100 balance in Insurance Expense and the $2,300 balance in Prepaid Insurance are ready to be presented on the financial statements.

The allocation process in Illustration 3–2 shows that another adjusting entry in 1997 transfers $1,200 from Prepaid Insurance to Insurance Expense. A third adjusting entry in 1998 transfers the remaining $1,100 to the expense account.

**Store Supplies.** Store supplies are another prepaid expense that is adjusted. For example, Clear Copy purchased $3,720 of store supplies in December and used some of them up during the month. Consuming these supplies created an expense equal to their cost. However, the daily consumption of the supplies was not recorded in the accounts because the information was not needed. Due to the fact that the account balances are not presented in financial statements until the end of the month, bookkeeping effort can be reduced by making only one adjusting entry to record the total cost of all supplies consumed in the month.

Because an income statement is to be prepared for December, the cost of the store supplies used during the month needs to be recognized as an expense. To learn the amount used, Terry Dow counts (or, takes an inventory of) the remaining unused supplies. Then, the cost of the remaining supplies is deducted from the cost of the purchased supplies. For example, suppose that Dow finds that $2,670 of supplies remain out of the $3,720 purchased in December. The $1,050 difference between these two amounts is the cost of the consumed supplies. This amount is the month's store supplies expense. This adjusting entry records the expense with a debit and reduces the asset account balance with an equal credit:

|  |  |  |  |  |
|---|---|---|---|---|
|  |  | *Adjustment b* |  |  |
| Dec. | 31 | Store Supplies Expense . . . . . . . . . . . . . . . . . . . . . . | 1,050.00 |  |
|  |  | Store Supplies . . . . . . . . . . . . . . . . . . . . . . . . . . . |  | 1,050.00 |
|  |  | *To record the expense created by using store supplies.* |  |  |

Posting the adjusting entry has the following effect on the accounts:

| Store Supplies | | | | Store Supplies Expense | | |
|---|---|---|---|---|---|---|
| Dec. 2 | 2,500 | Dec. 31 | 1,050 | Dec. 31 | 1,050 | |
| 6 | 1,100 | | | | | |
| 26 | 120 | | | | | |
| Total | 3,720 | Total | 1,050 | | | |
| | − 1,050 | | | | | |
| Balance | 2,670 | | | | | |

As a result, the balance of the store supplies account now equals the $2,670 cost revealed by the manager's inventory.

**Other Prepaid Expenses.**  Unlike the two previous examples, some prepaid expenses are both acquired and fully used up within a single accounting period. For example, a company usually pays monthly rent on the first day of each month. Every month, the payment creates a prepaid expense that fully expires by the end of the month. In these cases, the bookkeeper can ignore the fact that the payment creates an asset and record the payment with a debit to the expense account instead of the asset account. (These practices are described more completely in Appendix B at the end of this chapter.)

## Amortization[3]

In accounting, the term **capital assets** describes tangible long-lived assets that are used to produce or sell goods and services. Examples of capital assets are land, buildings, machines, vehicles, and professional libraries. Except for land, capital assets eventually wear out or otherwise lose their usefulness and value. Therefore, income statements should report the cost of using these assets as expenses during their useful lives. The expense created by allocating the original cost of assets is called **amortization.** Amortization expense is recorded with an adjusting entry similar to the entries to record the using up of prepaid expenses. However, the entry is slightly more complicated because a special account is used to record the reduced asset balance.

---

[3]In 1990, the revised *CICA Handbook*, section 3060, recommended use of the term *amortization* instead of *depreciation*, but the use of *depreciation* was not ruled out. Also, *fixed assets* was replaced by *capital assets*. It may take several years for the new terminology to be widely implemented by companies; thus, *depreciation* and *depletion* may continue in use for some time.

For example, Clear Copy uses copy equipment to earn revenue. This equipment's cost should be amortized to provide a complete income statement. Early in December, Clear Copy made two purchases of equipment for $20,000 and $6,000. Using information received from the manufacturer and other sources, Terry Dow predicts that the equipment will have a four-year useful life. Dow also predicts that the company will be able to sell the equipment for $8,000 at the end of the four years. Therefore, the net cost expected to expire over the useful life is $18,000 ($26,000 − $8,000). When this net cost is divided by the 48 months in the asset's predicted life, the result is an average monthly cost of $375 ($18,000/48). This average cost is recorded as amortization expense for each month with this adjusting entry:

| | | | | |
|---|---|---|---|---|
| | | *Adjustment c* | | |
| Dec. | 31 | Amortization Expense . . . . . . . . . . . . . . . . . . . . . . . | 375.00 | |
| | | Accumulated Amortization, Copy Equipment . . . . | | 375.00 |
| | | *To record the expense created by using the copying equipment.* | | |

Posting the adjusting entry has the following effect on the accounts:

| Copy Equipment | | |
|---|---|---|
| Dec. 3 | 20,000 | |
| 6 | 6,000 | |
| Total | 26,000 | |

| Amortization Expense, Copy Equipment | | |
|---|---|---|
| Dec. 31 | 375 | |

| Accumulated Amortization, Copy Equipment | | |
|---|---|---|
| | Dec. 31 | 375 |

After the entry is posted, the Copy Equipment account and its related Accumulated Amortization, Copy Equipment account together show the December 31 balance sheet amounts for this asset. The Amortization Expense, Copy Equipment account shows the amount of expense that will appear on the December income statement.

In most cases, a decrease in an asset account is recorded by entering a credit directly in the account. However, note in the illustrated accounts that this procedure is not followed in recording amortization. Instead, amortization is recorded in a **contra account.** A contra account's balance is subtracted from a related account's balance to provide more information than simply the net amount. In this example, the contra account is Accumulated Amortization, Copy Equipment.

Why are contra accounts used to record amortization? Contra accounts allow balance sheet readers to observe both the original cost of the assets and the estimated amount of amortization that has been charged to expense in the past. By knowing both the original cost and the accumulated amortization, decision makers can more completely assess the company's productive capacity and the potential need to replace the assets. For example, Clear Copy's balance sheet shows both the $26,000 original cost of the equipment and the $375 balance in the accumulated amortization contra account. This information lets statement users see that the equipment is almost new. In contrast, if Clear Copy simply reported the net remaining cost of $25,625, the users would not know whether the equipment is new or so old that it needs immediate replacement.

Note the words **accumulated amortization** in the title of the contra account. This reflects the fact that this account reports the total amount of amortization expense recognized in all prior periods since the assets were put into service. For example, the Copy Equipment and the Accumulated Amortization accounts would look like this on February 28, 1997, after three monthly adjusting entries:

| Copy Equipment | | Accumulated Amortization, Copy Equipment | |
|---|---|---|---|
| Dec. 3 | 20,000 | Dec. 31 | 375 |
| 6 | 6,000 | Jan. 31 | 375 |
| | | Feb. 28 | 375 |
| Total | 26,000 | Total | 1,125 |

These account balances would be presented on the February 28 balance sheet as follows:

| | |
|---|---|
| Copy equipment | $26,000 |
| Less accumulated amortization | 1,125 |
| Net | $24,875 |

Later chapters describe how other contra accounts are used in other situations.

## Unearned Revenues

An unearned revenue is a liability created when a customer's payment is received in advance of delivering the goods or services. For example, Clear Copy has unearned revenue. On December 26, Terry Dow agreed to provide copying services for a customer for the fixed fee of $1,500 per month. On that day, the customer paid the first two months' fees in advance to cover the period from December 27 to February 26. This entry records the cash receipt:

| Dec. | 26 | Cash | 3,000.00 | |
| | | Unearned Copy Services Revenue | | 3,000.00 |
| | | *Received advanced payment for copying services to be provided over two months.* | | |

This advance payment increased cash and created an obligation to do copying work over the next two months. By December 31, the business provided five days' service and earned one-sixth of the $1,500 revenue for the first month. This amount is $250 ($1,500/6). The company also discharged one-twelfth of the total $3,000 liability because five days is one-twelfth of two months. According to the *revenue recognition principle,* the $250 of revenue should appear on the December income statement. Notice that the event that caused the earning of revenue was simply the passage of time. There was no external transaction. The following adjusting entry updates the accounts by reducing the liability and recognizing the earned revenue:

| | | | | |
|---|---|---|---|---|
| | | *Adjustment d* | | |
| Dec. | 31 | Unearned Copy Services Revenue ................ | 250.00 | |
| | | Copy Services Revenue ($1,500/6) ........... | | 250.00 |
| | | *Earned revenue that was received in advance.* | | |

The accounts look like this after the entry is posted:

| Unearned Copy Services Revenue | | | | Copy Services Revenue | |
|---|---|---|---|---|---|
| Dec. 31 | 250 | Dec. 26 | 3,000 | Dec. 10 | 2,200 |
| | | | | 12 | 1,700 |
| | | | | 31 | 250 |

In effect, the adjusting entry transfers $250 of earned revenue from the liability account to the revenue account.

## Accrued Expenses

Most expenses are recorded when they are paid with cash. In making the journal entry to record the transaction, the credit to the Cash account is accompanied by a debit to the expense account. However, because some expenses incurred during the period have not been paid for, they may remain unrecorded at the end of an accounting period. These incurred but unpaid expenses are called **accrued expenses.** One typical example of an accrued expense is the unpaid wages earned by employees for work they have already completed.

**Accrued Salaries.** For example, Clear Copy's only employee earns $70 per day or $350 for a five-day workweek that begins on Monday and ends on Friday. The employee's salary is paid every two weeks on Friday. On the 12th and the 26th of December, these wages were paid, recorded in the journal, and posted to the ledger. The Salaries Expense and Cash accounts show these entries:

| **December 1997** | | | | | | |
|---|---|---|---|---|---|---|
| S | M | T | W | T | F | S |
| | 1 | 2 | 3 | 4 | 5 | 6 |
| 7 | 8 | 9 | 10 | 11 | 12 | 13 |
| 14 | 15 | 16 | 17 | 18 | 19 | 20 |
| 21 | 22 | 23 | 24 | 25 | 26 | 27 |
| 28 | 29 | 30 | 31 | | | |

| Cash | | | Salaries Expense | |
|---|---|---|---|---|
| Dec. 12 | 700 | Dec. 12 | 700 | |
| 26 | 700 | 26 | 700 | |

The calendar for December 1997 in the margin shows us that three working days (December 29, 30, and 31) come after the December 26 payday. Thus, the employee earned three days' salary at the close of business on Wednesday, December 31. Because this salary had not been paid, the expense was not recorded. But, the financial statements would be incomplete if they failed to report this additional expense and the liability to the employee for the unpaid salary. Therefore, this adjusting entry should be recorded on December 31 to produce a complete record of the company's expenses and liabilities:

| | | | | |
|---|---|---|---|---|
| | | *Adjustment e* | | |
| Dec. | 31 | Salaries Expense . . . . . . . . . . . . . . . . . . . . . . . . . . | 210.00 | |
| | | Salaries Payable . . . . . . . . . . . . . . . . . . . . . . . . | | 210.00 |
| | | *To record three days' accrued salary.* | | |

After this entry is posted, the Salaries Expense and liability accounts appear as follows:

| Salaries Expense | | | Salaries Payable | |
|---|---|---|---|---|
| Dec. 12 | 700 | | Dec. 31 | 210 |
| 26 | 700 | | | |
| 31 | **210** | | | |
| Total | 1,610 | | | |

As a result of this entry, $1,610 of salaries expense is reported on the income statement. In addition, the balance sheet reports a $210 liability to the employee.

**Accrued Interest Expense.**  Another typical accrued expense is interest incurred on accounts and notes payable. Interest expense is incurred simply with the passage of time. Therefore, unless interest is paid on the last day of the accounting period, some additional amount will have accrued since the previous payment. A company's financial statements will be incomplete unless this expense and additional liability are recorded. The adjusting entry for interest is similar to the one used to accrue the unpaid salary.

## Accrued Revenues

Many revenues are recorded when cash is received from the customer. Other revenues are recorded when goods and services are sold on credit. However, some earned revenues may remain unrecorded at the end of the accounting period. Although these **accrued revenues** are earned, they are unrecorded because the customer has not yet paid for them or the seller has not yet billed the customer. For example, suppose that Clear Copy agreed to provide copying services for a bank at a fixed fee of $2,700 per month. The terms of the agreement call for Clear Copy to provide services from the 12th of December, 1996, through the 11th of the following month. The bank will pay $2,700 cash to Clear Copy on January 11, 1997, when the service period is over.

As of December 31, 1996, 20 days of services have been provided to the bank. However, because Clear Copy has not yet been paid, it has not recorded the earning of the revenue. Because 20 days equal two-thirds of a month, Clear Copy has earned two-thirds of one month's fee, or $1,800 ($2,700 × 2/3). According to the *revenue recognition principle,* this revenue should be reported on the December income statement because it was earned in that month. In addition, the balance sheet should report that the bank owes the company $1,800. Clear Copy makes this adjusting entry to record the effects of the agreement:

|      |    | Adjustment f | | |
|------|----|--------------|---|---|
| Dec. | 31 | Accounts Receivable | 1,800.00 | |
|      |    | Copy Services Revenue | | 1,800.00 |
|      |    | *To record 20 days' accrued revenue.* | | |

The debit to the receivable reflects the fact that the bank owes Clear Copy for the provided services. After this entry is posted, the affected accounts look like this:

| Accounts Receivable | | | | | Copy Services Revenue | |
|---|---|---|---|---|---|---|
| Dec. 12 | 1,700 | Dec. 22 | 1,700 | | Dec. 10 | 2,200 |
| **31** | **1,800** | | | | 12 | 1,700 |
| | | | | | 31 | 250 |
| | | | | | **31** | **1,800** |
| | | | | | Balance | 5,950 |

Accounts receivable are reported on the balance sheet at $1,800, and $5,950 of revenues are reported on the income statement.

**Accrued Interest Income.** We mentioned earlier that interest is an accrued expense recorded with an adjusting entry. Interest is also an accrued revenue when a company is entitled to receive it from a debtor. If a company has notes or accounts receivable that produce interest income, the bookkeeper records an adjusting entry to recognize any accrued but uncollected interest revenue. The entry also records the interest receivable from the debtor as an asset.

Take time to read the As a Matter of Ethics case on page 139. It tells about pressure being applied to an accountant to omit some adjusting entries that are needed to present complete financial statements. Consider the situation and determine what you would do if you were in this accountant's place.

---

**Progress Check**

3-6    At the end of its 1996 fiscal year, Corona Company omitted an adjustment to record $200 of accrued service revenues. The effect of the error is to: *(a)* Overstate 1996 net income by $200; *(b)* Overstate 1996 revenues by $200; *(c)* Understate total assets by $200; *(d)* Overstate total assets by $200.

3-7    What is a contra account?

3-8    What is an accrued expense? Give an example.

3-9    How does an unearned revenue arise? Give an example of an unearned revenue.

---

## THE ADJUSTED TRIAL BALANCE

### LO 3

Prepare a schedule that includes the unadjusted trial balance, the adjustments, and the adjusted trial balance; use the adjusted trial balance to prepare financial statements; and prepare entries to record cash receipts and cash disbursements related to accrued assets and liabilities.

An **unadjusted trial balance** is prepared before adjustments have been recorded. As you might expect, an **adjusted trial balance** uses the account balances after the adjusting entries have been posted to the ledger. In Illustration 3–3, parallel columns show the unadjusted trial balance, the adjustments, and the adjusted trial balance for Clear Copy as of December 31, 1996. Notice that several new accounts have been added because of the adjusting entries. (The order of the accounts also has been changed to match the order of the account numbers listed inside the book's front and back covers.) Also notice that the letters in the adjustments columns identify the debits and credits that were recorded with adjusting entries presented earlier in the chapter.

## PREPARING FINANCIAL STATEMENTS FROM THE ADJUSTED TRIAL BALANCE

Chapter 2 explained that the trial balance summarizes the information in the ledger by showing the account balances. This summary is easier to work with than the entire ledger when preparing financial statements. The accountant uses the adjusted trial balance for this purpose because it includes the balances that should appear in the statements.

Illustrations 3–4 and 3–5 show how the account balances are transferred from the adjusted trial balance to the statements. For completeness, the trial balance includes the identification numbers for the accounts.

Because the amount of net income is used on the statement of changes in owner's equity, the first phase of the preparation process produces the company's income statement. The arrows in the lower section of Illustration 3–4 show how the balances of the revenue and expense accounts are transferred into the income statement. The revenue is listed on the statement first, and then the expenses. The total expenses are subtracted from the revenues to find the net income of $1,585.

**Illustration 3-3**  The Unadjusted Trial Balance, Adjustments, and Adjusted Trial Balance for Clear Copy as of December 31, 1996

| | Unadjusted Trial Balance | | Adjustments | | Adjusted Trial Balance | |
|---|---|---|---|---|---|---|
| Cash ...................... | 7,950 | | | | 7,950 | |
| Accounts receivable ............ | | | (f) 1,800 | | 1,800 | |
| Store supplies ............... | 3,720 | | | (b)1,050 | 2,670 | |
| Prepaid insurance .............. | 2,400 | | | (a) 100 | 2,300 | |
| Copy equipment ............. | 26,000 | | | | 26,000 | |
| Accumulated amortization, copy equipment ............. | | | | (c) 375 | | 375 |
| Accounts payable .............. | | 6,200 | | | | 6,200 |
| Salaries payable ............... | | | | (e) 210 | | 210 |
| Unearned copy services revenue .... | | 3,000 | (d) 250 | | | 2,750 |
| Terry Dow, capital ............. | | 30,000 | | | | 30,000 |
| Terry Dow, withdrawals .......... | 400 | | | | 400 | |
| Copy services revenue .......... | | 3,900 | | (d) 250 | | 5,950 |
| | | | | (f) 1,800 | | |
| Amortization expense, copy equipment ............. | | | (c) 375 | | 375 | |
| Salaries expense .............. | 1,400 | | (e) 210 | | 1,610 | |
| Insurance expense ............. | | | (a) 100 | | 100 | |
| Rent expense ................ | 1,000 | | | | 1,000 | |
| Store supplies expense .......... | | | (b)1,050 | | 1,050 | |
| Utilities expense .............. | 230 | | | | 230 | |
| Totals ..................... | 43,100 | 43,100 | 3,785 | 3,785 | 45,485 | 45,485 |

The second phase prepares the statement of changes in owner's equity. In developing this statement, the accountant combines the net income from the income statement with the balances of Terry Dow's capital and withdrawals accounts. The $30,000 capital account balance came from the initial investment in December. (In other situations, the accountant would have to analyze the capital account to identify the beginning balance and any new investments made during the period.) The bottom line of the statement shows the owner's equity on December 31.

The third phase of the preparation process is represented in Illustration 3–5. In this phase, the balances of the asset and liability accounts are transferred to the asset and liability sections of the balance sheet. Notice how the balance of the accumulated amortization account is shown as a deduction from the cost of the copy equipment. Also, notice that the December 31 balance of Terry Dow's capital is taken from the statement of changes in owner's equity. The $30,000 balance of the capital account cannot be used on the balance sheet because it does not include the changes in equity created by the month's revenues, expenses, and withdrawals. (The next chapter explains how the capital account is updated through the closing process.) The completed balance sheet shows the total cost of the company's assets, its total liabilities, and the owner's equity.

Illustration 3-4  Preparing the Income Statement and the Statement of Changes in Owner's Equity from the Adjusted Trial Balance

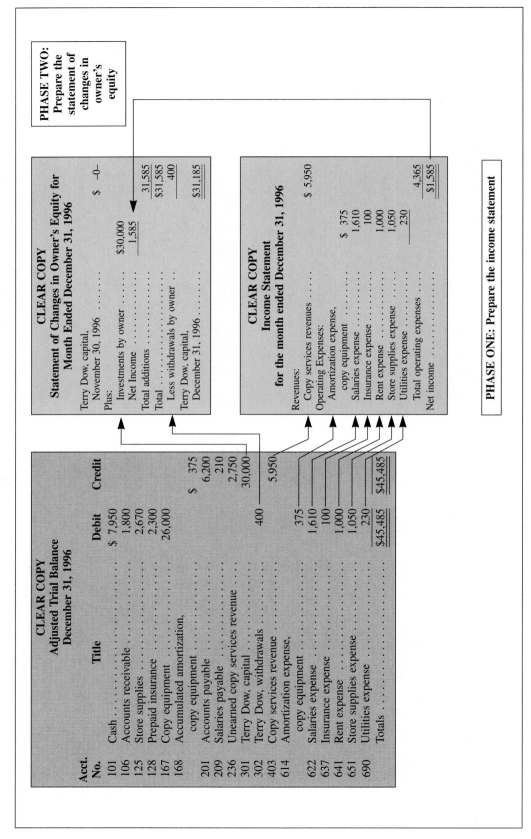

**PHASE TWO: Prepare the statement of changes in owner's equity**

**CLEAR COPY**
**Statement of Changes in Owner's Equity for**
**Month Ended December 31, 1996**

| | | |
|---|---:|---:|
| Terry Dow, capital, November 30, 1996 | | $ –0– |
| Plus: | | |
| Investments by owner | $30,000 | |
| Net Income | 1,585 | |
| Total additions | | 31,585 |
| Total | | $31,585 |
| Less withdrawals by owner | | 400 |
| Terry Dow, capital, December 31, 1996 | | $31,185 |

**CLEAR COPY**
**Income Statement**
**for the month ended December 31, 1996**

| | | |
|---|---:|---:|
| Revenues: | | |
| Copy services revenues | | $ 5,950 |
| Operating Expenses: | | |
| Amortization expense, copy equipment | $ 375 | |
| Salaries expense | 1,610 | |
| Insurance expense | 100 | |
| Rent expense | 1,000 | |
| Store supplies expense | 1,050 | |
| Utilities expense | 230 | |
| Total operating expenses | | 4,365 |
| Net income | | $1,585 |

**CLEAR COPY**
**Adjusted Trial Balance**
**December 31, 1996**

| Acct. No. | Title | Debit | Credit |
|---|---|---:|---:|
| 101 | Cash | $ 7,950 | |
| 106 | Accounts receivable | 1,800 | |
| 125 | Store supplies | 2,670 | |
| 128 | Prepaid insurance | 2,300 | |
| 167 | Copy equipment | 26,000 | |
| 168 | Accumulated amortization, copy equipment | | $ 375 |
| 201 | Accounts payable | | 6,200 |
| 209 | Salaries payable | | 210 |
| 236 | Unearned copy services revenue | | 2,750 |
| 301 | Terry Dow, capital | | 30,000 |
| 302 | Terry Dow, withdrawals | 400 | |
| 403 | Copy services revenue | | 5,950 |
| 614 | Amortization expense, copy equipment | 375 | |
| 622 | Salaries expense | 1,610 | |
| 637 | Insurance expense | 100 | |
| 641 | Rent expense | 1,000 | |
| 651 | Store supplies expense | 1,050 | |
| 690 | Utilities expense | 230 | |
| | Totals | $45,485 | $45,485 |

**PHASE ONE: Prepare the income statement**

**Illustration 3–5** Preparing the Balance Sheet from the Adjusted Trial Balance and the Statement of Changes in Owner's Equity

**CLEAR COPY**
**Adjusted Trial Balance**
**December 31, 1996**

| Acct. No. | Title | Debit | Credit |
|---|---|---|---|
| 101 | Cash | $ 7,950 | |
| 106 | Accounts receivable | 1,800 | |
| 125 | Store supplies | 2,670 | |
| 128 | Prepaid insurance | 2,300 | |
| 167 | Copy equipment | 26,000 | |
| 168 | Accumulated amortization, copy equipment | | $ 375 |
| 201 | Accounts payable | | 6,200 |
| 209 | Salaries payable | | 210 |
| 236 | Unearned copy services revenue | | 2,750 |
| 301 | Terry Dow, capital | | 30,000 |
| 302 | Terry Dow, withdrawals | 400 | |
| 403 | Copy services revenue | | 5,950 |
| 614 | Amortization expense, copy equipment | 375 | |
| 622 | Salaries expense | 1,610 | |
| 637 | Insurance expense | 100 | |
| 641 | Rent expense | 1,000 | |
| 651 | Store supplies expense | 1,050 | |
| 690 | Utilities expense | 230 | |
| | Totals | $45,485 | $45,485 |

**PHASE THREE: Prepare the balance sheet**

**CLEAR COPY**
**Balance Sheet**
**December 31, 1996**

**Assets**

| | | |
|---|---|---|
| Cash | | $ 7,950 |
| Accounts receivable | | 1,800 |
| Store supplies | | 2,670 |
| Prepaid insurance | | 2,300 |
| Copy equipment | $26,000 | |
| Less accumulated amortization | (375) | 25,625 |
| Total assets | | $40,345 |

**Liabilities**

| | | |
|---|---|---|
| Accounts payable | $ 6,200 | |
| Salaries payable | 210 | |
| Unearned copy services revenue | 2,750 | |
| Total liabilities | | $ 9,160 |

**Owner's Equity**

| | | |
|---|---|---|
| Terry Dow, capital, December 31, 1996 | | 31,185 |
| Total liabilities and owner's equity | | $40,345 |

**Statement of Changes in Owner's Equity (from Illustration 3–4)**

**REMOVING
ACCRUED
ASSETS AND
LIABILITIES
FROM THE
ACCOUNTS**

Revenues that are accrued at the end of an accounting period result in cash receipts from customers during the next period. In addition, expenses that were accrued at the end of an accounting period result in cash payments during the next period to settle the unpaid liabilities. This section explains how the accrued assets and accrued liabilities are removed from the accounts.

## Accrued Expenses

Earlier, Clear Copy recorded three days of accrued wages for its employee with this adjusting entry:

| | | | | |
|---|---|---|---|---|
| Dec. | 31 | Salaries Expense .......................... | 210.00 | |
| | | Salaries Payable ......................... | | 210.00 |
| | | *To record three days' accrued salary.* | | |

When the next payday comes on Friday, January 9, the following entry removes the accrued liability and records additional salaries expense for January:

| | | | | |
|---|---|---|---|---|
| Jan. | 9 | Salaries Payable (3 days at $70) ................ | 210.00 | |
| | | Salaries Expense (7 days at $70) ................ | 490.00 | |
| | | Cash ................................... | | 700.00 |
| | | *Paid two weeks' salary, including three days accrued in December* | | |

The first debit in the January 9 entry records the payment of the liability for the three days' salary accrued on December 31. The second debit records the salary for January's first seven working days (including the New Year's Day holiday) as an expense of the new accounting period. The credit records the total amount of cash paid to the employee.

## Accrued Revenue

On December 31, the following adjusting entry was made to record 20 days' accrued revenue earned under Clear Copy's contract with the bank:

| | | | | |
|---|---|---|---|---|
| Dec. | 31 | Accounts Receivable ....................... | 1,800.00 | |
| | | Copy Services Revenue ................... | | 1,800.00 |
| | | *To record 20 days' accrued revenue.* | | |

When the first month's fee is received on January 11, the company makes the following entry to eliminate the receivable and recognize the revenue earned in January:

| Jan. | 11 | Cash ...................................... | 2,700.00 | |
|------|----|---------------------------------------------|----------|----------|
| | | Accounts Receivable ..................... | | 1,800.00 |
| | | Copy Services Revenue ................... | | 900.00 |
| | | *Received cash for accrued and earned copy* | | |
| | | *services revenue.* | | |

The first credit in the entry records the collection of the receivable. The second credit records the earned revenue.

---

**Progress Check**

**3-10** The following information has been taken from Jones Company's unadjusted and adjusted trial balances:

| | Unadjusted | | Adjusted | |
|---|---|---|---|---|
| | **Debit** | **Credit** | **Debit** | **Credit** |
| Prepaid insurance .... | $6,200 | | $5,900 | |
| Salaries payable ...... | | | | $1,400 |

The adjusting entries must have included these items:
*a.* A $300 debit to Prepaid Insurance and a $1,400 credit to Salaries Payable.
*b.* A $300 credit to Prepaid Insurance and a $1,400 debit to Salaries Payable.
*c.* A $300 debit to Insurance Expense and a $1,400 debit to Salaries Expense.

**3-11** What types of accounts are taken from the adjusted trial balance to prepare an income statement?

**3-12** In preparing financial statements from an adjusted trial balance, which statement is prepared second?

**3-13** On December 31, 1996, Hall Company recorded $1,600 of accrued salaries. On January 5 (the next payday), salaries of $8,000 were paid. From this you know that: *(a)* The company uses cash basis accounting; *(b)* The January 5 entry includes a $6,400 credit to Cash; *(c)* The salaries expense assigned to 1997 is $6,400.

---

Up to this point, we have presented only **unclassified balance sheets.** (For example, see Illustration 3–5.) However, the information on a balance sheet is more useful if assets and liabilities are classified into relevant groups. Readers of these **classified balance sheets** have more information to use in making their decisions. For example, they can use the data to assess the likelihood that funds will be available to meet the liabilities when they become due.

Businesses do not all use the same system of classifying assets and liabilities on their balance sheets. However, most businesses classify them as shown in Illustration 3–6. Assets are classified as (1) current assets, (2) investments, (3) capital assets, and (4) intangible assets. Liabilities are either (1) current liabilities or (2) long-term liabilities. We explain the nature of these classes next.

## CLASSIFYING BALANCE SHEET ITEMS

**LO 4**

Define each asset and liability category for the balance sheet, prepare a classified balance sheet, and calculate the current ratio.

**Illustration 3–6**    A Classified Balance Sheet

**NATIONAL ELECTRICAL SUPPLY CO.**
**Balance Sheet**
**December 31, 1996**

### Assets

**Current assets:**

| | | |
|---|---:|---:|
| Cash | $  6,500 | |
| Temporary investments | 2,100 | |
| Accounts receivable | 4,400 | |
| Notes receivable | 1,500 | |
| Merchandise inventory | 27,500 | |
| Prepaid expenses | 2,400 | |
| Total current assets | | $ 44,400 |

**Investments:**

| | | |
|---|---:|---:|
| Chrysler Corporation common shares | $ 18,000 | |
| Land held for future expansion | 48,000 | |
| Total investments | | 66,000 |

**Capital assets:**
Plant and equipment:

| | | | |
|---|---:|---:|---:|
| Store equipment | $ 33,200 | | |
| Less accumulated amortization | 8,000 | $ 25,200 | |
| Buildings | $170,000 | | |
| Less accumulated amortization | 45,000 | 125,000 | |
| Land | | 73,200 | |
| Total plant and equipment | | | 223,400 |

**Intangible asset:**

| | | |
|---|---:|---:|
| Trademark | | 10,000 |
| Total assets | | $343,800 |

### Liabilities

**Current liabilities:**

| | | |
|---|---:|---:|
| Accounts payable | $ 15,300 | |
| Wages payable | 3,200 | |
| Notes payable | 3,000 | |
| Current portion of long-term liabilities | 7,500 | |
| Total current liabilities | | $ 29,000 |

**Long-term liabilities:**

| | | |
|---|---:|---:|
| Notes payable (net of current portion) | 150,000 | |
| Total liabilities | | $179,000 |

### Owner's Equity

| | |
|---|---:|
| B. Brown, capital | 164,800 |
| Total liabilities and owner's equity | $343,800 |

## Current Assets

**Current assets** are cash and other assets that are reasonably expected to be sold, collected, or consumed within one year or within the normal **operating cycle of the business,** whichever is longer. In addition to cash, current assets typically include temporary investments in marketable securities, accounts receivable, notes receivable, goods expected to be sold to customers (called *merchandise* or *inventory*), and prepaid expenses.

**The Operating Cycle.**  The length of a company's operating cycle depends on its activities. The diagrams in Illustration 3–7 represent the phases of operating cycles for service and merchandising companies. For a company that sells services, the operating cycle is the average time between paying the employees who perform the services and receiving the cash from customers. For a company that sells goods, the operating cycle is the average time between paying for the merchandise and receiving cash from customers.

Most operating cycles are shorter than one year. As a result, most companies use a one-year period in deciding which assets are current. However, a few companies have an operating cycle longer than one year. For example, a company may routinely allow customers to take several years to pay for their purchases. Some producers of beverages and other products allow their products to age for several years. In both cases, these companies use the longer operating cycle in deciding which assets are current.[4]

**Other Details.**  The balance sheet in Illustration 3–6 lists current assets first. This practice gives a prominent position to assets that are most easily converted into cash. Items within the current asset category are traditionally listed in the order of how quickly they will be converted to cash. Prepaid expenses are usually listed last because they will not be converted to cash.

A company's individual prepaid expenses are usually small compared to other assets on the balance sheet. As a result, they are often combined and shown as a single item. Thus, it is likely that the Prepaid expenses item in Illustration 3–6 includes such things as prepaid insurance, prepaid rent, office supplies, and store supplies.

## Investments

The second balance sheet classification is long-term investments. In many cases, notes receivable and investments in shares and bonds are not current assets because they will be held for more than one year (or one operating cycle). Investments also include land that is not being used in operations because it is held for future expansion. Notice that the temporary investments on the second line in Illustration 3–6 are current assets and are not presented in the Investments section. We explain the differences between temporary and long-term investments in a later chapter.

## Capital Assets

Earlier, we described capital assets as tangible long-lived assets that are used to produce or sell goods and services. Examples include equipment, vehicles, buildings, and land. Two key phrases in the definition are *long-lived* and *used to produce or sell goods and services.* Although it is tangible and has a long life, land held for future expansion is not a capital asset because it is not used to produce or sell goods and services.

The term *capital assets* is often used as a balance sheet caption. Other widely used titles for the same category are *Property, plant, and equipment*, or *Land, buildings, and equipment.* The order of the listing of the types of capital assets within the category varies among organizations.

---

[4]In these unusual situations, the companies provide supplemental information about their current assets and liabilities to allow users to compare them with other companies.

**Illustration 3–7**   The Phases of Operating Cycles for Companies that Sell Services and Merchandise

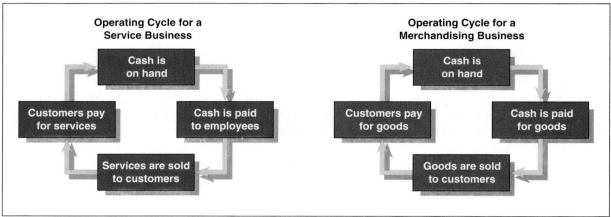

### Intangible Assets

Some assets that are used to produce or sell goods and services do not have a physical form. These assets are called **intangible assets.** Examples of intangible assets are goodwill, patents, trademarks, copyrights, and franchises. Their value comes from the privileges or rights granted to or held by the owner.

### Current Liabilities

Obligations due to be paid or liquidated within one year (or the operating cycle) are classified as **current liabilities.** Current liabilities are usually satisfied by paying out current assets. Typical current liabilities are accounts payable, notes payable, wages payable, taxes payable, interest payable, and unearned revenues. Also, any portion of a long-term liability due to be paid within one year (or a longer operating cycle) is a current liability. Illustration 3–6 shows how the current portion of long-term liabilities is usually described on a balance sheet. Unearned revenues are classified as current liabilities because they will be settled by delivering goods or services within the year (or the operating cycle). Different companies present current liabilities in different orders. Generally, the first position goes to the liabilities that will be paid first.

### Long-Term Liabilities

The second liability classification consists of **long-term liabilities.** These liabilities are not due to be paid within one year, or the operating cycle. Notes payable and bonds payable are usually long-term liabilities. If a company has both short- and long-term notes payable, it probably uses separate accounts for them in its ledger.

## EQUITY ON THE BALANCE SHEET

The format of the balance sheet's equity section depends on whether the company is a single proprietorship, a partnership, or a corporation.

## Single Proprietorships and Partnerships

If a business is a single proprietorship, the equity section consists of a single line showing the owner's equity as of the balance sheet date. For example, the balance sheet in Illustration 3–5 shows "Terry Dow, capital, December 31, 1996" and the amount of $31,185. When total liabilities exceed total assets, the negative equity amount (often called a *deficit*) is subtracted from total liabilities.

If a business is organized as a partnership, separate equity accounts are used for each partner. Changes in each partner's equity are reported in a statement of changes in partners' equity that is similar to the statement of changes in owner's equity. The balance sheet shows the equity of each partner in a format like this:

|  |  |
|---|---|
| **Partners' Equity** | |
| Shirley Tucker, capital . . . . | $17,300 |
| Mark Jackson, capital . . . . | 24,800 |
| Total partners' equity . . . . | $42,100 |

## Corporations

Corporations are established under provincial or federal laws. These laws may require the company's financial statements to distinguish between the equity created by investments from shareholders and the equity created by the corporation's net incomes less any reductions for **dividends.** A dividend is a distribution, generally a cash payment, made by a corporation to its shareholders. A cash dividend reduces the assets and the equity of a corporation in the same way that a withdrawal reduces the assets and equity of a proprietorship.

As described in Chapter 1, a corporation's total shareholders' equity is divided into **contributed capital** (also called *paid-in capital*) and **retained earnings.** Contributed capital is created by the shareholders' investments, and retained earnings are created by the corporation's profitable activities (cumulative net income less net losses and dividends). The components of shareholders' equity are usually shown on a corporate balance sheet like this:

|  |  |
|---|---|
| **Shareholders' Equity** | |
| Contributed capital: Common shares . . . | $400,000 |
| Retained earnings . . . . . . . . . . . . . . . . | 124,400 |
| Total shareholders' equity . . . . . . . . . . | $524,400 |

If a corporation issues only one kind of shares, they are called **common shares** or *share capital-common*. (Other types of classes or shares are described in Chapter 15.) The $400,000 amount assigned to common share capital in the example is the amount invested in the corporation by its original shareholders when they bought the shares from the corporation. The retained earnings of $124,400 represents the shareholders' equity arising from prior years' net incomes in excess of any net losses and dividends paid to the shareholders.

## ALTERNATIVE BALANCE SHEET FORMATS

Different companies choose different formats for their balance sheets. For example, the balance sheet in Illustration 1–7 (on p. 40) places the liabilities and shareholder's equity to the right of the assets. This format creates an **account form balance sheet.** If the items are arranged vertically, as shown in Illustration 3–6, the format creates a **report form balance sheet.** Both forms are widely used, and neither is considered more useful than the other.

## USING CODE NUMBERS FOR ACCOUNTS

We described a possible three-digit account numbering system in Chapter 2. In these systems, the code number assigned to an account not only identifies the account but also provides information about the account's financial statement category.

In the following simple system, the first digit in an account's number identifies its primary balance sheet or income statement category. For example, account numbers beginning with a 1 are assigned to asset accounts and account numbers beginning with a 2 are assigned to liability accounts. Under this system, the following numbers could be assigned to the accounts of a company that buys and sells merchandise:

| | |
|---|---|
| **101–199** | **Assets** |
| **201–299** | **Liabilities** |
| **301–399** | **Owner's Equity** (including withdrawals) |
| **401–499** | **Revenues** |
| **501–599** | **Cost of Goods Sold** (these accounts are described in Chapter 5) |
| **601–699** | **Operating Expenses** |
| **701–799** | **Gains** |
| **801–899** | **Losses** |

In this system, the second digit of each account number identifies its subclassification within the primary category, as follows:

| | |
|---|---|
| **101–199** | **Assets** |
| 101–139 | Current assets (second digit is 0, 1, 2, or 3) |
| 141–149 | Long-term investments (second digit is 4) |
| 151–179 | Capital assets (second digit is 5, 6, or 7) |
| 181–189 | Natural resources (second digit is 8) |
| 191–199 | Intangible assets (second digit is 9) |
| **201–299** | **Liabilities** |
| 201–249 | Current liabilities (second digit is 0, 1, 2, 3, or 4) |
| 251–299 | Long-term liabilities (second digit is 5, 6, 7, 8, or 9) |

Finally, the third digit completes the unique code for each account. For example, specific current asset accounts might be assigned the following numbers:

| | |
|---|---|
| **101–199** | **Assets** |
| 101–139 | Current assets |
| 101 | Cash |
| 106 | Accounts Receivable |

| 110 | Rent Receivable |
| 128 | Prepaid Insurance |

This code is used for the accounts listed inside the front and back covers of the book.

A three-digit account numbering system may be adequate for many smaller businesses. However, a numbering system for a more complex business might use four, five, or even more digits.

## USING THE INFORMATION— THE CURRENT RATIO

Most financial statement users find it helpful to evaluate a company's ability to pay its debts in the near future. This ability affects decisions by suppliers about allowing the company to buy on credit. It affects decisions by banks about lending money to the company and the terms of the loan, including the interest rate, due date, and any assets to be pledged as security against the loan. The ability to pay debts also affects a business owner's decisions about obtaining cash to pay existing debts when they come due.

The **current ratio** is widely used to describe the company's ability to pay its short-term obligations. It is calculated by dividing the current assets by the current liabilities:

$$\text{Current ratio} = \frac{\text{Current assets}}{\text{Current liabilities}}$$

Using the data for **Imperial Oil Limited,** presented at the beginning of the chapter, the current ratios at the end of 1994 and 1993 are calculated as follows:

$$\text{Current ratio} = \begin{array}{cc} 1994 & 1993 \\ \dfrac{\$2,797}{\$1,581} = 1.77 & \dfrac{\$2,899}{\$1,593} = 1.82 \end{array}$$

Note that the ratio decreased slightly from the end of 1993 to the end of 1994. Both values suggest that the company's short-term obligations could be satisfied with the short-term resources on hand. If the ratio were to be closer to one, the company might expect to face more difficulty in paying the liabilities. If the ratio were less than one, the company would be more likely to have difficulty because its current liabilities would be greater than its current assets.

---

### Progress Check

**3-14**  **Which of the following assets should be classified as current assets? Which should be classified as capital assets?**  *(a)* **Land used in operating the business;** *(b)* **Office supplies;** *(c)* **Receivables from customers due in 10 months;** *(d)* **Insurance protection for the next nine months;** *(e)* **Trucks used to provide services to customers;** *(f)* **Trademarks used in advertising the company's services.**

**3-15**  **Identify two examples of assets classified as investments on the balance sheet.**

**3-16**  **Which category of liabilities is used in the calculation of the current ratio?**

**3-17**  **On the balance sheet of a corporation, the shareholders' equity is divided into two categories. What are they?**

---

**SUMMARY OF
THE CHAPTER
IN TERMS OF
LEARNING
OBJECTIVES**

**LO 1. Explain why financial statements are prepared at the end of regular accounting periods, why the accounts must be adjusted at the end of each period, and why the accrual basis of accounting produces more useful income statements and balance sheets than the cash basis.** Companies prepare reports once each year. They also prepare interim financial statements because decision makers need information frequently and promptly. Adjusting entries are needed to capture information about unrecorded events that are not external transactions. The revenue recognition principle requires adjustments to ensure that revenue is reported when it is earned. The matching principle requires adjustments to ensure that expenses are reported in the same period as the revenue that was earned as a result of the expenses.

Accrual accounting is preferred to cash basis accounting because accrual accounting reports the economic effects of events when they occur, not when the cash flows happen. In addition to accrual basis financial statements, however, GAAP requires companies to report a statement of changes in financial position (SCFP) on a cash or cash equivalent basis. You will learn the preparation of the SCFP in Chapter 18.

**LO 2. Prepare adjusting entries for prepaid expenses, amortization, unearned revenues, accrued expenses, and accrued revenues.** Adjusting entries are used *(a)* to record expenses when prepaid expenses expire, *(b)* to record amortization expense as the cost of using plant and equipment assets, *(c)* to record revenues when the company converts unearned revenues to earned revenues, *(d)* to accrue expenses and related liabilities, and *(e)* to accrue revenues and related assets.

**LO 3. Prepare a schedule that includes the unadjusted trial balance, the adjustments, and the adjusted trial balance; use the adjusted trial balance to prepare financial statements; and prepare entries to record cash receipts and cash disbursements related to accrued assets and liabilities.** The effects of adjustments can be shown in a six-column schedule that presents the unadjusted trial balance in the first two columns, the adjusting entries in the next two columns, and the adjusted trial balance in the final two columns. The adjusted trial balance shows all ledger accounts, including assets, liabilities, revenues, expenses, and owner's equity. As a result, it can be used to prepare the income statement, the statement of changes in owner's equity, and the balance sheet.

Payments of accrued expenses in the next accounting period are recorded with a debit to the accrued liability and may include another debit for any additional expense incurred since the beginning of the new period. When accrued revenues are collected, the entry credits the previously recorded asset (a receivable) and may include another credit for any additional revenue earned during the new period.

**LO 4. Define each asset and liability category for the balance sheet, prepare a classified balance sheet, and calculate the current ratio.** Classified balance sheets usually report three categories of assets: current assets, investments, capital assets—tangible and intangible. The two categories of liabilities are current and long-term. Owner's equity for proprietorships and partners' equity for partnerships are reported by putting the capital account balances on the balance sheet. A corporation reports shareholders' equity as contributed capital and retained earnings. A company's current ratio describes its ability to pay its current liabilities out of its current assets. The value of the ratio equals the amount of the current assets divided by the current liabilities.

The following information relates to Best Plumbing Company on December 31, 1997. The company uses the calendar year as its annual reporting period.

## DEMONSTRATION PROBLEM

a.  The company's weekly payroll is $2,800, paid every Friday for a five-day workweek. December 31, 1997, falls on a Wednesday, but the employees will not be paid until Friday, January 2, 1998.

b.  Eighteen months earlier, on July 1, 1996, the company purchased equipment that cost $10,000 and had no salvage value. Its useful life is predicted to be five years.

c.  On October 1, 1997, the company agreed to work on a new housing project. For installing plumbing in 24 new homes, the company was paid $144,000 in advance. When the $144,000 cash was received on October 1, 1997, that amount was credited to the Unearned Plumbing Revenue account. Between October 1 and December 31, 1997, work on 18 homes was completed.

d.  On September 1, 1997, the company purchased a one-year insurance policy for $1,200. The transaction was recorded with a $1,200 debit to Prepaid Insurance.

### Required

1.  Prepare the adjusting entries needed on December 31, 1997, to record the previously unrecorded effects of the events.

2.  Complete the following table describing your adjusting entries. Your answer should indicate the amount entered in the listed accounts by each entry; the amount of the asset or liability that will appear on the December 31, 1997, balance sheet; and whether the item on the balance sheet will be a current asset, an item related to plant and equipment, a current liability, or a long-term liability:

| Entry | Account | Amount in the Entry | Amount on the Balance Sheet | Balance Sheet Category |
|-------|---------|---------------------|------------------------------|------------------------|
| a | Wages Payable | | | |
| b | Accumulated Amortization, Equipment | | | |
| c | Unearned Plumbing Revenue | | | |
| d | Prepaid Insurance | | | |

3.  Complete the following table describing your adjusting entries. Your answer should indicate how much the entry changed (if at all) the company's reported income, its reported total assets, and its reported total liabilities. If the change is a decrease, enter the amount in parentheses:

| Entry | Reported Net Income | Reported Total Assets | Reported Total Liabilities |
|-------|---------------------|-----------------------|-----------------------------|
| a | | | |
| b | | | |
| c | | | |
| d | | | |

*Planning the Solution*

- Analyze the information for each situation to determine which accounts need to be updated with an adjustment.
- Calculate the size of each adjustment and prepare the necessary journal entries.
- Show the amount entered by each adjustment in the designated accounts, determine the adjusted balance, and then determine the balance sheet classification that the account falls within.
- Determine each entry's effect on reported net income, reported total assets, and reported total liabilities.

*Solution to Demonstration Problem*

Adjusting journal entries.

| | | | | | |
|---|---|---|---|---|---|
| *a.* | Dec. | 31 | Wages Expense . . . . . . . . . . . . . . . . . . . . . . | 1,680.00 | |
| | | | Wages Payable . . . . . . . . . . . . . . . . . . . . | | 1,680.00 |
| | | | *To accrue wages for the last three days of the year ($2,800 × 3/5).* | | |
| *b.* | Dec. | 31 | Amortization Expense, Equipment . . . . . . . . | 2,000.00 | |
| | | | Accumulated Amortization, . . . . . . . . . . | | 2,000.00 |
| | | | Equipment . . . . . . . . . . . . . . . . . . | | |
| | | | *To record amortization expense for the full year ($10,000/5 = $2,000).* | | |
| *c.* | Dec. | 31 | Unearned Plumbing Revenue . . . . . . . . . . . . | 108,000.00 | |
| | | | Plumbing Services Revenue . . . . . . . . . . | | 108,000.00 |
| | | | *To recognize plumbing revenues earned ($144,000 × 18/24).* | | |
| *d.* | Dec. | 31 | Insurance Expense . . . . . . . . . . . . . . . . . . . | 400.00 | |
| | | | Prepaid Insurance . . . . . . . . . . . . . . . . . | | 400.00 |
| | | | *To adjust for the expired portion of insurance ($1,200 × 4/12).* | | |

| Entry | Account | Amount in the Entry | Amount on the Balance Sheet | Balance Sheet Category |
|---|---|---|---|---|
| *a* | Wages Payable | $1,680 cr | $1,680 | Current liability |
| *b* | Accumulated Amortization, Equipment | $2,000 cr | $3,000 | Plant and equipment |
| *c* | Unearned Plumbing Revenue | $108,000 dr | $36,000 | Current liability |
| *d* | Prepaid Insurance | $400 cr | $800 | Current asset |

| Entry | Reported Net Income | Reported Total Assets | Reported Total Liabilities |
|---|---|---|---|
| *a* | $(1,680) | no effect | $1,680 |
| *b* | $(2,000) | $(2,000) | no effect |
| *c* | $108,000 | no effect | $(108,000) |
| *d* | $(400) | $(400) | no effect |

# Recording Prepaid and Unearned Items in Income Statement Accounts

The discussion in Chapter 3 emphasized the fact that prepaid expenses are assets at the time they are purchased. Therefore, at the time of purchase, we recorded prepaid expenses with debits to asset accounts. Then, at the end of the accounting period, adjusting entries transferred the cost that had expired to expense accounts. We also recognized that some prepaid expenses are purchased and will fully expire before the end of the accounting period. In these cases, you can avoid having to make adjusting entries if you charge the prepaid items to expense accounts at the time of purchase.

Some companies follow a practice of recording all prepaid expenses with debits to expense accounts. Then, at the end of the accounting period, if any amounts remain unused or unexpired, adjusting entries are made to transfer the cost of the unused portions from the expense accounts to prepaid expense (asset) accounts. This practice is perfectly acceptable. The reported financial statements are exactly the same under either procedure.

To illustrate the differences between the two procedures, recall that on December 26, Clear Copy paid for 24 months of insurance coverage that began on December 1. We recorded that payment with a debit to an asset account but could have recorded a debit to an expense account. The alternatives are as follows:

## PREPAID EXPENSES

### LO 6

Explain why some companies record prepaid and unearned items in income statement accounts and prepare adjusting entries when this procedure is used.

|         |    |                                     | Payment Recorded as Asset | | Payment Recorded as Expense | |
|---------|----|-------------------------------------|-----------|----------|-----------|----------|
| Dec.    | 26 | Prepaid Insurance . . . . . . . . . . . . . | 2,400.00 |          |           |          |
|         |    | Cash . . . . . . . . . . . . . . . . . . |          | 2,400.00 |           |          |
|         | 26 | Insurance Expense . . . . . . . . . . . |          |          | 2,400.00  |          |
|         |    | Cash . . . . . . . . . . . . . . . . . . |          |          |           | 2,400.00 |

At the end of the accounting period (December 31), insurance protection for one month has expired. That means $2,400/24 = $100 of the asset expired and became an expense of December. The required adjusting entry depends on how the original payment was recorded. The alternative adjusting entries are:

| | | | Payment Recorded as Asset | | Payment Recorded as Expense | |
|---|---|---|---|---|---|---|
| Adjusting entries: | | | | | | |
| Dec. | 31 | Insurance Expense . . . . . . . . . . . . . | 100.00 | | | |
| | | Prepaid Insurance . . . . . . . . . . . | | 100.00 | | |
| | 31 | Prepaid Insurance . . . . . . . . . . . . . | | | 2,300.00 | |
| | | Insurance Expense . . . . . . . . . . | | | | 2,300.00 |

When these entries are posted to the accounts, you can see that the two alternative procedures give the same results. Regardless of which procedure is followed, the December 31 adjusted account balances show prepaid insurance of $2,300 and insurance expense of $100.

| **Payment Recorded as Asset** | | | | **Payment Recorded as Expense** | | | |
|---|---|---|---|---|---|---|---|
| **Prepaid Insurance** | | | | **Prepaid Insurance** | | | |
| Dec. 26 | 2,400 | Dec. 31 | 100 | Dec. 31 | 2,300 | | |
| | −100 | | | | | | |
| Bal. | 2,300 | | | | | | |

| **Insurance Expense** | | | | **Insurance Expense** | | | |
|---|---|---|---|---|---|---|---|
| Dec. 31 | 100 | | | Dec. 26 | 2,400 | Dec. 31 | 2,300 |
| | | | | | −2,300 | | |
| | | | | Bal. | 100 | | |

To continue the example for another month, assume that on January 1, Clear Copy paid $750 to purchase a second insurance policy. This policy provides protection for three months beginning January 1. Therefore, the total cost of unexpired insurance on January 1 was $2,300 + $750 = $3,050. On January 31, $250 of the second policy's cost (one month's worth) had expired. Since $100 of the first insurance policy and $250 of the second insurance policy expired during January, the adjusting entry on January 31 must be designed to report an insurance expense of $350 and a prepaid insurance asset of $3,050 − $350 = $2,700. Depending on how the original payments were recorded, the alternative adjusting entries are:

| | | | Payment Recorded as Asset | | Payment Recorded as Expense | |
|---|---|---|---|---|---|---|
| Adjusting entries: | | | | | | |
| Jan. | 31 | Insurance Expense . . . . . . . . . . . . . | 350.00 | | | |
| | | Prepaid Insurance . . . . . . . . . . . | | 350.00 | | |
| | 31 | Prepaid Insurance . . . . . . . . . . . . . | | | 400.00 | |
| | | Insurance Expense . . . . . . . . . . | | | | 400.00 |

Note that if the insurance payments are debited to an expense account, the required adjusting entry increases the Prepaid Insurance account balance $400, from $2,300 to $2,700. The credit in the entry reduces the Insurance Expense account debit balance from $750 to $350.

The procedures for recording unearned revenues are similar to those used to record prepaid expenses. Receipts of unearned revenues may be recorded with credits to liability accounts (as described in Chapter 3) or they may be recorded with credits to revenue accounts. The adjusting entries at the end of the period are different, depending on which procedure is followed. Nevertheless, either procedure is acceptable. The amounts reported in the financial statements are exactly the same, regardless of which procedure is used.

To illustrate the alternative procedures of recording unearned revenues, recall that on December 26, Clear Copy received $3,000 in payment for copying services to be provided over the two-month period beginning December 15. In Chapter 3, that receipt was recorded with a credit to a liability account. The alternative would be to record it with a credit to a revenue account. Both alternatives follow:

## UNEARNED REVENUES

| | | | Receipt Recorded as a Liability | Receipt Recorded as a Revenue |
|---|---|---|---|---|
| Dec. | 26 | Cash . . . . . . . . . . . . . . . . . . . . . . | 3,000.00 | |
| | | Unearned Copy Services Revenue . . . . . . . . . . . . . . . | 3,000.00 | |
| | 26 | Cash . . . . . . . . . . . . . . . . . . . . . . | | 3,000.00 |
| | | Copy Services Revenue . . . . . . . . | | 3,000.00 |

By the end of the accounting period (December 31), Clear Copy had earned $750 of this revenue. That means $750 of the liability had been satisfied. Depending on how the original receipt was recorded, the required adjusting entry is as follows:

| | | | Receipt Recorded as Liability | Receipt Recorded as Revenue |
|---|---|---|---|---|
| Adjusting entries: | | | | |
| Dec. | 31 | Unearned Copy Services Revenue . . | 750.00 | |
| | | Copy Services Revenue . . . . . . . | 750.00 | |
| | 31 | Copy Services Revenue . . . . . . . . | | 2,250.00 |
| | | Unearned Copy Services Revenue . . . . . . . . . . . . . . . | | 2,250.00 |

After these entries are posted, you can see that the two alternative procedures give the same results. Regardless of which procedure is followed, the December 31 adjusted account balances show unearned copy services revenue of $2,250 and copy services revenue of $750.

| Receipt Recorded as a Liability<br>Unearned Copy Services Revenue | | | Receipt Recorded as a Revenue<br>Unearned Copy Services Revenue | |
|---|---|---|---|---|
| Dec. 31        750 | Dec. 26           3,000 | | | Dec. 31           2,250 |
| | | −750 | | |
| | Bal.              2,250 | | | |

| Copy Services Revenue | | | Copy Services Revenue | | | |
|---|---|---|---|---|---|---|
| | Dec. 31 | 750 | Dec. 31 | 2,250 | Dec. 26 | 3,000 |
| | | | | | | −2,250 |
| | | | | | Bal. | 750 |

## SUMMARY OF APPENDIX B IN TERMS OF LEARNING OBJECTIVES

**LO 6.  Explain why some companies record prepaid and unearned items in income statement accounts and prepare adjusting entries when this procedure is used.** Because many prepaid expenses expire during the same period they are purchased, some companies choose to charge all prepaid expenses to expense accounts at the time they are purchased. When this is done, end-of-period adjusting entries are required to transfer any unexpired amounts from the expense accounts to appropriate asset accounts. Also, unearned revenues may be credited to revenue accounts at the time cash is received. If so, end-of-period adjusting entries are required to transfer any unearned amounts from the revenue accounts to appropriate unearned revenue accounts.

## GLOSSARY

**Account form balance sheet**  a balance sheet that is arranged so that the assets are listed on the left and the liability and owner's equity items are listed on the right. p. 150

**Accounting period**  the length of time into which the life of a business is divided for the purpose of preparing periodic financial statements. p. 128

**Accrual basis of accounting**  a system of accounting in which the adjustment process is used to assign revenues to the periods in which they are earned and to match expenses with revenues. p. 131

**Accrued expenses**  expenses incurred during an accounting period but that prior to end-of-period adjustments, remain unrecorded because payment is not due. p. 137

**Accrued revenues**  revenues earned during an accounting period but that, prior to end-of-period adjustments, remain unrecorded because payment has not been received. p. 138

**Accumulated amortization**  the total amount of amortization recorded against an asset or group of assets during the entire time the asset or assets have been owned. p. 136

**Adjusted trial balance**  a trial balance that shows the account balances after they have been revised to reflect the effects of end-of-period adjustments. p. 140

**Adjusting entry**  a journal entry made at the end of an accounting period for the purpose of assigning revenues to the period in which they are earned, assigning ex-

penses to the period in which the expiration of benefit is incurred, and to update related liability and asset accounts. p. 132

**Amortization**  the expiration of the usefulness of capital assets (plant, equipment, and intangibles), and the related process of allocating the cost of such assets to expense of the periods during which the assets are used. p. 134

**Capital assets**  tangible, long-lived assets held for use in the production or sale of other assets of services. p. 134

**Cash basis of accounting**  an accounting system in which revenues are reported in the income statement when cash is received and expenses are reported when cash is paid. p. 131

**Classified balance sheet**  a balance sheet that shows assets and liabilities grouped in meaningful subclasses. p. 145

**Common shares**  the name given to a corporation's shares when it issues only one kind or class of shares. p. 149

**Contra account**  an account the balance of which is subtracted from the balance of an associated account to show a more proper amount for the item recorded in the associated account. p. 135

**Contributed capital**  the portion of a corporation's equity that represents investments in the corporation by its shareholders. p. 149

**Current assets**  cash or other assets that are reasonably expected to be realized in cash or to be sold or consumed within one year or one operating cycle of the business, whichever is longer. p. 146

**Current liabilities**  obligations due to be paid or liquidated within one year or one operating cycle of the business, whichever is longer. p. 148

**Dividends**  a distribution, generally of assets, made by a corporation to its shareholders. p. 149

**Fiscal year**  any 12 consecutive months used by a business as its annual accounting period. p. 129

**Intangible assets**  economic benefits or resources without physical substance, the value of which stems from the privileges or rights that accrue to their owner. p. 148

**Interim financial reports**  financial reports of a business that are based on one-month or three-month accounting periods. p. 129

**Long-term liabilities**  obligations not due to be paid within one year or the current operating cycle of the business. p. 148

**Matching principle**  accounting requirements that expenses be reported in the same accounting period as the revenues that were earned as a result of the expenses. p. 130

**Natural business year**  the 12-month period that ends when the activities of a business are at their lowest point. p. 129

**Operating cycle of a business**  the average time a business takes to pay cash for salaries of employees or to pay for merchandise and then to receive cash from customers in exchange for the sale of the services or merchandise. pp. 146

**Plant and equipment**  same as capital assets. p. 147

**Report form balance sheet**  a balance sheet with a vertical format that shows the assets above the liabilities and the liabilities above the owner's equity. p. 150

**Retained earnings**  the portion of a corporation's equity that represents its cumulative net income less net losses and dividends. p.149

**Time period principle**  identifying the activities of a business as occurring during specific time periods such as months, or three-month periods, or years so that periodic financial reports of the business can be prepared. p. 128

**Unadjusted trial balance**  trial balance before adjustments have been recorded. p. 140

**Unclassified balance sheet**  a balance sheet that presents a single list of assets and a single list of liabilities with no attempt to divide them into classes. p. 145

---

## SYNONYMOUS TERMS

**Accumulated amortization**  allowance for amortization.

**Amortization**  depreciation.

**Capital assets**  property, plant, and equipment; land, buildings, and equipment; plant assets; fixed assets

**Common shares**  capital stock

---

*The letter*[B] *identifies the questions, quick studies, exercises, and problems that are based on Appendix B at the end of the chapter.*

---

## QUESTIONS

1. What type of business is most likely to select a fiscal year that corresponds to the natural business year instead of the calendar year?

2. What kind of assets require adjusting entries to record amortization?

3. What contra account is used when recording and reporting the effects of amortization? Why is it used?

4. How is an unearned revenue classified on the balance sheet?

5. What is an accrued revenue? Give an example.

6. What is the difference between the cash and accrual bases of accounting?

7. What classes of assets and liabilities are shown on a typical classified balance sheet?

8. What is a company's operating cycle?

9. What are the characteristics of capital assets?

10. When financial statements are prepared from an adjusted trial balance, why should the income statement be prepared first? What statement is prepared next?

11. Which accounting principles provide the basis for the adjustment process?

[B]12. Bee Company records revenues received in advance with credits to liability accounts, while Cee Company records revenues received in advance with credits to revenue accounts. Will these companies have differences in their financial statements because of this difference in their procedures? Why or why not?

---

# QUICK STUDY (Five-Minute Exercises)

**QS 3–1**
**(LO 1)**

In its first year of operations, Blaine Company earned $26,000 in revenues and received $22,000 cash from customers. The company incurred expenses of $15,000 but had not paid for $1,500 of them at year-end. In addition, Blaine prepaid $2,500 for expenses that would be incurred the next year. Calculate the first year's net income under a cash basis and calculate the first year's net income under an accrual basis.

**QS 3–2**
**(LO 2)**

In recording its transactions during the year, Founder Company records prepayments of expenses in asset accounts and receipts of unearned revenues in liability accounts. At the end of its annual accounting period, the company must make three adjusting entries. They are (a) to accrue salaries expense, (b) to adjust the Unearned Services Revenue account to recognize earned revenue, and (c) to record the earning of services revenue for which cash will be received the following period. For each of these adjusting entries, use the numbers assigned to the following accounts to indicate the correct account to be debited and the correct account to be credited.

| | |
|---|---|
| 1. Prepaid Salaries Expense | 5. Salaries Expense |
| 2. Cash | 6. Services Revenue Earned |
| 3. Salaries Payable | 7. Unearned Services Revenue |
| 4. Accounts Receivable | |

**QS 3–3**
**(LO 2)**

In making adjusting entries at the end of its accounting period, Fulmer Company failed to record $700 of insurance premiums that had expired. This cost had been initially debited to the Prepaid Insurance account. The company also failed to record accrued salaries payable of $400. As a result of these oversights, the financial statements for the reporting period will (a) understate net income by $400, (b) understate assets by $700, (c) overstate liabilities by $400, (d) understate expenses by $1,100.

**QS 3–4**
**(LO 3)**

The following information has been taken from Jones Company's unadjusted and adjusted trial balances:

| | Unadjusted | | Adjusted | |
|---|---|---|---|---|
| | **Debit** | **Credit** | **Debit** | **Credit** |
| Prepaid insurance . . . . | $6,200 | | $5,900 | |
| Salaries payable . . . . . | | | | $1,400 |

The adjusting entries must have included these items:

*a.* A $300 credit to Prepaid Insurance and a $1,400 debit to Salaries Payable.

*b.* A $300 debit to Insurance Expense and a $1,400 debit to Salaries Payable.

*c.* A $300 debit to Insurance Expense and a $1,400 debit to Salaries Expense.

Calculate Nickel Company's current ratio given the following information about its assets and liabilities:

**QS 3–5**
**(LO 4)**

| | |
|---|---|
| Accounts receivable ........ | $17,000 |
| Accounts payable .......... | 11,000 |
| Buildings ................ | 35,000 |
| Cash ................... | 4,000 |
| Long-term notes payable ..... | 20,000 |
| Office supplies ........... | 800 |
| Prepaid insurance ......... | 3,500 |
| Unearned services revenue .... | 3,000 |

Blalock Company initially records prepaid and unearned items in income statement accounts. In preparing adjusting entries at the end of the company's first accounting period:

**ᴮQS 3–6**
**(LO 6)**

*a.* Unpaid salaries will be recorded with a debit to Prepaid Salaries and a credit to Salaries Expense.

*b.* The cost of unused office supplies will be recorded with a debit to Supplies Expense and a credit to Office Supplies.

*c.* Unearned fees will be recorded with a debit to Consulting Fees Earned and a credit to Unearned Consulting Fees.

*d.* Earned but unbilled consulting fees will be recorded with a debit to Unearned Consulting Fees and a credit to Consulting Fees Earned.

*e.* None of the above is correct.

---

# EXERCISES

Prepare adjusting journal entries for the financial statements for the year ended December 31, 1996, for each of these independent situations:

**Exercise 3–1**
Adjusting entries for expenses
**(LO 2)**

*a.* The Supplies account had a $150 debit balance on January 1, 1996; $1,340 of supplies were purchased during the year; and the December 31, 1996, count showed that $177 of supplies are on hand.

*b.* The Prepaid Insurance account had a $2,800 debit balance at December 31, 1996, before adjusting for the costs of any expired coverage. An analysis of the company's insurance policies showed that $2,300 of coverage had expired.

*c.* The Prepaid Insurance account had a $3,500 debit balance at December 31, 1996, before adjusting for the costs of any expired coverage. An analysis of the company's insurance policies showed that $520 of unexpired insurance remained in effect.

*d.* Amortization on the company's equipment for 1996 was estimated to be $8,000.

*e.* Six months' property taxes are estimated to be $5,400. They have accrued since June 30, 1996, but are unrecorded and unpaid at December 31, 1996.

**Exercise 3–2**
Adjusting entries for accrued expenses
**(LO 2, 3)**

The Haywood Company has five part-time employees, and each earns $120 per day. They are normally paid on Fridays for work completed on Monday through Friday of the same week. They were all paid in full on Friday, December 28, 1996. The next week, all five of the employees worked only four days because New Year's Day was an unpaid holiday. Show the adjusting entry that would be recorded on Monday, December 31, 1996, and the journal entry that would be made to record paying the employees' wages on Friday, January 4, 1997.

**Exercise 3–3**
Identifying adjusting entries
**(LO 2)**

For each of these adjusting entries, enter the letter of the explanation that most closely describes the transaction in the blank space beside the entry:

*a.* To record the year's consumption of a prepaid expense.

*b.* To record accrued interest expense.

*c.* To record accrued income.

*d.* To record the year's amortization expense.

*e.* To record the earning of previously unearned income.

*f.* To record accrued salaries expense.

|  |  |  |
|---|---|---|
| ___ 1. Amortization Expense | 99,000.00 | |
|     Accumulated Amortization | | 99,000.00 |
| ___ 2. Insurance Expense | 6,000.00 | |
|     Prepaid Insurance | | 6,000.00 |
| ___ 3. Interest Receivable | 22,000.00 | |
|     Interest Earned | | 22,000.00 |
| ___ 4. Salaries Expense | 37,500.00 | |
|     Salaries Payable | | 37,500.00 |
| ___ 5. Interest Expense | 63,000.00 | |
|     Interest Payable | | 63,000.00 |
| ___ 6. Unearned Professional Fees | 86,000.00 | |
|     Professional Fees Earned | | 86,000.00 |

**Exercise 3–4**
Missing data in supplies expense calculations
**(LO 2)**

Determine the missing amounts in each of these four independent situations:

| | a. | b. | c. | d. |
|---|---|---|---|---|
| Supplies on hand—January 1 | $100 | $ 800 | $ 680 | ? |
| Supplies purchased during the year | 700 | 2,700 | ? | $12,000 |
| Supplies on hand—December 31 | 250 | ? | 920 | 1,600 |
| Supplies expense for the year | ? | 650 | 4,800 | 13,150 |

**Exercise 3–5**
Adjustments and payments of accrued items
**(LO 2, 3)**

The following three situations require adjusting journal entries to prepare financial statements as of June 30. For each situation, present the adjusting entry and the entry that would be made to record the payment of the accrued liability during July.

*a.* The total weekly salaries expense for all employees is $6,000. This amount is paid at the end of the day on Friday of each week with five working days. June 30 falls on Tuesday of this year, which means that the employees had worked two days since the last payday. The next payday is July 3.

*b.* The company has a $390,000 note payable that requires 0.8% interest to be paid each month on the 20th of the month. The interest was last paid on June 20 and the next payment is due on July 20.

*c.* On June 1, the company retained a lawyer at a flat monthly fee of $1,000. This amount is payable on the 12th of the following month

On March 1, 1996, a company paid a $32,400 premium on a three-year insurance policy for protection beginning on that date. Fill in the blanks in the following table:

| Balance Sheet Asset under the: | | | Insurance Expense under the: | | |
| --- | --- | --- | --- | --- | --- |
| | Accrual Basis | Cash Basis | | Accrual Basis | Cash Basis |
| 31/12/96 | $_____ | $_____ | 1996 | $_____ | $_____ |
| 31/12/97 | _____ | _____ | 1997 | _____ | _____ |
| 31/12/98 | _____ | _____ | 1998 | _____ | _____ |
| 31/12/99 | _____ | _____ | 1999 | _____ | _____ |
| | | | Total | $_____ | $_____ |

The owner of a duplex apartment building prepares annual financial statements based on a March 31 fiscal year.

a.   The tenants of one of the apartments paid five months' rent in advance on November 1, 1996. The monthly rental is $1,000 per month. Because more than one month's rent was paid in advance, the journal entry credited the Unearned Rent account when the payment was received. No other entry had been recorded prior to March 31, 1997. Give the adjusting journal entry that should be recorded on March 31, 1997.

b.   On January 1, 1997, the tenants of the other apartment moved in and paid the first month's rent. The $900 payment was recorded with a credit to the Rent Earned account. However, the tenants have not paid the rent for February or March. They have agreed to pay it as soon as possible. Give the adjusting journal entry that should be recorded on March 31, 1997.

c.   On April 3, 1997, the tenants described in part b paid $2,700 rent for February, March, and April. Give the journal entry to record the cash collection.

Use the following adjusted trial balance of the Hamburg Trucking Company to prepare (a) an income statement for the year ended December 31, 1996; (b) a statement of changes in owner's equity for the year ended December 31, 1996; and (c) an unclassified balance sheet as of December 31, 1996. The owner did not make any new investments during 1996.

| | Debit | Credit |
| --- | --- | --- |
| Cash | $ 5,500 | |
| Accounts receivable | 18,000 | |
| Office supplies | 2,000 | |
| Trucks | 180,000 | |
| Accumulated amortization, trucks | | $ 45,000 |
| Land | 75,000 | |
| Accounts payable | | 11,000 |
| Interest payable | | 3,000 |
| Long-term notes payable | | 52,000 |
| B. Hamburg, capital | | 161,000 |
| B. Hamburg, withdrawals | 19,000 | |
| Trucking fees earned | | 128,000 |
| Amortization expense, trucks | 22,500 | |
| Salaries expense | 60,000 | |
| Office supplies expense | 7,000 | |
| Repairs expense, trucks | 11,000 | |
| Total | $400,000 | $400,000 |

**Exercise 3–9**
Preparing a classified
balance sheet and
calculating the current
ratio
**(LO 4)**

Use the information provided in Exercise 3–8 to prepare a classified balance sheet for the Hamburg Trucking Company as of December 31, 1996. Determine the value of the current ratio as of the balance sheet date.

**Exercise 3–10**
Identifying the effects of
adjusting entries
**(LO 2, 3)**

Following are two income statements for the Carlton Financial Consulting Co. for the year ended December 31. The left column was prepared before any adjusting entries were recorded and the right column includes the effects of adjusting entries. Analyze the statements and prepare the adjusting entries that must have been recorded. Thirty percent of the additional consulting fees were earned but not billed and the other 70% were earned by performing services that the customers had paid for in advance.

**CARLTON FINANCIAL CONSULTING CO.**
**Income Statements**
**For Year Ended December 31**

|  | Before Adjustments | After Adjustments |
|---|---|---|
| Revenues: |  |  |
| Consulting fees earned . . . . . . . . . . . . . | $ 48,000 | $ 60,000 |
| Commissions earned . . . . . . . . . . . . . . | 85,000 | 85,000 |
| Total revenues . . . . . . . . . . . . . . . . . | $133,000 | $145,000 |
| Operating expenses: |  |  |
| Amortization expense, computers . . . . . |  | $ 3,000 |
| Amortization expense, office furniture . . |  | 3,500 |
| Salaries expense . . . . . . . . . . . . . . . . | $ 25,000 | 29,900 |
| Insurance expense . . . . . . . . . . . . . . . |  | 2,600 |
| Rent expense . . . . . . . . . . . . . . . . . . . | 9,000 | 9,000 |
| Office supplies expense . . . . . . . . . . . . |  | 960 |
| Advertising expense . . . . . . . . . . . . . . | 6,000 | 6,000 |
| Utilities expense . . . . . . . . . . . . . . . . | 2,500 | 2,640 |
| Total operating expenses . . . . . . . . . . . | $ 42,500 | $ 57,600 |
| Net income . . . . . . . . . . . . . . . . . . . . | $ 90,500 | $ 87,400 |

**Exercise 3–11**
Calculating the current
ratio
**(LO 4)**

Calculate the current ratio in each of the following cases:

|  | Current Assets | Current Liabilities |
|---|---|---|
| Case 1 . . . . . . . . . . . . . . . . . . . . . . . . | $84,000 | $31,000 |
| Case 2 . . . . . . . . . . . . . . . . . . . . . . . . | 96,000 | 75,000 |
| Case 3 . . . . . . . . . . . . . . . . . . . . . . . . | 45,000 | 48,000 |
| Case 4 . . . . . . . . . . . . . . . . . . . . . . . . | 84,500 | 82,600 |
| Case 5 . . . . . . . . . . . . . . . . . . . . . . . . | 65,000 | 97,000 |

**BExercise 3–12**
Adjustments for prepaid
items recorded in expense
and revenue accounts
**(LO 6)**

The Elder Painting Co. was organized on December 1 by Terry Elder. In setting up the bookkeeping procedures, Elder decided to debit expense accounts when the company prepays its expenses and to credit revenue accounts when customers pay for services in advance. Prepare journal entries for items *a* through *d* and adjusting entries as of December 31 for items *e* through *g:*

*a.*   Shop supplies were purchased on December 1 for $1,000.

*b.*   The company prepaid insurance premiums of $480 on December 2.

c. On December 15, the company received an advance payment of $4,000 from one customer for two painting projects.

d. On December 28, the company received $1,200 from a second customer for painting services to be performed in January.

e. By counting them on December 31, Elder determined that $640 of shop supplies were on hand.

f. An analysis of the insurance policies in effect on December 31 showed that $80 of insurance coverage had expired.

g. As of December 31, only one project had been completed. The fee for this particular project was $2,100.

The Falcon Company experienced the following events and transactions during March:

**BExercise 3–13**
Alternative procedures for revenues received in advance
**(LO 6)**

Mar. 1 Received $1,000 in advance of performing work for T. Carson.

5 Received $4,200 in advance of performing work for B. Gamble.

10 Completed the job for T. Carson.

16 Received $3,750 in advance of performing work for S. Curtin.

25 Completed the job for B. Gamble.

31 The job for S. Curtin is still unfinished.

a. Give journal entries (including any adjusting entry as of the end of the month) to record these events using the procedure of initially crediting the Unearned Fees account when a payment is received from a customer in advance of performing services.

b. Give journal entries (including any adjusting entry as of the end of the month) to record these events using the procedure of initially crediting the Fees Earned account when a payment is received from a customer in advance of performing services.

c. Under each method, determine the amount of earned fees that should be reported on the income statement for March and the amount of unearned fees that should appear on the balance sheet as of March 31.

## PROBLEMS

The Montgomery Company's annual accounting period ends on December 31, 1997. The following information concerns the adjusting entries to be recorded as of that date:

**Problem 3–1**
Adjusting journal entries
**(LO 2, 3)**

a. The Office Supplies account started the year with a $1,000 balance. During 1997, the company purchased supplies at a cost of $4,200, which was added to the Office Supplies account. The inventory of supplies on hand at December 31 had a cost of $880.

b. An analysis of the company's insurance policies provided these facts:

| Policy | Date of Purchase | Years of Coverage | Total Cost |
|---|---|---|---|
| 1 .... | April 1, 1996 | 2 | $5,280 |
| 2 .... | April 1, 1997 | 3 | 4,356 |
| 3 .... | August 1, 1997 | 1 | 900 |

The total premium for each policy was paid in full at the purchase date, and the Prepaid Insurance account was debited for the full cost.

c.   The company has five employees who earn a total of $700 in salaries for every working day. They are paid each Monday for their work in the five-day workweek ending on the preceding Monday. December 31, 1997, falls on Wednesday, and all five employees worked the first two days of the week. Because New Year's Day is a paid holiday, they will be paid salaries for five full days on Tuesday, January 6, 1998.

d.   The company purchased a building on August 1, 1997. The building cost $570,000 and is expected to have a $30,000 salvage value at the end of its predicted 30-year life.

e.   Because the company is not large enough to occupy the entire building, it arranged to rent some space to a tenant at $800 per month, starting on November 1, 1997. The rent was paid on time on November 1, and the amount received was credited to the Rent Earned account. However, the tenant has not paid the December rent. The company has worked out an agreement with the tenant, who has promised to pay both December's and January's rent in full on January 15. The tenant has agreed not to fall behind again.

f.   On November 1, the company also rented space to another tenant for $725 per month. The tenant paid five months' rent in advance on that date. The payment was recorded with a credit to the Unearned Rent account.

**Required**

1.   Use the information to prepare adjusting entries as of December 31, 1997.

2.   Prepare journal entries to record the subsequent cash transactions described in parts c and e.

**Problem 3–2**
Adjusting entries and the adjusted trial balance
**(LO 3, 4)**

Miller Realty's unadjusted trial balance on December 31, 1996, the end of its annual accounting period, is as follows:

**MILLER REALTY**
**Trial Balance**
**December 31, 1996**

| | | |
|---|---:|---:|
| Cash | $ 2,910 | |
| Prepaid insurance | 1,375 | |
| Office supplies | 435 | |
| Office equipment | 9,375 | |
| Accumulated amortization, office equipment | | $ 2,880 |
| Automobile | 19,150 | |
| Accumulated amortization, automobile | | 3,225 |
| Accounts payable | | 335 |
| Unearned management fees | | 675 |
| Don Miller, capital | | 16,700 |
| Don Miller, withdrawals | 27,900 | |
| Sales commissions earned | | 61,920 |
| Office salaries expense | 15,450 | |
| Advertising expense | 1,245 | |
| Rent expense | 7,200 | |
| Telephone expense | 695 | |
| Totals | $85,735 | $85,735 |

**Required**

1. Set up accounts for the items in the trial balance plus these additional accounts: Accounts Receivable; Office Salaries Payable; Management Fees Earned; Insurance Expense; Office Supplies Expense; Amortization Expense, Office Equipment; and Amortization Expense, Automobile. Enter the trial balance amounts in the accounts.

2. Use the information that follows to prepare and post adjusting entries:
   
   *a.* An examination of insurance policies shows $1,085 of expired insurance.
   
   *b.* An inventory shows $120 of unused office supplies on hand.
   
   *c.* Estimated annual amortization on the office equipment is $1,225.
   
   *d.* Estimated annual amortization on the automobile is $2,665.
   
   *e.* The December telephone bill arrived after the trial balance was prepared, and its $60 amount was not included in the trial balance amounts. Also, a $165 bill for newspaper advertising that had appeared in December was not included in the trial balance amounts.
   
   *f.* A client who was taking a tour around the world signed a contract with Miller Realty for the management of his apartment building. The contract calls for a $225 monthly fee, and management began on December 1. The client paid three months' fees in advance, and the amount paid was credited to the Unearned Management Fees account.
   
   *g.* Miller Realty agreed to manage the small office building of a second client for $250 per month payable at the end of each three months. The contract was signed on November 15, and one and one-half months' fees have accrued.
   
   *h.* The one office employee is paid weekly; and on December 31, two days' wages at $120 per day have accrued.

3. After posting the adjusting entries, prepare an adjusted trial balance, an income statement, a statement of changes in owner's equity, and a classified balance sheet. Miller's capital account balance of $16,700 consists of a $6,700 balance on December 31, 1995, plus a $10,000 investment during 1996.

Carl Carter owns and operates Carter Carpentry School. The school provides training to individuals who pay tuition directly to the business, and also offers extension training to groups in off-site locations. The school's unadjusted trial balance as of December 31, 1996, follows. Facts that require eight adjusting entries on December 31, 1996, are presented after the table:

**Problem 3–3**
Adjusting entries and financial statements
**(LO 3, 4)**

**CARTER CARPENTRY SCHOOL**
**Unadjusted Trial Balance**

| | | |
|---|---:|---:|
| Cash | $ 13,000 | |
| Accounts receivable | | |
| Teaching supplies | 5,000 | |
| Prepaid insurance | 7,500 | |
| Prepaid rent | 1,000 | |
| Professional library | 15,000 | |
| Accumulated amortization, professional library | | $ 4,500 |
| Equipment | 35,000 | |
| Accumulated amortization, equipment | | 8,000 |
| Accounts payable | | 18,000 |
| Salaries payable | | |
| Unearned extension fees | | 5,500 |
| Carl Carter, capital | | 31,800 |
| Carl Carter, withdrawals | 20,000 | |
| Tuition fees earned | | 51,000 |
| Extension fees earned | | 19,000 |
| Amortization expense, equipment | | |
| Amortization expense, professional library | | |
| Salaries expense | 24,000 | |
| Insurance expense | | |
| Rent expense | 11,000 | |
| Teaching supplies expense | | |
| Advertising expense | 3,500 | |
| Utilities expense | 2,800 | |
| Totals | $137,800 | $137,800 |

**Additional facts:**

a. An analysis of the company's policies shows that $1,500 of insurance coverage has expired.

b. An inventory shows that teaching supplies costing $1,300 are on hand at the end of the year.

c. The estimated annual amortization on the equipment is $6,000.

d. The estimated annual amortization on the professional library is $3,000.

e. The school offers off-campus services for specific employers. On November 1, the company agreed to do a special six-month course for a client. The contract calls for a monthly fee of $1,100, and the client paid the first five months' fees in advance. When the cash was received, the Unearned Extension Fees account was credited.

f. On October 15, the school agreed to teach a four-month class for an individual for $1,500 tuition per month payable at the end of the class. The services have been provided as agreed, and no payment has been received.

g. The school's only employee is paid weekly. As of the end of the year, two days' wages have accrued at the rate of $100 per day.

h. The balance in the Prepaid Rent account represents the rent for December.

**Required**

1. Enter the unadjusted trial balance in the first two columns of a six-column table like the one shown in Illustration 3–3.

2. Enter the adjusting entries in the Adjustments columns of the table. Identify the debits and credits of each entry with the letters in the list of additional facts. Complete the adjusted trial balance.

3. Prepare the company's income statement and statement of changes in owner's equity for 1996, and prepare the classified balance sheet as of December 31, 1996. The owner did not make additional investments in the business during the year.

In the following six-column table for the Decker Company, the first two columns contain the unadjusted trial balance for the company as of March 31, 1996. The last two columns contain the adjusted trial balance as of the same date.

**Problem 3–4**
Comparing the unadjusted and adjusted trial balances and preparing financial statements
**(LO 3, 4)**

| | Unadjusted Trial Balance | | Adjustments | | Adjusted Trial Balance | |
|---|---|---|---|---|---|---|
| Cash ............... | $ 13,500 | | | | $ 13,500 | |
| Accounts receivable .... | 6,000 | | | | 11,230 | |
| Office supplies ........ | 9,000 | | | | 1,500 | |
| Prepaid insurance ...... | 3,660 | | | | 2,440 | |
| Office equipment ...... | 36,000 | | | | 36,000 | |
| Accumulated amortization, office equipment ..... | | $ 6,000 | | | | $ 9,000 |
| Accounts payable ...... | | 4,650 | | | | 5,100 |
| Interest payable ....... | | | | | | 400 |
| Salaries payable ....... | | | | | | 3,300 |
| Unearned consulting fees . | | 8,000 | | | | 7,150 |
| Long-term notes payable . | | 22,000 | | | | 22,000 |
| Webster Decker, capital .. | | 14,210 | | | | 14,210 |
| Webster Decker, withdrawals ........ | 15,000 | | | | 15,000 | |
| Consulting fees earned .. | | 78,000 | | | | 84,080 |
| Amortization expense, office equipment ..... | | | | | 3,000 | |
| Salaries expense ....... | 35,500 | | | | 38,800 | |
| Interest expense ....... | 700 | | | | 1,100 | |
| Insurance expense ...... | | | | | 1,220 | |
| Rent expense ......... | 6,600 | | | | 6,600 | |
| Office supplies expense .. | | | | | 7,500 | |
| Advertising expense .... | 6,900 | | | | 7,350 | |
| Totals .............. | $132,860 | $132,860 | | | $145,240 | $145,240 |

**Required**

*Preparation component:*

1. Prepare the company's income statement and the statement of changes in owner's equity for the year ended March 31, 1996. The owner did not make any new investments during the year.

2. Prepare the company's classified balance sheet as of March 31, 1996.

3. Calculate the company's current ratio and debt ratio as of March 31, 1996.

*Analysis component:*

4. Analyze the differences between the unadjusted and adjusted trial balances to determine the adjustments that must have been made. Show the results of your analysis by inserting the adjusting journal entries that must have been recorded by the company in the two middle columns. Label each entry with a letter, and provide a short description of the purpose for recording it. (Use the Working Papers that accompany the text or recreate the table.)

**Problem 3–5**
Adjusting entries and the adjusted trial balance
**(LO 3, 4)**

The unadjusted trial balance of United Moving and Storage follows:

**UNITED MOVING AND STORAGE**
**Trial Balance**
**December 31, 1996**

| | | |
|---|---:|---:|
| Cash | $ 3,360 | |
| Accounts receivable | 815 | |
| Prepaid insurance | 5,370 | |
| Office supplies | 480 | |
| Investment in Trail, Inc., common shares | 25,000 | |
| Office equipment | 5,475 | |
| Accumulated amortization, office equipment | | $ 2,520 |
| Trucks | 66,300 | |
| Accumulated amortization, trucks | | 17,300 |
| Building | 207,000 | |
| Accumulated amortization, building | | 42,900 |
| Land | 26,250 | |
| Franchise | 20,000 | |
| Unearned storage fees | | 2,595 |
| Long-term notes payable | | 180,000 |
| Dennis Mead, capital | | 81,170 |
| Dennis Mead, withdrawals | 36,000 | |
| Revenue from moving services | | 135,170 |
| Storage fees earned | | 11,660 |
| Office salaries expense | 17,100 | |
| Drivers' and helpers' wages expense | 39,945 | |
| Gas, oil, and repairs expense | 4,020 | |
| Interest expense | 16,200 | |
| Totals | $473,315 | $473,315 |

**Required**

1. Set up accounts for the items in the trial balance plus these additional accounts: Salaries and Wages Payable; Insurance Expense; Office Supplies Expense; Amortization Expense, Office Equipment; Amortization Expense, Trucks; and Amortization Expense, Building. Enter the trial balance amounts in the accounts.

2. Use the information that follows to prepare and post adjusting entries:
   *a.* Insurance premiums of $4,225 expired during the year.
   *b.* An inventory shows $165 of unused office supplies on hand.
   *c.* Estimated amortization on the office equipment, $775; (*d*) on the trucks, $8,000; and (*e*) on the building, $9,300.

f.  Of the $2,595 balance in the Unearned Storage Fees account, $1,985 was earned by the year-end.

g.  Accrued storage fees earned but unrecorded at year-end totaled $515.

h.  There were $200 of earned but unrecorded office salaries and $1,135 of earned but unrecorded drivers' and helpers' wages at the year-end.

3.  Prepare an adjusted trial balance, an income statement for the year, a statement of changes in owner's equity, and a classified year-end balance sheet. Mead's $81,170 capital balance reflects the December 31, 1995, balance plus a January 15, 1996, investment of $30,000. A $9,000 installment on the long-term note payable is due within one year.

James Piper, a lawyer, has always kept his records on a cash basis; at the end of 1996, he prepared the following cash basis income statement:

**Problem 3–6**
Accrual basis income statement
**(LO 3)**

**JAMES PIPER, LAWYER**
**Income Statement**
**For Year Ended December 31, 1996**

| | |
|---|---|
| Revenues . . . . . . . . . . . . . . . . . . . | $95,500 |
| Expenses . . . . . . . . . . . . . . . . . . . | 40,450 |
| Net income . . . . . . . . . . . . . . . . | $ 55,050 |

In preparing the statement, the following amounts of prepaid, unearned, and accrued items were ignored at the end of 1995 and 1996:

| | End of | |
|---|---|---|
| | **1995** | **1996** |
| Prepaid expenses . . . . . | $ 2,310 | 1,800 |
| Accrued expenses . . . . | 2,595 | 3,270 |
| Unearned revenues . . . . | 3,300 | 5,430 |
| Accrued revenues . . . . | 4,550 | 3,660 |

**Required**

Under the assumptions that the 1995 prepaid expenses were consumed or expired in 1996, the 1995 unearned revenues were earned in 1996, and the 1995 accrued items were either paid or received in cash in 1996, prepare a 1996 accrual basis income statement for James Piper's law practice. Attach to your statement calculations showing how you arrived at each 1996 income statement amount.

**Problem 3–7**
Preparing financial
statements from the
adjusted trial balance and
computing ratios
**(LO 3, 4)**

This adjusted trial balance is for the Krumbell Wrecking Co. as of December 31, 1996:

| | Debit | Credit |
|---|---|---|
| Cash | $ 11,000 | |
| Accounts receivable | 22,000 | |
| Interest receivable | 5,000 | |
| Notes receivable (due in 90 days) | 80,000 | |
| Office supplies | 4,000 | |
| Trucks | 90,000 | |
| Accumulated amortization, trucks | | $ 36,000 |
| Equipment | 70,000 | |
| Accumulated amortization, equipment | | 5,000 |
| Land | 35,000 | |
| Accounts payable | | 44,000 |
| Interest payable | | 6,000 |
| Salaries payable | | 5,500 |
| Unearned wrecking fees | | 11,000 |
| Long-term notes payable | | 65,000 |
| W. Krumbell, capital | | 123,900 |
| W. Krumbell, withdrawals | 19,000 | |
| Wrecking fees earned | | 210,000 |
| Interest earned | | 8,000 |
| Amortization expense, trucks | 9,000 | |
| Amortization expense, equipment | 5,000 | |
| Salaries expense | 90,000 | |
| Wages expense | 16,000 | |
| Interest expense | 12,000 | |
| Office supplies expense | 13,000 | |
| Advertising expense | 25,000 | |
| Repairs expense, trucks | 8,400 | |
| Total | $514,400 | $514,400 |

**Required**

1. Use the information in the trial balance to prepare (*a*) the income statement for the year ended December 31, 1996 (under the assumption that the owner made no new investments during the year); (*b*) the statement of changes in owner's equity for the year ended December 31, 1996; and (*c*) the classified balance sheet as of December 31, 1996.

2. Calculate the following ratios for the company:

   *a.* Current ratio as of December 31, 1996.

   *b.* Debt ratio as of December 31, 1996.

The following events occurred for a company during the last two months of its fiscal year ended December 31:

Nov. 1  Paid $1,000 for future newspaper advertising.

    1  Paid $1,440 for insurance through October 31 of the following year.

    30  Received $2,200 for future services to be provided to a customer.

Dec. 1  Paid $1,800 for the services of a consultant, to be received over the next three months.

    15  Received $5,100 for future services to be provided to a customer.

Dec. 31 Of the advertising paid for on November 1, $600 worth had not yet been published by the newspaper.

31 Part of the insurance paid for on November 1 had expired.

31 Services worth $800 had not yet been provided to the customer who paid on November 30.

31 One-third of the consulting services paid for on December 1 had been received.

31 The company had performed $2,000 of the services that the customer had paid for on December 15.

**Required**

*Preparation component:*

1. Prepare entries for the above events under the approach that records prepaid expenses as assets and records unearned revenues as liabilities. Also, prepare adjusting entries at the end of the year.

2. Prepare journal entries under the approach that records prepaid expenses as expenses and records unearned revenues as revenues. Also, prepare adjusting entries at the end of the year.

*Analysis component:*

3. Explain why the alternative sets of entries in requirements 1 and 2 do not result in different financial statement amounts.

Carmen Tam purchased Pecan Grove, a mobile home park, last September 1, and she has operated it four months without keeping formal accounting records. However, she has deposited all receipts in the bank and has kept an accurate chequebook record of payments. An analysis of the cash receipts and payments follows:

**Problem 3–9**
Accrual basis income statement
**(LO 3, 5)**

|  | | Receipts | Payments |
|---|---|---|---|
| Investment | | $52,000 | |
| Purchased Pecan Grove: | | | |
|    Office equipment | $ 1,500 | | |
|    Buildings and improvements | 90,000 | | |
|    Land | 105,000 | | |
|    Total | $196,500 | | |
|    Less long-term note payable signed | 145,000 | | |
| Cash paid | | | $51,500 |
| Insurance premium paid | | | 1,140 |
| Office supplies purchased | | | 144 |
| Wages paid | | | 4,000 |
| Utilities paid | | | 450 |
| Property taxes paid | | | 1,500 |
| Owner's withdrawals of cash | | | 4,800 |
| Mobile home space rentals collected | | 19,380 | |
| Totals | | $71,380 | $63,534 |
| Cash balance, December 31 | | | 7,846 |
| Totals | | $71,380 | $71,380 |

Ms. Tam wants you to prepare an accrual basis income statement for the village for the four-month period she has operated the business, a statement of changes in owner's equity, and a December 31 balance sheet. You ascertain the following (T-accounts may be helpful in organizing the data):

The buildings and improvements were estimated to have a 25-year remaining life when purchased and at the end of that time will be wrecked. It is estimated that the sale of salvaged materials will just pay the wrecking costs and the cost of clearing the site. The office equipment is in good condition. At the time of purchase, Ms. Tam estimated she would use the equipment for three years and would then trade it in on new equipment of like kind. She thought $150 a fair estimate of what she would receive for the old equipment when she traded it in at the end of three years.

The $1,140 payment for insurance was for a policy taken out on September 1. The policy's protection was for one year beginning on that date. Ms. Tam estimates that one-third of the office supplies purchased have been used. She also says that the one employee of the park earns $50 per day for a five-day week that ends on Friday. The employee was paid last week but has worked four days, December 28 through 31, for which he has not been paid.

Included in the $19,380 of mobile home rentals collected is $360 received from a tenant for three months' rent beginning on December 1. Also, a tenant has not paid his $120 rent for the month of December.

The long-term note payable requires an annual payment of 12% interest on the beginning principal balance plus a $6,000 annual payment on the principal. The first payment is due next September 1. The property tax payment was for one year's taxes that were paid on October 1 for the tax year beginning on September 1, the day Ms. Tam purchased the business

**BProblem 3–10**
Recording prepayments
and unearned items in
income statement
accounts
**(LO 2, 6)**

Waivah Company debits expense accounts when recording prepaid expenses; it credits revenue accounts when recording unearned receipts. The following information was available on December 31, 1996, the end of the company's annual accounting period.

a. The Store Supplies account had a $340 debit balance at the beginning of the year, $1,250 of supplies were purchased during the year, and an inventory of unused supplies at the year-end totaled $620.

b. An examination of insurance policies showed two policies, as follows:

| Policy | Date of Purchase | Life of Policy | Cost |
|--------|------------------|----------------|------|
| 1 . . . | May 1, 1994 | 3 years | $2,340 |
| 2 . . . | October 1, 1996 | 2 years | 2,280 |

Insurance Expense was debited for the cost of each policy at the time of its purchase. However, the correct amount of Prepaid Insurance was recorded during the adjustment processes at the end of 1994 and 1995.

c. On October 15, 1996, Waivah Company agreed to provide consulting services to a client and received advance payment of $8,500. At year-end, the client agreed that three-fourths of the services had been provided.

d. The company occupies most of the space in its building but it also rents space to one tenant. The tenant agreed on November 1 to rent a small amount of space at $750 per month, and on that date paid three months' rent in advance.

e. The Office Supplies account had a $550 debit balance at the beginning of the year and $750 of supplies were purchased during the year. A year-end inventory of office supplies indicated that supplies amounting to $990 had been used during the year.

**Required**

Prepare adjusting journal entries dated December 31, 1996, prior to the preparation of annual financial statements. For item (b), prepare a separate adjusting entry for each insurance policy.

Review the information presented in paragraphs c, d, and e of Problem 3–1. Describe how each of the following errors from 1997 would affect the company's income statements for 1997 and 1998 and its balance sheets as of December 31, 1997, and 1998 (treat each case as independent from the others). None of the errors were repeated in 1998, but they remained undiscovered until well into 1999.

**Problem 3–11**
Analytical essay
**(LO 1, 2)**

1. The company mistakenly recorded the $1,400 of accrued salary expense described in part c as if the amount was only $1,000. However, the employees were paid the correct amount of $1,400 on January 6, 1998. At that time, the Salaries Payable account was debited for $1,000 and the remainder of the $3,500 payment to the employees was debited to the Salaries Expense account for 1998.

2. The company failed to record the $7,500 amortization expense on the building described in part d.

3. The company failed to record the $800 of accrued rent income described in part e. Instead, the revenue was recorded on January 15 as income earned in 1998.

On November 1, 1996, Carson Company and Winslow Company each paid $6,000 for six months' rent on their offices. Carson recorded its payment with a debit to the Prepaid Rent account. On the other hand, Winslow debited the Rent Expense account for $6,000. Both companies use calendar years as their accounting periods. Describe the differences between the adjusting entries the two companies should make on December 31, 1996. Be sure to explain how the two companies' different bookkeeping procedures affect the financial statements.

**ᴮProblem 3–12**
Analytical essay
**(LO 1, 2, 6)**

---

# SERIAL PROBLEM

(This comprehensive problem was introduced in Chapter 2 and continues in Chapters 4 and 5. If the Chapter 2 segment has not been completed, the assignment can begin at this point. However, you will need to use the facts presented on pages 119-20 in Chapter 2. Because of its length, this problem is most easily solved if you use the Working Papers that accompany this text.)

**Emerald Computer Services**

After the success of its first two months, Tracy Green has decided to continue operating Emerald Computer Services. (The transactions that occurred in these months are described in Chapter 2.) Before proceeding into December, Green adds these new accounts to the chart of accounts for the ledger:

| Account | No. |
|---|---|
| Accumulated Amortization, Office Equipment . . . . . . | 164 |
| Accumulated Amortization, Computer Equipment . . . | 168 |
| Wages Payable . . . . . . . . . . . . . . . . . . . . . . . . . . . | 210 |
| Unearned Computer Fees . . . . . . . . . . . . . . . . . . . | 233 |
| Amortization Expense, Office Equipment . . . . . . . . . | 612 |
| Amortization Expense, Computer Equipment . . . . . . | 613 |
| Insurance Expense . . . . . . . . . . . . . . . . . . . . . . . . | 637 |
| Rent Expense . . . . . . . . . . . . . . . . . . . . . . . . . . . . | 640 |
| Computer Supplies Expense . . . . . . . . . . . . . . . . . . | 652 |

**Required**

1. Prepare journal entries to record each of the following transactions for Emerald Computer Services. Post the entries to the accounts in the ledger.

2. Prepare adjusting entries to record the events described on December 31. Post the entries to the accounts in the ledger.

3. Prepare an adjusted trial balance as of December 31, 1996.

4. Prepare an income statement for the three months ended December 31, 1996.

5. Prepare a statement of changes in owner's equity for the three months ended December 31, 1996.

6. Prepare a balance sheet as of December 31, 1996.

Transactions and other data:

Dec. 3    Paid $700 to the Town Centre Mall for the company's share of mall advertising costs.

4    Paid $400 to repair the company's computer.

6    Received $2,500 from Alpha Printing Co. for the receivable from the prior month.

10    Paid Fran Sims for six days' work at the rate of $125 per day.

12    Notified by Alpha Printing Co. that Emerald's bid of $4,000 on a proposed project was accepted. The company paid an advance of $1,000.

13    Purchased $770 of computer supplies on credit from AAA Supply Co.

15    Sent a reminder to Fox Run Estates to pay the fee for services originally recorded on November 7.

19    Completed project for Delta Fixtures, Inc., and received $3,750 cash.

21    Paid $2,000 to Tracy Green as a cash withdrawal.

22–26    Took the week off for the holidays.

28    Received $1,900 from Fox Run Estates on their receivable.

29    Reimbursed Tracy Green for business usage of her automobile, 400 kilometres at $0.25 per km.

31    The following information was collected to be used in adjusting entries prior to preparing financial statements for the company's first three months:

   *a.*    The December 31 inventory of computer supplies was $480.

   *b.*    Three months have passed since the annual insurance premium was paid.

   *c.*    As of the end of the year, Fran Sims has not been paid for four days of work at the rate of $125 per day.

   *d.*    The computer is expected to have a four-year life with no salvage value.

   *e.*    The office equipment is expected to have a three-year life with no salvage value.

   *f.*    Prepaid rent for three of the four months has expired.

# PROVOCATIVE PROBLEMS

The 1996 and 1997 balance sheets for Phillips Law Practice reported the following assets and liabilities:

|  | 1996 | 1997 |
|---|---|---|
| Accounts receivable ... | $45,000 | $62,000 |
| Prepaid insurance ..... | 4,800 | 3,600 |
| Interest payable ...... | 5,750 | 9,250 |
| Unearned legal fees .... | 17,000 | 25,000 |

The company's records show that the following amounts of cash were spent and received during 1997:

| | |
|---|---|
| Cash spent to pay insurance premiums .. | $ 12,500 |
| Cash spent to pay interest ........... | 14,000 |
| Cash received on accounts receivable ... | 120,000 |
| Cash received in advance for legal fees .. | 108,000 |

Calculate the amounts to be reported on Phillips Law Practice's 1997 income statement for (a) insurance expense, (b) interest expense, and (c) total legal fees earned.

Early in January, Chris Williams created a new business called We-Fix-Anything. Unfortunately, Williams has not maintained any double-entry accounting records, although all cash receipts and disbursements have been carefully recorded. In addition, all unpaid invoices for the company's expenses and purchases are kept in a file until they are paid. The cash records have been summarized in this schedule:

| | | |
|---|---|---|
| Cash received: | | |
| Investment by owner ......... | $43,000 | |
| Customer repairs ............ | 66,000 | |
| Total ................... | | $109,000 |
| Cash paid: | | |
| Shop equipment ............ | $21,200 | |
| Repair supplies ............. | 25,000 | |
| Rent ..................... | 8,400 | |
| Insurance premiums ........ | 900 | |
| Newspaper advertising ........ | 2,000 | |
| Utility bills ................ | 1,600 | |
| Employee's wages ........... | 8,000 | |
| Chris Williams ............. | 20,000 | |
| Total cash payments ........ | | 87,100 |
| Cash balance as of December 31 .. | | $ 21,900 |

Williams wants to know the net income for the first year and the company's financial position at the end of the year. Provide this information by preparing an accrual basis income statement, a statement of changes in owner's equity, and a classified balance sheet. Also compute the current ratio and the debt ratio.

The following information will help you: The shop equipment was bought in January and is predicted to have a useful life of 10 years, with a $1,200 salvage value. There is a $4,000 unpaid invoice in the file; it is for supplies that have been purchased and received. An inventory shows that $8,200 of supplies are on hand at the end of the year. The shop space is rented for $600 per month under a five-year lease. The lease contract required Williams to pay the first and the final two months' rents in advance. The insurance premiums acquired two policies on January 2. The first is a one-year policy that cost $500, and the second is a two-year policy that cost $400. There are $190 of earned but unpaid wages and customers owe the shop $3,750 for services they have received.

**Provocative Problem 3–3**
Financial statement analysis case
**(LO 4)**

Geac

Refer to the financial statements and related information for Geac Computer Corporation Limited in Appendix I. Find the answers to the following questions by analyzing the information in the report.

1. Does the company present a classified balance sheet? What title is given to the financial statement?
2. Identify the classifications of assets presented on the balance sheet.
3. What is the total amount of accumulated depreciation and amortization as of April 30, 1994?
4. What is the company's current ratio at the end of its 1993 and 1992 fiscal years?

**Provocative Problem 3–4**
Ethical issues essay
**(LO 2, 3, 4, 6)**

Review the As a Matter of Ethics case on page 139. Describe the ethical dilemma faced by Bill Palmer and describe the alternative courses of action that he might take. Explain how your answer would differ given the following assumptions: (a) Palmer knows that the company's financial statements are not going to be audited; (b) Palmer knows that the president's bonus depends on the amount of income reported in the first year; and (c) Palmer's job depends on complying with the president's wishes.

# ANALYTICAL AND REVIEW PROBLEMS

**A & R Problem 3–1**

The Salaries Payable account of James Bay Company Limited appears below:

| Salaries Payable | | | |
|---|---|---|---|
| Entries during 1996 | 155,648 | Bal. Jan. 1, 1996 | 9,008 |
| | | Entries during 1996 | 155,360 |

The company records the salary expense and related liability at the end of each week and pays the employees on the last Friday of the month.

**Required**

Calculate:

1. Salary expense for 1996.
2. How much was paid to employees in 1996 for work done in 1995?
3. How much was paid to employees in 1996 for work done in 1996?
4. How much will be paid to employees in 1997 for work done in 1996?

The records for Jan Kauffman's home nursing business were kept on the cash basis instead of the accrual basis. However, the company is now applying for a loan and the bank wants to know what its net income for 1997 was under generally accepted accounting principles. Here is the income statement for 1997 under the cash basis:

**A & R Problem 3–2**

**KAUFFMAN'S HOME NURSING**
**Income Statement (Cash Basis)**
**For Year Ended December 31, 1997**

| | |
|---|---|
| Revenues . . . . . . . . . . . . . . . . . . | $175,000 |
| Expenses . . . . . . . . . . . . . . . . . . | 110,000 |
| Net income . . . . . . . . . . . . . . . . | $ 65,000 |

This additional information was gathered to help the accountant convert the income statement to the accrual basis:

| | As of 31/12/96 | As of 31/12/97 |
|---|---|---|
| Accrued revenues . . . . | $ 4,000 | $5,500 |
| Unearned revenues . . . . | 22,000 | 7,000 |
| Accrued expenses . . . . | 4,900 | 3,000 |
| Prepaid expenses . . . . . | 9,000 | 6,900 |

All prepaid expenses from the beginning of the year were consumed or expired, all unearned revenues from the beginning of the year were earned, and all accrued expenses and revenues from the beginning of the year were paid or collected.

**Required**

Prepare an accrual basis income statement for this business for 1997. Provide schedules that explain how you converted from cash revenues and expenses to accrual revenues and expenses.

## CONCEPT TESTER

Test your understanding of the concepts introduced in this chapter by completing the following crossword puzzle.

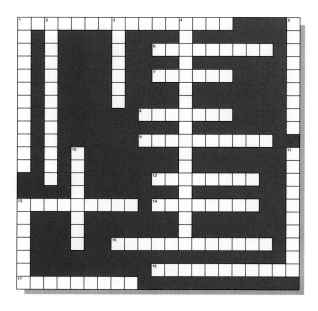

**Across Clues**

1. Time period covered by financial reports (2 words).
6. Distribution to shareholders.
7. An account, the balance of which is subtracted from the balance of the associated account.
8. Expenses incurred but unpaid.
9. Time period of twelve consecutive months (2 words).
12. Classification of liabilities to be paid beyond a year (2 words).
13. End of period entry to recognize revenue earned but unrecorded.
14. Principle that requires reporting of expenses in the same accounting period as resulting revenues.
15. Indicator of ability to pay short-term obligations (2 words).
16. Total of amortization recorded since acquisition of a capital asset.
17. Definition of unearned revenue.

**Down Clues**

1. Term recommended by AcSB instead of depreciation.
2. Long-term assets used by businesses (2 words).
3. Financial reports for one or three months.
4. Principle that requires reporting of revenues when earned (2 words).
5. Recognition of revenue when cash is received (2 words).
10. Trial balance that shows account balances after they have been revised by end-of-period procedure.
11. Balance sheet with meaningful groupings.
13. Basis of accounting for external financial statements.

# ANSWERS TO PROGRESS CHECKS

**3–1** *a*

**3–2** Interim financial statements are prepared to provide decision makers information frequently and promptly.

**3–3** The revenue recognition principle and the matching principle.

**3–4** No, the cash basis is not consistent with the matching principle because it does not always report expenses in the same period as the revenues that were earned as a result of the expenses.

**3–5** No expense is reported in 1997. Under the cash basis, the entire $4,800 is reported as expense in 1996 when the premium was paid.

**3–6** *c*

**3–7** The balance of a contra account is subtracted from the balance of a related account so that more complete information than simply the net amount is provided.

**3–8** An accrued expense is an incurred expense that is not recorded prior to adjusting entries because it has not been paid. An example is unpaid salaries earned by employees prior to the year-end.

**3–9** An unearned revenue arises when cash is received from a customer before the service is provided to the customer. Magazine subscription receipts are an example.

**3–10** *c*

**3–11** Revenue accounts and expense accounts.

**3–12** The statement of changes in owner's equity is prepared second.

**3–13** *c*

**3–14** Current assets: *b, c, d.*
Capital assets: *a, e.*

**3–15** Share investments that will be held longer than one year or the current operating cycle. Land held for plant expansion.

**3–16** Current liabilities.

**3–17** Contributed capital and retained earnings.

# The Work Sheet and the Closing Process

*A systematic approach is essential for efficient and accurate processing of large amounts of information. Whether work sheets are on paper or computerized, they help provide this structure. Proprietorships, partnerships, and corporations all use similar work sheets.*

**P**aralleling Karen White and Mark Smith's progress in the study of accounting was their continued interest in the examination of the annual report of Imperial Oil Limited. They reread the "Letter to Shareholders." On this reading they were particularly interested in the statement: "First, we intend to improve the sales mix by emphasizing more profitable products."

White and Smith have now completed the study of Chapter 3. They intend to use their newfound knowledge to test whether Imperial is indeed improving its profitability.

**IMPERIAL OIL LIMITED**
Selected financial data
(in millions)

|  | 1994 | 1993 | 1992 | 1991 | 1990 |
|---|---|---|---|---|---|
| Net earnings (income) .. | $ 359 | $ 279 | $ 195 | $ 162 | $ 256 |
| Revenue . . . . . . . . . . . | 9,011 | 8,903 | 9,147 | 9,502 | 11,303 |

## LEARNING OBJECTIVES

**After studying Chapter 4, you should be able to:**

1.  **Explain why work sheets are useful, prepare a work sheet for a service business, and prepare financial statements from the information in a work sheet.**

2.  **Explain why the temporary accounts are closed at the end of each accounting period and prepare closing entries and a post-closing trial balance for a service business.**

3.  **Describe each step in the accounting cycle.**

4.  **Calculate the profit margin ratio and describe what it reveals about a company's performance.**

5.  **Define or explain the words and phrases listed in the chapter glossary.**

**After studying Appendix C at the end of Chapter 4, you should be able to:**

6.  **Explain when and why reversing entries are used and prepare reversing entries.**

**After studying Appendix D at the end of Chapter 4, you should be able to:**

7.  **Explain the nature of a corporation's retained earnings and their relationship to the declaration of dividends.**

8.  **Prepare entries to record the declaration and payment of a dividend and to close the temporary accounts of a corporation.**

This chapter continues your study of the accounting process by describing procedures that the accountant performs at the end of each reporting period. You learn about an optional work sheet that accountants use to draft adjusting entries and the financial statements. Studying the work sheet allows you to get an overall perspective on the steps in the accounting cycle. The chapter also describes the closing process that prepares the revenue, expense, and withdrawals accounts for the next reporting period and updates the owner's capital account. In addition, the chapter describes the profit margin ratio that decision makers use to assess a company's performance.

## USING WORK SHEETS AT THE END OF ACCOUNTING PERIODS

**LO 1**

Explain why work sheets are useful, prepare a work sheet for a service business, and prepare financial statements from the information in a work sheet.

When organizing the information presented in formal reports to internal and external decision makers, accountants prepare numerous analyses and informal documents. These informal documents are important tools for accountants. Traditionally, they are called **working papers.** One widely used working paper is the **work sheet.** Normally, the work sheet is not distributed to decision makers. It is prepared and used by accountants.

## Why Study the Work Sheet?

As we stated previously, preparing a work sheet is an optional procedure. When a business has only a few accounts and adjustments, preparing a work sheet is not necessary. Also, computerized accounting systems provide financial statements without first generating a work sheet. Nevertheless, there are several reasons why an understanding of work sheets is helpful:

1. In a manual accounting system involving many accounts and adjustments, the work sheet helps the accountant avoid errors.

2. Studying the work sheet is an effective way for you to see the entire accounting process from beginning to end. In a sense, it gives a bird's-eye view of the process between the occurrence of economic events and the presentation of their effects in financial statements. This knowledge helps managers and other decision makers understand the information in the statements.

3. After a company has tentatively prepared its financial statements, the auditors of the statements often use a work sheet as a basis for planning and organizing the audit. Also, they may use a work sheet to reflect any additional adjustments that appear necessary as a result of the audit.

4. Accountants often use work sheets to prepare interim (monthly or quarterly) financial statements.

5. A modified form of the work sheet is sometimes used to show the effects of proposed transactions.

## Where Does the Work Sheet Fit into the Accounting Process?

In practice, the work sheet is an optional step in the accounting process that can simplify the accountant's efforts in preparing financial statements. When a work sheet is used, it is prepared before making the adjusting entries at the end of the reporting period. The work sheet gathers information about the accounts, the needed adjustments, and the financial statements. When it is finished, the work sheet contains information that is recorded in the journal and then presented in the statements.

Illustration 4–1 shows a blank work sheet. Notice that it has five sets of double columns for the

1. Unadjusted trial balance.
2. Adjustments.
3. Adjusted trial balance.
4. Income statement.
5. Statement of changes in owner's equity and the balance sheet.

**PREPARING THE WORK SHEET**

Note that a separate set of double columns is not provided for the statement of changes in owner's equity. Because that statement includes only a few items, they are simply listed with the balance sheet items. A work sheet can be completed manually or with a computer. In fact, the format is well-suited for using a spreadsheet program.

### Step 1—Enter the Unadjusted Trial Balance

Turn the first transparency over to create Illustration 4–2. This illustration shows how the accountant starts preparing the work sheet by listing the number and title of every account expected to appear on the company's financial statements. Then, the unadjusted debit or credit balances of the accounts are found in the ledger and recorded in the first two columns. Because these columns serve as the unadjusted trial balance, the totals of the columns should be equal.

Illustration 4–2 uses the information for Clear Copy from Chapter 2 to show step 1. The account balances include the effects of December's external transactions. They do not reflect any of the adjustments described in Chapter 3.

In some cases, the accountant determines later that additional accounts need to be inserted on the work sheet. If the work sheet is completed manually, the additional accounts are inserted below the initial list. If a computer spreadsheet program is used, the new lines are easily inserted between existing lines.

Because a later phase in the example requires two lines for the Copy Services Revenue account, Illustration 4–2 includes an extra blank line below that account. If this need is not anticipated when the work sheet is being prepared manually, the accountant can squeeze two entries on one line.

## Step 2—Enter the Adjustments and Prepare the Adjusted Trial Balance

Turn the next overlay page to create Illustration 4–3. The work sheet now appears as it would after step 2 is completed. Step 2 begins by entering adjustments for economic events that were not external transactions. These include adjustments for prepaid expenses, amortization, unearned revenues, accrued expenses, and accrued revenues. The illustration shows the six adjustments for Clear Copy that were explained in Chapter 3:

a.   Expiration of $100 of prepaid insurance.

b.   Consumption of $1,050 of store supplies.

c.   Amortization of copy equipment by $375.

d.   Earning of $250 of previously unearned revenue.

e.   Accrual of $210 of salaries owed to the employee.

f.   Accrual of $1,800 of revenue owed by a customer.

To be sure that equal debits and credits are entered, the components of each adjustment are identified on the work sheet with a letter. Some accountants explain the adjustments with a list at the bottom of the work sheet or on a separate page.[1] To test for accuracy, they add the totals of the two columns to confirm that they are equal.

After the adjustments are entered on the work sheet, the adjusted trial balance is prepared by combining the adjustments with the unadjusted balances. Debits and credits are combined just as they would be in determining an account's balance. For example, the Prepaid Insurance account in Illustration 4–3 has a $2,400 debit balance in the unadjusted trial balance. This is combined with the $100 credit entry (a) in the Adjustments columns to give the account a $2,300 debit balance in the adjusted trial balance. Salaries Expense has a $1,400 balance in the unadjusted trial balance and is combined with the $210 debit entry (e) in the Adjustments columns. When the debit balance is combined with the debit from the adjustment, the account

---

[1]Auditors' work sheets cross-reference each adjustment to a detailed analysis and other supporting evidence.

**USE THE FOLLOWING OVERLAYS (ILLUSTRATIONS 4-1 THROUGH 4-6) IN THE DISCUSSION OF WORKSHEETS.**

**CLEAR COPY CO.**
**Work Sheet**
**For Month Ended December 31, 1996**

← The heading should identify the entity, the document, and the time period.

| Account | | Unadjusted Trial Balance | | Adjustments | | Adjusted Trial Balance | | Income Statement | | Statement of Changes in Owner's Equity and Balance Sheet | |
|---|---|---|---|---|---|---|---|---|---|---|---|
| No. | Title | Dr. | Cr. | Dr. | Cr. | Dr. | Cr. | Dr. | Cr. | Dr. | Cr. |
| | | | | | | | | | | | |

The work sheet can be prepared manually or with a computer spreadsheet program.

The worksheet collects and summarizes the information used to prepare financial statements, adjusting entries, and closing entries.

**CLEAR COPY CO.**
**Income Statement**
**For Month Ended December 31,1996**

| | | |
|---|---:|---:|
| Revenues: | | |
| Copy services revenue . . . . . . . . . . . . . . . . | | $5,950 |
| Operating expenses: | | |
| Amortization expense, copy equipment . . . . | $ 375 | |
| Salaries expense . . . . . . . . . . . . . . . . . . . . . | 1,610 | |
| Insurance expense . . . . . . . . . . . . . . . . . . . | 100 | |
| Rent expense . . . . . . . . . . . . . . . . . . . . . . . | 1,000 | |
| Store supplies expense . . . . . . . . . . . . . . . . | 1,050 | |
| Utilities expense . . . . . . . . . . . . . . . . . . . . | 230 | |
| Total operating expenses . . . . . . . . . . . . . . | | 4,365 |
| Net income . . . . . . . . . . . . . . . . . . . . . . . . . | | $1,585 |

**CLEAR COPY CO.**
**Statement of Changes in Owner's Equity**
**For Month Ended December 31, 1996**

| | | |
|---|---:|---:|
| Terry Dow, capital, November 30, 1996 . . . . . . . | | $ 0 |
| Plus: | | |
| Investments by owner . . . . . . . . . . . . . . . . | $30,000 | |
| Net income . . . . . . . . . . . . . . . . . . . . . . . | 1,585 | 31,585 |
| Total . . . . . . . . . . . . . . . . . . . . . . . . . . . . . | | 31,585 |
| Less withdrawals by owner . . . . . . . . . . . . . . | | 400 |
| Terry Dow, capital, December 31, 1996 . . . . . . . | | $31,185 |

**CLEAR COPY CO.**
**Balance Sheet**
**December 31, 1996**

**Assets**

| | | |
|---|---:|---:|
| Cash . . . . . . . . . . . . . . . . . . . . . . . . . . . . . . . | | $ 7,950 |
| Accounts receivable . . . . . . . . . . . . . . . . . . . . . | | 1,800 |
| Store supplies . . . . . . . . . . . . . . . . . . . . . . . . . | | 2,670 |
| Prepaid insurance . . . . . . . . . . . . . . . . . . . . . . | | 2,300 |
| Copy equipment . . . . . . . . . . . . . . . . . . . . . . . | $26,000 | |
| Accumulated amortization, copy equipment . . . | (375) | 25,625 |
| Total assets . . . . . . . . . . . . . . . . . . . . . . . . . . | | $40,345 |

**Liabilities**

| | | |
|---|---:|---:|
| Accounts payable . . . . . . . . . . . . . . . . . . . . . . | | $ 6,200 |
| Salaries payable . . . . . . . . . . . . . . . . . . . . . . . | | 210 |
| Unearned copy services revenue . . . . . . . . . . . | | 2,750 |
| Total Liabilities . . . . . . . . . . . . . . . . . . . . . . . | | $ 9,160 |

**Owner's Equity**

| | | |
|---|---:|---:|
| Terry Dow, capital . . . . . . . . . . . . . . . . . . . . . | | 31,185 |
| Total liabilities and owner's equity . . . . . . . . . | | $40,345 |

has a $1,610 debit balance in the adjusted trial balance. The totals of the Adjusted Trial Balance columns should confirm that debits equal credits.

## Step 3—Extend the Adjusted Trial Balance Amounts to the Financial Statement Columns

Turn the third transparency over to create Illustration 4–4 and to see the effects of step 3. In this step, the accountant assigns each adjusted account balance to its financial statement. This is done by extending each amount to the appropriate column across the page. The revenue and expense balances are extended to the Income Statement columns. The asset, liability, and owner's capital and withdrawals account balances are extended to the Statement of Changes in Owner's Equity and Balance Sheet columns. Accounts with debit balances in the adjusted trial balance are extended to the Debit columns and accounts with credit balances are extended to the Credit columns.

Next, the columns are totaled. Notice that the paired column totals are not equal. This occurs because the sum of the expenses debit balances does not equal the sum of the revenue credit balances. This also creates an equal and opposite imbalance in the Statement of Changes in Owner's Equity and Balance Sheet columns. Step 4 deals with this imbalance.

## Step 4—Enter the Net Income (or Loss) and Balance the Financial Statement Columns

To see the completed work sheet, turn the final transparent overlay to create Illustration 4–5. Step 4 begins by entering Net income and Totals on the next two lines in the account title column. Next, the accountant computes the net income by finding the excess of the Income Statement Credit column total over the Debit column total. This amount is inserted on the net income line in the Debit column, and a new total is computed for each column. (If the initial total of the debits is greater than the initial total credits, the expenses exceed the revenues and the company has incurred a net loss. If so, the difference is entered in the Credit column instead of the Debit column.) The total debits and total credits in the Income Statement columns are now equal.

The accountant next enters the net income in the last Credit column of the work sheet. (If there is a net loss, it is entered in the last Debit column.) Notice that this entry causes the total debits in the last two columns to equal the total credits.

Even if all five pairs of columns balance, the work sheet may not be free of errors. For example, if the accountant incorrectly extends an asset account's balance to the Income Statement Debit column, the columns balance but net income is understated. Or, if an expense is extended to the Statement of Changes in Owner's Equity and Balance Sheet Debit column, the columns balance but the net income is overstated. Although these errors may not be immediately obvious, they are discovered when the accountant begins to actually prepare the financial statements. For example, it would be apparent that an asset does not belong on the income statement or that an expense does not belong on the balance sheet.

At this point, the work sheet is complete. If the accountant discovers new information or an error, the change can easily be included in the work sheet, especially if it is being prepared with a computer spreadsheet.

## PREPARING ADJUSTING ENTRIES FROM THE WORK SHEET

Entering the adjustments in the Adjustments columns of a work sheet does not get these adjustments into the ledger accounts. Therefore, after completing the work sheet, adjusting entries like the ones described in Chapter 3 must be entered in the General Journal and posted to the accounts in the ledger. The work sheet makes this easy because its Adjustments columns provide the information for these entries. If adjusting entries are prepared from the information in Illustration 4–3, you will see that they are the same adjusting entries we discussed in the last chapter.

## PREPARING FINANCIAL STATEMENTS FROM THE WORK SHEET

A work sheet is not a substitute for the financial statements. The work sheet is nothing more than a supporting tool that the accountant uses at the end of an accounting period to help organize the data. However, as soon as it is completed, the accountant uses the work sheet to prepare the financial statements.

The sequence is the same as we have seen before. The income statement is completed first. The net income is then combined with the owner's investments, withdrawals, and beginning capital balance on the statement of changes in owner's equity. In doing this, the accountant analyzes the owner's capital account to separate the beginning balance from any new investments made during the reporting period. Finally, the balance sheet is completed by using the ending balance of owner's equity from the statement of changes in owner's equity.

## WHY USE A WORK SHEET?

At this point, it should be clear that we ended up with exactly the same financial statements and adjusting entries that we developed in Chapter 3 without using a work sheet. So, why prepare a work sheet?

First, the example in this chapter is greatly simplified. Real companies have many more adjusting entries and accounts than Clear Copy. A work sheet makes it easier to organize all the additional information. As we mentioned earlier in the chapter, auditors often use work sheets to plan and organize their work. In fact, they may request that a company provide a work sheet showing the adjustments made prior to the audit.

Second, the work sheet can be used to prepare *interim* financial statements without recording the adjusting entries in the journal and ledger. Thus, a company can prepare statements each month or quarter and avoid taking the time to formally journalize and post the adjustments except once at the end of each year. All large companies with publicly traded ownership prepare interim financial reports, usually on a quarterly basis. Some of them also include summaries of the past year's quarterly data in their annual reports.

Also, companies may use a work sheet format to show the effects of proposed transactions. In doing this, they enter their adjusted financial statements amounts in the first two columns, arranging them to appear in the form of financial statements. Then, the proposed transactions are inserted in the second two columns. The extended amounts in the last columns show the effects of the proposed transactions on the financial statements. These final columns are called **pro forma statements,** because they show the statements as if the proposed transactions had already occurred.

Because the work sheet is an informal working paper, its format is not dictated by generally accepted accounting principles. For example, some accountants omit the Adjusted Trial Balance columns. Others use different work sheet columns to draft the *closing entries* described later in the chapter. Some work sheets have separate columns for the statement of changes in owner's equity and the balance sheet. The decision about which format is preferred rests with the accountant who creates the work sheet.

## ALTERNATE FORMATS OF THE WORK SHEET

---

**Progress Check**

*(Answers to Progress Checks are provided at the end of the chapter.)*

4-1    On a work sheet, the $99,400 salaries expense balance was incorrectly extended from the Adjusted Trial Balance column to the Statement of Changes in Owner's Equity and Balance Sheet Debit column. As a result of this error, *(a)* the Adjusted Trial Balance columns will not balance; *(b)* revenues on the work sheet will be understated; *(c)* net income on the work sheet will be overstated.

4-2    Where does the accountant obtain the amounts entered in the Unadjusted Trial Balance columns of the work sheet?

4-3    What is the advantage of using a work sheet to prepare adjusting entries?

4-4    From a 10-column work sheet, the accountant prepares the financial statements in what order?

---

After the financial statements are completed and the adjusting entries are recorded, the next step in the accounting cycle is to journalize and post **closing entries.** Closing entries are designed to transfer the end-of-period balances in the revenue, expense, and withdrawals accounts to the owner's capital account. These entries are necessary because:

## CLOSING ENTRIES

**LO 2**

Explain why the temporary accounts are closed at the end of each accounting period and prepare closing entries and a post-closing trial balance for a service business.

1. Revenues increase owner's equity, while expenses and withdrawals decrease owner's equity.

2. During an accounting period, these increases and decreases are temporarily accumulated in the revenue, expense, and withdrawals accounts rather than in the owner's capital account.

3. By transferring the effects of revenues, expenses, and withdrawals from the revenue, expense, and withdrawals accounts to the owner's capital account, closing entries install the correct end-of-period balance in the owner's capital account.

4. Closing entries also cause the revenue, expense, and withdrawals accounts to begin each new accounting period with zero balances.

Remember that an income statement reports the revenues earned and expenses incurred during one accounting period and is prepared from information recorded in the revenue and expense accounts. Also, the statement of changes in owner's equity reports the changes in the owner's capital account during one period and uses the information accumulated in the withdrawals account. Because the revenue, expense, and withdrawals accounts accumulate information for only one period and then must be ready to do the same thing the next period, they must start each period with zero balances.

To close the revenue and expense accounts, the accountant transfers their balances first to a summary account called **Income Summary.** Then, the Income Summary balance, which is the net income or loss, is transferred to the owner's capital account. Finally, the accountant transfers the owner's withdrawals account balance to the owner's capital account. After the closing entries are posted, the revenue, expense, Income Summary, and withdrawals accounts have zero balances. Thus, these accounts are said to be closed or cleared.

Illustration 4–7 diagrams the four entries that close the revenue, expense, Income Summary, and withdrawals accounts of Clear Copy on December 31, 1996. The preclosing balances of the accounts in the illustration are taken from the adjusted trial balance in Illustration 4–5.

**Entry 1.** The first closing entry transfers the credit balances in the revenue accounts to the Income Summary account. In general journal form, the entry is:

| | | | | |
|---|---|---|---|---|
| Dec. | 31 | Copy Services Revenue  . . . . . . . . . . . . . . . . . . . . | 5,950.00 | |
| | | Income Summary . . . . . . . . . . . . . . . . . . . . . . . | | 5,950.00 |
| | | *To close the revenue account and create the Income Summary account.* | | |

Note that this entry closes the revenue account by giving it a zero balance. If the company had several different revenue accounts, this entry would be a compound entry that included a debit to each of them. This clearing of the accounts allows them to be used to record new revenues in the upcoming year.

The Income Summary account is created especially for the closing process and is used only during that process. The $5,950 credit balance in Income Summary equals the total revenues for the year.

**Entry 2.** The second closing entry transfers the debit balances in the expense accounts to the Income Summary account. This step concentrates all the expense account debit balances in the Income Summary account. It also closes each expense account by giving it a zero balance. That allows it to be used to record new expenses in the upcoming year. The second closing entry for Clear Copy is:

| | | | | |
|---|---|---|---|---|
| Dec. | 31 | Income Summary  . . . . . . . . . . . . . . . . . . . . . . . . | 4,365.00 | |
| | | Amortization Expense, Copy Equipment  . . . . . . . | | 375.00 |
| | | Salaries Expense  . . . . . . . . . . . . . . . . . . . . . . . | | 1,610.00 |
| | | Insurance Expense . . . . . . . . . . . . . . . . . . . . . . | | 100.00 |
| | | Rent Expense . . . . . . . . . . . . . . . . . . . . . . . . . . | | 1,000.00 |
| | | Store Supplies Expense  . . . . . . . . . . . . . . . . . . | | 1,050.00 |
| | | Utilities Expense  . . . . . . . . . . . . . . . . . . . . . . . | | 230.00 |
| | | *To close the expense accounts.* | | |

Illustration 4–7 shows that posting this entry gives each expense account a zero balance and prepares it to accept entries for expenses in 1997. The entry also makes the balance of the Income Summary account equal to December's net income of

**Illustration 4-7**  Closing Entries for Clear Copy

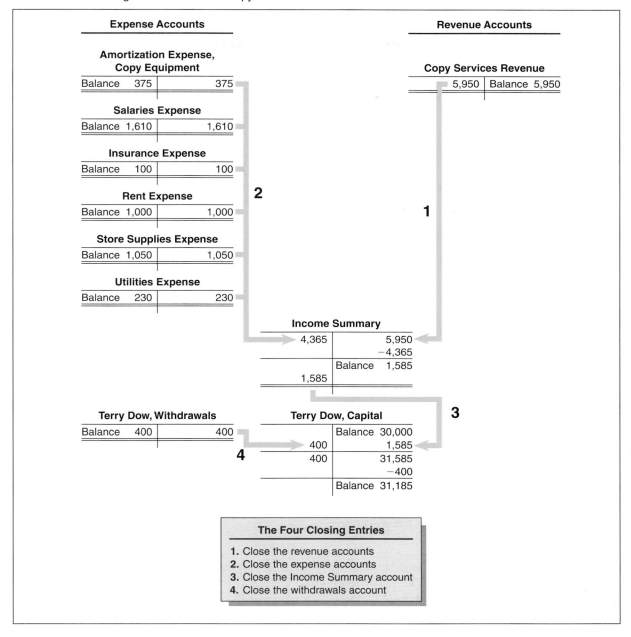

$1,585. In effect, all the debit and credit balances of the expense and revenue accounts have now been concentrated in the Income Summary account.

**Entry 3.**  The third closing entry transfers the balance of the Income Summary account to the owner's capital account. This entry closes the Income Summary account and adds the company's net income to the owner's capital account:

| Dec. | 31 | Income Summary  . . . . . . . . . . . . . . . . . . . . . . . . . | 1,585.00 | |
|------|----|--------------------------------------------|----------|----------|
| | |     Terry Dow, Capital . . . . . . . . . . . . . . . . . . . . . . | | 1,585.00 |
| | | *To close the Income Summary account and add the* | | |
| | | *net income to the capital account.* | | |

After this entry is posted, the Income Summary account has a zero balance. It will continue to have a zero balance until the closing process occurs at the end of the next year. The owner's capital account has been increased by the amount of the net income, but still does not include the effects of the withdrawal that occurred in December.

**Entry 4.**  The final closing entry transfers the debit balance of the withdrawals account to the capital account. This entry for Clear Copy is:

| Dec. | 31 | Terry Dow, Capital  . . . . . . . . . . . . . . . . . . . . . . . . | 400.00 | |
|------|----|--------------------------------------------|----------|----------|
| | |     Terry Dow, Withdrawals . . . . . . . . . . . . . . . . . . | | 400.00 |
| | | *To close the withdrawals account and reduce the* | | |
| | | *balance of the capital account.* | | |

This entry gives the withdrawals account a zero balance, which allows it to accumulate the next year's payments to the owner. It also reduces the capital account balance to the $31,185 amount reported on the balance sheet.

## SOURCES OF CLOSING ENTRY INFORMATION

The accountant can identify the accounts to be closed and the amounts to be used in the closing entries by referring to the individual revenue and expense accounts in the ledger. However, the work sheet provides this information in a more convenient format. To locate the information on the work sheet, look again at the income statement columns in Illustration 4–5. All accounts with balances in these columns are closed and the amounts in the work sheet are used in the closing entries. The balance of the owner's withdrawals account appears in the last debit column in the work sheet.

## THE POST-CLOSING TRIAL BALANCE

The six-column table in Illustration 4–8 summarizes the effects of the closing process. The first two columns contain the adjusted trial balance from the work sheet, with two additional lines for the Income Summary account. The next two columns present the closing entries, numbered (1) through (4). The last two columns contain the **post-closing trial balance,** which lists the balances of the accounts that were not closed.[2] These accounts represent the company's assets, liabilities, and owner's equity as of the end of 1996. These items and amounts are the same as those presented in the balance sheet in Illustration 4–6.

---

[2] Some accountants use work sheets that include these four columns instead of the financial statement columns. The financial statements are not changed by choosing one or the other.

**Illustration 4–8**   The Adjusted Trial Balance, Closing Entries, and Post-Closing Trial Balance for Clear Copy

| | Adjusted Trial Balance | | Closing Entries | | Post-Closing Trial Balance | |
|---|---|---|---|---|---|---|
| Cash . . . . . . . . . . . . . . . . . . . . . . | 7,950 | | | | 7,950 | |
| Accounts receivable . . . . . . . . . . . . | 1,800 | | | | 1,800 | |
| Store supplies . . . . . . . . . . . . . . . . | 2,670 | | | | 2,670 | |
| Prepaid insurance . . . . . . . . . . . . . | 2,300 | | | | 2,300 | |
| Copy equipment . . . . . . . . . . . . . . | 26,000 | | | | 26,000 | |
| Accumulated amortization, | | | | | | |
|   copy equipment . . . . . . . . . . . . . | | 375 | | | | 375 |
| Accounts payable . . . . . . . . . . . . . | | 6,200 | | | | 6,200 |
| Salaries payable . . . . . . . . . . . . . . | | 210 | | | | 210 |
| Unearned copy services revenue . . . . | | 2,750 | | | | 2,750 |
| Terry Dow, capital . . . . . . . . . . . . . | | 30,000 | (4) 400 | (3) 1,585 | | 31,185 |
| Terry Dow, withdrawals . . . . . . . . . | 400 | | | (4) 400 | | |
| Copy services revenue . . . . . . . . . . | | 5,950 | (1) 5,950 | | | |
| Amortization expense, | | | | | | |
|   copy equipment . . . . . . . . . . . . . | 375 | | | (2) 375 | | |
| Salaries expense . . . . . . . . . . . . . . | 1,610 | | | (2) 1,610 | | |
| Insurance expense . . . . . . . . . . . . . | 100 | | | (2) 100 | | |
| Rent expense . . . . . . . . . . . . . . . . | 1,000 | | | (2) 1,000 | | |
| Store supplies expense . . . . . . . . . . | 1,050 | | | (2) 1,050 | | |
| Utilities expense . . . . . . . . . . . . . . | 230 | | | (2) 230 | | |
| Income summary . . . . . . . . . . . . . . | | | (2) 4,365 | (1) 5,950 | | |
| | | | (3) 1,585 | | | |
| Totals . . . . . . . . . . . . . . . . . . . . . . | 45,485 | 45,485 | 12,300 | 12,300 | 40,720 | 40,720 |

Instead of preparing the six-column table in Illustration 4–8, the post-closing trial balance is often prepared as a separate two-column table, as in Illustration 4–9. Regardless of the format, the post-closing trial balance is the last step in the annual accounting process.

## Permanent (Real) Accounts and Temporary (Nominal) Accounts

Asset, liability, and owner's capital accounts are not closed as long as the company continues to own the assets, owe the liabilities, and have owner's equity. Because these accounts are not closed, they are called **permanent accounts** or **real accounts.** These accounts are permanent because they describe real conditions that are perceived to exist.

In contrast, the terms **temporary accounts** and **nominal accounts** describe the revenue, expense, Income Summary, and withdrawals accounts. These terms are used because the accounts are opened at the beginning of the year, used to record events, and then closed at the end of the year. These accounts are temporary because they describe nominal events or changes that have occurred rather than real conditions that continue to exist.

Illustration 4-9
Separate Post-Closing
Trial Balance for Clear
Copy

**The Post Closing Trial Balance**

| | | |
|---|---:|---:|
| Cash | $ 7,950 | |
| Accounts receivable | 1,800 | |
| Store supplies | 2,670 | |
| Prepaid insurance | 2,300 | |
| Copy equipment | 26,000 | |
| Accumulated amortization, copy equipment | | $ 375 |
| Accounts payable | | 6,200 |
| Salaries payable | | 210 |
| Unearned copy services revenue | | 2,750 |
| Terry Dow, capital | | 31,185 |
| Totals | $40,720 | $40,720 |

## THE LEDGER FOR CLEAR COPY

To complete the Clear Copy example, look at Illustration 4–10, the company's entire ledger as of December 31, 1996. Review the accounts and observe that the temporary accounts (the withdrawals account and all accounts with numbers greater than 400) have been closed.

## CLOSING ENTRIES FOR CORPORATIONS

Up to this point, our examples of closing entries have related to the activities and accounts of single proprietorships. However, closing entries for corporations are very similar. The first two closing entries are exactly the same. In other words, a corporation's revenue and expense accounts are closed to the Income Summary account. The last two entries are different.

Recall from Chapter 3 that a corporation's balance sheet presents the shareholders' equity as contributed capital and retained earnings. As a result, the third closing entry for a corporation closes the Income Summary account to the Retained Earnings account. For example, **Petro-Canada** reported a net income of $162 million in 1993, which means that was the credit balance in the Income Summary account after the revenue and expense accounts were closed. The company's third closing entry would have updated the Retained Earnings account as follows:

| | | | | |
|---|---|---|---:|---:|
| Dec. | 31 | Income Summary | 162,000,000.00 | |
| | | Retained Earnings | | 162,000,000.00 |
| | | *To close the Income Summary account and update Retained Earnings.* | | |

The fourth closing entry is also different because corporations use a Dividends Declared account instead of a withdrawals account. The accounting practices for dividends paid to shareholders are described in Appendix D and in Chapter 16. Coverage of corporations, at this point, is limited to closing entries. For a more complete coverage of partnership and corporation accounting refer to Appendix D at the end of this chapter and Chapters 14, 15 and 16.

**Illustration 4–10**  The Ledger for Clear Copy as of December 31, 1996 (after adjustments and closing entries have been posted)

**Asset Accounts:**

**Cash**          Acct. No. 101

| Date | | Expl. | Debit | Credit | Balance |
|---|---|---|---|---|---|
| 1996 | | | | | |
| Dec. | 1 | | 30,000 | | 30,000 |
| | 2 | | | 2,500 | 27,500 |
| | 3 | | | 20,000 | 7,500 |
| | 10 | | 2,200 | | 9,700 |
| | 12 | | | 1,000 | 8,700 |
| | 12 | | | 700 | 8,000 |
| | 22 | | 1,700 | | 9,700 |
| | 24 | | | 900 | 8,800 |
| | 24 | | | 400 | 8,400 |
| | 26 | | 3,000 | | 11,400 |
| | 26 | | | 2,400 | 9,000 |
| | 26 | | | 120 | 8,880 |
| | 26 | | | 230 | 8,650 |
| | 26 | | | 700 | 7,950 |

**Store Supplies**          Acct. No. 125

| Date | | Expl. | Debit | Credit | Balance |
|---|---|---|---|---|---|
| 1996 | | | | | |
| Dec. | 2 | | 2,500 | | 2,500 |
| | 6 | | 1,100 | | 3,600 |
| | 26 | | 120 | | 3,720 |
| | 31 | | | 1,050 | 2,670 |

**Prepaid Insurance**          Acct. No. 128

| Date | | Expl. | Debit | Credit | Balance |
|---|---|---|---|---|---|
| 1996 | | | | | |
| Dec. | 26 | | 2,400 | | 2,400 |
| | 31 | | | 100 | 2,300 |

**Accounts Receivable**          Acct. No. 106

| Date | | Expl. | Debit | Credit | Balance |
|---|---|---|---|---|---|
| 1996 | | | | | |
| Dec. | 12 | | 1,700 | | 1,700 |
| | 22 | | | 1,700 | 0 |
| | 31 | | 1,800 | | 1,800 |

**Copy Equipment**          Acct. No. 167

| Date | | Expl. | Debit | Credit | Balance |
|---|---|---|---|---|---|
| 1996 | | | | | |
| Dec. | 3 | | 20,000 | | 20,000 |
| | 6 | | 6,000 | | 26,000 |

**Accumulated Amortization, Copy Equipment**          Acct. No. 168

| Date | | Expl. | Debit | Credit | Balance |
|---|---|---|---|---|---|
| 1996 | | | | | |
| Dec. | 31 | | | 375 | 375 |

**Liability and Equity Accounts:**

**Accounts Payable**          Acct. No. 201

| Date | | Expl. | Debit | Credit | Balance |
|---|---|---|---|---|---|
| 1996 | | | | | |
| Dec. | 6 | | | 7,100 | 7,100 |
| | 24 | | 900 | | 6,200 |

**Unearned Copy Services Revenue**          Acct. No. 236

| Date | | Expl. | Debit | Credit | Balance |
|---|---|---|---|---|---|
| 1996 | | | | | |
| Dec. | 26 | | | 3,000 | 3,000 |
| | 31 | | 250 | | 2,750 |

**Salaries Payable**          Acct. No. 209

| Date | | Expl. | Debit | Credit | Balance |
|---|---|---|---|---|---|
| 1996 | | | | | |
| Dec. | 31 | | | 210 | 210 |

**Illustration 4–10**  *(concluded)*

### Terry Dow, Capital    Acct. No. 301

| Date | | Expl. | Debit | Credit | Balance |
|---|---|---|---|---|---|
| 1996 | | | | | |
| Dec. | 1 | | | 30,000 | 30,000 |
| | 31 | | | 1,585 | 31,585 |
| | 31 | | 400 | | 31,185 |

### Terry Dow, Withdrawals    Acct. No. 302

| Date | | Expl. | Debit | Credit | Balance |
|---|---|---|---|---|---|
| 1996 | | | | | |
| Dec. | 24 | | 400 | | 400 |
| | 31 | | | 400 | 0 |

**Revenue and Expense Accounts (including Income Summary):**

### Copy Services Revenue    Acct. No. 403

| Date | | Expl. | Debit | Credit | Balance |
|---|---|---|---|---|---|
| 1996 | | | | | |
| Dec. | 10 | | | 2,200 | 2,200 |
| | 12 | | | 1,700 | 3,900 |
| | 31 | | | 250 | 4,150 |
| | 31 | | | 1,800 | 5,950 |
| | 31 | | 5,950 | | 0 |

### Amortization Expense, Copy Equipment    Acct. No. 614

| Date | | Expl. | Debit | Credit | Balance |
|---|---|---|---|---|---|
| 1996 | | | | | |
| Dec. | 31 | | 375 | | 375 |
| | 31 | | | 375 | 0 |

### Salaries Expense    Acct. No. 622

| Date | | Expl. | Debit | Credit | Balance |
|---|---|---|---|---|---|
| 1996 | | | | | |
| Dec. | 12 | | 700 | | 700 |
| | 26 | | 700 | | 1,400 |
| | 31 | | 210 | | 1,610 |
| | 31 | | | 1,610 | 0 |

### Insurance Expense    Acct. No. 637

| Date | | Expl. | Debit | Credit | Balance |
|---|---|---|---|---|---|
| 1996 | | | | | |
| Dec. | 31 | | 100 | | 100 |
| | 31 | | | 100 | 0 |

### Rent Expense    Acct. No. 641

| Date | | Expl. | Debit | Credit | Balance |
|---|---|---|---|---|---|
| 1996 | | | | | |
| Dec. | 12 | | 1,000 | | 1,000 |
| | 31 | | | 1,000 | 0 |

### Store Supplies Expense    Acct. No. 651

| Date | | Expl. | Debit | Credit | Balance |
|---|---|---|---|---|---|
| 1996 | | | | | |
| Dec. | 31 | | 1,050 | | 1,050 |
| | 31 | | | 1,050 | 0 |

### Utilities Expense    Acct. No. 690

| Date | | Expl. | Debit | Credit | Balance |
|---|---|---|---|---|---|
| 1996 | | | | | |
| Dec. | 26 | | 230 | | 230 |
| | 31 | | | 230 | 0 |

### Income Summary    Acct. No. 901

| Date | | Expl. | Debit | Credit | Balance |
|---|---|---|---|---|---|
| 1996 | | | | | |
| Dec. | 31 | | | 5,950 | 5,950 |
| | 31 | | 4,365 | | 1,585 |
| | 31 | | 1,585 | | 0 |

**Progress Check**

**4–5    When closing entries are prepared:**
   *a.* **The accounts for expenses, revenues, and the owner's withdrawals are closed to the Income Summary account.**
   *b.* **The final balance of the Income Summary account equals net income or net loss for the period.**
   *c.* **All temporary accounts have zero balances when the process is completed.**

**4–6    Why are revenue and expense accounts called temporary? Are there any other temporary accounts?**

**4–7    What accounts are listed on the post-closing trial balance?**

**4–8    What account is used by a corporation to close the Income Summary account?**

Chapters 2, 3, and 4 have described the accounting procedures that are completed during each reporting period. They begin with recording external transactions in the journal and end with preparing the post-closing trial balance. Because these steps are repeated each period, they are often called the **accounting cycle.** A flow

## A REVIEW OF THE ACCOUNTING CYCLE

LO 3
Describe each step in the accounting cycle.

| | Step | Description |
|---|---|---|
| 1. | **Journalizing** | Analyzing transactions and recording debits and credits in a journal. |
| 2. | **Posting** | Copying the debits and credits from the journal entries to the accounts in the ledger. |
| 3. | **Preparing an unadjusted trial balance** | Summarizing the ledger accounts and partially testing clerical accuracy. (If a work sheet is used, this is done on the work sheet.) |
| 4. | **Completing the work sheet (optional)** | Identifying the effects of adjustments on the financial statements before entering them in the ledger and posting them to the accounts; also drafting the adjusted trial balance, extending the adjusted amounts to the appropriate financial statement columns, and determining the size of the net income or net loss. |
| 5. | **Adjusting the accounts** | Identifying necessary adjustments to bring the account balances up to date; journalizing and posting entries to record the adjustments in the accounts. (If the work sheet is prepared, the information in the adjustments columns is used for the entries.) |
| 6. | **Preparing the financial statements** | Using the information on the adjusted trial balance (or the work sheet) to prepare an income statement, a statement of changes in owner's equity, a balance sheet, and a statement of changes in financial position. (Techniques for preparing the changes in financial position statement are described in Chapter 18.) |
| 7. | **Closing the temporary accounts** | Preparing journal entries to close the revenue, expense, and withdrawals accounts and to update the owner's capital (or retained earnings) account. These entries are posted to the ledger. |
| 8. | **Preparing a post-closing trial balance** | Testing the clerical accuracy of the adjusting and closing procedures. |

**Illustration 4-11**   The Accounting Cycle

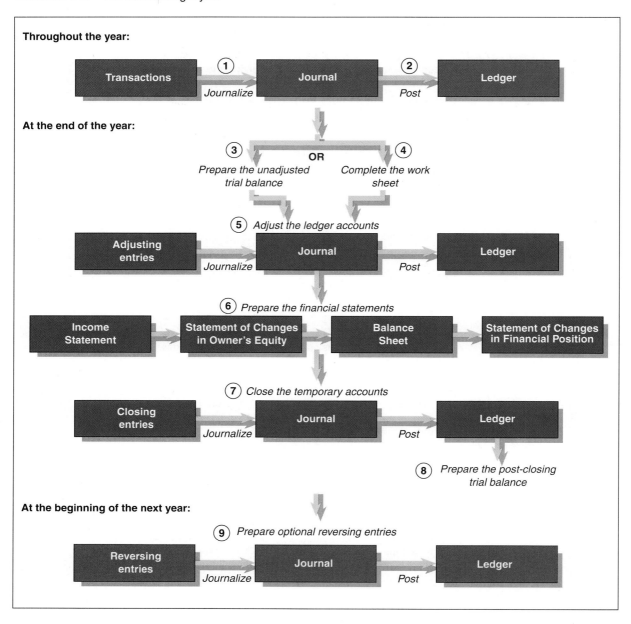

chart in Illustration 4–11 shows the steps in order. Steps 1 and 2 take place every day as the company engages in business transactions. The other steps are completed at the end of the accounting period. Review this illustration and the list of the steps to be sure that you understand how each one helps accountants provide useful information in the financial statements.

Illustration 4–11 also identifies an optional ninth step of making reversing entries at the beginning of the following period. These entries are described in Appendix C, which begins on page 204.

## A Practical Point

Normally, accountants are not able to make all of the adjusting and closing entries on the last day of the fiscal year. Information about the economic events that require adjustments often is not available until after several days or even a few weeks. As a result, the adjusting and closing entries are recorded later but dated as of the last day of the year. This means the financial statements reflect what is known on the date that they are prepared instead of what was known on the financial statement date.

For example, a company might receive a utility bill on January 14 for costs incurred from December 1 through December 31. Upon receiving the bill, the company's accountant records the expense and the payable as of December 31. The income statement for December reflects the full expense and the December 31 balance sheet includes the payable, even though the exact amounts were not actually known on December 31.

---

**Progress Check**

4-9    **The steps in the accounting cycle** (a) **are concluded by preparing a post-closing trial balance;** (b) **are concluded by preparing a balance sheet; or** (c) **begin with preparing the unadjusted trial balance.**

4-10    **At what point in the accounting cycle is the work sheet prepared?**

---

**USING THE INFORMATION— THE PROFIT MARGIN**

**LO 4**
Calculate the profit margin ratio and describe what it reveals about a company's performance.

By now, it should be clear that accountants go to great lengths to ensure that a company's financial statements reflect up-to-date information about its assets, liabilities, revenues, and expenses. A primary goal of this effort is to provide information that helps internal and external decision makers evaluate the results achieved in the reporting period. This includes evaluating management's success in generating profits. The information may suggest ways to achieve better results and also helps users predict future results.

In using accounting information to evaluate the results of operations, one widely used ratio relates the company's net income to its sales. The ratio is called the **profit margin** or the **return on sales,** and is calculated with this formula:

$$\text{Profit margin} = \frac{\text{Net income}}{\text{Revenues}}$$

In effect, this ratio measures the average portion of each dollar of revenue that ends up as profit.

Recall from the beginning of the chapter that Karen White and Mark Smith desired to test whether Imperial Oil Limited was improving its profitability. The company's profit margins during several years were:

---

(in millions)

|  | 1994 | 1993 | 1992 | 1991 | 1990 |
|---|---|---|---|---|---|
| Net revenue (income) . . . . | $ 359 | $ 279 | $ 195 | $ 162 | $ 256 |
| Revenue . . . . . . . . . . . . . | 9,011 | 8,903 | 9,147 | 9,502 | 11,303 |
| Profit margin . . . . . . . . . | 4.0% | 3.1% | 2.1% | 1.7% | 2.3% |

---

Note the positive trend in Imperial's profit margin in the last three years. However, this may be less favourable because the company's sales volume decreased 20% during the same period. Consequently, one may conclude that although the trend in Imperial's profit margin is favourable, you cannot conclude that the absolute values are good without further investigation, such as comparisons with other companies in the same industry.

---

**Progress Check**

4–11    The profit margin is the ratio between a company's net income and total   *(a)* expenses;   *(b)* assets;   *(c)* liabilities; or   *(d)* revenues.

4–12    If a company had a profit margin of 22.5% and net income of $1,012,500, what was the total amount of its revenues for the reporting period?

---

## SUMMARY OF THE CHAPTER IN TERMS OF LEARNING OBJECTIVES

**LO 1.  Explain why work sheets are useful, prepare a work sheet for a service business, and prepare financial statements from the information in a work sheet.** Accountants often use work sheets at the end of an accounting period in the process of preparing adjusting entries, the adjusted trial balance, and the financial statements. The work sheet is only a tool for accountants and is not distributed to investors or creditors. The work sheet described in this chapter has five pairs of columns for the unadjusted trial balance, the adjustments, the adjusted trial balance, the income statement, and the statement of changes in owner's equity and the balance sheet. Other formats are used in practice.

The income statement is prepared from the Income Statement columns of the work sheet by taking the revenues from the Credit column and the expenses from the Debit column. The net income is the difference between the debits and credits. The statement of changes in owner's equity combines the preclosing balance of the capital account (including the beginning balance plus any new investments), the net income from the Income Statement columns, and the owner's withdrawals. The balance sheet combines all assets, contra assets, and liabilities from the last two columns of the work sheet with the ending balance of owner's equity presented in the statement of changes in owner's equity.

**LO 2.  Explain why the temporary accounts are closed at the end of each accounting period and prepare closing entries and a post-closing trial balance for a service business.** The temporary accounts are closed at the end of each accounting period for two reasons. First, this process updates the owner's equity account to include the effects of all economic events recorded for the year. Second, it prepares the revenue, expense, and withdrawals accounts for the next reporting period by giving them zero balances. The revenue and expense account balances are initially transferred to the Income Summary account, which is then closed to the owner's capital account. Finally, the withdrawals account is closed to the capital account.

**LO 3.  Describe each step in the accounting cycle.** The accounting cycle consists of eight steps: (1) journalizing external transactions and (2) posting the entries during the year, and at the end of the year: (3) preparing either an unadjusted trial balance or (4) a work sheet, (5) preparing and posting adjusting entries, (6) preparing the financial statements, (7) preparing and posting closing entries, and (8) preparing the post-closing trial balance.

**LO 4. Calculate the profit margin ratio and describe what it reveals about a company's performance.** The profit margin ratio describes a company's income earning activities by showing the period's net income as a percentage of total revenue. It is found by dividing the reporting period's net income by the revenue for the same period. The ratio can be usefully interpreted only in light of additional facts about the company and its industry.

This six-column table shows the December 31, 1996, adjusted trial balance of Westside Appliance Repair Company:

**DEMONSTRATION PROBLEM**

| | Adjusted Trial Balance | | Closing Entries | | Post-Closing Trial Balance | |
|---|---|---|---|---|---|---|
| Cash ......................... | 83,300 | | | | | |
| Notes receivable ................. | 60,000 | | | | | |
| Prepaid insurance ............... | 19,000 | | | | | |
| Prepaid rent .................... | 5,000 | | | | | |
| Equipment ..................... | 165,000 | | | | | |
| Accumulated amortization, equipment .. | | 52,000 | | | | |
| Accounts payable ................. | | 37,000 | | | | |
| Long-term notes payable ........... | | 58,000 | | | | |
| B. Westside, capital .............. | | 173,500 | | | | |
| B. Westside, withdrawals .......... | 25,000 | | | | | |
| Repair services revenue ........... | | 294,000 | | | | |
| Interest earned .................. | | 6,500 | | | | |
| Amortization expense, equipment ..... | 26,000 | | | | | |
| Wages expense .................. | 179,000 | | | | | |
| Rent expense ................... | 47,000 | | | | | |
| Insurance expense .............. | 7,000 | | | | | |
| Interest expense ................ | 4,700 | | | | | |
| Income summary ................ | | | | | | |
| Totals ....................... | 621,000 | 621,000 | | | | |
| | | | | | | |

The beginning balance of the capital account was $140,500, and the owner invested $33,000 cash in the company on June 15, 1996.

**Required**

1. Prepare closing entries for Westside Appliance Repair Co.
2. Complete the six-column schedule.
3. Post the closing entries to this capital account:

| | **B. Westside, Capital** | | | **Account No. 301** | |
|---|---|---|---|---|---|
| **Date** | **Explanation** | **Debit** | **Credit** | **Balance** | |
| 1996 | | | | | |
| Jan.   1 | Beginning balance | | | 140,500.00 | |
| June 15 | New investment | | 33,000.00 | 173,500.00 | |

• Prepare entries to close the revenue accounts to Income Summary, to close the expense accounts to Income Summary, to close Income Summary to the capital account, and to close the withdrawals account to the capital account.

*Planning the Solution*

- Enter the four closing entries in the second pair of columns in the six-column schedule, and then extend the balances of the asset and liability accounts to the third pair of columns.

- Enter the post-closing balance of the capital account in the last column. Examine the totals of the columns to verify that they are equal.

- Post the third and fourth closing entries to the capital account.

*Solution to Demonstration Problem*

1.

| | | | | |
|---|---|---|---:|---:|
| Dec. | 31 | Repair Services Revenue . . . . . . . . . . . . . . . . . . . . . . | 294,000.00 | |
| | | Interest Earned . . . . . . . . . . . . . . . . . . . . . . . . . . . | 6,500.00 | |
| | | Income Summary . . . . . . . . . . . . . . . . . . . . . . . | | 300,500.00 |
| | | *To close the revenue accounts and create the Income Summary account.* | | |
| | 31 | Income Summary . . . . . . . . . . . . . . . . . . . . . . . . . | 263,700.00 | |
| | | Amortization Expense, Equipment . . . . . . . . . . . | | 26,000.00 |
| | | Wages Expense . . . . . . . . . . . . . . . . . . . . . . . . . | | 179,000.00 |
| | | Rent Expense . . . . . . . . . . . . . . . . . . . . . . . . . . . | | 47,000.00 |
| | | Insurance Expense . . . . . . . . . . . . . . . . . . . . . . . | | 7,000.00 |
| | | Interest Expense . . . . . . . . . . . . . . . . . . . . . . . . | | 4,700.00 |
| | | *To close the expense accounts.* | | |
| | 31 | Income Summary . . . . . . . . . . . . . . . . . . . . . . . . . | 36,800.00 | |
| | | B. Westside, Capital . . . . . . . . . . . . . . . . . . . . . . | | 36,800.00 |
| | | *To close the Income Summary account and add the net income to the capital account.* | | |
| | 31 | B. Westside, Capital . . . . . . . . . . . . . . . . . . . . . . . | 25,000.00 | |
| | | B. Westside, Withdrawals . . . . . . . . . . . . . . . . | | 25,000.00 |
| | | *To close the withdrawals account and reduce the balance of the capital account.* | | |

2.

| | Adjusted Trial Balance | | Closing Entries | | Post-Closing Trial Balance | |
|---|---|---|---|---|---|---|
| Cash ......................... | 83,300 | | | | 83,300 | |
| Notes receivable ................. | 60,000 | | | | 60,000 | |
| Prepaid insurance ................ | 19,000 | | | | 19,000 | |
| Prepaid rent .................... | 5,000 | | | | 5,000 | |
| Equipment ..................... | 165,000 | | | | 165,000 | |
| Accumulated amortization, equipment .. | | 52,000 | | | | 52,000 |
| Accounts payable ................ | | 37,000 | | | | 37,000 |
| Long-term notes payable ........... | | 58,000 | | | | 58,000 |
| B. Westside, capital ............... | | 173,500 | (4) 25,000 | (3) 36,800 | | 185,300 |
| B. Westside, withdrawals ........... | 25,000 | | | (4) 25,000 | | |
| Repair services revenue ............ | | 294,000 | (1) 294,000 | | | |
| Interest earned ................. | | 6,500 | (1) 6,500 | | | |
| Amortization expense, equipment ...... | 26,000 | | | (2) 26,000 | | |
| Wages expense .................. | 179,000 | | | (2) 179,000 | | |
| Rent expense ................... | 47,000 | | | (2) 47,000 | | |
| Insurance expense ................ | 7,000 | | | (2) 7,000 | | |
| Interest expense ................. | 4,700 | | | (2) 4,700 | | |
| Income summary ................ | | | (2) 263,700 | (1) 300,500 | | |
| ............................ | | | (3) 36,800 | | | |
| Totals ...................... | 621,000 | 621,000 | 626,000 | 626,000 | 332,300 | 332,300 |

3.

**B. Westside, Capital**                                    Account No. 301

| Date | | Explanation | Debit | Credit | Balance |
|---|---|---|---|---|---|
| 1996 | | | | | |
| Jan. | 1 | Beginning balance | | | 140,500.00 |
| June | 15 | New investment | | 33,000.00 | 173,500.00 |
| Dec. | 31 | Net income | | 36,800.00 | 210,300.00 |
| | 31 | Withdrawals | 25,000.00 | | 185,300.00 |

# Reversing Entries

LO 6
Explain when and why reversing entries are used and prepare reversing entries.

**Reversing entries** are optional entries that relate to accrued assets and liabilities created by adjusting entries at the end of a reporting period. Reversing entries are used for the practical purpose of simplifying a company's bookkeeping process.

Illustration C–1 shows how reversing entries work. The top of the diagram shows the adjusting entry that Clear Copy recorded on December 31, 1996, for the employee's earned but unpaid salary. The entry recorded three days' salary to increase December's total salary expense to $1,610. The entry also recognized a liability of $210. The expense is reported on December's income statement and the expense account is closed. As a result, the ledger on January 1, 1997, reflects a $210 liability and a zero balance in the Salaries Expense account. At this point, the choice is made between using or not using reversing entries.

## BOOKKEEPING WITHOUT REVERSING ENTRIES

The path down the left side of Illustration C–1 was described in Chapter 3. When the next payday occurs on January 9, the bookkeeper records the payment with a compound entry that debits both the expense and liability accounts. Posting the entry creates a $490 balance in the expense account and reduces the liability account balance to zero because the debt has been settled.

The disadvantage of this approach is the complex entry on January 9. Paying the accrued liability causes the entry to differ from the routine entries made on all other paydays. To construct the proper entry on January 9, the bookkeeper must be informed of the effect of the adjusting entry. Reversing entries overcome this disadvantage.

## BOOKKEEPING WITH REVERSING ENTRIES

The right side of Illustration C–1 shows how a reversing entry on January 1 overcomes the disadvantage of the complex January 9 entry. The reversing entry is the exact opposite of the adjusting entry recorded on December 31. In other words, the Salaries Payable liability is debited for $210, with the result that the account has a zero balance after the entry is posted. Technically, the Salaries Payable account now understates the liability, but no problem exists because financial statements will not be prepared before the liability is settled on January 9.

The credit to the Salaries Expense account is unusual because it gives the account an *abnormal credit balance*. This account's balance is also temporary and does not cause a problem because financial statements will not be prepared before January 9.

As a result of the reversing entry, the January 9 entry to record the payment is simple. Notice that it debits the Salaries Expense account for the full $700 paid. This entry is the same as all other entries made to record 10 days' salary for the employee.

Look next at the accounts on the lower right side of Illustration C–1. After the payment entry is posted, the Salaries Expense account has the $490 balance that

**Illustration C–1**   Reversing Entries for Accrued Expenses

*Accrue salaries expense on December 31, 1996*

Salaries Expense ————————— 210
    Salaries Payable ————————— 210

**Salaries Expense**

| Date | Expl. | Debit | Credit | Balance |
|------|-------|-------|--------|---------|
| 1996 | | | | |
| Dec. 12 | (7) | 700 | | 700 |
| 26 | (16) | 700 | | 1,400 |
| 31 | (e) | 210 | | 1,610 |

**Salaries Payable**

| Date | Expl. | Debit | Credit | Balance |
|------|-------|-------|--------|---------|
| 1996 | | | | |
| Dec. 31 | (e) | | 210 | 210 |

*No reversing entry recorded on January 1, 1997*

NO ENTRY

**Salaries Expense**

| Date | Expl. | Debit | Credit | Balance |
|------|-------|-------|--------|---------|
| 1997 | | | | |

**Salaries Payable**

| Date | Expl. | Debit | Credit | Balance |
|------|-------|-------|--------|---------|
| 1996 | | | | |
| Dec. 31 | (e) | | 210 | 210 |
| 1997 | | | | |

*Reversing entry recorded on January 1, 1997*

Salaries Payable ————————— 210
    Salaries Expense ————————— 210

**Salaries Expense**

| Date | Expl. | Debit | Credit | Balance |
|------|-------|-------|--------|---------|
| 1997 | | | | |
| Jan. 1 | | | 210 | (210) |

**Salaries Payable**

| Date | Expl. | Debit | Credit | Balance |
|------|-------|-------|--------|---------|
| 1996 | | | | |
| Dec. 31 | (e) | | 210 | 210 |
| 1997 | | | | |
| Jan. 1 | | 210 | | 0 |

*Pay the accrued and current salaries on January 9, the first payday in 1997*

Salaries Expense ————————— 490
Salaries Payable ————————— 210
    Cash ————————— 700

**Salaries Expense**

| Date | Expl. | Debit | Credit | Balance |
|------|-------|-------|--------|---------|
| 1997 | | | | |
| Jan. 9 | | 490 | | 490 |

**Salaries Payable**

| Date | Expl. | Debit | Credit | Balance |
|------|-------|-------|--------|---------|
| 1996 | | | | |
| Dec. 31 | (e) | | 210 | 210 |
| 1997 | | | | 0 |
| Jan. 9 | | 210 | | |

Salaries Expense ————————— 700
    Cash ————————— 700

**Salaries Expense**

| Date | Expl. | Debit | Credit | Balance |
|------|-------|-------|--------|---------|
| 1997 | | | | |
| Jan. 1 | | 700 | 210 | (210) |
| Jan. 9 | | | | 490 |

**Salaries Payable**

| Date | Expl. | Debit | Credit | Balance |
|------|-------|-------|--------|---------|
| 1996 | | | | |
| Dec. 31 | (e) | | 210 | 210 |
| 1997 | | | | 0 |
| Jan. 1 | | 210 | | |

Under both approaches, the expense and liability accounts have
the same balances after the subsequent payment on January 9:

Salaries Expense ————————— $ 490
Salaries Payable ————————— $ 0

it should have to reflect seven days' salary of $70 per day. The zero balance in the Salaries Payable account is now correct. Then, the lower section of the illustration shows that the expense and liability accounts have exactly the same balances whether reversing occurs or not.

As a general rule, adjusting entries that create new asset or new liability accounts are the best candidates for reversing.

**SUMMARY OF APPENDIX C IN TERMS OF LEARNING OBJECTIVES**

**LO 6.  Explain when and why reversing entries are used and prepare reversing entries.** Optional reversing entries can be applied to accrued assets and liabilities, including accrued interest earned, accrued interest expense, accrued taxes, and accrued salaries or wages. The goal of reversing entries is to simplify subsequent journal entries. The financial statements are not affected by the choice. Reversing entries are used simply as a matter of convenience in bookkeeping.

# Accounting for Partnerships and Corporations

In the early chapters we use the "Proprietorship Approach," that is, the accounting model is based on a single proprietor. Accounting for partnerships and corporations is discussed in detail in Chapters 14, 15, and 16. Appendix D to this chapter facilitates those individuals who desire to introduce accounting for partnerships and corporations at this stage.

**PARTNERSHIP ACCOUNTING**

Accounting for a partnership is like accounting for a single proprietorship except for transactions that directly affect the partners' capital and withdrawals accounts. These transactions require a capital account and a withdrawals account for each partner. To close the Income Summary account, make a compound entry that allocates to each partner his or her share of the net income or loss such as the following:

| | | | | |
|---|---|---|---|---|
| Dec. | 31 | Income Summary . . . . . . . . . . . . . . . . . . . . . . . . . . . . | 7,000.00 | |
| | |     Julie Ehlers, Capital . . . . . . . . . . . . . . . . . . . . . . . | | 3,000.00 |
| | |     Megan Brinkoeter, Capital . . . . . . . . . . . . . . . . . | | 4,000.00 |
| | |       *To close the Income Summary account.* | | |

**CORPORATE ACCOUNTING**

**LO 7**
Explain the nature of a corporation's retained earnings and their relationship to the declaration of dividends.

Accounting for a corporation also differs from that of a single proprietorship for transactions that affect the equity accounts of the corporation. The accounts of a corporation are designed to distinguish between equity resulting from amounts invested in the corporation by its shareholders and equity resulting from earnings. This distinction is important because a corporation generally cannot pay a legal dividend unless it has shareholders' equity resulting from earnings. In making the distinction, two kinds of shareholders' equity accounts are kept: (1) *contributed capital accounts* and (2) *retained earnings accounts.* Amounts invested in a corporation (contributed) by its shareholders are shown in contributed capital accounts such as the Common Share account. Shareholders' equity resulting from earnings is shown in a retained earnings account.

To demonstrate corporate accounting, assume that five persons secured a certificate of incorporation for a new corporation. Each invested $10,000 in the corporation by buying 1,000 of its common shares. The corporation's entry to record their investments is

| Jan. | 5 | Cash .................................. | 50,000.00 | |
| | | Common Shares ...................... | | 50,000.00 |
| | | *Issued 5,000 common shares for cash.* | | |

If during its first year the corporation earned $20,000, the entry to close its Income Summary account is

| Dec. | 31 | Income Summary .......................... | 20,000.00 | |
| | | Retained Earnings ..................... | | 20,000.00 |
| | | *To close the Income Summary account.* | | |

If these are the only entries that affected the Common Shares and Retained Earnings accounts during the first year, the corporation's year-end balance sheet will show the shareholders' equity as follows:

**Shareholders' Equity**

| | |
|---|---|
| Share capital–common: 5,000 shares outstanding . . | $50,000 |
| Retained earnings ...................... | 20,000 |
| Total shareholders' equity ................. | $70,000 |

Because a corporation is a separate legal entity, the names of its shareholders usually are of little interest to a balance sheet reader and are not shown in the equity section. However, in this case, the section does show that the net asset or equity of the corporation is $70,000. Of this amount, $50,000 resulted from the issuance of shares to the shareholders and $20,000 was the result of net income that has not been paid out as dividends.

Perhaps the concept of retained earnings would be clearer if the balance sheet item were labeled "Shareholders' equity resulting from earnings." However, the retained earnings caption is commonly used; it does not represent a specific amount of cash or any other asset. These are shown in the asset section of the balance sheet. Retained earnings represent the shareholders' equity resulting from earnings.

**LO 8**

Prepare entries to record the declaration and payment of a dividend and to close the temporary accounts of a corporation.

To continue, assume that on January 10 of the corporation's second year, its board of directors met and by vote declared a $1 per share dividend payable on February 1 to the January 25 **shareholders of record** (shareholders according to the corporation's records). The entry to record the declaration of the dividend is as follows:

| Jan. | 10 | Cash Dividends Declared .................... | 5,000.00 | |
| | | Common Dividend Payable ................ | | 5,000.00 |
| | | *Declared a $1 per share dividend.* | | |

The **Cash Dividends Declared**[1] account is a temporary account that serves the same function for a corporation as does a withdrawals account for a proprietorship. At the end of each period, the Cash Dividends Declared account is closed to Retained Earnings. The entry to record the payment of the dividend is as follows:

| Feb. | 01 | Common Dividend Payable .................... | 5,000.00 | |
|------|----|-----|-----|-----|
| | | Cash ................................. | | 5,000.00 |
| | | *Paid the dividend declared on January 10.* | | |

Note from the two entries that the dividend declaration reduces shareholders' equity and increases liabilities, while the payment of the dividend reduces the corporation's assets and liabilities. The net result is to reduce assets and shareholders' equity just as a withdrawal of cash by the owner of a single proprietorship reduces assets and the owner's equity.

A cash dividend is normally paid by mailing cheques to the shareholders. Also, in this case, three dates are normally involved in a dividend declaration and payment. They are (1) the **date of declaration**, (2) the **date of record**, and (3) the **date of payment**. On the date of declaration, the dividend becomes a liability of the corporation. However, if some shareholders sell their shares to new investors in time for the new shareholders to be listed in the corporation's records on the date of record, the new shareholders will receive the dividend on the date of payment. Otherwise, the dividend will be paid to the old shareholders.

A dividend must be formally voted by a corporation's board of directors. Also, courts have generally held that the board is the final judge of when a dividend should be paid. Therefore, shareholders have no right to a dividend until it is declared. However, as soon as a cash dividend is declared, it becomes a liability of the corporation, normally a current liability, and must be paid. Furthermore, shareholders have the right to sue and force payment of a cash dividend once it is declared.

If during its second year (1996) the corporation suffered a $7,000 net loss, the entries to close its Income Summary and Dividends Declared accounts are:

| 1996 | | | | |
|------|----|-----|-----|-----|
| Dec. | 31 | Retained Earnings ........................... | 7,000.00 | |
| | | Income Summary ........................... | | 7,000.00 |
| | | *To close the Income Summary account.* | | |
| | 31 | Retained Earnings ........................... | 5,000.00 | |
| | | Cash Dividends Declared ..................... | | 5,000.00 |
| | | *To close the Cash Dividends Declared account.* | | |

Now assume that during 1997, the corporation paid no dividends but suffered a net loss of $14,000. The entry to close the Income Summary account at the end of 1997 is

---

[1] Some corporations prefer to debit retained earnings directly at the time of dividend declaration. The Cash Dividend Declared account is used to illustrate the parallelism in accounting for withdrawals in proprietorships and partnerships and dividends in corporate accounting.

| | | | | | |
|---|---|---|---|---|---|
| 1997 | | | | | |
| Dec. | 31 | Retained Earnings ......................... | | 14,000.00 | |
| | | Income Summary ....................... | | | 14,000.00 |
| | | *To close the Income Summary account.* | | | |

Posting these entries has the following effects on the Retained Earnings account:

Retained Earnings            Acct. No. 318

| Date | | Explanation | PR | Debit | Credit | Balance | |
|---|---|---|---|---|---|---|---|
| 1995 | | | | | | | |
| Dec. | 31 | Net income | G4 | | 20,000.00 | 20,000.00 | |
| 1996 | | | | | | | |
| Dec. | 31 | Net loss | G5 | 7,000.00 | | 13,000.00 | |
| | 31 | Cash dividends declared | G7 | 5,000.00 | | 8,000.00 | |
| 1997 | | | | | | | |
| Dec. | 31 | Net loss | G9 | 14,000.00 | | 6,000.00 | Dr. |

Due to the dividend and the net losses, the Retained Earnings account has a $6,000 debit balance. A debit balance in a Retained Earnings account indicates a negative amount of retained earnings. A corporation with a negative amount of retained earnings is said to have a **deficit**. A deficit may be shown on a corporation's balance sheet as follows:

Shareholders' Equity

| | |
|---|---|
| Share capital–common: 5,000 shares outstanding  .. | $50,000 |
| Deduct retained earnings deficit  .............. | (6,000) |
| Total shareholders' equity .................. | $44,000 |

In most jurisdictions, a corporation with a deficit is not allowed to pay a cash dividend. This legal requirement is intended to protect the creditors of the corporation. Because a corporation is a separate legal entity, it is responsible for its own debts. However, the corporation's shareholders normally are not responsible for the corporation's debts. Therefore, if a corporation's creditors are to be paid, they must be paid from the corporation's assets. By making dividends illegal when there is a deficit, a corporation in financial difficulty is prevented from paying its assets in dividends and leaving nothing for payment of its creditors. (You will learn more about partnerships and corporations in Chapters 14, 15, and 16.)

**SUMMARY OF APPENDIX D IN TERMS OF LEARNING OBJECTIVES**

**LO 7. Explain the nature of a corporation's retained earnings and their relationship to the declaration of dividends.** Retained earnings is the total amount of net incomes a corporation has earned since it was organized, less the total of losses and the total of dividends declared.

**LO 8. Prepare entries to record the declaration and payment of a dividend and to close the temporary accounts of a corporation.** Dividend declarations are recorded with a debit to a temporary account called Dividends Declared and a credit to a liability account. Payment in cash is recorded like any other liability.

# GLOSSARY

**Accounting cycle** eight recurring steps performed each accounting period, starting with recording transactions in the journal and continuing through the post-closing trial balance. p. 197

**Cash Dividends Declared** a temporary account that serves the same function for a corporation as does a withdrawals account for a proprietorship and that is closed to Retained Earnings at the end of each accounting period. p. 209

**Closing entries** journal entries recorded at the end of each accounting period to prepare the revenue, expense, and withdrawals accounts for the upcoming year and update the owner's capital account for the events of the year just finished. p. 189

**Date of declaration** the date on which a dividend is declared by vote of a corporation's board of directors. p. 209

**Date of payment** the date on which a dividend liability of a corporation is satisfied by mailing cheques to the shareholders. p. 209

**Date of record** the date on which the shareholders who are listed in a corporation's records are determined to be those who will receive a dividend. p. 209

**Deficit** a negative amount (debit balance) of retained earnings. p. 210

**Income Summary** the special account used only in the closing process to temporarily hold the amounts of revenues and expenses before the net difference is added to (or subtracted from) the owner's capital account or the Retained Earnings account for a corporation. p. 190

**Nominal accounts** another name for *temporary accounts*. p. 193

**Permanent accounts** accounts that are used to describe assets, liabilities, and owner's equity; they are not closed as long as the company continues to own the assets, owe the liabilities, or have owner's equity; the balances of these accounts appear on the balance sheet. p. 193

**Post-closing trial balance** a trial balance prepared after the closing entries have been posted; the final step in the accounting cycle. p. 192

**Profit margin** the ratio of a company's net income to its revenues; measures the average proportion of each dollar of revenue that ends up as profit. p. 199

**Pro forma statements** statements that show the effects of the proposed transactions as if the transactions had already occurred. p. 188

**Real accounts** another name for *permanent accounts*. p. 193

**Return on sales** another name for *profit margin*. p. 199

**Reversing entries** optional entries recorded at the beginning of a new year that prepare the accounts for simplified journal entries subsequent to accrual adjusting entries. p. 204

**Shareholders of record** the shareholders of a corporation as reflected in the records of the corporation. p. 208

**Temporary accounts** accounts that are used to describe revenues, expenses, and owner's withdrawals; they are closed at the end of the reporting period. p. 193

**Work sheet** a 10-column spreadsheet used to draft a company's unadjusted trial balance, adjusting entries, adjusted trial balance, and financial statements; an optional step in the accounting process. p. 184

**Working papers** analyses and other informal reports prepared by accountants when organizing the useful information presented in formal reports to internal and external decision makers. p. 184

# SYNONYMOUS TERMS

**Permanent accounts** real accounts; balance sheet accounts

**Temporary accounts** nominal accounts

*The letters C and D identify the questions, quick studies, exercises, and problems based on Appendixes C and D at the end of the chapter.*

# QUESTIONS

1. What tasks are performed with the work sheet?
2. Why are the debit and credit entries in the Adjustments columns of the work sheet identified with letters?

3.  What internal document is produced by combining the amounts in the Unadjusted Trial Balance columns with the amounts in the Adjustments columns of the work sheet?

4.  What two purposes are accomplished by recording closing entries?

5.  What are the four closing entries?

6.  What accounts are affected by closing entries? What accounts are not affected?

7.  Describe the similarities and differences between adjusting and closing entries.

8.  What is the purpose of the Income Summary account?

9.  Explain whether an error has occurred if a post-closing trial balance includes an Amortization Expense, Building account.

C10.  How are the financial statements of a company affected by the accountant's choice to use or not use reversing entries?

C11.  How do reversing entries simplify a company's bookkeeping efforts?

C12.  If a company accrued unpaid salaries expense of $500 at the end of a fiscal year, what reversing entry could be made? When would it be made?

---

# QUICK STUDY (Five-Minute Exercises)

**QS 4–1**
**(LO 1)**

In preparing a work sheet, indicate the financial statement debit column to which a normal balance of each of the following accounts should be extended. Use IS for the Income Statement Debit column and BS for the Statement of Changes in Owner's Equity or Balance Sheet Debit column.

1.  Accounts receivable
2.  Owner, withdrawals
3.  Prepaid insurance
4.  Insurance expense
5.  Equipment
6.  Amortization expense, equipment

**QS 4–2**
**(LO 1)**

The following information is from the work sheet for Pursley Company as of December 31, 1996. Using this information, determine the amount that should be reported for A. Pursley, capital on the December 31, 1996, balance sheet.

|  | Income Statement | | Statement of Changes in Owner's Equity and Balance Sheet | |
|---|---|---|---|---|
|  | Dr. | Cr. | Dr. | Cr. |
| A. Pursley, capital |  |  |  | 50,000 |
| A. Pursley, withdrawals . . . . |  |  | 32,000 |  |
| Totals . . . . . . . . . . . . . . . | 125,000 | 184,000 |  |  |

**QS 4–3**
**(LO 2)**

Using the information presented in QS 4–2, prepare the entries to close the Income Summary and the withdrawals accounts.

**QS 4–4**
**(LO 3)**

List the following steps of the accounting cycle in the proper order:

a.  Preparing the post-closing trial balance.
b.  Journalizing and posting adjusting entries.
c.  Preparing the unadjusted trial balance.
d.  Journalizing and posting closing entries.
e.  Journalizing transactions.
f.  Posting the transaction entries.
g.  Preparing the financial statements.
h.  Completing the work sheet.

Gruene Corporation had net income of $75,850 and revenue of $410,000 for the year ended December 31, 1996. Calculate Gruene's profit margin.

QS 4–5
(LO 4)

On December 31, 1996, Ace Management Co. prepared an adjusting entry for $9,800 of earned but unrecorded rent revenue. On January 20, 1997, Ace received rent payments in the amount of $15,500. Assuming Ace uses reversing entries, prepare the 1997 entries pertaining to the rent transactions.

CQS 4–6
(LO 6)

# EXERCISES

These accounts are from the Adjusted Trial Balance columns in a company's 10-column work sheet. In the blank space beside each account, write the letter of the appropriate financial statement column to which a normal account balance should be extended.

Exercise 4–1
Extending adjusted
account balances on a
work sheet
(LO 1)

A. Debit column for the income statement

B. Credit column for the income statement

C. Debit column for the statement of changes in owner's equity and balance sheet

D. Credit column for the statement of changes in owner's equity and balance sheet

___ 1. R. Jefferson, Withdrawals

___ 2. Interest Earned

___ 3. Accumulated Amortization, Machinery

___ 4. Service Fees Revenue

___ 5. Accounts Receivable

___ 6. Rent Expense

___ 7. Amortization Expense, Machinery

___ 8. Accounts Payable

___ 9. Cash

___ 10. Office Supplies

___ 11. R. Jefferson, Capital

___ 12. Wages Payable

___ 13. Machinery

___ 14. Insurance Expense

___ 15. Interest Expense

___ 16. Interest Receivable

Use the following information from the Adjustments columns of a 10-column work sheet to prepare adjusting journal entries:

Exercise 4–2
Preparing adjusting
entries from work sheet
information
(LO 1)

|  |  | Adjustments | |
| No. | Title | Debit | Credit |
| --- | --- | --- | --- |
| 109 | Interest receivable | (d) 380 | |
| 124 | Office supplies | | (b) 1,350 |
| 128 | Prepaid insurance | | (a) 1,000 |
| 164 | Accumulated amortization, office equipment | | (c) 3,500 |
| 209 | Salaries payable | | (e) 660 |
| 409 | Interest earned | | (d) 380 |
| 612 | Amortization expense, office equipment | (c) 3,500 | |
| 620 | Office salaries expense | (e) 660 | |
| 636 | Insurance expense, office equipment | (a) 432 | |
| 637 | Insurance expense, store equipment | (a) 568 | |
| 650 | Office supplies expense | (b) 1,350 | |
| | Totals | 6,890 | 6,890 |

The following unadjusted trial balance contains the accounts and balances of the Fine Painting Co. as of December 31, 1996, the end of its fiscal year:

Exercise 4–3
Preparing a work sheet
(LO 1)

| No. | Title | Debit | Credit |
|-----|-------|-------|--------|
| 101 | Cash ....................... | $18,000 | |
| 126 | Supplies ..................... | 12,000 | |
| 128 | Prepaid insurance ............... | 2,000 | |
| 167 | Equipment ................... | 23,000 | |
| 168 | Accumulated amortization, equipment . | | $ 6,500 |
| 209 | Salaries payable ................ | | |
| 301 | B. Fine, capital ................. | | 31,900 |
| 302 | B. Fine, withdrawals ............. | 6,000 | |
| 404 | Services revenue ................ | | 36,000 |
| 612 | Amortization expense, equipment ..... | | |
| 622 | Salaries expense ................ | 11,000 | |
| 637 | Insurance expense ............... | | |
| 640 | Rent expense ................. | 2,400 | |
| 652 | Supplies expense ................ | | |
| | Totals ...................... | $74,400 | $74,400 |

**Required**

Use the following information about the company's adjustments to complete a 10-column work sheet for the company:

a. The cost of expired insurance coverage was $300.

b. The cost of unused supplies on hand at the end of the year was $1,600.

c. Amortization of the equipment for the year was $3,250.

d. Earned but unpaid salaries at the end of the year were $250.

**Exercise 4–4**
Adjusting and closing entries
**(LO 2)**

Use the information in Exercise 4–3 to prepare adjusting and closing journal entries for Fine Painting Co. (It is helpful but not mandatory to solve Exercise 4–3 first.)

**Exercise 4–5**
Completing the income statement columns and preparing closing entries
**(LO 1, 2)**

These partially completed Income Statement columns from a 10-column work sheet are for the Winston Sail'em Boat Rental Company. Use the information to determine the amount that should be entered on the Net income line of the work sheet. In addition, draft closing entries for the company. The owner's name is C. Winston, and the preclosing balance of the withdrawals account is $18,000.

| | Debit | Credit |
|---|-------|--------|
| Rent earned ................ | | 99,000 |
| Salaries expense ............ | 35,300 | |
| Insurance expense ........... | 4,400 | |
| Dock rental expense .......... | 12,000 | |
| Boat supplies expense ........ | 6,220 | |
| Amortization expense, boats .... | 21,500 | |
| Totals .................... | | |
| Net income ................ | | |
| Totals .................... | | |

**Exercise 4–6**
Extending accounts in the work sheet
**(LO 1)**

The Adjusted Trial Balance columns of a 10-column work sheet for the Plummer Plumbing Co. follow. Complete the work sheet by extending the account balances into the appropriate financial statement columns and by entering the amount of net income for the reporting period.

| No. | Title | Adjusted Trial Balance | |
|-----|-------|------------------------|--|
| 101 | Cash ......................... | $ 8,200 | |
| 106 | Accounts receivable ............. | 24,000 | |
| 153 | Trucks ....................... | 41,000 | |
| 154 | Accumulated amortization, trucks .... | | $ 16,500 |
| 193 | Franchise .................... | 30,000 | |
| 201 | Accounts payable .............. | | 14,000 |
| 209 | Salaries payable ............... | | 3,200 |
| 233 | Unearned fees ................ | | 2,600 |
| 301 | F. Plummer, capital ............. | | 64,500 |
| 302 | F. Plummer, withdrawals .......... | 14,400 | |
| 401 | Plumbing fees earned ........... | | 79,000 |
| 611 | Amortization expense, trucks ....... | 11,000 | |
| 622 | Salaries expense ............... | 31,500 | |
| 640 | Rent expense ................. | 12,000 | |
| 677 | Miscellaneous expenses .......... | 7,700 | |
| | Totals ...................... | $179,800 | $179,800 |
| | Net income ................... | | |
| | Totals ...................... | | |

The adjusted trial balance for Plummer Plumbing Co. follows. Prepare a table with two columns under each of the following headings: Adjusted Trial Balance, Closing Entries, and Post-Closing Trial Balance. Complete the table by providing four closing entries and the post-closing trial balance.

**Exercise 4–7**
Preparing closing entries and the post-closing trial balance
**(LO 2)**

| No. | Title | Adjusted Trial Balance | |
|-----|-------|------------------------|--|
| 101 | Cash ......................... | $ 8,200 | |
| 106 | Accounts receivable ............. | 24,000 | |
| 153 | Trucks ....................... | 41,000 | |
| 154 | Accumulated amortization, trucks .... | | $ 16,500 |
| 193 | Franchise .................... | 30,000 | |
| 201 | Accounts payable .............. | | 14,000 |
| 209 | Salaries payable ............... | | 3,200 |
| 233 | Unearned fees ................ | | 2,600 |
| 301 | F. Plummer, capital ............. | | 64,500 |
| 302 | F. Plummer, withdrawals .......... | 14,400 | |
| 401 | Plumbing fees earned ........... | | 79,000 |
| 611 | Amortization expense, trucks ....... | 11,000 | |
| 622 | Salaries expense ............... | 31,500 | |
| 640 | Rent expense ................. | 12,000 | |
| 677 | Miscellaneous expenses .......... | 7,700 | |
| 901 | Income summary ............... | | |
| | Totals ...................... | $179,800 | $179,800 |

The following balances of the retained earnings and temporary accounts are for High Ridge, Inc., from its adjusted trial balance:

**Exercise 4–8**
Closing entries for a corporation
**(LO 2)**

| | Debit | Credit |
|-|-------|--------|
| Retained earnings ............ | | $43,200 |
| Services revenue ............. | | 62,000 |
| Interest earned .............. | | 5,800 |
| Salaries expense ............. | $23,500 | |
| Insurance expense ............ | 4,050 | |
| Rental expense .............. | 6,400 | |
| Supplies expense ............ | 3,100 | |
| Amortization expense, trucks .... | 10,600 | |

**Required**

*a.* Prepare the closing entries for this corporation.

*b.* Determine the amount of retained earnings to be reported on the company's balance sheet.

**Exercise 4–9**
Preparing and posting
closing entries
**(LO 2, 3)**

Open the following T-accounts with the provided balances. Prepare closing journal entries and post them to the accounts.

| B. Holley, Capital | | | | Rent Expense | | |
|---|---|---|---|---|---|---|
| | | Dec. 31 | 44,000 | Dec. 31 | 9,600 | |

| B. Holley, Withdrawals | | | | Salaries Expense | | |
|---|---|---|---|---|---|---|
| Dec. 31 | 21,000 | | | Dec. 31 | 24,000 | |

| Income Summary | | | | Insurance Expense | | |
|---|---|---|---|---|---|---|
| | | | | Dec. 31 | 3,500 | |

| Services Revenue | | | | Amortization Expense | | |
|---|---|---|---|---|---|---|
| | | Dec. 31 | 77,000 | Dec. 31 | 15,000 | |

**Exercise 4–10**
Calculating the profit
margin
**(LO 4)**

Use the following information to calculate the profit margin for each case:

| | Net Income | Revenue |
|---|---|---|
| *a.* | $ 1,745 | $ 10,540 |
| *b.* | 48,372 | 131,651 |
| *c.* | 55,102 | 84,262 |
| *d.* | 27,513 | 450,266 |
| *e.* | 39,632 | 144,638 |

**CExercise 4–11**
Reversing entries
**(LO 6)**

The following information was used to prepare adjusting entries for the Maritime Company as of August 31, the end of the company's fiscal year:

*a.* The company has earned $3,000 of unrecorded service fees.

*b.* The expired portion of prepaid insurance is $2,400.

*c.* The earned portion of the Unearned Fees account balance is $1,700.

*d.* Amortization expense for the office equipment is $3,300.

*e.* Employees have earned but have not been paid salaries of $2,250.

**Required**

Prepare the reversing entries that would simplify the bookkeeping effort for recording subsequent events related to these adjustments.

**CExercise 4–12**
Reversing entries
**(LO 6)**

The following two conditions existed for Lomax Company on September 30, 1996, the end of its fiscal year:

a. Lomax rents a building from its owner for $2,400 per month. By a prearrangement, the company delayed paying September's rent until October 5. On this date, the company paid the rent for both September and October.

b. Lomax rents space in a building it owns to a tenant for $655 per month. By pre-arrangement, the tenant delayed paying the September rent until October 8. On this date, the tenant paid the rent for both September and October.

**Required**

1. Prepare the adjusting entries that Lomax should record for these situations as of September 30.

2. Assuming that Lomax does not use reversing entries, prepare journal entries to record Lomax's payment of rent on October 5 and the collection of rent on October 8 from Lomax's tenant.

3. Assuming that Lomax does use reversing entries, prepare those entries and the journal entries to record Lomax's payment of rent on October 5 and the collection of rent on October 8 from Lomax's tenant.

A corporation debited Cash Dividends Declared for $50,000 during the year ended December 31. The items that follow appeared in the Income Statement columns of the work sheet prepared at year-end. Prepare closing journal entries for the corporation.

<sup>D</sup>**Exercise 4–13**
Closing entries for a corporation
**(LO 8)**

| | Income Statement | |
|---|---|---|
| | Debit | Credit |
| Services revenue ................. | | 285,700 |
| Office salaries expense ............. | 187,000 | |
| Rent expense .................... | 18,000 | |
| Insurance expense ............... | 4,400 | |
| Office supplies expense ........... | 400 | |
| Amortization expense, office equipment . . | 5,100 | |
| | 214,900 | 285,700 |
| Net income .................... | 70,800 | |
| | 285,700 | 285,700 |

1. On a sheet of notepaper, open the following T-accounts: Cash, Accounts Receivable, Equipment, Notes Payable, Common Dividend Payable, Common Shares, Retained Earnings, Income Summary, Cash Dividends Declared, Services Revenue, and Operating Expenses.

<sup>D</sup>**Exercise 4–14**
Recording corporate transactions in T-accounts
**(LO 8)**

2. Record directly in the T-accounts these transactions of a new corporation:
   a. Issued common shares for $150,000 cash.
   b. Purchased equipment for $146,500 cash.
   c. Sold and delivered $30,000 of services on credit.
   d. Collected $27,000 of accounts receivable.
   e. Paid $18,000 of operating expenses.
   f. Declared cash dividends of $7,500.
   g. Paid the dividends declared in (f).
   h. Purchased $12,000 of additional equipment, giving $5,000 in cash and a $7,000 promissory note.
   i. Closed the revenue accounts, (j) the expense accounts, (k) Income Summary, and (l) Cash Dividends Declared.

3.  Answer these questions:

    a.  Does the corporation have retained earnings?

    b.  Does it have any cash?

    c.  If the corporation has retained earnings, why does it not also have cash?

    d.  Can the corporation legally declare additional cash dividends?

    e.  Can it pay additional cash dividends?

    f.  What does the balance of the Notes Payable account tell the financial statement reader about the makeup of the corporation's assets?

    g.  Explain what the balance of the Common Shares account represents.

    h.  Explain what the balance of the Retained Earnings account represents.

# PROBLEMS

**Problem 4–1**
The work sheet, adjusting and closing entries, financial statements, and profit margin
**(LO 1, 2, 4)**

Dunagin's Repairs opened for business on January 1, 1996. By the end of the year, the company's unadjusted trial balance appeared as follows:

**DUNAGIN'S REPAIRS**
**Unadjusted Trial Balance**
**December 31, 1996**

| No. | Title | Debit | Credit |
|---|---|---|---|
| 101 | Cash | $ 3,000 | |
| 124 | Office supplies | 3,800 | |
| 128 | Prepaid insurance | 2,650 | |
| 167 | Equipment | 48,000 | |
| 168 | Accumulated amortization, equipment | | |
| 201 | Accounts payable | | $ 12,000 |
| 210 | Wages payable | | |
| 301 | R. Dunagin, capital | | 30,000 |
| 302 | R. Dunagin, withdrawals | 15,000 | |
| 401 | Repair fees earned | | 77,750 |
| 612 | Amortization expense, equipment | | |
| 623 | Wages expense | 36,000 | |
| 637 | Insurance expense | | |
| 640 | Rent expense | 9,600 | |
| 650 | Office supplies expense | | |
| 690 | Utilities expense | 1,700 | |
| | Totals | $119,750 | $119,750 |

**Required**

*Preparation component:*

1.  Enter the unadjusted trial balance on a 10-column work sheet and complete the work sheet using this information:

    a.  An inventory of the office supplies at the end of the year showed that $700 of supplies were on hand.

    b.  The cost of expired insurance coverage was $660.

    c.  The year's amortization on the equipment was $4,000.

    d.  The earned but unpaid wages at the end of the year were $500.

2. Present the adjusting entries and closing entries as they would appear in the journal.

3. Use the information in the work sheet to prepare an income statement, a statement of changes in owner's equity, and a classified balance sheet.

4. Determine the company's profit margin.

*Analysis component:*

5. Assume that the facts presented in requirement 1 differ as follows:

   *a.* None of the $2,650 prepaid insurance had expired.

   *b.* There were no earned but unpaid wages at the end of the year.

   Describe the changes in the financial statements that would result from these assumptions.

This unadjusted trial balance is for Blue Max Construction as of the end of its fiscal year. The beginning balance of the owner's capital account was $12,660 and the owner invested another $15,000 cash in the company during the year.

**Problem 4–2**
Work sheet, journal entries, financial statements, and profit margin
**(LO 1, 2, 4)**

### BLUE MAX CONSTRUCTION
#### Unadjusted Trial Balance
#### September 30, 1997

| No. | Title | Debit | Credit |
|---|---|---|---|
| 101 | Cash ......................... | $ 18,000 | |
| 126 | Supplies ...................... | 9,400 | |
| 128 | Prepaid insurance ................ | 6,200 | |
| 167 | Equipment .................... | 81,000 | |
| 168 | Accumulated amortization, equipment .. | | $ 20,250 |
| 201 | Accounts payable ................ | | 4,800 |
| 203 | Interest payable ................. | | |
| 208 | Rent payable ................... | | |
| 210 | Wages payable .................. | | |
| 213 | Estimated business taxes payable ...... | | |
| 251 | Long-term notes payable ........... | | 25,000 |
| 301 | T. Morrison, capital .............. | | 27,660 |
| 302 | T. Morrison, withdrawals ........... | 36,000 | |
| 401 | Construction fees earned ........... | | 140,000 |
| 612 | Amortization expense, equipment ..... | | |
| 623 | Wages expense .................. | 41,000 | |
| 633 | Interest expense ................. | 1,500 | |
| 637 | Insurance expense ................ | | |
| 640 | Rent expense ................... | 13,200 | |
| 652 | Supplies expense ................ | | |
| 683 | Business taxes expense ............ | 5,000 | |
| 684 | Repairs expense ................. | 2,510 | |
| 690 | Utilities expense ................ | 3,900 | |
| | Totals ...................... | $217,710 | $217,710 |

**Required**

1. Prepare a 10-column work sheet for 1997, starting with the unadjusted trial balance and including these additional facts:

   *a.* The inventory of supplies at the end of the year had a cost of $2,500.

   *b.* The cost of expired insurance for the year is $4,000.

   *c.* Annual amortization on the equipment is $9,000.

*d.* The September utilities expense was not included in the trial balance because the bill arrived after it was prepared. Its $400 amount needs to be recorded.

*e.* The company's employees have earned $1,500 of accrued wages.

*f.* The lease for the office requires the company to pay total rent for the year equal to 10% of the company's annual revenues. The rent is paid to the building owner with monthly payments of $1,100. If the annual rent exceeds the total monthly payments, the company must pay the excess before October 31. If the total is less than the amount previously paid, the building owner will refund the difference by October 31.

*g.* Additional business taxes of $800 have been assessed on the company but have not been paid or recorded in the accounts.

*h.* The long-term note payable bears interest at 1% per month, which the company is required to pay by the 10th of the following month. The balance of the Interest Expense account equals the amount paid during the year. The interest for September has not yet been paid or recorded. In addition, the company is required to make a $5,000 payment on the note on November 30, 1997.

2. Use the work sheet to prepare the adjusting and closing entries.

3. Prepare an income statement, a statement of changes in owner's equity, and a classified balance sheet. Calculate the company's profit margin for the year.

4. Analyze the following independent errors and describe how each would affect the 10-column work sheet. Explain whether the error is likely to be discovered in completing the work sheet and, if not, the effect of the error on the financial statements.

*a.* The adjustment for supplies consumption credited Supplies for $2,500 and debited the same amount to Supplies Expense.

*b.* When completing the adjusted trial balance in the work sheet, the $18,000 cash balance was incorrectly entered in the Credit column.

**Problem 4–3**
End-of-period accounting procedures
**(LO 1, 2, 3)**

The unadjusted trial balance of Doc's Delivery Service is as follows:

**DOC'S DELIVERY SERVICE**
**Unadjusted Trial Balance**
**December 31, 1996**

| | | |
|---|---:|---:|
| Cash | $ 785 | |
| Accounts receivable | 1,000 | |
| Prepaid insurance | 3,415 | |
| Office supplies | 365 | |
| Prepaid rent | 375 | |
| Office equipment | 3,690 | |
| Accumulated amortization, office equipment | | $ 855 |
| Delivery equipment | 22,185 | |
| Accumulated amortization, delivery equipment | | 4,725 |
| Accounts payable | | 1,335 |
| Unearned delivery service revenue | | 825 |
| Mark Welby, capital | | 34,355 |
| Mark Welby, withdrawals | 18,000 | |
| Delivery service revenue | | 62,325 |
| Rent expense | 3,750 | |
| Telephone expense | 515 | |
| Office salaries expense | 15,090 | |
| Delivery wages expense | 30,480 | |
| Gas, oil, and repairs expense | 4,770 | |
| Totals | $104,420 | $104,420 |

**Required**

1. Enter the unadjusted trial balance on a work sheet form and complete the work sheet using the information that follows:

   *a.* Expired insurance on the office equipment, $165, and on the delivery equipment, $2,665.

   *b.* An inventory showed $180 of unused office supplies on hand.

   *c.* Estimated amortization on the office equipment, $435, and (*d*) on the delivery equipment, $3,495.

   *e.* In December 1995, the company had prepaid the January 1996 rent for garage and office space occupied by the delivery service. This amount appears as the balance of the Prepaid Rent account. Rents for February through November were paid each month and debited to the Rent Expense account. As of December 31, 1996, the December rent had not been paid.

   *f.* The delivery service has contracts with three stores for the delivery of packages on a fixed-fee basis. Two of the stores made advance payments on their contracts, and the amounts paid were credited to the Unearned Delivery Service Revenue account. An examination of the contracts shows that $480 of the $825 paid was earned by the end of the accounting period. The third store's contract provides for a $380 monthly fee to be paid at the end of each month's service. One-half of a month's revenue has accrued on this contract but it is unrecorded.

   *g.* A $125 bill for repairs to a delivery truck during December arrived in the mail after the trial balance was prepared. The bill is unpaid and unrecorded.

   *h.* Office salaries, $60, and delivery wages, $145, have accrued but are unpaid and unrecorded.

2. Prepare an income statement, a statement of changes in owner's equity, and a classified balance sheet.

3. Journalize adjusting and closing entries.

4. Post the adjusting and closing entries to the accounts and prepare a post-closing trial balance. (If the working papers are not being used, omit this requirement.)

Your examination of the books of Dr. Milton Vacon, a local general practitioner, revealed that his nurse/secretary followed the cash basis of accounting in all matters with the exception of equipment. The equipment, which cost $42,000 at the time Dr. Vacon started practice (January 2, 1995), was set up as an asset and to date has not been amortized. The equipment had an estimated useful life of 10 years at which time it could be sold for an estimated $2,000. Upon further examination you were able to identify the relevant data as follows:

**Problem 4–4**
Financial statement preparation
**(LO 1)**

| | 1995 | 1996 | 1997 |
|---|---|---|---|
| Reported income | $91,000 | $96,000 | $89,000 |
| Supplies on hand at year-end | 500 | 300 | 1,200 |
| Wages not paid at year-end | 1,600 | 1,800 | 1,500 |
| Billings to the Provincial Hospital Insurance during December for which a cheque has not been received | 10,000 | 8,000 | 12,000 |
| Miscellaneous expenses owing at year-end | 1,300 | 1,700 | 1,200 |
| Cash on hand and in bank at year-end | 6,000 | 5,000 | 8,000 |

**Required**

1. Compute the correct net income for each year using the accrual basis of accounting (show all supporting calculations).

2.  Prepare the December 31, 1997, balance sheet. (Assume there were no other asset or liability accounts than the ones given above).

**Problem 4–5**
All steps in the accounting cycle (covers two accounting cycles)
**(LO 1, 2, 3)**

Tami Martin opened a real estate office she called Martin Realty. During May she completed these transactions:

May  3   Invested in the real estate agency $3,000 in cash and an automobile having a $15,000 fair value.

   3   Rented furnished office space and paid one month's rent, $750.

   4   Purchased office supplies for cash, $225.

   8   Paid the premium on a one-year insurance policy, $1,080.

   14   Paid the salary of the office secretary for two weeks, $600.

   16   Sold a house and collected an $8,010 commission.

   28   Paid the salary of the office secretary for two weeks, $600.

   31   Paid the May telephone bill, $75.

   31   Paid for gas and oil used in the agency car during May, $90.

### Required Work for May

1.  Open these accounts: Cash; Prepaid Insurance; Office Supplies; Automobile; Accumulated Depreciation, Automobile; Salaries Payable; Tami Martin, Capital; Tami Martin, Withdrawals; Income Summary; Commissions Earned; Rent Expense; Salaries Expense; Gas, Oil, and Repairs Expense; Telephone Expense; Insurance Expense; Office Supplies Expense; and Amortization Expense, Automobile.

2.  Prepare and post journal entries to record the transactions.

3.  Prepare an unadjusted trial balance on a work sheet form and complete the work sheet using the following information:

    *a.*   Two-thirds of a month's insurance has expired.

    *b.*   An inventory shows $185 of unused office supplies remaining.

    *c.*   Estimated amortization on the automobile, $250.

    *d.*   Earned but unpaid salary of the office secretary, $60.

4.  Prepare an income statement and a statement of changes in owner's equity for May, and prepare a May 31 classified balance sheet.

5.  Journalize and post adjusting and closing entries.

6.  Prepare a post-closing trial balance.

During June, Tami Martin completed these transactions:

June  1   Paid the June rent on the office space, $750.

   4   Purchased additional office supplies for cash, $45.

   11   Paid the salary of the office secretary for two weeks, $600.

   15   Tami Martin withdrew $3,000 cash from the business for personal use.

   18   Sold a building lot and collected a $2,200 commission.

   25   Paid the salary of the office secretary for two weeks, $600.

   30   Paid for gas and oil used in the agency car during June, $80.

   30   Paid the June telephone bill, $65.

### Required Work for June

1.  Prepare and post journal entries to record the transactions.

2. Prepare an unadjusted trial balance on a work sheet form and complete the work sheet using the following information:

   a. One month's insurance has expired.

   b. An office supplies inventory shows $185 of unused supplies.

   c. Estimated amortization on the automobile, $250.

   d. Earned but unpaid secretary's salary, $180.

3. Prepare an income statement and a statement of changes in owner's equity for June and prepare a June 30 classified balance sheet.

4. Journalize and post adjusting and closing entries.

5. Prepare a post-closing trial balance.

On June 1, Jo Farr created a new travel agency called International Tours. These events occurred during the company's first month:

**Problem 4–6**
Performing the steps in the accounting cycle
**(LO 1, 2, 3)**

June 1    Farr created the new company by investing $20,000 cash and computer equipment worth $30,000.

2    The company rented furnished office space by paying $1,600 rent for the first month.

3    The company purchased $1,200 of office supplies for cash.

10    The company paid $3,600 for the premium on a one-year insurance policy.

14    The owner's assistant was paid $800 for two weeks' salary.

24    The company collected $6,800 of commissions from airlines on tickets obtained for customers.

28    The assistant was paid another $800 for two weeks' salary.

29    The company paid the month's $750 telephone bill.

30    The company paid $350 cash to repair the company's computer.

30    The owner withdrew $1,425 cash from the business.

The company's chart of accounts included these accounts:

| | | | |
|---|---|---|---|
| 101 | Cash | 405 | Commissions Earned |
| 106 | Accounts Receivable | 612 | Amortization Expense, Computer Equipment |
| 124 | Office Supplies | | |
| 128 | Prepaid Insurance | 622 | Salaries Expense |
| 167 | Computer Equipment | 637 | Insurance Expense |
| 168 | Accumulated Amortization, Computer Equipment | 640 | Rent Expense |
| | | 650 | Office Supplies Expense |
| 209 | Salaries Payable | 684 | Repairs Expense |
| 301 | J. Farr, Capital | 688 | Telephone Expense |
| 302 | J. Farr, Withdrawals | 901 | Income Summary |

**Required**

1. Use the balance-column format to create each of the listed accounts.

2. Prepare journal entries to record the transactions for June and post them to the accounts.

3. Prepare a 10-column work sheet that starts with the unadjusted trial balance as of June 30. Use the following information to draft the adjustments for the month:

   a. Two-thirds of one month's insurance coverage was consumed.

   b. There were $800 of office supplies on hand at the end of the month.

    *c.*  Amortization on the computer equipment was estimated to be $825.

    *d.*  The assistant had earned $160 of unpaid and unrecorded salary.

    *e.*  The company had earned $1,750 of commissions that had not yet been billed.

    Complete the remaining columns of the worksheet.

4.  Prepare journal entries to record the adjustments drafted on the work sheet and post them to the accounts.

5.  Prepare an income statement, a statement of changes in owner's equity, and a balance sheet.

6.  Prepare journal entries to close the temporary accounts and post them to the accounts.

7.  Prepare a separate post-closing trial balance.

**Problem 4–7**
**Financial reporting**
**problem**
**(LO 1)**

The following balance sheet was prepared at the end of the company's fiscal year:

**TENDER TUNES**
**Balance Sheet**
**December 31, 1996**

**Assets**

| | | |
|---|---:|---:|
| Current assets: | | |
|   Cash | | $ 6,500 |
|   Office supplies | | 1,500 |
|   Prepaid insurance | | 600 |
|   Total current assets | | 8,600 |
| Capital assets: | | |
|   Automobiles | $42,000 | |
|   Accumulated amortization, automobiles | (17,000) | $25,000 |
|   Office equipment | $40,000 | |
|   Accumulated amortization, office equipment | (13,500) | 26,500 |
|   Total capital assets | | 51,500 |
| Total assets | | $60,100 |

**Liabilities**

| | |
|---|---:|
| Current liabilities: | |
|   Accounts payable | $ 4,200 |
|   Interest payable | 400 |
|   Salaries payable | 1,100 |
|   Unearned fees | 1,800 |
|   Total current liabilities | $ 7,500 |
| Noncurrent liabilities: | |
|   Long-term notes payable | 40,000 |
| Total liabilities | $47,500 |

**Owner's Equity**

| | |
|---|---:|
| Charlie Griffin, capital | 12,600 |
| Total liabilities and owner's equity | $60,100 |

The company's accountant also prepared and posted the following adjusting and closing entries:

| | | | | |
|---|---|---|---:|---:|
| Dec. | 31 | Insurance Expense | 800.00 | |
| | |     Prepaid Insurance | | 800.00 |
| | | *To record consumed insurance coverage.* | | |

| 31 | Office Supplies Expense .............. | 4,100.00 | |
|---|---|---|---|
| | Office Supplies ................. | | 4,100.00 |
| | *To record consumed office supplies.* | | |

| 31 | Amortization Expense, Automobiles ....... | 8,500.00 | |
|---|---|---|---|
| | Accumulated Amortization, | | |
| | Automobiles ................. | | 8,500.00 |
| | *To record amortization on automobiles.* | | |

| 31 | Amortization Expense, Office Equipment ... | 3,500.00 | |
|---|---|---|---|
| | Accumulated Amortization, | | |
| | Office Equipment .............. | | 3,500.00 |
| | *To record amortization on equipment.* | | |

| 31 | Unearned Fees ..................... | 730.00 | |
|---|---|---|---|
| | Fees Earned ................... | | 730.00 |
| | *To record earning of fees paid in advance.* | | |

| 31 | Salaries Expense ................... | 1,100.00 | |
|---|---|---|---|
| | Salaries Payable ................. | | 1,100.00 |
| | *To record accrued salaries.* | | |

| 31 | Interest Expense ................... | 400.00 | |
|---|---|---|---|
| | Interest Payable ................. | | 400.00 |
| | *To record accrued interest expense.* | | |

| 31 | Fees Earned ..................... | 61,000.00 | |
|---|---|---|---|
| | Income Summary ............... | | 61,000.00 |
| | *To close the revenue account and open the Income Summary account.* | | |

| 31 | Income Summary ................... | 45,960.00 | |
|---|---|---|---|
| | Amortization Expense, Automobiles ... | | 8,500.00 |
| | Amortization Expense, Office Equipment | | 3,500.00 |
| | Salaries Expense ................ | | 15,000.00 |
| | Interest Expense ................. | | 3,200.00 |
| | Insurance Expense ............... | | 800.00 |
| | Rent Expense ................... | | 7,200.00 |
| | Office Supplies Expense ........... | | 4,100.00 |
| | Gas, Oil, and Repairs Expense ....... | | 2,350.00 |
| | Telephone Expense .............. | | 1,310.00 |
| | *To close the expense accounts.* | | |

| 31 | Income Summary ................... | 15,040.00 | |
|---|---|---|---|
| | Charlie Griffin, Capital ........... | | 15,040.00 |
| | *To close Income Summary.* | | |

| 31 | Charlie Griffin, Capital ............... | 16,000.00 | |
|---|---|---|---|
| | Charlie Griffin, Withdrawals ........ | | 16,000.00 |
| | *To close withdrawals account.* | | |

Use the information in the balance sheet and the journal entries to complete a 10-column work sheet. (The five steps should be completed in reverse order.)

The unadjusted trial balance for Milton's Pool Parlor as of December 31, 1996, follows:

**MILTON'S POOL PARLOR**
**December 31, 1996**

| | Unadjusted Trial Balance | |
|---|---:|---:|
| Cash .......................... | $ 11,000 | |
| Accounts receivable ................ | | |
| Supplies ....................... | 4,500 | |
| Equipment ...................... | 150,000 | |
| Accumulated amortization, equipment .... | | $ 15,000 |
| Interest payable .................... | | |
| Salaries payable .................... | | |
| Unearned membership fees ............ | | 24,000 |
| Notes payable .................... | | 50,000 |
| U. Milton, capital .................. | | 58,250 |
| U. Milton, withdrawals .............. | 30,000 | |
| Membership fees earned .............. | | 90,000 |
| Amortization expense, equipment ....... | | |
| Salaries expense ................... | 38,000 | |
| Interest expense ................... | 3,750 | |
| Supplies expense .................. | | |
| Totals ........................ | $237,250 | $237,250 |

**Required**

1. Prepare a six-column table with two columns under each of the following headings: Unadjusted Trial Balance, Adjustments, and Adjusted Trial Balance. Complete the table by entering adjustments that reflect the following information:

   a. As of December 31, employees have earned $800 of unpaid and unrecorded wages. The next payday is January 4, and the total wages to be paid will be $1,200.

   b. The cost of supplies on hand at December 31 is $1,800.

   c. The note payable requires an interest payment to be made every three months. The amount of unrecorded accrued interest at December 31 is $1,250, and the next payment is due on January 15. This payment will be $1,500.

   d. An analysis of the unearned membership fees shows that $16,000 remains unearned at December 31.

   e. In addition to the membership fees included in the revenue account balance, the company has earned another $12,000 in fees that will be collected on January 21. The company is also expected to collect $7,000 on the same day for new fees earned during January.

   f. Amortization expense for the year is $15,000.

2. Prepare journal entries for the adjustments drafted in the six-column table.

3. Prepare journal entries to reverse the effects of the adjusting entries that involve accruals.

4. Prepare journal entries to record the cash payments and collections that are described for January.

Leeward Service Company's unadjusted trial balance on December 31, 1996, the end of its annual accounting period, is as follows:

CProblem 4–9
Adjusting, closing, and reversing entries
(LO 2, 6)

**LEEWARD SERVICE COMPANY**
**Unadjusted Trial Balance**
**December 31, 1996**

| | | |
|---|---:|---:|
| Cash | $ 73,725 | |
| Notes receivable | 37,500 | |
| Office supplies | 4,200 | |
| Land | 45,000 | |
| Unearned service fees | | $ 18,000 |
| Notes payable | | 90,000 |
| J. Boat, capital | | 37,500 |
| J. Boat, withdrawals | 60,000 | |
| Service fees earned | | 267,000 |
| Interest earned | | 2,550 |
| Rent earned | | 12,375 |
| Salaries expense | 193,500 | |
| Insurance expense | 4,950 | |
| Interest expense | 8,550 | |
| Totals | $427,425 | $427,425 |

Information necessary to prepare adjusting entries is as follows:

a. Employees, who are paid $7,500 every two weeks, have earned $5,250 since the last payment. The next payment of $7,500 will be on January 4.

b. Leeward rents office space to a tenant who has paid only $450 of the $1,125 rent for December. On January 12, the tenant will pay the remainder along with the rent for January.

c. An inventory of office supplies discloses $675 of unused supplies.

d. Premiums for insurance against injuries to employees are paid monthly. The $450 premium for December will be paid January 12.

e. Leeward owes $90,000 on a note payable that requires quarterly payments of accrued interest. The quarterly payments of $2,700 each are made on the 15th of January, April, July, and October.

f. An analysis of Leeward's service contracts with customers shows that $6,300 of the amount customers have prepaid remains unearned.

g. Leeward has a $37,500 note receivable on which interest of $175 has accrued. On January 22, the note and the total accrued interest of $575 will be repaid to Leeward.

h. Leeward has earned but unrecorded revenue for $8,250 for services provided to a customer who will pay for the work on January 24. At that time, the customer will also pay $3,100 for services Leeward will perform in early January.

### Required

1. Prepare adjusting journal entries.
2. Prepare closing journal entries.
3. Prepare reversing entries.
4. Prepare journal entries to record the January 1997 cash receipts and cash payments identified in the above information.

On December 31, 1996, the Castle Rock Company recorded a $10,000 liability to its employees for wages earned in 1996 that will be paid on January 5, the first pay day in 1997. In addition, they will receive another $5,000 for wages earned in 1997. The accountant did

CProblem 4–10
Analytical Essay
(LO 6)

not prepare a reversing entry as of January 1, 1997, but did not inform the bookkeeper about the liability accrued for the wages. As a result, the bookkeeper recorded a $15,000 debit to Wages Expense on January 5, and a $15,000 credit to Cash.

Describe the effects of this error on the financial statements for 1996. Describe any erroneous account balances that will exist during 1997. Suggest a reasonable point in time at which the error would be discovered.

**Problem 4–11**
Analytical Essay
**(LO 6)**

On December 31, 1996, the Big Rock Company recorded a $15,000 liability to its employees for wages earned in 1996 that will be paid on January 5, the first pay day in 1997. In addition, they will receive another $7,500 for wages earned in 1997. The accountant did not prepare a reversing entry as of January 1, 1997, but did not inform the bookkeeper about the liability accrued for the wages. As a result, the bookkeeper recorded a $22,500 debit to Wages Expense on January 5, and a $22,500 credit to Cash.

Also in 1996, two-thirds of work was completed on a contract the total value of which was $30,000. On completion of the contract in 1997, the bookkeeper recorded $30,000 debit to cash and a $30,000 credit to contract revenue. No account was taken in 1996 of the work on the contract.

Describe the effects of these errors on the financial statements for 1996. Describe any erroneous account balances that will exist during 1997. Suggest a reasonable point in time at which the errors would be discovered.

**ᴰProblem 4–12**
Closing entries for
partnerships and
corporations
**(LO 8)**

Carol Boyce, Sarah Reed, and John Hudson started a business on January 7, 1995, and each invested $75,000 in the business. During 1995, the business lost $30,240, and during 1996, it earned $83,550. On January 5, 1997, the three owners agreed to pay out to themselves $36,000 of the accumulated earnings of the business. On January 9, 1997, the $36,000 was paid out.

### Required

1.  Assume that the business is a partnership and the partners share net incomes and net losses equally. Give the entries to record the investments and to close the Income Summary account at the end of 1995 and again at the end of 1996. Also assume that the partners shared equally in the $36,000 of earnings paid out. Give the entry to record the withdrawals.

2.  Assume that the business is organized as a corporation and that each owner invested $75,000 in it by buying 7,500 of its common shares. Give the entry to record the investments. Also, give the entries to close the Income Summary account at the end of 1995 and again at the end of 1996 and to record the declaration and payment of the $1.60 per share dividend. (Ignore corporate income taxes and assume that the three owners are the corporation's board of directors.)

**ᴰProblem 4–13**
Closing entries for
partnerships and
corporations
**(LO 8)**

On January 7, 1995, John Aspen, Sarah Khan, and Paul Glen started a business in which John Aspen invested $10,000. Sarah Khan invested $20,000, and Paul Glen invested $40,000. During 1995, the business lost $70,000; and during 1996, it earned $24,500. On January 5, 1997, the three business owners agreed to pay out to themselves $14,000 of the accumulated earnings of the business, and on January 10, the $14,000 was paid out.

### Required

1.  Assume that the business is a partnership and that the partners share net incomes and net losses in proportion to their investments. Give the entries to record the

investments and to close the Income Summary account at the end of 1995 and again at the end of 1996. Also assume that the partners paid out the accumulated earnings in proportion to their investments. Give the entry to record the withdrawals.

2. Assume that the business is organized as a corporation and that the owners invested in the corporation by buying its common shares at $5 per share, with John Aspen buying 2,000 shares, Sarah Khan buying 4,000 shares, and Paul Glen buying 8,000 shares. Give the entry to record the investments. Also, give the entries to close the Income Summary account at the end of 1995 and again at the end of 1996. Then give the entries to record the declaration and payment of the $1 per share dividend. (Ignore corporation income taxes and assume the investors are the corporation's board of directors.)

# SERIAL PROBLEM

*(The first two segments of this comprehensive problem were in Chapters 2 and 3, and the final segment is presented in Chapter 5. If the Chapter 2 and 3 segments have not been completed, the assignment can begin at this point. However, you should use the facts on pages 119–120 in Chapter 2 and pages 175–176 in Chapter 3. Because of its length, this problem is most easily solved if you use the Working Papers that accompany this text.)*

**Emerald Computer Services**

The transactions of Emerald Computer Services for October through December 1996 have been recorded in the problem segments in Chapters 2 and 3, as well as the year-end adjusting entries. Prior to closing the revenue and expense accounts for 1996, the accounting system is modified to include the Income Summary account, which is given the number 901.

**Required**

1. Record and post the appropriate closing entries.
2. Prepare a post-closing trial balance.

# PROVOCATIVE PROBLEMS

During his second year in college, Wesley Smith inherited Strongarm Moving Service when his father died. He immediately dropped out of school and took over management of the business. At the time he took over, Wesley recognized he knew little about accounting. However, he reasoned that since the business performed its services strictly for cash, if the cash of the business increased, the business was doing OK. Therefore, he was pleased as he watched the cash balance grow from $2,100 when he took over to $25,715 at year-end. Furthermore, since he had withdrawn $30,000 from the business to buy a new car and to pay personal expenses, he reasoned that the business must have earned $48,850 during the year. He arrived at $48,850 by adding the $23,615 increase in cash to the $30,000 he had withdrawn from the business. Wesley was shocked when he received the income statement that follows and learned that the business had earned less than the amounts withdrawn.

**Provocative Problem 4–1**
Strongarm Moving Service
**(Review problem)**

**STRONGARM MOVING SERVICE**
**Income Statement**
**For Year Ended December 31, 1996**

| | | |
|---|---:|---:|
| Revenue from moving services . . . . . . . . . . | | $120,565 |
| Operating expenses: | | |
|    Salaries and wages expense . . . . . . . . . . . | $54,825 | |
|    Gas, oil, and repairs expense . . . . . . . . . | 4,835 | |
|    Telephone expense . . . . . . . . . . . . . . . . . | 525 | |
|    Taxes expense . . . . . . . . . . . . . . . . . . . . | 3,710 | |
|    Insurance expense . . . . . . . . . . . . . . . . . | 3,485 | |
|    Office supplies expense . . . . . . . . . . . . . | 375 | |
|    Amortization expense, office equipment . . | 600 | |
|    Amortization expense, trucks . . . . . . . . . | 9,375 | |
|    Amortization expense, building . . . . . . . . | 7,500 | |
|    Total operating expenses . . . . . . . . . . . . | | 85,230 |
| Net income . . . . . . . . . . . . . . . . . . . . . . . . | | $ 35,335 |

After thinking about the statement for several days, Wesley asked you to explain how, in a year in which the cash increased $18,850 and he withdrew $30,000, the business earned only $35,335. In examining the accounts of the business, you note that accrued salaries and wages payable at the beginning of the year were $185 but increased to $575 at year's end. Also, the accrued taxes payable were $675 at the beginning of the year but had increased to $715 at year-end. Also, the balance of the Prepaid Insurance account was $300 less and the balance of the Office Supplies account was $75 less at the end of the year than at the beginning. However, except for the changes in these accounts, the change in cash, and the changes in the balances of the accumulated amortization accounts, there were no other changes in the balances of the concern's asset and liability accounts between the beginning of the year and the end. Back your explanation with a calculation that accounts for the increase in the business's cash.

**Provocative Problem
4–2
Red River Car Wash
(LO 1, 2, 3)**

Use the following information to complete a 10-column work sheet for Red River Car Wash. Instead of the usual column headings, use the following headings on the work sheet:

Unadjusted Trial Balance: Debit and Credit

Adjustments: Debit and Credit

Adjusted Trial Balance: Debit and Credit

Closing Entries: Debit and Credit

Post-Closing Trial Balance: Debit and Credit

**Unadjusted Trial Balance**

| No. | Title | Debit | Credit |
|---|---|---|---|
| 101 | Cash | $ 3,200 | |
| 106 | Accounts receivable | 500 | |
| 126 | Soap supplies | 6,000 | |
| 128 | Prepaid insurance | 2,100 | |
| 167 | Equipment | 15,000 | |
| 168 | Accumulated amortization, equipment | | $ 4,000 |
| 201 | Accounts payable | | 1,350 |
| 210 | Salaries payable | | |
| 301 | K. McGowan, capital | | 25,900 |
| 302 | K. McGowan, withdrawals | 13,500 | |
| 401 | Fees earned | | 44,450 |
| 612 | Amortization expense, equipment | | |
| 623 | Wages expense | 18,000 | |
| 637 | Insurance expense | | |
| 640 | Rent expense | 6,000 | |
| 652 | Soap supplies expense | | |
| 690 | Utilities expense | 11,400 | |
| 901 | Income summary | | |
| | Totals | $75,700 | $75,700 |

Use this information for the adjustments:

*a.* Three customers owe the company $550 for services provided but not billed.

*b.* A count of the supplies shows that $3,700 has been consumed.

*c.* The insurance coverage expired at the rate of $35 per month for 12 months.

*d.* The annual amortization expense for the equipment is $2,000.

*e.* December's utility costs of $135 were not included in the unadjusted trial balance.

*f.* The employees had earned $623 of accrued wages as of December 31.

As the end of the calendar year is approaching, Controller Jerry James is getting the Woodward Company's accounting department ready to prepare the annual financial statements. One concern is the expense of the services provided by an external consultant under a three-month contract that runs from November 30, 1996, through February 28, 1997. The total fee for the contract is based on the hours of the consultant's time, with the result that the total fee is not known.

**Provocative Problem 4–3**
**Woodward Company (LO 3)**

The controller is concerned that the company's financial statements could not be prepared until March because the amount of consulting expense will not be known until then. To avoid this problem, the controller has asked you to prepare a letter to Pat Patterson, the consultant, that would ask for a progress report by the end of the first week of January. This report would specifically identify the hours and charges that will be billed for the consultant's time in December.

Draft the letter that will be sent to Patterson requesting this information. It will be signed by the controller on December 15, 1996.

Review the consolidated balance sheet and the consolidated statement of operations of Geac Computer Corporation Limited in Appendix I at the end of this book. Assume that a ledger account exists for each item in these statements. Prepare the closing entries and a post-closing trial balance for the company as of April 30, 1994. (Note: Check "Notes to Consolidated Financial Statements" for contra account balances.)

**Provocative Problem 4–4**
**Financial statement analysis case (LO 4)**

# ANALYTICAL AND REVIEW PROBLEMS

**A & R Problem 4–1**

The owner of Dynamo Stores has come to you for assistance because his bookkeeper has just moved to another city. The following is the only information his bookkeeper left him.

(1)  Balance sheets as of December 31, 1996 and 1997.

|             | 1996      | 1997      |
|-------------|-----------|-----------|
| Assets      | $150,000  | $120,000  |
| Liabilities | $ 45,000  | $ 30,000  |
| Capital     | 105,000   | 90,000    |
|             | $150,000  | $120,000  |

(2)  The owner withdrew $75,000 in 1997 for his personal use.

(3)  The business incurred total expenses of $120,000 for 1997, of which $90,000 was for wages and $30,000 for advertising.

**Required**

1.  Compute the total revenue and net income for 1997.
2.  Prepare closing or clearing entries for 1997 (omit narratives).

**A & R Problem 4–2**

The partially completed work sheet for the current fiscal year of Sandy's Delivery Service appears below:

**Required**

1.  Complete the work sheet.
2.  Journalize the adjusting and closing entries (omit narratives).

**SANDY'S DELIVERY SERVICE**
**Work Sheet**
**For the Year Ended December 31, 1996**

| Account Titles | Trial Balance Dr. | Cr | Adjustments Dr. | Cr. | Adjusted Trial Balance Dr. | Cr. | Income Statement Dr. | Cr. | Balance Sheet Dr. | Cr. |
|---|---|---|---|---|---|---|---|---|---|---|
| Cash | 10,650 | | | | | | | | | |
| Accounts receivable | 5,000 | | | | 6,000 | | | | | |
| Supplies on hand | 2,400 | | | | | | | | 600 | |
| Prepaid insurance | 2,400 | | | | | | | | | |
| Prepaid rent | 1,800 | | | | | | | | | |
| Delivery trucks | | | | | 40,000 | | | | | |
| Accounts payable | | 3,130 | | | | 3,130 | | | | |
| Unearned delivery fees | | 3,500 | | | | | | | | 2,000 |
| Sandra Berlasty, capital, Dec. 31, 1996 | | 50,000 | | | | | | | | |
| Sandra Berlasty, drawing | 3,000 | | | | | | | | | |
| Delivery service revenue | | 15,700 | | | | | | | | |
| Advertising expense | 600 | | | | | | | | | |
| Gas and oil expense | 680 | | | | | | | | | |
| Salaries expense | 5,600 | | | | | | | | | |
| Utilities expense | 200 | | | | | | | | | |
| | 72,330 | 72,330 | | | | | | | | |
| Insurance expense | | | | | | | 800 | | | |
| Rent expense | | | | | 900 | | | | | |
| Supplies expense | | | | | | | | | | |
| Amortization expense—delivery trucks | | | | | | | | | | |
| Accumulated amortization—delivery trucks | | | | | | | | | | 2,000 |
| Accrued salaries payable | | | | | | | | | | 400 |
| | | | | | | | | | | |
| Net income | | | | | | | | | | |
| | | | | | | | | | | |
| | | | | | | | | | | |

# CONCEPT TESTER

Test your understanding of the concepts introduced in this chapter by completing the following crossword puzzle.

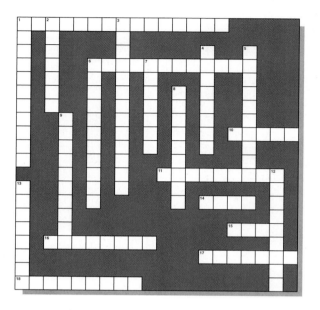

**Across Clues**

1. Recurring steps performed each accounting period (2 words).
6. Ratio of net income to revenue (2 words).
10. Number of recurring steps performed each accounting period.
11. Term used to describe asset, liability and owner equity accounts.
14. Another name for permanent accounts.
15. Balance in nominal accounts after posting closing entries.
16. Trial balance that shows account balances revised by end-of-period procedure.
17. Another name for temporary accounts.
18. Distribution to shareholders.

**Down Clues**

1. Total amount of amortization recorded against an asset.
2. End-of-period entries to render zero balances in nominal accounts.
3. Special account used only in the closing process (2 words).
4. Financial statements that show the effects of proposed transactions as if the transactions had already ocurred.
5. Assets with no physical form.
6. Trial balance that tests the accuracy of adjusting and closing procedure (2 words).
7. Financial statements prepared at intervals during a fiscal period.
8. A 10-column spreadsheet (2 words).
9. Balance sheet with meaningful groupings of assets and liabilities.
12. Term used to describe revenue, expense, and other withdrawal accounts.
13. Trial balance that shows account balances revised by end-of-period procedure.

# COMPREHENSIVE PROBLEM

Following is the unadjusted trial balance of Piper's Plumbing and Heating as of November 30, 1996. The account balances include the effects of transactions during the first 11 months of the year.

**Piper's Plumbing and Heating (Review of Chapters 1–4)**

### PIPER'S PLUMBING AND HEATING
### Unadjusted Trial Balance
### November 30, 1996

| No. | Title | Debit | Credit |
|---|---|---|---|
| 101 | Cash | $ 17,000 | |
| 124 | Office supplies | 9,400 | |
| 126 | Repair supplies | 86,500 | |
| 128 | Prepaid insurance | 2,400 | |
| 153 | Trucks | 82,000 | |
| 154 | Accumulated amortization, trucks | | $ 40,000 |
| 173 | Building | 185,000 | |
| 174 | Accumulated amortization, building | | 32,000 |
| 201 | Accounts payable | | 13,500 |
| 210 | Wages payable | | |
| 233 | Unearned heating fees | | 3,700 |
| 301 | Bill Piper, capital | | 174,600 |
| 302 | Bill Piper, withdrawals | 30,000 | |
| 401 | Plumbing fees earned | | 180,000 |
| 402 | Heating fees earned | | 95,000 |
| 606 | Amortization expense, building | | |
| 611 | Amortization expense, trucks | | |
| 623 | Wages expense | 65,000 | |
| 637 | Insurance expense | | |
| 650 | Office supplies expense | | |
| 652 | Repair supplies expense | | |
| 669 | Gas, oil, and repairs expense | 13,500 | |
| 672 | General and administrative expenses | 48,000 | |
| | Totals | $538,800 | $538,800 |

The following transactions occurred during December 1996:

Dec. 2 Received $1,000 for completed heating work.

5 Paid $11,325 on accounts payable.

6 Paid $4,100 insurance premium in advance.

7 Received $3,300 cash for plumbing work completed.

10 Purchased $1,500 of repair supplies on credit.

14 Paid $3,000 for wages earned December 1 to 14.

17 Purchased $325 of office supplies on credit.

21 Received $2,200 cash for plumbing work completed and $14,000 cash for heating work.

24 Paid $1,430 for truck repairs related to an accident.

28 Paid $3,300 for wages earned December 15 to 28.

30 Received $600 cash for plumbing work completed and $4,500 cash for heating work.

**Required**

1. Use the balance column format to create the accounts listed in the November 30 trial balance. Enter the unadjusted November 30 balances in the accounts.

2. Prepare and post journal entries to record the transactions for December; omit entering the account numbers in the posting reference column.

3. Prepare a 10-column work sheet as of December 31. Start by entering the unadjusted balances from the accounts as of that date. Continue by entering adjustments for the following items, and then complete the rest of the work sheet.

   a. At the end of the year, the office supplies inventory was $730.

   b. At the end of the year, the repair supplies inventory was $7,600.

   c. At the end of the year, the unexpired portion of the prepaid insurance was $3,800.

   d. Annual amortization on the trucks was $20,000.

   e. Annual amortization on the building was $5,000.

   f. At the end of the year, the employees had earned $990 in accrued wages.

   g. At the end of the year, the balance of unearned heating fees was $600.

4. Prepare adjusting journal entries and post them to the accounts.

5. Prepare an income statement and a statement of changes in owner's equity for 1996 and a balance sheet as of December 31, 1996. The owner did not make any new investments during the year.

6. Prepare closing journal entries and post them to the accounts.

7. Prepare a post-closing trial balance.

## ANSWERS TO PROGRESS CHECKS

4–1   c

4–2   The amounts in the Unadjusted Trial Balance columns are taken from the account balances in the ledger.

4–3   The work sheet offers the advantage of providing an overview of the information in the accounts and helps accountants organize the data.

4–4   Income statement, statement of changes in owner's equity, balance sheet.

4–5   c

4–6   Revenue and expense accounts are called temporary because they are opened and closed every reporting period. The Income Summary and owner's withdrawals accounts are also temporary accounts.

4–7   Permanent accounts are listed on the post-closing trial balance. These accounts include the asset, liability, and owner's capital accounts.

4–8   A corporation closes the Income Summary account to the Retained Earnings account.

4–9   a

4–10   A work sheet is prepared at the end of the reporting period after all transactions have been journalized and posted, but before adjustments have been recorded.

4–11   d

4–12   Profit margin = Net income/Total revenue. Therefore, Total revenue = Net income/Profit margin. Total revenue = $1,012,500/22.5% = $4,500,000.

# Accounting for Merchandising Activities

*Many companies earn profits by buying merchandise and selling it to customers. Accounting helps managers to determine the amount of income earned by these companies and the cost of the inventory they have on hand.*

*K*aren White and Mark Smith's continued interest in Imperial Oil Limited brought them back to both the company's financial statements and the section in Chapter 3 discussing the current ratio. They focused on the part that stated: "The current ratio is widely used to describe the company's ability to pay its short-term obligations." White and Smith then examined the composition of Imperial's current assets and the level of current liabilities, presented in the table below:

White and Smith left the school library wondering how items such as "Inventories of crude oil and products" and "materials, supplies and prepaid expenses" could be used to pay the current liabilities. They intended to raise this issue in their next accounting class.

| IMPERIAL OIL LIMITED (in millions) December 31 | 1994 | 1993 |
|---|---|---|
| **Current assets:** | | |
| Cash | $ 409 | $ 605 |
| Marketable securities at cost | 859 | 874 |
| Accounts receivable | 1,045 | 889 |
| Inventories of crude oil and products | 384 | 402 |
| Materials, supplies and prepaid expenses | 100 | 129 |
| Total current assets | $2,797 | $2,899 |
| Total current liabilities | $1,581 | $1,593 |

## LEARNING OBJECTIVES

**After studying Chapter 5, you should be able to:**

1. **Describe merchandising activities, analyze their effects on financial statements, and record sales of merchandise.**
2. **Describe how the ending inventory and the cost of goods sold are determined with perpetual and periodic inventory accounting systems.**
3. **Describe various formats for income statements and prepare closing entries for a merchandising business.**
4. **Complete a work sheet that includes the inventory-related accounts.**
5. **Calculate the acid-test ratio and describe what it reveals about a company's liquidity.**
6. **Define or explain the words and phrases in the chapter glossary.**

**After studying Appendix E at the end of Chapter 5, you should be able to:**

7. **Explain an adjusting entry approach to recording the change in the Merchandise Inventory account.**

The first four chapters in this book used only service companies as examples of businesses that prepare financial statements. This chapter introduces some of the business and accounting practices used by companies that engage in merchandising activities. These companies buy goods and then resell them to customers. This chapter shows how the financial statements describe the special transactions and assets related to these activities. In particular, you will learn about the additional financial statement elements created by merchandising activities. To help you understand where the information comes from, we describe how accountants close the accounts of merchandising companies and design income statements.

## THE NATURE OF MERCHANDISING ACTIVITIES

**LO 1**

Describe merchandising activities, analyze their effects on financial statements, and record sales of merchandise.

The first four chapters have described the financial statements and accounting records of Clear Copy. Because it provides services to its customers, Clear Copy is a service company. Other examples of service companies include **Greyhound Lines Inc.; Air Canada; Price Waterhouse;** and **Richardson Greenshields of Canada Limited**. In return for services provided to its customers, a service company receives commissions, fares, or fees as revenue. Its net income for a reporting period is the difference between its revenues and the operating expenses incurred in providing the services.

In contrast, a merchandising company earns net income by buying and selling **merchandise,** which consists of goods that the company acquires for the purpose of reselling them to customers.[1] To achieve a net income, the revenue from selling the merchandise needs to exceed not only the cost of the merchandise sold to customers but also the company's other operating expenses for the reporting period.

---

[1]A merchandising company can be either a wholesaler or a retailer. Wholesalers buy goods from manufacturers and sell them to retailers or other wholesalers. Retailers buy goods from wholesalers and sell them to individual customers.

The accounting term for the revenues from selling merchandise is *sales* and the term used to describe the expense of buying and preparing the merchandise is *cost of goods sold.*[2] The company's other expenses are often called *operating expenses.* This condensed income statement for Meg's Mart shows you how these three elements of net income are related to each other:

**MEG'S MART**
**Condensed Income Statement**
**For Year Ended December 31, 1997**

| | |
|---|---|
| Net sales | $314,700 |
| Cost of goods sold | (230,400) |
| Gross profit from sales | $ 84,300 |
| Total operating expenses | (62,800) |
| Net income | $ 21,500 |

This income statement tells us that Meg's Mart sold goods to its customers for $314,700. The company acquired those goods at a total cost of $230,400. As a result, it earned $84,300 of **gross profit,** which is the difference between the net sales and the cost of goods sold. In addition, the company incurred $62,800 of operating expenses and achieved $21,500 of net income for the year.

A merchandising company's balance sheet includes an additional element that is not on the balance sheet of a service company. In Illustration 5–1, we present the classified balance sheet for Meg's Mart. Notice that the current asset section includes an item called **merchandise inventory.** Even though they also have inventories of supplies, most companies simply refer to merchandise on hand as *inventory.* This asset consists of goods the company owns on the balance sheet date and holds for the purpose of selling to its customers. The $21,000 amount listed for the inventory is the costs incurred to buy the goods, ship them to the store, and otherwise make them ready for sale.

The next sections of the chapter provide more information about these unique elements of the financial statements for merchandising companies.

This schedule shows how Meg's Mart calculates its *net sales* for 1997:

**TOTAL REVENUE FROM SALES**

**MEG'S MART**
**Calculation of Net Sales**
**For Year Ended December 31, 1997**

| | | |
|---|---|---|
| Sales | | $321,000 |
| Less: Sales returns and allowances | $2,000 | |
| Sales discounts | 4,300 | 6,300 |
| Net sales | | $314,700 |

[2]Many service companies also use the word *sales* to describe their revenues.

**Illustration 5–1**
Classified Balance
Sheet for a
Merchandising
Company

**MEG'S MART**
**Balance Sheet**
**December 31, 1997**

**Assets**

Current assets:
    Cash . . . . . . . . . . . . . . . . . . . . . . .     $ 8,200
    Accounts receivable . . . . . . . . . . . .     11,200
    Merchandise inventory . . . . . . . . . .     21,000
    Prepaid expenses . . . . . . . . . . . . .     1,100
    Total current assets . . . . . . . . . . . . .             $41,500
Capital assets:
    Office equipment . . . . . . . . . . . . . .   $ 4,200
        Less accumulated amortization . . . .   1,400   $ 2,800
    Store equipment . . . . . . . . . . . . . . .   $30,000
        Less accumulated amortization . . . .   6,000   24,000
    Total capital assets . . . . . . . . . . . . .            26,800
Total assets . . . . . . . . . . . . . . . . . . .             $68,300

**Liabilities**

Current liabilities:
    Accounts payable . . . . . . . . . . . . . .     $16,000
    Salaries payable . . . . . . . . . . . . . . .     800
    Total liabilities . . . . . . . . . . . . . . . .           $16,800

**Owner's Equity**

Meg Harlowe, capital . . . . . . . . . . . . .         51,500
Total liabilities and
    owner's equity . . . . . . . . . . . . . . .         $68,300

The components of this calculation are described in the following paragraphs.

## Sales

The sales item in this calculation is the total cash and credit sales made by the company during the year. Each cash sale was rung up on one of the company's cash registers. At the end of each day, the total cash sales for the day were recorded with a journal entry like this one for November 3:

| | | | | |
|---|---|---|---|---|
| Nov. | 3 | Cash . . . . . . . . . . . . . . . . . . . . . . . . . . . . . . . . . . . . . . | 1,205.00 | |
| | |     Sales . . . . . . . . . . . . . . . . . . . . . . . . . . . . . . . . . . . . | | 1,205.00 |
| | |     *Sold merchandise for cash.* | | |

This entry records the fact that the cash received from customers represents sales revenue earned by the company.

    In addition, a journal entry would be prepared each day to record the credit sales made on that day. For example, this entry records $450 of credit sales on November 3:

| Nov. | 3 | Accounts Receivable . . . . . . . . . . . . . . . . . . . . . . . | 450.00 | |
| | | Sales . . . . . . . . . . . . . . . . . . . . . . . . . . . . . . . . | | 450.00 |
| | | *Sold merchandise on credit.* | | |

This entry records the increase in the company's assets in the form of the accounts receivable and records the revenue from the credit sales.[3]

## Sales Returns and Allowances

To meet their customers' needs, most companies allow customers to return any unsuitable merchandise for a full refund. If a customer keeps the unsatisfactory goods and is given a partial refund of the selling price, the company is said to have provided a sales *allowance.* Either way, returns and allowances involve dissatisfied customers and the possibility of lost future sales. To monitor the extent of these problems, managers need information about actual returns and allowances. Thus, many accounting systems record returns and allowances in a separate *contra-revenue* account like the one used in this entry to record a $200 cash refund:

| Nov. | 3 | Sales Returns and Allowances . . . . . . . . . . . . . . . . . | 200.00 | |
| | | Cash . . . . . . . . . . . . . . . . . . . . . . . . . . . . . . . . | | 200.00 |
| | | *Customer returned defective merchandise.* | | |

The company could record the refund with a debit to the Sales account. Although this would provide the same measure of net sales, it would not provide information that the manager can use to monitor the refunds and allowances. By using the Sales Returns and Allowances contra account, the information is readily available. To simplify the reports provided to external decision makers, published income statements usually omit this detail and present only the amount of net sales.

## Sales Discounts

When goods are sold on credit, the expected amounts and dates of future payments need to be clearly stated to avoid misunderstandings. The **credit terms** for a sale describe the amounts and timing of payments that the buyer agrees to make in the future. The specific terms usually reflect the ordinary practices of most companies in the industry. For example, companies in one industry might expect to be paid 10 days after the end of the month in which a sale occurred. These credit terms would be stated on sales invoices or tickets as "n/10 EOM," with the abbreviation **EOM** standing for "end of the month." In another industry, invoices may normally be due and payable 30 calendar days after the invoice date. These terms are abbreviated as "n/30," and the 30-day period is called the **credit period.**

When the credit period is long, the seller often grants a **cash discount** if the customer pays promptly. These early payments are desirable because the seller re-

---

[3]Chapter 8 describes how stores account for sales to customers who use third-party credit cards, such as those issued by banks.

ceives the cash more quickly and can use it to carry on its activities. In addition, prompt payments reduce future efforts and costs of billing customers. These advantages are usually worth the cost of offering the discounts.

If cash discounts for early payment are granted, they are described in the credit terms on the invoice. For example, the terms of 2/10, n/60 mean that a 60-day credit period passes before full payment is due. However, to encourage early payment, the seller allows the buyer to deduct 2% of the invoice amount from the payment if it is made within 10 days of the invoice date. The **discount period** is the period in which the reduced payment can be made.

At the time of a credit sale, the seller does not know that the customer will pay within the discount period and take advantage of a cash discount. As a result, the discount is usually not recorded until the customer pays within the discount period. For example, suppose that Meg's Mart completed a credit sale on November 12 at a gross selling price of $100, subject to terms of 2/10, n/60. This entry records the sale:

| Nov. | 12 | Accounts Receivable ....................... | 100.00 | |
| | | Sales ............................... | | 100.00 |
| | | *Sold merchandise under terms of 2/10, n/60.* | | |

Even though the customer may pay less than the gross price, the entry records the receivable and the revenue as if the full amount will be collected.

In fact, the customer has two alternatives. One option is to wait 60 days until January 11 and pay the full $100. If this is done, Meg's Mart records the collection as follows:

| Jan. | 11 | Cash ................................. | 100.00 | |
| | | Accounts Receivable .................... | | 100.00 |
| | | *Collected account receivable.* | | |

The customer's other option is to pay $98 within a 10-day period that runs through November 22. If the customer pays on November 22, Meg's Mart records the collection with this entry:

| Nov. | 22 | Cash ................................. | 98.00 | |
| | | Sales Discounts ....................... | 2.00 | |
| | | Accounts Receivable .................... | | 100.00 |
| | | *Received payment for the November 12 sale less the discount.* | | |

Cash discounts granted to customers are called **sales discounts.** Because management needs to monitor the amount of cash discounts to assess their effectiveness and their cost, they are recorded in a contra-revenue account called Sales Discounts.

The balance of this account is deducted from the balance of the Sales account when calculating the company's net sales. Although information about the amount of discounts is useful internally, it is seldom reported on income statements distributed to external decision makers.

---

**Progress Check**
*(Answers to Progress Checks are provided at the end of the chapter.)*

5-1    Which of the following items is not unique to the financial statements of merchandising companies? *(a)* Cost of goods sold; *(b)* Accounts receivable; *(c)* Merchandise inventory.

5-2    What is a merchandising company's gross profit?

5-3    Why are sales returns and allowances and sales discounts recorded in contra-revenue accounts instead of in the Sales account? Is this information likely to be reported outside the company?

5-4    How long are the credit and discount periods under credit terms of 2/10, n/60?

---

A merchandising company's balance sheet includes a current asset called *inventory* and its income statement includes the item called *cost of goods sold*. Both of these items are affected by the company's merchandise transactions. The amount of the asset on the balance sheet equals the cost of the inventory on hand at the end of the fiscal year. The amount of the cost of goods sold is the cost of the merchandise that was sold to customers during the year.

Two different inventory accounting systems may be used to collect information about the cost of the inventory on hand and the cost of goods sold. They are described in the following paragraphs.

## Periodic and Perpetual Inventory Systems

The two basic types of inventory accounting systems are called *perpetual* and *periodic*. As suggested by their name, **perpetual inventory systems** maintain a continuous record of the amount of inventory on hand. This perpetual record is maintained by adding the cost of each newly purchased item to the inventory account and subtracting the cost of each sold item from the account. When an item is sold, its cost is recorded in the Cost of Goods Sold account. Whenever posting is up to date during the period, users of perpetual systems can determine the cost of merchandise on hand by looking at the balance of the inventory account. They can also determine the cost of goods sold thus far during the period by referring to the Cost of Goods Sold account.

Before computers were used widely, perpetual systems were generally applied only by businesses that made a limited number of sales each day, such as automobile dealers or major appliance stores. Because there were relatively few transactions, the perpetual accounting system could be operated efficiently. However, the availability of improved technology has greatly increased the number of companies that use perpetual systems.

Under **periodic inventory systems,** a company does not continuously update its records of the quantity and cost of goods that are on hand or sold. Instead, the company simply records the cost of new merchandise in a temporary *Purchases*

**MEASURING INVENTORY AND COST OF GOODS SOLD**

LO 2

Describe how the ending inventory and the cost of goods sold are determined with perpetual and periodic inventory accounting systems.

account. When merchandise is sold, only the revenue is recorded. Then, when financial statements are prepared, the company takes a *physical inventory* by counting the quantities of merchandise on hand. The total cost is determined by relating the quantities to records that show each item's original cost. This total cost is then used to determine the cost of goods sold.

Traditionally, periodic systems were used by companies such as drug and department stores that sold large quantities of low-valued items. Without computers and scanners, it was not feasible for accounting systems to track such small items as toothpaste, pain killers, clothing, and housewares through the inventory and into the customers' hands.

Although perpetual systems are now more affordable, they are still not used by all merchandising companies. As a result, it will be helpful for you to understand how periodic systems work. In addition, studying periodic systems will help you visualize the flow of goods through inventory without having to learn the more complicated sequence of journal entries used in perpetual systems. (More information on perpetual systems is provided in Chapter 9. However, at this stage you may wish to consider journal-entry comparison of the two systems: comparison is provided in the footnote at the bottom of this page.[4])

## CALCULATING THE COST OF GOODS SOLD WITH A PERIODIC INVENTORY SYSTEM

As mentioned earlier, a store that uses a periodic inventory system does not record the cost of merchandise items when they are sold. Rather, the accountant waits until the end of the reporting period and determines the cost of all the goods sold during the period. To make this calculation, the accountant must have information about:

1.  The cost of merchandise on hand at the beginning of the period.
2.  The cost of merchandise purchased during the period.
3.  The cost of unsold goods on hand at the end of the period.

Look at Illustration 5–2 to see how this information can be used to measure the cost of goods sold for Meg's Mart.

In Illustration 5–2, note that Meg's Mart had $251,400 of goods available for sale during the period. They were available because the company had $19,000 of goods on hand when the period started and purchased an additional $232,400 of goods during the year.

The available goods either were sold during the period or on hand at the end of the period. Because the count showed that $21,000 were on hand at the end of the year, we can conclude that $230,400 must have been sold. This schedule presents the calculation:

---

| **Periodic**[4] | | | **Perpetual** | | |
|---|---|---|---|---|---|
| Purchase of goods: | | | Inventory .............. | xxx | |
| Purchases ................. | xxx | |     Accounts payable ...... | | xxx |
|     Accounts payable ........ | | xxx | Accounts receivable ........ | xxx | |
| Sales of goods: | | |     Sales .............. | | xxx |
| Accounts receivable | xxx | | Cost of goods sold ........ | xxx | |
|     Sales ................. | | xxx |     Inventory ............ | | xxx |

No entry; the impact of the cost of the goods is via an end-of-period update of inventory and the closing of purchases and related accounts.

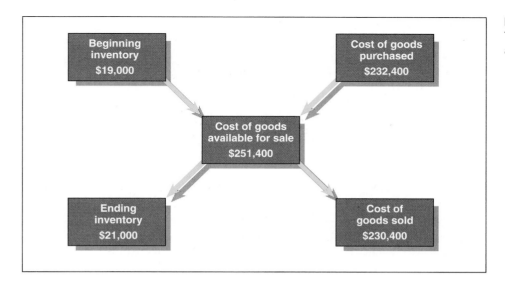

**Illustration 5-2**
The Flow of Goods
and Costs through
Inventory

**MEG'S MART**
**Calculation of Cost of Goods Sold**
**For Year Ended December 31, 1997**

| | |
|---|---|
| Beginning inventory . . . . . . . . . . . . | $ 19,000 |
| Cost of goods purchased . . . . . . . . | 232,400 |
| Cost of goods available for sale . . . . | $251,400 |
| Less ending inventory . . . . . . . . . . | (21,000) |
| Cost of goods sold . . . . . . . . . . . . | $230,400 |

Note that if any three of the items in this calculation are known, they can be used to calculate the fourth. For example, **Example** Corporation's 1996 annual report disclosed the following information:

| | |
|---|---|
| Beginning merchandise inventories . . . . | $2,269 million |
| Ending merchandise inventories . . . . . . | 1,579 million |
| Cost of sales . . . . . . . . . . . . . . . . . . . | $6,717 million |

The cost of Example's purchases during 1996 can be calculated as follows:

| | |
|---|---|
| Ending merchandise inventories . . . . . . . . . . . | $1,579 million |
| Cost of sales . . . . . . . . . . . . . . . . . . . . . . . | 6,717 million |
| Cost of goods that must have been available for sale . . . . . . . . . . . . . . . . . . . | $8,296 million |
| Less beginning merchandise inventories . . . . . . | 2,269 million |
| Cost of goods purchased . . . . . . . . . . . . . . . . | $6,027 million |

The following paragraphs explain how the accounting system accumulates the information that the accountant needs to make these calculations.

## Measuring and Recording Merchandise Inventory

Because a new reporting period starts as soon as the old period ends, the ending inventory of one period is always the beginning inventory of the next. When a periodic inventory system is used, the dollar amount of the ending inventory is determined by (1) counting the unsold items in the store and the stockroom, (2) multiplying the counted quantity of each type of good by its cost, and (3) adding all the costs of the different types of goods. The cost of goods sold is found by subtracting the cost of the ending inventory from the cost of the goods available for sale.

Through the closing process described later in the chapter, the periodic system records the cost of the ending inventory in the *Merchandise Inventory* account. The balance in this account is not changed during the next accounting period. In fact, entries are made to the Merchandise Inventory account only at the end of the period. Thus, neither the purchases of new merchandise nor the cost of goods sold is entered in the Merchandise Inventory account. As a result, as soon as any goods are purchased or sold in the current period, the account no longer shows the cost of the merchandise on hand. Because the account's balance describes the beginning inventory of the period, it cannot be used on a new balance sheet without being updated by the closing entries described later in this chapter.

## Recording the Cost of Purchased Merchandise

To determine the cost of purchased merchandise, the gross purchase price must be adjusted for the effects of (1) any cash discounts provided by the suppliers, (2) any returns and allowances for unsatisfactory items received from the suppliers, and (3) any freight costs paid by the buyer to get the goods into the buyer's inventory. For example, the cost of the goods purchased by Meg's Mart for 1997 is calculated as follows:

**MEG'S MART**
**Calculation of Cost of Goods Purchased**
**For Year Ended December 31, 1997**

| | | |
|---|---:|---:|
| Purchases ........................ | | $235,800 |
| Less: Purchases returns and allowances .... | $1,500 | |
| Purchases discounts ............. | 4,200 | 5,700 |
| Net purchases ...................... | | $230,100 |
| Add transportation-in ................ | | 2,300 |
| Cost of goods purchased ............. | | $232,400 |

The following paragraphs explain how these amounts are accumulated in the accounts.

**The Purchases Account.** Under a periodic inventory system, the cost of merchandise bought for resale is debited to a temporary account called *Purchases*. For example, Meg's Mart records a $1,200 credit purchase of merchandise on November 2 with this entry:

| Nov. | 2 | Purchases ................................ | 1,200.00 | |
|------|---|---------------------------------------------|----------|----------|
|      |   | Accounts Payable ....................... |          | 1,200.00 |
|      |   | *Purchased merchandise on credit, invoice* | | |
|      |   | *dated November 2, terms 2/10, n/30.* | | |

The Purchases account accumulates the cost of all merchandise bought during a period. The account is a holding place for information used at the end of the period to calculate the cost of goods sold.

**Trade Discounts.** When a manufacturer or wholesaler prepares a catalogue of the items it offers for sale, each item is given a **list price,** which is also called a *catalogue price.* The list price generally is not the intended selling price of the item. Instead, the intended selling price equals the list price reduced by a given percentage called a **trade discount.**

The amount of the trade discount usually depends on whether the buyer is a wholesaler, a retailer, or the final consumer. For example, a wholesaler that buys large quantities is granted a larger discount than a retailer that buys smaller quantities. Regardless of its amount, a trade discount is a reduction in a list price that is applied to determine the actual sales price of the goods to a customer.

Trade discounts are commonly used by manufacturers and wholesalers to change selling prices without republishing their catalogues. When the seller wants to change the selling prices, it can notify its customers merely by sending them a new set of trade discounts to apply to the catalogue prices.

Because list prices are not intended to reflect the negotiated sales value of the merchandise, neither the buyer nor the seller enters the list prices and the trade discounts in their accounts. Instead, they record the actual sales price (the list price less the trade discount). For example, if a manufacturer deducts a 40% trade discount on an item listed in its catalogue at $2,000, the selling price is $1,200, which is [$2,000 − (40% × $2,000)]. The seller records the credit sale as follows:

| Nov. | 2 | Accounts Receivable ........................ | 1,200.00 | |
|------|---|-----------------------------------------------|----------|----------|
|      |   | Sales ................................. |          | 1,200.00 |
|      |   | *Sold merchandise on credit.* | | |

The buyer also records the purchase at $1,200. For example, see the previous entry to record the purchase by Meg's Mart.

**Purchases Discounts.** When stores buy merchandise on credit, they may be offered cash discounts for paying within the discount period. The buyer refers to these cash discounts as **purchases discounts.** When the buyer pays within the discount period, the accounting system records a credit to a contra-purchases account called *Purchases Discounts.* The following entry uses this account to record the payment for the merchandise purchased on November 2:

### As a Matter of Ethics

Renee Fleck was recently hired by Mid-Mart, a medium-size retailing company that purchases most of its merchandise on credit. She overlapped on the new job for several days with the outgoing employee in her position, Martin Hull, so that he could help her learn the ropes.

One of Fleck's responsibilities is to see that the payables are paid promptly to maintain the company's credit standing with its suppliers and to take advantage of all cash discounts. Hull told Fleck that the current system has accomplished both goals easily and has also made another contribution to the company's profits. He explained that the computer system has been programmed to prepare cheques for amounts net of the cash discounts. Even though the cheques are dated as of the last day of the discount period, they are not mailed until five days later. Because the accounts are always paid, the company has had virtually no trouble with its suppliers. "It's simple," Hull explained to Fleck. "We get the free use of the cash for an extra five days, and who's going to complain? Even when somebody does, we just blame the computer system and the people in the mail room."

A few days later, Hull had departed and Fleck assumed her new duties. The first invoice that she examined had a 10-day discount period on a $10,000 purchase. The transaction occurred on April 9 subject to terms of 2/10, n/30. Fleck had to decide whether she should mail the $9,800 cheque on April 19 or wait until the 24th.

| Nov. | 12 | Accounts Payable ......................... | 1,200.00 | |
|---|---|---|---|---|
| | | Purchases Discounts (2% × $1,200) ......... | | 24.00 |
| | | Cash ................................. | | 1,176.00 |
| | | *Paid for the purchase of November 2 less the discount.* | | |

By recording the amount of discounts taken in a separate contra account, the accountant can help managers keep track of the company's performance in taking advantage of discounts. For example, if all purchases are made on credit and all suppliers offer a 2% discount, the balance of the Purchases Discounts contra account should equal 2% of the balance of the Purchases account. If the accountant did not use the contra account, the $24 credit entry would be recorded as a reduction of the Purchases account balance. As a result, it would be more difficult to determine whether discounts were taken.

The accountant uses the balance of the Purchases Discounts account to compute the net cost of the purchases for the period. However, published financial statements usually do not include this calculation because it is useful only for managers.

**A Cash Management Technique.** To ensure that discounts are not missed, most companies set up a system to pay all invoices within the discount period. Furthermore, careful cash management ensures that no invoice is paid until the last day of the discount period. A helpful technique for reaching both of these goals is to file each invoice in such a way that it automatically comes up for payment on the last day of its discount period. For example, a simple manual system uses 31 folders, one for each day in the month. After an invoice is recorded in the journal, it is placed in the file folder for the last day of its discount period. Thus, if the last day of an invoice's discount period is November 12, it is filed in folder number 12. Then, the invoice and any other invoices in the same folder are removed and paid on November 12. Computerized systems can accomplish the same result by using a code that identifies the last date in the discount period. When that date is reached, the computer automatically provides a reminder that the account should be paid. Another way a company can gain more control over purchase discounts is by using the *net method of recording purchases*. This method is discussed in Chapter 7.

Read the As a Matter of Ethics case and consider what you would do if you were faced with the situation it describes.

**Purchases Returns and Allowances.**  Sometimes, merchandise received from a supplier is not acceptable and must be returned. In other cases, the purchaser may keep imperfect but marketable merchandise because the supplier grants an allowance, which is a reduction in the purchase price.

Even though the seller does not charge the buyer for the returned goods or gives an allowance for imperfect goods, the buyer incurs costs in receiving, inspecting, identifying, and possibly returning defective merchandise. The occurrence of these costs can be signaled to the manager by recording the cost of the returned merchandise or the seller's allowance in a separate contra-purchases account called *Purchases Returns and Allowances*. For example, this journal entry is recorded on November 14 when Meg's Mart returns defective merchandise for a $265 refund of the original purchase price:

| Nov. | 14 | Accounts Payable . . . . . . . . . . . . . . . . . . . . . . . . . | 265.00 | |
|------|----|-------------------------------------------------------------------|--------|--------|
| | | Purchases Returns and Allowances . . . . . . . . . . . | | 265.00 |
| | | *Returned defective merchandise.* | | |

As we described for Purchases Discounts, the accountant uses the balance of the Purchases Returns and Allowances account to compute the net cost of goods purchased during the period. However, published financial statements generally do not include this detailed information.

**Discounts and Returned Merchandise.**  If part of a shipment of goods is returned within the discount period, the buyer can take the discount only on the remaining balance of the invoice. For example, suppose that Meg's Mart is offered a 2% cash discount on $5,000 of merchandise. Two days later, the company returns $800 of the goods before the invoice is paid. When the liability is paid within the discount period, Meg's Mart can take the 2% discount only on the $4,200 balance. Thus, the discount is $84 (2% $\times$ $4,200) and the cash payment must be $4,116 ($4,200 − $84).

**Transportation Costs.**  Depending on the terms negotiated with its suppliers, a company may be responsible for paying the shipping costs for transporting the acquired goods to its own place of business. Because these costs are necessary to make the goods ready for sale, the cost principle requires them to be added to the cost of the purchased goods.

The freight charges could be recorded with a debit to the Purchases account. However, more complete information about these costs is provided to management if they are debited to a special supplemental account called *Transportation-In*. The accountant adds this account's balance to the net purchase price of the acquired goods to find the total cost of goods purchased. (See the schedule on page 246.)

The use of this account is demonstrated by the following entry, which records a $75 freight charge for incoming merchandise:

| Nov. | 24 | Transportation-In ........................... | 75.00 | |
|------|----|-----------------------------------------------|-------|-------|
| | | Cash ................................... | | 75.00 |
| | | *Paid freight charges on purchased merchandise.* | | |

Because detailed information about freight charges is relevant only for managers, it is seldom found in external financial statements.

Freight paid to bring purchased goods into the inventory is accounted for separately from freight paid on goods sent to customers. The shipping cost of incoming goods is included in the cost of goods sold, while the shipping cost for outgoing goods is a selling expense.

**Identifying Ownership Responsibilities and Risks.** When a merchandise transaction is planned, the buyer and seller need to establish which party will be responsible for paying any freight costs and which will bear the risk of loss during transit.

The basic issue to be negotiated is the point at which ownership is transferred from the buyer to the seller. The place of the transfer is called the **FOB** point, which is the abbreviation for the phrase, *free on board*. The meaning of different FOB points is explained by the diagram in Illustration 5–3.

Under an *FOB shipping point* agreement (also called *FOB factory*), the buyer accepts ownership at the seller's place of business. As a result, the buyer is responsible for paying the shipping costs and bears the risk of damage or loss while the goods are in shipment. In addition, the goods are part of the buyer's inventory while they are in transit because the buyer already owns them.

Alternatively, an *FOB destination* agreement causes ownership of the goods to pass at the buyer's place of business. If so, the seller is responsible for paying the shipping charges and bears the risk of damage or loss in transit. Furthermore, the seller should not record the sales revenue until the goods arrive at the destination because the transaction is not complete before that point in time.

**Compaq Computer Corporation** originally shipped all of its products under FOB factory agreements. However, customers' shipping companies proved to be undependable in picking up shipments at scheduled times and caused backups at the plant, missed deliveries, and disappointed end users. The company changed its agreements to FOB destination and cleared up these problems.

## Debit and Credit Memoranda

Buyers and sellers often find they need to adjust the amount that is owed between them. For example, purchased merchandise may not meet specifications, unordered goods may be received, different quantities may be received than were ordered and billed, and billing errors may occur.

**Illustration 5-3**   Identifying Ownership Responsibilities and Risks

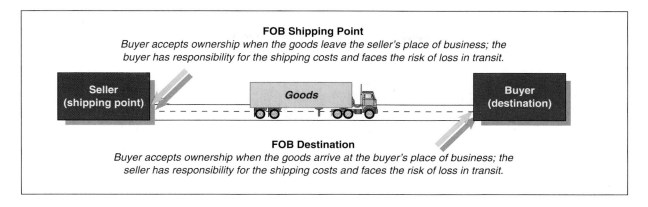

In some cases, the original balance can be adjusted by the buyer without a negotiation. For example, a seller may make an error on an invoice. If the buying company discovers the error, it can make its own adjustment and notify the seller by sending a **debit memorandum** or a **credit memorandum.** A debit memorandum is a business document that informs the recipient that the sender has *debited* the account receivable or payable. It provides the notification with words like these: "We debit your account," followed by the amount and an explanation. On the other hand, a credit memorandum informs the recipient that the sender has credited the receivable or payable. See Illustration 5–4 for two situations that involve these documents.

The debit memorandum in Illustration 5–4 is based on a case in which a buyer initially records an invoice as an account payable and later discovers an error by the seller that overstated the total bill by $100. The buyer corrects the balance of its liability and formally notifies the seller of the mistake with a debit memorandum reading: "We have debited your account for $100 because of an error." Additional information is provided about the invoice, its date, and the nature of the error. The buyer sends a *debit* memorandum because the correction debits the account payable to reduce its balance. The buyer's debit to the payable is offset by a credit to the Purchases account.

When the seller receives its copy of the debit memorandum, it records a *credit* to the buyer's account receivable to reduce its balance. An equal debit is recorded in the Sales account. Neither company uses a contra account because the adjustment was created by an error.

In other situations, an adjustment can be made only after negotiations between the buyer and the seller. For example, suppose that a buyer claims that some merchandise does not meet specifications. The amount of the allowance to be given by the seller can be determined only after discussion. Assume that a buyer accepts delivery of merchandise and records the transaction with a $750 debit to the Purchases account and an equal credit to Accounts Payable. Later, the buyer discovers that some of the merchandise is flawed. After a phone call, the seller agrees to grant a $250 allowance against the original purchase price.

The seller records the allowance with a debit to the Sales Returns and Allowances contra account and a credit to Accounts Receivable. Then, the seller formally

**Illustration 5–4**   The Use of Debit and Credit Memoranda

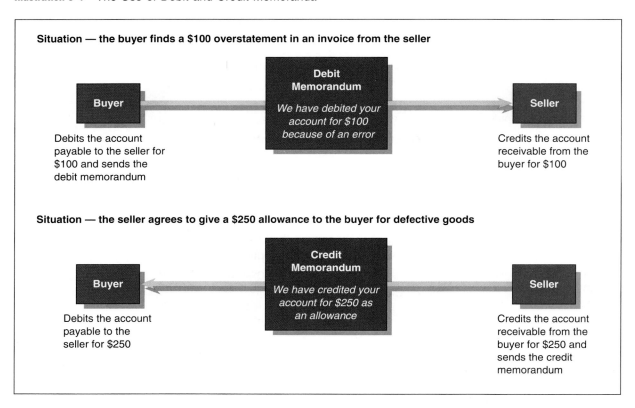

notifies the buyer of the allowance with a credit memorandum. A *credit* memorandum is used because the adjustment credited the receivable to reduce its balance. When the buyer receives the credit memorandum, it debits Accounts Payable and credits Purchases Returns and Allowances.

## Inventory Shrinkage

Merchandising companies lose merchandise in a variety of ways, including shoplifting and deterioration while an item is on the shelf or in the warehouse. These losses are called **shrinkage.**

Even though perpetual inventory systems track all goods as they move into and out of the company, they are not able to directly measure shrinkage. However, these systems allow the accountant to calculate shrinkage by comparing a physical count with recorded quantities.

Because periodic inventory systems do not identify quantities on hand, they cannot provide direct measures of shrinkage. In fact, all that they can determine is the cost of the goods on hand and the goods that passed out of the inventory. The amount that passed out includes the cost of goods sold, stolen, or destroyed. For example, suppose that shoplifters took merchandise that cost $500. Because the goods were not on hand for a physical count, the ending inventory's cost is $500 smaller than it would have been. As a result, the $500 is included in the cost of the goods sold.

Chapter 9 describes perpetual systems and how they provide more complete information about shrinkage. Chapter 9 also describes how an accountant can estimate shrinkage when a periodic system is used.

---

**Progress Check**

**5–5**  Which of the following items is subtracted from the list price of merchandise to determine the actual sales price? *(a)* Freight-in; *(b)* Trade discount; *(c)* Purchases discount; *(d)* Purchases return and/or allowance.

**5–6**  How is the cost of goods sold determined with a periodic inventory accounting system?

**5–7**  What is the meaning of the abbreviation *FOB?* What is the meaning of the term *FOB destination?*

---

## ALTERNATIVE INCOME STATEMENT FORMATS

**LO 3**

Describe various formats for income statements and prepare closing entries for a merchandising business.

Generally accepted accounting principles do not require companies to use exactly the same financial statement formats. In fact, practice shows that many different formats are used. This section of the chapter describes several possible formats that Meg's Mart could use for its income statement.

In Illustration 5–5, we present a **classified income statement** that would probably be distributed only to the company's managers because of the details that it includes. The sales and cost of goods sold sections are the same as the calculations presented earlier in the chapter. The difference between the net sales and cost of goods sold is the gross profit for the year.

Also notice that the operating expenses section classifies the expenses into two categories. **Selling expenses** include the expenses of promoting sales through displaying and advertising the merchandise, making sales, and delivering goods to customers. **General and administrative expenses** support the overall operations of a business and include the expenses of activities such as accounting, human resource management, and financial management.

Some expenses may be divided between categories because they contribute to both activities. For example, Illustration 5–5 reflects the fact that Meg's Mart divided the total rent expense of $9,000 for its store building between the two categories. Ninety percent ($8,100) was selling expense and the remaining 10% ($900) was general and administrative expense.[5] The cost allocation should reflect an economic relationship between the prorated amounts and the activities. For example, the allocation in this case could be based on relative rental values.

In Illustration 5–6, we use the **multiple-step income statement** format that is sometimes used in external reports. The only difference between this format and the one in Illustration 5–5 is that it leaves out the detailed calculations of net sales and cost of goods sold. The format is called multiple-step because it shows several intermediate totals between sales and net income.

In contrast, we present a **single-step income statement** for Meg's Mart in Illustration 5–7. This simpler format includes cost of goods sold as an operating

---

[5]These expenses can be recorded in a single account or in two separate accounts. If they are recorded in one account, the accountant allocates its balance between the two expenses when preparing the statements.

**Illustration 5–5**  Classified Income Statement for Internal Use

**MEG'S MART**
**Income Statement**
**For Year Ended December 31, 1997**

| | | | |
|---|---|---:|---:|
| Sales | | | $321,000 |
| Less: Sales returns and allowances | | $2,000 | |
| Sales discounts | | 4,300 | 6,300 |
| Net sales | | | $314,700 |
| Cost of goods sold: | | | |
| Merchandise inventory, December 31, 1996 | | $19,000 | |
| Purchases | $235,800 | | |
| Less: Purchases returns and allowances | $1,500 | | |
| Purchases discounts | 4,200 | 5,700 | |
| Net purchases | | $230,100 | |
| Add transportation-in | | 2,300 | |
| Cost of goods purchased | | 232,400 | |
| Goods available for sale | | $251,400 | |
| Merchandise inventory, December 31, 1997 | | 21,000 | |
| Cost of goods sold | | | 230,400 |
| Gross profit from sales | | | $ 84,300 |
| Operating expenses: | | | |
| Selling expenses: | | | |
| Amortization expense, store equipment | $ 3,000 | | |
| Sales salaries expense | 18,500 | | |
| Rent expense, selling space | 8,100 | | |
| Store supplies expense | 1,200 | | |
| Advertising expense | 2,700 | | |
| Total selling expenses | | $33,500 | |
| General and administrative expenses: | | | |
| Amortization expense, office equipment | $ 700 | | |
| Office salaries expense | 25,300 | | |
| Insurance expense | 600 | | |
| Rent expense, office space | 900 | | |
| Office supplies expense | 1,800 | | |
| Total general and administrative expenses | | 29,300 | |
| Total operating expenses | | | 62,800 |
| Net income | | | $ 21,500 |

expense and presents only one intermediate total for total operating expenses. Many companies use this format in their published financial statements.

In practice, many companies use formats that combine some of the features of both the single- and multiple-step statements. As long as the income statement elements are presented logically, management can choose the format that it wants to use.[6]

---

[6]Later chapters describe other possible elements, such as extraordinary gains and losses, that must be presented in specified locations on the income statement.

Illustration 5–6
Multiple-Step Income
Statement

**MEG'S MART**
**Income Statement**
**For Year Ended December 31, 1997**

| | | |
|---|---:|---:|
| Net sales | | $314,700 |
| Cost of goods sold | | 230,400 |
| Gross profit from sales | | $ 84,300 |
| Operating expenses: | | |
| Selling expenses: | | |
| Amortization expense, store equipment . . . $ 3,000 | | |
| Sales salaries expense 18,500 | | |
| Rent expense, selling space 8,100 | | |
| Store supplies expense 1,200 | | |
| Advertising expense 2,700 | | |
| Total selling expenses | $33,500 | |
| General and administrative expenses: | | |
| Amortization expense, office equipment . . $ 700 | | |
| Office salaries expense 25,300 | | |
| Insurance expense 600 | | |
| Rent expense, office space 900 | | |
| Office supplies expense 1,800 | | |
| Total general and administrative expenses . | 29,300 | |
| Total operating expenses | | 62,800 |
| Net income | | $ 21,500 |

Illustration 5–7
Single-Step Income
Statement

**MEG'S MART**
**Income Statement**
**For Year Ended December 31, 1997**

| | | |
|---|---:|---:|
| Net sales | | $314,700 |
| Cost of goods sold | $230,400 | |
| Selling expenses | 33,500 | |
| General and administrative expenses | 29,300 | |
| Total operating expenses | | 293,200 |
| Net income | | $ 21,500 |

## CLOSING ENTRIES FOR MERCHANDISING COMPANIES

To help you understand how information flows through the accounting system into the financial statements, we now discuss the process for closing the temporary accounts of merchandising companies. The process is demonstrated with data from the adjusted trial balance for Meg's Mart in Illustration 5–8. In addition, the accountant knows from a physical count that the cost of the ending inventory is $21,000.

The trial balance includes these unique accounts for merchandising activities: Merchandise Inventory, Sales, Sales Returns and Allowances, Sales Discounts, Purchases, Purchases Returns and Allowances, Purchases Discounts, and Transportation-In. Their presence in the ledger causes the four closing entries to be slightly different from the ones described in Chapter 4.

Illustration 5–8
Adjusted Trial Balance

**MEG'S MART**
**Adjusted Trial Balance**
**December 31, 1997**

| | | |
|---|---:|---:|
| Cash | $ 8,200 | |
| Accounts receivable | 11,200 | |
| Merchandise inventory | 19,000 | |
| Office supplies | 550 | |
| Store supplies | 250 | |
| Prepaid insurance | 300 | |
| Office equipment | 4,200 | |
| Accumulated amortization, office equipment | | $ 1,400 |
| Store equipment | 30,000 | |
| Accumulated amortization, store equipment | | 6,000 |
| Accounts payable | | 16,000 |
| Salaries payable | | 800 |
| Meg Harlowe, capital | | 34,000 |
| Meg Harlowe, withdrawals | 4,000 | |
| Sales | | 321,000 |
| Sales returns and allowances | 2,000 | |
| Sales discounts | 4,300 | |
| Purchases | 235,800 | |
| Purchases returns and allowances | | 1,500 |
| Purchases discounts | | 4,200 |
| Transportation-in | 2,300 | |
| Amortization expense, store equipment | 3,000 | |
| Amortization expense, office equipment | 700 | |
| Office salaries expense | 25,300 | |
| Sales salaries expense | 18,500 | |
| Insurance expense | 600 | |
| Rent expense, office space | 900 | |
| Rent expense, selling space | 8,100 | |
| Office supplies expense | 1,800 | |
| Store supplies expense | 1,200 | |
| Advertising expense | 2,700 | |
| Totals | $384,900 | $384,900 |

## Entry 1—Record the Ending Inventory and Close the Temporary Accounts that Have Credit Balances

The first entry adds the $21,000 cost of the ending inventory to the balance of the Merchandise Inventory account. It also closes the temporary accounts that have credit balances, including the Sales account and the two contra-purchases accounts. The first closing entry for Meg's Mart is:

| | | | | |
|---|---|---|---:|---:|
| Dec. | 31 | Merchandise Inventory | 21,000.00 | |
| | | Sales | 321,000.00 | |
| | | Purchases Returns and Allowances | 1,500.00 | |
| | | Purchases Discounts | 4,200.00 | |
| | | Income Summary | | 347,700.00 |
| | | *To close temporary accounts with credit balances and record the ending inventory.* | | |

Posting this entry gives zero balances to the three temporary accounts that had credit balances in the adjusted trial balance. It also momentarily increases the balance of the Merchandise Inventory account to $40,000. However, the next entry reduces the balance of this account.

## Entry 2—Remove the Beginning Inventory and Close the Temporary Accounts that Have Debit Balances

The second entry subtracts the cost of the beginning inventory from the Merchandise Inventory account. It also closes the temporary accounts that have debit balances, including the expense accounts, the two contra-sales accounts, the Purchases account, and the Transportation-In account. The second closing entry for Meg's Mart is:

| | | | | |
|---|---|---|---|---|
| Dec. | 31 | Income Summary | 326,200.00 | |
| | | Merchandise Inventory | | 19,000.00 |
| | | Sales Returns and Allowances | | 2,000.00 |
| | | Sales Discounts | | 4,300.00 |
| | | Purchases | | 235,800.00 |
| | | Transportation-In | | 2,300.00 |
| | | Amortization Expense, Store Equipment | | 3,000.00 |
| | | Amortization Expense, Office Equipment | | 700.00 |
| | | Office Salaries Expense | | 25,300.00 |
| | | Sales Salaries Expense | | 18,500.00 |
| | | Insurance Expense | | 600.00 |
| | | Rent Expense, Office Space | | 900.00 |
| | | Rent Expense, Selling Space | | 8,100.00 |
| | | Office Supplies Expense | | 1,800.00 |
| | | Store Supplies Expense | | 1,200.00 |
| | | Advertising Expense | | 2,700.00 |
| | | *To close temporary accounts with debit balances and to remove the beginning inventory balance.* | | |

Posting this entry reduces the balance of the Merchandise Inventory account to $21,000, which is the amount determined by the physical count on December 31, 1997. It also gives zero balances to the 14 temporary accounts that had debit balances.

After posting the first two closing entries, the Merchandise Inventory account appears as follows:

**Merchandise Inventory**                        **Acct. No.** 119

| Date | | Explanation | Debit | Credit | Balance |
|---|---|---|---|---|---|
| 1996 Dec. | 31 | Ending balance for 1996 | | | 19,000.00 |
| 1997 Dec. | 31 | First closing entry | 21,000.00 | | 40,000.00 |
| | 31 | Second closing entry | | 19,000.00 | 21,000.00 |

As mentioned earlier in the chapter, the $21,000 balance will remain unchanged throughout 1998 until the accounts are closed at the end of that year.

## Entry 3—Close the Income Summary Account to the Owner's Capital Account

The third closing entry for a merchandising company is the same as the third closing entry for a service company. It closes the Income Summary account and updates the balance of the owner's capital account. The third closing entry for Meg's Mart is:

| Dec. | 31 | Income Summary ......................... | 21,500.00 | |
|------|----|------------------------------------------|-----------|-----------|
| | | Meg Harlowe, Capital .................... | | 21,500.00 |
| | | *To close the Income Summary account.* | | |

The $21,500 amount in the entry is the net income reported on the income statement.

## Entry 4—Close the Owner's Withdrawals Account to the Owner's Capital Account

The fourth closing entry for a merchandising company is the same as the fourth closing entry for a service company. It closes the owner's withdrawals account and reduces the balance of the owner's capital account to the amount shown on the balance sheet. The fourth closing entry for Meg's Mart is:

| Dec. | 31 | Meg Harlowe, Capital ..................... | 4,000.00 | |
|------|----|-------------------------------------------|----------|----------|
| | | Meg Harlowe, Withdrawals ................ | | 4,000.00 |
| | | *To close the withdrawals account.* | | |

When this entry is posted, all the temporary accounts are cleared and ready to record events in 1998. In addition, the owner's capital account has been fully updated to reflect the events of 1997.

**Progress Check**

**5–8**  Which of the following accounts is not unique to a merchandising company? *(a)* Merchandise Inventory; *(b)* Purchases Returns and Allowances; *(c)* Advertising Expense; *(d)* Transportation-In; *(e)* Purchases.

**5–9**  Which income statement format shows the detailed calculations of net sales and cost of goods sold? Which format does not present any intermediate totals (other than total expenses)?

**5–10**  Which of the four closing entries includes a credit to Merchandise Inventory?

Illustration 5–9 presents a version of the work sheet that the accountant for Meg's Mart could prepare in the process of developing its 1997 financial statements. It differs in two ways from the 10-column work sheet described in Chapter 4.

The first difference is the deletion of the adjusted trial balance columns. Many accountants delete these columns simply to reduce the size of the work sheet. This has nothing to do with the fact that Meg's Mart is a retail business. The omission of the columns causes the accountant to first compute the adjusted balances and then extend them directly into the financial statement columns.

The second difference appears on the line for the Merchandise Inventory account. The unadjusted trial balance includes the beginning inventory balance of $19,000. This amount is extended into the Debit column for the income statement. Then, the ending balance is entered in the Credit column for the income statement and the Debit column for the balance sheet. This step allows the cost of goods sold to be included in net income while the correct ending balance is included for the balance sheet.

The adjustments in the work sheet reflect the following economic events:

*(a)* Expiration of $600 of prepaid insurance.
*(b)* Consumption of $1,200 of store supplies.
*(c)* Consumption of $1,800 of office supplies.
*(d)* Amortization of the store equipment for $3,000.
*(e)* Amortization of the office equipment for $700.
*(f)* Accrual of $300 of unpaid office salaries and $500 of unpaid store salaries.

Once the adjusted amounts are extended into the financial statement columns, the accountant uses the information to develop the company's financial statements.

You have learned in this chapter that a company's current assets may include a merchandise inventory. Thus, you can understand that a major part of a company's current assets may not be available immediately for paying its existing liabilities. The inventory must be sold and the resulting accounts receivable must be collected before cash is available. As a result, the current ratio (which we described in Chapter 3) may not be an adequate indicator of a company's ability to pay its current liabilities.

Another measure that financial statement users often use to evaluate a company's ability to settle its current debts with its existing assets is the **acid-test ratio.** The acid-test ratio is similar to the current ratio, but differs because it excludes the less liquid current assets. The acid-test ratio is calculated just like the current ratio except that its numerator omits inventory and prepaid expenses. The remaining current assets (cash, temporary investments, and receivables) are called the company's *quick assets*. The formula for the ratio is

$$\text{Acid-test ratio} = \frac{\text{Quick assets}}{\text{Current liabilities}}$$

Recall the discussion of **Imperial Oil Limited** at the beginning of the chapter. The acid-test ratios for Imperial Oil are computed as follows:

## A WORK SHEET FOR A MERCHANDISING COMPANY

**LO 4**

Complete a work sheet for a merchandising company and explain the difference between the closing entry and adjusting entry approaches to updating the Merchandise Inventory account.

## USING THE INFORMATION— THE ACID-TEST RATIO

**LO 5**

Calculate the acid-test ratio and describe what it reveals about a company's liquidity.

**Illustration 5–9** Work Sheet for Meg's Mart for the Year Ended December 31, 1997

| No. | Account | Unadjusted Trial Balance Dr. | Cr. | Adjustments Dr. | Cr. | Income Statement Dr. | Cr. | Statement of Changes in Owner's Equity and Balance Sheet Dr. | Cr. |
|---|---|---|---|---|---|---|---|---|---|
| 101 | Cash | 8,200 | | | | | | 8,200 | |
| 106 | Accounts receivable | 11,200 | | | | | | 11,200 | |
| 119 | **Merchandise inventory** | **19,000** | | | | **19,000** | **21,000** | **21,000** | |
| 124 | Office supplies | 2,350 | | | (c) 1,800 | | | 550 | |
| 125 | Store supplies | 1,450 | | | (b) 1,200 | | | 250 | |
| 128 | Prepaid insurance | 900 | | | (a) 600 | | | 300 | |
| 163 | Office equipment | 4,200 | | | | | | 4,200 | |
| 164 | Accum. amort., office equipment | | 700 | | (e) 700 | | | | 1,400 |
| 165 | Store equipment | 30,000 | | | | | | 30,000 | |
| 166 | Accum. amort., store equipment | | 3,000 | | (d) 3,000 | | | | 6,000 |
| 201 | Accounts payable | | 16,000 | | | | | | 16,000 |
| 209 | Salaries payable | | | | (f) 800 | | | | 800 |
| 301 | Meg Harlowe, capital | | 34,000 | | | | | | 34,000 |
| 302 | Meg Harlowe, withdrawals | 4,000 | | | | | | 4,000 | |
| 413 | Sales | | 321,000 | | | | 321,000 | | |
| 414 | Sales returns and allowances | 2,000 | | | | 2,000 | | | |
| 415 | Sales discounts | 4,300 | | | | 4,300 | | | |
| 505 | Purchases | 235,800 | | | | 235,800 | | | |
| 506 | Purchases returns and allowances | | 1,500 | | | | 1,500 | | |
| 507 | Purchases discounts | | 4,200 | | | | 4,200 | | |
| 508 | Transportation-in | 2,300 | | | | 2,300 | | | |
| 612 | Amort. expense, store equipment | | | (d) 3,000 | | 3,000 | | | |
| 613 | Amort. expense, office equipment | | | (e) 700 | | 700 | | | |
| 620 | Office salaries expense | 25,000 | | (f) 300 | | 25,300 | | | |
| 621 | Sales salaries expense | 18,000 | | (f) 500 | | 18,500 | | | |
| 637 | Insurance expense | | | (a) 600 | | 600 | | | |
| 641 | Rent expense, office space | 900 | | | | 900 | | | |
| 642 | Rent expense, selling space | 8,100 | | | | 8,100 | | | |
| 650 | Office supplies expense | | | (c) 1,800 | | 1,800 | | | |
| 651 | Store supplies expense | | | (b) 1,200 | | 1,200 | | | |
| 655 | Advertising expense | 2,700 | | | | 2,700 | | | |
| | Totals | 380,400 | 380,400 | 8,100 | 8,100 | 326,200 | 347,700 | 79,700 | 58,200 |
| | Net income | | | | | 21,500 | | | 21,500 |
| | Totals | | | | | 347,700 | 347,700 | 79,700 | 79,700 |

| | | End of Year | |
|---|---|---|---|
| **Acid-Test Ratios** | | **1994** | **1993** |
| ($409 + $859 + $1,045)/$1,581 | . . . . . . | 1.5 | |
| ($605 + $874 + $899)/$1,593 | . . . . . . . | | 1.5 |

In contrast, the current ratios (current assets/current liabilities) for Imperial Oil have these values:

| Current Ratios | End of Year | |
| | 1994 | 1993 |
|---|---|---|
| $2,797/$1,581 . . . . . . | 1.8 | |
| $2,899/$1,593 . . . . . . | | 1.8 |

A traditional rule of thumb is that an acid-test ratio value of at least 1.0 suggests the company is not likely to face a liquidity crisis in the near future. However, a value less than 1.0 may not be threatening if the company can generate enough cash from sales or the accounts payable are not due until later in the year. On the other hand, a value more than 1.0 may hide a liquidity crisis if the payables are due at once but the receivables will not be collected until late in the year. These possibilities reinforce the point that a single ratio is seldom enough to indicate strength or weakness. However, it can identify areas that the analyst should look into more deeply.

**Progress Check**

**5-11** Which assets are defined as quick assets for the purpose of calculating the acid-test ratio? *(a)* Cash, temporary investments, and prepaid expenses; *(b)* Merchandise inventory and prepaid expenses; *(c)* Merchandise inventory and temporary investments; *(d)* Cash, temporary investments, and receivables.

**5-12** Which ratio is a more strict test of a company's ability to meet its obligations in the very near future, the acid-test ratio or the current ratio?

**SUMMARY OF THE CHAPTER IN TERMS OF LEARNING OBJECTIVES**

**LO 1. Describe merchandising activities, analyze their effects on financial statements, and record sales of merchandise.** Merchandising companies purchase and sell products. Their financial statements include the cost of the merchandise inventory in the current assets on the balance sheet and sales and cost of goods sold on the income statement. The difference between sales and cost of goods sold is called gross profit.

The seller of merchandise records the sale at the list price less any trade discount. Any returns or allowances are recorded in a contra account to provide information to the manager. When cash discounts from the sales price are offered and the customers pay within the discount period, the seller records the discounts in a contra-sales account.

**LO 2. Describe how the ending inventory and the cost of goods sold are determined with perpetual and periodic inventory accounting systems.** A perpetual inventory system continuously tracks the cost of goods on hand and the cost of goods sold. A periodic system merely accumulates the cost of goods purchased during the year and does not provide continuous information about the cost of the inventory or the sold goods. At year-end, the cost of the inventory is determined and used to calculate the cost of goods sold. The cost of goods available for sale equals the beginning inventory plus the cost of goods purchased. The cost of goods sold equals the cost of goods available for sale minus the cost of the ending inventory. The cost of goods purchased is affected by purchases discounts, purchases returns and allowances, and transportation-in. These amounts are recorded in con-tra and supplemental accounts to provide information to management. The contra and supplemental accounts are seldom reported in external statements.

**LO 3. Describe various formats for income statements and prepare clos-ing entries for a merchandising business.** Companies have flexibility in choos-ing formats for their income statements. Internal statements show more details, in-cluding the calculations of net sales and the cost of goods sold. Classified income statements describe expenses incurred in different activities. Multiple-step state-ments include several intermediate totals and single-step statements do not.

In the closing entry approach, the Merchandise Inventory account is updated in the process of making closing entries. The ending inventory amount is added to the account as part of the entry that closes the income statement accounts with credit balances. The beginning inventory amount is removed from the account as part of the entry that closes the income statement accounts with debit balances.

**LO 4. Complete a work sheet that includes the inventory-related accounts.** The work sheet for a merchandising company uses special entries to update the in-ventory. The beginning inventory balance is extended into the Income Statement Debit column and the cost of the ending inventory is entered in the Income State-ment Credit column and Balance Sheet Debit column. Many accountants omit the adjusted trial balance columns to reduce the size of the work sheet.

**LO 5. Calculate the acid-test ratio and describe what it reveals about a company's liquidity.** The acid-test ratio is used to assess a company's ability to pay its current liabilities with its existing quick assets (cash, temporary investments, and receivables). The costs of the merchandise inventory and prepaid expenses are not included in the numerator. A ratio value equal to or greater than one is usually considered to be adequate.

**DEMONSTRATION PROBLEM**

Use the following adjusted trial balance and additional information to complete the re-quirements:

**YE OLDE JUNQUE AND STUFF**
**Adjusted Trial Balance**
**December 31, 1997**

| | | |
|---|---:|---:|
| Cash | $ 19,000 | |
| Merchandise inventory | 52,000 | |
| Store supplies | 1,000 | |
| Equipment | 40,000 | |
| Accumulated amortization, equipment | | $ 16,500 |
| Accounts payable | | 8,000 |
| Salaries payable | | 1,000 |
| Ann Teak, capital | | 69,000 |
| Ann Teak, withdrawals | 8,000 | |
| Sales | | 320,000 |
| Sales discounts | 20,000 | |
| Purchases | 147,000 | |
| Purchases discounts | | 12,000 |
| Transportation-in | 11,000 | |
| Amortization expense | 5,500 | |
| Salaries expense | 60,000 | |
| Insurance expense | 12,000 | |
| Rent expense | 24,000 | |
| Store supplies expense | 6,000 | |
| Advertising expense | 21,000 | |
| Totals | $426,500 | $426,500 |

A physical count shows that the cost of the year's ending inventory is $50,000.

**Required**

1. Prepare schedules that calculate the company's net sales and cost of goods sold for the year.
2. Present a single-step income statement for 1997.
3. Prepare closing entries.

- The calculation of net sales deducts discounts from sales. The calculation of cost of goods sold adds the cost of goods purchased for the year to the beginning inventory and then subtracts the cost of the ending inventory.

- To prepare the single-step income statement, find the net sales and then list the operating expenses. Use the cost of goods sold number calculated in the first requirement.

- The first closing entry debits the inventory account for the cost of the ending inventory and debits all temporary accounts with credit balances. The second closing entry credits the inventory account with the cost of the beginning inventory and credits all temporary accounts with debit balances. The third entry closes the Income Summary account to the owner's capital account, and the fourth closing entry closes the owner's withdrawals account to the owner's capital account.

*Planning the Solution*

1.

| | | |
|---|---:|---:|
| Sales | | $320,000 |
| Less sales discounts | | (20,000) |
| Net sales | | $300,000 |
| Beginning inventory | | $ 52,000 |
| Purchases | $147,000 | |
| Less purchases discounts | (12,000) | |
| Plus transportation-in | 11,000 | |
| Cost of goods purchased | | 146,000 |
| Cost of goods available for sale | | $198,000 |
| Less ending inventory | | (50,000) |
| Cost of goods sold | | $148,000 |

*Solution to Demonstration Problem*

2.

**YE OLDE JUNQUE AND STUFF**
**Income Statement**
**For Year Ended December 31, 1997**

| | | |
|---|---:|---:|
| Net sales | | $300,000 |
| Operating expenses: | | |
| Cost of goods sold | $148,000 | |
| Amortization expense | 5,500 | |
| Salaries expense | 60,000 | |
| Insurance expense | 12,000 | |
| Rent expense | 24,000 | |
| Store supplies expense | 6,000 | |
| Advertising expense | 21,000 | |
| Total expenses | | 276,500 |
| Net income | | $ 23,500 |

3.

| Dec. | 31 | Merchandise Inventory | 50,000.00 | |
| | | Sales | 320,000.00 | |
| | | Purchases Discounts | 12,000.00 | |
| | | Income Summary | | 382,000.00 |
| | | *To close temporary accounts with credit balances and record the ending inventory.* | | |
| Dec. | 31 | Income Summary | 358,500.00 | |
| | | Merchandise Inventory | | 52,000.00 |
| | | Sales Discounts | | 20,000.00 |
| | | Purchases | | 147,000.00 |
| | | Transportation-In | | 11,000.00 |
| | | Amortization Expense | | 5,500.00 |
| | | Salaries Expense | | 60,000.00 |
| | | Insurance Expense | | 12,000.00 |
| | | Rent Expense | | 24,000.00 |
| | | Store Supplies Expense | | 6,000.00 |
| | | Advertising Expense | | 21,000.00 |
| | | *To close temporary accounts with debit balances and to remove the beginning inventory balance.* | | |
| Dec. | 31 | Income Summary | 23,500.00 | |
| | | Ann Teak, Capital | | 23,500.00 |
| | | *To close the Income Summary account.* | | |
| Dec. | 31 | Ann Teak, Capital | 8,000.00 | |
| | | Ann Teak, Withdrawals | | 8,000.00 |
| | | *To close the withdrawals account.* | | |

# The Adjusting Entry Approach to Recording the Change in the Merchandise Inventory Account

In the previous sections, the change in the Merchandise Inventory account was recorded in the process of making closing entries. This closing entry approach is widely used in practice. However, it is not the only bookkeeping method that can be applied at the end of the year. Another approach is to record the change in the Merchandise Inventory account with adjusting entries. When this approach is followed, the first two closing entries do not include changes in the Merchandise Inventory account. This adjusting entry approach is preferred by some accountants. It is also used by many computerized accounting systems that do not allow the Merchandise Inventory account (a permanent account) to be changed in the closing process.

**LO 7**

Explain an adjusting entry approach to recording the change in the Merchandise Inventory account.

## The Adjusting Entries

Under the adjusting entry approach, Meg's Mart removes the beginning balance from the Merchandise Inventory account by recording this adjusting entry at the end of 1997:

| Dec. | 31 | Income Summary .......................... | 19,000.00 | |
|------|----|--------------------------------------------|-----------|-----------|
| | | Merchandise Inventory ................... | | 19,000.00 |
| | | *To remove the beginning balance from the* | | |
| | | *Merchandise Inventory account.* | | |

The second adjusting entry produces the correct ending balance in the Merchandise Inventory account:

| Dec. | 31 | Merchandise Inventory ..................... | 21,000.00 | |
|------|----|--------------------------------------------|-----------|-----------|
| | | Income Summary ......................... | | 21,000.00 |
| | | *To insert the correct ending balance into the* | | |
| | | *Merchandise Inventory account.* | | |

265

After this entry is posted, the Merchandise Inventory account has a $21,000 debit balance. In addition, the Income Summary account has a $2,000 credit balance.

## The Closing Entries

If the two adjusting entries for inventory are used, the closing entries differ only by not including the Merchandise Inventory account. Thus, Meg's Mart records the following two closing entries for 1997 under the adjusting entry approach:

| Dec. | 31 | Sales | 321,000.00 | |
| | | Purchases Returns and Allowances | 1,500.00 | |
| | | Purchases Discounts | 4,200.00 | |
| | |     Income Summary | | 326,700.00 |
| | | *To close temporary accounts with credit balances.* | | |

| Dec. | 31 | Income Summary | 307,200.00 | |
| | |     Sales Returns and Allowances | | 2,000.00 |
| | |     Sales Discounts | | 4,300.00 |
| | |     Purchases | | 235,800.00 |
| | |     Transportation-In | | 2,300.00 |
| | |     Amortization Expense, Store Equipment | | 3,000.00 |
| | |     Amortization Expense, Office Equipment | | 700.00 |
| | |     Office Salaries Expense | | 25,300.00 |
| | |     Sales Salaries Expense | | 18,500.00 |
| | |     Insurance Expense | | 600.00 |
| | |     Rent Expense, Office Space | | 900.00 |
| | |     Rent Expense, Selling Space | | 8,100.00 |
| | |     Office Supplies Expense | | 1,800.00 |
| | |     Store Supplies Expense | | 1,200.00 |
| | |     Advertising Expense | | 2,700.00 |
| | | *To close temporary accounts with debit balances.* | | |

The third and fourth entries are the same as before, although now the amount debited to the Income Summary account is based on four previous entries instead of two:

| Dec. | 31 | Income Summary | 21,500.00 | |
| | |     Meg Harlowe, Capital | | 21,500.00 |
| | | *To close the Income Summary account.* | | |
| Dec. | 31 | Meg Harlowe, Capital | 4,000.00 | |
| | |     Meg Harlowe, Withdrawals | | 4,000.00 |
| | | *To close the withdrawals account.* | | |

**The Adjusting Entry Approach and the Work Sheet.** If the accountant uses the adjusting entry approach to update the inventory account, the two adjustments are included in the adjustments columns in the work sheet, and a line for the Income Summary account is inserted at the bottom of the work sheet.

**Progress Check**

**5–13** In which of the following columns is the ending inventory entered on the work sheet when the closing entry approach is used to record the change in inventory? *(a)* Unadjusted Trial Balance Debit Column; *(b)* Adjustments Debit column; *(c)* Income Statement Debit column; *(d)* Income Statement Credit column; *(e)* Balance Sheet Credit column.

**5–14** Will the reported amounts of ending inventory and net income differ if the adjusting entry approach to recording the change in inventory is used instead of the closing entry approach?

**LO 7. Explain an adjusting entry approach to recording the change in the Merchandise Inventory account.** The adjusting entry approach to recording the ending inventory in the accounts uses two adjusting entries that remove the beginning cost from and add the ending cost to the Merchandise Inventory account. This approach is often used in computer systems.

**SUMMARY OF APPENDIX E IN TERMS OF LEARNING OBJECTIVE**

## GLOSSARY

**Acid-test ratio** a ratio used to assess the company's ability to settle its current debts with its existing assets; it is the ratio between a company's quick assets (cash, temporary investments, and receivables) and its current liabilities. p. 259

**Cash discount** a reduction in a debt that is granted by a seller to a purchaser in exchange for the purchaser's making payment within a specified period of time called the discount period. p. 241

**Classified income statement** an income statement format that classifies items in significant groups and shows detailed calculations of sales and cost of goods sold. p. 253

**Credit memorandum** a notification that the sender has entered a credit in the recipient's account maintained by the sender. p. 251

**Credit period** the time period that can pass before a customer's payment is due. p. 241

**Credit terms** the description of the amounts and timing of payments that a buyer agrees to make in the future. p. 241

**Debit memorandum** a notification that the sender has entered a debit in the recipient's account maintained by the sender. p. 251

**Discount period** the time period in which a cash discount is available. p. 242

**EOM** the abbreviation for *end-of-month*; used to describe credit terms for some transactions. p. 241

**FOB** the abbreviation for *free on board;* the designated point at which ownership of goods passes to the buyer; FOB shipping point (or factory) means that the buyer pays the shipping costs and FOB destination means that the seller pays the shipping costs. p. 250

**General and administrative expenses** expenses that support the overall operations of a business and include the expenses of such activities as providing accounting services, human resource management, and financial management. p. 253

**Gross profit** the difference between net sales and the cost of goods sold. p. 239

**List price** the nominal price of an item before any trade discount is deducted. p. 247

**Merchandise** goods acquired for the purpose of reselling them to customers. p. 238

**Merchandise inventory** goods a company owns on any given date and holds for the purpose of selling them to its customers. p. 239

**Multiple-step income statement** an income statement format that shows several intermediate totals between sales and net income. p. 253

**Periodic inventory system** a method of accounting that records the cost of inventory purchased but does not track the quantity on hand or sold to customers; the records are updated periodically to reflect the results of physical counts of the items on hand. p. 243

**Perpetual inventory system** a method of accounting that maintains continuous records of the amount of inventory on hand and sold. p. 243

**Purchases discount** a cash discount taken against an amount owed to a supplier of goods. p. 247

**Sales discount** a cash discount taken by customers against an amount owed to the seller. p. 242

**Selling expenses** the expenses of promoting sales by displaying and advertising the merchandise, making sales, and delivering goods to customers. p. 253

**Shrinkage** inventory losses that occur as a result of shoplifting or deterioration. p. 252

**Single-step income statement** an income statement format that does not present intermediate totals other than total expenses. p. 253

**Trade discount** a reduction below a list or catalogue price that is negotiated in setting the selling price of goods. p. 247

---

## SYNONYMOUS TERMS

**Actual sales price** invoice price
**FOB factory** FOB shipping point
**Gross profit** gross margin

**List price** catalogue price
**Merchandise** goods

---

*The letter E identifies the questions, quick studies, exercises, and problems based on Appendix E at the end of the chapter.*

---

## QUESTIONS

1. What item on the balance sheet is unique to merchandising companies? What items on the income statement are unique to merchandising companies?

2. Explain how a business can earn a gross profit on its sales and still have a net loss.

3. Why would a company offer a cash discount?

4. What is the difference between a sales discount and a purchases discount?

5. In counting the ending inventory, an employee omitted the contents of one shelf that contained merchandise with a cost of $2,300. How would this omission affect the company's balance sheet and income statement?

6. Distinguish between cash discounts and trade discounts. Is the amount of a trade discount on purchased merchandise recorded in the Purchases Discounts account?

7. Why would a company's manager be concerned about the quantity of its purchases returns if its suppliers allow unlimited returns?

8. What do the sender and the recipient of a debit memorandum record in their accounts?

9. What is the difference between single-step and multiple-step income statement formats?

10. Does the beginning or ending inventory appear on the unadjusted trial balance of a company that uses a periodic inventory system?

11. How and when is cost of goods sold determined in a store that uses a periodic inventory system?

12. When is the cost of goods sold recorded when a company uses a perpetual inventory system?

13. Why should the manager of a business be interested in the amount of its sales returns and allowances?

14. Since sales returns and allowances are subtracted from sales on the income statement, why not save the effort of this subtraction by debiting all such returns and allowances directly to the Sales account?

# QUICK STUDY (Five-Minute Exercises)

Calculate net sales and gross profit in each of the following situations:

QS 5–1
(LO 1)

|  | a | b | c | d |
|---|---|---|---|---|
| Sales | $125,000 | $505,000 | $33,700 | $256,700 |
| Sales discounts | 3,200 | 13,500 | 300 | 4,000 |
| Sales returns and allowances | 19,000 | 3,000 | 6,000 | 600 |
| Cost of goods sold | 67,600 | 352,700 | 22,300 | 123,900 |

A company purchased merchandise that cost $165,000 during the year that just ended. Determine the company's cost of goods sold in each of the following four situations:

QS 5–2
(LO 2)

a. There were no beginning or ending inventories.

b. There was a beginning inventory of $35,000 and no ending inventory.

c. There was a $30,000 beginning inventory and a $42,000 ending inventory.

d. There was no beginning inventory but there was a $21,000 ending inventory.

Given the following accounts with normal year-end balances, prepare the entry to close the income statement accounts that have debit balances (entry 2):

QS 5–3
(LO 3)

| | |
|---|---|
| Merchandise inventory | $ 34,800 |
| Jan Dean, capital | 115,300 |
| Jan Dean, withdrawals | 4,000 |
| Sales | 157,200 |
| Sales returns and allowances | 3,500 |
| Sales discounts | 1,700 |
| Purchases | 102,000 |
| Purchases returns and allowances | 8,100 |
| Purchases discounts | 2,000 |
| Transportation-in | 5,400 |
| Amortization expense | 7,300 |
| Salaries expense | 29,500 |
| Miscellaneous expenses | 1,900 |

Refer to the information in QS 5–3. Prepare the entry to close the income statement accounts that have debit balances (entry 2) assuming the business uses the adjusting entry approach to record the change in merchandise inventory.

EQS 5–4
(LO 4)

Use the following information to calculate the acid-test ratio:

QS 5–5
(LO 5)

| | |
|---|---|
| Cash | $1,000 |
| Accounts receivable | 2,500 |
| Inventory | 6,000 |
| Prepaid expenses | 500 |
| Accounts payable | 3,750 |
| Other current liabilities | 1,250 |

# EXERCISES

**Exercise 5–1**
**Merchandising terms**
**(LO 1, 2)**

Insert the letter for each term in the blank space beside the definition that it most closely matches:

A. Cash discount       E. FOB shipping point       H. Purchases discount

B. Credit period       F. Gross profit       I. Sales discount

C. Discount period       G. Inventory       J. Trade discount

D. FOB destination

_____ 1. An agreement that ownership of goods is transferred at the buyer's place of business.

_____ 2. The time period in which a cash discount is available

_____ 3. The difference between net sales and the cost of goods sold.

_____ 4. A reduction in a receivable or payable that is granted if it is paid within the discount period.

_____ 5. A cash discount taken against an amount owed to a supplier of goods.

_____ 6. An agreement that ownership of goods is transferred at the seller's place of business.

_____ 7. A reduction below a list or catalogue price that is negotiated in setting the selling price of goods.

_____ 8. A cash discount taken by customers against an amount owed to the seller.

_____ 9. The time period that can pass before a customer's payment is due.

_____ 10. The goods that a company owns and expects to sell to its customers.

**Exercise 5–2**
**Calculating cost of goods sold**
**(LO 2)**

Determine each of the missing numbers in the following situations:

| | a | b | c |
|---|---|---|---|
| Purchases | $45,000 | $80,000 | $61,000 |
| Purchases discounts | 2,000 | ? | 1,300 |
| Purchases returns and allowances | 1,500 | 3,000 | 2,200 |
| Transportation-in | ? | 7,000 | 8,000 |
| Beginning inventory | 3,500 | ? | 18,000 |
| Cost of goods purchased | 44,700 | 79,000 | ? |
| Ending inventory | 2,200 | 15,000 | ? |
| Cost of goods sold | ? | 83,200 | 68,260 |

**Exercise 5–3**
**Recording journal entries for merchandise transactions**
**(LO 2)**

Prepare journal entries to record the following transactions for a retail store:

March   2   Purchased merchandise from Alfa Company under the following terms: $1,800 invoice price, 2/15, n/60, FOB factory.

       3   Paid $125 for shipping charges on the purchase of March 2.

       4   Returned to Alfa Company unacceptable merchandise that had an invoice price of $300.

      17   Sent a cheque to Alfa Company for the March 2 purchase, net of the discount and the returned merchandise.

March 18 Purchased merchandise from Bravo Company under the following terms: $2,500 invoice price, 2/10, n/30, FOB destination.

21 After brief negotiations, received a credit memorandum from Bravo Company granting a $700 allowance on the purchase of March 18.

28 Sent a cheque to Bravo Company paying for the March 18 purchase, net of the discount and the allowance.

On May 12, Wilcox Company accepted delivery of $20,000 of merchandise and received an invoice dated May 11, with terms of 3/10, n/30, FOB Garner Company's factory. When the goods were delivered, Wilcox Company paid $185 to Express Shipping Service for the delivery charges on the merchandise. The next day, Wilcox Company returned $800 of defective goods to the seller, which received them one day later. On May 21, Wilcox Company mailed a cheque to Garner Company for the amount owed on that date. It was received the following day.

**Exercise 5–4**
Analyzing and recording merchandise transactions and returns
**(LO 1, 2)**

**Required**

a. Present the journal entries that Wilcox Company should record for these transactions.

b. Present the journal entries that Garner Company should record for these transactions.

Sandra's Store purchased merchandise from a manufacturer with an invoice price of $11,000 and credit terms of 3/10, n/60, and paid within the discount period.

**Exercise 5–5**
Analyzing and recording merchandise transactions and discounts
**(LO 1, 2)**

**Required**

a. Prepare the journal entries that the purchaser should record for the purchase and payment.

b. Prepare the journal entries that the seller should record for the sale and collection.

c. Assume that the buyer borrowed enough cash to pay the balance on the last day of the discount period at an annual interest rate of 8% and paid it back on the last day of the credit period. Calculate how much the buyer saved by following this strategy. (Use a 365-day year.)

The following information appeared in a company's income statement:

**Exercise 5–6**
Calculating expenses and cost of goods sold
**(LO 1, 2)**

| | |
|---|---:|
| Sales | $300,000 |
| Sales returns | 15,000 |
| Sales discounts | 4,500 |
| Beginning inventory | 25,000 |
| Purchases | 180,000 |
| Purchases returns and allowances | 6,000 |
| Purchases discounts | 3,600 |
| Transportation-in | 11,000 |
| Gross profit from sales | 105,000 |
| Net income | 55,000 |

**Required**

Calculate the (a) total operating expenses, (b) cost of goods sold, and (c) ending inventory.

**Exercise 5–7**
**Calculating expenses**
**and income**
**(LO 1, 2)**

Fill in the blanks in the following income statements. Identify any losses by putting the amount in parentheses.

|  | a | b | c | d | e |
|---|---|---|---|---|---|
| Sales | $40,000 | $85,000 | $24,000 | $  ? | $59,000 |
| Cost of goods sold: |  |  |  |  |  |
| Beginning inventory | $ 4,000 | $ 6,200 | $ 5,000 | $ 3,500 | $ 6,400 |
| Purchases | 24,000 | ? | ? | 16,000 | 14,000 |
| Ending inventory | ? | (5,400) | (6,000) | (3,300) | ? |
| Cost of goods sold | $22,700 | $31,800 | $  ? | $  ? | $14,000 |
| Gross profit | $  ? | $  ? | $ 2,500 | $22,800 | $  ? |
| Expenses | 6,000 | 21,300 | 8,100 | 1,300 | 15,000 |
| Net income (loss) | $  ? | $31,900 | $ (5,600) | $21,500 | $  ? |

**Exercise 5–8**
**Multiple-step income**
**statement and other**
**calculations**
**(LO 3)**

The following accounts and balances are taken from the year-end adjusted trial balance of the Vintage Shop, a single proprietorship. Use the information in these columns to complete the requirements.

|  | Debit | Credit |
|---|---|---|
| Merchandise inventory | $ 28,000 |  |
| Sales |  | $425,000 |
| Sales returns and allowances | 16,500 |  |
| Sales discounts | 4,000 |  |
| Purchases | 240,000 |  |
| Purchases returns and allowances |  | 18,000 |
| Purchases discounts |  | 2,000 |
| Transportation-in | 6,000 |  |
| Selling expenses | 35,000 |  |
| General and administrative expenses | 95,000 |  |

The count of the ending inventory shows that its cost is $37,000.

**Required**

a.  Calculate the company's net sales for the year.

b.  Calculate the company's cost of goods purchased for the year.

c.  Calculate the company's cost of goods sold for the year.

d.  Prepare a multiple-step income statement for the year that lists net sales, cost of goods sold, gross profit, the operating expenses, and net income.

**Exercise 5–9**
**Classified income**
**statement**
**(LO 3)**

Use the information provided in Exercise 5–8 to prepare a classified income statement that shows the calculations of net sales and cost of goods sold.

**Exercise 5–10**
**Closing entries**
**(LO 3)**

The Vintage Shop described in Exercise 5–8 is owned and operated by Otto Vintage. The ending balance of Vintage's withdrawals account is $25,000. Prepare four closing entries for this company. Post the entries to a balance column account for Merchandise Inventory that includes the beginning balance.

The Vintage Shop described in Exercise 5–8 is owned and operated by Otto Vintage. The ending balance of Vintage's withdrawals account is $25,000. Assume that the company uses the adjusting entry approach to update its inventory account. Prepare adjusting and closing journal entries for this company, and post them to a balance column account for Merchandise Inventory that includes the beginning balance.

EExercise 5–11
Adjusting entry approach
(LO 7)

The following closing entries for Fox Fixtures Co. were made on March 31, the end of its annual accounting period:

Exercise 5–12
Preparing reports from closing entries
(LO 3)

| 1. | Merchandise Inventory | 11,000.00 | |
|---|---|---|---|
| | Sales | 445,000.00 | |
| | Purchases Returns and Allowances | 22,000.00 | |
| | Purchases Discounts | 11,400.00 | |
| | Income Summary | | 489,400.00 |
| | *To close temporary accounts with credit balances and record the ending inventory.* | | |
| 2. | Income Summary | 453,300.00 | |
| | Merchandise Inventory | | 15,000.00 |
| | Sales Returns and Allowances | | 25,000.00 |
| | Sales Discounts | | 16,000.00 |
| | Purchases | | 286,000.00 |
| | Transportation-In | | 8,800.00 |
| | Selling Expenses | | 69,000.00 |
| | General and Administrative Expenses | | 33,500.00 |
| | *To close temporary accounts with debit balances and to remove the beginning inventory balance.* | | |

**Required**

Use the information in the closing entries to prepare:

*a.* A calculation of net sales.

*b.* A calculation of cost of goods purchased.

*c.* A calculation of cost of goods sold.

*d.* A multiple-step income statement for the year that lists net sales, cost of goods sold, gross profit, the operating expenses, and net income.

The following unadjusted trial balance was taken from the ledger of Johnson's Newsstand at the end of its fiscal year. (To reduce your effort, the account balances are relatively small.)

Exercise 5–13
Preparing a work sheet for a merchandising proprietorship
(LO 4)

**JOHNSON'S NEWSSTAND**
**Unadjusted Trial Balance**
**December 31**

| No. | Title | Debit | Credit |
|---|---|---|---|
| 101 | Cash . . . . . . . . . . . . . . . . . . . . . | $ 3,700 | |
| 106 | Accounts receivable . . . . . . . . . . | 1,800 | |
| 119 | Merchandise inventory . . . . . . . . | 1,200 | |
| 125 | Store supplies . . . . . . . . . . . . . | 600 | |
| 201 | Accounts payable . . . . . . . . . . | | $ 140 |
| 209 | Salaries payable . . . . . . . . . . . . | | |
| 301 | Tod Johnson, capital . . . . . . . . | | 5,785 |
| 302 | Tod Johnson, withdrawals . . . . . . | 375 | |
| 413 | Sales . . . . . . . . . . . . . . . . . . . . | | 6,000 |
| 414 | Sales returns and allowances . . . . | 145 | |
| 505 | Purchases . . . . . . . . . . . . . . . . | 3,200 | |
| 506 | Purchases discounts . . . . . . . . . . | | 125 |
| 507 | Transportation-in . . . . . . . . . . . . | 80 | |
| 622 | Salaries expense . . . . . . . . . . . . | 700 | |
| 640 | Rent expense . . . . . . . . . . . . . . | 250 | |
| 651 | Store supplies expense . . . . . . . . | | |
| | Totals . . . . . . . . . . . . . . . . . . | $12,050 | $12,050 |

**Required**

Use the preceding information and the following additional facts to complete an eight-column work sheet for the company (do not include columns for the adjusted trial balance).

*a.* The ending inventory of store supplies was $450.

*b.* Accrued salaries at the end of the year were $60.

*c.* The ending merchandise inventory was $1,360.

**Exercise 5–14**
**Acid-test ratio**
**(LO 5)**

Calculate the current and acid-test ratios in each of the following cases:

| | Case X | Case Y | Case Z |
|---|---|---|---|
| Cash . . . . . . . . . . . . . . . . | $ 800 | $ 910 | $1,100 |
| Temporary investments . . . . | | | 500 |
| Receivables . . . . . . . . . . . . | | 990 | 800 |
| Inventory . . . . . . . . . . . . . | 2,000 | 1,000 | 4,000 |
| Prepaid expenses . . . . . . . . | 1,200 | 600 | 900 |
| Total current assets . . . . . . . | $4,000 | $3,500 | $7,300 |
| Current liabilities . . . . . . . . | $2,200 | $1,100 | $3,650 |

# PROBLEMS

**Problem 5–1**
**Journal entries for merchandising activities**
**(LO 1, 2)**

Prepare general journal entries to record the following transactions of the Belton Company and determine the cost of goods purchased and net sales for the month. (Use a separate account for each receivable and payable; for example, record the purchase on July 1 in Accounts Payable—Jones Co.)

July  1  Purchased merchandise from the Jones Company for $3,000 under credit terms of 1/15, n/30, FOB factory.

July 2   Sold merchandise to Terra Co. for $800 under credit terms of 2/10, n/60, FOB shipping point.

3   Paid $100 for freight charges on the purchase of July 1.

8   Sold $1,600 of merchandise for cash.

9   Purchased merchandise from the Keene Co. for $2,300 under credit terms of 2/15, n/30, FOB destination.

12   Received a $200 credit memorandum acknowledging the return of merchandise purchased on July 9.

13   Received the balance due from the Terra Co. for the credit sale dated July 2, net of the discount.

16   Paid the balance due to the Jones Company within the discount period.

19   Sold merchandise to Urban Co. for $1,250 under credit terms of 2/10, n/60, FOB shipping point.

21   Issued a $150 credit memorandum to Urban Co. for an allowance on goods sold on July 19.

22   Received a debit memorandum from Urban Co. for an error that overstated the total invoice by $50.

24   Paid the Keene Co. the balance due after deducting the discount.

30   Received the balance due from the Urban Co. for the credit sale dated July 19, net of the discount.

31   Sold merchandise to Terra Co. for $5,000 under credit terms of 2/10, n/60, FOB shipping point.

Prepare general journal entries to record the following transactions of Schafer Merchandising:

**Problem 5–2**
Journal entries for merchandising transactions
**(LO 1, 2)**

Oct. 1   Purchased merchandise on credit, terms 2/10, n/30, $7,200.

2   Sold merchandise for cash, $750.

7   Purchased merchandise on credit, terms 2/10, n/30, $5,250, FOB the seller's factory.

7   Paid $225 cash for freight charges on the merchandise shipment of the previous transaction.

8   Purchased delivery equipment on credit, $12,000.

12   Sold merchandise on credit, terms 2/15, 1/30, n/60, $3,000.

13   Received a $750 credit memorandum for merchandise purchased on October 7 and returned for credit.

13   Purchases office supplies on credit, $240, n/30.

15   Sold merchandise on credit, terms 2/10, 1/30, n/60, $2,100.

15   Paid for the merchandise purchased on October 7, less the return and the discount.

16   Received a credit memorandum for unsatisfactory office supplies purchased on October 13 and returned, $60.

19   Issued a $210 credit memorandum to the customer who purchased merchandise on October 15 and returned a portion for credit.

25   Received payment for the merchandise sold on October 15, less the return and applicable discount.

27   The customer of October 12 paid for the purchase of that date, less the applicable discount.

31   Paid for the merchandise purchased on October 1.

**Problem 5–3**
Income statements and
closing entries
**(LO 1, 2, 3)**

On December 31, 1996, the end of Seaside Sales' annual accounting period, the financial statement columns of its work sheet appeared as follows:

| | Income Statement | | Balance Sheet | |
|---|---|---|---|---|
| | **Debit** | **Credit** | **Debit** | **Credit** |
| Merchandise inventory .............. | 69,330 | 66,545 | 66,545 | |
| Other assets ...................... | | | 487,785 | |
| Debra Kelso, capital .............. | | | | 200,000 |
| Liabilities ....................... | | | | 312,370 |
| Debra Kelso, withdrawals ........... | | | 50,000 | |
| Sales .......................... | | 963,720 | | |
| Sales returns and allowances .......... | 5,715 | | | |
| Sales discounts ................... | 14,580 | | | |
| Purchases ....................... | 651,735 | | | |
| Purchases returns and allowances ....... | | 2,730 | | |
| Purchases discounts ............... | | 8,970 | | |
| Transportation-in ................. | 9,205 | | | |
| Sales salaries expense .............. | 80,080 | | | |
| Rent expense, selling space .......... | 33,000 | | | |
| Store supplies expense ............. | 1,620 | | | |
| Amortization expense, store equipment . . . | 8,910 | | | |
| Office salaries expense ............. | 65,945 | | | |
| Rent expense, office space ........... | 3,000 | | | |
| Office supplies expense ............. | 735 | | | |
| Insurance expense ................. | 3,390 | | | |
| Amortization expense, office equipment . . | 2,760 | | | |
| | 950,005 | 1,041,965 | 604,330 | 512,370 |
| Net income ..................... | 91,960 | | | 91,960 |
| | 1,041,965 | 1,041,965 | 604,330 | 604,330 |

**Required**

1. Prepare a 1996 classified, multiple-step income statement for Seaside, showing in detail the expenses and the items that make up cost of goods sold.

2. Prepare compound closing entries for Seaside.

3. Open a Merchandise Inventory account and enter a December 31, 1995, balance of $69,330. Then post those portions of the closing entries that affect the account.

4. Prepare a single-step income statement. Condense each revenue and expense category into a single item.

The December 31, 1996, year-end, unadjusted trial balance of the ledger of Eastman Store, a single proprietorship business, is as follows:

**Problem 5–4**
Proprietorship work
sheet, income statement,
and closing entries
(LO 2, 3, 4)

**EASTMAN STORE**
**Unadjusted Trial Balance**
**December 31, 1996**

| | | |
|---|---:|---:|
| Cash | $ 7,305 | |
| Merchandise inventory | 47,000 | |
| Store supplies | 1,715 | |
| Office supplies | 645 | |
| Prepair insurance | 3,840 | |
| Store equipment | 57,735 | |
| Accumulated amortization, store equipment | | $ 9,575 |
| Office equipment | 14,130 | |
| Accumulated amortization, office equipment | | 3,670 |
| Accounts payable | | 4,680 |
| Bob Eastman, capital | | 93,585 |
| Bob Eastman, withdrawals | 31,500 | |
| Sales | | 478,850 |
| Sales returns and allowances | 3,185 | |
| Sales discounts | 5,190 | |
| Purchases | 331,315 | |
| Purchases returns and allowances | | 1,845 |
| Purchases discounts | | 4,725 |
| Transportation-in | 2,810 | |
| Sales salaries expense | 34,710 | |
| Rent expense, selling space | 24,000 | |
| Advertising expense | 1,220 | |
| Store supplies expense | –0– | |
| Amortization expense, store equipment | –0– | |
| Office salaries expense | 27,630 | |
| Rent expense, office space | 3,000 | |
| Office supplies expense | –0– | |
| Insurance expense | –0– | |
| Amortization expense, office equipment | –0– | |
| Totals | $596,930 | $596,930 |

**Required**

1. Copy the unadjusted trial balance on a work sheet form and complete the work sheet using the following information:

   a. Store supplies inventory, $385.

   b. Office supplies inventory, $180.

   c. Expired insurance, $2,765.

   d. Amortization on the store equipment, $5,865.

   e. Amortization on the office equipment, $1,755.

   f. Ending merchandise inventory, $48,980.

2. Journalize closing entries for the store.

3. Open a balance column Merchandise Inventory account and enter a December 31, 1995, balance of $47,000. Then post those portions of the closing entries that affect the account.

The following amounts appeared on the Gershwin Company's adjusted trial balance as of October 31, the end of its fiscal year:

|  | Debit | Credit |
|---|---|---|
| Merchandise inventory .......... | $ 25,000 |  |
| Other assets ................... | 140,000 |  |
| Liabilities ..................... |  | $ 37,000 |
| G. Gershwin, capital ............ |  | 117,650 |
| G. Gershwin, withdrawals ........ | 17,000 |  |
| Sales ........................ |  | 210,000 |
| Sales returns and allowances ....... | 15,000 |  |
| Sales discounts ................ | 2,250 |  |
| Purchases .................... | 90,000 |  |
| Purchases returns and allowances .... |  | 4,300 |
| Purchases discounts ............. |  | 1,800 |
| Transportation-in ............... | 3,100 |  |
| Sales salaries expense ............ | 28,000 |  |
| Rent expense, selling space ........ | 10,000 |  |
| Store supplies expense ........... | 3,000 |  |
| Advertising expense ............ | 18,000 |  |
| Office salaries expense ........... | 16,000 |  |
| Rent expense, office space ......... | 2,500 |  |
| Office supplies expense ........... | 900 |  |
| Totals ...................... | $370,750 | $370,750 |

A physical count shows that the cost of the ending inventory is $27,000.

**Required**

1. Calculate the company's net sales for the year.

2. Calculate the company's cost of goods purchased for the year.

3. Calculate the company's cost of goods sold for the year.

4. Present a multiple-step income statement that lists the company's net sales, cost of goods sold, and gross profit, as well as the components and amounts of selling expenses and general and administrative expenses.

5. Present a condensed single-step income statement that lists these expenses: cost of goods sold, selling expenses, and general and administrative expenses.

**Problem 5–6**
Closing entries and interpreting information about discounts and returns
**(LO 1, 3)**

Use the data for the Gershwin Company in Problem 5–5 to meet the following requirements:

**Required**

*Preparation component:*

1. Prepare closing entries for the company as of October 31.

*Analysis component:*

2. All of the company's purchases were made on credit and the suppliers uniformly offer a 3% discount. Does it appear that the company's cash management system is accomplishing the goal of taking all available discounts?

3. In prior years, the company has experienced a 4% return rate on its sales, which means that approximately 4% of its gross sales were for items that were eventually returned outright or that caused the company to grant allowances to customers. How does this year's record compare to prior years' results?

Refer to the Gershwin Company data in Problem 5-5 and notice that the adjusted trial balance reflects the closing entry approach to account for merchandise inventory. Now assume that the company has decided to switch to the adjusting entry approach.

**EProblem 5–7**
Adjusting entries,
closing entries, and
interpreting information
about discounts and
returns
**(LO 1, 3, 4)**

**Required**

*Preparation component:*

1. Prepare adjusting entries to update the Merchandise Inventory account at October 31 and then prepare closing entries for the company as of October 31.

*Analysis component:*

2. All of the company's purchases were made on credit and the suppliers uniformly offer a 2.1% discount. Does it appear that the company's cash management system is accomplishing the goal of taking all available discounts?

3. In prior years, the company has experienced a 9% return rate on its sales, which means that approximately 9% of its gross sales were for items that were eventually returned outright or that caused the company to grant allowances to customers. How does this year's record compare to prior years' results?

The following unadjusted trial balance was prepared at the end of the fiscal year for Ruth's Place:

**Problem 5–8**
Work sheet, income
statements, and acid-test
ratio
**(LO 3, 4, 5)**

### RUTH'S PLACE
### Unadjusted Trial Balance
### December 31

| | | | |
|---|---|---:|---:|
| 101 | Cash | $ 4,000 | |
| 119 | Merchandise inventory | 9,900 | |
| 125 | Store supplies | 5,000 | |
| 128 | Prepaid insurance | 2,000 | |
| 165 | Store equipment | 45,000 | |
| 166 | Accumulated amortization, store equipment | | $ 6,000 |
| 201 | Accounts payable | | 8,000 |
| 301 | Ruth Helm, capital | | 35,200 |
| 302 | Ruth Helm, withdrawals | 3,500 | |
| 413 | Sales | | 90,000 |
| 415 | Sales discounts | 1,000 | |
| 505 | Purchases | 38,000 | |
| 506 | Purchases returns and allowances | | 800 |
| 508 | Transportation-in | 1,800 | |
| 612 | Amortization expense, store equipment | | |
| 622 | Salaries expense | 16,000 | |
| 637 | Insurance expense | | |
| 640 | Rent expense | 5,000 | |
| 651 | Store supplies expense | | |
| 655 | Advertising expense | 8,800 | |
| | Totals | $140,000 | $140,000 |

**Required**

1. Use the unadjusted trial balance and the following information to prepare an eight-column work sheet for the company:

   *a.* The ending inventory of store supplies is $650.

   *b.* Expired insurance for the year is $1,200.

*c.* Amortization expense for the year is $9,000.

*d.* The ending merchandise inventory is $11,500.

2. Prepare a detailed multiple-step income statement that would be used by the store's owner.

3. Prepare a single-step income statement that would be provided to decision makers outside the company.

4. Compute the company's current and acid-test ratios as of December 31.

**Problem 5–9**
Proprietorship work sheet, financial statements, and closing entries
**(LO 1, 2, 4)**

The unadjusted trial balance of Classic Threads on December 31, 1996, the end of the annual accounting period, is as follows:

**CLASSIC THREADS**
**Unadjusted Trial Balance**
**December 31, 1996**

| | | |
|---|---:|---:|
| Cash | $ 10,275 | |
| Accounts receivable | 22,665 | |
| Merchandise inventory | 51,845 | |
| Store supplies | 2,415 | |
| Office supplies | 775 | |
| Prepaid insurance | 3,255 | |
| Store equipment | 61,980 | |
| Accumulated amortization, store equipment | | $ 10,830 |
| Office equipment | 12,510 | |
| Accumulated amortization, office equipment | | 2,825 |
| Accounts payable | | 8,310 |
| Salaries payable | | –0– |
| Sally Fowler, capital | | 106,015 |
| Sally Fowler, withdrawals | 15,000 | |
| Sales | | 562,140 |
| Sales returns and allowances | 5,070 | |
| Purchases | 385,085 | |
| Purchases returns and allowances | | 1,820 |
| Purchases discounts | | 4,710 |
| Transportation-in | 5,125 | |
| Sales salaries expense | 43,220 | |
| Rent expense, selling space | 20,250 | |
| Store supplies expense | –0– | |
| Amortization expense, store equipment | –0– | |
| Office salaries expense | 48,330 | |
| Rent expense, office space | 8,850 | |
| Office supplies expense | –0– | |
| Insurance expense | –0– | |
| Amortization expense, office equipment | –0– | |
| Totals | $696,650 | $696,650 |

**Required**

1. Copy the unadjusted trial balance on a work sheet form and complete the work sheet using the information that follows:

*a.* Ending store supplies inventory, $445.

*b.* Ending office supplies inventory, $225.

*c.* Expired insurance, $2,805.

*d.* Amortization on the store equipment, $5,415.

*e.* Amortization on the office equipment, $1,485.

*f.* Accrued sales salaries payable, $445; and accrued office salaries payable, $210.

*g.* Ending merchandise inventory, $54,365.

2. Prepare a multiple-step income statement showing in detail the expenses and the items that make up cost of goods sold.

3. Prepare a statement of changes in owner's equity. On December 31, 1995, the Sally Fowler, Capital account had a balance of $36,015. Early in 1996, Ms. Fowler invested an additional $70,000 in the business.

4. Prepare a year-end classified balance sheet with the prepaid expenses combined.

5. Prepare adjusting and closing entries.

Briefly explain why a company's manager would want the accounting system to record a customer's return of unsatisfactory goods in the Sales Returns and Allowances account instead of the Sales account. In addition, explain whether the information would be useful for external decision makers.

**Problem 5–10**
Analytical Essay
**(LO 1)**

A retail company's accountant recently compiled the cost of the ending merchandise inventory to use in preparing the financial statements. In developing the measure, the accountant did not know that $10,000 of incoming goods had been shipped by a supplier on December 31 under an FOB factory agreement. These goods had been recorded as a purchase, but they were not included in the physical count because they were not on hand. Explain how this overlooked fact would affect the company's financial statements and these ratios: debt ratio, current ratio, profit margin, and acid-test ratio.

**Problem 5–11**
Analytical Essay
**(LO 2)**

# SERIAL PROBLEM

*(The first three segments of this comprehensive problem were presented in Chapters 2, 3, and 4. If those segments have not been completed, the assignment can begin at this point. However, the student will need to use the facts presented on pages 119–20 in Chapter 2, pages 175–76 in Chapter 3, and page 229 in Chapter 4. Because of its length, this problem is most easily solved if students use the Working Papers that accompany this text.)*

**Emerald Computer Services**

Earlier segments of this problem have described how Tracy Green created Emerald Computer Services on October 1, 1996. The company has been successful, and its list of customers has started to grow. To accommodate the growth, the accounting system is ready to be modified to set up separate accounts for each customer. The following list of customers includes the account number used for each account and any balance as of the end of 1996. Green decided to add a fourth digit with a decimal point to the 106 account number that had been used for the single Accounts Receivable account. This modification allows the existing chart of accounts to continue being used. The list also shows the balances that two customers owed as of December 31, 1996:

| Account | No. | Dec. 31 Balance |
|---|---|---|
| Alpha Printing Co. | 106.1 | |
| Bravo Productions | 106.2 | |
| Charles Company | 106.3 | $ 900 |
| Delta Fixtures, Inc. | 106.4 | |
| Echo Canyon Ranch | 106.5 | |
| Fox Run Estates | 106.6 | $1,000 |
| Golf Course Designs, Inc. | 106.7 | |
| Hotel Pollo del Mar | 106.8 | |
| Indiana Manuf. Co. | 106.9 | |

In response to frequent requests from customers, Green has decided to begin selling computer software. The company will extend credit terms of 1/10, n/30 to customers who purchase merchandise. No cash discount will be available on consulting fees. The following additional accounts were added to the General Ledger to allow the system to account for the company's new merchandising activities:

| Account | No. |
|---|---|
| Merchandise Inventory | 119 |
| Sales | 413 |
| Sales Returns and Allowances | 414 |
| Sales Discounts | 415 |
| Purchases | 505 |
| Purchases Returns and Allowances | 506 |
| Purchases Discounts | 507 |
| Transportation-In | 508 |

Because the accounting system does not use reversing entries, all revenue and expense accounts have zero balances as of January 1, 1997.

**Required**

1. Prepare journal entries to record each of the following transactions for Emerald Computer Services.

2. Post the journal entries to the accounts in the company's General Ledger. (Use asset, liability, and capital accounts that start with the balance as of December 31, 1996.)

3. Prepare a six-column table similar to Illustration 3–3 that presents the unadjusted trial balance, the March 31 adjustments, and the adjusted trial balance.

   Do not prepare closing entries and do not journalize the adjusting entries or post them to the ledger.

4. Prepare an interim income statement for the three months ended March 31, 1997. Use a detailed multiple-step format that shows calculations of net sales, total revenues, cost of goods sold, total expenses, and net income.

5. Prepare an interim statement of changes in owner's equity for the three months ended March 31, 1997.

6. Prepare an interim balance sheet as of March 31, 1997.

Transactions:

Jan. 4   Paid Fran Sims for five days, including one day in addition to the four unpaid days from the prior year.

     6   Tracy Green invested an additional $12,000 cash in the business.

     7   Purchased $2,800 of merchandise from SoftHead Co. on terms of 1/10, n/30, FOB shipping point.

     8   Received $1,000 from Fox Run Estates as final payment on its account.

   10   Completed 5-day project for Alpha Printing Co. and billed them $3,000, which is the total price of $4,000 less the advance payment of $1,000.

   13   Sold merchandise with a retail value of $2,100 to Delta Fixtures, Inc., with terms of 1/10, n/30, FOB shipping point.

   14   Paid $350 for freight charges on the merchandise purchased on January 7.

   16   Received $1,500 cash from Golf Course Designs, Inc., for computer services.

   17   Paid SoftHead Co. for the purchase on January 7, net of the discount.

Jan. 21    Delta Fixtures, Inc., returned $200 of defective merchandise from its purchase on January 13.

      22    Received the balance due from Delta Fixtures, Inc., net of the discount and the credit for the returned merchandise.

      23    Returned defective merchandise to SoftHead Co. and accepted credit against future purchases. Its cost, net of the discount, was $198.

      26    Sold $2,900 of merchandise on credit to Hotel Pollo del Mar.

      28    Purchased $4,000 of merchandise from SoftHead Co. on terms of 1/10, n/30, FOB destination.

      29    Received a $198 credit memo from SoftHead Co. concerning the merchandise returned on January 23.

      31    Paid Fran Sims for 10 days' work.

Feb.  1    Paid $2,250 to the Town Hall Mall for another three months' rent.

      3    Paid SoftHead Co. for the balance due, net of the cash discount, less the $198 amount in the credit memo.

      4    Paid $400 to the local newspaper for advertising.

     11    Received the balance due from Alpha Printing Co. for fees billed on January 10.

     16    Paid $2,000 to Tracy Green as a withdrawal.

     23    Sold $1,600 of merchandise on credit to Golf Course Designs, Inc.

     26    Paid Fran Sims for 8 days' work.

     27    Reimbursed Tracy Green's business automobile usage for 600 km. at $0.25 per kilometre.

Mar.  8    Purchased $1,200 of computer supplies from AAA Supply Co. on credit.

      9    Received the balance due from Golf Course Designs, Inc., for merchandise sold on February 23.

     15    Repaired the company's computer at the cost of $430.

     16    Received $2,130 cash from Indiana Manuf. Co. for computing services.

     19    Paid the full amount due to AAA Supply Co. including amounts created on December 13 and March 8.

     24    Billed Bravo Productions for $2,950 of computing services.

     25    Sold $900 of merchandise on credit to Echo Canyon Ranch.

     30    Sold $1,110 of merchandise on credit to Charles Company.

     31    Reimbursed Tracy Green's business automobile usage for 400 km. at $0.25 per kilometre.

Information for the March 31 adjustments and financial statements:

*a.*    The March 31 inventory of computing supplies is $670.

*b.*    Three more months have passed since the company purchased the annual insurance policy at the cost of $1,440.

*c.*    Fran Sims has not been paid for 7 days of work.

*d.*    Three months have passed since any prepaid rent cost has been transferred to expense.

*e.*    Amortization on the computer for January through March is $750.

*f.*    Amortization on the office equipment for January through March is $500.

*g.*    The March 31 inventory of merchandise is $2,182.

# PROVOCATIVE PROBLEMS

**Provocative Problem 5–1**

Financial Reporting Problem

**(LO 1, 2, 3)**

Wanda Wonder, the owner of the WonderFull Store, has operated the company for several years but has never used an accrual accounting system. To have more useful information, Wonder has engaged you to help prepare an income statement for 1997. Based on data that you have gathered from the cash-basis accounting system and other documents, you have been able to prepare the following balance sheets as of the beginning and end of 1997:

|  | December 31 | |
|---|---|---|
|  | **1996** | **1997** |
| Cash ...................... | $ 5,400 | $ 42,250 |
| Accounts receivable ........... | 18,500 | 22,600 |
| Merchandise inventory ......... | 39,700 | 34,000 |
| Equipment (net of amortization) ... | 87,000 | 56,000 |
| Total assets ................ | $150,600 | $154,850 |
| Accounts payable ............. | $ 28,300 | $ 36,250 |
| Wages payable ............... | 2,200 | 1,700 |
| Wanda Wonder, capital ......... | 120,100 | 116,900 |
| Total liabilities and owner's equity .. | $150,600 | $154,850 |

The store's cash records also provided the following facts for 1997:

| | |
|---|---|
| Amount collected on accounts receivable  .. | $339,900 |
| Payments for: | |
| Accounts payable.................. | 198,050 |
| Employees' wages ................. | 52,000 |
| All other operating expenses .......... | 29,000 |
| Withdrawals by the owner ........... | 24,000 |

You have determined that all merchandise purchases and sales were made on credit, and that no equipment was either purchased or sold during the year.

Use the preceding information to calculate the amounts of the company's sales, cost of goods purchased, cost of goods sold, amortization expense, and wages expense for 1997. Then, prepare a multiple-step income statement that shows the company's gross profit.

**Provocative Problem 5–2**

Nan's Nursery

**(LO 1, 2, 3)**

Nan Hall and Mike Linden were partners in a nursery. They disagreed, closed the business, and ended their partnership. In settlement for her partnership interest, Nan Hall received an inventory of trees, plants, and garden supplies having a $22,500 cost. Since there was nothing practical she could do with the inventory except open a new nursery, she did so by investing the inventory and $18,000 in cash. She used $15,000 of the cash to buy equipment, and she opened for business on May 1. During the succeeding eight months, she paid out $63,750 to creditors for additional trees, plants, and garden supplies and $21,000 in operating expenses. She also withdrew $15,000 for personal expenses, and at the year-end, she prepared the balance sheet that follows:

**NAN'S NURSERY**
**Balance Sheet**
**December 31, 1996**

| | | | | |
|---|---|---|---|---|
| Cash . . . . . . . . . . . . . . . . | | $ 8,550 | Accounts payable (all for | |
| Merchandise inventory . . . | | 26,650 | merchandise) . . . . . . . . . | $ 3,300 |
| Equipment . . . . . . . . . . . . | $ 15,000 | | Nan Hall, capital . . . . . . . . | 45,700 |
| Less amortization . . . . . . . | 1,200 | 13,800 | Total liabilities and | |
| Total assets . . . . . . . . . . . | | $49,000 | owner's equity | $49,000 |

Based on the information given, prepare calculations to determine the net income earned by the business, the cost of goods sold, and the amount of its sales. Then prepare an income statement showing the result of the nursery's operations during its first eight months.

Phil Potter worked in the National Bank for 20 years, until his aunt died, leaving him a sizable estate. After sitting around long enough to get bored and see his bank balance dwindle, Phil decided to open a retail paint store. When he started the business on July 1, 1996, Valley Hills had no such store, and it appeared to Phil that the business would succeed.

On July 1, Phil deposited $53,500 in a bank account under the name Phil's Paints. He then paid $12,000 cash for store equipment, which he expected to last 10 years before it became valueless. He also bought merchandise for $37,500 cash, and paid $3,600 in advance for six months' rent.

Phil estimated that most paint stores marked their goods for sale at prices averaging 35% above cost. In other words, an item that cost $10.00 was marked for sale at $13.50. But to entice customers, he decided to mark his merchandise for sale at 30% above cost. Since his overhead would be low, he thought this would still leave a new income equal to 10% of sales.

On December 31, 1996, six months after opening his store, Phil has come to you for advice. He thinks business has been good. However, he doesn't quite understand why his cash balance has fallen to $1,200.

In talking with Phil and examining his records, you determine that the inventory was replaced three times during the six months, each time at a cost of $37,500. All merchandise suppliers have been paid except for $10,850, which is not yet due. A full stock of merchandise (cost of $37,500) is on hand and customers owe Phil $29,100. In addition to the rend paid in advance, Phil paid $14,700 for other expenses.

Prepare an income statement for the business covering the six-month period ended December 31, a statement of changes in owner's equity, a December 31, 1996, balance sheet, and a statement that explains the $1,200 cash balance by showing the cash receipts and cash disbursements during the six months ended December 31.

*Provocative Problem 5–3*
*Phil's Paints*
**(LO 1, 3)**

Use the financial statements for Geac Computer Corporation Limited in Appendix I at the end of the book to find the answers to these questions:

a.  Although Geac manufactures most of the goods that it sells, assume that the amounts reported for inventories and cost of sales* were all purchased ready for resale and then calculate the total cost of goods purchased during the fiscal year ended April 30, 1994.

b.  Calculate the current and acid-test ratios as of the end of the 1994 and 1993 fiscal years. Comment on what you find.

*Use "costs, excluding amounts shown below" as cost of sales.

*Provocative Problem 5–4*
*Financial statement analysis case*
**(LO 1, 5)**
**Geac**

Describe the problem faced by Renee Fleck in the As a Matter of Ethics case on page 248 and evaluate her alternative courses of action.

*Provocative Problem 5–5*
*Ethical issue essay*

# ANALYTICAL AND REVIEW PROBLEMS

**A & R Problem 5–1**        The partially completed work sheet of Incomplete Data Company appears below:

**INCOMPLETE DATA COMPANY**
**Work Sheet for the Year Ended December 31, 1996**

| Account Titles | Trial Balance | | Adjustments | | Income Statement | | Balance Sheet | |
|---|---|---|---|---|---|---|---|---|
| | Debit | Credit | Debit | Credit | Debit | Credit | Debit | Credit |
| Cash ...................... | 34,780 | | | | | | | |
| Accounts receivable .............. | | | | | | | 4,600 | |
| Merchandise inventory ............ | | | | | 31,400 | 26,400 | | |
| Prepaid fire insurance ........... | 720 | | | | | | 480 | |
| Prepaid rent ................... | 4,800 | | | | | | | |
| Office equipment ............... | | | | | | | 12,000 | |
| Accum. amort.—office equipment ..... | | 4,500 | | | | | | |
| Accounts payable ............... | | 8,000 | | | | | | |
| Clay Camp, capital .............. | | 22,000 | | | | | | |
| Clay Camp, drawing ............. | | | | | | | 20,000 | |
| Sales ...................... | | 300,000 | | | | | | |
| Sales returns and allowances ....... | | | | | 1,000 | | | |
| Purchases .................... | 199,200 | | | | | | | |
| Purchases returns and allowances ..... | | | | | | 1,400 | | |
| Advertising expense .............. | 1,000 | | | | | | | |
| Supplies expense ................ | 1,800 | | | | | | | |
| Salaries expense ............... | 23,200 | | | | | | | |
| Utilities expense ............... | 1,400 | | | | | | | |
| | | | | | | | | |
| Fire insurance expense ........... | | | | | | | | |
| Rent expense ................... | | | | | 2,400 | | | |
| Amort. expense—office equipment .... | | | | | 1,500 | | | |
| Salaries payable ............... | | | | | | | | 660 |

**Required**

1.  Complete the work sheet for the year ended December 31, 1996.

The following are the selected data for the Allen Sales Company for the year 1997.    **A & R Problem 5–2**

1    Selected closing entries:

| | | |
|---|---:|---:|
| Income Summary | 273,000 | |
| Purchases Returns and Allowances | 2,500 | |
| Purchases | | 180,000 |
| Freight-In | | 4,000 |
| Purchase Discounts Lost | | 200 |
| Sales Salaries Expense | | 40,000 |
| Advertising Expense | | 10,000 |
| Rent Expense, Office Space | | 8,000 |
| Delivery Expense | | 4,800 |
| Office Salaries Expense | | 26,000 |
| Amortization, Office Equipment | | 2,000 |
| Miscellaneous Expense | | 500 |
| To close expense and other nominal accounts | | |
| G. Allen, Capital | 28,000 | |
| G. Allen, Withdrawals | | 28,000 |
| To close the withdrawals account. | | |

2.  G. Allen follows the practice of withdrawing half of the annual net income from the business.

3.  There were no sales returns and allowances for the year. However, sales discounts amounted to $2,000.

4.  Inventories:

December 31, 1996—$25,000

December 31, 1997—$20,000

**Required**

1. Compute the amount of net income for 1997.

2. Compute the amount of sales for 1997.

3. Prepare a classified income statement for 1997.

# CONCEPT TESTER

Test your understanding of the concepts introduced in this chapter by completing the following crossword puzzle.

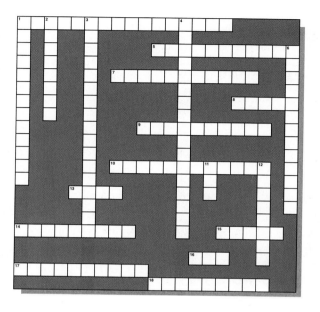

**Across Clues**

1. Freight charges on goods purchased (2 words).

5. Amounts and timing of payments agreed to by buyers (2 words).

7. Goods bought and sold to others.

8. Term for revenues from selling of merchandise.

9. Income statement format (2 words).

10. Income statement format that discloses gross profit (2 words).

13. Expense of buying and preparing goods sold (abbreviation).

14. Inventory method that recognizes COGS at time of sale.

15. Synonymous term for merchandise.

16. Legal arrangement for identifying location at which title to goods is transferred (abbreviation).

17. Balance sheet that identifies current assets, capital assets, etc.

18. Collection of goods waiting to be sold to customers.

**Down Clues**

1. Reduction from catalogue price (2 words).

2. Ratio of quick assets to current liabilities (2 words).

3. Cash discount taken against amount owed to supplier (2 words).

4. Total of selling and general administration expenses (2 words).

6. Cash discount taken by customers (2 words).

11. Credit terms (abbreviation).

12. Inventory method which fails to identify amount of shrinkage.

## ANSWERS TO PROGRESS CHECKS

5–1  *b*

5–2  Gross profit is the difference between net sales and cost of goods sold.

5–3  Keeping sales returns and allowances and sales discounts separate from sales makes useful information readily available to managers for internal monitoring and decision making. This information is not likely to be reported outside the company because it would not be useful for external decision makers.

5–4  Under credit terms of 2/10, n/60, the credit period is 60 days and the discount period is 10 days.

5–5  *b*

5–6  With a periodic inventory system, the cost of goods sold is determined at the end of an accounting period by adding the cost of goods purchased to the beginning inventory and subtracting the ending inventory.

5–7  FOB means free on board. The term *FOB destination* means that the seller does not transfer ownership of the goods to the buyer until they arrive at the buyer's place of business. Thus, the seller is responsible for paying the shipping charges and bears the risk of damage during shipment.

5–8  *c*

5–9  The classified income statement; the single-step income statement.

5–10  The second closing entry, which closes the income statement accounts with debit balances, includes a credit to Merchandise Inventory to remove the beginning inventory amount.

5–11  *d*

5–12  The acid-test ratio.

5–13  *d*

5–14  Both approaches will report the same ending inventory and net income.

# CHAPTER 6

# Accounting Systems

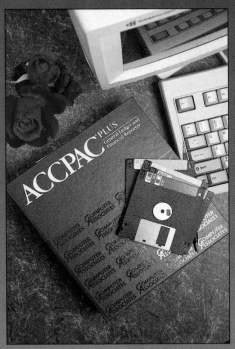

*As businesses grow, the number of transactions becomes very large. To handle this load, companies use special accounting methods and records. Today, most companies use the powerful capabilities of computers to achieve accurate and fast information processing.*

Karen White's friends operated O'Natural, a small business that sells nutritional supplements. During 1995, sales revenue amounted to $37,600. Upon learning that Karen was studying accounting, they invited her to examine their record-keeping system. Upon examination of the accounting records, Karen was amazed at how closely the rather simple system followed what she had learned in the first five chapters of her textbook. She found a single sales and purchases account and a number of asset, liability, and owner's equity accounts.

That evening Karen shared her experience with Mark Smith and the two wondered how complex a system a company such as Imperial Oil Limited needs, with sales over $9 billion and the level of detail the financial statements provide, especially in the notes to the statements. They wondered how this information can be captured by Imperial's accounting system and whether management decisions for a small business might be better served by a more complex accounting system.

**Imperial Oil Limited—1994**
(amounts in millions)

| | |
|---|---:|
| Total revenues: | |
| Natural resources | $ 854 |
| Petroleum products | 7,313 |
| Chemicals | 759 |
| Corporate and other | 85 |
| Total revenues | $ 9,011 |

## LEARNING OBJECTIVES

**After studying Chapter 6, you should be able to:**

1. **Describe the five basic components of an accounting system.**
2. **Describe the types of computers used in large and small accounting systems, the role of software in those systems, and the different approaches to inputting and processing data, including the use of networking.**
3. **Explain special journals and controlling accounts, use them to record transactions, and explain how to test the posting of entries to the Accounts Receivable and Accounts Payable subsidiary ledgers.**
4. **Explain the use of special and general journals in accounting for sales and goods and services taxes and sales returns and allowances, and explain how sales invoices can serve as a Sales Journal.**
5. **Explain the nature and use of business segment information.**
6. **Define or explain the words and phrases listed in the chapter glossary.**

Even in a small business such as O'Natural, a large amount of information must be processed through the accounting system. Thus, the accounting system should be designed to process the information efficiently. As you study this chapter, you will learn some general concepts to follow in designing an efficient accounting system. The chapter begins by explaining the basic components of an accounting system, whether it is a manual or computer-based system. After considering some of the special characteristics of computer-based systems, the chapter then explains some of the labour-saving procedures employed in manual systems. These include efficient ways of processing routine transactions such as credit sales, cash receipts, credit purchases, and cash disbursements.

## THE COMPONENTS OF AN ACCOUNTING SYSTEM

LO 1

Describe the five basic components of an accounting system.

**Accounting systems** consist of people, forms, procedures, and equipment. These systems must be designed to capture data about the transactions of the entity and to generate from that data a variety of financial, managerial, and tax accounting reports. Because all accounting systems must accomplish these same broad objectives, both manual and computerized accounting systems include the same basic components. However, computer-based systems provide more accuracy, speed, efficiency, and convenience.

The five common components of manual and computerized accounting systems are:

- Source documents.
- Input devices.
- Data processor.
- Data storage.
- Output devices.

Illustration 6–1 shows the relationships between these five components.

**Illustration 6–1**    The Components of an accounting System

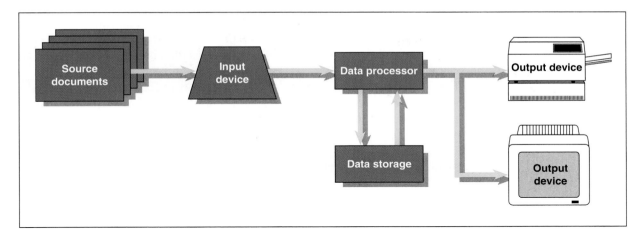

## Source Documents

Chapter 2 described some of the business papers that companies use in the process of completing transactions. These business papers are called *source documents* because they provide a basis for making accounting entries. In other words, they provide the data that are entered in and processed by the accounting system. You are no doubt familiar with some kinds of source documents such as bank statements and cheques received from other parties. Other examples of source documents include invoices from suppliers, billings to customers, and employee earnings records.

In manual accounting systems, source documents consist of paper documents. Paper documents are also very important for computerized systems, but some source documents take other forms. For example, some companies send invoices directly from their own computers to their customers' computers. The source documents in this case are computer files.

Accurate source documents are important for the proper functioning of an accounting system. If the information going into the system is faulty and incomplete, the information coming out of the system will also be faulty and incomplete. (In computer jargon, the results of defective input are described as garbage in, garbage out.)

## Input Devices

The second component of an accounting system is one or more **input devices.** As shown in Illustration 6–1, an input device transfers the information from source documents to the data processing component of the accounting system. In a computer-based system, this often involves converting the data on the source documents from a written form into electronic signals. In addition to transferring data from source documents to the data processor, input devices are used to tell the data processing component how to process the data.

In prior chapters, you used an input device when you solved exercises and problems by recording the effects of transactions with journal entries. If you recorded transactions using the *SPATS* supplement that accompanies this text, you used the keyboard of a computer as the input device. When you recorded transactions using pencil and paper, you were using these items as the input device for a manual accounting system.

The most common input device for a computer-based accounting system is a keyboard. System operators use keyboards to transfer data from the source documents into the computer. Another input device is a *bar code reader* like those used in grocery and other retail stores. With a bar code reader, the clerk merely moves purchased items over the reader, which picks up their code numbers and sends the data to the computer. Other input devices include *scanners* that read words and numbers directly from source documents.

In both manual and computer systems, companies promote clerical accuracy by using routine procedures to input data. Also, controls should be in place to ensure that only authorized individuals can input data to the accounting system. Such controls help protect the integrity of the system and also allow incorrect input to be traced back to its source.

## Data Processor

The third component of an accounting system is the **data processor** which interprets, manipulates, and summarizes recorded information so it can be used in analyses and reports. In manual systems, the primary data processor is the accountant's brain. However, the manual processing of data is not entirely a mental process. That is, the accountant uses the journal, the ledger, the working papers, and such procedures as posting to convert the journal entry data into more useful information. Of course, few if any accounting systems are completely manual. For example, calculators are essential equipment for manual systems.

As a result of technical developments over the last two decades, many manual accounting systems have been replaced by computer-based systems. The data processor in a computer-based system includes both *hardware* and *software*. Hardware is the machinery that performs the steps called for by the software. The software consists of computer programs that specify the operations to be performed on the data. Software actually controls the whole system, including input, file management, processing, and output.

## Data Storage

**Data storage** is an essential component of both manual and computer-based systems. As data is inputted and processed, it must be saved so it can be used as output or processed further. This stockpile of data (a database) should be readily accessible so periodic financial reports can be compiled quickly. In addition, data storage should support the preparation of special purpose reports that managers may request. The accounting database also serves as the primary source of information auditors use when they audit the financial statements. Companies also maintain files of source documents for use by auditors and to clear up errors or disputes.

In manual systems, data storage consists of files of paper documents. However, with a computer-based system, most of the data is stored on floppy diskettes, hard disks, or magnetic tapes. As a result of recent improvements, these devices can store very large amounts of data. For example, floppy diskettes can hold up to two megabytes of information (one megabyte is roughly equivalent to 500 double-spaced typed pages). Small digital-audio-tape (DAT) cassettes can hold hundreds of megabytes of information. Some hard disks can hold thousands of megabytes (1,000 megabytes is a gigabyte). Because of the recent improvements in data storage, accounting systems now can store much more detailed and extensive databases than was possible in the past. As a result, managers have much more information available to help them plan and control business activities.

In a computer-based system, data storage can be on-line (usually on a hard disk), which means that the data can be accessed whenever it is needed by the software. In contrast, when data is stored off-line, the data cannot be accessed until the computer operator inserts a disk or a magnetic tape into a drive.

Generally, we do not use the concepts of on-line and off-line storage in reference to manual accounting systems. However, one might argue that in a manual system, only the data stored in the accountant's brain is on-line; everything else is off-line.

## Output Devices

The fifth component of an accounting system is the **output devices.** These allow information to be taken out of the system and placed in the hands of its users. Examples of output include bills to customers, cheques payable to suppliers and employees, financial statements, and a variety of other internal reports.

For computer-based systems, the most common output devices are video screens and printers. Other output devices include telephones or direct phone line connections to the computer systems of suppliers or customers. When requests for output are entered, the data processor searches the database for the needed data, organizes it in the form of a report, and sends the information to an output device.

Depending on the output device, the information may be displayed on a screen, printed on paper, or expressed as a voice over the telephone. For example, a bank customer may call to find out the balance in his or her chequing account. If a touch-tone telephone serves as an input/output device, a recording may ask the customer to enter appropriate identifying information including the number of the account. With this input, the computer searches the database for the information and sends it back over the telephone. If the telephone is not used as an input/output device, the bank employee who answers the phone inputs the information request using a keyboard. The employee then reads the output on a video screen and relays it over the phone to the customer.

Another kind of output involves paying employees without writing paycheques. Instead, the company's computer system may send the payroll data directly to the computer system of the company's bank. Thus, the output of the company's system is an electronic fund transfer (EFT) from the company's bank account to the employees' bank accounts. The output device in this instance is the connection or interface between the computer systems of the company and the bank. Large companies are increasingly using EFTs. In other situations, the company's computer outputs the payroll data on a magnetic tape or disk. The tape or disk is then used by the bank to transfer the funds to the employees' bank accounts.

In addition to the preceding forms of output, many situations require printed output that computer systems produce on laser, impact, or ink-jet printers.

For companies using manual accounting systems, the production of output involves physically searching the records to find the needed data and then organizing it in a written report.

---

**Progress Check**
*(Answers to Progress Checks are provided at the end of the chapter.)*

6-1    Which one of the following components of an accounting system is not likely to include paper documents? *(a)* Source documents; *(b)* Data processor; *(c)* Data storage; *(d)* Output devices.

6-2    What does the data processor component of an accounting system accomplish?

6-3    What uses are made of the data that are stockpiled in the data storage component of an accounting system?

---

## SMALL AND LARGE COMPUTER-BASED SYSTEMS

**LO 2**

Describe the types of computers used in large and small accounting systems, the role of software in those systems, and the different approaches to inputting and processing data, including the use of networking.

The world has seen radical changes in the use of computers since the first Apple computer was sold in 1980. Many of you are already proficient users of personal computers (PCs) such as those produced by **International Business Machines Corporation (IBM)** or by **Apple Computer, Inc.** These computers (often called *microcomputers*) are physically small, easy to operate, and increasingly inexpensive.

Although the use of microcomputers in business has greatly expanded in recent years, many companies also use larger computers called *mainframes*. These machines are able to process huge quantities of accounting data quickly. In addition, they help businesses perform other important tasks such as analyzing the results of market research, compiling shareholder information, and doing engineering design work for products and production lines. These computers include the AS series of machines produced by IBM and the VAX family manufactured by **Digital Equipment Corporation (DEC)**.

## CUSTOM-DESIGNED AND OFF-THE-SHELF PROGRAMS

Regardless of its size and speed, every computer does nothing more than execute instructions that are organized as programs. A program consists of a series of very specific instructions for obtaining data from input or storage, processing it, returning it to storage for later use, and sending it to an output device to produce a report.

Illustration 6–2 presents a flowchart of the steps that a computer program might use to process a stack of customer orders for merchandise. When this program is executed in a normal situation, the system creates a shipping order that identifies the products to be sent to customers. If a shipment causes the quantity on hand to fall below the minimum level, the system generates a purchase order to be approved by a manager. If the quantity on hand is less than the customer ordered, the system produces a partial shipping order as well as a report to the customer that the remainder is on back order. Then, if replacements have not been ordered already, the system produces a purchase order. If no units of the desired product are on hand, the system notifies the customer of the back order and issues a purchase

**Illustration 6–2**   Flowchart for an Order-Processing Program

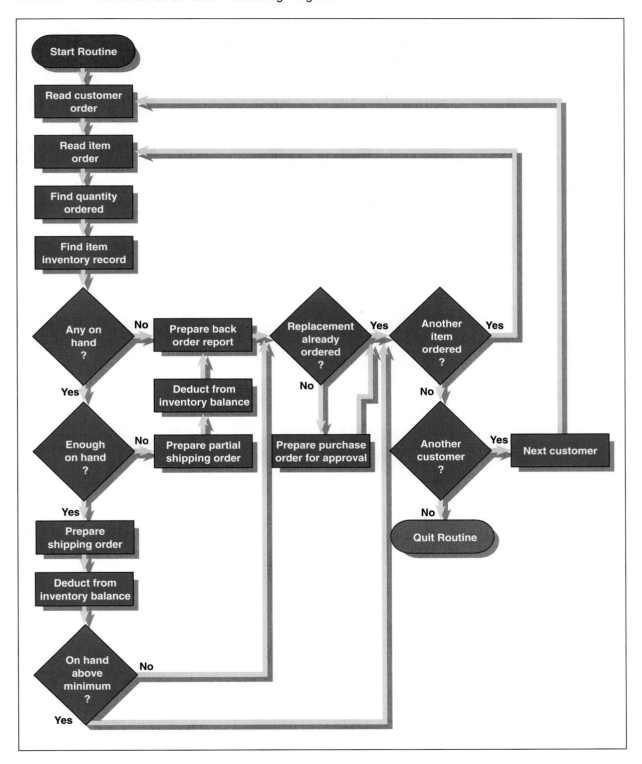

## As a Matter of Opinion

Lorrie L. King, BBA, CA

*Mrs. King graduated from Wilfrid Laurier University with her Honours Bachelor of Business Administration degree in 1986. She received her Chartered Accountant designation in 1987. She currently works in Toronto for the public accounting firm, Arthur Andersen in their Enterprise Group which provides audit, tax and consulting services to family-owned and mid-sized organizations. She has also worked in private industry as a controller for a computer software company. She is the Treasurer of the Toronto Venture Group and a member of the Institute of Chartered Accountants of Ontario.*

The advent of microcomputers, local area networks and user friendly software have made it a virtual necessity for companies, regardless of size, to use computer systems in their accounting functions. This has allowed small businesses to eliminate much of the mechanical drudgery in their financial recordkeeping and allowed them to create their financial records much more quickly. But accounting software can be deceptively simple. Many programs do not have built in internal controls to ensure that transactions are captured properly or do not provide audit trails to allow users to track their transactions readily. Accounting programs must also be set up properly at the outset or the financial data that is created may be meaningless. All of these factors can lead to disaster if there is no one in the business with accounting expertise.

Even sophisticated computer systems cannot replace sound accounting knowledge. Many transactions require judgements to be made that can only be made by humans with a clear understanding of the transaction. Similarly, humans trained in accounting and analysis can detect input errors that the computer would rarely, if ever, identify.

Today's accountant must have skills in both areas; computer applications and accounting knowledge. It is important to understand how computer systems work in order to use them effectively without having to pay costly computer consultants every time there is a problem. However, one must never assume that the computer does everything correctly and that is why strong accounting skills are still a necessity in today's complex business environment.

---

order, unless one already exists. The system follows this process for each item ordered by each customer until the stack of orders is exhausted.

Despite the apparent complexity of the instructions in Illustration 6–2, this routine is actually incomplete. For example, it does not update the accounting records for sales and accounts receivable, nor does it deal with cash and trade discounts that might be offered to customers.

In the early days of computer systems, each program had to be custom designed using a programming language such as COBOL or FORTRAN. Since then, programmers have developed more flexible and easier-to-use languages. However, programming is a skill that only a limited number of people need to master. Instead, the expanded used of microcomputers has resulted in an increasing variety of off-the-shelf programs that are ready to be used.

Some off-the-shelf programs are general, multipurpose applications that accomplish a variety of different tasks. These programs include familiar word processor programs (such as Microsoft Word® and WordPerfect®), spreadsheet programs (such as Quattro®Pro, Microsoft Excel®, and Lotus® 1-2-3®), and database management programs (such as dBase®).

Other off-the-shelf programs are designed to meet very specific needs of users. These programs include a large number of accounting programs such as AccPac for Windows®, CA Simply Accounting®, AccPac 2000, DacEasy® Accounting, Peachtree® Complete Accounting, and Great Plains® Accounting Series. Off-the-shelf programs are designed to be so user-friendly they guide users through the input steps and then ask which reports are desired.

Many of the off-the-shelf accounting programs save time and minimize errors because they operate as *integrated* systems. In an integrated system, actions taken in one part of the system also produce results in related parts.

For example, when a credit sale is recorded in an integrated system, several parts of the system are updated with one or two simple commands. First, the system stores transaction data (as in a journal) so that you can review the entire entry at a later time. Second, it updates the Cash and Accounts Receivable accounts. Third, it updates a detailed record of the amount owed by the customer. Fourth, it might update a detailed record of the products held for sale to show the number of units sold and the number that remain on hand.

Computers and integrated software programs have dramatically reduced the bookkeeping tasks in accounting. However, do not think that computers have eliminated the need for accountants. Nor should you conclude that success in business no longer requires a knowledge of accounting. The need for accountants and accounting knowledge is created by the need for information, not by the need for pencil and paper. Accountants continue to be in demand because their expertise is necessary to determine what information ought to be produced and what data should be used to produce it. Accountants are also needed to analyze and explain the output. Furthermore, writing new, improved programs requires a knowledge of accounting.

In short, the value of accounting knowledge does not disappear just because mechanical steps are done with a computer. You still need to understand the effects of events on the company and how they are reflected in financial statements and management reports.

## BATCH AND ON-LINE SYSTEMS

Accounting systems also differ in how the input is entered and processed. With **batch processing,** the source documents are accumulated for a period of time and then processed all at the same time, such as once a day, week, or month. By comparison, with **on-line processing,** data are entered and processed as soon as source documents are available. As a result, the database is immediately updated.

The disadvantage of batch processing is that the database is not kept up to date during the times that source documents are being accumulated. In many situations, however, companies use batch processing because the database requires only periodic updating. For example, records used in sending bills to customers may require updating only once each month.

On-line processing has the advantage of keeping the database always up to date. However, it is more expensive because the software is more complicated and because it usually requires a much larger investment in hardware. On-line processing applications include airline reservations, credit card records, and rapid response mail-order processing.

## COMPUTER NETWORKS

In many circumstances, firms create advantages by linking or networking computers with each other. **Computer networks** allow different users to share access to the same data and the same programs. A relatively small computer network is called a *local area network (LAN)*. This type of network links the machines within an office by special *hard-wired* hookups. For example, many universities have networks in their computer labs. Larger computer networks that are spread over long distances communicate over telephone lines by using *modems.*

In some cases, the need for information requires very large networks. Examples include the system used by **Federal Express Corporation** for tracking its packages and billing its customers and the system used by **The Bay** for monitoring inventory levels in each of its stores. These networks involve many computers (desktops and mainframes) and satellite communications to gather information and to provide ready access to the database from all locations.

We now turn to a discussion of some of the labour-saving procedures used to process transactions in manual systems. However, remember that accounting systems have similar purposes whether they are computer-based or manual in operation. Thus, your understanding of computer-based systems will be improved when you understand manual procedures.

**Progress Check**

6-4 In a computer-based accounting system:
   a. The accounting software is more efficient if it operates as an integrated system.
   b. The need for accountants is nearly eliminated.
   c. Data about transactions must be entered with on-line processing.
   d. The accountant must have the ability to program the computer.

6-5 What advantages do computer systems offer over manual systems?

6-6 Which of the following allows different computer users to access the same data and programs? (a) On-line processing; (b) Electronic Fund Transfers; (c) Bar code readers; (d) Local area networks.

## SPECIAL JOURNALS

The General Journal is a flexible journal in which you can record any transaction. However, each debit and credit entered in a General Journal must be individually posted. As a result, a firm that uses a General Journal to record all the transactions of its business requires much time and labour to post the individual debits and credits.

One way to reduce the writing and the posting labour is to divide the transactions of a business into groups of similar transactions and to provide a separate **special journal** for recording the transactions in each group. For example, most of the transactions of a merchandising business fall into four groups: sales on credit, purchases on credit, cash receipts, and cash disbursements. When a special journal is provided for each group, the journals are:

LO 3

Explain special journals and controlling accounts, use them to record transactions, and explain how to test the posting of entries to the Accounts Receivable and Accounts Payable subsidiary ledgers.

1. A Sales Journal for recording credit sales.
2. A Purchases Journal for recording credit purchases.
3. A Cash Receipts Journal for recording cash receipts.
4. A Cash Disbursements Journal for recording cash payments.
5. A General Journal for the miscellaneous transactions not recorded in the special journals and also for adjusting, closing, and correcting entries.

The following illustrations show how special journals save time in journalizing and posting transactions. They do this by providing special columns for accumulating the debits and credits of similar transactions. These journals allow you to post the amounts entered in the special columns as column totals rather than as individual amounts. For example, you can save posting labour if you record credit sales for a month in a Sales Journal like the one at the top of Illustration 6–3. As the illustration shows, you do not post the credit sales to the general ledger accounts until the end of the month. Then, you calculate the total sales for the month and post the total as one debit to Accounts Receivable and as one credit to Sales. Only seven sales are recorded in the illustrated journal. However, if you assume the 7 sales represent 700 sales, you can better appreciate the posting labour saved by making only one debit to Accounts Receivable and one credit to Sales.

The special journal in Illustration 6–3 is also called a **columnar journal** because it has columns for recording the date, the customer's name, the invoice number, and the amount of each credit sale. Only credit sales are recorded in it, and they are recorded daily with the information about each sale placed on a separate line. Normally, the information is taken from a copy of the sales ticket or invoice prepared at the time of the sale. However, before discussing the journal further, you need to understand the role played by subsidiary ledgers.

## KEEPING A SEPARATE ACCOUNT FOR EACH CREDIT CUSTOMER

In previous chapters, when we recorded credit sales, we debited a single account called Accounts Receivable. However, when a business has more than one credit customer, the accounts must show how much each customer has purchased, how much each customer has paid, and how much remains to be collected from each customer. To provide this information, businesses with credit customers must maintain a separate Account Receivable for each customer.

One possible way of keeping a separate account for each customer would be to keep all of these accounts in the same ledger that contains the financial statement accounts. However, this usually is not done. Instead, the ledger that contains the financial statement accounts, now called the **General Ledger,** continues to hold a single Accounts Receivable account. Then, a supplementary record is established in which a separate account is maintained for each customer. This supplementary record is called the **Accounts Receivable Ledger.** This subsidiary ledger may exist on tape or disk storage in a computerized system. In a manual system, the Accounts Receivable Ledger may take the form of a book or tray that contains the customer accounts. In either case, the customer accounts in the subsidiary ledger are kept separate from the Accounts Receivable account in the General Ledger.

Understand that when debits (or credits) to Accounts Receivable are posted twice (once to Accounts Receivable and once to the customer's account), this does not

**Illustration 6–3**    Posting from the Sales Journal

| Sales Journal | | | | Page 3 |
|---|---|---|---|---|
| **Date** | **Account Debited** | **Invoice Number** | **PR** | **Amount** |
| Feb. 2 | James Henry .................................. | 307 | √ | 450.00 |
| 7 | Albert Smith .................................. | 308 | √ | 500.00 |
| 13 | Sam Moore .................................. | 309 | √ | 350.00 |
| 15 | Paul Roth .................................. | 310 | √ | 200.00 |
| 22 | James Henry .................................. | 311 | √ | 225.00 |
| 25 | Frank Booth .................................. | 312 | √ | 175.00 |
| 28 | Albert Smith .................................. | 313 | √ | 250.00 |
| 28 | Total—Accounts Receivable, Dr.; Sales, Cr. ............... | | | 2,150.00 |
| | | | | (106/413) |

Individual amounts are posted daily to the sub-sidiary ledger.

Total is posted at the end of the month to the general ledger accounts.

**Accounts Receivable Ledger**

**Frank Booth**

| Date | PR | Debit | Credit | Balance |
|---|---|---|---|---|
| Feb. 25 | S3 | 175.00 | | 175.00 |

**James Henry**

| Date | PR | Debit | Credit | Balance |
|---|---|---|---|---|
| Feb. 2 | S3 | 450.00 | | 450.00 |
| 22 | S3 | 225.00 | | 675.00 |

**Sam Moore**

| Date | PR | Debit | Credit | Balance |
|---|---|---|---|---|
| Feb. 13 | S3 | 350.00 | | 350.00 |

**Paul Roth**

| Date | PR | Debit | Credit | Balance |
|---|---|---|---|---|
| Feb. 15 | S3 | 200.00 | | 200.00 |

**Albert Smith**

| Date | PR | Debit | Credit | Balance |
|---|---|---|---|---|
| Feb. 7 | S3 | 500.00 | | 500.00 |
| 28 | S3 | 250.00 | | 750.00 |

**General Ledger**

**Accounts Receivable**        No. 106

| Date | PR | Debit | Credit | Balance |
|---|---|---|---|---|
| Feb. 28 | S3 | 2,150.00 | | 2,150.00 |

**Sales**        No. 413

| Date | PR | Debit | Credit | Balance |
|---|---|---|---|---|
| Feb. 28 | S3 | | 2,150.00 | 2,150.00 |

Note that the customer accounts are in a subsidiary ledger and the financial statement accounts are in the **General Ledger.**
Explanation columns are omitted from the accounts due to a lack of space.

**Illustration 6–4**   The Accounts Receivable Controlling Account and Subsidiary Ledger

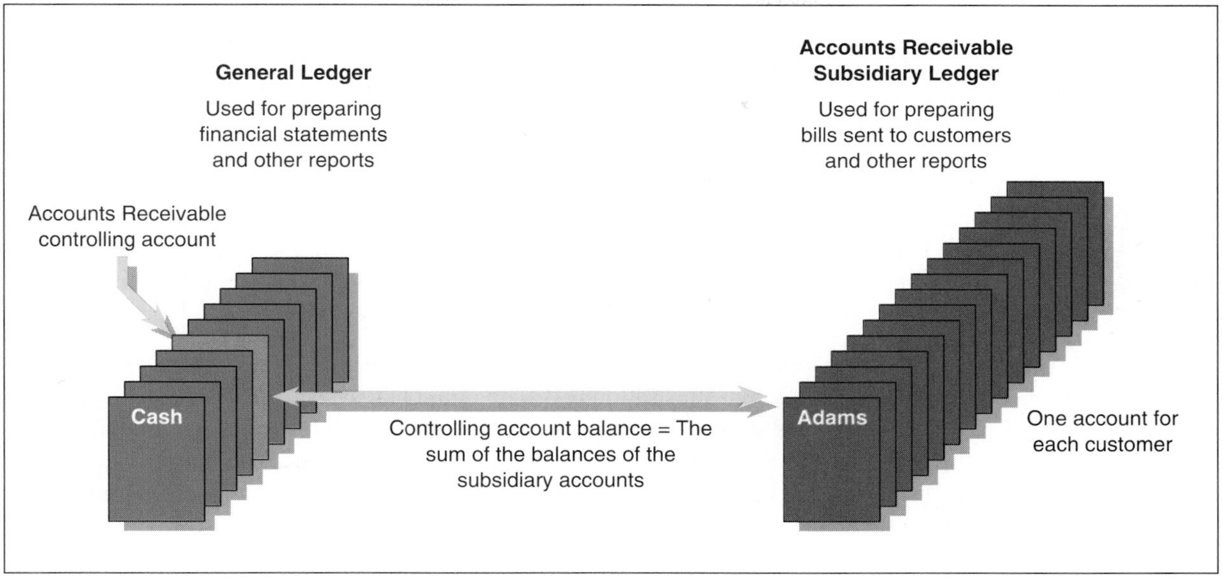

violate the requirement that debits equal credits. The equality of debits and credits is maintained in the General Ledger. The Accounts Receivable Ledger is simply a supplementary record that provides detailed information concerning each customer.

Illustration 6–4 shows the relationship between the Accounts Receivable controlling account and the accounts in the subsidiary ledger. Note that after all items are posted, the balance in the Accounts Receivable account should equal the sum of the balances in the customers' accounts. As a result, the Accounts Receivable account controls the Accounts Receivable Ledger and is called a **controlling account.** Since the Accounts Receivable Ledger is a supplementary record controlled by an account in the General Ledger, it is called a **subsidiary ledger.** After posting is completed, if the Accounts Receivable balance does not equal the sum of the customer account balances, you know an error has been made.

The Accounts Receivable account and the Accounts Receivable Ledger are not the only examples of controlling accounts and subsidiary ledgers. Most companies buy on credit from several suppliers. As a result, a company must keep a separate account for each creditor. To accomplish this, the firm maintains an Accounts Payable controlling account in the General Ledger and a separate account for each creditor in a subsidiary **Accounts Payable Ledger.** The controlling account, subsidiary ledger, and columnar journal techniques demonstrated thus far with accounts receivable also apply to the creditor accounts. The only difference is that a Purchases Journal and a Cash Disbursements Journal are used to record most of the transactions that affect these accounts. You will learn about these journals later in the chapter.

Another situation in which a subsidiary ledger often is used involves equipment. For example, a company with many items of office equipment might keep only one Office Equipment account in its General Ledger. This account would control a subsidiary ledger in which each item of equipment is recorded in a separate account.

## MAINTAINING A SEPARATE RECORD FOR EACH ACCOUNT PAYABLE

Recall from the beginning of the chapter the detailed sales information **Imperial Oil** presented in its 1994 annual report. The presentation included the revenue of each major business segment. However, Imperial Oil's accounting system undoubtedly keeps far more detailed sales records than reflected in the annual report. In fact, the company sells thousands of different products and no doubt is able to analyze the sales performance of each one of them.

To some extent, this kind of detail is captured by having many different general ledger sales accounts. However, it also may be captured by using supplementary records that function like subsidiary ledgers. In fact, the concept of a subsidiary ledger may be applied in many different ways to ensure that the accounting system captures sufficient details to support possible analyses managers may want to make.

## POSTING THE SALES JOURNAL

When customer accounts are maintained in a subsidiary ledger, a Sales Journal is posted as shown in Illustration 6–3. The individual sales recorded in the Sales Journal are posted each day to the proper customer accounts in the Accounts Receivable Ledger. These daily postings keep the customer accounts up-to-date. This is important in granting credit because the person responsible for granting credit should know the amount the credit-seeking customer currently owes. The source of this information is the customer's account; if the account is not up-to-date, an incorrect decision may be made.

Note the check marks in the Sales Journal's Posting Reference column. They indicate that the sales recorded in the journal were individually posted to the customer accounts in the Accounts Receivable Ledger. Check marks rather than account numbers are used because customer accounts may not be numbered. When the accounts are not numbered, they are arranged alphabetically in the Accounts Receivable Ledger so they can be located easily.

In addition to the daily postings to customer accounts, the Sales Journal's Amount column is totaled at the end of the month. Then, the total is debited to Accounts Receivable and credited to Sales. The credit records the month's revenue from charge sales. The debit records the resulting increase in accounts receivable.

## IDENTIFYING POSTED AMOUNTS

When posting several journals to ledger accounts, you should indicate in the Posting Reference column before each posted amount the journal and the page number of the journal from which the amount was posted. Indicate the journal by using its initial. Thus, items posted from the Cash Disbursements Journal carry the initial *D* before their journal page numbers in the Posting Reference columns. Likewise, items from the Cash Receipts Journal carry the letter *R*. Those from the Sales Journal carry the initial *S*. Items from the Purchases Journal carry the initial *P*, and from the General Journal, the letter *G*.

---

**Progress Check**

6–7    When special journals are used:
   *a.* A General Journal is not used.
   *b.* All cash payments by cheque are recorded in the Cash Disbursements Journal.
   *c.* All purchase transactions are recorded in the Purchases Journal.
   *d.* All sales transactions are recorded in the Sales Journal.

6–8    Why does a columnar journal save posting labour?

**6-9** How can debits and credits remain equal when credit sales to customers are posted twice (once to Accounts Receivable and once to the customer's account)?

**6-10** How can you identify the journal from which a particular amount in a ledger account was posted?

A Cash Receipts Journal that is designed to save labour through posting column totals must be a multicolumn journal. A multicolumn journal is necessary because different accounts are credited when cash is received from different sources. For example, the cash receipts of a store normally fall into three groups: (1) cash from credit customers in payment of their accounts, (2) cash from cash sales, and (3) cash from other sources. Note in Illustration 6–5 that a special column is provided for the credits that result when cash is received from each of these sources.

## Cash from Credit Customers

When a Cash Receipts Journal similar to Illustration 6–5 is used to record cash received in payment of a customer's account, the customer's name is entered in the journal's Account Credited column. The amount credited to the customer's account is entered in the Accounts Receivable Credit column, and the debits to Sales Discounts and Cash are entered in the journal's last two columns.

Look at the Accounts Receivable Credit column. First, observe that this column contains only credits to customer accounts. Second, the individual credits are posted daily to the customer accounts in the subsidiary Accounts Receivable Ledger. Third, the column total is posted at the end of the month as a credit to the Accounts Receivable controlling account. This is the normal recording and posting procedure when using special journals and controlling accounts with subsidiary ledgers. Transactions are normally entered in a special journal column. Then, the individual amounts are posted to the subsidiary ledger accounts and the column totals are posted to the general ledger accounts.

## Cash Sales

After cash sales are entered on one or more cash registers and totaled at the end of each day, the daily total is recorded with a debit to Cash and a credit to Sales. When using a Cash Receipts Journal like Illustration 6–5, the debits to Cash are entered in the Cash Debit column, and the credits in a special column headed Sales Credit. By using a separate Sales Credit column, the bookkeeper can post the total cash sales for a month as a single amount, the column total. (Although cash sales are normally journalized daily based on the cash register reading, cash sales are journalized only once each week in Illustration 6–5 to shorten the illustration.)

At the time they record daily cash sales in the Cash Receipts Journal, some bookkeepers, as in Illustration 6–5, place a check mark in the Posting Reference (PR) column to indicate that no amount is individually posted from that line of the journal. Other bookkeepers use a double check ($\sqrt{\sqrt{}}$) to distinguish amounts that are not posted to customer accounts from amounts that are posted.

## Miscellaneous Receipts of Cash

Most cash receipts are from collections of accounts receivable and from cash sales. However, other sources of cash include borrowing money from a bank or selling

CASH RECEIPTS JOURNAL

**LO 3**

Explain special journals and controlling accounts, use them to record transactions, and explain how to test the posting of entries to the Accounts Receivable and Accounts Payable subsidiary ledgers.

**Illustration 6–5**  Posting from the Cash Receipts Journal

| Cash Receipts Journal | | | | | | | | Page 2 |
|---|---|---|---|---|---|---|---|---|
| Date | Account Credited | Explanation | PR | Other Accounts Credit | Accts. Rec. Credit | Sales Credit | Sales Discounts Debit | Cash Debit |
| Feb. 7 | Sales ......... | Cash sales ...... | √ | | | 4,450.00 | | 4,450.00 |
| 12 | James Henry ... | Invoice, Feb. 2 ... | √ | | 450.00 | | 9.00 | 441.00 |
| 14 | Sales ......... | Cash sales ...... | √ | | | 3,925.00 | | 3,925.00 |
| 17 | Albert Smith ... | Invoice, Feb. 7 ... | √ | | 500.00 | | 10.00 | 490.00 |
| 20 | Notes Payable .. | Note to bank .... | 245 | 1,000.00 | | | | 1,000.00 |
| 21 | Sales ......... | Cash sales ...... | √ | | | 4,700.00 | | 4,700.00 |
| 23 | Sam Moore .... | Invoice, Feb. 13 .. | √ | | 350.00 | | 7.00 | 343.00 |
| 25 | Paul Roth ..... | Invoice, Feb. 15 .. | √ | | 200.00 | | 4.00 | 196.00 |
| 28 | Sales ......... | Cash sales ...... | √ | | | 4,225.00 | | 4,225.00 |
| 28 | Totals ....... | | | 1,000.00 | 1,500.00 | 17,300.00 | 30.00 | 19,770.00 |
| | | | | (√) | (106) | (413) | (415) | (101) |

Individual amounts in the Other Accounts Credit and Accounts Receivable Credit columns are posted daily.

Total is not posted.

Totals posted at the end of the month.

**Accounts Receivable Ledger**

**Frank Booth**

| Date | PR | Debit | Credit | Balance |
|---|---|---|---|---|
| Feb. 25 | S3 | 175.00 | | 175.00 |

**James Henry**

| Date | PR | Debit | Credit | Balance |
|---|---|---|---|---|
| Feb. 2 | S3 | 450.00 | | 450.00 |
| 12 | R2 | | 450.00 | -0- |
| 22 | S3 | 225.00 | | 225.00 |

**Sam Moore**

| Date | PR | Debit | Credit | Balance |
|---|---|---|---|---|
| Feb. 13 | S3 | 350.00 | | 350.00 |
| 23 | R2 | | 350.00 | -0- |

**Paul Roth**

| Date | PR | Debit | Credit | Balance |
|---|---|---|---|---|
| Feb. 15 | S3 | 200.00 | | 200.00 |
| 25 | R2 | | 200.00 | -0- |

**Albert Smith**

| Date | PR | Debit | Credit | Balance |
|---|---|---|---|---|
| Feb. 7 | S3 | 500.00 | | 500.00 |
| 17 | R2 | | 500.00 | -0- |
| 28 | S3 | 250.00 | | 250.00 |

**General Ledger**

**Cash**  No. 101

| Date | PR | Debit | Credit | Balance |
|---|---|---|---|---|
| Feb. 28 | R2 | 19,770.00 | | 19,770.00 |

**Accounts Receivable**  No. 106

| Date | PR | Debit | Credit | Balance |
|---|---|---|---|---|
| Feb. 28 | S3 | 2,150.00 | | 2,150.00 |
| 28 | R2 | | 1,500.00 | 650.00 |

**Notes Payable**  No. 245

| Date | PR | Debit | Credit | Balance |
|---|---|---|---|---|
| Feb. 20 | R2 | | 1,000.00 | 1,000.00 |

**Sales**  No. 413

| Date | PR | Debit | Credit | Balance |
|---|---|---|---|---|
| Feb. 28 | S3 | | 2,150.00 | 2,150.00 |
| 28 | R2 | | 17,300.00 | 19,450.00 |

**Sales Discounts**  No. 415

| Date | PR | Debit | Credit | Balance |
|---|---|---|---|---|
| Feb. 28 | R2 | 30.00 | | 30.00 |

unneeded assets. The Other Accounts Credit column is for receipts that do not occur often enough to warrant a separate column. In most companies, the items entered in this column are few and are posted to a variety of general ledger accounts. As a result, postings are less apt to be omitted if these items are posted daily.

The Cash Receipts Journal's Posting Reference column is used only for daily postings from the Other Accounts and Accounts Receivable columns. The account numbers in the Posting Reference column indicate items that were posted to general ledger accounts. The check marks indicate either that an item (like a day's cash sales) was not posted or that an item was posted to the subsidiary Accounts Receivable Ledger.

## Month-End Postings

At the end of the month, the amounts in the Accounts Receivable, Sales, Sales Discounts, and Cash columns of the Cash Receipts Journal are posted as column totals. However, the transactions recorded in any journal must result in equal debits and credits to general ledger accounts. Therefore, to be sure that the total debits and credits in a columnar journal are equal, the bookkeeper must *crossfoot* the column totals before posting them. To *foot* a column of numbers is to add it. To crossfoot, add the debit column totals and add the credit column totals; then compare the two sums for equality. For Illustration 6–5, the column totals appear as follows:

| Debit Columns | | Credit Columns | |
|---|---|---|---|
| Sales discounts debit .... | $   30 | Other accounts credit ....... | $  1,000 |
| Cash debit ........... | 19,770 | Accounts receivable credit .... | 1,500 |
| | | Sales credit ............. | 17,300 |
| Total ............... | $19,800 | Total .................. | $19,800 |

After crossfooting the journal to confirm that debits equal credits, the bookkeeper posts the totals of the last four columns as indicated in each column heading. Because the individual items in the Other Accounts column are posted daily, the column total is not posted. Note in Illustration 6–5 the check mark below the Other Accounts column. The check mark indicates that the column total was not posted. The account numbers of the accounts to which the remaining column totals were posted are in parentheses below each column.

Posting items daily from the Other Accounts column with a delayed posting of the offsetting items in the Cash column (total) causes the General Ledger to be out of balance during the month. However, this does not matter because posting the Cash column total causes the offsetting amounts to reach the General Ledger before the trial balance is prepared.

## POSTING RULE

Now that we have explained the procedures for posting from two different journals to a subsidiary ledger and its controlling account, the rule that governs all such postings should be clear. The rule for posting to a subsidiary ledger and its controlling account is: *The controlling account must be debited periodically for an amount or amounts equal to the sum of the debits that have already been posted to the subsidiary ledger, and it must be credited periodically for an amount or amounts equal to the sum of the credits that have already been posted to the subsidiary ledger.*

# PURCHASES JOURNAL

A Purchases Journal with one money column can be used to record purchases of merchandise on credit. However, a Purchases Journal usually is more useful if it is a multicolumn journal in which all credit purchases on account are recorded. Such a journal may have columns similar to those in Illustration 6–6. In the illustrated journal, the invoice date and terms together indicate the date on which payment for each purchase is due. The Accounts Payable Credit column is used to record the amounts credited to each creditor's account. These amounts are posted daily to the individual creditor accounts in a subsidiary Accounts Payable Ledger.

In Illustration 6–6, note that each line of the Account column shows the subsidiary ledger account that should be posted for the amount in the Accounts Payable Credit column. The Account column also shows the general ledger account to be debited when a purchase involves an amount recorded in the Other Accounts Debit column.

In this illustration, note the separate column provided for purchases of office supplies on credit. A separate column such as this is useful whenever several transactions involve debits to a particular account. The Other Accounts Debit column in Illustration 6–6 allows the Purchases Journal to be used for all purchase transactions involving credits to Accounts Payable. The individual amounts in the Other Accounts Debit column typically are posted daily to the indicated general ledger accounts.

At the end of the month, all of the column totals except the Other Accounts Debit column are posted to the appropriate general ledger accounts. After this is done, the balance in the Accounts Payable controlling account should equal the sum of the account balances in the subsidiary Accounts Payable Ledger.

# THE CASH DISBURSEMENTS JOURNAL OR CHEQUE REGISTER

The Cash Disbursements Journal, like the Cash Receipts Journal, has columns so that you can post repetitive debits and credits in column totals. The repetitive cash payments involve debits to the Accounts Payable controlling account and credits to both Purchases Discounts and Cash. Most companies usually purchase merchandise on credit. Therefore, a Purchases column is not needed. Instead, the occasional cash purchase is recorded as shown on line 2 of Illustration 6–7.

Observe that the illustrated journal has a column headed Cheque Number (Ch. No.). To gain control over cash disbursements, all payments except for very small amounts should be made by cheque.[1] The cheques should be prenumbered by the printer and should be entered in the journal in numerical order with each cheque's number in the column headed Ch. No. This makes it possible to scan the numbers in the column for omitted cheques. When a Cash Disbursements Journal has a column for cheque numbers, it is often called a **Cheque Register.**

The individual amounts in the Other Accounts Debit column of a Cash Disbursements Journal are normally posted to the appropriate general ledger accounts on a daily basis. The individual amounts in the Accounts Payable Debit column are also posted daily to the named creditors' accounts in the subsidiary Accounts Payable Ledger. At the end of the month, the bookkeeper crossfoots the column totals and posts the Accounts Payable Debit column total to the Accounts Payable

---

[1] In Chapter 7, we discuss a system that is used to control small payments made with currency and coins.

**Illustration 6-6**   Posting from the Purchases Journal

## Purchases Journal          Page 1

| Date | Account | Date of Invoice | Terms | PR | Purchases Debit | Office Supplies Debit | Other Accounts Debit | Accounts Payable Credit |
|------|---------|-----------------|-------|-----|-----------------|-----------------------|----------------------|-------------------------|
| Feb. 3 | Horn Supply Co. ......... | Feb. 2 | n/30 | √ | 275.00 | 75.00 | | 350.00 |
| 5 | Acme Mfg. Co. .......... | Feb. 5 | 2/10,n/30 | √ | 200.00 | | | 200.00 |
| 13 | Wycoff & Co. ........... | Feb. 10 | 2/10,n/30 | √ | 150.00 | | | 150.00 |
| 20 | Smith & Co. ............ | Feb. 18 | 2/10,n/30 | √ | 300.00 | | | 300.00 |
| 25 | Acme Mfg. Co. .......... | Feb. 24 | 2/10,n/30 | √ | 100.00 | | | 100.00 |
| 28 | Store Supplies/HAG Co. .... | Feb. 28 | n/30 | 125/√ | 125.00 | 25.00 | 75.00 | 225.00 |
| 28 | Totals ................ | | | | 1,150.00 | 100.00 | 75.00 | 1,325.00 |
| | | | | | (505) | (124) | (√) | (201) |

These totals are posted at the end of the month.

Individual amounts in the Other Accounts Debit and Accounts Payable Credit columns are posted daily.

### General Ledger

**Office Supplies**     No. 124

| Date | PR | Debit | Credit | Balance |
|------|-----|-------|--------|---------|
| Feb. 28 | P1 | 100.00 | | 100.00 |

**Store Supplies**     No. 125

| Date | PR | Debit | Credit | Balance |
|------|-----|-------|--------|---------|
| Feb. 28 | P1 | 75.00 | | 75.00 |

**Accounts Payable**     No. 201

| Date | PR | Debit | Credit | Balance |
|------|-----|-------|--------|---------|
| Feb. 28 | P1 | | 1,325.00 | 1,325.00 |

**Purchases**     No. 505

| Date | PR | Debit | Credit | Balance |
|------|-----|-------|--------|---------|
| Feb. 28 | P1 | 1,150.00 | | 1,150.00 |

### Accounts Payable Ledger

**Acme Mfg. Company**

| Date | PR | Debit | Credit | Balance |
|------|-----|-------|--------|---------|
| Feb. 5 | P1 | | 200.00 | 200.00 |
| 25 | P1 | | 100.00 | 300.00 |

**HAG Company**

| Date | PR | Debit | Credit | Balance |
|------|-----|-------|--------|---------|
| Feb. 28 | P1 | | 225.00 | 225.00 |

**Horn Supply Company**

| Date | PR | Debit | Credit | Balance |
|------|-----|-------|--------|---------|
| Feb. 3 | P1 | | 350.00 | 350.00 |

**Smith & Company**

| Date | PR | Debit | Credit | Balance |
|------|-----|-------|--------|---------|
| Feb. 20 | P1 | | 300.00 | 300.00 |

**Wycoff & Company**

| Date | PR | Debit | Credit | Balance |
|------|-----|-------|--------|---------|
| Feb. 13 | P1 | | 150.00 | 150.00 |

**Illustration 6-7**   Posting from the Cash Disbursements Journal

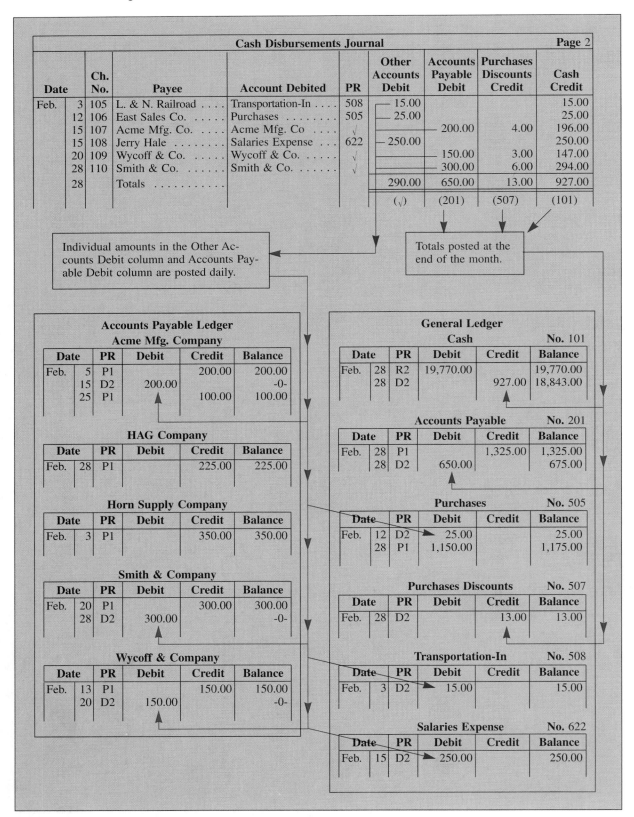

controlling account. Then, the Purchases Discounts Credit column total is posted to the Purchases Discounts account and the Cash Credit column total is posted to the Cash account. The Other Accounts column total is not posted.

Periodically, after all posting is completed, the account balances in the General Ledger and the subsidiary ledgers should be tested for accuracy. To do this, the bookkeeper first prepares a trial balance of the General Ledger to confirm that debits equal credits. If the trial balance balances, the accounts in the General Ledger, including the controlling accounts, are assumed to be correct. Second, the subsidiary ledgers are tested by preparing schedules of accounts receivable and accounts payable.

**TESTING THE ACCURACY OF THE LEDGERS**

A **schedule of accounts payable** is prepared by listing the accounts in the Accounts Payable Ledger with their balances and calculating the sum of the balances. If the total is equal to the balance of the Accounts Payable controlling account, the accounts in the Accounts Payable Ledger are presumably correct. Illustration 6–8 shows a schedule of accounts payable drawn from the Accounts Payable Ledger of Illustration 6–7.

A **schedule of accounts receivable** is prepared in the same way as a schedule of accounts payable. Also, if its total equals the balance of the Accounts Receivable controlling account, you can assume the accounts in the Accounts Receivable Ledger are correct.

Illustration 6–9 provides a schematic look at the flow of accounting information from the source documents through to the general ledger and trial balance. This flow of information is essentially the same whether a manual or computerized accounting system is being used. The advantage of a computerized system is in its accuracy since the posting of the amounts to the accounts, the accumulation of balances, and the production of the financial statements are done automatically by the program. This assumes, of course, that the initial identification of the accounts and the entering of the amounts are done accurately. A solid knowledge of accounting is still necessary whether a manual or computerized system is being used.

**Progress Check**

6–11    When special journals and controlling accounts with subsidiary ledgers are used, which of the following is not true?
   a. Transactions are first entered in the appropriate special journal.
   b. All column totals, except Other Accounts, are posted to the general ledger accounts at month-end.
   c. Individual transactions in the Other Accounts columns are posted to the appropriate general ledger accounts at month-end.

6–12    What is the rule for posting to a subsidiary ledger and its controlling account?

6–13    To test the accuracy of amounts posted to Accounts Receivable and Accounts Payable controlling accounts and their subsidiary ledgers:
   a. Prepare a trial balance of the General Ledger accounts.
   b. Foot and crossfoot the column totals in the journals.
   c. Prepare schedules of accounts receivable and accounts payable.
   d. Both a and c.

Illustration 6-8
Schedule of
Accounts Payable,
December 31

| | |
|---|---:|
| Acme Mfg. Company . . . . | $100 |
| HAG Company . . . . . . . . | 225 |
| Horn Supply Company . . . . | 350 |
| Total accounts payable . . . . | $675 |

## SALES AND GOODS AND SERVICES TAXES

**LO 4**

Explain how sales and goods and services taxes are recorded in special journals, how sales invoices can serve as a Sales Journal, and how sales returns and allowances are recorded.

## Provincial Sales Tax

All provinces except Alberta require retailers to collect a provincial sales tax (**PST**) from their customers and to periodically remit this tax to the appropriate provincial authority. When special journals are used, a column is provided for PST in the Sales Journal and the Cash Receipts Journal. A record of PST is obtained by recording in the PST column the appropriate amount of PST on cash sales (Cash Receipts Journal) and sales on account (Sales Journal). It should be noted that not all sales are subject to PST.

## Goods and Services Tax

The goods and services tax (**GST**) is a 7% tax on almost all goods and services provided in Canada. It is a federal tax on the consumer. However, unlike the PST, businesses pay GST up front but generally receive a full credit or refund for all GST paid. Ultimately, only the final consumer bears the burden of this tax. This is because businesses collect GST on sales, but since they receive full credit for GST paid on their purchases, they only remit the difference to the appropriate federal authority. To illustrate the collection and payment of GST consider the following example.

LM Company assembles riding mowers. It pays $200 for materials which are subject to GST of $14. LM pays the $14 to its suppliers who remit the $14 to Revenue Canada. LM now has a $14 GST credit, that is, prepaid GST.

LM sells the mower to KD Company, a dealer, for $500 and collects $35 in GST. LM remits the $35, minus the $14 input credit, that is, the GST paid to its suppliers. KD now has a $35 GST credit, that is, prepaid GST.

KD sells the mower to CC, the consumer, for $800 and collects $56 in GST. KD remits the $56, minus the $35 GST credit to Revenue Canada.

To summarize:

| | GST Paid | GST Collected | GST Remitted |
|---|---:|---:|---:|
| Materials supplier | | $14 | $14 |
| LM Company | $14 | 35 | 21 |
| KD Company | 35 | 56 | 21 |
| CC (the consumer) | 56 | | $56 |

The total GST remitted is $56, the same amount that CC, the consumer, paid. The supplier, and LM and KD companies act as collection agents, collecting the tax along each stage of the process.

**Illustration 6-9** Flow of Accounting Information

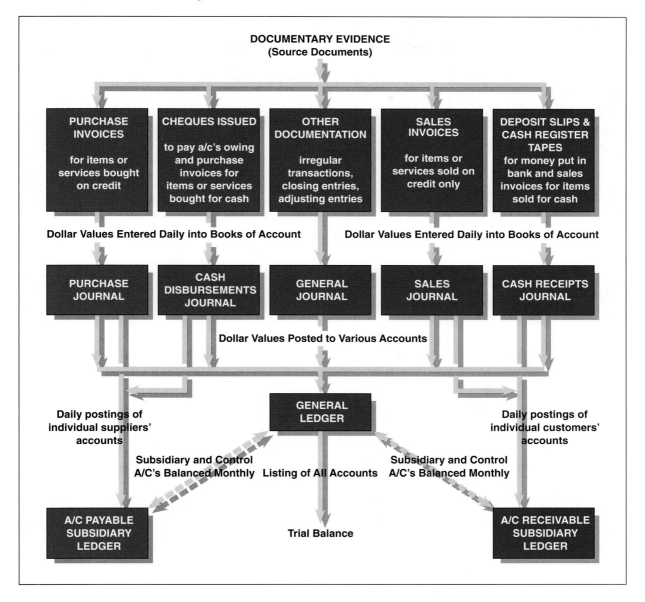

To facilitate the recording of GST, special GST (credit) columns must be pro-vided not only in the Sales Journal and the Cash Receipts Journal, as in the case of PST, but also GST (debit) columns in the Purchases Journal and Cash Dis-bursements Journal. To illustrate, assume that Berlasty Company uses specialized journals shown in Illustration 6–10. The following transactions were completed and recorded during December:

Dec. 1   Purchases on account, $1,000 from Jason Supply, terms n/30.
    3   Paid transportation on the Dec. 1 purchase, $30.

**Illustration 6-10**  Special Journals with PST and GST Columns as Applicable

### Purchases Journal

| Date | Account Credited | Terms | PR | Accounts Payable Credit | Purchases Debit | Office Supplies Debit | GST Payable Debit |
|------|-----------------|-------|-----|------------------------|-----------------|----------------------|-------------------|
| Dec. 1 | Jason Supply | n/30 | | 1,070.00 | 1,000.00 | | 70.00 |
| | | | | | | | 70.00 |
| | | | | | | | (225) |

### Cash Disbursements Journal

| Date | Ch. No. | Account Debited | PR | Other Accounts Debit | GST Payable Debit | Accts. Payable Debit | Purch. Disc. Credit | Cash Credit |
|------|---------|-----------------|-----|---------------------|-------------------|---------------------|--------------------|-------------|
| Dec. 3 | 256 | Transportation-in | | 30.00 | 2.10 | | | 32.10 |
| 9 | 257 | Purchases | | 500.00 | 35.00 | | | 535.00 |
| 28 | 258 | Accts. Pay/Jason Supply | | | | 1,070.00 | | 1,070.00 |
| | | | | 530.00 | 37.10 | 1,070.00 | | 1,637.10 |
| | | | | | (225) | | | |

### Sales Journal

| Date | Account Debited | Invoice No. | PR | Acct. Rec. Debit | PST Payable Credit | GST Payable Credit | Sales Credit |
|------|-----------------|-------------|-----|-----------------|--------------------|--------------------|--------------|
| Dec. 30 | S. Burns | 2734 | | 2,260.00 | 120.00 | 140.00 | 2,000.00 |
| | | | | | (224) | (225) | |

### Cash Receipts Journal

| Date | Account Credited | Explanation | PR | Other Accounts Credit | Accts. Rec. Credit | PST Payable Credit | GST Payable Credit | Sales Credit | Cash Debit |
|------|-----------------|-------------|-----|----------------------|--------------------|--------------------|--------------------|--------------|-----------|
| Dec. 15 | | | | | | 96.00 | 84.00 | 1,200.00 | 1,380.00 |
| | | | | | | (224) | (225) | | |

Dec. 9   Purchases for cash, $500.

1   Cash sale, $1,200 (subject to PST and GST).

28   Paid for the Dec. 1 purchase.

30   Sales to S. Burns on account, $2,000 ($1,500 subject to PST and $2,000 subject to GST).

After the posting is completed, as described earlier in the chapter, the PST and GST T-accounts would appear as follows:

| PST (224) | | | GST (225) | | | | |
|-----------|---|--------|-----------|-------|--------|-----|--------|
| | SJ | 120.00 | PJ | 70.00 | SJ | | 140.00 |
| | CRJ | 96.00 | CDJ | 37.10 | CRS | | 84.00 |
| Balance | | 216.00 | Balance | | | | 116.90 |

On December 31, PST payable amounts to $216 and GST payable amounts to $116.90. The computation of GST is not uniform throughout the country. In some of the provinces, the computation is as illustrated above, that is, PST and GST are computed as a percentage of the selling price. In other provinces, PST is initially computed as a percentage of the selling price and GST is computed as a percentage of the total of the selling price plus the PST. It should also be noted that while GST is a 7% federal tax, thus uniform in each of the provinces, PST is a provincial tax and differs in percentage from province to province. The preceding discussion is based on Ontario's PST of 8%.

In Illustration 6–10, one account was used to record GST on purchases and on sales. Some accountants prefer to record GST on purchases in a Prepaid GST account and GST on sales in a GST Payable account. Thus, if two accounts are used in Illustration 6–10, the GST Payable Debit column in the Purchases Journal and the Cash Disbursements Journal would be changed to Prepaid GST. The Sales Journal and the Cash Receipts Journal would remain as illustrated. The use of one or two accounts to account for GST is a matter of preference; the final result is the same.

## Remittance of GST

The GST is administered by Revenue Canada Customs and Excise. Remittance is accompanied by a Goods and Services Tax Return shown in Illustration 6–11.

Frequency of filing returns is dependent on the size of the business. Large businesses (annual sales in excess of $6 million) are required to file GST returns monthly. Medium size businesses (annual sales of $500,000 to $6 million) are required to file quarterly. Small businesses (annual sales up to $500,000) have the option of filing annually but paying quarterly installments. GST for a period must be remitted to Revenue Canada by the end of the month following the month (quarter) collected.

**SALES INVOICES AS A SALES JOURNAL**

To save labour, some retailers avoid using Sales Journals for credit sales. Instead, they post each sales invoice total directly to the customer's account in the subsidiary Accounts Receivable Ledger. Then, they place copies of the invoices in numerical order in a binder. At the end of the month, they total all the invoices of that month and make a general journal entry to debit Accounts Receivable and credit Sales for the total. In effect, the bound invoice copies act as a Sales Journal. Such a procedure is known as direct posting of sales invoices.

**SALES RETURNS**

A business that has only a few sales returns may record them in a General Journal with an entry like the following:

| | | | | | |
|---|---|---|---|---|---|
| Oct. | 17 | Sales Returns and Allowances .................. | 414 | 17.50 | |
| | | Accounts Receivable—George Ball ........... | 106/√ | | 17.50 |
| | | *Customer returned merchandise.* | | | |

The debit of the entry is posted to the Sales Returns and Allowances account. The credit is posted to both the Accounts Receivable controlling account and to

**Illustration 6–11**    Goods and Services Tax Return

Revenue Canada / Revenu Canada
Customs and Excise / Douanes et Accise

PROTECTED WHEN COMPLETED
PROTÉGÉ UNE FOIS REMPLI

**GOODS AND SERVICES TAX RETURN (Non-personalized)**
**DÉCLARATION DE LA TAXE SUR LES PRODUITS ET SERVICES (non personnalisée)**

Prescribed by the Minister of National Revenue under subsection 238(4) of the Excise Tax Act / Prescrit par le ministre du Revenu national en vertu du paragraphe 238(4) de la Loi sur la taxe d'accise

This return is for use by a GST registrant, or by a person who is required to remit tax where a personalized return is not available for the reporting period.

Cette formule doit être utilisée par les inscrits ou par toute personne tenue de verser la taxe lorsqu'une déclaration personnalisée n'est pas disponible pour la période de déclaration.

● To complete this form, please refer to the Instructions on the back.
Pour remplir cette formule, voir les renseignements au verso de la déclaration.

GST Account Number / Numéro de compte TPS: A 1 2 3 4 9 7 3 4

Reporting Period / Période de déclaration: From/du 95 10 01 To/au 95 12 31
Due Date / Date d'échéance: 96 01 31

Name of Individual or Entity / Raison sociale ou nom: BERLASTY COMPANY

Trading Name if Different from Above / Nom commercial s'il diffère de la raison sociale ou du nom

Mailing Address (No., Street and Apt. Number) / Adresse postale (n°, rue, app.): 125 SUNSET AVENUE

City / Ville: WINDSOR

Province: ONTARIO

Postal Code / Code postal: N9B 3P4

Name of the person we may contact concerning your return / Nom de la personne avec qui nous pouvons communiquer concernant votre déclaration: SANDRA BERLASTY

Telephone No. / N° de téléphone: (519) 253-4232

Personal information provided on this form is protected under the provisions of the Privacy Act and is maintained in Personal Information Bank RCC/P-PU-065.

Les renseignements personnels fournis dans cette formule sont protégés en vertu de la Loi sur la protection des renseignements personnels et sont conservés dans le Répertoire des renseignements personnels RND/P-PU-065.

**SECTION TWO - TAX CALCULATIONS**
**PARTIE DEUX - CALCULS DE LA TAXE**

| | | |
|---|---|---|
| GST Collectible / TPS perceptible | 103 | 2 2 4 0 0 |
| GST Adjustments / Redressements de la TPS | 104 | 0 |
| Input Tax Credit (ITC) / Crédit de taxe sur les intrants (CTI) | 106 | – 1 0 7 1 0 |
| ITC Adjustments / Redressements du CTI | 107 | 0 |

**SECTION ONE - PERIOD SUMMARY**
**PARTIE UN - SOMMAIRE DE LA PÉRIODE**

| | | |
|---|---|---|
| Total Taxable Supplies (sales and other revenue) / Total des fournitures taxables (ventes et autres recettes) | 101 | 3 2 0 0 0 0 |
| Total Purchases / Total des achats | 102 | 1 5 3 0 0 0 |
| Paid by instalments / Payée par acomptes provisionnels | 110 | 0 |
| Rebates / Remboursements | 111 | 0 |

Add Lines 103 and 104 / Additionnez les montants des lignes 103 et 104 — 105

Add Lines 106 and 107 / Additionnez les montants des lignes 106 et 107 — 108

Subtract Line 108 from Line 105 (indicate if negative amount) / Soustrayez le montant de la ligne 108 de celui de la ligne 105 (indiquez s'il s'agit d'un montant négatif) — 109

Add Lines 110 and 111 / Additionnez les montants des lignes 110 et 111 — 112

Subtract Line 112 from Line 109 (indicate if negative amount) / Soustrayez le montant de la ligne 112 de celui de la ligne 109 (indiquez s'il s'agit d'un montant négatif) — 113

Total GST and Adjustments for Period / Total de la TPS et des redressements pour cette période: 2 2 4 0 0

Total ITCs and Adjustments / Total du CTI et des redressements: – 1 0 7 1 0

**NET TAX - TAXE NETTE**: 1 1 6 9 0

Total Other Credits - Total des autres crédits: 0

**BALANCE - SOLDE**: 1 1 6 9 0

OR / OU

Refund Claimed / Remboursement demandé — 114

Payment Enclosed / Paiement inclus — 115: 1 1 6 9 0

If the balance is negative claim a refund, otherwise remit the amount owing. A balance of less than $1.00 will neither be charged nor refunded. All registrants must file a return regardless of the balance. Do not staple or paper clip.

Si le montant du solde est négatif, demandez un remboursement. S'il est positif, vous devez remettre le montant inscrit. Les soldes inférieurs à 1,00 $ ne sont ni exigés ni remboursés. Tous les inscrits doivent produire une déclaration, peu importe le montant du solde. N'utilisez ni agrafes ni trombones.

I hereby certify that the information given in this return and in any documents attached is true, correct and complete in every respect and that I am authorized to sign on behalf of the registrant.

J'atteste que les renseignements fournis dans cette déclaration et dans tout document qui y serait joint sont vrais, exacts et complets sous tous les rapports et que je suis autorisé à signer au nom de l'inscrit.

▶ IT IS A SERIOUS OFFENCE TO MAKE A FALSE RETURN.
LA PRODUCTION D'UNE DÉCLARATION FAUSSE EST UNE INFRACTION GRAVE.

Name / Nom: Sandra Berlasty
Title / Titre: Treasurer
Authorized Signature / Signature autorisée: Sandra Berlasty
Date: January 31, 1996

GST 62 (90/11)

**PART 1: DETACH AND FORWARD TO PROCESSING CENTRE**
**PARTIE 1: DÉTACHEZ ET FAITES PARVENIR AU CENTRE DE TRAITEMENT DES DONNÉES**

the customer's account. Note the account number and the check mark, 106/√, in the PR column on the credit line. This indicates that both the Accounts Receivable controlling account in the General Ledger and the George Ball account in the Accounts Receivable Ledger were credited for $17.50. Both were credited because the balance of the controlling account in the General Ledger will not equal the sum of the customer account balances in the subsidiary ledger unless both are credited.

**Illustration 6-12**

| | | Sales Returns and Allowances Journal | | | | |
|---|---|---|---|---|---|---|
| Date | | Account Credited | Explanation | Credit Memo No. | PR | Amount |
| Oct. | 7 | Robert Moore ...... | Defective merchandise ....... | 203 | √ | 10.00 |
| | 14 | James Warren ...... | Defective merchandise ....... | 204 | √ | 12.00 |
| | 18 | T. M. Jones ........ | Not ordered ............. | 205 | √ | 6.00 |
| | 23 | Sam Smith ........ | Defective merchandise ...... | 206 | √ | 18.00 |
| | 31 | Sales Returns and Allowances, Dr.; Accts. Receivable, Cr. | | | | 46.00 |
| | | | | | | (414/106) |

A company with a large number of sales returns can save posting labour by recording them in a special Sales Returns and Allowances Journal similar to Illustration 6–12. Note that this is in keeping with the idea that a company can design and use a special journal for any group of similar transactions if there are enough transactions to warrant the journal. When using a Sales Returns and Allowances Journal to record returns, the amounts in the journal are posted daily to the customers' accounts. Then, at the end of the month, the journal total is posted as a debit to Sales Returns and Allowances and as a credit to Accounts Receivable.

## GENERAL JOURNAL ENTRIES

When special journals are used, a General Journal is always necessary for adjusting, closing, and correcting entries and for a few transactions that cannot be recorded in the special journals. Some of these transactions are purchases returns, purchases of plant assets financed by notes payable, and if a Sales Returns and Allowances Journal is not provided, sales returns.

---

**Progress Check**

6-14 If sales taxes must be recorded and special journals are used: *(a)* The sales taxes must be recorded in the General Journal. *(b)* A separate column for sales taxes should be included in the Cash Receipts Journal and the Sales Journal. *(c)* A special Sales Taxes Journal should be used.

6-15 What is direct posting of sales invoices?

6-16 If a company uses special journals for sales, purchases, cash receipts, and cash disbursements, why does it need a General Journal?

---

## USING THE INFORMATION— BUSINESS SEGMENTS

The accounting system a company uses is more complicated when a company is large and operates in more than one line of business. When information is provided about each **business segment** of the company, outside users of the financial statements can gain a better understanding of the overall business. A business segment is a portion of the company that can be separately identified by the products or services that it provides or a geographic market that it serves.

LO 5

Explain the nature and
use of business
segment information.

Companies that have securities traded in public markets must publish segment information if they have material operations in more than one industry.[2] The required information for each segment includes:

1. Revenues or net sales.
2. Operating profits.
3. Capital expenditures.
4. Depreciation and amortization expense.
5. Identifiable assets.

In addition, they may be required to report (1) a geographical distribution of sales and (2) sales to each major customer that accounts for 10% or more of total sales.

Look again at the net sales information for **Imperial Oil** presented on page 291. This is a typical example of business segment information. Note that the company identified three primary segments: natural resources, petroleum products, and chemicals. In addition, the company reported its geographic distribution of sales.

The usefulness of segment information comes from the fact that different industries and geographical areas often face different levels of risk, profitability, and opportunities for growth. The information helps financial statement readers gain insight about the performance of the segments and the dependence of the entire company on the profits derived from each of the segments.

---

**Progress Check**

6-17    **The requirements for segment information include presenting each segment's:**
        *(a)* **Revenues;**  *(b)* **Operating expenses;**  *(c)* **Income taxes;**  *(d)* **Capital expenditures;**  *(e)* **Both *a* and *d*.**

---

**SUMMARY OF THE CHAPTER IN TERMS OF LEARNING OBJECTIVES**

**LO 1. Describe the five basic components of an accounting system.** The components of accounting systems include source documents, input devices, the data processor, data storage, and output devices. Both manual and computerized systems must have all five components.

**LO 2. Describe the types of computers used in large and small accounting systems, the role of software in those systems, and the different approaches to inputting and processing data, including the use of networking.** Depending on the complexity of a company's accounting system, the computers used may be large mainframe computers or smaller microcomputers. If a mainframe computer is used, the software that provides the computer instructions is likely to be custom made for the company. However, an increasing variety of off-the-shelf programs are available, especially for microcomputers. There are many different ways to set up computer systems, including batch and on-line processing, and computer networks.

**LO 3. Explain special journals and controlling accounts, use them to record transactions, and explain how to test the posting of entries to the Accounts Receivable and Accounts Payable subsidiary ledgers.** Columnar journals are designed so that repetitive debits or credits are entered in separate columns. A typical set of special journals includes a Sales Journal, a Purchases Journal, a Cash

---

[2]*CICA Handbook*, section 1700, "Segmented Information" paragraph .33.

Receipts Journal, and a Cash Disbursements Journal (or Cheque Register). Any transactions that cannot be entered in the special journals are entered in the General Journal.

When many accounts of the same type are required, such as an account receivable for each credit customer, they usually are kept in a separate subsidiary ledger. Then, a single controlling account is maintained in the General Ledger. After all transactions are posted to the accounts in the subsidiary ledger and to the controlling account, the controlling account balance should equal the sum of the account balances in the subsidiary ledger.

**LO 4.** **Explain the use of special and general journals in accounting for sales taxes and sales returns and allowances, and explain how sales invoices can serve as a Sales Journal.** To record PST and GST, the Sales Journal and the Cash Receipts Journal should include separate PST and GST Payable columns. When sales invoices substitute for a Sales Journal, the customer accounts in the Accounts Receivable Ledger are posted directly from the sales invoices. Copies of the invoices for each month are then bound and totaled as a basis for recording the sales in the General Ledger. Sales returns and allowances may be recorded in the General Journal, or a special journal for sales returns and allowances may be used. GST paid by the firm is recorded in the Purchases Journal.

**LO 5.** **Explain the nature and use of business segment information.** Public companies with material operations in more than one industry must provide separate information for each segment. The information includes revenues, operating profits, capital expenditures, amortization, and identifiable assets. It also includes a geographical distribution of sales and sales to major customers.

---

# GLOSSARY

**Accounting system** the people, forms, procedures, and equipment that are used to capture data about the transactions of an entity and to generate from that data a variety of financial, managerial, and tax accounting reports. p. 292

**Accounts Payable Ledger** a subsidiary ledger that contains a separate account for each party that grants credit on account to the entity. p. 303

**Accounts Receivable Ledger** a subsidiary ledger that contains an account for each credit customer. p. 301

**Batch processing** an approach to inputting data that accumulates source documents for a period such as a day, week, or month and inputs all of them at the same time. p. 299

**Business segment** a portion of a company that can be separately identified by the products or services that it provides or a geographic market that it serves. p. 317

**Cheque Register** a book of original entry for recording cash payments by cheque. p. 308

**Columnar journal** a book of original entry having columns, each of which is designated as the place for

entering specific data about each transaction of a group of similar transactions. p. 301

**Computer network** a system in which computers are linked with each other so that different users on different computers can share access to the same data and the same programs. p. 299

**Controlling account** a general ledger account the balance of which (after posting) equals the sum of the balances of the accounts in a related subsidiary ledger. p. 303

**Data processor** the component of an accounting system that interprets, manipulates, and summarizes the recorded information so that it can be used in analyses and reports. p. 294

**Data storage** the component of an accounting system that keeps the inputted data in a readily accessible manner so that financial reports can be drawn from it efficiently. p. 294

**General Ledger** the ledger that contains the financial statement accounts of a business. p. 301

**GST (Goods and Services Tax)**   a federal tax on the consumer on almost all goods and services. p. 312

**Input device**   a means of transferring information from source documents to the data processing component of an accounting system. p. 293

**On-line processing**   an approach to inputting data whereby the data on each source document is inputted as soon as the document is available. p. 299

**Output devices**   the means by which information is taken out of the accounting system and made available for use. p. 295

**PST (Provincial Sales Tax)**   a tax collected by retailers on customer purchases. p. 312

**Schedule of accounts payable**   a list of the balances of all the accounts in the Accounts Payable Ledger that is summed to show the total amount of accounts payable outstanding. p. 311

**Schedule of accounts receivable**   a list of the balances of all the accounts in the Accounts Receivable Ledger that is summed to show the total amount of accounts receivable outstanding. p. 311

**Special journal**   a book of original entry that is designed and used for recording only a specified type of transaction. p. 300

**Subsidiary ledger**   a group of accounts that show the details underlying the balance of a controlling account in the General Ledger. p. 303

## QUESTIONS

1. What are the five basic components of an accounting system?

2. What are source documents? Give some examples.

3. What is the purpose of an input device? Give some examples of input devices for computer systems.

4. What is the difference between data that is stored off-line and data that is stored on-line?

5. What purpose is served by the output devices of an accounting system?

6. What is the difference between batch and on-line processing?

7. When special journals are used, separate special journals normally are used to record each of four different types of transactions. What are these four types of transactions?

8. Why should sales to and receipts of cash from credit customers be recorded and posted daily?

9. Both credits to customer accounts and credits to miscellaneous accounts are individually posted from a Cash Receipts Journal similar to the one in Illustration 6–5. Why not put both kinds of credits in the same column and thus save journal space?

10. What procedures allow copies of a company's sales invoices to be used as a Sales Journal?

11. When a general journal entry is used to record a returned credit sale, the credit of the entry must be posted twice. Does this cause the trial balance to be out of balance? Why or why not?

12. Look in Appendix I at Geac Computer's financial statements. What amount of operating income in 1994 came from operations in Europe? What geographic area generated the largest operating income?

## QUICK STUDY (Five-Minute Exercises)

Identify the role in an accounting system played by each of the lettered items by assigning a number from the list on the left:

1. Source documents          _____ a. Bar code reader
2. Input devices             _____ b. Filing cabinet
3. Data processor            _____ c. Bank statement
4. Data storage              _____ d. Calculator
5. Output devices            _____ e. Computer keyboard
                             _____ f. Floppy diskette
                             _____ g. Computer monitor
                             _____ h. Invoice from a supplier
                             _____ i. Computer hardware and software
                             _____ j. Computer printer

Fill in the blanks:

a. Personal computers, often called _____, are physically small, easy to operate, and increasingly inexpensive.

b. Off-the-shelf programs designed so that actions taken in one part of the system also produce results in related parts are known as _____ systems.

c. With _____ processing, source documents are accumulated for a period of time and then processed all at the same time, such as once a day, week, or month.

d. A computer _____ allows different computer users to share access to the same data and programs.

Sampson Iron Works uses a Sales Journal, a Purchases Journal, a Cash Receipts Journal, a Cash Disbursements Journal, and a General Journal. Sampson recently completed the following transactions. List the transaction letters and next to each letter give the name of the journal in which the transaction should be recorded.

a. Paid a creditor.                    e. Borrowed money from the bank.
b. Sold merchandise for cash.          f. Purchased shop supplies on credit.
c. Purchased merchandise on credit.    g. Paid an employee's salary.
d. Sold merchandise on credit.

The Nostalgic Book Shop uses a Sales Journal, a Purchases Journal, a Cash Receipts Journal, a Cash Disbursements Journal, and a General Journal. The following transactions occurred during the month of November. Journalize the November transactions that should be recorded in the General Journal.

Nov. 2   Purchased merchandise on credit for $1,900 from the Randolph Co., terms 2/10, n/30.

Nov. 12   The owner, I. M. Nowalski, contributed an automobile worth $13,500 to the business.

16   Sold merchandise on credit to W. Ryder for $1,100, terms n/30.

19   W. Ryder returned $90 of merchandise originally purchased on November 16.

28   Returned $170 of defective merchandise to the Randolph Co. from the November 2 purchase.

**QS 6–5**
**(LO 5)**

A company with publicly traded securities operates in more than one industry. Which of the following items of information about each business segment must the company report?

| | | | |
|---|---|---|---|
| a. | Revenues | e. | Capital expenditures |
| b. | Net sales | f. | Amortization and depreciation |
| c. | Operating profits | g. | Cash flows |
| d. | Operating expenses | h. | Identifiable assets |

# EXERCISES

**Exercise 6–1**
The Sales Journal
**(LO 3)**

Fletcher's Frozen Foods uses a Sales Journal, a Purchases Journal, a Cash Receipts Journal, a Cash Disbursements Journal, and a General Journal. The following transactions occurred during the month of February:

Feb. 2   Sold merchandise to M. Stohl for $356 cash, Invoice No. 5703.

5   Purchased merchandise on credit from Campbell Company, $2,035.

7   Sold merchandise to E. Jason for $950, terms 2/10, n/30, Invoice No. 5704.

8   Borrowed $5,000 by giving a note to the bank.

12   Sold merchandise to L. Patrick for $223, terms n/30, Invoice No. 5705.

16   Received $931 from E. Jason to pay for the purchase of February 7.

19   Sold used store equipment to Green Acres for $500.

25   Sold merchandise to P. Sumo for $428, terms n/30, Invoice No. 5706.

**Required**

On a sheet of notebook paper, draw a Sales Journal like the one that appears in Illustration 6–3. Journalize the February transactions that should be recorded in the Sales Journal.

**Exercise 6–2**
The Cash Receipts
Journal
**(LO 3)**

Landmark Map Company uses a Sales Journal, a Purchases Journal, a Cash Receipts Journal, a Cash Disbursements Journal, and a General Journal. The following transactions occurred during the month of September:

Sept. 3   Purchased merchandise on credit for $2,900 from Pace Supply Co.

7   Sold merchandise on credit to N. Jamal for $800, subject to a $16 sales discount if paid by the end of the month.

9   Borrowed $1,750 by giving a note to the bank.

13   Received a capital contribution of $3,500 from R. Galindo, the owner of the company.

18   Sold merchandise to T. Byrd for $199 cash.

22   Paid Pace Supply $2,900 for the merchandise purchased on September 3.

Sept. 27  Received $784 from N. Jamal in payment of the September 7 purchase.

30  Paid salaries of $1,500.

**Required**

On a sheet of notebook paper, draw a multicolumn Cash Receipts Journal like the one that appears in Illustration 6–5. Journalize the September transactions that should be recorded in the Cash Receipts Journal.

Gem Industries uses a Sales Journal, a Purchases Journal, a Cash Receipts Journal, a Cash Disbursements Journal, and a General Journal. The following transactions occurred during the month of July:

**Exercise 6–3**
**The Purchases Journal**
**(LO 3)**

July  1  Purchased merchandise on credit for $7,190 from Angel, Inc., terms n/30.

8  Sold merchandise on credit to H. Baruk for $1,300, subject to a $26 sales discount if paid by the end of the month.

10  J. Powers, the owner of the business, contributed $2,500 cash to the business.

14  Purchased store supplies from Steck & Vaughn on credit for $145, terms n/30.

17  Purchased office supplies on credit from King Mart for $310, terms n/30.

24  Sold merchandise to V. Valdi for $467 cash.

28  Purchased store supplies from Hadlock's for $79 cash.

29  Paid Angel, Inc., $7,190 for the merchandise purchased on July 1.

**Required**

On a sheet of notebook paper, draw a multicolumn Purchases Journal like the one that appears in Illustration 6–6. Journalize the July transactions that should be recorded in the Purchases Journal.

Neon Art Supply uses a Sales Journal, a Purchases Journal, a Cash Receipts Journal, a Cash Disbursements Journal, and a General Journal. The following transactions occurred during the month of March:

**Exercise 6–4**
**The Cash Disbursements Journal**
**(LO 3)**

Mar.  3  Purchased merchandise for $1,850 on credit from Paige, Inc., terms 2/10, n/30.

9  Issued Cheque No. 210 to Mott & Son to buy store supplies for $369.

12  Sold merchandise on credit to C. Klempt for $625, terms n/30.

17  Issued Cheque No. 211 for $1,000 to repay a note payable to City Bank.

20  Purchased merchandise for $4,700 on credit from LeBeck's, terms 2/10, n/30.

29  Issued Cheque No. 212 to LeBeck's to pay the amount due for the purchase of March 20, less the discount.

31  Paid salary of $1,500 to B. Eldon by issuing Cheque No. 213.

31  Issued Cheque No. 214 to Paige, Inc., to pay the amount due for the purchase of March 3.

**Required**

On a sheet of notebook paper, draw a multicolumn Cash Disbursements Journal like the one that appears in Illustration 6–7. Journalize the March transactions that should be recorded in the Cash Disbursements Journal.

**Exercise 6–5**
Special journal
transactions
**(LO 3)**

Simonetti Pharmacy uses the following journals: Sales Journal, Purchases Journal, Cash Receipts Journal, Cash Disbursements Journal, and General Journal. On June 5, Simonetti purchased merchandise priced at $15,000, subject to credit terms of 2/10, n/30. On June 14, the pharmacy paid the net amount due. However, in journalizing the payment, the bookkeeper debited Accounts Payable for $15,000 and failed to record the cash discount. Cash was credited for the actual amount paid. In what journals would the June 5 and the June 14 transactions have been recorded? What procedure is likely to discover the error in journalizing the June 14 transaction?

**Exercise 6–6**
Posting to subsidiary
ledger accounts
**(LO 3)**

At the end of May, the Sales Journal of Cowtown Leather Goods appeared as follows:

**Sales Journal**

| Date | | Account Debited | Invoice Number | PR | Amount |
|---|---|---|---|---|---|
| May | 6 | Bud Smith ................................ | 190 | | 1,780.00 |
| | 10 | Don Holly ................................ | 191 | | 2,040.00 |
| | 17 | Sandy Ford ................................ | 192 | | 960.00 |
| | 25 | Don Holly ................................ | 193 | | 335.00 |
| | 31 | Total ................................ | | | 5,115.00 |

Cowtown also had recorded the return of merchandise with the following entry:

| May | 20 | Sales Returns and Allowances ................. | 165.00 | |
|---|---|---|---|---|
| | | Accounts Receivable—Sandy Ford ........... | | 165.00 |
| | | *Customer returned merchandise.* | | |

**Required**

1. On a sheet of notebook paper, open a subsidiary Accounts Receivable Ledger that has a T-account for each customer listed in the Sales Journal. Post to the customer accounts the entries in the Sales Journal and any portion of the general journal entry that affects a customer's account.

2. Open a General Ledger that has T-accounts for Accounts Receivable, Sales, and Sales Returns and Allowances. Post the Sales Journal and any portion of the general journal entry that affects these accounts.

3. Prepare a list or schedule of the accounts in the subsidiary Accounts Receivable Ledger and add their balances to show that the total equals the balance in the Accounts Receivable controlling account.

**Exercise 6–7**
Accounts Receivable
Ledger
**(LO 3, 4)**

Skillern Company posts its sales invoices directly and then binds the invoices to make them into a Sales Journal. Sales are subject to a 10% Provincial Sales Tax and the 7% Goods and Services Tax. Skillern had the following sales during January:

| Jan. | 2 | Jay Newton ..... | $ 3,600 |
|---|---|---|---|
| | 8 | Adrian Carr .... | 6,100 |
| | 10 | Kathy Olivas .... | 13,400 |
| | 14 | Lisa Mack ..... | 20,500 |
| | 20 | Kathy Olivas .... | 11,200 |
| | 29 | Jay Newton ..... | 7,300 |
| | | Total ......... | $62,100 |

## Required

1. On a sheet of notebook paper, open a subsidiary Accounts Receivable Ledger having a T-account for each customer. Post the invoices to the subsidiary ledger.

2. Give the general journal entry to record the end-of-month total of the Sales Journal.

3. Open an Accounts Receivable controlling account and a Sales account and post the general journal entry.

4. Prepare a list or schedule of the accounts in the subsidiary Accounts Receivable Ledger and add their balances to show that the total equals the balance in the Accounts Receivable controlling account.

Following are the condensed journals of Tip-Top Trophy Shop. The journal column headings are incomplete in that they do not indicate whether the columns are debit or credit columns.

**Exercise 6–8**

Posting from special journals and subsidiary ledgers to T-accounts (LO 3)

### Sales Journal

| Account | Amount |
|---|---|
| Jack Heinz . . . . . . . . . . . . . | 2,700 |
| Trudy Stone . . . . . . . . . . . . | 7,400 |
| Wayne Day . . . . . . . . . . . . . | 3,000 |
| Total . . . . . . . . . . . . . . . | 13,100 |

### Purchases Journal

| Account | Amount |
|---|---|
| Frasier Corp. . . . . . . . . . . . | 3,400 |
| Sultan, Inc. . . . . . . . . . . . . | 6,500 |
| McGraw Company . . . . . . . . | 1,700 |
| Total . . . . . . . . . . . . . . . | 11,600 |

### General Journal

| | | | | |
|---|---|---|---|---|
| ... | .. | Sales Returns and Allowances . . . . . . . . . . . . . . . . . | 400.00 | |
| .. | .. | Accounts Receivable—Jack Heinz . . . . . . . . . . . . | | 400.00 |
| ... | .. | Accounts Payable—Frasier Corp. . . . . . . . . . . . . . . | 850.00 | |
| .. | .. | Purchases Returns and Allowances . . . . . . . . . . . . | | 850.00 |

### Cash Receipts Journal

| Account | Other Accounts | Accounts Receivable | Sales | Sales Discounts | Cash |
|---|---|---|---|---|---|
| Jack Heinz . . . . . . . . . . . . | | 2,300 | | 46 | 2,254 |
| Sales . . . . . . . . . . . . . . . | | | 1,950 | | 1,950 |
| Notes Payable . . . . . . . . . . | 3,500 | | | | 3,500 |
| Sales . . . . . . . . . . . . . . . | | | 525 | | 525 |
| Trudy Stone . . . . . . . . . . . | | 7,400 | | 148 | 7,252 |
| Store Equipment . . . . . . . . | 200 | | | | 200 |
| Totals . . . . . . . . . . . . . . | 3,700 | 9,700 | 2,475 | 194 | 15,681 |

### Cash Disbursements Journal

| Account | Other Accounts | Accounts Payable | Purchases Discounts | Cash |
|---|---|---|---|---|
| Prepaid Insurance . . . . . . . . | 960 | | | 960 |
| Sultan, Inc. . . . . . . . . . . . | | 6,500 | 195 | 6,305 |
| Frasier Corp. . . . . . . . . . . | | 2,550 | 51 | 2,499 |
| Store Equipment . . . . . . . . . | 1,570 | | | 1,570 |
| Totals . . . . . . . . . . . . . . | 2,530 | 9,050 | 246 | 11,334 |

**Required**

1. Prepare T-accounts on notebook paper for the following general ledger and subsidiary ledger accounts. Separate the accounts of each ledger group as follows:

| **General Ledger Accounts** | **Accounts Receivable Ledger Accounts** |
|---|---|
| Cash | Wayne Day |
| Accounts Receivable | Jack Heinz |
| Prepaid Insurance | Trudy Stone |
| Store Equipment | |
| Accounts Payable | |
| Notes Payable | |
| Sales | **Accounts Payable Ledger Accounts** |
| Sales Returns and Allowances | Frasier Corp. |
| Sales Discounts | McGraw Company |
| Purchases | Sultan, Inc. |
| Purchases Returns and Allowances | |
| Purchases Discounts | |

2. Without referring to any of the illustrations in the chapter that show complete column headings for the journals, post the journals to the proper T-accounts.

**Exercise 6–9**
Errors related to the Purchases Journal
**(LO 3, 4)**

A company that records credit purchases in a Purchases Journal and records purchases returns in its General Journal made the following errors. List each error by letter, and opposite each letter tell when the error should be discovered:

a. Made an addition error in determining the balance of a creditor's account.

b. Made an addition error in totaling the Office Supplies column of the Purchases Journal.

c. Posted a purchases return to the Accounts Payable account and to the creditor's account but did not post to the Purchases Returns and Allowances account.

d. Posted a purchases return to the Purchases Returns and Allowances account and to the Accounts Payable account but did not post to the creditor's account.

e. Correctly recorded a $4,000 purchase in the Purchases Journal but posted it to the creditor's account as a $400 purchase.

# PROBLEMS

**Problem 6–1**
Special journals, subsidiary ledgers, schedule of accounts receivable
**(LO 3)**

Niagara Company completed these transactions during April of the current year:

Apr. 2  Purchased merchandise on credit from Flott Company, invoice dated April 2, terms 2/10, n/60, $13,300.

3  Sold merchandise on credit to Linda Hobart, Invoice No. 760, $2,000. (The terms of all credit sales are 2/10, n/30.)

3  Purchased office supplies on credit from Whitewater Inc., $1,380. Invoice dated April 2, terms n/10 EOM.

4  Issued Cheque No. 587 to *Northern Times* for advertising expense, $815.

5  Sold merchandise on credit to Paul Abrams, Invoice No. 761, $6,000.

6  Received an $85 credit memorandum from Whitewater Inc. for office supplies received on April 3 and returned for credit.

9  Purchased store equipment on credit from Cooper's Supply, invoice dated April 9, terms n/10 EOM, $11,125.

Apr. 11　Sold merchandise on credit to Kelly Schaefer, Invoice No. 762, $9,500.

　　12　Issued Cheque No. 588 to Flott Company in payment of its April 2 invoice, less the discount.

　　13　Received payment from Linda Hobart for the April 3 sale, less the discount.

　　13　Sold merchandise on credit to Linda Hobart, Invoice No. 763, $4,100.

　　14　Received payment from Paul Abrams for the April 5 sale, less the discount.

　　16　Issued Cheque No. 589, payable to Payroll, in payment of the sales salaries for the first half of the month, $9,750. Cashed the cheque and paid the employees.

　　16　Cash sales for the first half of the month were $50,840. (Cash sales are usually recorded daily from the cash register readings. However, they are recorded only twice in this problem to reduce the repetitive transactions.)

　　17　Purchased merchandise on credit from Sprague Company, invoice dated April 16, terms 2/10, n/30, $12,750.

　　18　Borrowed $40,000 from First Provincial Bank by giving a long-term note payable.

　　20　Received payment from Kelly Schaefer for the April 11 sale, less the discount.

　　20　Purchased store supplies on credit from Cooper's Supply, invoice dated April 19, terms n/10 EOM, $730.

　　23　Received a $400 credit memorandum from Sprague Company for defective merchandise received on April 17 and returned.

　　23　Received payment from Linda Hobart for the April 13 sale, less the discount.

　　25　Purchased merchandise on credit from Flott Company, invoice dated April 24, terms 2/10, n/60, $10,375.

　　26　Issued Cheque No. 590 to Sprague Company in payment of its April 16 invoice, less the return and the discount.

　　27　Sold merchandise on credit to Paul Abrams, Invoice No. 764, $3,070.

　　27　Sold merchandise on credit to Kelly Schaefer, Invoice No. 765, $5,700.

　　30　Issued Cheque No. 591, payable to Payroll, in payment of the sales salaries for the last half of the month, $9,750.

　　30　Cash sales for the last half of the month were $70,975.

## Required

*Preparation component:*

1. Open the following general ledger accounts: Cash, Accounts Receivable, Long-Term Notes Payable, Sales, and Sales Discounts. Also open subsidiary accounts receivable ledger accounts for Paul Abrams, Linda Hobart, and Kelly Schaefer.

2. Prepare a Sales Journal and a Cash Receipts Journal like the ones illustrated in this chapter.

3. Review the transactions of Niagara Company and enter those transactions that should be journalized in the Sales Journal and those that should be journalized in the Cash Receipts Journal. Ignore any transactions that should be journalized in a Purchases Journal, a Cash Disbursements Journal, or a General Journal.

4. Post the items that should be posted as individual amounts from the journals. (Normally, such items are posted daily; but since they are few in number in this problem you are asked to post them only once.)

5. Foot and crossfoot the journals and make the month-end postings.

6.   Prepare a trial balance of the General Ledger and test the accuracy of the subsidiary ledger by preparing a schedule of accounts receivable.

*Analysis component:*

7.   Assume that the sum of the account balances on the schedule of accounts receivable does not equal the balance of the controlling account in the General Ledger. Describe the steps you would go through to discover the error(s).

**Problem 6–2**

Special journals, subsidiary ledgers, schedule of accounts payable
**(LO 3, 4)**

On March 31, Niagara Company had a cash balance of $167,000 and a Long-Term Notes Payable balance of $167,000. The April transactions of Niagara Company included those listed in Problem 6–1.

**Required**

1.   Open the following general ledger accounts: Cash, Office Supplies, Store Supplies, Store Equipment, Accounts Payable, Long-Term Notes Payable, Purchases, Purchases Returns and Allowances, Purchases Discounts, Sales Salaries Expense, and Advertising Expense. Enter the March 31 balances of Cash and Long-Term Notes Payable ($167,000 each).

2.   Open subsidiary accounts payable ledger accounts for Cooper's Supply, Flott Company, Sprague Company, and Whitewater Inc.

3.   Prepare a General Journal and a Cash Disbursements Journal like the ones illustrated in this chapter. Prepare a Purchases Journal with a debit column for purchases, a debit column for other accounts, and a credit column for accounts payable.

4.   Review the April transactions of Niagara Company and enter those transactions that should be journalized in the General Journal, the Purchases Journal, or the Cash Disbursements Journal. Ignore any transactions that should be journalized in a Sales Journal or Cash Receipts Journal.

5.   Post the items that should be posted as individual amounts from the journals. (Normally, such items are posted daily; but since they are few in number in this problem you are asked to post them only once.)

6.   Foot and crossfoot the journals and make the month-end postings.

7.   Prepare a trial balance and a schedule of accounts payable.

**Problem 6–3**

Special journals, subsidiary ledgers, trial balance
**(LO 3, 4)**

*(If the Working Papers that accompany this text are not being used, omit this problem.)*

It is December 16 and you have just taken over the accounting work of Outdoor Outfitters, whose annual accounting periods end each December 31. The company's previous accountant journalized its transactions through December 15 and posted all items that required posting as individual amounts, as an examination of the journals and ledgers in the Working Papers will show.

The company completed these transactions beginning on December 16:

Dec. 16   Sold merchandise on credit to Ambrose Fielder, Invoice No. 916, $7,700. (Terms of all credit sales are 2/10, n/30.)

17   Received a $1,040 credit memorandum from Weathers Company for merchandise received on December 15 and returned for credit.

17   Purchased office supplies on credit from Gray Supply Company, $615. Invoice dated December 16, terms n/10 EOM.

Dec. 18    Received a $40 credit memorandum from Gray Supply Company for office supplies received on December 17 and returned for credit.

     20    Issued a credit memorandum to Amy Oakley for defective merchandise sold on December 15 and returned for credit, $500.

     21    Purchased store equipment on credit from Gray Supply Company, invoice dated December 21, terms n/10 EOM, $6,700.

     22    Received payment from Ambrose Fielder for the December 12 sale less the discount.

     23    Issued Cheque No. 623 to Sunshine Company in payment of its December 15 invoice less the discount.

     24    Sold merchandise on credit to Wilson Wilde, Invoice No. 917, $1,200.

     24    Issued Cheque No. 624 to Weathers Company in payment of its December 15 invoice less the return and the discount.

     25    Received payment from Amy Oakley for the December 15 sale less the return and the discount.

     26    Received merchandise and an invoice dated December 25, terms 2/10, n/60, from Sunshine Company, $8,100.

     29    Sold a neighboring merchant five boxes of file folders (office supplies) for cash at cost, $50.

     30    Marlin Levy, the owner of Outdoor Outfitters, used Cheque No. 625 to withdraw $2,500 cash from the business for personal use.

     31    Issued Cheque No. 626 to Jamie Forster, the company's only sales employee, in payment of her salary for the last half of December, $1,620.

     31    Issued Cheque No. 627 to Countywide Electric Company in payment of the December electric bill, $510.

     31    Cash sales for the last half of the month were $29,600. (Cash sales are usually recorded daily but are recorded only twice in this problem to reduce the repetitive transactions.)

**Required**

1. Record the transactions in the journals provided.

2. Post to the customer and creditor accounts and also post any amounts that should be posted as individual amounts to the general ledger accounts. (Normally, these amounts are posted daily, but they are posted only once by you in this problem because they are few in number.)

3. Foot and crossfoot the journals and make the month-end postings.

4. Prepare a December 31 trial balance and test the accuracy of the subsidiary ledgers by preparing schedules of accounts receivable and payable.

The Flutie Company completed these transactions during March of the current year:

Mar. 2    Sold merchandise on credit to Leroy Hazzard, Invoice No. 854, $15,800. (Terms of all credit sales are 2/10, n/30.)

     3    Purchased office supplies on credit from Arnot Company, $1,120. Invoice dated March 3, terms n/10 EOM.

     3    Sold merchandise on credit to Sam Segura, Invoice No. 855, $9,200.

**Problem 6–4**
Special journals, subsidiary ledgers, trial balance
**(LO 3)**

| Mar. 5 | Received merchandise and an invoice dated March 3, terms 2/10, n/30, from Defore Industries, $42,600. |
|---|---|
| 6 | Borrowed $36,000 by giving Commerce Bank a long-term promissory note payable. |
| 9 | Purchased office equipment on credit from Jett Supply, invoice dated March 9, terms n/10 EOM, $20,850. |
| 10 | Sold merchandise on credit to Marjorie Cobb, Invoice No. 856, $4,600. |
| 12 | Received payment from Leroy Hazzard for the March 2 sale less the discount. |
| 13 | Sent Defore Industries Cheque No. 416 in payment of its March 3 invoice less the discount. |
| 13 | Received payment from Sam Segura for the March 3 sale less the discount. |
| 14 | Received merchandise and an invoice dated March 13, terms 2/10, n/30, from the Welch Company, $31,625. |
| 15 | Issued Cheque No. 417, payable to Payroll, in payment of sales salaries for the first half of the month, $15,900. Cashed the cheque and paid the employees. |
| 15 | Cash sales for the first half of the month were $134,680. (Normally, cash sales are recorded daily; however, they are recorded only twice in this problem to reduce the repetitive entries.) |
| 15 | *Post to the customer and creditor accounts and also post any amounts that should be posted as individual amounts to the general ledger accounts. (Normally, such items are posted daily; but you are asked to post them on only two occasions in this problem because they are few in number.)* |
| 16 | Purchased store supplies on credit from Arnot Company, $1,670. Invoice dated March 16, terms n/10 EOM. |
| 17 | Received a credit memorandum from the Welch Company for unsatisfactory merchandise received on March 14 and returned for credit, $2,425. |
| 19 | Received a credit memorandum from Jett Supply for office equipment received on March 9 and returned for credit, $630. |
| 20 | Received payment from Marjorie Cobb for the sale of March 10 less the discount. |
| 23 | Issued Cheque No. 418 to the Welch Company in payment of its invoice of March 13 less the return and the discount. |
| 27 | Sold merchandise on credit to Marjorie Cobb, Invoice No. 857, $13,910. |
| 28 | Sold merchandise on credit to Sam Segura, Invoice No. 858, $5,315. |
| 31 | Issued Cheque No. 419, payable to Payroll, in payment of sales salaries for the last half of the month, $15,900. Cashed the cheque and paid the employees. |
| 31 | Cash sales for the last half of the month were $144,590. |
| 31 | *Post to the customer and creditor accounts and post any amounts that should be posted as individual amounts to the general ledger accounts.* |
| 31 | *Foot and crossfoot the journals and make the month-end postings.* |

**Required**

1. Open the following general ledger accounts: Cash, Accounts Receivable, Office Supplies, Store Supplies, Office Equipment, Accounts Payable, Long-Term Notes Payable, Sales, Sales Discounts, Purchases, Purchases Returns and Allowances, Purchases Discounts, and Sales Salaries Expense.

2. Open the following accounts receivable ledger accounts: Marjorie Cobb, Leroy Hazzard, and Sam Segura.

3. Open the following accounts payable ledger accounts: Arnot Company, Defore Industries, Jett Supply, and the Welch Company.

4. Enter the transactions in a Sales Journal, a Purchases Journal, a Cash Receipts Journal, a Cash Disbursements Journal, and a General Journal similar to the ones illustrated in this chapter. Post when instructed to do so.

5. Prepare a trial balance and test the accuracy of the subsidiary ledgers by preparing schedules of accounts receivable and payable.

Small Company uses a Cash Disbursements Journal similar to the one shown in Illustration 6–7. In the process of crossfooting the journal at the end of the current month, the company's bookkeeper found that the sum of the debits did not equal the sum of the credits. Describe the procedures you would follow to discover the reason why the journal does not crossfoot correctly.

**Problem 6–5**
Analytical essay
**(LO 3)**

Lorber's is a merchandising company that uses the special journals described in this chapter. At the end of the accounting period, the bookkeeper for the company prepared a trial balance and a schedule of accounts receivable. The trial balance is in balance but the sum of the account balances on the schedule of accounts receivable does not equal the balance in the controlling account. Describe the procedures you would follow to discover the reason for the imbalance between the controlling account and the total shown on the schedule of accounts receivable.

**Problem 6–6**
Analytical essay
**(LO 2)**

Youngstown Company completed these transactions during May of the current year:

May 1   Issued Cheque No. 101 to *The Weekly Journal* for advertising expense, $1,080.

  2   Purchased merchandise on credit from Barclay Company, invoice dated May 1, terms 2/10, n/60, $6,500.

  4   Sold merchandise on credit to Mark Loftis, Invoice No. 203, $6,500. (The terms of all credit sales are 2/10, n/60.)

  4   Purchased on credit from Nixen Company merchandise, $7,050; and store supplies, $750. Invoice dated May 4, terms n/10 EOM.

  5   Sold merchandise on credit to Helen Stone, Invoice No. 204, $12,300.

  6   Received a $525 credit memorandum from Nixen Company for unsatisfactory merchandise received on May 4 and returned for credit.

  8   Purchased store equipment on credit from Rexor Company, invoice dated May 8, terms n/10 EOM, $17,400.

  10   Issued Cheque No. 102 to Barclay Company in payment of its May 1 invoice, less the discount.

  12   Sold merchandise on credit to Regina Niser, Invoice No. 205, $4,650.

  14   Received payment from Mark Loftis for the May 4 sale, less the discount.

  15   Issued Cheque No. 103, payable to Payroll, in payment of the sales salaries for the first half of the month, $4,875. Cashed the cheque and paid the employees.

  15   Sold merchandise on credit to Mark Loftis, Invoice No. 206, $7,350.

  15   Cash sales for the first half of the month, $14,835. (Cash sales are usually recorded daily from the cash register readings. However, they are recorded only twice in this problem to reduce the repetitive transactions.)

**Problem 6–7**
Special journals and subsidiary ledgers
**(LO 3)**

May 15   Received payment from Helen Stone for the May 5 sale, less the discount.

16   Purchased merchandise on credit from Long Company, invoice dated May 16, terms 2/10, n/60, $8,250.

18   Borrowed $15,000 from Pioneer Trust Bank by giving a note payable.

22   Received payment from Regina Niser for the May 12 sale, less the discount.

23   Received a $300 credit memorandum from Long Company for defective merchandise received on May 16 and returned.

24   Purchased on credit from Rexor Company merchandise, $4,410; and store supplies, $540. Invoice dated May 23, terms n/10 EOM.

25   Received payment from Mark Loftis for the May 15 sale, less the discount.

26   Purchased merchandise on credit from Barclay Company, invoice dated May 25, terms 2/10, n/60, $3,900.

26   Issued Cheque No. 104 to Long Company in payment of its May 16 invoice, less the return and the discount.

27   Sold merchandise on credit to Helen Stone, Invoice No. 207, $5,085.

29   Sold merchandise on credit to Regina Niser, Invoice No. 208, $3,495.

31   Issued Cheque No. 105, payable to Payroll, in payment of the sales salaries for the last half of the month, $4,875.

31   Cash sales for the last half of the month were $20,820.

### Required

1.   Open the following general ledger accounts: Cash, Accounts Receivable, Notes Payable, Sales, and Sales Discounts. Also open subsidiary accounts receivable ledger accounts for Mark Loftis, Regina Niser, and Helen Stone.

2.   Prepare a Sales Journal and a Cash Receipts Journal like the ones illustrated in this chapter.

3.   Review the transactions of Youngstown Company and enter those transactions that should be journalized in the Sales Journal and those that should be journalized in the Cash Receipts Journal. Ignore any transactions that should be posted in a Purchases Journal, a Cash Disbursements Journal, or a General Journal.

4.   Post the items that should be posted as individual amounts from the journals. (Normally, such items are posted daily; but since they are few in number, in this problem you are asked to post them only once.)

5.   Foot and crossfoot the journals and make the month-end postings.

6.   Prepare a trial balance of the General Ledger and test the accuracy of the subsidiary ledger by preparing a schedule of accounts receivable.

**Problem 6–8**
Special journals,
subsidiary ledgers,
schedule of
accounts payable
**(LO 3, 4)**

On April 30, Youngstown Company had a cash balance of $30,000 and a Notes Payable balance of $30,000. The May transactions of Youngstown Company included those listed in Problem 6–7.

### Required

1.   Open the following general ledger accounts: Cash, Store Supplies, Office Supplies, Store Equipment, Notes Payable, Accounts Payable, Purchases, Purchases Returns and Allowances, Purchases Discounts, Sales Salaries Expense, and Advertising Expense. Enter the April 30 balances of Cash and Notes Payable ($30,000 each).

2. Open subsidiary accounts payable ledger accounts for Barclay Company, Long Company, Nixen Company, and Rexor Company.

3. Prepare a General Journal, a Purchases Journal, and a Cash Disbursements Journal like the ones illustrated in this chapter.

4. Review the May transactions of Youngstown Company and enter those transactions that should be journalized in the General Journal, the Purchases Journal, or the Cash Disbursements Journal. Ignore any transactions that should be posted in a Sales Journal or Cash Receipts Journal.

5. Post the items that should be posted as individual amounts from the journals. (Normally, such items are posted daily; but since they are few in number, in this problem you are asked to post them only once.)

6. Foot and crossfoot the journals and make the month-end postings.

7. Prepare a trial balance and a schedule of accounts payable.

*(If the working papers that accompany this text are not being used, omit this problem.)*

**Problem 6–9**
Special journals, subsidiary ledgers, and a trial balance
**(LO 3)**

It is January 19, and you have just taken over the accounting work of Crowe Company, a concern operating with annual accounting periods that end each January 31. The company's previous accountant journalized its transactions through January 18 and posted all items that required posting as individual amounts, as an examination of the journals and ledgers in the booklet of working papers will show.

The company completed these transactions beginning on January 19:

Jan. 19 Sold merchandise on credit to Brenda Simms, Invoice No. 741, $8,300. (Terms of all credit sales are 2/10, n/60.)

20 Received a $685 credit memorandum from Younger Company for merchandise received on January 17 and returned for credit.

20 Purchased on credit from Reed Suppliers merchandise, $7,350; store supplies, $1,080; and office supplies, $745. Invoice dated January 19, terms n/10 EOM.

22 Issued a credit memorandum to Sam Trent for defective merchandise sold on January 18 and returned for credit, $445.

23 Received a $270 credit memorandum from Reed Suppliers for office supplies received on January 20 and returned for credit.

23 Purchased store equipment on credit from Reed Suppliers, invoice dated January 22, terms n/10 EOM, $9,925.

24 Sold merchandise on credit to Frank Urich, Invoice No. 742, $11,135.

25 Issued Cheque No. 450 to Younger Company in payment of its January 15 invoice less the return and the discount.

25 Received payment from Brenda Simms for the January 15 sale less the discount.

26 Issued Cheque No. 451 to Vax Company in payment of its January 16 invoice less a 2% discount.

28 Received merchandise and an invoice dated January 28, terms 2/10, n/60, from Vax Company, $12,750.

28 Received payment from Sam Trent for the January 18 sale less the return and the discount.

30 Sold a neighbouring merchant a carton of computer ribbons (store supplies) for cash at cost, $405.

Jan. 31   Issued Cheque No. 452 to Valley Power Company in payment of the January hydro bill, $2,495.

31   Issued Cheque No. 453 to Max Davis, the company's only sales employee, in payment of her salary for the last half of January, $1,440.

31   Cash sales for the last half of the month, $54,510. (Cash sales are usually recorded daily but are recorded only twice in this problem in order to reduce the repetitive transactions.)

31   Susan Linder, the owner of Crowe Company, used Cheque No. 454 to withdraw $7,500 cash from the business for personal use.

**Required**

1.   Record the transactions in the journals provided.

2.   Post to the customer and creditor accounts and also post any amounts that should be posted as individual amounts to the general ledger accounts. (Normally, these amounts are posted daily, but they are posted only once by you in this problem because they are few in number.)

3.   Foot and crossfoot the journals and make the month-end postings.

4.   Prepare a January 31 trial balance and test the accuracy of the subsidiary ledgers by preparing schedules of accounts receivable and payable.

**Problem 6–10**
Special journals,
preparing and proving
the trial balance
**(LO 3)**

Jarrett Company completed these transactions during October of the current year: Sales are subject to a 10% PST and the 7% GST.

Oct.  2   Borrowed $36,000 by giving Regional Bank a promissory note payable.

3   Received merchandise and an invoice dated October 1, terms 2/10, n/60, from Bradley Company, $12,600.

4   Purchased on credit from Abell Company merchandise, $10,950; store supplies, $450; and office supplies, $225. Invoice dated October 3, terms n/10 EOM.

5   Sold merchandise on credit to Omar Hanes, Invoice No. 520, $9,300. (Terms of all credit sales are 2/10, n/60.)

6   Purchased office equipment on credit from Telecore Company, invoice dated October 5, terms n/10 EOM, $14,550.

9   Sold merchandise on credit to Leigh Rogers, Invoice No. 521, $8,850.

10   Sent Bradley Company Cheque No. 312 in payment of its October 1 invoice less the discount.

11   Received merchandise and an invoice dated October 10, terms 2/10, n/60, from Thomas Company, $12,900.

15   Received payment from Omar Hanes for the October 5 sale less the discount.

15   Issued Cheque No. 313, payable to Payroll, in payment of sales salaries for the first half of the month, $7,200. Cashed the cheque and paid the employees.

15   Cash sales for the first half of the month, $44,700. (Normally, cash sales are recorded daily; however, they are recorded only twice in this problem to reduce the number of repetitive entries.)

15   *Post to the customer and creditor accounts and also post any amounts that should be posted as individual amounts to the general ledger accounts. (Normally, such items are posted daily; but you are asked to post them on only two occasions in this problem because they are few in number.)*

Oct. 16   Sold merchandise on credit to Carl Chase, Invoice No. 522, $10,850.

18   Purchased on credit from Abell Company merchandise, $5,475; store supplies, $525; and office supplies, $420. Invoice dated October 17, terms n/10 EOM.

19   Received payment from Leigh Rogers for the October 9 sale less the discount.

20   Received a credit memorandum from Thomas Company for unsatisfactory merchandise received on October 10 and returned for credit, $1,200.

20   Issued Cheque No. 314 to Thomas Company in payment of its invoice of October 10 less the return and the discount.

23   Sold merchandise on credit to Carl Chase, Invoice No. 523, $7,050.

26   Received payment from Carl Chase for the sale of October 16 less the discount.

27   Received a credit memorandum from Telecore Company for office equipment received on December 6 and returned for credit, $750.

28   Sold merchandise on credit to Leigh Rogers, Invoice No. 524. $6,150.

31   Issued Cheque No. 315, payable to Payroll, in payment of sales salaries for the last half of the month, $7,200. Cashed the cheque and paid the employees.

31   Cash sales for the last half of the month, $50,550.

31   *Post to the customer and creditor accounts and post any amounts that should be posted as individual amounts to general ledger accounts.*

31   Foot and crossfoot the journals and make the month-end postings.

### Required

1. Open the following general ledger accounts: Cash, Accounts Receivable, Store Supplies, Office Supplies, Office Equipment, Notes Payable, Accounts Payable, Sales, Sales Discounts, Purchases, Purchases Returns and Allowances, Purchases Discounts, and Sales Salaries Expense.

2. Open the following accounts receivable ledger accounts: Carl Chase, Omar Hanes, Leigh Rogers.

3. Open the following accounts payable ledger accounts: Abell Company, Bradley Company, Telecore Company, and Thomas Company.

4. Enter the transactions in a Sales Journal, a Purchases Journal, a Cash Receipts Journal, a Cash Disbursements Journal, and a General Journal similar to the ones illustrated in this chapter. Post when instructed to do so.

5. Prepare a trial balance and test the accuracy of the subsidiary ledgers by preparing schedules of accounts receivable and payable.

Short Company uses a Cash Receipts Journal similar to the one shown in Illustration 6–5. In the process of crossfooting the journal at the end of the current month, the company's bookkeeper found that the sum of the debits did not equal the sum of the credits. Describe the procedures you would follow in an effort to discover the reason why the journal does not crossfoot correctly.

**Problem 6–11**
Analytical essay
**(LO 3)**

Ferber's is a merchandising company that uses the special journals described in this chapter. At the end of the accounting period, the bookkeeper for the company prepared a trial balance and a schedule of accounts payable. The trial balance is in balance but the sum of the account balances on the schedule of accounts payable does not equal the balance in the controlling account. Describe the procedures you would follow to discover the reason for the imbalance between the controlling account and the total shown on the schedule of accounts payable.

**Problem 6–12**
Analytical essay
**(LO 2)**

# PROVOCATIVE PROBLEM

**Provocative Problem
6–1**

**Ethical issues essay**

Review the As a Matter of Ethics case presented on page 299. Discuss the problem faced by the public accountant and the factors the public accountant should consider in deciding on a course of action.

# ANALYTICAL AND REVIEW PROBLEM

**A & R Problem 6–1**

The following problem is designed to test your ability in the use of special journals and subsidiary ledgers. The special journals of James Bay Department Store are reproduced below, followed by a number of representative transactions that occurred during the period. The money columns in the journals are numbered to minimize clerical work in recording each transaction.

| Accounts Receivable Debit | Sales Credit | | | | | | PST Credit | GST Credit |
|---|---|---|---|---|---|---|---|---|
| | Men's Clothing | Women's Clothing | Appliances | Furniture | Bargain Basement | Other Departments | | |
| 1 | 2 | 3 | 4 | 5 | 6 | 7 | 8 | 9 |

| Cash Debit | Sales Discounts Debit | Sales Credit | | | | | | Accounts Receivable Credit | Other Accounts Credit | PST Credit | GST Credit |
|---|---|---|---|---|---|---|---|---|---|---|---|
| | | Men's Clothing | Women's Clothing | Appli-ances | Furni-ture | Bargain Basement | Other Departments | | | | |
| 10 | 11 | 12 | 13 | 14 | 15 | 16 | 17 | 18 | 19 | 20 | 21 |

| Purchases Debit | | | | | | Prepaid GST Debit | Accounts Payable Credit |
|---|---|---|---|---|---|---|---|
| Men's Clothing | Women's Clothing | Appliances | Furniture | Bargain Basement | Other Departments | | |
| 22 | 23 | 24 | 25 | 26 | 27 | 28 | 29 |

| Accounts Payable Debit | Supplies Expense Debit | Other Accounts Debit | Prepaid GST Debit | Cash Credit |
|---|---|---|---|---|
| 30 | 31 | 32 | 33 | 34 |

| Debit | Credit |
|---|---|
| 35 | 36 |

Transactions (*Note:* All sales are subject to a provincial sales tax (PST) of 8% and the federal goods and services tax (GST) of 7%.)

| | Debit | Credit |
|---|---|---|

*a.* Borrowed $37,500 from Great Northern Bank on note payable.

*b.* Sale on account $450 to J.C. Snead—Men's Clothing.

*c.* Sale for cash of baked goods—$15.

*d.* Purchases of $11,250 on account of goods—Bargain Basement from Lonbec Co.

*e.* Purchases of $12,300 on account of Appliances from Canlec Inc.

*f.* Sale on account $2,100 of Furniture to Gates Brown.

*g.* Sale for cash $1,500 less 5% discount—Appliances.

*h.* Collection of account receivable from Cec Oak, $900.

*i.* Payment of account payable to J.T. Inglis, $6,300.

*j.* J.C. Snead returned for credit a shirt that had a flaw—$60.

## Required

1. Identify each of the journals.
2. Journalize by indicating the column number in the spaces provided after each transaction. For example: Purchase for cash of supplies (immediately expensed).

| Debit | Credit |
|---|---|
| 31, 33 | 34 |
| | |

3. Indicate how the data in the special journals are posted to various accounts by filling in the spaces provided with the following posting possibilities.

    *a.* Posted as a *debit* to some General Ledger account.

    *b.* Posted as a *debit* to some subsidiary ledger account.

    *c.* Posted as a *credit* to some General Ledger account.

    *d.* Posted as a *credit* to some subsidiary ledger account.

    *e.* Not posted.

*Note:* The numbers in parentheses are the identification numbers for the money columns of the special journals. For example: (31) money column.

| | Posted as |
|---|---|
| (00) Total of column (34) Example | e |
| *a.* Total of column 1. | |
| *b.* Detail items of column 3. | |
| *c.* Detail items of column 8. | |
| *d.* Total of column 9. | |
| *e.* Detail items of column 17. | |
| *f.* Total of column 20. | |
| *g.* Total of column 26. | |
| *h.* Detail items of column 27. | |
| *i.* Detail items of column 32. | |
| *j.* Detail items of column 1. | |
| *k.* Total of column 19. | |
| *l.* Detail items of column 18. | |
| *m.* Total of column 29. | |
| *n.* Total of column 5. | |
| *o.* Detail items of column 10. | |
| *p.* Detail items of column 21. | |

---

# COMPREHENSIVE PROBLEM

**Regis Company**
**(LO 3, 4)**

*(If the Working Papers that accompany this text are not available, omit this comprehensive problem.)*

Assume it is Monday, August 1, the first business day of the month, and you have just been hired as the accountant for Regis Company, which operates with monthly accounting periods. All of the company's accounting work has been completed through the end of July and its ledgers show July 31 balances. During your first month on the job, you record the following transactions:

Aug. 1  Issued Cheque No. 1236 to Republic Management Co. in payment of the August rent, $2,650. (Use two lines to record the transaction. Charge 80% of the rent to Rent Expense, Selling Space and the balance to Rent Expense, Office Space.)

2  Sold merchandise on credit to L&M Company, Invoice No. 5725, $4,300. (The terms of all credit sales are 2/10, n/30.)

2  Issued a $125 credit memorandum to Prime, Inc., for defective merchandise sold on July 28 and returned for credit. The total selling price (gross) was $3,375.

3  Received a $570 credit memorandum from Signature Products for merchandise received on July 29 and returned for credit.

4  Purchased on credit from Discount Supplies: merchandise, $26,480; store supplies, $410; and office supplies, $59. Invoice dated August 4, terms n/10 EOM.

5  Received payment from Prime, Inc., for the remaining balance from the sale of July 28 less the August 2 return and the discount.

8  Issued Cheque No. 1237 to Signature Products to pay for the $5,070 of merchandise received on July 29 less the August 3 return and a 2% discount.

9  Sold store supplies to the merchant next door at cost for cash, $250.

10  Purchased office equipment on credit from Discount Supplies, invoice dated August 10, terms n/10 EOM, $2,910.

11  Received payment from L&M Company for the August 2 sale less the discount.

11  Received merchandise and an invoice dated August 10, terms 2/10, n/30, from Mayfair Corp., $6,300.

12  Received a $610 credit memorandum from Discount Supplies for defective office equipment received on August 10 and returned for credit.

15  Issued Cheque No. 1238, payable to Payroll, in payment of sales salaries, $3,800, and office salaries, $2,250. Cashed the cheque and paid the employees.

15  Cash sales for the first half of the month, $42,300. (Such sales are normally recorded daily. They are recorded only twice in this problem to reduce the repetitive entries.)

15  *Post to the customer and creditor accounts. Also, post individual items that are not included in column totals at the end of the month to the general ledger accounts. (Such items are normally posted daily, but you are asked to post them only twice each month because they are few in number.)*

Aug. 16   Sold merchandise on credit to L&M Company, Invoice No. 5726, $2,850.

17   Received merchandise and an invoice dated August 14, terms 2/10, n/60, from Tranh Industries, $9,750.

19   Issued Cheque No. 1239 to Mayfair Corp. in payment of its August 10 invoice less the discount.

22   Sold merchandise on credit to Anchor Services, Invoice No. 5727, $4,900.

23   Issued Cheque No. 1240 to Tranh Industries in payment of its August 14 invoice less the discount.

24   Purchased on credit from Discount Supplies: merchandise, $5,800; store supplies, $450; and office supplies, $200. Invoice dated August 24, terms n/10 EOM.

25   Received merchandise and an invoice dated August 23, terms 2/10, n/30, from Signature Products, $2,200.

26   Sold merchandise on credit to Franzetti Corp., Invoice No. 5728, $10,150.

26   Issued Cheque No. 1241 to HP&L in payment of the July electric bill, $918.

29   The owner of Regis Company, Walt Regis, used Cheque No. 1242 to withdraw $5,000 from the business for personal use.

30   Received payment from Anchor Services for the August 22 sale less the discount.

30   Issued Cheque No. 1243, payable to Payroll, in payment of sales salaries, $3,800, and office salaries, $2,250. Cashed the cheque and paid the employees.

31   Cash sales for the last half of the month were $47,180.

31   *Post to the customer and creditor accounts. Also, post individual items that are not included in column totals at the end of the month to the general ledger accounts.*

31   Foot and crossfoot the journals and make the month-end postings.

## Required

1.   Enter the transactions in the appropriate journals and post when instructed to do so.

2.   Prepare a trial balance in the Trial Balance columns of the provided work sheet form and complete the work sheet using the following information:

   *a.*   Expired insurance, $395.

   *b.*   Ending store supplies inventory, $1,880.

   *c.*   Ending office supplies inventory, $360.

   *d.*   Estimated amortization of store equipment, $405.

   *e.*   Estimated amortization of office equipment, $235.

   *f.*   Ending merchandise inventory, $126,000.

3.   Prepare a multiple-step classified August income statement, an August statement of changes in owner's equity, and an August 31 classified balance sheet.

4.   Prepare and post adjusting and closing entries.

5.   Prepare a post-closing trial balance. Also prepare a list of the Accounts Receivable Ledger accounts and a list of the Accounts Payable Ledger accounts. Total the balances of each to confirm that the totals equal the balances in the controlling accounts.

## CONCEPT TESTER (LO 5)

Test your understanding of the concepts introduced in this chapter by completing the following crossword puzzle.

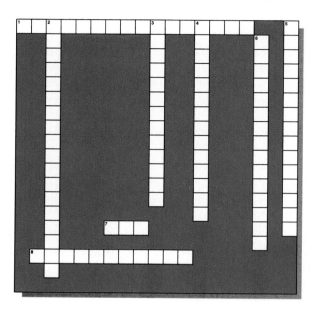

### Across Clues

1. The means by which data is captured and reports are generated (2 words).

7. A federal tax on the consumer.

8. Means of transferring information from source documents to an accounting system (2 words).

### Down Clues

2. The portion of the general ledger that represents the sum of the balances in the subsidiary ledger (2 words).

3. The book that contains the financial statement accounts (2 words).

4. A book of original entry designed for recording specified transactions (2 words).

5. Accumulating source data for a period of time and inputting them at the same time (2 words).

6. The portion of a company that can be separately identified (2 words).

# ANSWERS TO PROGRESS CHECKS

**6–1** *b*

**6–2** The data processor component interprets, manipulates, and summarizes the recorded information so that it can be used in analyses and reports.

**6–3** The data that is saved in data storage is used to prepare periodic financial reports, to prepare special-purpose reports for managers, and to provide a source of information for independent auditors.

**6–4** *a*

**6–5** Compared to manual systems, computer systems offer more accuracy, speed, efficiency, and convenience.

**6–6** *d*

**6–7** *b*

**6–8** Columnar journals allow you to accumulate repetitive debits and credits and post them as column totals rather than as individual amounts.

**6–9** The equality of debits and credits is still maintained within the General Ledger. The subsidiary ledger containing the customer's individual account is used only for supplementary information.

**6–10** The initial and page number of the journal from which the amount was posted is entered in the Posting Reference column of the ledger account next to the amount.

**6–11** *c*

**6–12** The controlling account must be debited periodically for an amount or amounts equal to the sum of the debits to the subsidiary ledger, and it must be credited periodically for an amount or amounts equal to the sum of the credits to the subsidiary ledger.

**6–13** *d*

**6–14** *b*

**6–15** This refers to the procedure of using copies of sales invoices as a Sales Journal. Each invoice total is posted directly to the customer's account, and all the invoices are totaled at month-end for posting to the General Ledger accounts.

**6–16** The General Journal would still be needed for adjusting, closing, and correcting entries, and for miscellaneous transactions such as sales returns, purchases returns, and plant asset purchases.

**6–17** *e*

# Accounting for Cash and the Principles of Internal Control

*Because almost all business activities involve cash, it must be carefully controlled. Internal control systems are designed to make accounting information dependable and to help companies avoid misplacing or misusing their assets.*

t the outset of the lecture on Chapter 7, Karen White and Mark Smith's instructor took time to review the fundamental, or basic, accounting system as covered in the first six chapters and to preview some of the interesting topics that will be coming up. She challenged the students to review financial reports of different companies to reinforce their "book learning" and promised to bring to their attention selections she found on topics such as fraud, internal control, temporary investments, inventory pricing, accounting for capital assets and liabilities, and so on.

Her first handout discussed the rise worldwide of white-collar crimes, which cause substantial financial loss and even bankruptcy in some cases. The "Insurance Bureau of Canada estimates that its industry loses about $1 billion annually and the banking industry probably suffers similar losses" due to fraud.[1] In a case involving a $60,000 embezzlement from a church, an analysis of the facts attributed the fraud to the governing board's lack of basic accounting knowledge. In another case, a salesperson with access to the assets and to shipping, receiving, and invoicing documents defrauded the company of $3 million. Other news reports indicate that a wide range of business entities—medical offices, travel agencies, retail operations, utility companies, major unions—are victims of substantial embezzlement. In addition, accounting literature indicates that small businesses and not-for-profit organizations often have weak internal control structures that leave them vulnerable to embezzlement.

---

[1]Gordon Arnault, "Corporate Fraud Is a Growth Industry," *Globe and Mail,* January 17, 1995, p. B28.

## LEARNING OBJECTIVES

**After studying Chapter 7, you should be able to:**

1. Explain the concept of liquidity and the difference between cash and cash equivalents.

2. Explain why internal control procedures are needed in a large organization and state the broad principles of internal control.

3. Describe internal control procedures used to protect cash received from cash sales, cash received through the mail, and cash disbursements.

4. Explain the operation of a petty cash fund and be able to prepare journal entries to record petty cash fund transactions.

5. Explain why the bank balance and the book balance of cash should be reconciled and be able to prepare a reconciliation.

6. Explain how recording invoices at net amounts helps gain control over cash discounts taken, and calculate days' sales uncollected.

7. Define or explain the words and phrases listed in the chapter glossary.

Cash is an asset that every business owns and uses. Most organizations own at least some assets known as cash equivalents, which are very similar to cash. In studying this chapter, you will learn the general principles of internal control and the specific principles that guide businesses in managing and accounting for cash. It is management's responsibility to set up the policies and procedures to ensure the safeguarding of business assets, including cash. In order to do so, management and employees of organizations should understand and be able to apply basic principles of internal control. If these internal control principles had been followed by the victims described on the previous page, many of the entities might have been saved from financial loss.

The chapter shows you how to establish and use a petty cash fund and how to reconcile a chequing account. Also, you will learn a method of accounting for purchases that helps management determine whether cash discounts on purchases are being lost and, if so, how much has been lost.

## CASH, CASH EQUIVALENTS, AND THE CONCEPT OF LIQUIDITY

**LO 1**

Explain the concept of liquidity and the difference between cash and cash equivalents.

In previous chapters, you learned that a company can own many different kinds of assets such as accounts receivable, merchandise inventory, equipment, buildings, and land. These assets all have value, but most of them are not easily used as a means of payment when buying other assets, acquiring services, or paying off liabilities. Usually, cash must be used as the method of payment. Another way to state this is to say that cash is more *liquid* than these other assets.

In more general terms, the **liquidity** of an asset refers to how easily the asset can be converted into other types of assets or be used to buy services or satisfy obligations. All assets can be evaluated in terms of their relative liquidity. Assets such as cash are said to be **liquid assets** because they can be converted easily into other types of assets or used to buy services or pay liabilities.

As you know, a company needs more than valuable assets to stay in business. That is, the company must own some liquid assets so that bills are paid on time and purchases can be made for cash when necessary.

For financial accounting, the asset *cash* includes not only currency and coins but also amounts on deposit in bank accounts, including chequing accounts (sometimes called demand deposits) and some savings accounts (also called time deposits). In addition, cash includes items that are acceptable for deposit in those accounts, especially customers' cheques made payable to the company.

To increase their return, many companies invest their idle cash balances in assets called **cash equivalents**. These assets are short-term, or temporary, investments that are highly liquid, that is, readily convertible into cash and relatively insensitive to interest and market rate fluctuations. Examples of cash equivalents include short-term investments in treasury bills, commercial paper (short-term corporate notes payable), and money market funds.

Because cash equivalents are so similar to cash, most companies combine them with cash as a single item on the balance sheet. For example, **Canadian Pacific Limited's** balance sheet on December 31, 1993, reported the following:

---

Cash and temporary investments  . . . .  $1,667.7 (million)

---

Canadian Pacific Limited has classified its temporary investments as a cash equivalent.

As you would expect, cash is an important asset for every business. Because cash is so important, companies need to be careful about keeping track of it. They also need to carefully control access to cash by employees and others who might want to take it for their own use. A good accounting system supports both goals. It can keep track of how much cash is on hand, and it helps control who has access to the cash. Because of the special importance of cash, this chapter describes the practices companies follow to account for and protect cash.

The importance of accounting for cash and cash equivalents is highlighted by the fact that a complete set of financial statements includes a statement of changes in financial position, or statement of cash flows. That statement identifies the types of activities that caused changes in cash and cash equivalents. You learn more about that statement in Chapter 18.

---

**Progress Check**
*(Answers to Progress Checks are provided at the end of the chapter.)*

7-1  Why does a company need to own liquid assets?

7-2  Why does a company own cash equivalent assets in addition to cash?

7-3  Which of the following assets should be classified as a cash equivalent?  *(a)* Land purchased as an investment;  *(b)* Accounts receivable;  *(c)* Common shares purchased as a long-term investment;  *(d)* A 90-day Treasury bill issued by the Canadian government.

---

## INTERNAL CONTROL

**LO 2**

Explain why internal control procedures are needed in a large organization and state the broad principles of internal control.

In a small business, the manager often controls the entire operation through personal supervision and direct participation in all its activities. For example, he or she commonly buys all the assets and services used in the business. The manager also hires and supervises all employees, negotiates all contracts, and signs all cheques. As a result, the manager knows from personal contact and observation whether the business actually received the assets and services for which the cheques were written. However, as a business grows, it becomes increasingly difficult to maintain this close personal contact. At some point, the manager must delegate responsibilities and rely on formal procedures rather than personal contact in controlling the operations of the business.

The procedures a company uses to control its operations make up its **internal control system.** A properly designed internal control system encourages adherence to prescribed managerial policies. In doing so, it promotes efficient operations and protects the assets from waste, fraud, and theft. The system also helps ensure that accurate and reliable accounting data are produced.

Specific internal control procedures vary from company to company and depend on such factors as the nature of the business and its size. However, the same broad principles of internal control apply to all companies. These broad principles are:

1.  Clearly establish responsibilities.
2.  Maintain adequate records.
3.  Insure assets and bond employees.
4.  Separate record-keeping and custody over assets.
5.  Divide responsibility for related transactions.
6.  Use mechanical devices whenever feasible.
7.  Perform regular and independent reviews.

We discuss these seven principles in the following paragraphs. Throughout, we describe how various internal control procedures prevent fraud and theft. Remember, however, that these procedures are needed to ensure that the accounting records are complete and accurate.

### Clearly Establish Responsibilities

To have good internal control, responsibility for each task must be clearly established and assigned to one person. When responsibility is not clearly spelled out, it is difficult to determine who is at fault when something goes wrong. For example, if two sales clerks share access to the same cash register and there is a shortage, it may not be possible to tell which clerk is at fault. Neither can prove that he or she did not cause the shortage. To prevent this problem, one clerk should be given responsibility for making all change. Alternately, the business can use a register with separate cash drawers for each operator.

### Maintain Adequate Records

A good record-keeping system helps protect assets and ensures that employees follow prescribed procedures. Reliable records are also a source of information that management uses to monitor the operations of the business. For example, if detailed records of manufacturing equipment and tools are maintained, items are unlikely to be lost or otherwise disappear without any discrepancy being noticed. As another example, expenses and other expenditures are less likely to be debited to the wrong accounts if a comprehensive chart of accounts is established and followed carefully. If the chart is not in place or is not used correctly, management may never discover that some expenses are excessive.

Numerous preprinted forms and internal business papers should be designed and properly used to maintain good internal control. For example, if sales slips are properly designed, sales personnel can record the needed information efficiently without errors or delays to customers. And, if all sales slips are prenumbered and controlled, each salesperson can be held responsible for the sales slips issued to him or her. As a result, a salesperson is not able to pocket cash by making a sale and destroying the sales slip. Computerized point-of-sale systems can achieve the same control results.

## Insure Assets and Bond Key Employees

Assets should be covered by adequate casualty insurance, and employees who handle cash and negotiable assets should be bonded. An employee is said to be *bonded* when the company purchases an insurance policy, or a bond, against losses from theft by that employee. Bonding clearly reduces the loss suffered by a theft. It also tends to discourage theft because bonded employees know that an impersonal bonding company must be dealt with when a theft is discovered.

## Separate Record-Keeping and Custody over Assets

A fundamental principle of internal control is that the person who has access to or is otherwise responsible for an asset should not maintain the accounting record for that asset. When this principle is followed, the custodian of an asset, knowing that a record of the asset is being kept by another person, is not as likely to misplace, steal, or waste the asset. And, the record-keeper, who does not have access to the asset, has no reason to falsify the record. As a result, two people would have to agree to commit a fraud (called *collusion*) if the asset were stolen and the theft concealed in the records. Because collusion is necessary, the fraud is less likely to happen.

## Divide Responsibility for Related Transactions

Responsibility for a transaction or a series of related transactions should be divided between individuals or departments so that the work of one acts as a check on the other. However, this principle does not call for duplication of work. Each employee or department should perform an unduplicated portion.

For example, responsibility for placing orders, receiving the merchandise, and paying the vendors should not be given to one individual or department. Doing so creates a situation in which mistakes and perhaps fraud are more likely to occur. Having a different person check incoming goods for quality and quantity may encourage more care and attention to detail than having it done by the person who placed the order. And designating a third person to approve the payment of the invoice offers additional protection against error and fraud. Finally, giving a fourth person the authority to actually write cheques adds another measure of protection.

## Use Mechanical Devices Whenever Feasible

Cash registers, cheque protectors, time clocks, and mechanical counters are examples of control devices that should be used whenever feasible. A cash register with a locked-in tape makes a record of each cash sale. A cheque protector perforates the amount of a cheque into its face, and makes it difficult to change the amount. A time clock registers the exact time an employee arrives on the job and the exact time the employee departs. Using mechanical change and currency counters is faster and more accurate than counting by hand and reduces the possibility of loss.

## Perform Regular and Independent Reviews

Even a well-designed internal control system has a tendency to deteriorate as time passes. Changes in personnel and computer equipment present opportunities for shortcuts and other omissions. The stress of time pressures tends to bring about the same results. Thus, regular reviews of internal control systems are needed to be sure that the standard procedures are being followed. Where possible, these reviews should be performed by internal auditors who are not directly involved in operations. From their independent perspective, internal auditors can evaluate the overall efficiency of operations as well as the effectiveness of the internal control system.

Many companies also have audits by independent auditors who are public accountants. After testing the company's financial records, the public accountants give an opinion as to whether the company's financial statements are presented fairly in accordance with generally accepted accounting principles. However, before public accountants decide on how much testing they must do, they evaluate the effectiveness of the internal control system. When making their evaluation, they can find areas for improvement and offer suggestions.

## COMPUTERS AND INTERNAL CONTROL

The broad principles of internal control should be followed for both manual and computerized accounting systems. However, computers have several important effects on internal control. Perhaps the most obvious is that computers provide rapid access to large quantities of information. As a result, management's ability to monitor and control business operations can be greatly improved.

### Computers Reduce Processing Errors

Computers reduce the number of errors in processing information. Once the data are entered correctly, the possibility of mechanical and mathematical errors is largely eliminated. On the other hand, data entry errors may occur because the process of entering data may be more complex in a computerized system. Also, the lack of human involvement in later processing may cause data entry errors to go undiscovered.

### Computers Allow More Extensive Testing of Records

The regular review and audit of computerized records can include more extensive testing because information can be accessed so rapidly. To reduce costs when manual methods are used, managers may select only small samples of data to test. But, when computers are used, large samples or even complete data files can be reviewed and analyzed.

## Computerized Systems May Limit Hard Evidence of Processing Steps

Because many data processing steps are performed by the computer, fewer items of documentary evidence may be available for review. However, computer systems can create additional evidence by recording more information, such as who made entries and even when they were made. And, the computer can be programmed to require the use of passwords before making entries so that access to the system is limited. Therefore, internal control may depend more on reviews of the design and operation of the computerized processing system and less on reviews of the documents left behind by the system.

## Separation of Duties Must Be Maintained

Because computerized systems are so efficient, companies often need fewer employees. This savings carries the risk that the separation of critical responsibilities may not be maintained. In addition, companies that use computers need employees with special skills to program and operate them. The duties of such employees must be controlled to minimize undetected errors and the risk of fraud. For example, better control is maintained if the person who designs and programs the system does not serve as the operator. Also, control over programs and files related to cash receipts and disbursements should be separated. To prevent fraud, cheque-writing activities should not be controlled by the computer operator. However, achieving a suitable separation of duties can be especially difficult in small companies that have only a few employees.

Recall from the first page of the chapter the case in which $3 million was embezzled. The salesperson in that case had access to both the assets and the documents. Similar access to both the cash and the records may result in cash being embezzled.

---

**Progress Check**

7-4    The broad principles of internal control require that:
   *a.* Responsibility for a series of related transactions (such as placing orders for, receiving, and paying for merchandise) should be given to one person so that responsibility is clearly assigned.
   *b.* Responsibility for specific tasks should be shared by more than one employee so that one serves as a check on the other.
   *c.* Employees who handle cash and negotiable assets should be bonded.

7-5    What are some of the effects of computers on internal control?

---

Now that we have covered the principles of good internal control in general, it is helpful to see how they are applied to cash, the most liquid of all assets. A good system of internal control for cash should provide adequate procedures for protecting both cash receipts and cash disbursements. In the procedures, three basic guidelines should always be observed:

**INTERNAL CONTROL FOR CASH**

LO 3

Describe internal control procedures used to protect cash received from cash sales, cash received through the mail, and cash disbursements.

1.  Duties should be separated so that people responsible for actually handling cash are not responsible for keeping the cash records.
2.  All cash receipts should be deposited in the bank, intact, each day.
3.  All cash payments should be made by cheque.

The reason for the first principle is that a division of duties helps avoid errors. It also requires two or more people to collude if cash is to be embezzled (stolen) and the theft concealed in the accounting records. One reason for the second guideline is that the daily deposit of all receipts produces a timely independent test of the accuracy of the count of the cash received and the deposit. It also helps prevent loss or theft and keeps an employee from personally using the money for a few days before depositing it.

Finally, if all payments are made by cheque, the bank records provide an independent description of cash disbursements. This arrangement also tends to prevent thefts of cash. (One exception to this principle allows small disbursements of currency and coins to be made from a petty cash fund. Petty cash funds are discussed later in this chapter.) Note especially that the daily intact depositing of receipts and making disbursements by cheque allows you to use the bank records as a separate and external record of essentially all cash transactions. Later in the chapter, you learn how to use bank records to confirm the accuracy of your own records.

The exact procedures used to achieve control over cash vary from company to company. They depend on such factors as company size, number of employees, the volume of cash transactions, and the sources of cash. Therefore, the procedures described in the following paragraphs illustrate many but not all situations.

## Cash from Cash Sales

Cash sales should be recorded on a cash register at the time of each sale. To help ensure that correct amounts are entered, each register should be placed so that customers can read the amounts displayed. Also, clerks should be required to ring up each sale before wrapping the merchandise and should give the customer a receipt. Finally, each cash register should be designed to provide a permanent, locked-in record of each transaction. In some systems, the register is directly connected to a computer. The computer is programmed to accept cash register transactions and enter them in the accounting records. In other cases, the register simply prints a record of each transaction on a paper tape locked inside the register.

We stated earlier that custody over cash should be separated from record-keeping for cash. For cash sales, this separation begins with the cash register. The salesclerk who has access to the cash in the register should not have access to its locked-in record. At the end of each day, the salesclerk should count the cash in the register, record the result, and turn over the cash and this record of the count to an employee in the cashier's office. The employee in the cashier's office, like the salesclerk, has access to the cash and should not have access to the computerized accounting records (or the register tape). A third employee, preferably from the accounting department, examines the computerized record of register transactions (or the register tape) and compares its total with the cash receipts reported by the cashier's office. The computer record (or register tape) becomes the basis for the journal entry to record cash sales. Note that the accounting department employee has access to the records for cash but does not have access to the actual cash. The salesclerk and the employee from the cashier's office have access to the cash but not to the accounting records. Thus, their accuracy is automatically checked, and none of them can make a mistake or divert any cash without the difference being revealed.

## Cash Received through the Mail

Control of cash that comes in through the mail begins with the person who opens the mail. Preferably, two people should be present when the mail is opened. One should make a list (in triplicate) of the money received. The list should record each sender's name, the amount, and the purpose for which the money was sent. One copy is sent to the cashier with the money. A second copy goes to the accounting department. A third copy is kept by the clerk who opened the mail. The cashier deposits the money in the bank, and the bookkeeper records the amounts received in the accounting records. Then, when the bank balance is reconciled by a fourth person (this process is discussed later in the chapter), errors or fraud by the clerk, the cashier, or the bookkeeper are detected. They will be detected because the bank's record of the amount of cash deposited and the records of three people must agree. Note how this arrangement makes errors and fraud nearly impossible, unless the employees enter into collusion. If the clerk does not report all receipts accurately, the customers will question their account balances. If the cashier does not deposit all receipts intact, the bank balance does not agree with the bookkeeper's cash balance. The bookkeeper and the fourth person who reconciles the bank balance do not have access to cash and, therefore, have no opportunity to divert any to themselves. Thus, undetected errors and fraud are made highly unlikely.

## Cash Disbursements

The previous discussions clearly show the importance of gaining control over cash from sales and cash received through the mail. Most large embezzlements, however, are actually accomplished through payments of fictitious invoices. Therefore, controlling cash disbursements is perhaps even more critical than controlling cash receipts.

As described earlier, the key to controlling cash disbursements is to require all expenditures to be made by cheque, except very small payments from petty cash. And, if authority to sign cheques is assigned to some person other than the business owner, that person should not have access to the accounting records. This separation of duties helps prevent an employee from concealing fraudulent disbursements in the accounting records.

In a small business, the manager usually signs cheques and normally knows from personal contact that the items being paid for were actually received. However, this arrangement is impossible in a larger business. Instead, internal control procedures must be substituted for personal contact. The procedures are designed to assure the cheque signer that the obligations to be paid were properly incurred and should be paid. Often these controls are achieved through a voucher system.

**Illustration 7-1**   The Accumulation of Documents in the Voucher

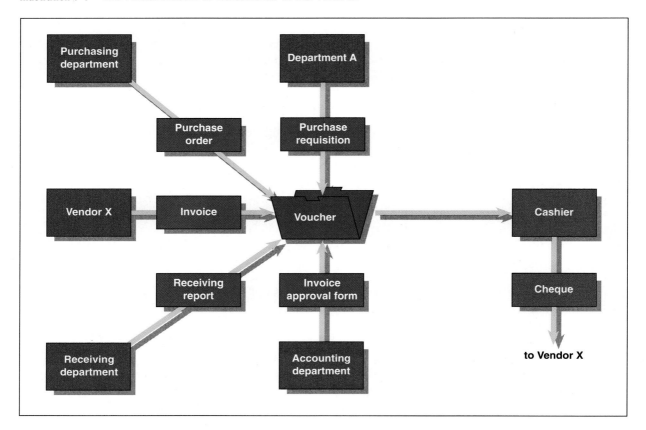

## THE VOUCHER SYSTEM AND CONTROL

A **voucher system** is a set of procedures designed to control the incurrence of obligations and disbursements of cash. This kind of system:

1.  Establishes procedures for incurring obligations that result in cash disbursements, such as permitting only authorized individuals to make purchase commitments.

2.  Provides established procedures for verifying, approving, and recording these obligations.

3.  Permits cheques to be issued only in payment of properly verified, approved, and recorded obligations.

4.  Requires that every obligation be recorded at the time it is incurred and that every purchase be treated as an independent transaction, complete in itself.

A good voucher system produces these results for every transaction, even if several purchases are made from the same company during a month or other billing period.

When a voucher system is used, control over cash disbursements begins as soon as the company incurs an obligation that will result in cash being paid out. A key factor in making the system work is that only specified departments and individuals are authorized to incur such obligations. Managers should also limit the kind of obligations that each department or individual can incur. For example, in a large retail store, only a specially created purchasing department should be authorized to incur obligations through merchandise purchases. In addition, the procedures for purchasing, receiving, and paying for merchandise should be divided among several departments. These departments include the one that originally requested the purchase, the purchasing department, the receiving department, and the accounting department. To coordinate and control the responsibilities of these departments, several different business papers are used. Illustration 7–1 shows how these papers are accumulated in a **voucher.** A voucher is an internal business paper that is used to accumulate other papers and information needed to control the disbursement of cash and to ensure that the transaction is properly recorded. The following explanation of each paper going into the voucher will show you how companies use this system to gain control over cash disbursements for merchandise purchases.

## Purchase Requisition

In a large retail store, department managers generally are not allowed to place orders directly with suppliers. If each manager could deal directly with suppliers, the amount of merchandise purchased and the resulting liabilities would not be well controlled. Therefore, to gain control over purchases and the resulting liabilities, department managers usually are required to place all orders through the purchasing department. When merchandise is needed, the department managers inform the purchasing department of their needs by preparing and signing a **purchase requisition** shown in Illustration 7–2. On the requisition, the manager lists the merchandise needed by the department and requests that it be purchased. Two copies of the purchase requisition are sent to the Purchasing Department. The manager of the requisitioning department (identified in Illustration 7–1 as Department A) keeps a third copy as a backup. The purchasing department sends one copy to the accounting department. When it is received, the accounting department creates a new voucher.

## Purchase Order

A **purchase order** is a business paper used by the purchasing department to place an order with the seller, or **vendor,** which usually is a manufacturer or wholesaler. The purchase order such as the one shown in Illustration 7–3 authorizes the vendor to ship the ordered merchandise at the stated price and terms.

When a purchase requisition is received by the purchasing department, it prepares at least four copies of a purchase order. The copies are distributed as follows:

> **Copy 1** is sent to the vendor as a request to purchase and as authority to ship the merchandise.

**Illustration 7-2** Purchase Requisition

SUGGESTED SUPPLIER & ADDRESS

**PURCHASE REQUISITION**

**Albert Distributing Company**

**NOTE:** (1) REQUISITIONER TO COMPLETE ALL UNSHADED AREAS.
(2) SUBMIT ALL QUOTATIONS WITH REQUISITION.

ORDERED FROM

| | |
|---|---|
| REQUISITIONED BY: | EXT. |
| DELIVER TO: | EXT. |
| DEPARTMENT: | |
| BLDG/RM | |

| DATE REQUISITIONED (D \| M \| Y) | DATE REQUIRED (D \| M \| Y) | SHIP VIA | F.O.B. | RC | TERMS ☐ 2%-10 ☐ N-30 |
|---|---|---|---|---|---|
| | | | | | |

FOR FEDERAL AND PROVINCIAL TAX PURPOSES PLEASE GIVE A BRIEF OUTLINE OF THE **END USE** ▶

| ITEM | QUANTITY | REF. NO. | DESCRIPTION | DUTY | ANNEX CODE | G.S.T. | PROV. TAX | UNIT PRICE | AMOUNT |
|---|---|---|---|---|---|---|---|---|---|
| | | | | | | | | | |
| | | | | | | | | | |
| | | | | | | | | | |
| | | | | | | | | | |
| | | | | | | | | | |
| | | | | | | | | | |
| | | | | | | | | | |
| | | | | | | | | | |
| | | | | | | | | | |
| | | | | | | | | | |
| | | | | | | | | | |
| | | | | | | | | | |
| | | | | | | | | | |
| | | | | | | | | | |
| | | | | | | | | | |
| | | | | | | | | | |
| | | | | | | | | | |
| | | | | | | | | | |
| | | | | | | | | | |
| | | | | | | | | | |

**IF** THIS EQUIPMENT REQUIRES INSTALLATION OR SERVICE CONNECTION (e.g. PLUMBING, ELECTRICAL) PLEASE INDICATE ☐ YES ☐ NO

DUTY: A EXEMPT; B INCL IF APP.; C NOT APP.

GOODS & SERVICES TAX: D TAXABLE; E EXEMPT; F ZERO RATED; G INCLUDED

PROVINCIAL SALES TAX: H APP. P.S.T. INCL; I LIC; J NOT APP.; K EXEMPT RESEARCH; L EXEMPT PROD.; M PLUS

| | |
|---|---|
| AMOUNT | |
| G.S.T. | |
| P.S.T. | |
| TOTAL | |

| ACCOUNT NUMBER | COMMITTED AMOUNT |
|---|---|
| | |
| | |
| | |

**AUTHORIZED SIGNATURE**

PURCHASE ORDER NUMBER:

**Illustration 7–3**   Purchase Order

**Albert Distributing Company**
365 Albert Street
Waterloo, Ontario N2L 3C5
(519) 884-8457

**PURCHASE ORDER**
**No.  335**

THIS NUMBER MUST APPEAR ON ALL
CORRESPONDENCE, INVOICES,
SHIPPING PAPERS AND PACKAGES.
(519) 884-8457

**SEND INVOICE ONLY TO:**
365 Albert Street, Waterloo, Ont. N2L 3C5

VENDOR _____         SHIP TO _____

| DATE | DATE TO BE SHIPPED | SHIP VIA | C.O.D. TERMS | FREIGHT TERMS | ADV. ALLOWANCE | SPECIAL ALLOWANCE |
|---|---|---|---|---|---|---|
| | | | | | | |

| ORDERED | PRODUCT NO. | DESCRIPTION | COST EACH | |
|---|---|---|---|---|
| | | | | |
| | | | | |
| | | | | |
| | | | | |
| | | | | |
| | | | | |
| | | | | |
| | | | | |
| | | | | |

**PURCHASE CONDITIONS**

1. Supplier will be responsible for extra freight cost on partial shipment; unless prior permission is obtained.
2. Please acknowledge this order.
3. Please notify us immediately if you are unable to complete order by date specified.

4. All items must be individually packed.
5. **Our purchase order no. must appear on all invoice packages & correspondence.**

**IF NOT SHIPPED BY**_____ **, CANCEL ORDER.**        _____
PURCHASING AGENT

**VENDOR COPY**

**Copy 2,** with a copy of the purchase requisition attached, is sent to the accounting department, where it is used in approving the payment of the invoice for the purchase; this copy is shown in Illustration 7–1.

**Copy 3** is sent to the department originally issuing the requisition to inform its manager that the action has been taken.

**Copy 4** is retained on file by the purchasing department.

## Invoice

An **invoice** such as the one in Illustration 7–4 is an itemized statement of goods prepared by the vendor that lists the customer's name, the items sold, the sales prices, and the terms of sale. In effect, the invoice is the bill sent to the buyer by the seller. (From the vendor's point of view, it is a *sales invoice*.) The vendor sends the invoice to the buyer or **vendee,** who treats it as a *purchase invoice*. On receiving a purchase order, the vendor ships the ordered merchandise to the buyer and mails a copy of the invoice that covers the shipment. The goods are delivered to the buyer's receiving department and the invoice is sent directly to the buyer's accounting department, where it is placed in the voucher. Illustration 7–1 also presents this document flow.

## Receiving Report

Most large companies maintain a special department that receives all merchandise or other purchased assets. When each shipment arrives, this receiving department counts the goods and checks them for damage and agreement with the purchase order. Then, it prepares four or more copies of a **receiving report.** An example of a receiving report is shown in Illustration 7–5. This report is a form used within the business to notify the appropriate persons that ordered goods were received and to describe the quantities and condition of the goods. As shown in Illustration 7–1, one copy is sent to the accounting department and placed in the voucher. Copies are also sent to the original requisitioning department and the purchasing department to notify them that the goods have arrived. The receiving department retains a copy in its files.

## Invoice Approval Form

After the receiving report arrives, the accounting department should have copies of these papers on file in the voucher:

1. The *purchase requisition* listing the items to be ordered.
2. The *purchase order* listing the merchandise that was actually ordered.
3. The *invoice* showing the quantity, description, price, and total cost of the goods shipped by the seller.
4. The *receiving report* listing the quantity and condition of the items actually received by the buyer.

With the information on these papers, the accounting department is in a position to make an entry recording the purchase and to approve its eventual payment before the end of the discount period. In approving the invoice for payment, the accounting department checks and compares the information on all the papers. To facilitate the checking procedure and to ensure that no step is omitted, the department commonly uses an **invoice approval form.** (See Illustration 7–6.) This form is a document on which the accounting department notes that it has performed each step in the process of checking an invoice and approving it for recording and payment. An invoice approval form may be a separate business paper that is filed in

**Illustration 7-4    Sales Invoice**

**SALE INVOICE**

**Albert Distributing Company**
365 Albert Street
Waterloo, Ontario N2L 3C5
(519) 884-8457

**INVOICE NO. 730**

S
O
L
D
T
O

FIRM NAME _____

ATTENTION OF _____

_____
ADDRESS

CITY                PROVINCE            POSTAL CODE

Invoice Date _____

Prepared By _____

Credit Terms _____

Customer Purchase Order

Number _____

Date _____

Signed By _____

Shipment Date _____

Shipped Via _____

Bill of Lading No. _____

BO
DO
NO
SO

BO = Back order — will be shipped shortly.
DO = Being shipped direct from factory.
NO = Not available — item no longer stocked.
SO = Similar item substituted.

| QUANTITY ORDERED | PRODUCT NUMBER | DESCRIPTION | QUANTITY SHIPPED | UNIT PRICE | EXTENSION |
|---|---|---|---|---|---|
| | | | | | |
| | | | | | |
| | | | | | |
| | | | | | |
| | | | | | |
| | | | | | |
| | | | | | |
| | | | | | |
| | | | | | |
| | | | | | |

| | | |
|---|---|---|
| TOTAL SALE | | |
| GST | | |
| PST | | |
| TOTAL | | |
| CUSTOMER ACCT. NO. | | |
| INVOICE VERIFIED BY | | |

**IMPORTANT:**    **ALL RETURNS MUST BE MADE WITHIN 10 DAYS AND ACCOM-PANIED BY AN INVOICE COPY AND PACKED IN THE ORIGINAL CARTON.**

**CUSTOMER**

**Illustration 7-5**   Receiving Report

## RECEIVING REPORT

**Albert Distributing Company**
365 Albert Street
Waterloo, Ontario N2L 3C5
(519) 884-8457

NO. **73**

| DATE | | PURCHASE ORDER NO. OR RETURN REQUEST NO. |
|---|---|---|
| | 19 | |

| RECEIVED FROM | PREPAID |
|---|---|
| ADDRESS | COLLECT |

| FREIGHT CARRIER | FREIGHT BILL NO. |
|---|---|

| | QUANTITY | ITEM NO. | DESCRIPTION |
|---|---|---|---|
| 1. | | | |
| 2. | | | |
| 3. | | | |
| 4. | | | |
| 5. | | | |
| 6. | | | |
| 7. | | | |
| 8. | | | |
| 9. | | | |
| 10. | | | |
| 11. | | | |
| 12. | | | |

REMARKS: CONDITIONS, ETC.

| RECEIVED BY | DELIVERED TO |
|---|---|

**BE SURE TO
MAKE THIS RECORD
ACCURATE AND COMPLETE**

| | By | Date |
|---|---|---|
| Purchase order number | ____ | ____ |
| Requisition check | ____ | ____ |
| Purchase order check | ____ | ____ |
| Receiving report check | ____ | ____ |
| Invoice check: | | |
|     Price approval | ____ | ____ |
|     Calculations | ____ | ____ |
|     Terms | ____ | ____ |
| Approved for payment | ____ | ____ |

**Illustration 7–6**

An Invoice Approval Form

the voucher or it may be preprinted on the voucher. It also may be stamped on the invoice. For clarity, the flowchart in Illustration 7–1 shows the form as a separate document.

As each step in the checking procedure is finished, the clerk initials the invoice approval form and records the current date. Initials in each space on the form indicate that the following administrative actions have been taken:

1. **Requisition check** . . . . . . . The items on the invoice were actually requisitioned, as shown on the copy of the purchase requisition.

2. **Purchase order check** . . . . The items on the invoice were actually ordered, as shown on the copy of the purchase order.

3. **Receiving report check** . . . The items on the invoice were actually received, as shown on the copy of the receiving report.

4. **Invoice check:**
   **Price approval** . . . . . . . . . The invoice prices are stated as agreed with the vendor.
   **Calculations** . . . . . . . . . . The invoice has no mathematical errors.
   **Terms** . . . . . . . . . . . . . . The terms are stated as agreed with the vendor.

## The Voucher

After an invoice is checked and approved, the voucher is complete. At this point, the voucher is a record that summarizes the transaction. The voucher shows that the transaction has been certified as correct and authorizes its recording as an obligation of the buyer. The voucher also contains approval for paying the obligation on the appropriate date. Of course, the actual physical form used for vouchers varies substantially from company to company. In general, they are designed so that the invoice and other documents from which they are prepared are placed inside the voucher, which is often a folder. The information printed on the inside of a typical voucher is shown in Illustration 7–7, and the information on the outside is shown in Illustration 7–8.

The preparation of a voucher requires a clerk to enter the specified information in the proper blanks. The information is taken from the invoice and all the supporting documents filed inside the voucher. Once the steps are completed, the voucher is sent to the appropriate authorized individual, who completes one final

**Illustration 7-7**
Inside of a Voucher

VALLEY SUPPLY COMPANY     Voucher No. _93–767_
Vancouver, B.C.

Date _____Oct. 1, 1996_____
Pay to ___A. B. Seay Wholesale Company_____
City____New Westminster_____     Province ___British Columbia_____

For the following: (attach all invoices and supporting papers)

| Date of Invoice | Terms | Invoice Number and Other Details | Amount |
|---|---|---|---|
| Sept. 30, 1996 | 2/10, n/60 | Invoice No. C-11756<br>Less discount<br>Net amount payable | 800.00<br>16.00<br>784.00 |

Payment approved

_____N.O.Neal_____
Auditor

**Illustration 7-8**
Outside of a Voucher

Voucher No. _93–767_

ACCOUNTING DISTRIBUTION

| Account Debited | Amount |
|---|---|
| Purchases | 800.00 |
| Transportation-In | |
| Store Supplies | |
| Office Supplies | |
| Sales Salaries | |
| Other | |
| | |
| | |
| | |
| | |
| Total Vouch. Pay. Cr. | 800.00 |

Due date _____October 10, 1996_____

Pay to __A. B. Seay Wholesale Company__
City___New Westminster_____
Province ___British Columbia_____

Summary of charges:
Total charges _____800.00____
Discount _____16.00____
Net payment _____784.00____

Record of payment:
Paid _____
Cheque No. _____

review of the information, approves the accounts and amounts to be debited (called the *accounting distribution*), and approves the voucher for recording.

After a voucher is approved and recorded, it is filed until its due date, when it is sent to the cashier's office for payment. Here, the person responsible for issuing cheques relies on the approved voucher and its signed supporting documents as proof that the obligation was properly incurred and should be paid. As described earlier, the purchase requisition and purchase order attached to the voucher confirm that the purchase was authorized. The receiving report shows that the items were received, and the invoice approval form verifies that the invoice was checked for errors. As a result, there is little chance for error. There is even less chance for fraud without collusion, unless all the documents and signatures are forged.

Under a voucher system, obligations should be approved for payment and recorded as liabilities as soon as possible after they are incurred. As shown in the example, this practice should be followed for all purchases. It also should be followed for all expenses. For example, when a company receives a monthly telephone bill, the charges (especially long-distance calls) should be examined for accuracy. A voucher should be prepared, and the telephone bill should be filed inside the voucher. The voucher then is recorded with a journal entry. If the amount is due at once, a cheque should be issued. Otherwise, the voucher should be filed for payment on the due date.

The requirement that vouchers be prepared for expenses as they are incurred helps ensure that every expense payment is approved only when adequate information is available. However, invoices or bills for such things as equipment repairs are sometimes not received until weeks after the work is done. If no records of the repairs exist, it may be difficult to determine whether the invoice or bill correctly states the amount owed. Also, if no records exist, it may be possible for a dishonest employee to arrange with an outsider for more than one payment of an obligation, or for payment of excessive amounts, or for payment for goods and services not received. A properly functioning voucher system helps prevent all of these undesirable results. A voucher system may also be computerized. However, similar controls must be instituted to ensure that orders and payments are properly authorized. The major difference is that the records would be computer-generated instead of being manually created.

## THE VOUCHER SYSTEM AND EXPENSES

### Progress Check

**7-6**  **Regarding internal control procedures for cash receipts:**
   *a.* **All cash disbursements, other than from petty cash, should be made by cheque.**
   *b.* **An accounting employee should count the cash received from sales and promptly deposit the receipts.**
   *c.* **Mail containing cash receipts should be opened by an accounting employee who is responsible for recording and depositing the receipts.**

**7-7**  **Do all companies need a voucher system? At what approximate point in a company's growth would you recommend installing a voucher system?**

A basic principle for controlling cash disbursements requires that all disbursements be made by cheque. However, an exception to this rule is made for *petty cash disbursements.* Every business must make many small payments for items such as postage, express charges, repairs, and small items of supplies. If firms made such payments by cheque, they would end up writing many cheques for small amounts. This arrangement would be both time consuming and expensive. Therefore, to avoid writing cheques for small amounts, a business should establish a petty cash fund and use the money in this fund to make payments like those listed earlier.

Establishing a petty cash fund requires estimating the total amount of small payments likely to be made during a short period, such as a month. Then, a cheque is drawn by the company cashier's office for an amount slightly in excess of this estimate. This cheque is recorded with a debit to the Petty Cash account (an asset) and a credit to Cash. The cheque is cashed, and the currency is turned over to a

## THE PETTY CASH FUND

LO 4

Explain the operation of a petty cash fund and be able to prepare journal entries to record petty cash fund transactions.

member of the office staff designated as the *petty cashier.* This person is responsible for the safekeeping of the cash, for making payments from this fund, and for keeping accurate records.

The petty cashier should keep the petty cash in a locked box in a safe place. As each disbursement is made, the person receiving payment signs a *petty cash receipt* (see Illustration 7–9). The receipt is then placed in the petty cashbox with the remaining money. Under this system, the sum of all the receipts plus the remaining cash should always equal the amount of the fund. For example, a $100 petty cash fund could have *(a)* $100 in cash, *(b)* $80 in cash and $20 in receipts, or *(c)* $10 in cash and $90 in receipts. Notice that each disbursement reduces the cash and increases the sum of the receipts in the petty cashbox. When the cash is nearly gone, the fund should be reimbursed. This provides internal control over the petty cash fund since only one person is responsible for each petty cash fund, and the total of the cash and receipts must equal the amount of the fund.

To reimburse the fund, the petty cashier presents the receipts to the company cashier. The company cashier stamps all receipts *paid* so that they cannot be reused, retains them, and gives the petty cashier a cheque for their sum. When this cheque is cashed and the proceeds returned to the cashbox, the money in the box is restored to its original amount, and the fund is ready to begin a new cycle of operations.

At the time a cheque is written to reimburse the petty cash fund, the petty cashier should sort the paid receipts according to the type of expense or other accounts to be debited in recording payments from the fund. Each group is then totaled, and the totals are used in making the entry to record the reimbursement.

## ILLUSTRATION OF A PETTY CASH FUND

To avoid writing numerous cheques for small amounts, a company established a petty cash fund on November 1, designating one of its office clerks, Carl Burns, as petty cashier. A $75 cheque was drawn, cashed, and the proceeds turned over to Burns. The following entry recorded the cheque:

| | | | | |
|---|---|---|---|---|
| Nov. | 1 | Petty Cash . . . . . . . . . . . . . . . . . . . . . . . . . . . . . . . . . | 75.00 | |
| | | Cash . . . . . . . . . . . . . . . . . . . . . . . . . . . . . . . . . | | 75.00 |
| | | *Established a petty cash fund.* | | |

Notice that this entry transfers $75 from the regular Cash account to the Petty Cash account. After the petty cash fund is established, the Petty Cash account is not debited or credited again unless the size of the total fund is changed. For example, the fund should be increased if it is being exhausted and reimbursed too frequently. Another entry like the preceding one would be made to record an increase in the size of the fund. That is, there would be a debit to Petty Cash and credit to Cash for the amount of the increase. If the fund is too large, some of the money in the fund should be redeposited in the chequing account. Such a reduction in the fund is recorded with a debit to Cash and a credit to Petty Cash.

Illustration 7-9
A Petty Cash Receipt

No ___- 1 -___                                            $___$10.00___

RECEIVED OF PETTY CASH

Date___Nov. 2___ 19_96_

For __Washing windows__

Charge to_____Miscellaneous expenses_____

Approved by                          Received by

CaB                                  Bob Tone

TOPS-Form 3008

During November, Carl Burns, the petty cashier, made several payments from the petty cash fund. Each time, he asked the person who received payment to sign a receipt. On November 27, after making a $26.50 payment for repairs to an office computer, Burns noticed that only $3.70 cash remained in the fund. Therefore, he summarized and totaled the petty cash receipts as shown in Illustration 7–10. Then, he gave the summary and the petty cash receipts to the company cashier in exchange for a $71.30 cheque to reimburse the fund. Burns cashed the cheque, put the $71.30 proceeds in the petty cashbox, and was ready to make additional payments from the fund. The reimbursing cheque is recorded with the following journal entry:

| | | | | |
|------|----|-----------------------------------------------|-------|-------|
| Nov. | 27 | Miscellaneous Expenses ........................ | 46.50 | |
| | | Transportation-In ............................ | 15.05 | |
| | | Delivery Expense ............................ | 5.00 | |
| | | Office Supplies .............................. | 4.75 | |
| | | Cash .................................. | | 71.30 |
| | | *Reimbursed petty cash.* | | |

Information for this entry came from the petty cashier's summary of payments. Note that the debits in the entry record the petty cash payments. Even if the petty cash fund is not low on funds at the end of an accounting period, it may be reimbursed at that time to record the expenses in the proper period. Otherwise, the financial statements show an overstated petty cash asset and understated expenses or assets that were paid for out of petty cash. (Of course, the amounts involved are seldom if ever significant to users of the financial statements.)

Illustration 7-10
Summary of Petty
Cash Payments

| | | |
|---|---|---|
| Miscellaneous expenses: | | |
| Nov. 2, washing windows . . . . . . . . . . . . . . | $10.00 | |
| Nov. 17, washing windows . . . . . . . . . . . . . | 10.00 | |
| Nov. 27, computer repairs . . . . . . . . . . . . . | 26.50 | $46.50 |
| Transportation-in: | | |
| Nov. 5, delivery of merchandise purchased . . . | $ 6.75 | |
| Nov. 20, delivery of merchandise purchased . . | 8.30 | 15.05 |
| Delivery expense: | | |
| Nov. 18, customer's package delivered . . . . . . | | 5.00 |
| Office supplies: | | |
| Nov. 15, purchased office supplies . . . . . . . . . | | 4.75 |
| Total . . . . . . . . . . . . . . . . . . . . . . . . . . . . . . | | $71.30 |

# CASH OVER AND SHORT

Sometimes, a petty cashier fails to get a receipt for a payment. Then, when the fund is reimbursed, he or she may forget the purpose of the expenditure. This mistake causes the fund to be short. If, for whatever reason, the petty cash fund is short at reimbursement time, the shortage is recorded as an expense in the reimbursing entry with a debit to the **Cash Over and Short account.** This account is an income statement account that records the income effects of cash overages and cash shortages arising from omitted petty cash receipts and from errors in making change.

Errors in making change are discovered when there are differences between the cash in a cash register and the record of the amount of cash sales. Even though a cashier is careful, some customers may be given too much or too little change. As a result, at the end of a day, the actual cash from a cash register may not equal the cash sales rung up. For example, assume that a cash register shows cash sales of $550 but the actual count of cash in the register is $555. The entry to record the cash sales and the overage would be:

| Nov. | 23 | Cash . . . . . . . . . . . . . . . . . . . . . . . . . . . . . . . . . . . . . | 555.00 | |
|---|---|---|---|---|
| | | Cash Over and Short . . . . . . . . . . . . . . . . . . . . . . | | 5.00 |
| | | Sales . . . . . . . . . . . . . . . . . . . . . . . . . . . . . . . . . | | 550.00 |
| | | *Day's cash sales and overage.* | | |

On the other hand, if there were a shortage of cash in the register on the next day, the entry to record cash sales and the shortage would look like the following:

| Nov. | 24 | Cash . . . . . . . . . . . . . . . . . . . . . . . . . . . . . . . . . . . . . | 621.00 | |
|---|---|---|---|---|
| | | Cash Over and Short . . . . . . . . . . . . . . . . . . . . . . . . | 4.00 | |
| | | Sales . . . . . . . . . . . . . . . . . . . . . . . . . . . . . . . . . | | 625.00 |
| | | *Day's cash sales and shortage.* | | |

## As a Matter of Ethics

Nancy Tucker is an internal auditor for a large corporation and is in the process of making surprise counts of three $200 petty cash funds in various offices in the headquarters building. She arrived at the office of one of the fund custodians shortly before lunch while he was on the telephone. Tucker explained the purpose of her visit, and the custodian asked politely that she come back after lunch so that he could finish the business he was conducting by long distance. She agreed and returned around 1:30. The custodian opened the petty cash box and showed her nine new $20 bills with consecutive serial numbers plus receipts that totaled $20. Would you suggest that the auditor take any further action or comment on these events in her report to management?

Because customers are more likely to dispute being shortchanged, the Cash Over and Short account usually has a debit balance by the end of the accounting period. Because it is a debit, this balance represents an expense. This expense may be shown on the income statement as a separate item in the general and administrative expense section. Or, because the amount is usually small, you can combine it with other small expenses and report them as a single item called *miscellaneous expenses*. If Cash Over and Short has a credit balance at the end of the period, it usually is included as part of *miscellaneous revenues* on the income statement.

---

### Progress Check

**7-8**   Why are some cash payments made from a petty cash fund?

**7-9**   Why should a petty cash fund be reimbursed at the end of an accounting period?

**7-10**   What are two results of reimbursing the petty cash fund?

---

## RECONCILING THE BANK BALANCE

LO 5

Explain why the bank balance and the book balance of cash should be reconciled and be able to prepare a reconciliation.

At least once every month, banks send depositors bank statements that show the activity in their accounts during the month. Different banks use a variety of formats for their bank statements. However, all of them include the following items of information in one place or another:

1.   The balance of the depositor's account at the beginning of the month.
2.   Deposits and any other amounts added to the account during the month.
3.   Cheques and any other amounts deducted from the account during the month.
4.   The account balance at the end of the month.

Of course, all this information is presented as it appears in the bank's records. Examine Illustration 7–11, an example of a typical bank statement, to find the four items just listed.

Enclosed with the monthly statement are the depositor's **canceled cheques** and any debit or credit memoranda that have affected the account. Canceled cheques are cheques that the bank has paid and deducted from the customer's account during the month. Additional deductions that may appear on the bank statement for an individual include withdrawals through automatic teller machines (ATM withdrawals) and periodic payments arranged in advance by the depositor.[2] Other de-

---

[2]Because of the need to make all disbursements by cheque, most business chequing accounts do not allow ATM withdrawals.

**Illustration 7-11    A Typical Bank Statement**

# LONDON BANK LB

| VALLEY COMPANY | | LONDON BANK |
| 39 MAPLE STREET | | NOV 30 |
| LONDON, ONTARIO | | DAILY |
| K2M 4K6 | | INTEREST |
| | | ACCOUNT |

| BRANCH | ACCOUNT NUMBER | BALANCE FORWARD |
| LONDON MAIN | 007–500865 | 7,502.02 |

| DATE | SYMBOL | WITHDRAWALS | DEPOSITS | BALANCE |
|------|--------|-------------|----------|---------|
| OCT 31 | 756 | 1,102.31 | | 6,399.71 |
| OCT 31 | 757 | 179.00 | | 6,220.71 |
| NOV 02 | NBD | | 20,000.00 | 26,220.71 |
| NOV 02 | 755 | 835.17 | | 25,385.54 |
| NOV 03 | PL | 250.00 | | 25,135.54 |
| NOV 04 | 759 | 1,116.00 | | 24,019.54 |
| NOV 08 | 749 | 32.00 | | 23,987.54 |
| NOV 08 | 747 | 4,212.00 | | 19,775.54 |
| NOV 09 | 751 | 50.00 | | 19,725.54 |
| NOV 10 | 762 | 1,906.81 | | 17,818.73 |
| NOV 14 | PL | 250.00 | | 17,568.73 |
| NOV 14 | 764 | 940.43 | | 16,628.30 |
| NOV 14 | 750 | 113.78 | | 16,514.52 |
| NOV 15 | CM | | 2,075.05 | 18,589.57 |
| NOV 15 | 770 | 10,000.00 | | 8,589.57 |
| NOV 15 | 763 | 267.29 | | 8,322.28 |
| NOV 15 | 767 | 86.46 | | 8,235.82 |
| NOV 17 | 766 | 125.00 | | 8,110.82 |
| NOV 17 | 769 | 164.00 | | 7,946.82 |
| NOV 21 | 765 | 89.78 | | 7,857.04 |
| NOV 23 | 771 | 150.00 | | 7,707.04 |
| NOV 24 | 768 | 178.29 | | 7,528.75 |
| NOV 30 | INT | | 78.89 | 7,607.64 |
| NOV 30 | S/C | 1.00 | | 7,606.64 |

### EXPLANATION OF SYMBOLS

Each transaction is identified by one of the following symbols.
Talk to your branch staff if you have any questions.

| | | | | | |
|---|---|---|---|---|---|
| AID | Investment Certificate Interest | INT | Interest | OBC | Other Bank Service Charge |
| CHQ | Cheque | JCW | Johnny Cash Withdrawal | PAY | Payroll Deposit |
| CM | Miscellaneous Credit | MCM | Merchant MasterCard Credit | PL | Loan Payment |
| COR | Correction | MDM | Merchant MasterCard Debit | PWR | Powerline Payment |
| CSB | Canada Savings Bond Transaction | MTC | MasterTeller Service Charge | RTD | Returned Item |
| DEP | Deposit | MTG | Mortgage Payment | SC | Service Charge |
| DM | Miscellaneous Debit | MTW | MasterTeller Withdrawal | SDB | Safe Deposit Box Payment |
| ECM | Electronic Funds Credit | NBD | No Book Deposit | WD | Withdrawal |
| EDM | Electronic Funds Debit | NBW | No Book Withdrawal | | |
| ICW | Interac Withdrawal | NRT | Non Resident Tax | | |

ductions from the depositor's account may include service charges and fees assessed by the bank, customers' cheques deposited that prove to be uncollectible, and corrections of previous errors. Except for the service charges, the bank notifies the depositor of the deduction in each case with a debit memorandum at the time that the bank reduces the balance. For completeness, a copy of each debit memorandum is usually sent with the monthly statement.[3]

In addition to deposits made by the depositor, the bank may add amounts to the depositor's account. Examples of additions would be amounts the bank has collected on behalf of the depositor and corrections of previous errors. Credit memoranda notify the depositor of all additions when they are first recorded. For completeness, a copy of each credit memorandum may be sent with the monthly statement.

Another item commonly added to the bank balance on the statement is interest earned by the depositor. Some chequing accounts pay the depositor interest based on the average cash balance maintained in the account. The bank calculates the amount of interest earned and credits it to the depositor's account each month. In Illustration 7–11, note that the bank credited $78.89 of interest to the account of Valley Company. (The methods used to calculate interest are discussed in the next chapter.)

When the business deposits all receipts intact and when all payments (other than petty cash payments) are drawn from the chequing account, the bank statement is a device for proving the accuracy of the depositor's cash records. The test of the accuracy begins by preparing a **bank reconciliation;** this analysis explains the difference between the balance of a chequing account in the depositor's records and the balance on the bank statement and is a critical element of internal control for cash.

## Need for Reconciling the Bank Balance

For virtually all chequing accounts, the balance on the bank statement does not agree with the balance in the depositor's accounting records. Therefore, to prove the accuracy of both the depositor's records and those of the bank, you must *reconcile* the two balances. In other words, you must explain or account for the differences between them.

Numerous factors cause the bank statement balance to differ from the depositor's book balance. Some are:

1. **Outstanding cheques.** These cheques were written (or drawn) by the depositor, deducted on the depositor's records, and sent to the payees. However, they did not reach the bank for payment and deduction before the statement date.

2. **Unrecorded deposits.** Companies often make deposits at the end of each business day, after the bank is closed. These deposits made in the bank's night depository are not recorded by the bank until the next business day. Therefore, a deposit placed in the night depository on the last day of the month cannot appear on the bank statement for that month. In addition, deposits mailed to the bank toward the end of the month may be in transit and unrecorded when the statement is prepared.

---

[3]A depositor's account is a liability on the bank's records. Thus, a deposit increases the account balance, and the bank records it with a *credit* to the account. Debit memos from the bank produce *credits* on the depositor's books, and credit memos lead to *debits*.

3.  **Charges for uncollectible items and for service.** Occasionally, a company deposits a customer's cheque that bounces, or turns out to be uncollectible. Usually, the balance in the customer's account is not large enough to cover the cheque. In these cases, the cheque is called a nonsufficient funds (NSF) cheque. In other situations, the customer's account has been closed. In processing deposited cheques, the bank credits the depositor's account for the full amount. Later, when the bank learns that the cheque is uncollectible, it debits (reduces) the depositor's account for the amount of the cheque. Also, the bank may charge the depositor a fee for processing the uncollectible cheque. At the same time, the bank notifies the depositor of each deduction by mailing a debit memorandum. Although each deduction should be recorded by the depositor on the day the debit memorandum is received, sometimes an entry is not made until the bank reconciliation is prepared.

    Other charges to a depositor's account that a bank might report on the bank statement include the printing of new cheques. Also, the bank may assess a monthly service charge for maintaining the account. Notification of these charges is *not* provided until the statement is mailed.

4.  **Credits for collections and for interest.** Banks sometimes act as collection agents for their depositors by collecting promissory notes and other items. When the bank collects an item, it deducts a fee and adds the net proceeds to the depositor's account. At the same time, it sends a credit memorandum to notify the depositor of the transaction. As soon as the memorandum is received, it should be recorded by the depositor. However, these items may remain unrecorded until the time of the bank reconciliation.

    Many bank accounts earn interest on the average cash balance in the account during the month. If an account earns interest, the bank statement includes a credit for the amount earned during the past month. Notification of earned interest is provided only by the bank statement.

5.  **Errors.** Regardless of care and systems of internal control for automatic error detection, both banks and depositors make errors. Errors by the bank may not be discovered until the depositor completes the bank reconciliation. Also, the depositor's errors often are not discovered until the balance is reconciled.

## Steps in Reconciling the Bank Balance

To obtain the benefits of separated duties, an employee who does not handle cash receipts, process cheques, or maintain cash records should prepare the bank reconciliation. In preparing to reconcile the balance, this employee must gather information from the bank statement and from other sources in the records. The person who performs the reconciliation must do the following:

*   Compare the deposits listed on the bank statement with the deposits shown in the accounting records. Identify any discrepancies and determine which is correct. Make a list of any errors or unrecorded deposits.
*   Examine all other credits on the bank statement and determine whether each was recorded in the books. These items include collections by the bank, correction of previous bank statement errors, and interest earned by the depositor. List any unrecorded items.

- Compare the canceled cheques listed on the bank statement with the actual cheques returned with the statement. For each cheque, make sure that the correct amount was deducted by the bank and that the returned cheque was properly charged to the company's account. List any discrepancies or errors.
- Compare the canceled cheques listed on the bank statement with the cheques recorded in the books. (To make this process easier, the bank statement normally lists canceled cheques in numerical order.) Prepare a list of any outstanding cheques.

  Although an individual may occasionally write a cheque and fail to record it in the books, companies with reasonable internal controls rarely if ever write a cheque without recording it. Nevertheless, prepare a list of any canceled cheques unrecorded in the books.
- Determine whether any outstanding cheques listed on the previous month's bank reconciliation are not included in the canceled cheques listed on the bank statement. Prepare a list of any of these cheques that remain outstanding at the end of the current month. Send this list to the cashier's office for follow-up with the payees to see if the cheques were actually received.
- Examine all other debits to the account shown on the bank statement and determine whether each was recorded in the books. These include bank charges for newly printed cheques, NSF cheques, and monthly service charges. List those not yet recorded.

When this information has been gathered, the employee can complete the reconciliation like the one in Illustration 7–12 by using these steps:

1. Start with the bank balance of the cash account.
2. Identify and list any unrecorded deposits and any bank errors that understated the bank balance. Add them to the bank balance.
3. Identify and list any outstanding cheques and any bank errors that overstated the bank balance. Subtract them from the bank balance.
4. Compute the adjusted balance. This amount is also called the correct or reconciled balance.
5. Start with the book balance of the cash account.
6. Identify and list any unrecorded credit memoranda from the bank (perhaps for the proceeds of a collected note), interest earned, and any errors that understated the balance. Add them to the book balance.
7. Identify and list any unrecorded debit memoranda from the bank (perhaps for a NSF cheque from a customer), service charges, and any errors that overstated the book balance. Subtract them from the book balance.
8. Compute the reconciled balance. This is also the correct balance.
9. Verify that the two adjusted balances from steps 4 and 8 are equal. If so, they are reconciled. If not, check for mathematical accuracy and for any missing data.

When the reconciliation is complete, the employee should send a copy to the accounting department so that any needed journal entries can be recorded. For

**Illustration 7-12**
A Typical Bank
Reconciliation

| MOUNTAIN COMPANY |
|---|
| **Bank Reconciliation** |
| **October 31, 1996** |

| | | | | |
|---|---|---|---|---|
| ①Bank statement balance . . . . | $2,050.00 | ⑤Book balance . . . . . . . . . . . | | $1,404.58 |
| ②Add: | | ⑥Add: | | |
| Deposit of October 31 . . . | 145.00 | Proceeds of note less | | |
| | | collection fee . . . . . . . . | $ 485.00 | |
| | | Interest earned . . . . . . . . | 8.42 | |
| | | Total . . . . . . . . . . . . . . . | $ 493.42 | |
| Total . . . . . . . . . . . . . . . . . | $2,195.00 | Total . . . . . . . . . . . . . . . . . | | $1,898.00 |
| ③Deduct: | | ⑦Deduct: | | |
| Outstanding checks: | | NSF check plus service | | |
| No. 124 . . . . . . . . . . . . . | $ 150.00 | charge . . . . . . . . . . . . | $ 30.00 | |
| No. 126 . . . . . . . . . . . | 200.00 | Check printing charge . . . . | 23.00 | |
| Total . . . . . . . . . . . . . . | $ 350.00 | Total . . . . . . . . . . . . . . | $ 53.00 | |
| ④Reconciled balance . . . . . . . | $1,845.00 | ⑧Reconciled balance . . . . . . . | | $1,845.00 |

⑨The two balances both equal $1,845.00

example, entries are needed to record any unrecorded debit and credit memoranda and any of the company's mistakes. Another copy should go to the cashier's office, especially if the bank has made an error that needs to be corrected.

**ILLUSTRATION OF A BANK RECONCILIATION**

We can illustrate a bank reconciliation by preparing one for Mountain Company as of October 31. In preparing to reconcile the bank account, the Mountain Company employee gathered the following facts:

- The bank balance shown on the bank statement was $2,050.
- The cash balance according to the accounting records was $1,404.58.
- A $145 deposit was placed in the bank's night depository on October 31 and was unrecorded by the bank when the bank statement was mailed.
- Enclosed with the bank statement was a copy of a credit memorandum showing that the bank had collected a note receivable for the company on October 23. The note's proceeds of $500 (less a $15 collection fee) were credited to the company's account. This credit memorandum had not been recorded by the company.
- The bank statement also showed a credit of $8.42 for interest earned on the average cash balance in the account. Because there had been no prior notification of this item, it had not been recorded on the company's books.
- A comparison of canceled cheques with the company's books showed that two cheques were outstanding—No. 124 for $150 and No. 126 for $200.
- Other debits on the bank statement that had not been previously recorded on the books included *(a)* a $23 charge for cheques printed by the bank; and *(b)* an NSF (nonsufficient funds) cheque for $20 plus the related processing

fee of $10. The NSF cheque had been received from a customer, Frank Green, on October 16 and had been included in that day's deposit.

Illustration 7–12 shows the bank reconciliation that reflects these items. The numbers in the circles beside the various parts of the reconciliation correspond to the numbers of the steps listed earlier.

Preparing a bank reconciliation helps locate any errors made by either the bank or the depositor. It also identifies unrecorded items that should be recorded on the company's books. For example, in Mountain Company's reconciliation, the adjusted balance of $1,845.00 is the correct balance as of October 31, 1996. However, at that date, Mountain Company's accounting records show a $1,404.58 balance. Therefore, journal entries must be made to increase the book balance to the correct balance. This process requires four entries. The first is:

| Nov. | 2 | Cash ..................................... | 485.00 | |
|------|---|-------------------------------------------|--------|--------|
| | | Collection Expense .......................... | 15.00 | |
| | | Notes Receivable ......................... | | 500.00 |
| | | *To record the collection fee and proceeds of a note collected by the bank.* | | |

This entry records the net proceeds of Mountain Company's note receivable that had been collected by the bank, the expense of having the bank perform that service, and the reduction in the Notes Receivable account.

The second entry records the interest credited to Mountain Company's account by the bank:

| Nov. | 2 | Cash ..................................... | 8.42 | |
|------|---|-------------------------------------------|------|------|
| | | Interest Earned ......................... | | 8.42 |
| | | *To record interest earned on the average cash balance maintained in the chequing account.* | | |

Interest earned is a revenue, and the entry recognizes both the revenue and the related increase in Cash.

The third entry records the NSF cheque that was returned as uncollectible. The $20 cheque was received from Green in payment of his account and deposited. The bank charged $10 for handling the NSF cheque and deducted $30 from Mountain Company's account. Therefore, the company must reverse the entry made when the cheque was received and also record the $10 processing fee:

| Nov. | 2 | Accounts Receivable—Frank Green .............. | 30.00 | |
|------|---|-----------------------------------------------|-------|-------|
| | | Cash ................................. | | 30.00 |
| | | *To charge Frank Green's account for his NSF cheque and for the bank's fee.* | | |

This entry reflects the fact that Mountain Company followed customary business practice and added the NSF $10 fee to Green's account. Thus, it will try to collect the entire $30 from Green.

The fourth entry debits Miscellaneous Expenses for the cheque printing charge. The entry is:

| Nov. | 2 | Miscellaneous Expenses ...................... | 23.00 | |
| | | Cash ................................... | | 23.00 |
| | | *Cheque printing charge.* | | |

After these entries are recorded, the balance of cash is increased to the correct amount of $1,845.00 ($1,404.58 + $485.00 + $8.42 − $30.00 − $23.00)

---

**Progress Check**

**7-11    What is a bank statement?**

**7-12    What is the meaning of the phrase *to reconcile a bank balance*?**

**7-13    Why should you reconcile the bank statement balance of cash and the depositor's book balance of cash?**

**7-14    List items that commonly affect the bank side of a reconciliation and indicate if the items are added or subtracted.**

**7-15    List items that commonly affect the book side of a reconciliation and indicate if the items are added or subtracted.**

---

## OTHER INTERNAL CONTROL PROCEDURES

**LO 6**

Explain how recording invoices at net amounts helps gain control over cash discounts taken, and calculate days' sales uncollected.

Internal control principles apply to every phase of a company's operations including merchandise purchases, sales, cash receipts, cash disbursements, and owning and operating plant assets. Many of these procedures are discussed in later chapters. At this point, we consider a way that a company can gain more control over *purchases discounts.*

Recall that entries such as the following have recorded the receipt and payment of an invoice for a purchase of merchandise:

| Oct. | 2 | Purchases ................................. | 1,000.00 | |
| | | Accounts Payable ........................ | | 1,000.00 |
| | | *Purchased merchandise, terms 2/10, n/60.* | | |
| | 12 | Accounts Payable ........................... | 1,000.00 | |
| | | Purchases Discounts ..................... | | 20.00 |
| | | Cash ................................. | | 980.00 |
| | | *Paid the invoice of October 2.* | | |

These entries reflect the **gross method of recording purchases.** That is, the invoice was recorded at its gross amount of $1,000 before considering the cash discount. Many companies record invoices in this way. However, the **net method of recording purchases** records invoices at their *net* amounts (after cash discounts). This method is widely thought to provide more useful information to management.

To illustrate the net method, assume that a company purchases merchandise with a $1,000 invoice price, and terms of 2/10, n/60. On receiving the goods, the purchasing company deducted the offered $20 discount from the gross amount and recorded the purchase at the $980 net amount:

| Oct. | 2 | Purchases . . . . . . . . . . . . . . . . . . . . . . . . . . . . . . . . . . | 980.00 | |
|------|---|--------------------------------------------------------------------------|--------|--------|
| | |     Accounts Payable . . . . . . . . . . . . . . . . . . . . . . . | | 980.00 |
| | | *Purchased merchandise on credit.* | | |

If the invoice for this purchase is paid within the discount period, the entry to record the payment debits Accounts Payable and credits Cash for $980. However, if payment is not made within the discount period and the discount is *lost,* an entry such as the following must be made either before or when the invoice is paid:

| Dec. | 1 | Discounts Lost . . . . . . . . . . . . . . . . . . . . . . . . . . . . . | 20.00 | |
|------|---|--------------------------------------------------------------------------|--------|--------|
| | |     Accounts Payable . . . . . . . . . . . . . . . . . . . . . . . | | 20.00 |
| | | *To record the discount lost.* | | |

A cheque for the full $1,000 invoice amount is then written, recorded, and mailed to the creditor.[4]

## Advantage of the Net Method

When invoices are recorded at *gross* amounts, the amount of discounts taken is deducted from the balance of the Purchases account on the income statement to arrive at the cost of merchandise purchased. However, the amount of any lost discounts does not appear in any account or on the income statement. Therefore, lost discounts may not come to the attention of management.

On the other hand, when purchases are recorded at *net* amounts, the amount of discounts taken does not appear on the income statement. Instead, an expense for **discounts lost** is brought to management's attention through its appearance on the income statement as an operating expense.

Recording invoices at their net amounts supplies management with useful information about the amount of discounts missed through oversight, carelessness, or some other reason. Thus, this practice gives management better control over the people responsible for paying bills on time so that cash discounts can be taken. When the accounts record the fact that discounts are missed, someone has to explain why. As a result, it is likely that fewer discounts are lost through carelessness.

---

[4]Alternatively, the lost discount can be recorded with the late payment in a single entry.

Many companies attract customers by selling to them on credit. As a result, cash flows from customers are postponed until the accounts receivable are collected. To evaluate the liquidity of a company's assets, investors want to know how quickly the company converts its accounts receivable into cash. One way financial statement users evaluate the liquidity of the receivables is to look at the **days' sales uncollected.** This is calculated by taking the ratio between the present balance of receivables and the credit sales over the preceding year, and then multiplying by the number of days in the year. Since the amount of credit sales usually is not reported, net sales is typically used in the calculation. Thus, the formula for the calculation is:

$$\text{Days' sales uncollected} = \frac{\text{Accounts receivable}}{\text{Net sales}} \times 365$$

For example, assume Meg's Mart had accounts receivable of $11,200 at the end of 1996 and net sales of $314,700 for the year. By dividing $11,200 by $314,700, we find that the receivables balance represents 3.56% of the year's sales. Because there are 365 days in a year, the $11,200 balance is 3.56% of 365 days of sales, or 13 days of sales.

The number of days' sales uncollected is used as an estimate of how much time is likely to pass before cash receipts from credit sales equal the amount of the existing accounts receivable. In evaluating this number, financial statement users should compare it to days' sales uncollected calculations for other companies in the same industry. In addition, they may make comparisons between the current and prior periods. To illustrate such a comparison, selected data from the 1993 annual reports of two toy manufacturing companies are used to compute days' sales uncollected:

| (*in thousands*) | TYCO | | MATTEL | |
|---|---|---|---|---|
| Accounts Receivable | $\dfrac{\$219,036}{\$730,179} \times 365$ | | $\dfrac{\$580,313}{\$2,704,448} \times 365$ | |
| Net Sales | | | | |
| Days' Sales Uncollected | 110 days | | 78 days | |

If **TYCO Toys, Inc.'s** management made the preceding comparison, the resulting figures might motivate them to investigate how this compares to last year and how they could improve this ratio. Continuation of a financially sound business requires continuous monitoring of the liquidity of the firm's assets.

---

**Progress Check**

7-16   **When invoices are recorded at net amounts:**
   *a.* **The amount of purchases discounts taken is not recorded in a separate account.**
   *b.* **Purchases discounts taken are recorded in a Purchases Discounts account.**
   *c.* **The cash expenditures for purchases will always be less than if the invoices are recorded at gross amounts.**

7-17   **Why is the days' sales uncollected calculation usually based on net sales instead of credit sales?**

---

**LO 1. Explain the concept of liquidity and the difference between cash and cash equivalents.** The liquidity of an asset refers to how easily the asset can be converted into other types of assets or used to buy services or satisfy obligations. Cash is the most liquid asset. To increase their return, companies may invest their idle cash balances in cash equivalents. These investments are readily convertible to a known amount of cash with market values that are relatively insensitive to interest rate changes. In evaluating the liquidity of a company, financial statement users may calculate days' sales uncollected.

**LO 2. Explain why internal control procedures are needed in a large organization and state the broad principles of internal control.** Internal control systems are designed to encourage adherence to prescribed managerial policies. In doing so, they promote efficient operations and protect assets against theft or misuse. They also help ensure that accurate and reliable accounting data are produced. Principles of good internal control include establishing clear responsibilities, maintaining adequate records, insuring assets and bonding employees, separating record-keeping and custody of assets, dividing responsibilities for related transactions, using mechanical devices whenever feasible, and performing regular independent reviews of internal control practices.

**LO 3. Describe internal control procedures used to protect cash received from cash sales, cash received through the mail, and cash disbursements.** To maintain control over cash, custody must be separated from record-keeping for cash. All cash receipts should be deposited intact in the bank on a daily basis, and all payments (except for minor petty cash payments) should be made by cheque. A voucher system helps maintain control over cash disbursements by ensuring that payments are made only after full documentation and approval.

**LO 4. Explain the operation of a petty cash fund and be able to prepare journal entries to record petty cash fund transactions.** The petty cashier, who should be a responsible employee, makes small payments from the petty cash fund and obtains signed receipts for the payments. The Petty Cash account is debited when the fund is established or increased in size. Petty cash disbursements are recorded with a credit to cash whenever the fund is replenished.

**LO 5. Explain why the bank balance and the book balance of cash should be reconciled and be able to prepare a reconciliation.** A bank reconciliation is produced to prove the accuracy of the depositor's and the bank's records. In completing the reconciliation, the bank statement balance is adjusted for such items as outstanding cheques and unrecorded deposits made on or before the bank statement date but not reflected on the statement. The depositor's cash account balance is adjusted to the correct balance. The difference arises from such items as service charges, collections the bank has made for the depositor, and interest earned on the average chequing account balance.

**LO 6. Explain how recording invoices at net amounts helps gain control over cash discounts taken, and calculate days' sales uncollected.** When the net method of recording invoices is used, missed cash discounts are reported as an expense in the income statement. In contrast, when the gross method is used, discounts taken are reported as reductions in the cost of the purchased goods. Therefore, the net method directs management's attention to instances where the company failed to take advantage of discounts.

**SUMMARY OF THE CHAPTER IN TERMS OF LEARNING OBJECTIVES**

**DEMONSTRATION PROBLEM**

**Reconciliation of Phillip Company's bank account as of May 31:**

| | | | | |
|---|---|---|---|---|
| Bank statement balance | $2,304.75 | Book balance | | $2,268.32 |
| Add: | | | | |
| Deposit of May 30 | 245.62 | | | |
| Total | 2,550.37 | | | |
| Deduct: | | Deduct: | | |
| Outstanding cheques: | | NSF cheque plus service charge | 56.75 | |
| No. 376 | 185.30 | Bank service charges | 18.65 | |
| No. 382 | 172.15 | | | |
| Total | 357.45 | Total | 75.40 | |
| Reconciled balance | $2,192.92 | Reconciled balance | | $2,192.92 |

**Summary of Phillip Company's bank statement for the month of June:**

| Date | Symbol | Withdrawl | Deposit | Balance |
|---|---|---|---|---|
| May 31 | Balance forward | | | 2,304.75 |
| June 2 | NBD | | 245.62 | 2,550.37 |
| June 3 | 376 | 185.30 | | 2,365.08 |
| June 5 | 383 | 250.00 | | 2,115.07 |
| June 10 | NBD | | 385.70 | 2,500.77 |
| June 12 | 384 | 48.90 | | 2,451.87 |
| June 14 | 385 | 152.30 | | 2,299.57 |
| June 18 | 387 | 113.78 | | 2,185.79 |
| June 20 | NBD | | 462.95 | 2,648.74 |
| June 22 | 389 | 238.95 | | 2,409.79 |
| June 25 | 386 | 138.40 | | 2,271.39 |
| June 26 | 382 | 172.15 | | 2,099.24 |
| June 29 | 391 | 74.20 | | 2,025.04 |
| June 30 | SC | 15.70 | | 2,009.34 |

**Summary of June Cheque Register:**

| Date | No. | Amount |
|---|---|---|
| June | | |
| 2 | 383 | $ 250.00 |
| 5 | 384 | 48.90 |
| 6 | 385 | 152.30 |
| 8 | 386 | 138.40 |
| 10 | 387 | 113.78 |
| 12 | 388 | 186.30 |
| 15 | 389 | 238.95 |
| 16 | 390 | 146.40 |
| 20 | 391 | 74.20 |
| 26 | 392 | 106.70 |
| 29 | 393 | 164.80 |
| Total | | $1,620.73 |

**Summary of June Cash Receipts:**

| Date | Amount |
|---|---|
| June | |
| 9 | $ 385.70 |
| 18 | 462.95 |
| 29 | 220.85 |
| Total | $1,069.50 |

**Book cash balance, June 30:**

| | |
|---|---|
| Book balance, May 31 | $2,192.92 |
| Add receipts | 1,069.50 |
| Total | 3,262.42 |
| Deduct cheques | 1,620.73 |
| Book balance, June 30 | $1,641.69 |

**Required**

Prepare a bank reconciliation and any necessary journal entries for Phillip Company for the month of June.

- Examine the previous month's bank reconciliation for any items that should be carried over to the current month.
- Compare the deposits in the accounting records with the deposits in the bank statement.
- Examine any other credits in the bank statement.
- Compare the canceled cheques in the bank statement with the cheques recorded in the books.
- Examine any other debits in the bank statement.
- Calculate and compare the reconciled bank balance and the reconciled book balance.

*Planning the Solution*

Reconciliation of Phillip Company's bank account as of June 30:

*Solution to Demonstration Problem*

| | | | | |
|---|---|---|---|---|
| Bank statement balance ...... | $2,009.34 | Book balance .............. | | .$1,641.69 |
| Add: | | | | |
|   Deposit of June 29 ........ | 220.85 | | | |
|   Total ................ | 2,230.19 | | | |
| Deduct: | | Deduct: | | |
|   Outstanding cheques: | |   Bank service charge ....... | 15.70 | |
|     No. 388 ............. | 186.30 | | | |
|     No. 390 ............. | 146.40 | | | |
|     No. 392 ............. | 106.70 | | | |
|     No. 393 ............. | 164.80 | | | |
|   Total ................ | 604.20 | | | |
| Reconciled balance ........ | $1,625.99 | Reconciled balance .......... | | .$1,625.99 |

Journal entry:

| | | | | |
|---|---|---|---|---|
| June | 30 | Miscellaneous expense ...................... | 15.70 | |
| | |   Cash .................................... | | 15.70 |
| | |    *Bank charges.* | | |

# GLOSSARY

**Bank reconciliation**  an analysis that explains the difference between the balance of a chequing account shown in the depositor's records and the balance shown on the bank statement. p. 367

**Canceled cheques**  cheques that the bank has paid and deducted from the customer's account during the month. p. 365

**Cash equivalents**  temporary liquid investments that can be easily and quickly converted to cash.  p. 345

**Cash Over and Short account**  an income statement account used to record cash overages and cash shortages arising from omitted petty cash receipts and from errors in making change. p. 364

**Days' sales uncollected**  the number of days of average credit sales volume accumulated in the accounts receivable balance, calculated as the product of 374 times the ratio of the accounts receivable balance divided by credit (or net) sales. p. 374

**Discounts lost**  an expense resulting from failing to take advantage of cash discounts on purchases. p. 373

**Gross method of recording purchases**  a method of recording purchases at the full invoice price without deducting any cash discounts. p. 372

**Internal control system**  procedures adopted by a business to encourage adherence to prescribed managerial policies; in doing so, the system also promotes operational efficiencies and protects the business assets from waste, fraud, and theft, and helps ensure that accurate and reliable accounting data are produced. p. 346

**Invoice**  an itemized statement prepared by the vendor that lists the customer's name, the items sold, the sales prices, and the terms of sale. p. 356

**Invoice approval form**  a document on which the accounting department notes that it has performed each step in the process of checking an invoice and approving it for recording and payment. p. 356

**Liquid asset**  an asset, such as cash, that is easily converted into other types of assets or used to buy services or pay liabilities. p. 344

**Liquidity**  a characteristic of an asset that refers to how easily the asset can be converted into another type of asset or used to buy services or satisfy obligations. p. 344

**Net method of recording purchases**  a method of recording purchases at the full invoice price less any cash discounts. p. 373

**Outstanding cheques**  cheques that were written (or drawn) by the depositor, deducted on the depositor's records, and sent to the payees; however, they had not reached the bank for payment and deduction before the statement date. p. 367

**Purchase order**  a business paper used by the purchasing department to place an order with the vendor; authorizes the vendor to ship the ordered merchandise at the stated price and terms. p. 353

**Purchase requisition**  a business paper used to request that the Purchasing Department buy the needed merchandise or other items. p. 352

**Receiving report**  a form used within the business to notify the appropriate persons that ordered goods were received and to describe the quantities and condition of the goods. p. 356

**Vendee**  the buyer or purchaser of goods or services. p. 356

**Vendor**  the seller of goods or services, usually a manufacturer or wholesaler. p. 353

**Voucher**  an internal business paper used to accumulate other papers and information needed to control the disbursement of cash and to ensure that the transaction is properly recorded. p. 352

**Voucher system**  a set of procedures designed to control the incurrence of obligations and disbursements of cash. p. 352

## SYNONYMOUS TERMS

**Chequing account**  demand deposit.
**Invoice**  bill.
**Purchase order**  P.O.
**Savings account**  time deposit.

**Unrecorded deposits**  deposits in transit.
**Vendee**  buyer.
**Vendor**  seller.
**Write a cheque**  draw a cheque.

## QUESTIONS

1. Which of the following assets is most liquid? Which is least liquid? Merchandise inventory, building, accounts receivable, cash.
2. List the seven broad principles of internal control.
3. Why should the person who keeps the record of an asset not be the person responsible for custody of the asset?
4. Internal control procedures are important in every business, but at what stage in the development of a business do they become critical?
5. Why should responsibility for a sequence of related transactions be divided among different departments or individuals?

6. Why should all receipts be deposited intact on the day of receipt?
7. When merchandise is purchased for a large store, why are department managers not permitted to deal directly with suppliers?
8. When a disbursing officer issues a cheque for a large business, he or she usually cannot know from personal contact that the assets, goods, or services being paid for were received by the business or that the purchase was properly authorized. However, if the company has an internal control system, the officer can depend on it. Exactly which documents does the officer depend on to tell that the purchase

was authorized and that the goods were actually received?

9. Why are some cash payments made from a petty cash fund?

10. What is a petty cash receipt? Who signs a petty cash receipt?

11. Why should you reconcile the bank statement balance of cash and the depositor's book balance of cash?

12. Geac Computer Corporation Limited's consolidated statement of changes in financial position (see Appendix I) describes the changes in cash that occurred during the year ended April 30, 1994. What amount was provided (or used) by investing activities and what amount was provided (or used) by financing activities?

**Geac**

## QUICK STUDY (Five-Minute Exercises)

What is the difference between the terms *liquidity* and *cash equivalent?*

QS 7–1
(LO 1)

*a.* What is the main objective of internal control and how is it accomplished?

*b.* Why should record-keeping for assets be separated from custody over the assets?

QS 7–2
(LO 2)

In a good system of internal control for cash that provides adequate procedures for protecting both cash receipts and cash disbursements, three basic guidelines should always be observed. What are these guidelines?

QS 7–3
(LO 3)

*a.* The Petty Cash Fund of the No-Fear Ski Club was established at $50. At the end of the month, the fund contained $4.35 and had the following receipts: film rental $12.50, refreshments for meetings $20.15 (both expenditures to be classified as Entertainment Expenses), postage $4.00, and printing $9.00. Prepare the journal entries to record *(a)* the establishment of the fund; *(b)* the reimbursement at the end of the month.

*b.* Explain when the Petty Cash account would be credited in a journal entry.

QS 7–4
(LO 4)

*a.* Identify whether each of the following items affects the bank or book side of the reconciliation and indicate if the amount represents an addition or a subtraction.

QS 7–5
(LO 5)

(1) Bank service charges.

(2) Outstanding cheques.

(3) Debit memos.

(4) Unrecorded deposits.

(5) Interest on average monthly balance.

(6) NSF cheques.

(7) Credit memos.

*b.* Which of the previous items require a journal entry?

Which accounting method uses a Discounts Lost account and what is the advantage of this method?

QS 7–6
(LO 6)

Refer to Geac Computer financial statements in Appendix I. What was the difference in the number of days' sales collected in 1994 and 1993? According to this ratio analysis, is Geac's collection of receivables improving? Explain your answer.

QS 7–7
(LO 6)

**Geac**

# EXERCISES

**Exercise 7–1**
Analyzing internal
control
**(LO 2)**

Seinfeld Company is a young business that has grown rapidly. The company's bookkeeper, who was hired two years ago, left town suddenly after the company's manager discovered that a great deal of money had disappeared over the past 18 months. An audit disclosed that the bookkeeper had written and signed several cheques made payable to the bookkeeper's sister, and then recorded the cheques as salaries expense. The sister, who cashed the cheques but had never worked for the company, left town with the bookkeeper. As a result, the company incurred an uninsured loss of $123,000.

Evaluate Seinfeld Company's internal control system and indicate which principles of internal control appear to have been ignored in this situation.

**Exercise 7–2**
Recommending internal
control procedures
**(LO 2, 3)**

What internal control procedures would you recommend in each of the following situations?

*a.* An antique store has one employee who is given cash and sent to garage sales each weekend. The employee pays cash for merchandise to be resold at the antique store.

*b.* Fun in the Sun has one employee who sells sun visors and beach chairs at the beach. Each day, the employee is given enough visors and chairs to last through the day and enough cash to make change. The money is kept in a box at the stand.

**Exercise 7–3**
Internal control over cash
receipts
**(LO 2, 3)**

Some of Carver Company's cash receipts from customers are sent to the company in the mail. Carver's bookkeeper opens the letters and deposits the cash received each day. What internal control problem is inherent in this arrangement? What changes would you recommend?

**Exercise 7–4**
Petty cash fund
**(LO 4)**

A company established a $400 petty cash fund on March 1. One week later, on March 8, the fund contained $74.50 in cash and receipts for these expenditures: postage, $73.00; transportation-in, $38.00; miscellaneous expenses, $122.00; and store supplies, $92.50.

Prepare the journal entries to *(a)* establish the fund and *(b)* reimburse it on March 8. *(c)* Now assume that the fund was not only reimbursed on March 8 but also increased to $600 because it was exhausted so quickly. Give the entry to reimburse the fund and increase it to $600.

**Exercise 7–5**
Petty cash fund
**(LO 4)**

A company established a $300 petty cash fund on May 9. On May 31, the fund had $123.20 in cash and receipts for these expenditures: transportation-in, $24.20; miscellaneous expenses, $66.10; and store supplies, $84.90. The petty cashier could not account for the $1.60 shortage in the fund. Prepare *(a)* the May 9 entry to establish the fund and *(b)* the May 31 entry to reimburse the fund and reduce it to $225.

**Exercise 7–6**
Bank reconciliation
**(LO 5)**

Cisco Company deposits all receipts intact on the day received and makes all payments by cheque. On April 30, 1996, after all posting was completed, its Cash account showed a $9,540 debit balance. However, Cisco's April 30 bank statement showed only $7,881 on deposit in the bank on that day. Prepare a bank reconciliation for Cisco, using the following information:

*a.* Outstanding cheques, $1,440.

*b.* Included with the April canceled cheques returned by the bank was a $15 debit memorandum for bank services.

c.   Cheque No. 658, returned with the canceled cheques, was correctly drawn for $327 in payment of the utility bill and was paid by the bank on April 22. However, it had been recorded with a debit to Utilities Expense and a credit to Cash as though it were for $372.

d.   The April 30 cash receipts, $3,129, were placed in the bank's night depository after banking hours on that date and were unrecorded by the bank at the time the April bank statement was prepared.

Give the journal entries that Cisco Company should make as a result of having prepared the bank reconciliation in the previous exercise.

**Exercise 7–7**
Adjusting entries resulting from bank reconciliation
**(LO 5)**

Complete the following bank reconciliation by filling in the missing amounts:

**Exercise 7–8**
Completion of bank reconciliation
**(LO 5)**

### SAZAR COMPANY
### Bank Reconciliation
### September 30, 1996

| | | | |
|---|---|---|---|
| Bank statement balance ...... | $19,260 | Book balance of cash ...... | $  ? |
| Add: | | Add: | |
| Deposit of September 30 .... | $ 8,575 | Collection of note ....... | $15,000 |
| Bank error ............. | ? | Interest earned ......... | 450 |
| Total ................ | $  ? | Total ............... | $  ? |
| Total ................... | $27,915 | Total ................ | $23,640 |
| Deduct: | | Deduct: | |
| Outstanding cheques ....... | ? | NSF cheque ........... | $   550 |
| | | Recording error ........ | ? |
| | | Service charge ......... | 20 |
| | | Total ............... | $  ? |
| Reconciled balance ......... | $23,010 | Reconciled balance ........ | $  ? |

Tiny's Toys had the following transactions during the month of September. Prepare entries to record the transactions assuming Tiny's Toys records invoices (a) at gross amounts and (b) at net amounts.

**Exercise 7–9**
Recording invoices at gross or net amounts
**(LO 6)**

Sept.   3   Received merchandise purchased at a $3,150 invoice price, invoice dated August 31, terms 2/10, n/30.

8   Received a $650 credit memorandum (invoice price) for merchandise received on September 3 and returned for credit.

15   Received merchandise purchased at a $7,000 invoice price, invoice dated September 13, terms 2/10, n/30.

22   Paid for the merchandise received on September 15, less the discount.

29   Paid for the merchandise received on September 3. Payment was delayed because the invoice was mistakenly filed for payment today. This error caused the discount to be lost. The filing error occurred after the credit memorandum received on September 8 was attached to the invoice dated August 31.

**Exercise 7–10**
Liquidity of accounts
receivable
**(LO 6)**

Electric Services Company reported net sales for 1995 and 1996 of $345,000 and $520,000. The end-of-year balances of accounts receivable were December 31, 1995, $30,000; and December 31, 1996, $76,000. Calculate the days' sales uncollected at the end of each year and describe any changes in the apparent liquidity of the company's receivables.

# PROBLEMS

**Problem 7–1**
Establishing, reimbursing,
and increasing petty cash
fund
**(LO 4)**

Serrapede's Trading Company completed the following petty cash transactions during July of the current year:

July  1  Drew a $250 cheque, cashed it, and gave the proceeds and the petty cashbox to Tom Albertson, the petty cashier.

3  Purchased stationery, $37.00.

11  Paid $12.50 postage to express mail a contract to a customer.

14  Paid $11.25 COD charges on merchandise purchased for resale.

17  Paid $29.00 for stamps.

19  Purchased paper for the copy machine, $16.25.

22  Reimbursed Sarah Oliver, the manager of the business, $24.00 for business car usage.

24  Paid $37.50 COD charges on merchandise purchased for resale.

26  Paid City Delivery $12.00 to deliver merchandise sold to a customer.

31  Albertson sorted the petty cash receipts by accounts affected and exchanged them for a cheque to reimburse the fund for expenditures. However, there was only $65.35 in cash in the fund, and he could not account for the shortage. In addition, the size of the petty cash fund was increased to $300.

**Required**

*Preparation component:*

1.  Prepare a journal entry to record establishing the petty cash fund.

2.  Prepare a summary of petty cash payments that has these categories: Office supplies, Postage expense, Transportation-in, Auto expense, and Delivery expense. Sort the payments into the appropriate categories and total the expenses in each category.

3.  Prepare the journal entry to record the reimbursement and the increase of the fund.

*Analysis component:*

4.  Assume that the July 31 transaction reimbursed but did not increase the size of the fund. Also assume that when the payments from petty cash were recorded, the company's bookkeeper made an entry in the following general form:

| July | 31 | xxxxxxxxxxx (Expense) ...................... | xxx | |
| | | xxxxxxxxxxx (Expense) ...................... | xxx | |
| | | xxxxxxxxxxx (Asset) ....................... | xxx | |
| | |     Petty Cash ............................. | | xxx |

Explain why this entry is not correct. Also explain the effects of the error on the General Ledger and on the balance sheet.

The Thayer Company has only a General Journal in its accounting system and uses it to record all transactions. However, the company recently set up a petty cash fund to facilitate payments of small items. The following petty cash transactions were noted by the petty cashier as occurring during October (the last month of the company's fiscal year):

**Problem 7–2**
Petty cash fund;
reimbursement and
analysis of errors
**(LO 4)**

Oct.  2  Received a company cheque for $275 to establish the petty cash fund.

16  Received a company cheque to replenish the fund for the following expenditures made since October 2 and to increase the fund to $375.

   a. Payment of $63.50 to *Travis Times* for an advertisement in the newspaper.

   b. Purchased postage stamps for $58.

   c. Purchased office supplies for $70.75.

   d. Payment of $75 for janitorial service.

   e. Discovered that $12.35 remained in the petty cashbox.

31  The petty cashier noted that $182.20 remained in the fund. Having decided that the October 16 increase in the fund was too large, received a company cheque to replenish the fund for the following expenditures made since October 16 but causing the fund to be reduced to $325.

   f. Reimbursement to office manager for business travel, $36.

   g. Purchased office supplies for $57.80.

   h. Paid $52 to Austin Trucking Co. to deliver merchandise sold to a customer.

   i. Payment of $47 COD delivery charges on merchandise purchased for resale.

**Required**

1.  Prepare journal entries to record the establishment of the fund on October 2 and its replenishments on October 16 and on October 31.

2.  Explain how the company's financial statements would be affected if the petty cash fund is not replenished and no entry is made on October 31. (Hint: The amount of office supplies that appears on a balance sheet is determined by a physical count of the supplies on hand.)

The following information was available to reconcile Kramer Company's book cash balance with its bank statement balance as of March 31, 1996:

**Problem 7–3**
Preparation of bank
reconciliation and
recording adjustments
**(LO 5)**

a.  The March 31 cash balance according to the accounting records was $24,789, and the bank statement balance for that date was $34,686.

b.  Cheque No. 573 for $834 and Cheque No. 582 for $300, both written and entered in the accounting records in March, were not among the canceled cheques returned. Two cheques, No. 531 for $1,761 and No. 542 for $285, were outstanding on February 28 when the bank and book statement balances were last reconciled. Cheque No. 531 was returned with the March canceled cheques but Cheque No. 542 was not.

c.  When the March cheques were compared with entries in the accounting records, it was found that Cheque No. 567 had been correctly drawn for $1,925 to pay for office supplies but was erroneously entered in the accounting records as though it were drawn for $1,952.

d.  Two debit memoranda were included with the returned cheques and were un-recorded at the time of the reconciliation. One of the debit memoranda was for $570 and dealt with an NSF cheque for $555 that had been received from a customer, Barbara White, in payment of her account. It also assessed a $15 fee for processing. The second debit memorandum covered cheque printing and was for $67. These transactions were not recorded by Kramer before receiving the statement.

e.  A credit memorandum indicated that the bank had collected a $15,000 note receivable for the company, deducted a $15 collection fee, and credited the balance to the company's account. This transaction was not recorded by Kramer before receiving the statement.

f.  The March 31 cash receipts, $5,897, had been placed in the bank's night depository after banking hours on that date and did not appear on the bank statement.

**Required**

*Preparation component:*

1.  Prepare a bank reconciliation for the company as of March 31.

2.  Prepare the general journal entries necessary to bring the company's book balance of cash into conformity with the reconciled balance.

*Analysis component:*

3.  Explain the nature of the messages conveyed by a bank to one of its depositors when the bank sends a debit memo and a credit memo to the depositor.

**Problem 7–4**
Preparation of bank reconciliation
**(LO 5)**

Milton Vacon, the controller of the Dartmouth Corporation provided the following information.

**Reconciliation of Dartmouth Corporation's bank account as of May 31:**

| | | | | | |
|---|---:|---|---|---:|
| Bank statement balance | $12,304.75 | | Book balance | $12,568.32 |
| Add: | | | | |
| Deposit of Apr. 30 | 2,245.62 | | | |
| Total | 14,550.37 | | | |
| Deduct: | | | Deduct: | |
| Outstanding cheques: | | | NSF cheque plus service charge | 356.75 |
| No. 876 | 1,185.30 | | Bank service charges | 18.65 |
| No. 882 | 1,172.15 | | | |
| Total | $ 2,357.45 | | Total | 375.40 |
| Reconciled balance | $12,192.92 | | Reconciled balance | $12,192.92 |

**Summary of Dartmouth Corporation's bank statement for the month of June:**

| Date | Symbol | Withdrawl | Deposit | Balance |
|---|---|---|---|---|
| May 31 | Balance forward | | | 12,304.75 |
| June 2 | NBD | | 2,245.62 | 14,550.37 |
| June 3 | 876 | 1,185.30 | | 13,365.07 |
| June 5 | 883 | 2,250.00 | | 11,115.07 |
| June 10 | NBD | | 2,385.70 | 13,500.77 |
| June 12 | 884 | 848.90 | | 12,651.87 |
| June 14 | 885 | 1,152.30 | | 11,499.57 |
| June 18 | 887 | 1,113.78 | | 10.385.79 |
| June 20 | NBD | | 2,462.95 | 12,848.74 |
| June 22 | 889 | 1,238.95 | | 11,609.79 |
| June 25 | 886 | 1,138.40 | | 10,471.39 |
| June 26 | 882 | 1,172.15 | | 9,299.24 |
| June 29 | 891 | 874.20 | | 8,425.04 |
| June 30 | SC | 45.70 | | 8,379.34 |

**Summary of June Cheque Register:**

| Date | No. | Amount |
|---|---|---|
| June | | |
| 2 | 883 | $ 2,250.00 |
| 5 | 884 | 848.90 |
| 6 | 885 | 1,152.30 |
| 8 | 886 | 1,138.40 |
| 10 | 887 | 2,113.78 |
| 12 | 888 | 1,186.30 |
| 15 | 889 | 1,238.95 |
| 16 | 890 | 1,146.40 |
| 20 | 891 | 974.20 |
| 26 | 892 | 1,106.70 |
| 29 | 893 | 1,164.80 |
| Total | | $14,320.73 |

**Summary of June Cash Receipts:**

| Date | Amount |
|---|---|
| June | |
| 9 | $ 2,385.70 |
| 18 | 2,462.95 |
| 29 | 2,220.85 |
| Total | $ 7,069.50 |

**Book cash balance, June 30:**

| | |
|---|---|
| Book balance, May 31 | $12,192.92 |
| Add receipts | 7,069.50 |
| Total | 19,262.42 |
| Deduct cheques | 14,320.73 |
| Book balance, June 30 | $ 4,941.69 |

**Required**

Prepare a bank reconciliation for Dartmouth Corporation for the month of June.

Mountainview Co. reconciled its bank and book statement balances of cash on October 31 and showed two cheques outstanding at that time, No. 1388 for $1,597 and No. 1393 for $745. The following information was available for the November 30, 1996, reconciliation:

*From the November 30 bank statement:*

| | |
|---|---|
| Balance of previous statement on October 31, 1996 . . . . . . . . . . . . . . . . . . . . . . | 27,418.00 |
| 5 Deposits and other credits totaling . . . . . . . . . . . . . . . . . . . . . . . . . . . . . | 17,176.00 |
| 9 Cheques and other debits totaling . . . . . . . . . . . . . . . . . . . . . . . . . . . . . | 16,342.00 |
| Current balance as of November 30, 1996 . . . . . . . . . . . . . . . . . . . . . . . . . . | 28,252.00 |

**Problem 7–5**
Preparation of bank reconciliation and recording adjustments
**(LO 5)**

===============Chequing Account Transactions===============

| Date | Amount | Transaction Description |
|------|--------|-------------------------|
| Nov. 5 | 1,698.00 + | Deposit |
| 12 | 3,426.00 + | Deposit |
| 17 | 905.00 − | NSF cheque |
| 21 | 6,297.00 + | Deposit |
| 25 | 3,618.00 + | Deposit |
| 30 | 17.00 + | Interest |
| 30 | 2,120.00 + | Credit memorandum |

| Date | Cheque No. | Amount | Date | Cheque No. | Amount |
|------|-----------|--------|------|-----------|--------|
| Nov. 3 | 1388 | 1,597.00 | Nov. 22 | 1404 | 3,185.00 |
| 7 | 1401* | 4,363.00 | 20 | 1405 | 1,442.00 |
| 4 | 1402 | 1,126.00 | 28 | 1407* | 329.00 |
| 22 | 1403 | 614.00 | 29 | 1409* | 2,781.00 |

*Indicates a skip in cheque sequence

*From Mountainview Co.'s accounting records:*

**Cash**                                        **Account No.** 101

| Date | | Explanation | PR | Debit | Credit | Balance |
|------|--|-------------|----|----|--------|---------|
| Oct. | 31 | Balance | | | | 25,076.00 |
| Nov. | 30 | Total receipts | R12 | 17,474.00 | | 42,550.00 |
| | 30 | Total disbursements | D23 | | 15,537.00 | 27,013.00 |

**Cash Receipts Deposited**

| Date | | Cash Debit |
|------|--|------------|
| Nov. 5 | | 1,698.00 |
| 12 | | 3,426.00 |
| 21 | | 6,297.00 |
| 25 | | 3,618.00 |
| 30 | | 2,435.00 |
| | | 17,474.00 |

**Cash Disbursements**

| Cheque No. | | Cash Credit |
|-----------|--|-------------|
| 1401 | | 4,363.00 |
| 1402 | | 1,126.00 |
| 1403 | | 614.00 |
| 1404 | | 3,135.00 |
| 1405 | | 1,442.00 |
| 1406 | | 1,322.00 |
| 1407 | | 329.00 |
| 1408 | | 425.00 |
| 1409 | | 2,781.00 |
| | | 15,537.00 |

Cheque No. 1404 was correctly drawn for $3,185 to pay for computer equipment; however, the bookkeeper misread the amount and entered it in the accounting records with a debit to Computer Equipment and a credit to Cash as though it were for $3,135.

The NSF cheque was originally received from a customer, Jerry Skyles, in payment of his account. Its return was not recorded when the bank first notified the company. The credit memorandum resulted from the collection of a $2,150 note for Mountainview by the bank. The bank had deducted a $30 collection fee. The collection has not been recorded.

**Required**

1. Prepare a November 30 bank reconciliation for the company.

2. Prepare the general journal entries needed to adjust the book balance of cash to the reconciled balance.

The July 31, 1996, credit balance in the Sales account of Cardina Company showed it had sold merchandise for $147,000 during the month. The concern began July with a $280,700 merchandise inventory and ended the month with a $237,000 inventory. It had incurred $34,300 of operating expenses during the month, and it had also recorded the following transactions:

Problem 7–6
Recording invoices at gross or net amounts
(LO 6)

2 Received merchandise purchased at a $6,300 invoice price, invoice dated June 27, terms 2/10, n/30.

5 Received a $1,300 credit memorandum (invoice price) for merchandise received on July 2 and returned for credit.

10 Received merchandise purchased at a $14,000 invoice price, invoice dated July 8, terms 2/10, n/30.

14 Received merchandise purchased at a $7,800 invoice price, invoice dated July 12, terms 2/10, n/30.

17 Paid for the merchandise received on July 10, less the discount.

21 Paid for the merchandise received on July 14, less the discount.

27 Paid for the merchandise received on July 2. Payment was delayed because the invoice was mistakenly filed for payment today. This error caused the discount to be lost. The filing error occurred after the credit memorandum received on July 5 was attached to the invoice dated June 27.

**Required**

1. Assume that Cardina Company records invoices at gross amounts.
   a. Prepare General Journal entries to record the transactions.
   b. Prepare a July income statement.
2. Assume that Cardina Company records invoices at net amounts.
   a. Prepare General Journal entries to record the transactions.
   b. Prepare a July income statement.

In Problem 7–1, several of the transactions involved payments of cash from a petty cash fund. Nevertheless, the entry to record these payments does not include a credit to Petty Cash. Explain why this is true. Under what circumstances would the entry to record payments from the petty cash fund include a credit to Petty Cash?

Problem 7–7
Analytical essay
(LO 4)

The bank statement in Problem 7–5 discloses three places where the canceled cheques returned with the bank statement are not numbered sequentially. In other words, some of the prenumbered cheques in the sequence are missing. There are several possible situations that would explain why the canceled cheques returned with a bank statement might not be numbered sequentially. Describe three situations, each of which is a possible explanation of why the canceled cheques returned with a bank statement are not numbered sequentially.

Problem 7–8
Analytical essay
(LO 5)

A concern completed the following petty cash transactions during October of the current year:

Problem 7–9
Establishing and reimbursing petty cash fund
(LO 4)

Oct. 2 Drew a $125 cheque, cashed it, and turned the proceeds and the petty cashbox over to Norm Bowers, an office clerk who was to act as petty cashier.

5 Paid $9.15 parcel post charges on merchandise sold to a customer and delivered by mail.

8 Purchased office supplies with petty cash, $14.50.

9 Paid $28.35 from petty cash for repairs to an office copier.

Oct. 12  Paid $10 COD delivery charges on merchandise purchased for resale.

15  Paid Mercury Delivery Service $11.25 to deliver merchandise sold to a customer.

21  Gave Dennis Moore, the owner of the business, $20 from petty cash for personal use.

23  Paid $12.55 COD delivery charges on merchandise purchased for resale.

27  Dennis Moore, owner of the business, signed a petty cash receipt and took $12 from petty cash for lunch money.

30  Norm Bowers exchanged his paid petty cash receipts for a cheque reimbursing the fund for expenditures and a shortage of cash in the fund that he could not account for. He reported a cash balance of $2.20 in the fund.

### Required

1.  Prepare a general journal entry to record the cheque establishing the petty cash fund.

2.  Prepare a summary of petty cash payments that has these categories: Office supplies, Transportation-in, Delivery expense, Withdrawals, and Miscellaneous expenses. Sort the payments into the appropriate categories, total the expenses in each category, and prepare the general journal entry to reimburse the fund.

**Problem 7–10**
Establishing,
reimbursing,
and increasing
petty cash fund
**(LO 4)**

A business completed these petty cash transactions:

May  4  Drew a $75 cheque to establish a petty cash fund, cashed it, and turned the proceeds and the petty cashbox over to Gayle Bates, an office worker who was appointed petty cashier.

6  Paid $12.55 parcel post charges on merchandise sold to a customer and delivered by mail.

8  Paid $14 to have the office windows washed.

11  Purchased office supplies with petty cash, $25.25.

12  Susan Dixon, owner of the business, signed a petty cash receipt and took $8 from petty cash for coffee money.

14  Paid $13.20 COD delivery charges on merchandise purchased for resale.

15  Gayle Bates noted that only $2 remained in the petty cashbox. Thus, she sorted the petty cash receipts in terms of the accounts affected and exchanged the receipts for a cheque to reimburse the fund. However, since the fund had been exhausted so quickly, the cheque was made sufficiently large to increase the size of the fund to $150.

18  Paid $35 from petty cash for minor repairs to an office machine.

20  Paid $12.75 COD delivery charges on merchandise purchased for resale.

22  Paid A. M. Delivery Service $15.20 to deliver merchandise sold to a customer.

26  Purchased office supplies with petty cash, $18.

27  Susan Dixon, owner of the business, signed a petty cash receipt and took $15 from petty cash for lunch money.

June  1  Paid $16.50 COD delivery charges on merchandise purchased for resale.

5  Purchased paper clips and pencils with petty cash, $10.80.

10  Paid $18.75 COD delivery charges on merchandise purchased for resale.

12  Gayle Bates sorted the petty cash receipts and exchanged them for a cheque to replenish the fund for expenditures and, since there was only $1.50 in cash in the fund, for the unexplained shortage.

**Required**

1. Prepare a general journal entry to record the cheque establishing the petty cash fund.

2. Prepare a summary of petty cash payments prior to May 15 that has these categories: Delivery expense, Office supplies, Miscellaneous expenses, Withdrawals, and Transportation-in. Sort the payments into the appropriate categories and total each category. Prepare a similar summary of petty cash payments after May 15.

3. Prepare entries to reimburse the fund and increase its size on May 15 and to reimburse the fund on June 12.

The accounting system used by the Franklin Company requires that all entries be journalized in a General Journal. To facilitate payments of small items, Franklin Company recently established a petty cash fund. The following transactions involving the petty cash fund occurred during August (the last month of the company's fiscal year):

**Problem 7–11**
Petty cash fund;
reimbursement and
analysis of errors
**(LO 4)**

Aug. 3 A company cheque for $200 was drawn and made payable to the petty cashier to establish the petty cash fund.

　14 A company cheque was drawn to replenish the fund for the following expenditures made since August 1 and to increase the fund to $300:

　　*a.* Purchased postage stamps for $44.

　　*b.* Payment of $42.30 to Meeks Trucking for delivery of merchandise to customers.

　　*c.* Gave Beth Rogers, owner of the business, $50 for personal use.

　　*d.* Paid $60.50 to Appliance Company for repairs of office equipment.

　　*e.* Discovered that only $1.20 remained in the petty cashbox.

　31 The petty cashier noted that $2.60 remained in the fund. Having decided that the August 14 increase in the fund was not large enough, a company cheque was drawn to replenish the fund for the following expenditures made since August 14 and to increase it to $350:

　　*a.* Payment of $97.25 for office supplies to support the company's computer.

　　*b.* Payment of $52.15 for items classified as miscellaneous general expense.

　　*c.* Payment of $63 for janitorial service.

　　*d.* Payment of $85 to Southern Advertising Company for a space advertisement in a weekly newsletter.

**Required**

1. Prepare general journal entries to record the establishment of the fund on August 3 and its replenishments on August 14 and on August 31.

2. If Franklin Company had failed to replenish the petty cash fund on August 31, what would have been the effect on net income for the fiscal year ended August 31 and on total assets on August 31? Explain your answer. (Hint: The amount of Office Supplies to appear on a balance sheet is determined by a physical count of the supplies on hand.)

The following information was available to reconcile Golf Company's book balance of cash with its bank statement balance as of February 28:

**Problem 7–12**
Preparation of bank
reconciliation and
recording adjustments
**(LO 5)**

*a.* After all posting was completed on February 28, the company's Cash account had a $7,180 debit balance, but its bank statement showed a $9,415 balance.

b.  Cheques No. 217 for $353 and No. 222 for $709 were outstanding on the January 31 bank reconciliation. Cheque No. 222 was returned with the February canceled cheques, but Cheque No. 217 was not.

c.  In comparing the canceled cheques returned with the bank statement with the entries in the accounting records, it was found that Cheque No. 297 for the purchase of office equipment was correctly drawn for $724 but was entered in the accounting records as though it were for $742. It was also found that Cheque No. 331 for $482 and Cheque No. 333 for $240, both drawn in February, were not among the canceled cheques returned with the statement.

d.  A credit memorandum enclosed with the bank statement indicated that the bank had collected a $3,600 noninterest-bearing note for the concern, deducted a $24 collection fee, and had credited the remainder to the concern's account.

e.  A debit memorandum for $464 listed a $452 NSF cheque plus a $12 NSF charge. The cheque had been received from a customer, Jan Bellors, and was among the canceled cheques returned.

f.  Also among the canceled cheques was an $18 debit memorandum for bank services. None of the memoranda had been recorded.

g.  The February 28 cash receipts, $1,952, were placed in the bank's night depository after banking hours on that date, and their amount did not appear on the bank statement.

**Required**

1.  Prepare a bank reconciliation for the company.
2.  Prepare entries in general journal form to bring the company's book balance of cash into conformity with the reconciled balance.

**Problem 7–13**
Preparation of bank reconciliation
**(LO 5)**

Cindy Estelle, the controller of the Burnaby Corporation provided the following information.

**Reconciliation of Burnaby Corporation's bank account as of October 31:**

| | | | | | |
|---|---|---|---|---|---|
| Bank statement balance ..... | $ 9,843.80 | | Book balance ............ | | $10,054.69 |
| Add: | | | | | |
| Deposit of Oct. 30 ....... | 1,796.50 | | | | |
| Total ............... | 11,640.30 | | | | |
| Deduct: | | | Deduct: | | |
| Outstanding cheques: | | | NSF cheque plus service | | |
| No. 537 ............ | 948.24 | | charge ............. | | 285.40 |
| No. 542 ............ | 937.72 | | Bank service charges ..... | | 14.95 |
| Total ............... | $ 1,885.96 | | Total ................ | | 300.35 |
| Reconciled balance ....... | $ 9,754.34 | | Reconciled balance ....... | | $ 9,754.34 |

**Summary of Burnaby Corporation's bank statement for the month of November:**

| Date | Symbol | Withdrawl | Deposit | Balance |
|---|---|---|---|---|
| Oct 31 | Balance forward | | | 9,843.80 |
| Nov 2 | NBD | | 1,796.50 | 11,640.30 |
| Nov 3 | 536 | 948.24 | | 10,692.06 |
| Nov 5 | 543 | 1,800.00 | | 8,892.06 |
| Nov 10 | NBD | | 1,908.56 | 10,800.62 |
| Nov 12 | 544 | 679.12 | | 10,121.50 |
| Nov 14 | 545 | 921.84 | | 9,199.66 |
| Nov 18 | 547 | 891.02 | | 8,308.64 |
| Nov 20 | NBD | | 1,970.36 | 10,279.00 |
| Nov 22 | 549 | 991.16 | | 9,287.84 |
| Nov 25 | 546 | 910.72 | | 8,377.12 |
| Nov 26 | 542 | 937.72 | | 7,439.40 |
| Nov 29 | 551 | 699.36 | | 6,740.04 |
| Nov 30 | SC | 36.50 | | 6,703.54 |

**Summary of June Cheque Register:**

| Date | No. | Amount |
|---|---|---|
| Nov | | |
| 2 | 543 | $ 1,800.00 |
| 5 | 544 | 679.12 |
| 6 | 545 | 921.84 |
| 8 | 546 | 910.72 |
| 10 | 547 | 891.02 |
| 12 | 548 | 949.04 |
| 15 | 549 | 991.16 |
| 16 | 550 | 917.12 |
| 20 | 551 | 699.36 |
| 26 | 552 | 885.36 |
| 29 | 553 | 931.84 |
| Total | | $10,576.58 |

**Summary of June Cash Receipts:**

| Date | Amount |
|---|---|
| Nov | |
| 9 | $ 1,908.56 |
| 18 | 1,970.36 |
| 29 | 1,776.58 |
| Total | 5,655.50 |

Book cash balance, June 30:

| | |
|---|---|
| Book balance, May 31 | $ 9,754.34 |
| Add receipts | 5,655.50 |
| Total | 15,409.84 |
| Deduct cheques | 10,576.58 |
| Book balance, June 30 | $ 4,833.26 |

**Required**

Prepare a bank reconciliation for Burnaby Corporation for the month of November.

---

# PROVOCATIVE PROBLEMS

The Commerce Company has enjoyed rapid growth since it was created several years ago. Last year, for example, its sales exceeded $4 million. However, its purchasing procedures have not kept pace with its growth. A plant supervisor or department head who needs raw materials, plant assets, or supplies telephones a request to the purchasing department manager. The purchasing department manager then prepares a purchase order in duplicate, sends one copy to the company selling the goods, and keeps the other copy in the files. When the seller's invoice is received, it is sent directly to the purchasing department. When the goods

**Provocative Problem
7–1
Analytical Essay
(LO 2, 3)**

arrive, receiving department personnel count and inspect the items and prepare only one copy of a receiving report, which is then sent to the purchasing department. The purchasing department manager attaches the receiving report and the file copy of the purchase order to the invoice. If all is in order, the invoice is stamped *approved for payment* and signed by the purchasing department manager. The invoice and its supporting documents then are sent to the accounting department to be recorded and filed until due. On its due date, the invoice and its supporting documents are sent to the office of the company treasurer, and a cheque is prepared and mailed. The number of the cheque is entered on the invoice and the invoice is sent to the accounting department for an entry to record its payment.

Do the procedures of Commerce make it fairly easy for someone in the company to initiate the payment of fictitious invoices by the company? If so, who is most likely to commit the fraud and what would that person have to do to receive payment of a fictitious invoice? What changes should be made in the company's purchasing procedures, and why should each change be made?

**Provocative Problem 7–2**
Business communications case
**(LO 5)**

On March 26, Summerfield Office Supply received Miles Brokaw's cheque number 629, dated March 24, in the amount of $1,420. The cheque was to pay for merchandise Brokaw had purchased on February 25. The merchandise was shipped from Summerfield's office at 1715 Westgate Boulevard, Toronto, Ontario M5H 1A2 to Brokaw's home at 823 Congress, Mississauga, Ontario L5H 1K4. On March 27, Summerfield's cashier deposited the cheque in the company's bank account. The bank returned the cheque to Summerfield with the March 31 bank statement. Also included was a debit memorandum indicating that Brokaw's cheque was returned for nonsufficient funds and the bank was charging Summerfield a $25 NSF processing fee. Immediately after reconciling the bank statement on April 2, Marla Decker, Summerfield's accountant, asks you to write a letter for her signature using the company's letterhead stationery. Your letter to Brokaw should explain the amount owed and request prompt payment.

**Provocative Problem 7–3**
Financial statement analysis case
**(LO 1, 6)**

For this problem, turn to the financial statements of Geac Computer Corporation Limited, in Appendix I. Use the information presented in the financial statements to answer these questions:

1. For both 1994 and 1993, determine the total amount of cash and short-term investments that Geac held at the end of the year. Determine the percentage that this amount represents of total current assets, total current liabilities, total shareholders' equity, and total assets.

2. For 1994, use the information in the statement of changes in financial position to determine the percentage change between the beginning of the year and end of the year holding of cash and cash equivalents.

3. What was the number of days' sales uncollected at the end of the 1994 fiscal year and at the end of the 1993 fiscal year?

**Provocative Problem 7–4**
Ethical issue essay

Review the As a Matter of Ethics case on page 365. Discuss the nature of the problem faced by Nancy Tucker and evaluate the alternative courses of action she should consider.

# ANALYTICAL AND REVIEW PROBLEMS

The bank statement for October arrived in Friday's mail. You were especially anxious to receive the statement as one of your assignments was to prepare a bank reconciliation for the Saturday meeting. You got around to preparing the reconciliation rather late in the afternoon and found all the necessary data with the exception of the bank balance. The bottom portion of the bank statement was smudged, and several figures, including the balance, were obliterated. A telephone call to the bank was answered by a recording with the information that the bank was closed until 10 A.M. Monday. Since the reconcilation had to be prepared, you decided to plug in the bank balance.

In preparation, you assembled the necessary material as follows:

a. Cash balance per books was $6,800.

b. From the canceled cheques returned by the bank you determined that six cheques remained outstanding. The total of these cheques was $2,700.

c. In checking the canceled cheques you noted that Cheque No. 274 was properly made for $418 but was recorded in the cash disbursement journal as $481. The cheque was in payment of an account.

d. Included with the bank statement were two memoranda; the credit memorandum was for collection of a note for $1,200 and $90 of interest thereon and the debit memorandum was for $12 of bank charges.

e. While you were sorting the canceled cheques, one of the cheques caught your attention. You were astounded by the similarity of name with that of your company and the similarity of the cheques. The cheque was for $620 and was obviously in error charged to your company's account.

f. From the deposit book you determined that a $2,500 deposit was made after hours on October 31.

## Required

1. Prepare a bank reconciliation statement as of October 31 (plug in the indicated bank balance).

2. Prepare the necessary journal entries.

**A & R Problem 7–2**   Your assistant prepared the following bank reconciliation statement. Obviously the statement is unacceptable and the task of preparing a proper reconciliation falls upon you.

### BRANDON COMPANY
### Bank Reconciliation
### May 31, 1996

| | | |
|---|---:|---:|
| Balance per books May 31 ................................. | | $ 8,000 |
| Add: | | |
|    Note collected ....................................... | $1,000 | |
|    Interest on note ....................................... | 110 | |
|    Deposit in transit .................................... | 2,455 | 3,565 |
| | | 11,565 |
| Deduct: | | |
|    Bank charges ........................................ | 10 | |
|    NSF cheque ......................................... | 400 | |
|    Outstanding cheques ................................. | 1,800 | |
|    Error in Cheque No. 78 issued for $872 and recorded | | |
|     in the books as $827 ............................... | 45 | 2,255 |
| Indicated bank balance ................................. | | 9,310 |
| Balance per bank statement .............................. | | 8,000 |
| Discrepancy ........................................... | | $ 1,310 |

### Required

1. Prepare a proper bank reconciliation showing the true cash balance.
2. Prepare the necessary journal entries.

**A & R Problem 7–3**   Wanda White acquired a sports equipment distribution business with a staff of six salespersons and two clerks. Because of the trust that Wanda had in her employees—after all, they were all her friends and just like members of the family—she believed that an honour system in regard to the operation of the petty cash fund was adequate. Consequently, Wanda placed $300 in a coffee jar, which, for convenience, was kept in a cupboard in the common room. All employees had access to the petty cash fund and withdrew amounts as required. No vouchers were required for withdrawals. As required, additional funds were placed in the coffee jar and the amount of the replenishment was charged to "miscellaneous selling expense."

### Required

1. From the internal control point of view, discuss the weaknesses of the petty cash fund operation and suggest steps necessary for improvement.
2. Does the petty cash fund operation as described above violate any of the generally accepted accounting principles? If yes, which and how is the principle(s) violated?

# CONCEPT TESTER

Test your understanding of the concepts introduced in this chapter by completing the following crossword puzzle.

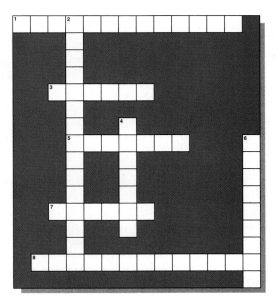

**Across Clues**

1. A business paper that tells a vendor to ship ordered merchandise at the stated terms (2 words).
3. The seller of goods or services.
5. A statement showing the items sold, price, and terms given by a vendor to a customer.
7. The buyer or purchaser of goods or services.
8. An expense resulting from failing to take a cash discount on purchases (2 words).

**Down Clues**

2. Investments convertible to a known amount of cash, without undue risk (2 words).
4. Business paper used to accumulate information needed to control disbursements of cash.
6. Asset characteristic; refers to how quickly the asset can be used to pay for other assets.

# ANSWERS TO PROGRESS CHECKS

7–1   A company needs to own liquid assets to be able to acquire other assets, buy services, and pay its obligations.

7–2   A company owns cash equivalents because they earn more income than cash does.

7–3   d

7–4   c

7–5   Computers reduce processing errors, allow more extensive testing of records, tend to limit the amount of hard evidence of processing steps that is available, and highlight the importance of maintaining a separation of duties.

7–6   a

7–7   Not necessarily. A voucher system should be used when the manager can no longer control the purchasing procedures through personal supervision and direct participation in the activities of the business.

7–8   If all cash payments were made by cheque, numerous cheques for small amounts would be written. Because this practice would be expensive and often would take too long, a petty cash fund is established to avoid writing cheques for small amounts.

7–9   If the petty cash fund is not reimbursed at the end of an accounting period, the transactions for which petty cash expenditures were made are unrecorded in the accounts and the asset petty cash

is overstated. However, these amounts are seldom large enough to affect the financial statements.

7–10   When the petty cash fund is reimbursed, the petty cash transactions are recorded in the accounts. The reimbursement also allows the fund to continue being used for its intended purpose.

7–11   A bank statement is a report prepared by the bank that describes the activity in a depositor's account.

7–12   To reconcile a bank balance means to explain the difference between the cash balance in the depositor's accounting records and the balance on the bank statement.

7–13   The purpose of the bank reconciliation is to determine if any errors have been made by the bank or by the depositor and to determine if the bank has completed any transactions affecting the depositor's account that the depositor has not recorded.

7–14   Outstanding cheques—subtracted
Unrecorded deposits—added

7–15   Bank services charges—subtracted
Debit memos—subtracted
NSF cheques—subtracted
Interest earned—added
Credit memos—added

7–16   a

7–17   The calculation is based on net sales because the amount of credit sales normally is not known by statement readers.

# CHAPTER 8

# Temporary Investments and Receivables

*Companies rarely operate in today's economy without extending credit to customers. By being careful in granting credit, a business can increase sales without incurring high costs. Accounting information helps managers assess the risk and the success of their credit decisions.*

aren White and Mark Smith have been asked to look at Imperial Oil Limited's (Esso) financial statements and, in particular, their amounts of temporary investments and receivables. Information from the company's balance sheet follows:

**IMPERIAL OIL LIMITED**
**(in millions)**
**December 31, 1994**

|  | Current Assets |
|---|---|
| Marketable securities at cost . . . . . . . . | $ 859 |
| Accounts Receivable . . . . . . . . . . . . . . | 1,045 |
| Total Current Assets . . . . . . . . . . . . . . | $2,797 |

Esso's marketable securities and accounts receivable represent 68% of the firm's total current assets. Sound financial management of these assets is vital to ensure future liquidity and growth potential. Accounting for these highly liquid assets provides important information to help managers assess the risk and success of their decisions regarding these assets. Economic conditions causing many businesses and consumers to take longer to pay their bills and an increasing amount of defaults due to bankruptcies have made receivables management a top priority today.

# LEARNING OBJECTIVES

**After studying Chapter 8, you should be able to:**

1. **Prepare journal entries to account for temporary investments and explain how lower of cost or market is reported on such investments.**

2. **Prepare entries to account for credit card and debit card sales.**

3. **Prepare entries to account for transactions with credit customers, including accounting for bad debts under the allowance method and the direct write-off method.**

4. **Calculate the interest on promissory notes and prepare entries to record the receipt of promissory notes and their payment or dishonour.**

5. **Explain how receivables can be converted into cash before they are due and calculate accounts receivable turnover.**

6. **Define or explain the words and phrases listed in the chapter glossary.**

The focus of the prior chapter was on accounting for cash, the most liquid of all assets. This chapter continues the discussion of liquid assets by focusing on temporary, or short-term, investments, accounts receivable, and short-term notes receivable. You will learn about current business trends relating to receivables and about accounting regulations for temporary investments. You will then be better able to understand and use the financial statement information related to these current assets.

Because companies use cash to acquire assets and to pay expenses and obligations, good managers plan to maintain a cash balance large enough to meet expected payments plus some surplus for unexpected needs. Also, idle cash balances may exist during some months of each year because of seasonal fluctuations in sales volume. Rather than leave these idle cash balances in chequing accounts that pay little or no interest, most companies invest them in securities that earn higher returns.

## TEMPORARY INVESTMENTS

**LO 1**

Prepare journal entries to account for temporary investments and explain how lower of cost or market is reported on such investments.

Recall from Chapter 7 that cash equivalents are investments that can be easily converted into a known amount of cash; generally, they mature within a relatively short time period. Some investments of idle cash balances do not meet the criteria of cash equivalents but, nevertheless, are classified as current assets. Although these **temporary investments,** or **short-term investments,** do not qualify as cash equivalents, they serve a similar purpose. Like cash equivalents, temporary investments can be converted into cash easily and are an available source of cash to satisfy the needs of current operations. Management usually expects to convert them into cash within one year or the current operating cycle of the business, whichever is longer.[1]

Temporary investments may be made in the form of government or corporate debt obligations (called *debt securities*) or in the form of shares (called *equity securities*). Some investments in debt securities mature within one year or the current operating cycle of the business and will be held until they mature. Other securities that do not mature in the short term can be classified as current assets only if they

---

[1]*CICA Handbook,* section 1510, "Current Assets and Current Liabilities," par. .01.

are marketable. In other words, the reporting company must be able to sell them without excessive delays.

In the notes to their financial statements, companies usually give their definition of cash equivalents and short-term investments. **Corel Corporation,** for example, includes this note:

> Short-term investments are stated at the lower of cost or market. Short-term investments of $52,114,000 and $68,629,000 at November 30, 1992 and 1993, respectively, included with cash consisted principally of government securities, commercial paper, bankers' acceptances, letter loan agreements, term deposit certificates and bearer deposit notes. The carrying amount approximates fair value because of the short maturity of those instruments.

When temporary investments are purchased, you should record them at cost. For example, assume that on January 10 Alpha Company purchased Ford Motor Company's short-term notes payable for $40,000. Alpha's entry to record the transaction is:

| | | | | |
|---|---|---|---|---|
| Jan. | 10 | Temporary Investments  . . . . . . . . . . . . . . . . . . . . . . | 40,000.00 | |
| | |     Cash  . . . . . . . . . . . . . . . . . . . . . . . . . . . . . . . . . | | 40,000.00 |
| | |     *Bought $40,000 of Ford Motor Company notes due* | | |
| | |     *May 10.* | | |

Assume that these notes mature on May 10 and that the cash proceeds are $40,000 plus $1,200 interest. When the receipt is recorded, this entry credits the interest to a revenue account:

| | | | | |
|---|---|---|---|---|
| May | 10 | Cash . . . . . . . . . . . . . . . . . . . . . . . . . . . . . . . . . . . . | 41,200.00 | |
| | |     Temporary Investments  . . . . . . . . . . . . . . . . . . . | | 40,000.00 |
| | |     Interest Earned  . . . . . . . . . . . . . . . . . . . . . . . . . | | 1,200.00 |
| | |     *Received cash proceeds from matured notes.* | | |

To determine the cost of an investment, you must include any commissions paid. For example, assume that on June 2, 1996, Bailey Company purchased 1,000 shares of Northern Telecom common stock as a temporary investment. The purchase price was 30⅛ ($30.125 per share) plus a $625 broker's commission. The entry to record the transaction is:[2]

| | | | | |
|---|---|---|---|---|
| June | 2 | Temporary Investments  . . . . . . . . . . . . . . . . . . . . . . | 30,750.00 | |
| | |     Cash  . . . . . . . . . . . . . . . . . . . . . . . . . . . . . . . . . | | 30,750.00 |
| | |     *Bought 1,000 shares of Nortel stock at 30⅛ plus $625* | | |
| | |     *broker's commission.* | | |

---

[2]Share prices are quoted on stock exchanges on the basis of dollars and ⅛ dollars per share. For example, a stock quoted at 23⅛ sold for $23.125 per share and one quoted at 36½ sold for $36.50 per share.

Notice that the commission is not recorded in a separate account.

When cash dividends are received on shares held as an investment, they are credited to a revenue account, as follows:

| Dec. | 12 | Cash ...................................... | 1,000.00 | |
| | | Dividends Earned ...................... | | 1,000.00 |
| | | *Received dividend of $1 per share on 1,000 shares of Nortel stock.* | | |

When a company sells a temporary investment, it records the difference between its cost and the cash proceeds from the sale as a gain or loss. For example, assume that on December 20, 1996, Bailey Company sells 500 shares of Nortel for 28¼ per share less a $120 commission. Bailey receives cash proceeds from the sale of $14,005, or [(500 × $28.25) − $120]. Bailey's cost of the sold shares is $15,375, or one half of the $30,750 original cost of the 1,000 shares. The following entry records the sale:

| Dec. | 20 | Cash ...................................... | 14,005.00 | |
| | | Loss on Sale of Temporary Investments ........... | 1,370.00 | |
| | | Temporary Investments ................... | | 15,375.00 |
| | | *Sold 500 Nortel shares at 28¼ less $120 broker's commission.* | | |

## Reporting Temporary Investments in the Financial Statements

Temporary investments in marketable securities should be reported on the balance sheet at the **lower of cost or market (LCM)**. To calculate the lower of cost or market, the *total* cost of all marketable securities held as temporary investments (called the *portfolio*) is compared with the *total* market value of the portfolio. Comparison on an item-by-item basis is normally not done.

For example, assume that Bailey Company did not have any temporary investments prior to its purchase of the Nortel shares on June 2, 1996. Later during 1996, Bailey Company purchased two other temporary investments in marketable securities. On December 31, 1996, the lower of cost or market is determined by comparing the total cost and total market value of the entire portfolio, as follows:

| Temporary Investments | Cost | Market | LCM |
|---|---|---|---|
| Alcan Aluminium common shares ..... | $42,600 | $43,500 | |
| Imperial Oil common shares ........ | 30,500 | 28,200 | |
| Northern Telecom common shares .... | 15,375 | 14,500 | |
| Total ........................ | $88,475 | $86,200 | $86,200 |

The difference between the $88,475 cost and the $86,200 market value amounts to a $2,275 loss of market value.

Since all of the temporary investments were purchased during 1996, this $2,275 market value decline occurred entirely during 1996. The following adjusting entry on December 31, 1996, records the loss:

| 1996 | | | | | |
|------|----|-------------------------------------------------------------|----------|----------|
| Dec. | 31 | Loss on Market Decline of Temporary Investments   . . . | 2,275.00 | |
| | | Allowance to Reduce Temporary Investments | | |
| | | to Market.  . . . . . . . . . . . . . . . . . . . . . . . | | 2,275.00 |
| | | *To record the decline in value of the investments* | | |
| | | *below their original cost.* | | |

The Loss on Market Decline of Temporary Investments account is closed to Income Summary and is reported on the income statement. The Allowance to Reduce Temporary Investments to Market account is a contra asset account. Its balance is subtracted from the total cost of the temporary investments so that on the balance sheet they are reported at the lower of cost or market. For example, the Bailey Company would report its temporary investments as follows:

Current assets:
    Cash and cash equivalents . . . . . . . . . .   $xx,xxx
    Temporary investments, at lower of
        cost or market (cost is $88,475) . . . .   86,200

In this example, notice that the $2,275 loss recorded during 1996 is equal to the December 31, 1996, balance in the allowance account. This occurs because we have assumed that no investments were owned prior to 1996. Therefore, the allowance account had a zero balance on December 31, 1995.

If an additional loss occurs in a future year, the allowance account balance after recording that loss probably will not equal the amount of that loss. To see why this is true, assume that on December 31, 1997, the total cost of Bailey Company's temporary investments portfolio is $108,475 and the total market value is $104,700 (assume additions to the investment portfolio during 1997). In other words, market value is $3,775 less than cost. Because the allowance account already has a credit balance of $2,275 as a result of the adjusting entry made on December 31, 1996, the adjusting entry to record the 1997 loss is:

| 1997 | | | | | |
|------|----|-------------------------------------------------------------|----------|----------|
| Dec. | 31 | Loss on Market Decline of Temporary Investments   . . . | 1,500.00 | |
| | | Allowance to Reduce Temporary Investments   . . . . | | |
| | | to Market.  . . . . . . . . . . . . . . . . . . . . . . . | | 1,500.00 |
| | | *To record the market decline during 1997.* | | |

Thus, the loss recorded in 1997 is $1,500 and the December 31, 1997, balance in the allowance account is $3,775.

Because temporary investments in marketable equity securities must be reported at the *lower* of cost or market, market value increases above cost are not recorded as gains until the investments are sold. However, if a portfolio of temporary investments has been written down to a market value below cost, later increases in market value up to the original cost are reported on the income statement.[3]

For example, assume that on December 31, 1998, the market value of Bailey Company's temporary investments is $500 less than cost. Since the allowance account had a credit balance of $3,775 at the end of 1997, the December 31, 1998, adjusting entry is:

| 1998 | | | | | |
|------|---|---|---|---|---|
| Dec. | 31 | Allowance to Reduce Temporary Investments to Market . . | 3,275.00 | |
| | | Recovery of Market Value Decline, Temporary | | |
| | | Investments . . . . . . . . . . . . . . . . . . . . . . . . . . . . | | 3,275.00 |
| | | *To adjust the allowance account from $3,775 to $500.* | | |

Notice that the only entries that change the allowance (contra asset) account balance are the end-of-period adjusting entries. The entries to record purchases and sales of investments during a period do not affect the allowance account.

If cost and market are about the same, a company can just report the investments at cost. For example, the 1994 balance sheet for Moore Corporation Limited shows this information:

---

Current assets:
   Short-term securities, at cost which
      approximates market value  . . . . . . . .    $246,481,000

---

Some people criticize the lower of cost or market method because it is a departure from the *cost principle*. In recent years, however, an increasing number of people have criticized LCM because it does not record all changes in value, including increases above the original cost. In fact, the CICA's Accounting Standards Board is developing a new Handbook section for financial instruments which recommends that temporary investments be reported at market value, whether higher or lower than cost. However, it is not expected that the Canadian standards will change before 1997. Until then we will continue to use LCM.

---

**Progress Check**

*(Answers to Progress Checks are provided at the end of the chapter.)*

8-1  **How are temporary investments reported on the balance sheet—at cost or market values?**

---

[3]Canadian GAAP is unclear about reversing previous losses when the allowance method is used. General practice appears to accept these recoveries on the basis that they reverse previous increases to the allowance account. Generally, if the direct method is used, any recoveries would not be included.

**8-2   Normally, how often would an adjusting entry to record LCM be entered?**

**8-3   What happens when a previously written-down portfolio increases?**

---

In addition to cash, cash equivalents, and temporary investments, the liquid assets of a business include receivables that result from credit sales to customers. In the following sections, we discuss the procedures to account for sales when customers use credit cards issued by banks or credit card companies. Then, we focus on accounting for credit sales when a business grants credit directly to its customers. This situation requires the company (1) to maintain a separate account receivable for each customer and (2) to account for bad debts that result from credit sales. In addition, we discuss how to account for notes receivable, many of which arise from extending credit to customers.

**CREDIT SALES AND RECEIVABLES**

Many customers use credit cards such as Visa, MasterCard, or American Express to charge purchases from various businesses. Other retail businesses such as **Eaton's** or **The Bay** issue their own in-house charge cards. This practice gives the customers the ability to make purchases without carrying cash or writing cheques. It also allows them to defer their payments to the credit card company. Further, once credit is established with the credit card company, the customer does not have to open an account with each store. Finally, customers who use credit cards can make single monthly payments instead of several to different creditors.

**CREDIT CARD SALES**

LO 2

Prepare entries to account for credit card sales.

Another method of paying for purchases is through the use of a **debit card**. A debit card, such as Interac, is similar to a credit card but the customer enters an authorization code at the point of sale and the amount of the purchase is electronically transferred by the bank from the customer's bank account to the merchant's bank account. Accounting for these transactions is similar to the accounting for credit card sales which is illustrated below.

There are good reasons why businesses allow customers to use credit cards instead of maintaining their own accounts receivable. First, the business does not have to evaluate the credit standing of each customer or make decisions about who should get credit and how much. Second, the business avoids the risk of extending credit to customers who cannot or do not pay. Instead, this risk is faced by the credit card company. Third, the business typically receives cash from the credit card company sooner than it would if it granted credit directly to its customers. Fourth, a variety of credit options for customers offers a potential increase in sales volume.

In dealing with some credit cards, usually those issued by banks such as Visa or MasterCard, the business deposits a copy of each credit card sales receipt in its bank account just like it deposits a customer's cheque. Thus, the business receives a credit to its chequing account without delay. Other credit cards, such as American Express, require the business to send a copy of each receipt to the credit card company. Until payment is received, the business has an account receivable from the credit card company. In return for the services provided by the credit card company, a business pays a fee ranging from 2% to 5% of credit card sales. This charge is deducted from the credit to the chequing account or the cash payment to the business.

The procedures used in accounting for credit card sales depend on whether cash is received immediately on deposit or is delayed until paid by the credit card company. If cash is received immediately, as would be the case for a debit card payment, the entry to record $100 of credit or debit card sales with a 4% fee is:

| | | | | |
|---|---|---|---|---|
| Jan. | 25 | Cash . . . . . . . . . . . . . . . . . . . . . . . . . . . . . . . . . . . . . . . | 96.00 | |
| | | Credit Card Expense . . . . . . . . . . . . . . . . . . . . . . . | 4.00 | |
| | | Sales . . . . . . . . . . . . . . . . . . . . . . . . . . . . . . . | | 100.00 |
| | | *To record credit/debit card sales less a 4% credit card expense.* | | |

If the business must send the receipts to the credit card company and wait for payment, this entry on the date of the sales records them:

| | | | | |
|---|---|---|---|---|
| Jan. | 25 | Accounts Receivable, Credit Card Company . . . . . . . . . | 100.00 | |
| | | Sales . . . . . . . . . . . . . . . . . . . . . . . . . . . . . . . . | | 100.00 |
| | | *To record credit card sales.* | | |

When cash is received from the credit card company, the entry to record the receipt and the deduction of the fee is:

| | | | | |
|---|---|---|---|---|
| Feb. | 10 | Cash . . . . . . . . . . . . . . . . . . . . . . . . . . . . . . . . . . . . | 96.00 | |
| | | Credit Card Expense . . . . . . . . . . . . . . . . . . . . . . . | 4.00 | |
| | | Accounts Receivable—Credit Card Co . . . . . . . . | | 100.00 |
| | | *To record cash receipt less 4% credit card expense.* | | |

In the last two entries, notice that the credit card expense was not recorded until cash was received from the credit card company. This practice is merely a matter of convenience. By following this procedure, the business avoids having to calculate and record the credit card expense each time sales are recorded. Instead, the expense related to many sales can be calculated once and recorded when cash is received. However, the *matching principle* requires reporting credit card expense in the same period as the sale. Therefore, if the sale and the cash receipt occur in different periods, you must accrue and report the credit card expense in the period of the sale by using an adjusting entry at the end of the year. For example, this year-end adjustment accrues $24 of credit card expense on a $600 receivable that the Credit Card Company has not yet paid.

| | | | | |
|---|---|---|---|---|
| Dec. | 31 | Credit Card Expense . . . . . . . . . . . . . . . . . . . . . . . . . | 24.00 | |
| | | Accounts Receivable—Credit Card Company . . . . | | 24.00 |
| | | *To accrue credit card expense that is unrecorded at the end of the year.* | | |

Then, the following entry records the cash collection in January:

| | | | | |
|---|---|---|---|---|
| Jan. | 5 | Cash . . . . . . . . . . . . . . . . . . . . . . . . . . . . . . . . . . . . | 576.00 | |
| | | Accounts Receivable—Credit Card Company . . . . | | 576.00 |
| | | *To record collection of the amount due from Credit Card Company.* | | |

Some firms report credit card expense in the income statement as a type of discount that is deducted from sales to get net sales. Other companies classify it as a selling expense or even as an administrative expense. Arguments can be made for all three alternatives but there is little practical difference in the result.

---

**Progress Check**

**8–4** In recording credit card sales, when do you debit Accounts Receivable and when do you debit Cash?

**8–5** When are credit card expenses recorded in situations where sales receipts must be accumulated before they can be sent to the credit card company? When are these expenses incurred?

**8–6** If payment for a credit card sale has not been received by the end of the accounting period, how do you account for the credit card expense associated with that sale?

---

## MAINTAINING A SEPARATE ACCOUNT FOR EACH CREDIT CUSTOMER

**LO 3**

Prepare entries to account for transactions with credit customers, including accounting for bad debts under the allowance method and the direct write-off method.

In previous chapters, we recorded credit sales by debiting a single Accounts Receivable account. However, a business with more than one credit customer must design its accounting system to show how much each customer has purchased, how much each customer has paid, and how much remains to be collected from each customer. This information provides the basis for sending bills to the customers. To have this information on hand, businesses that extend credit directly to their customers must maintain a separate account receivable for each of them.

One possible way of keeping a separate account for each customer would be to include all of these accounts in the same ledger that contains the financial statement accounts. However, this approach usually is not used because there are too many customers. Recall from Chapter 6 that the **General Ledger,** which is the ledger that contains the financial statement accounts, has only a single Accounts Receivable account. A supplementary record is established in which a separate account is maintained for each customer. This supplementary record is the **Accounts Receivable Ledger.**

Illustration 8–1 shows the relationship between the Accounts Receivable account in the General Ledger and the individual customer accounts in the Accounts Receivable Ledger. In Part A of Illustration 8–1, notice that the $3,000 sum of the two balances in the Accounts Receivable Ledger is equal to the balance of the Accounts Receivable account in the General Ledger as of February 1. To maintain this relationship, each time that credit sales are posted with a debit to the Accounts Receivable account in the General Ledger, they are also posted with debits to the appropriate

**Illustration 8-1**   The Accounts Receivable Account and the Accounts Receivable Ledger

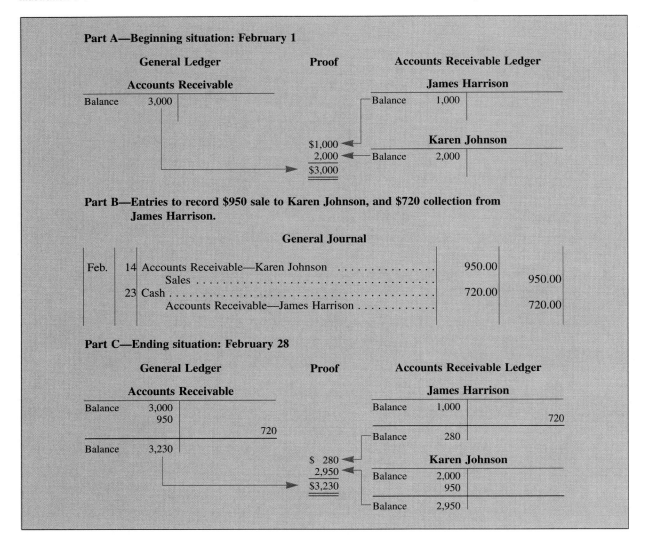

customer accounts in the Accounts Receivable Ledger. Also, cash receipts from credit customers must be posted with credits to both the Accounts Receivable account in the General Ledger and to the appropriate customer accounts.

Part B shows the general journal entry to record a credit sale on February 14 to customer Karen Johnson. It also shows the entry to record the collection of $720 from James Harrison.

Part C presents the General Ledger account and the Accounts Receivable Ledger as of February 28. Notice how the General Ledger account shows the effects of the sales and the collection, and that it has a $3,230 balance. The same events are reflected in the accounts for the two customers: Harrison now has a balance of only $280, and Johnson owes $2,950. The $3,230 sum of their accounts equals the debit balance of the General Ledger account.

Note that posting debits or credits to Accounts Receivable twice does not violate the requirement that debits equal credits. The equality of debits and credits is maintained *in the General Ledger*. The Accounts Receivable Ledger is simply a supplementary record that provides detailed information concerning each customer.

Because the balance in the Accounts Receivable account is always equal to the sum of the balances in the customers' accounts, the Accounts Receivable account is said to control the Accounts Receivable Ledger and is an example of a **controlling account.** And, the Accounts Receivable Ledger is an example of a supplementary record that is controlled by an account in the General Ledger; this kind of supplementary record is called a **subsidiary ledger.**

The Accounts Receivable account and the Accounts Receivable Ledger are not the only examples of controlling accounts and subsidiary ledgers. Most companies buy on credit from several suppliers and must use a controlling account and subsidiary ledger for accounts payable. Another example might be an Office Equipment account that would control a subsidiary ledger in which the cost of each item of equipment is recorded in a separate account.

## BAD DEBTS

When a company grants credit to its customers, there usually are a few who do not pay what they promised. The accounts of such customers are called **bad debts.** These bad debt amounts that cannot be collected are an expense of selling on credit.

You might ask why merchants sell on credit if it is likely that some of the accounts prove to be uncollectible. The answer is that they believe granting credit will increase revenues and profits. They are willing to incur bad debt losses if the net effect is to increase sales and profits. Therefore, bad debt losses are an expense of selling on credit that is incurred to increase sales.

The reporting of bad debts expense on the income statement is governed by the *matching principle*. This principle requires that the expenses from bad debts be reported in the same accounting period as the revenues they helped produce.

## MATCHING BAD DEBT EXPENSES WITH SALES

Managers realize that some portion of credit sales result in bad debts. However, the fact that a specific credit sale will not be collected does not become apparent until later. If a customer fails to pay within the credit period, most businesses send out several repeat billings and make other efforts to collect. Usually, they do not accept the fact that the customer is not going to pay until every reasonable means of collection has been exhausted. In many cases, this point may not be reached until one or more accounting periods after the period in which the sale was made. Thus, matching this expense with the revenue it produced requires the company to estimate its unknown amount at the end of the year. The **allowance method of accounting for bad debts** accomplishes this matching of bad debts expense with revenues.

## ALLOWANCE METHOD OF ACCOUNTING FOR BAD DEBTS

At the end of each accounting period, the allowance method of accounting for bad debts requires estimating the total bad debts expected to result from the period's sales. An allowance is then provided for the loss. This method has two advantages: (1) the expense is charged to the period in which the revenue is recognized; and (2) the accounts receivable are reported on the balance sheet at the estimated amount of cash to be collected.

## Recording the Estimated Bad Debts Expense

Under the allowance method of accounting for bad debts, you calculate the estimated bad debts expense at the end of each accounting period. Then, you record it with an adjusting entry. For example, assume that Fritz Company had credit sales of $300,000 during the first year of its operations. At the end of the year, $20,000 remains uncollected. Based on the experience of similar businesses, Fritz Company estimates that $1,500 of accounts receivable will be uncollectible. This estimated expense is recorded with the following adjusting entry:

| Dec. | 31 | Bad Debts Expense .......................... | 1,500.00 | |
|------|----|-----------------------------------------------|----------|----------|
| | | Allowance for Doubtful Accounts ............ | | 1,500.00 |
| | | *To record the estimated bad debts.* | | |

The debit in this entry causes the expense to appear on the income statement of the year in which the sales were made. As a result, the estimated $1,500 expense of selling on credit is matched with the $300,000 of revenue it helped produce.

Note that the credit of the entry is to a contra account called **Allowance for Doubtful Accounts.** A contra account must be used because at the time of the adjusting entry, you do not know which customers will not pay. Therefore, because specific bad accounts are not identifiable at the time of the adjusting entry, they cannot be removed from the subsidiary Accounts Receivable Ledger. Because the customer accounts are left in the subsidiary ledger, the controlling account for Accounts Receivable cannot be reduced. Instead, the Allowance for Doubtful Accounts account *must* be credited.

## Bad Debts in the Accounts and in the Financial Statements

The process of evaluating customers and approving them for credit usually is not assigned to the selling department of a business. Otherwise, given the primary objective of increasing sales, the selling department might not use good judgment in approving customers for credit. Because the sales department is not responsible for granting credit, it should not be held responsible for bad debts expense. Therefore, bad debts expense often appears on the income statement as an administrative expense rather than a selling expense.

Recall from the previous example that Fritz Company has $20,000 of outstanding accounts receivable at the end of its first year of operations. Thus, after the bad debts adjusting entry is posted, the company's Accounts Receivable and Allowance for Doubtful Accounts accounts show these balances:

| **Accounts Receivable** | | **Allowance for Doubtful Accounts** | |
|-------------------------|--|-------------------------------------|--|
| Dec. 31    20,000 | | | Dec. 31    1,500 |

The Allowance for Doubtful Accounts credit balance of $1,500 has the effect of reducing accounts receivable (net of the allowance) to their estimated **realizable**

**value.** The term *realizable value* means the expected proceeds from converting the assets into cash. Although $20,000 is legally owed to Fritz Company by all of its customers, only $18,500 is likely to be realized in cash collections from customers.

When the balance sheet is prepared, the allowance for doubtful accounts is subtracted from the accounts receivable to show the amount expected to be realized from the accounts. For example, this information could be reported as follows:

| | | |
|---|---:|---:|
| Current assets: | | |
| Cash and cash equivalents .............. | | $11,300 |
| Temporary investments, at lower of cost or | | |
| market (cost is $16,200) .............. | | 14,500 |
| Accounts receivable ................... | $20,000 | |
| Less allowance for doubtful accounts ...... | (1,500) | 18,500 |
| Merchandise inventory ................. | | 52,700 |
| Prepaid expenses ..................... | | 1,100 |
| Total current assets ................... | | $98,100 |

In this example, compare the presentations of temporary investments and accounts receivable, and note that contra accounts are subtracted in both cases. Even though the contra account to the Temporary Investments account is not shown on the statement, you can easily determine that its balance is $1,700 by comparing the $16,200 cost with the $14,500 net amount. Sometimes, the contra account to Accounts Receivable is presented in a similar fashion, as follows:

| | |
|---|---:|
| Accounts receivable (net of $1,500 estimated uncollectible accounts) ................. | $18,500 |

## Writing Off a Bad Debt

When specific accounts are identified as uncollectible, they are written off against the Allowance for Doubtful Accounts. For example, after spending a year trying to collect from Jack Vale, the Fritz Company finally decided that his $100 account was uncollectible and made the following entry to write it off:

| | | | | |
|---|---|---|---:|---:|
| Jan. | 23 | Allowance for Doubtful Accounts ............... | 100.00 | |
| | | Accounts Receivable—Jack Vale ............ | | 100.00 |
| | | *To write off an uncollectible account.* | | |

Posting the credit of the entry to the Accounts Receivable account removes the amount of the bad debt from the controlling account. Posting it to the Jack Vale account removes the amount of the bad debt from the subsidiary ledger. By removing it from the subsidiary ledger, Fritz Company avoids the cost of sending additional bills to Vale. After the entry is posted, the general ledger accounts appear as follows:

| Accounts Receivable | | | | | Allowance for Doubtful Accounts | | |
|---|---|---|---|---|---|---|---|
| Dec. 31 | 20,000 | | | | | Dec. 31 | 1,500 |
| | | Jan. 23 | 100 | Jan. 23 | 100 | | |

Notice two aspects of the entry and the accounts. First, although bad debts are an expense of selling on credit, the allowance account is debited in the write-off. The expense account is not debited. The expense account is not debited because the estimated expense was previously recorded at the end of the period in which the sale occurred. At that time, the expense was estimated and recorded with an adjusting entry.

Second, although the write-off removed the amount of the account receivable from the ledgers, it did not affect the estimated realizable value of Fritz Company's net accounts receivable, as the following tabulation shows:

| | Before | After |
|---|---|---|
| Accounts receivable ................. | $20,000 | $19,900 |
| Less allowance for doubtful accounts .... | 1,500 | 1,400 |
| Estimated realizable accounts receivable .... | $18,500 | $18,500 |

Thus, neither total assets nor net income are affected by the decision to write off a specific account. However, both total assets and net income are affected by the recognition of the year's bad debts expense in the adjusting entry. Again, a primary purpose of writing off a specific account is to avoid the cost of additional collection efforts. Also, the *conservatism principle* would indicate that the accounts receivable should only include those amounts that are reasonably expected to be collected.

## Bad Debt Recoveries

When a customer fails to pay and the account is written off, his or her credit standing is jeopardized. Therefore, the customer may choose to voluntarily pay all or part of the amount owed after the account is written off as uncollectible. This payment helps restore the credit standing. Thus, when this event happens, it should be recorded in the customer's subsidiary account where the information will be retained for use in future credit evaluations.

When a company collects an account that was previously written off, it makes two journal entries. The first reverses the original write-off and reinstates the customer's account. The second entry records the collection of the reinstated account. For example, assume that on August 15 Jack Vale pays in full the account that Fritz Company had previously written off. The entries to record the bad debt recovery are:

| Aug. | 15 | Accounts Receivable—Jack Vale ................ | 100.00 | |
| | | Allowance for Doubtful Accounts ............ | | 100.00 |
| | | *To reinstate the account of Jack Vale written off on January 23.* | | |
| | 15 | Cash ..................................... | 100.00 | |
| | | Accounts Receivable—Jack Vale ............. | | 100.00 |
| | | *Received full payment of account.* | | |

In this case, Jack Vale paid the entire amount previously written off. In other situations, the customer may pay only a portion of the amount owed. The question then arises of whether the entire balance of the account should be returned to accounts receivable or just the amount paid. The answer is a matter of judgment. If you believe the customer will later pay in full, the entire amount owed should be returned. However, only the amount paid should be returned if you believe that no more will be collected.

---

**Progress Check**

8-7   In meeting the requirements of the matching principle, why must bad debts expenses be estimated?

8-8   What term describes the balance sheet valuation of accounts receivable less the allowance for doubtful accounts?

8-9   Why is estimated bad debts expense credited to a contra account rather than to the Accounts Receivable controlling account?

---

As you already learned, the allowance method of accounting for bad debts requires an adjusting entry at the end of each accounting period to record management's estimate of the bad debts expense for the period. That entry takes the following form:

**ESTIMATING THE AMOUNT OF BAD DEBTS EXPENSE**

| Dec. | 31 | Bad Debts Expense ........................... | ???? | |
| | | Allowance for Doubtful Accounts ............. | | ???? |
| | | *To record the estimated bad debts.* | | |

How does a business determine the amount to record in this entry? There are two alternative approaches. One focuses on the income statement relationship between bad debts expense and sales. The other focuses on the balance sheet relationship between accounts receivable and allowance for doubtful accounts. Both alternatives require a careful analysis of past experience.

## Estimating Bad Debts by Focusing on the Income Statement

The income statement approach to estimating bad debts is based on the idea that some particular percentage of a company's credit sales for the period will become uncollectible.[4] Hence, in the income statement, the amount of bad debts expense should equal that amount.

For example, suppose that Baker Company had credit sales of $400,000 in 1996. Based on past experience and the experience of similar companies, Baker Company estimates that 0.6% of credit sales will be uncollectible. Using this prediction, Baker Company can expect $2,400 of bad debts expense to result from the year's sales ($400,000 × 0.006 = $2,400). The adjusting entry to record this estimated expense is:

| Dec. | 31 | Bad Debts Expense . . . . . . . . . . . . . . . . . . . . . . . . . . . . | 2,400.00 | |
| | | Allowance for Doubtful Accounts . . . . . . . . . . . . . | | 2,400.00 |
| | | *To record the estimated bad debts.* | | |

This entry does not mean the December 31, 1996, balance in Allowance for Doubtful Accounts will be $2,400. A $2,400 balance would occur only if the account had a zero balance immediately prior to posting the adjusting entry. For several reasons, however, the unadjusted balance of Allowance for Doubtful Accounts is not likely to be zero.

First, unless Baker Company began business during the current year, the Allowance for Doubtful Accounts would have had a credit balance at the beginning of the year. The beginning-of-year credit balance would have resulted from entries made in past years to record estimated bad debts expense and to write off uncollectible accounts. The cumulative effect of these entries would show up as a credit balance at the beginning of the current year.

Second, because bad debts expense must be estimated each year, the total amount of expense recorded in past years is not likely to equal the amounts that were written off as uncollectible. Although annual expense estimates are based on past experience, some residual difference between recorded expenses and amounts written off should be expected to show up in the unadjusted Allowance for Doubtful Accounts balance.

Third, some of the amounts written off as uncollectible during the current year probably relate to credit sales made during the current year. These debits affect the unadjusted Allowance for Doubtful Accounts balance. In fact, they may cause the account to have a debit balance prior to posting the adjusting entry for bad debts expense.

For these reasons, you should not expect the Allowance for Doubtful Accounts to have an unadjusted balance of zero at the end of the year. As we stated earlier, this means that the adjusted balance reported on the balance sheet normally does not equal the amount of expense reported on the income statement.

Remember that expressing bad debts expense as a percentage of sales is an estimate based on past experience. As new experience is gained over time, the percentage used may appear to have been too large or too small. When this happens, a different rate should be used in future periods.

---

[4]Note that the factor to be considered is *credit* sales. Naturally, cash sales do not produce bad debts, and they generally should not be used in the calculation. However, if cash sales are relatively small compared to credit sales, there is no practical difference in the result.

## Estimating Bad Debts by Focusing on the Balance Sheet

The balance sheet approach to estimating bad debts is based on the idea that some portion of the end-of-period accounts receivable balance will not be collected. From this point of view, the goal of the bad debts adjusting entry is to make the Allowance for Doubtful Accounts balance equal to the portion of outstanding accounts receivable estimated to be uncollectible. To obtain this required balance in the Allowance for Doubtful Accounts account, simply compare its balance before the adjustment with the required balance. The difference between the two is debited to Bad Debts Expense and credited to Allowance for Doubtful Accounts. Estimating the required balance of the Allowance account can be done in two ways: (1) by using the simplified approach and (2) by aging the accounts receivable.

**The Simplified Balance Sheet Approach.** Using the simplified balance sheet approach, a company estimates that a certain percentage of its outstanding receivables will prove to be uncollectible. This estimated percentage is based on past experience and the experience of similar companies. It also may be affected by current conditions such as recent prosperity or economic difficulties faced by the firm's customers. Then, the total dollar amount of all outstanding receivables is multiplied by the estimated percentage to determine the estimated dollar amount of uncollectible accounts. This amount must appear in the balance sheet as the balance of the Allowance for Doubtful Accounts. To put this balance in the account, you must prepare an adjusting entry that debits Bad Debts Expense and credits Allowance for Doubtful Accounts. The amount of the adjustment is the amount necessary to provide the required balance in Allowance for Doubtful Accounts.

For example, assume that Baker Company (of the previous illustration) has $50,000 of outstanding accounts receivable on December 31, 1996. Past experience suggests that 5% of the outstanding receivables are uncollectible. Thus, after the adjusting entry is posted, the Allowance for Doubtful Accounts should have a $2,500 credit balance (5% of $50,000). Assume that before the adjustment the account appears as follows:

**Allowance for Doubtful Accounts**

|          |     |     | Dec. 31, 1995, balance | 2,000 |
|----------|-----|-----|------------------------|-------|
| Feb.  6  | 800 |     |                        |       |
| July  10 | 600 |     |                        |       |
| Nov. 20  | 400 |     |                        |       |
|          |     |     | Unadjusted balance     | 200   |

The $2,000 beginning balance appeared on the December 31, 1995, balance sheet. During 1996, accounts of specific customers were written off on February 6, July 10, and November 20. As a result, the account has a $200 credit balance prior to the December 31, 1996, adjustment. The adjusting entry to give the Allowance the required $2,500 balance is:

| Dec. | 31 | Bad Debts Expense . . . . . . . . . . . . . . . . . . . . . . . . . | 2,300.00 |          |
|------|----|-------------------------------------------------------------------|----------|----------|
|      |    | Allowance for Doubtful Accounts . . . . . . . . . . . . . |          | 2,300.00 |
|      |    | *To record the estimated bad debts.* |          |          |

After this entry is posted, the Allowance has a $2,500 credit balance, as shown here:

**Allowance for Doubtful Accounts**

|              |     |                          |       |
|--------------|-----|--------------------------|-------|
|              |     | Dec. 31, 1995, balance   | 2,000 |
| Feb.   6     | 800 |                          |       |
| July  10     | 600 |                          |       |
| Nov. 20      | 400 |                          |       |
|              |     | Unadjusted balance       | 200   |
|              |     | Dec. 31                  | 2,300 |
|              |     | Dec. 31, 1996, balance   | 2,500 |

**Aging Accounts Receivable.** Both the income statement approach and the simplified balance sheet approach use knowledge gained from past experience to estimate the amount of bad debts expense. Another balance sheet approach produces a more refined estimate based on past experience and on information about current conditions.

This method involves **aging of accounts receivable.** Under this method, each account receivable is examined in the process of estimating the amount that is uncollectible. Specifically, the receivables are classified by how long they have been outstanding. Then, estimates of uncollectible amounts are made under the assumption that the longer an amount is outstanding, the more likely it will be uncollectible.

To age the accounts receivable outstanding at the end of the period, you must examine each account and classify the outstanding amounts by how much time has passed since they were created. The selection of the classes to be used depends on the judgment of each company's management. However, the classes are often based on 30-day (or one month) periods. After the outstanding amounts have been classified (or aged), past experience is used to estimate a percentage of each class that will become uncollectible. These percentages are applied to the amounts in the classes to determine the required balance of the Allowance for Doubtful Accounts. The calculation is completed by setting up a schedule like the one in Illustration 8–2 for Baker Company.

In Illustration 8–2, notice that each customer's account is listed with its total balance. Then, each balance is allocated to five categories based on the age of the unpaid charges that make up the balance. (In computerized systems, this allocation is done automatically.) When all accounts have been aged, the amounts in each category are totaled and multiplied by the estimated percentage of uncollectible accounts for each category. The reasonableness of the percentages used must be reviewed regularly and frequently reflect reactions to the state of the economy.

For example, in Illustration 8–2, Baker Company is owed $3,500 that is 31 to 60 days past due. Baker's management estimates that 10% of the amounts in this age category will not be collected. Thus, the dollar amount of uncollectible accounts in this category is $350 ($3,500 × 10%). The total in the first column tells us that the adjusted balance in Baker Company's Allowance for Doubtful Accounts should be $2,290 ($740 + $325 + $350 + $475 + $400). Because the Allowance has an unadjusted credit balance of $200, the aging of accounts receivable approach requires the following change in its balance:

**Illustration 8-2**    Estimating Bad Debts by Aging the Accounts

**BAKER COMPANY**
**Schedule of Accounts Receivable by Age**
**December 31, 1996**

| Customer's Name | Total | Not Due | 1 to 30 Days Past Due | 31 to 60 Days Past Due | 61 to 90 Days Past Due | Over 90 Days Past Due |
|---|---|---|---|---|---|---|
| Charles Abbot . . . . . . . | $ 450.00 | $ 450.00 | | | | |
| Frank Allen . . . . . . . . | 710.00 | | | $ 710.00 | | |
| George Arden . . . . . . . | 500.00 | 300.00 | $ 200.00 | | | |
| Paul Baum . . . . . . . . . | 740.00 | | | | $ 100.00 | $ 640.00 |
| ZZ Services . . . . . . . . | 1,000.00 | 810.00 | 190.00 | | | |
| Totals . . . . . . . . . . . . | $49,900.00 | $37,000.00 | $6,500.00 | $3,500.00 | $1,900.00 | $1,000.00 |
| Rate . . . . . . . . . . . . . | | × 2% | × 5% | × 10% | × 25% | × 40% |
| Estimated uncollectible amounts . . . | $ 2,290.00 | $ 740.00 | $ 325.00 | $ 350.00 | $ 475.00 | $ 400.00 |

Unadjusted balance  . . . .  $  200 credit
Required balance  . . . . . .  2,290 credit
Required adjustment . . . .  $2,090 credit

As a result, Baker should record the following adjusting entry:

| | | | | |
|---|---|---|---|---|
| Dec. | 31 | Bad Debts Expense . . . . . . . . . . . . . . . . . . . . . . . . . . | 2,090.00 | |
| | |     Allowance for Doubtful Accounts . . . . . . . . . . . . | | 2,090.00 |
| | |     *To record the estimated bad debts.* | | |

For instructional purposes, suppose that Baker's Allowance had an unadjusted *debit* balance of $500. In this case, the calculation of the adjustment amount and the entry would be:

Unadjusted balance  . . . .  $  500 debit
Required balance  . . . . . .  2,290 credit
Required adjustment . . . .  $2,790 credit

| | | | | |
|---|---|---|---|---|
| Dec. | 31 | Bad Debts Expense . . . . . . . . . . . . . . . . . . . . . . . . . . | 2,790.00 | |
| | |     Allowance for Doubtful Accounts . . . . . . . . . . . . | | 2,790.00 |
| | |     *To record the estimated bad debts.* | | |

Recall from page 411 that when the income statement approach was used, Baker's bad debts expense for 1996 was estimated to be $2,400. When the simplified balance sheet approach was used (see page 413), the estimate was $2,300. And when aging of accounts receivable was used the first time, the estimate was $2,090. Do not be surprised that the amounts are different; after all, each approach is only an estimate of what will prove to be true. However, the aging of accounts receivable is based on a more detailed examination of specific outstanding accounts and is usually the most reliable.[5]

## DIRECT WRITE-OFF METHOD OF ACCOUNTING FOR BAD DEBTS

The allowance method of accounting for bad debts satisfies the requirements of the *matching principle*. Therefore, it is the method that should be used in most cases. However, another method may be suitable under certain limited circumstances. Under this **direct write-off method of accounting for bad debts,** no attempt is made to estimate uncollectible accounts or bad debts expense at the end of each period. In fact, no adjusting entry is made. Instead, bad debts expense is recorded when specific accounts are written off as uncollectible. For example, note the following entry to write off a $52 uncollectible account:

| Nov. | 23 | Bad Debts Expense ........................ | 52.00 | |
|------|----|-------------------------------------|-------|-------|
| | | Accounts Receivable—Dale Hall ............. | | 52.00 |
| | | *To write off the uncollectible account under the direct write-off method.* | | |

The debit of the entry charges the uncollectible amount directly to the current year's Bad Debts Expense account. The credit removes the balance of the account from the subsidiary ledger and from the controlling account.

If an account previously written off directly to Bad Debts Expense is later collected in full, the following entries record the recovery:

| Mar. | 11 | Accounts Receivable—Dale Hall ............... | 52.00 | |
|------|----|-------------------------------------|-------|-------|
| | | Bad Debts Expense ...................... | | 52.00 |
| | | *To reinstate the account of Dale Hall previously written off.* | | |
| | 11 | Cash ................................... | 52.00 | |
| | | Accounts Receivable—Dale Hall ............. | | 52.00 |
| | | *In full payment of account.* | | |

Sometimes an amount previously written off directly to Bad Debts Expense is recovered in the year following the write-off. If there is no balance in the Bad Debts Expense account from previous write-offs and no other write-offs are expected, the

---

[5]In many cases, the aging analysis is supplemented with information about specific customers that allows management to decide whether those accounts should be classified as uncollectible. This information often is supplied by the sales and credit department managers.

credit portion of the entry recording the recovery can be made to a Bad Debt Recoveries revenue account.

The direct write-off method usually mismatches revenues and expenses. The mismatch occurs because bad debts expense is not recorded until an account becomes uncollectible, which often does not occur during the same period as the credit sale. Despite this weakness, the direct write-off method may be used when a company's bad debts expenses are very small in relation to other financial statement items such as total sales and net income. In such cases, the direct write-off method is justified by the *materiality principle,* which we explain next.

## THE MATERIALITY PRINCIPLE

The basic idea of the **materiality principle** is that the requirements of accounting principles may be ignored if the effect on the financial statements is unimportant to their users. In other words, failure to follow the requirements of an accounting principle is acceptable when the failure does not produce an error or misstatement large enough to influence a financial statement reader's judgment of a given situation.

## INSTALLMENT ACCOUNTS AND NOTES RECEIVABLE

Many companies allow their credit customers to make periodic payments over several months. When this is done, the selling company's assets may be in the form of **installment accounts receivable** or notes receivable. As is true for other accounts receivable, the evidence behind installment accounts receivable includes sales slips or invoices that describe the sales transactions. A note receivable, on the other hand, is a written document that promises payment and is signed by the customer. In either case, when payments are made over several months or if the credit period is long, the customer is usually charged interest. Although the credit period of installment accounts and notes receivable may be more than one year, they should be classified as current assets if the company regularly offers customers such terms.

Generally, creditors prefer notes receivable over accounts receivable when the credit period is long and the receivable relates to a single sale for a fairly large amount. Notes also can replace accounts receivable when customers ask for additional time to pay their past-due accounts. In these situations, creditors prefer notes to accounts receivable for legal reasons. If a lawsuit is needed to collect from a customer, a note represents a clear written acknowledgment by the debtor of the debt, its amount, and its terms. Banks and finance companies often use installment accounts, notes receivable, or similar instruments in dealings with their customers.

---

**Progress Check**

**D & C Boutiques International estimated that, based on an aging of accounts receivable, $6,142 would be uncollectible. The year-end December 31, 1995 balance of the allowance account is a credit of $440.**

8-10  **Prepare the year-end adjusting entry.**

8-11  **Using the following information, prepare the appropriate journal entries:**
**On January 10, 1996, the $300 account of customer Felix Arthur was determined uncollectible. On April 12, 1996, Felix Arthur paid the account that was determined uncollectible on January 10, 1996.**

---

**Illustration 8-3**
A Promissory Note

| | | |
|---|---|---|
| _$1,000.00_ | _Winnipeg, Manitoba_ | _March 9, 1996_ |

_Thirty days_ after date _I, Hugo Brown_ promise to pay to

the order of _Frank Tomlinson_

_One thousand and no / 100_ - - - - - - - - - - - - - - - - - - - - - - - - - - - - - - - - - - - - - - - - - - - dollars

for value received with interest at _12%_

payable at _National Bank of Winnipeg, Manitoba_

_Hugo Brown_

## PROMISSORY NOTES

**LO 4**

Calculate the interest on promissory notes and prepare entries to record the receipt of promissory notes and their payment or dishonour.

A **promissory note** is an unconditional written promise to pay a definite sum of money on demand or at a fixed or determinable future date. In the promissory note shown in Illustration 8–3, Hugo Brown promises to pay Frank Tomlinson or to his order (that is, according to Tomlinson's instructions) a definite sum of money ($1,000), called the **principal of the note** at a fixed future date (April 8, 1996). As the one who signed the note and promised to pay it at maturity, Hugo Brown is the **maker of the note.** As the person to whom the note is payable, Frank Tomlinson is the **payee of the note.** To Hugo Brown, the illustrated note is a liability called a _note payable._ To Frank Tomlinson, the same note is an asset called a _note receivable._

The Hugo Brown note bears **interest** at 12%. Interest is the charge assessed for the use of money. To a borrower, interest is an expense. To a lender, it is a revenue. The rate of interest that a note bears is stated on the note.

### Calculating Interest

Unless otherwise stated, the rate of interest on a note is the rate charged for the use of the principal for one year. The formula for calculating interest is:

$$\begin{array}{ccccccc} \text{Principal} & & \text{Annual} & & \text{Time of the} & & \\ \text{of the} & \times & \text{rate of} & \times & \text{note expressed} & = & \text{Interest} \\ \text{note} & & \text{interest} & & \text{in years} & & \end{array}$$

For example, interest on a $1,000, 12%, six-month note is calculated as:

$$\$1,000 \times 12\% \times \frac{6}{12} = \$60$$

The **maturity date of a note** is the day on which the note (principal and interest) must be repaid. Many notes mature in less than a full year, and the period covered by them often is expressed in days. When the time of a note is expressed in days, the maturity date is the specified number of days after the note's date. As a simple example, a one-day note dated June 15 matures and is due on June 16. Also, a 90-day note dated July 10 matures on October 8. This October 8 due date is calculated as follows:

| | |
|---|---:|
| Number of days in July . . . . . . . . . . . . . . . . . . . . . . . . . . | 31 |
| Minus the date of the note . . . . . . . . . . . . . . . . . . . . . . . | 10 |
| Gives the number of days the note runs in July . . . . . . . . . . . | 21 |
| Add the number of days in August . . . . . . . . . . . . . . . . . . . | 31 |
| Add the number of days in September . . . . . . . . . . . . . . . . | 30 |
| Total through September 30 . . . . . . . . . . . . . . . . . . . . . . . | 82 |
| Days in October needed to equal the 90-day time of the note, also the maturity date of the note (October 8) . . . . . . | 8 |
| Total time the note runs in days . . . . . . . . . . . . . . . . . . . . | 90 |

In other situations, the period of a note is expressed in months. In these cases, the note matures and is payable in the month of its maturity on the same day of the month as its original date. For example, a three-month note dated July 10 is payable on October 10.

The amount of interest for a 90-day note with interest at 12% is calculated as follows:[6]

$$\text{Interest} = \text{Principal} \times \text{Rate} \times \frac{\text{Exact days}}{365}$$

or

$$\text{Interest} = \$1,000 \times 12\% \times \frac{90}{365} = \$29.59$$

## Recording the Receipt of a Note

To simplify record-keeping, notes receivable are usually recorded in a single Notes Receivable account. Only one account is needed because the individual original notes are on hand. Therefore, the maker, rate of interest, due date, and other information may be learned by examining each note.[7]

When a company receives a note at the time of a sale, an entry such as this one is recorded:

| | | | | |
|---|---|---|---:|---:|
| Dec. | 5 | Notes Receivable . . . . . . . . . . . . . . . . . . . . . . . . . . | 650.00 | |
| | | Sales . . . . . . . . . . . . . . . . . . . . . . . . . . . . . . . . | | 650.00 |
| | | *Sold merchandise, terms six-month, 9% note.* | | |

A business also may accept a note from an overdue customer as a way of granting a time extension on the past-due account receivable. When this happens, the business may collect part of the past-due balance in cash. This partial payment

---

[6]Specific types of note may legally allow for three days of grace. For example, a 90-day note becomes due and payable on the 93rd day, and interest is calculated for 93 days. Because it is common practice that notes are due and payable on a specified date, illustrations are based on the time period specified on the face of the note. Unless otherwise instructed, you are to solve problems using the specific number of days and a 365-day year.

[7]If the company holds a large number of notes, it may be more efficient to set up a controlling account and a subsidiary ledger.

forces a concession from the customer, reduces the customer's debt (and the seller's risk), and produces a note for a smaller amount. For example, Symplex Company agrees to accept $232 in cash and a $600, 60-day, 15% note from Joseph Cook to settle his $832 past-due account. Symplex makes the following entry to record the receipt of the cash and note:

| Oct. | 5 | Cash ..................................... | 232.00 | |
| | | Notes Receivable .......................... | 600.00 | |
| | |     Accounts Receivable—Joseph Cook .......... | | 832.00 |
| | | *Received cash and a note in settlement of an account.* | | |

When Cook pays the note on the due date, Symplex records the receipt as follows:

| Dec. | 4 | Cash ..................................... | 614.79 | |
| | |     Notes Receivable ......................... | | 600.00 |
| | |     Interest Earned ......................... | | 14.79 |
| | | *Collected the Joseph Cook note including interest of* | | |
| | | *$600 × 15% × 60/365.* | | |

## Dishonoured Notes Receivable

Sometimes, the maker of a note is not able to pay the note at maturity. When a note's maker is unable or refuses to pay at maturity, the note is said to be dishonoured. This act of **dishonouring a note** does not relieve the maker of the obligation to pay. Furthermore, the payee should use every legitimate means to collect. However, collection may require lengthy legal proceedings.

The usual practice is to have the balance of the Notes Receivable account show only the amount of notes that have not matured. Therefore, when a note is dishonoured, you should remove the amount of the note from the Notes Receivable account and charge it back to an account receivable from its maker. To illustrate, Symplex Company holds an $800, 12%, 60-day note of George Hart. At maturity, Hart dishonours the note. To remove the dishonoured note from the Notes Receivable account, the company makes the following entry:

| Oct. | 14 | Accounts Receivable—George Hart .............. | 815.78 | |
| | |     Interest Earned ......................... | | 15.78 |
| | |     Notes Receivable ........................ | | 800.00 |
| | | *To charge the account of George Hart for his* | | |
| | | *dishonoured note including interest of* | | |
| | | *$800 × 12% × 60/365.* | | |

Charging a dishonoured note back to the account of its maker serves two purposes. First, it removes the amount of the note from the Notes Receivable account, leaving in the account only notes that have not matured. It also records the dishonoured note in the maker's account. The second purpose is important. If the maker of the dishonoured note again applies for credit in the future, his or her account will show all past dealings, including the dishonoured note. Restoring the account also reminds the business to continue collection efforts.

Note that Hart owes both the principal and the interest. Therefore, the entry records the full amount owed in Hart's account and credits the interest to Interest Earned. This procedure assures that the interest will be included in future efforts to collect from Hart.

## End-of-Period Adjustments

When notes receivable are outstanding at the end of an accounting period, the accrued interest should be calculated and recorded. This procedure recognizes the interest revenue when it is earned and recognizes the additional asset owned by the note's holder. For example, on December 16, Perry Company accepted a $3,000, 60-day, 12% note from a customer in granting an extension on a past-due account. When the company's accounting period ends on December 31, $14.79 of interest will have accrued on this note ($3,000 $\times$ 12% $\times$ 15/365). The following adjusting entry records this revenue:

| Dec. | 31 | Interest Receivable ........................... | 14.79 | |
|------|----|-----------------------------------------------|-------|-------|
| | | Interest Earned .......................... | | 14.79 |
| | | *To record accrued interest.* | | |

The adjusting entry causes the interest earned to appear on the income statement of the period in which it was earned. It also causes the interest receivable to appear on the balance sheet as a current asset.

## Collecting Interest Previously Accrued

When the note is collected, Perry Company's entry to record the cash receipt is:

| Feb. | 14 | Cash ...................................... | 3,059.18 | |
|------|----|----------------------------------------------|----------|----------|
| | | Interest Earned .......................... | | 44.39 |
| | | Interest Receivable ...................... | | 14.79 |
| | | Notes Receivable ........................ | | 3,000.00 |
| | | *Received payment of a note and its interest.* | | |

Observe that the entry's credit to Interest Receivable records collection of the interest accrued at the end of the previous period. Only the $44.39 of interest earned between January 1 and February 14 is recorded as revenue.

**ALTERNATIVE METHOD OF INTEREST CALCULATION**

In calculating interest in the foregoing examples, the "exact," or proper, method was used. For classroom purposes, however, instructors may prefer to use a less accurate simplified method of interest calculation in order to focus on comprehension rather than on lengthy procedural calculation. To simplify interest calculations, the following assumptions are made:

1.  Treat a year as having 360 days divided into 12 months of 30 days each.
2.  Use the exact days of the note; that is, do not give consideration to the days of grace.

Thus, interest on a 90-day, 12%, $1,500 note is calculated as:

$$\$1,500 \times \frac{12}{100} \times \frac{90}{360} = \$45$$

To facilitate the use of the alternative method of interest calculation, certain exercises and problems may be designated for use of this method.

---

**Progress Check**

**8-12**   **White Corporation purchased $7,000 of merchandise from Stamford Company on December 16, 1995. Stamford accepted White's $7,000, 90-day, 12% note as payment. Assuming Stamford's annual accounting period ends on December 31 and it does not make reversing entries, prepare entries for Stamford Company on December 16, 1995, and December 31, 1995.**

**8-13**   **Based on the facts in 8-12, prepare the March 16, 1996, entry assuming White dishonours the note.**

---

## CONVERTING RECEIVABLES INTO CASH BEFORE THEY ARE DUE

**LO 5**

Explain how receivables can be converted into cash before they are due and calculate accounts receivable turnover.

Many companies grant credit to customers and then hold the receivables until they are paid by the customers. However, some companies convert receivables into cash without waiting until they are due. This is done either by selling the receivables or by using them as security for a loan. In certain industries such as textiles and furniture, this has been a common practice for years. More recently, the practice has spread to other industries, in particular the apparel industry. More small businesses are using sale of receivables as a source of cash, especially those selling to other businesses and government agencies that often delay payment.

### Selling Accounts Receivable

A business may sell its accounts receivable to a finance company or bank. The buyer, which is called a *factor,* charges the seller a *factoring fee* and then collects the receivables as they come due. By incurring the factoring fee cost, the seller receives the cash earlier and passes the risk of bad debts to the factor. The seller also avoids the cost of billing and accounting for the receivables.

For example, assume that a business sells $20,000 of its accounts receivable and is charged a 2% factoring fee. The seller records the sale with the following entry:

| Aug. | 15 | Cash ................................. | 19,600.00 | |
|------|----|---------------------------------------|-----------|-----------|
| | | Factoring Fee Expense ...................... | 400.00 | |
| | | Accounts Receivable ..................... | | 20,000.00 |
| | | *Sold accounts receivable for cash, less a 2% factoring fee.* | | |

Factoring has become big business today with 90% of the factoring industry's business coming from textile and apparel businesses.

## Pledging Accounts Receivable as Security for a Loan

When a business borrows money and pledges its accounts receivable as security for the loan, the business records the loan with an entry such as the following:

| Aug. | 20 | Cash ..................................... | 35,000.00 | |
|------|----|-------------------------------------------|-----------|-----------|
| | | Notes Payable ........................... | | 35,000.00 |
| | | *Borrowed money on a note secured by the pledge of accounts receivable.* | | |

Under the pledging arrangement, the risk of bad debts is not transferred to the lender. The borrower retains ownership of the receivables. However, if the borrower defaults on the loan, the creditor has the right to be paid from the cash receipts as the accounts receivable are collected.

Because pledged receivables are committed as security for a loan from a particular creditor, the borrower's financial statements should disclose the fact that accounts receivable have been pledged. For example, the following note to the financial statements provides the necessary information: "Accounts receivable in the amount of $40,000 are pledged as security for a $35,000 note payable to Western National Bank."

## Discounting Notes Receivable

Notes receivable also can be converted into cash before they mature, usually by discounting the notes receivable at a bank. This discounting might be done for a number of reasons; perhaps the most common is to allow the holder to avoid having to borrow money by signing its own note. When a note receivable is discounted, the owner endorses and delivers the note to the bank in exchange for cash. The bank holds the note to maturity and then collects its maturity value from the original maker.

To illustrate, assume that on May 28, Symplex Company received a $1,200, 60-day, 12% note dated May 27 from John Owen. It held the note until June 2 and then discounted it at the bank at 14%. Since the maturity date of this note is July 26, the bank must wait 54 days after discounting the note to collect from Owen. These 54 days are called the **discount period,** which is the number of days between the date on which a note is discounted at the bank and its maturity date. The discount period is calculated for this note as follows:

| | | |
|---|---|---|
| Original period of the note in days ...... | | 60 |
| Less time held by Symplex Company: | | |
| Number of days in May .......... | 31 | |
| Less the date of the note. ........ | 27 | |
| Days held in May .............. | 4 | |
| Days held in June .............. | 2 | |
| Total days held by Symplex ....... | | 6 |
| Discount period in days ............. | | 54 |

At the end of the discount period, the bank expects to collect the maturity value of this note from Owen. The **maturity value of a note** is its principal plus any interest due on its maturity date. The maturity value of the Owen note is

---

| | |
|---|---:|
| Principal of the note . . . . . . . . . . . . . . . . | $1,200.00 |
| Interest on $1,200 for 60 days at 12% . . . . | 23.67 |
| Maturity value . . . . . . . . . . . . . . . . . . . . | $1,223.67 |

---

In calculating the interest or discount to be charged, banks traditionally base their discount on the maturity value of the note. In this case, we assume the bank has a 14% **discount rate,** which is the rate of interest it charges for lending money by discounting a note. Therefore, in discounting this note, the bank deducts 54 days' interest at 14% from the note's maturity value and gives Symplex Company the remainder. The amount of interest deducted in advance is called the **bank discount,** and the remainder is called the **proceeds of the discounted note.** The bank discount and the proceeds are calculated as follows:

---

| | |
|---|---:|
| Maturity value of the note . . . . . . . . . . . . . . . . . . . . | $1,223.67 |
| Less discount on $1,223.67 for 54 days at 14% . . . . | 25.35* |
| Proceeds . . . . . . . . . . . . . . . . . . . . . . . . . . . . . . . . . | $1,198.32 |

*$1,223.67 × .14 × ($\frac{54}{365}$) = $25.35

---

In this case, the proceeds, $1,198.32, are $1.68 less than the $1,200 principal amount of the note. Therefore, Symplex makes this entry to record the discount transaction:

| | | | | |
|---|---|---|---:|---:|
| June | 2 | Cash . . . . . . . . . . . . . . . . . . . . . . . . . . . . . . . . . . . . | 1,198.32 | |
| | | Interest Expense . . . . . . . . . . . . . . . . . . . . . . . . . . . . | 1.68 | |
| | |     Notes Receivable . . . . . . . . . . . . . . . . . . . . . . . . | | 1,200.00 |
| | | *Discounted the John Owen note for 54 days at 14%.* | | |

In this entry, note that the $23.67 of interest Symplex would have earned by holding the note to maturity is offset against the $25.35 discount charged by the bank. The $1.68 difference is debited to Interest Expense.

In the situation just described, the principal of the discounted note exceeded the proceeds. However, in other cases, the proceeds can exceed the principal. When this happens, the difference is credited to Interest Earned. For example, suppose that instead of discounting the John Owen note on June 2, Symplex discounted it on June 26 at 14%. Therefore, the discount period is 30 days, the discount is $14.08, and the proceeds of the note are $1,209.59, calculated as follows:

| Maturity value of the note . . . . . . . . . . . . . . . . . . . . . | $1,223.67 |
| Less discount on $1,223.67 for 30 days at 14% . . . . | 14.08* |
| Proceeds . . . . . . . . . . . . . . . . . . . . . . . . . . . . . . . . | $1,209.59 |

*$1,223.67 × .14 × (³⁰⁄₆₅) = $14.08

Because the proceeds exceed the principal, the transaction is recorded as follows:

| June | 26 | Cash . . . . . . . . . . . . . . . . . . . . . . . . . . . . . . . . . . | 1,209.59 | |
| | | Interest Earned . . . . . . . . . . . . . . . . . . . . . . . . . | | 9.59 |
| | | Notes Receivable . . . . . . . . . . . . . . . . . . . . . . . . | | 1,200.00 |
| | | *Discounted the John Owen note for 30 days at 14%.* | | |

Notes receivable may be discounted with recourse or without recourse. If a note is discounted with recourse and the original maker of the note fails to pay the bank when the note matures, the original payee of the note must pay. Thus, a company that discounts a note with recourse has a contingent liability until the bank is paid. A **contingent liability** is an obligation to make a future payment if, and only if, an uncertain future event actually occurs. The company should disclose the contingent liability in its financial statements with a note such as: "The company is contingently liable for a $50,000 note receivable discounted with recourse." When a note is discounted *without recourse,* the bank assumes the risk of a bad debt loss and the original payee does not have a contingent liability.

The disclosure of contingent liabilities in the notes is consistent with the **full-disclosure principle.** This principle requires financial statements (including the notes) to present all relevant information about the operations and financial position of the entity. A company should report any facts important enough to affect a statement reader's evaluation of the company's operations, financial position, or cash flows. This principle does not require companies to report excessive detail. It simply means that significant information should not be withheld and that enough information should be provided to make the reports understandable. Examples of items that are reported to satisfy the full-disclosure principle include the following:

**FULL-DISCLOSURE PRINCIPLE**

**Contingent Liabilities.** In addition to discounted notes, a company should disclose any items for which the company is contingently liable. Examples are possible additional tax assessments, debts of other parties that the company has guaranteed, and unresolved lawsuits against the company. Information about these facts helps users predict events that might affect the company.

**Long-Term Commitments under Contracts.** A company should disclose that it has signed a long-term lease requiring material annual payments, even though the obligation does not appear in the accounts. Also, a company should reveal that it has pledged certain of its assets as security for loans. These facts show statement readers that the company has restricted its flexibility. For example, the **Onex Corporation** reported the following in its December 31, 1994 Annual Report:

**15. COMMITMENTS AND CONTINGENCIES**

a) The estimated total cost to complete approved capital projects of the operating companies at December 31, 1994 is approximately $23,500,000.

b) Outstanding letters of credit of the operating companies amount to $83,300,000 at December 31, 1994. The letters of credit form part of the operating bank credit lines of the companies. Floating-charge debentures on the companies' assets and a pledge of assets form part of the security for these bank credit lines.

**Accounting Methods Used.** When more than one accounting method can be applied, a company must describe the one it uses, especially when the choice can materially affect reported net income.[8] For example, a company must describe the methods it uses to account for inventory and amortization. (These methods are explained in future chapters.) This information helps users understand how the company determines its net income.

## USING THE INFORMATION— ACCOUNTS RECEIVABLE TURNOVER

In Chapter 7, you learned how to calculate *days' sales uncollected,* which provides information about the short-term liquidity of a company. In evaluating short-term liquidity, you also may want to calculate **accounts receivable turnover.** The formula for this ratio is:

$$\text{Accounts receivable turnover} = \frac{\text{Net sales}}{\text{Average accounts receivable}}$$

Recall that days' sales uncollected relates to the accounts receivable balance at the end of the year. In contrast, notice that the denominator in the turnover formula is the average accounts receivable balance during the year. The average is often calculated as:

$$\frac{(\text{The beginning balance} + \text{The ending balance})}{2}$$

This method of estimating the average balance provides a useful result if the seasonal changes in the accounts receivable balances during the year are not too large.

Accounts receivable turnover indicates how often the company converted its average accounts receivable balance into cash during the year. Thus, a turnover of 12 suggests that the average accounts receivable balance was converted into cash 12 times during the year.

Accounts receivable turnover also provides useful information for evaluating how efficient management has been in granting credit to produce revenues. A ratio that is high in comparison with competing companies suggests that management should consider using more liberal credit terms to increase sales. A low ratio suggests that management should consider less liberal credit terms and more aggressive collection efforts to avoid an excessive investment in accounts receivable. The following data was extracted from 1994 annual reports of two companies to illustrate the calculations and comparisons:

---

[8]*CICA Handbook,* section 1505, "Disclosure of Accounting Policies," par. .09.

**Anchor Lamina Inc.** (In thousands)

$$\text{Accounts receivable turnover} = \frac{\$74,693}{(\$11,446 + \$14,471)/2} = 5.76 \text{ times}$$

**Magna International Inc.** (In millions)

$$\text{Accounts receivable turnover} = \frac{\$3,568.5}{(\$314.6 + \$536.5)/2} = 8.39 \text{ times}$$

---

**Progress Check**

**8-14** A garment manufacturer is short of cash but has substantial accounts receivable. What alternatives are available for gaining cash from the accounts receivable prior to receiving payments from the credit customers? Show the entry that would be made for each alternative.

**8-15** What does a low accounts receivable turnover ratio indicate? Should a low turnover ratio cause concern? Why or why not?

---

**SUMMARY OF THE CHAPTER IN TERMS OF LEARNING OBJECTIVES**

**LO 1. Prepare journal entries to account for temporary investments and explain how lower of cost or market is reported on such investments.** Temporary investments are recorded at cost; dividends and interest on the investments are recorded in appropriate income statement accounts. On the balance sheet, temporary investments are reported at lower of cost or market. Write-downs to market are credited to a contra account, the Allowance to Reduce Temporary Investments to Market, and the loss is reported in the income statement.

**LO 2. Prepare entries to account for credit card or debit card sales.** When credit card or debit card receipts are deposited in a bank account, the credit card expense is recorded at the time of the deposit. When credit card receipts must be submitted to the credit card company for payment, Accounts Receivable is debited for the sales amount. Then, credit card expense is recorded when cash is received from the credit card company. However, any unrecorded credit card expense should be accrued at the end of each accounting period.

**LO 3. Prepare entries to account for transactions with credit customers, including accounting for bad debts under the allowance method and the direct write-off method.** Under the allowance method, bad debts expense is recorded with an adjustment at the end of each accounting period that debits the expense and credits the Allowance for Doubtful Accounts. The amount of the adjustment is determined by focusing on either (*a*) the income statement relationship between bad debts expense and credit sales or (*b*) the balance sheet relationship between accounts receivable and the Allowance for Doubtful Accounts. The latter approach may involve using a simple percentage relationship or aging the accounts. Uncollectible accounts are written off with a debit to the Allowance for Doubtful Accounts. The direct write-off method charges Bad Debts Expense when accounts are written off as uncollectible. This method is suitable only when the amount of bad debts expense is immaterial.

**LO 4. Calculate the interest on promissory notes and prepare entries to record the receipt of promissory notes and their payment or dishonour.** Interest rates are typically stated in annual terms. When a note's time to maturity is more or less than one year, the amount of interest on the note must be determined by expressing the time as a fraction of one year and multiplying the note's principal by that fraction and the annual interest rate. Dishonoured notes are credited to Notes Receivable and debited to Accounts Receivable and to the account of the maker.

**LO 5. Explain how receivables can be converted into cash before they are due and calculate accounts receivable turnover.** To obtain cash from receivables before they are due, a company may sell accounts receivable to a factor, who charges a factoring fee. Also, a company may borrow money by signing a note payable that is secured by pledging the accounts receivable. Notes receivable may be discounted at a bank, with or without recourse. The full-disclosure principle requires companies to disclose the amount of accounts receivable that have been pledged and the contingent liability for notes discounted with recourse.

## DEMONSTRATION PROBLEM

Garden Company had the following transactions during 1996:

May    8    Purchased 300 common shares of Canadian Pacific as a temporary investment. The cost of $40 per share plus $975 in broker's commissions was paid in cash.

July   14   Wrote off a $750 account receivable arising from a sale several months ago. (Garden Company uses the allowance method.)

Aug.   15   Accepted a $2,000 down payment and a $10,000 note receivable from a customer in exchange for an inventory item that normally sells for $12,000. The note was dated August 15, bears 12% interest, and matures in six months.

Sept.  2    Sold 100 shares of Canadian Pacific at $47 per share, and continued to hold the other 200 shares. The broker's commission on the sale was $225.

Sept.  15   Received $9,850 in return for discounting without recourse the $10,000 note (dated August 15) at the local bank.

Dec.   2    Purchased 400 common shares of Magna International for $60 per share plus $1,600 in commissions. The shares are to be held as a temporary investment.

### Required

1. Prepare journal entries to record these transactions on the books of Garden Company.

2. Prepare adjusting journal entries as of December 31, 1996, for the following items (assume 1996 is the first year of operations):

   a. The market prices of the securities held by Garden Company are $48 per share for the Canadian Pacific shares, and $55 per share for the Magna International shares.

   b. Bad debts expense is estimated by an aging of accounts receivable. The unadjusted balance of the Allowance for Doubtful Accounts account is a $1,000 debit, while the required balance is estimated to be a $20,400 credit.

- Examine each item to determine which accounts are affected, and produce the needed journal entries.
- With respect to the year-end adjustments, adjust temporary investments to LCM and record the bad debts expense.

1.

| | | | | |
|---|---|---|---|---|
| May | 8 | Temporary Investments . . . . . . . . . . . . . . . . . . . . . . . . | 12,975.00 | |
| | | Cash . . . . . . . . . . . . . . . . . . . . . . . . . . . . . . . | | 12,975.00 |
| | | *Purchased 300 shares of Canadian Pacific. Cost is (300 × $40) + $975.* | | |
| July | 14 | Allowance for Doubtful Accounts . . . . . . . . . . . . . . | 750.00 | |
| | | Accounts Receivable . . . . . . . . . . . . . . . . . . . | | 750.00 |
| | | *Wrote off an uncollectible account.* | | |
| Aug. | 15 | Cash . . . . . . . . . . . . . . . . . . . . . . . . . . . . . . . . | 2,000.00 | |
| | | Notes Receivable . . . . . . . . . . . . . . . . . . . . . . . | 10,000.00 | |
| | | Sales . . . . . . . . . . . . . . . . . . . . . . . . . . . . . . | | 12,000.00 |
| | | *Sold merchandise to customer for $2,000 cash and $10,000 note receivable.* | | |
| Sept. | 2 | Cash . . . . . . . . . . . . . . . . . . . . . . . . . . . . . . . . | 4,475.00 | |
| | | Gain on Sale of Investment . . . . . . . . . . . . . . . | | 150.00 |
| | | Temporary Investments . . . . . . . . . . . . . . . . . . | | 4,325.00 |
| | | *Sold 100 shares of Canadian Pacific for $47 per share less a $225 commission. The original cost is $12,975 × 100/300.* | | |
| | 15 | Cash . . . . . . . . . . . . . . . . . . . . . . . . . . . . . . . . | 9,850.00 | |
| | | Interest Expense . . . . . . . . . . . . . . . . . . . . . . . . | 150.00 | |
| | | Notes Receivable . . . . . . . . . . . . . . . . . . . . . . | | 10,000.00 |
| | | *Discounted note receivable dated August 15.* | | |

| | |
|---|---|
| Principal . . . . . . . . . . . . . . . . . . . . . . . . . . . . . . . . . . . . . . . . . | $10,000 |
| Interest earned ($10,000 × 12% × $\frac{1}{12}$) . . . . . . . . . . . . . . . . | 100 |
| | $10,100 |
| Proceeds (given) . . . . . . . . . . . . . . . . . . . . . . . . . . . . . . . | 9,850 |
| Discounting fee . . . . . . . . . . . . . . . . . . . . . . . . . . . . . . . . | $ 250 |

Note: Months are used in the calculation because the time period of the note was expressed in months.

| Dec. | 2 | Temporary Investments ....................... | 25,600.00 | |
|---|---|---|---|---|
| | | Cash .................................. | | 25,600.00 |
| | | *Purchased 400 shares of Magna International for $60 per share plus $1,600 in commissions.* | | |
| | 31 | Loss on Temporary Investments ............... | 2,650.00 | |
| | | Allowance to Reduce Temporary Investments to Market ................................ | | 2,650.00 |
| | | *To reflect market values of temporary investments.* | | |

| Temporary Investments | Shares | Cost per Share | Total Cost | Market Value per Share | Total Market Value | Difference |
|---|---|---|---|---|---|---|
| Canadian Pacific .... | 200 | $43.25 | $ 8,650 | $48.00 | $ 9,600 | |
| Magna International .. | 400 | 64.00 | 25,600 | 55.00 | 22,000 | |
| Total ............. | | | $34,250 | | $31,600 | $2,650 |

| | 31 | Bad Debts Expense .......................... | 21,400.00 | |
|---|---|---|---|---|
| | | Allowance for Doubtful Accounts ............. | | 21,400.00 |
| | | *To adjust the allowance account from $1,000 debit balance to $20,400 credit balance.* | | |

# GLOSSARY

**Accounts Receivable Ledger** a supplementary record (also called a subsidiary ledger) having an account for each customer. p. 405

**Accounts receivable turnover** a measure of how long it takes a company to collect its accounts, calculated by dividing credit sales (or net sales) by the average accounts receivable balance. p. 426

**Aging of accounts receivable** a process of classifying accounts receivable by how long they have been outstanding for the purpose of estimating the amount of uncollectible accounts. p. 414

**Allowance for Doubtful Accounts** a contra asset account with a balance equal to the estimated amount of accounts receivable that will be uncollectible. p. 408

**Allowance method of accounting for bad debts** an accounting procedure that (1) estimates and reports bad debt expense from credit sales during the period of the sales, and (2) reports accounts receivable at the amount of cash proceeds that is expected from their collection (their estimated realizable value). p. 407

**Bad debts** accounts receivable from customers that are not collected; the amount is an expense of selling on credit. p. 407

**Bank discount** the amount of interest deducted in advance by the bank when discounting a note. p. 424

**Contingent liability** an obligation to make a future payment if, and only if, an uncertain future event actually occurs. p. 425

**Controlling account** a general ledger account with a balance that is always equal to the sum of the balances in a related subsidiary ledger. p. 407

**Debit card** card issued by a bank or similar financial institution to allow consumers to pay for purchases by a bank transfer authorized at point of sale. p. 403

**Direct write-off method of accounting for bad debts** a method that makes no attempt to estimate uncollectible accounts or bad debts expense at the end of each period; instead, when an account is found to be uncollectible, it is written off directly to Bad Debts Expense; this method is generally considered to be inferior to the allowance method. p. 416

**Discount period** the number of days between the day on which a note is discounted at the bank and its maturity date. p. 423

**Discount rate**  the rate of interest a bank charges for lending money by discounting a note. p. 424

**Dishonouring a note**  failure by a promissory note's maker to pay the amount due at maturity. p. 420

**Full-disclosure principle**  the accounting principle that requires financial statements (including the footnotes) to contain all relevant information about the operations and financial position of the entity; it also requires that the information be presented in an understandable manner. p. 425

**General Ledger**  the ledger that contains all the financial statement accounts of an organization. p. 405

**Installment accounts receivable**  accounts receivable that allow the customer to make periodic payments over several months and that typically earn interest for the seller. p. 417

**Interest**  the charge assessed for the use of money. p. 418

**Lower of cost or market (LCM)**  the required method of reporting temporary investments at the lower of the total cost of the securities (called the *portfolio*) or their total market value at the balance sheet date. p. 400

**Maker of a note**  one who signs a note and promises to pay it at maturity. p. 418

**Materiality principle**  the idea that the requirements of an accounting principle may be ignored if the effect on the financial statements is unimportant to their users. p. 417

**Maturity date of a note**  the date on which a note and any interest are due and payable. p. 418

**Maturity value of a note**  its principal plus any interest due on its maturity date. p. 424

**Payee of a note**  the one to whom a promissory note is made payable. p. 418

**Principal of a note**  the amount that the signer of a promissory note agrees to pay back when it matures, not including the interest. p. 418

**Proceeds of the discounted note**  the maturity value of a discounted note minus the interest deducted in advance by the bank. p. 424

**Promissory note**  an unconditional written promise to pay a definite sum of money on demand or at a fixed or determinable future date. p. 418

**Realizable value**  the expected proceeds from converting assets into cash. p. 408

**Short-term investments**  another name for *temporary investments*. p. 398

**Subsidiary ledger**  a collection of accounts (other than general ledger accounts) that contains the details underlying the balance of a controlling account in the General Ledger. p. 407

**Temporary investments**  investments that can be converted into cash quickly (but less quickly than cash equivalents), and that management intends to sell as a source of cash to satisfy the needs of current operations; temporary investments include such things as government or corporate debt obligations and marketable equity securities. p. 398

---

## SYNONYMOUS TERMS

**Allowance for doubtful accounts**  allowance for bad debts.

**Common shares**  common stock

**Credit sales**  charge sales.

**Debt obligations**  debt securities.

**Equity investment**  share or stock investment.

**Maker of a note**  borrower.

**Payee of a note**  lender.

**Preferred shares**  preferred stock.

**Shareholders' equity**  stockholders' equity.

**Stocks**  equity securities.

**Temporary investments**  short-term investments.

---

## QUESTIONS

1. Under what conditions should investments be classified as current assets?

2. If a temporary investment in securities cost $6,780 and was sold for $7,500, how should the difference between the two amounts be recorded?

3. On a balance sheet, what valuation must be reported for temporary investments in securities?

4. If a company purchases temporary investments in securities for the first time, and their fair (market) values fall below cost, what account is credited for the amount of the unrealized loss?

5. If temporary investments that have been written down increase in value, how is the increase in value accounted for?

6.  How do businesses benefit from allowing their customers to use credit cards?

7.  Explain why writing off a bad debt against the allowance account does not reduce the estimated realizable value of a company's accounts receivable.

8.  Why does the Bad Debts Expense account usually not have the same adjusted balance as the Allowance for Doubtful Accounts?

9.  Why does the direct write-off method of accounting for bad debts commonly fail to match revenues and expenses?

10. What is the essence of the accounting principle of materiality?

11. Why might a business prefer a note receivable to an account receivable?

12. Review the consolidated balance sheets of Geac Computer Corporation presented in Appendix I. Assuming the company records all of its receivables in one controlling account, what was the balance of that account on April 30, 1994?

# QUICK STUDY (Five-Minute Exercises)

**QS 8–1**
**(LO 1)**

On January 20, Smythe and O'Shea Co. made a temporary investment in 100 common shares of Computer Links. The purchase price was $62^1/_5$ and the broker's fee was $200. March 20, they received $2 per share in dividends. Prepare the January 20 and March 20 journal entries.

**QS 8–2**
**(LO 1)**

During this year, Balzarini Associates acquired temporary investments securities at a cost of $46,000. At December 31 year-end, these securities had a market (fair) value of $44,000.

a.  Prepare the necessary year-end adjustment.

b.  Explain how each account used in requirement *a* would affect or be reported in the financial statements.

**QS 8–3**
**(LO 2)**

Journalize the following transactions:

a.  Sold $2,000 in merchandise on Visa credit cards. The sales receipts were deposited in our business account. Visa charges us a 5% fee.

b.  Sold $5,000 on miscellaneous credit cards. Cash will be received within two weeks and a 4% fee will be charged.

**QS 8–4**
**(LO 3)**

Arnold Equipment Co. uses the allowance method to account for uncollectibles. On March 1, they wrote off a $4,000 account of a customer, Trukin Co. On May 1, they received a $1,000 payment from Trukin Co.

a.  Make the appropriate entry or entries for March 1.

b.  Make the appropriate entry or entries for May 1.

**QS 8–5**
**(LO 3)**

The year-end trial balance of Harpson Co. shows Accounts Receivable of $164,000, Allowance for Doubtful Accounts of $200 (credit), Sales of $600,000. Uncollectibles are estimated to be 1.5% of outstanding Accounts Receivable.

a.  Prepare the December 31 year-end adjustment.

b.  What amount would have been used in the year-end adjustment if the allowance account had a year-end debit balance of $100?

c.  Assume the same facts as presented above except Harpson Co. estimated uncollectibles as 1% of sales. What amount would be used in the adjustment?

On May 2, 1996, Building Corp. received a $9,000, 90-day, 12% note from a customer Sean Conrad as payment on account. Prepare the May 2 and maturity date entries assuming the note is honoured by Conrad.

QS 8–6
(LO 4)

The December 31 trial balance shows a $5,000 balance in Notes Receivable. This balance is from one note dated December 1, with a period of 120 days and 9% interest. Prepare the December 31 and maturity date entries assuming the note is honoured.

QS 8–7
(LO 4)

The following facts were extracted from Orion Corp's comparative balance sheets:

QS 8–8
(LO 5)

|  | 1996 | 1995 |
|---|---|---|
| Accounts receivable . . . . . | $ 514,000 | $ 426,000 |
| Sales (net) . . . . . . . . . . . . | 1,600,000 | 1,200,000 |

Compute the Accounts Receivable turnover for 1996.

---

# EXERCISES

Prepare general journal entries to record the following transactions involving Best Plumbing's temporary investments, all of which occurred during 1996.

Exercise 8–1
Transactions involving
temporary investments
(LO 1)

a.   On April 15, paid $90,000 to purchase $90,000 of Westside Company's short-term (60-day) notes payable, which are dated April 15, and pay interest at an 8% rate.

b.   On May 10, bought 600 shares of Algoma Steel common shares at 10 1/2 plus a $126 brokerage fee.

c.   On June 15, received a cheque from Westside Company in payment of the principal and 60 days' interest on the notes purchased in transaction a.

d.   On June 25, paid $75,000 to purchase Stockard Corporation's 7% notes payable, $75,000 principal value, due June 25, 1996.

e.   On August 16, received a $1.25 per share cash dividend on the Algoma Steel common shares purchased in transaction b.

f.   On September 3, sold 300 shares of Algoma Steel common shares for $15 per share, less a $90 brokerage fee.

g.   On December 26, received a cheque from Stockard Corporation for six months' interest on the notes purchased in transaction d.

On December 31, 1996, Compustat Company held the following temporary investments in securities:

Exercise 8–2
Recording LCM of
temporary investments
(LO 1)

|  | Cost | Market Value |
|---|---|---|
| Anchor Lamina Inc. common shares  . . . . | $37,200 | $41,100 |
| Dofasco Inc. common shares . . . . . . . . . . | 50,400 | 48,500 |
| Northern Telecom Ltd. common shares . . . | 69,600 | 63,900 |
| Union Gas Ltd. common shares . . . . . . . . | 85,500 | 84,100 |

Compustat had no temporary investments prior to 1996. Prepare the December 31 adjusting entry to record the change in market value of the investments.

**Exercise 8–3**
Adjusting the temporary investment account to reflect changes in market value
**(LO 1)**

Rexlon Company's annual accounting period ends on December 31. The cost and market value of the company's temporary investments in marketable securities were as follows:

|  | Total Cost | Total Market Value |
|---|---|---|
| Temporary investments: |  |  |
| On December 31, 1995 . . . . . . . . . . . . | $56,250 | $52,500 |
| On December 31, 1996 . . . . . . . . . . . . | 63,750 | 68,125 |

Prepare the December 31, 1996, adjusting entry to update the market values of the temporary investments.

**Exercise 8–4**
Credit card transactions
**(LO 2)**

Nickels Company allows customers to use two credit cards in charging purchases. With the Dominion Bank card, Nickels receives an immediate credit on depositing sales receipts in its chequing account. Dominion Bank assesses a 3% service charge for credit card sales. The second credit card that Nickels accepts is Canacard. Nickels sends their accumulated receipts to Canacard on a weekly basis and is paid by Canacard approximately 15 days later. Canacard charges 2.5% of sales for using its card. Prepare entries in journal form to record the following credit card transactions of Nickels Company:

May  4    Sold merchandise for $2,500, accepting the customers' Dominion Bank cards. At the end of the day, the Dominion Bank card receipts were deposited in the company's account at the bank.

     5    Sold merchandise for $550, accepting the customer's Canacard.

    12    Mailed $9,520 of credit card receipts to Canacard, requesting payment.

    28    Received Canacard's cheque for the May 12 billing, less the normal service charge.

**Exercise 8–5**
Subsidiary ledger accounts
**(LO 3)**

Littlefield Corporation recorded the following transactions during April 1996:

| Apr. | 2 | Accounts Receivable—Barbara Fowler . . . . . . . . . . . . | 2,500.00 |  |
|---|---|---|---|---|
|  |  | Sales . . . . . . . . . . . . . . . . . . . . . . . . . . . . . |  | 2,500.00 |
|  | 10 | Accounts Receivable—Robert Guerrero . . . . . . . . . . . . | 260.00 |  |
|  |  | Sales . . . . . . . . . . . . . . . . . . . . . . . . . . . . . |  | 260.00 |
|  | 18 | Accounts Receivable—Chris Layton . . . . . . . . . . . . . | 1,800.00 |  |
|  |  | Sales . . . . . . . . . . . . . . . . . . . . . . . . . . . . . |  | 1,800.00 |
|  | 23 | Sales Returns and Allowances . . . . . . . . . . . . . . . . . | 562.00 |  |
|  |  | Accounts Receivable—Chris Layton . . . . . . . . . . . |  | 562.00 |
|  | 30 | Accounts Receivable—Barbara Fowler . . . . . . . . . . . . . | 1,125.00 |  |
|  |  | Sales . . . . . . . . . . . . . . . . . . . . . . . . . . . . . |  | 1,125.00 |

**Required**

1. Open a General Ledger having T-accounts for Accounts Receivable, Sales, and Sales Returns and Allowances. Also, open a subsidiary Accounts Receivable Ledger having a T-account for each customer. Post the preceding entries to the general ledger accounts and the customer accounts.

2. List the balances of the accounts in the subsidiary ledger, total the balances, and compare the total with the balance of the Accounts Receivable controlling account.

On December 31, at the end of its annual accounting period, a company estimated its bad debts as one-fourth of 1% of its $1,240,000 of credit sales made during the year, and made an addition to its Allowance for Doubtful Accounts equal to that amount. On the following February 3, management decided the $1,390 account of Colin Smith was uncollectible and wrote it off as a bad debt. Two months later, on April 2, Smith unexpectedly paid the amount previously written off. Give the journal entries required to record these events.

**Exercise 8–6**
Allowance for doubtful accounts
**(LO 3)**

At the end of each year, a company uses the simplified balance sheet approach to estimate bad debts. On December 31, 1996, it has outstanding accounts receivable of $176,600 and estimates that 3.5% will be uncollectible. (*a*) Give the entry to record bad debts expense for 1996 under the assumption that the Allowance for Doubtful Accounts had a $1,470 credit balance before the adjustment. (*b*) Give the entry under the assumption that the Allowance for Doubtful Accounts has a $1,235 debit balance before the adjustment.

**Exercise 8–7**
Bad debts expense
**(LO 3)**

Prepare journal entries to record these transactions:

**Exercise 8–8**
Dishonour of a note
**(LO 4)**

Aug. 12  Accepted a $4,500, three-month, 10% note dated today from Clive Nelson in granting a time extension on his past-due account.

Nov. 12  Nelson dishonoured his note when presented for payment.

Dec. 31  After exhausting all legal means of collecting, wrote off the account of Nelson against the Allowance for Doubtful Accounts.

On March 31, Jester Company had accounts receivable in the amount of $82,500. Prepare journal entries to record the following transactions for April. Also, prepare any notes to the April 30 financial statements that should be reported as a result of these transactions.

**Exercise 8–9**
Selling and pledging accounts receivable
**(LO 5)**

Apr.  5  Sold merchandise to customers on credit, $23,600.

     8  Sold $6,800 of accounts receivable to Union Bank. Union Bank charges a 1.5% fee.

    17  Received payments from customers, $5,200.

    24  Borrowed $15,000 from Union Bank, pledging $22,000 of accounts receivable as security for the loan.

The following information is from the financial statements of Fine Furniture Company:

**Exercise 8–10**
Accounts receivable turnover
**(LO 5)**

|  | 1996 | 1995 | 1994 |
|---|---|---|---|
| Net sales ...................... | $1,080,000 | $860,000 | $750,000 |
| Accounts receivable (December 31)  .... | 81,900 | 80,100 | 76,800 |

Calculate Fine Furniture's accounts receivable turnover for 1995 and 1996. Compare the two results and give a possible explanation for any significant change.

---

# PROBLEMS

Ridgeway Company had no temporary investments on December 31, 1995, but had the following transactions involving temporary investments during 1996:

**Problem 8–1**
Accounting for temporary investments
**(LO 1)**

Jan. 15  Paid $250,000 to buy six-month, Treasury bills, $250,000 principal amount, 6%, dated January 15.

Feb.  7  Purchased 3,000 Royal Bank common shares at $59^{1}/_{2}$ plus a $3,570 brokerage fee.

Feb.   19    Purchased 1,200 Imperial Oil common shares at $62^1/_4$ plus a $1,494 brokerage fee.

Mar.   1    Paid $50,000 for Treasury notes, $50,000 principal amount, 9%, dated March 1, 1996, due March 1, 1997.

        26    Purchased 2,000 Abitibi Price common shares at $43^3/_8$ plus a $1,250 brokerage fee.

June   1    Received a $1.60 per share cash dividend on the Royal Bank common shares.

        17    Sold 1,200 Royal Bank common shares at 76 less a $912 brokerage fee.

July   17    Received a cheque for the principal and accrued interest on the Treasury bills that matured on July 15.

Aug.   5    Received a $3.10 per share cash dividend on the Imperial Oil common shares.

Sept.   1    Received a cheque for six months' interest on the Treasury notes purchased on March 1.

        1    Received a $1.75 per share cash dividend on the remaining Royal Bank common shares owned.

Nov.   5    Received a $2.95 per share cash dividend on the Imperial Oil common shares.

On December 31, 1996, the market prices of the equity securities held by Ridgeway Company were Royal Bank, $61^7/_8$; Imperial Oil, $50^5/_8$; and Abitibi Price, $33^1/_2$.

### Required

1.  Prepare General Journal entries to record the preceding transactions.
2.  Prepare a schedule to calculate the lower of cost or market of Ridgeway's temporary investments in marketable equity securities.
3.  Prepare adjusting entries, if necessary, to record accrued interest on Ridgeway Company's investments in debt obligations and to reduce the marketable equity securities to the lower of cost or market.

**Problem 8–2**
Credit sales and credit cards sales
**(LO 2)**

Werner Company allows a few customers to make purchases on credit. Other customers may use either of two credit cards. The First Bank deducts a 2% service charge for sales on its credit card but immediately credits the chequing account of its commercial customers when credit card receipts are deposited. Werner deposits the First Bank credit card receipts at the close of each business day.

When customers use the National Credit card, Werner Company accumulates the receipts for several days and then submits them to the National Credit Company for payment. National deducts a 3% service charge and usually pays within one week of being billed.

Werner Company completed the following transactions:

Aug.   2    Sold merchandise on credit to L. L. Terry for $985. (Terms of all credit sales are 2/15, n/60; all sales are recorded at the gross price.)

        3    Sold merchandise for $3,980 to customers who used their First Bank credit cards. Sold merchandise for $4,300 to customers who used their National Credit cards.

        5    Sold merchandise for $2,460 to customers who used their National Credit cards.

        7    Wrote off the account of R. Brown against Allowance for Doubtful Accounts. The $278 balance in Brown's account stemmed from a credit sale in December of last year.

Aug. 8 The National Credit card receipts accumulated since August 3 were submitted to the credit card company for payment.

    17 Received L. L. Terry's cheque paying for the purchase of August 2.

    19 Received the amount due from National Credit Company.

**Required**

Prepare General Journal entries to record the preceding transactions and events.

On December 31, 1996, Hallmart Company's records showed the following results for the year:

**Problem 8–3**
Estimating bad debts expense
**(LO 3)**

| | |
|---|---|
| Cash sales . . . . | $ 601,250 |
| Credit sales . . . . | 1,178,000 |

In addition, the unadjusted trial balance included the following items:

| | |
|---|---|
| Accounts receivable . . . . . . . . . . . . | $356,700 debit |
| Allowance for doubtful accounts . . . . | 5,250 debit |

**Required**

1. Prepare the adjusting entry needed on the books of Hallmart to recognize bad debts under each of the following independent assumptions:

    *a.* Bad debts are estimated to be 1% of total sales.

    *b.* Bad debts are estimated to be 2% of credit sales.

    *c.* An analysis suggests that 5% of outstanding accounts receivable on December 31, 1996, will become uncollectible.

2. Show how Accounts Receivable and the Allowance for Doubtful Accounts would appear on the December 31, 1996, balance sheet given the facts in requirement 1*(b)*.

3. Show how Accounts Receivable and the Allowance for Doubtful Accounts would appear on the December 31, 1996, balance sheet given the facts in requirement 1*(c)*.

Artex Company had credit sales of $1.3 million in 1996. On December 31, 1996, the company's Allowance for Doubtful Accounts had a credit balance of $6,700. The accountant for Artex has prepared a schedule of the December 31, 1996, accounts receivable by age, and on the basis of past experience has estimated the percentage of the receivables in each age category that will become uncollectible. This information is summarized as follows:

**Problem 8–4**
Aging accounts receivable
**(LO 3)**

| December 31, 1996 Accounts Receivable | Age of Accounts Receivable | Expected Percentage Uncollectible |
|---|---|---|
| $365,000 | Not due (under 30 days) | 1.00% |
| 177,000 | 1 to 30 days past due | 2.50 |
| 38,000 | 31 to 60 days past due | 7.75 |
| 20,000 | 61 to 90 days past due | 45.00 |
| 6,000 | over 90 days past due | 70.00 |

**Required**

*Preparation component:*

1. Calculate the amount that should appear in the December 31, 1996, balance sheet as the Allowance for Doubtful Accounts.

2. Prepare the journal entry to record bad debts expense for 1996.

*Analysis component:*

3.  On June 30, 1997, Artex concluded that a customer's $1,875 receivable (created in 1996) was uncollectible and that the account should be written off. What effect will this action have on Artex's 1997 net income? Explain your answer.

**Problem 8–5**
Recording accounts receivable transactions and bad debt adjustments **(LO 3)**

Gilcrest Company began operations on January 1, 1996. During the next two years, the company completed a number of transactions involving credit sales, accounts receivable collections, and bad debts. These transactions are summarized as follows:

### 1996

*a.*  Sold merchandise on credit for $817,500, terms n/30.

*b.*  Wrote off uncollectible accounts receivable in the amount of $12,500.

*c.*  Received cash of $476,500 in payment of outstanding accounts receivable.

*d.*  In adjusting the accounts on December 31, concluded that 1.5% of the outstanding accounts receivable would become uncollectible.

### 1997

*e.*  Sold merchandise on credit for $1,017,000, terms n/30.

*f.*  Wrote off uncollectible accounts receivable in the amount of $19,200.

*g.*  Received cash of $788,500 in payment of outstanding accounts receivable.

*h.*  In adjusting the accounts on December 31, concluded that 1.5% of the outstanding accounts receivable would become uncollectible.

**Required**

Prepare journal entries to record the 1996 and 1997 summarized transactions of Gilcrest and the adjusting entries to record bad debts expense at the end of each year.

**Problem 8–6**
Journalizing notes receivable and bad debt transactions **(LO 4)**

Prepare General Journal entries to record these transactions and events experienced by Ethyl Company:

Jan.   8   Accepted a $4,250, 60-day, 10% note dated this day in granting a time extension on the past-due account of Pat Wilkins.

Mar.   9   Pat Wilkins paid the maturity value of his $4,250 note.

11   Accepted a $4,950, 60-day, 11% note dated this day in granting a time extension on the past-due account of Paula Mathers.

May   10   Paula Mathers dishonoured her note when presented for payment.

17   Accepted a $3,000, 90-day, 13% note dated May 15 in granting a time extension on the past-due account of Elmer Mayes.

25   Discounted the Elmer Mayes note at the bank at 15%.

Aug.   16   Because the company had not received a notice protesting the Elmer Mayes note, assumed that it had been paid.

17   Accepted a $2,250, 60-day, 11% note dated August 15 in granting a time extension on the past-due account of Steve Rollins.

Sept.   8   Discounted the Steve Rollins note at the bank at 13%.

Oct.   15   Received notice protesting the Steve Rollins note. Paid the bank the maturity value of the note plus a $30 protest fee.

16   Received a $6,150, 60-day, 12% note dated this day from Martha Watson in granting a time extension on her past-due account.

Nov. 15  Discounted the Martha Watson note at the bank at 15%.

Dec. 16  Received notice protesting the Martha Watson note. Paid the bank the maturity value of the note plus a $30 protest fee.

27  Received payment from Martha Watson of the maturity value of her dishonoured note, the protest fee, and interest on both for 12 days beyond maturity at 12%.

31  Wrote off the accounts of Paula Mathers and Steve Rollins against Allowance for Doubtful Accounts.

Prepare General Journal entries to record the following transactions of Waterloo Company:

**Problem 8–7**
Analysis and journalizing of notes receivable transactions
**(LO 5)**

1996

Dec. 11  Accepted a $7,500, 60-day, 12% note dated this day in granting Fred Calhoun a time extension on his past-due account.

31  Made an adjusting entry to record the accrued interest on the Fred Calhoun note.

31  Closed the Interest Earned account.

1997

Jan. 10  Discounted the Fred Calhoun note at the bank at 14%.

Feb. 10  Received notice protesting the Fred Calhoun note. Paid the bank the maturity value of the note plus a $30 protest fee.

Mar. 5  Accepted a $2,250, 11%, 60-day note dated this day in granting a time extension on the past-due account of Donna Reed.

29  Discounted the Donna Reed note at the bank at 15%.

May 7  Because no notice protesting the Donna Reed note had been received, assumed that it had been paid.

June 9  Accepted a $3,375, 60-day, 10% note dated this day in granting a time extension on the past-due account of Jack Miller.

Aug. 8  Received payment of the maturity value of the Jack Miller note.

11  Accepted a $4,000, 60-day, 10% note dated this day in granting Roger Addison a time extension on his past-due account.

31  Discounted the Roger Addison note at the bank at 13%.

Oct. 12  Received notice protesting the Roger Addison note. Paid the bank the maturity value of the note plus a $30 protest fee.

Nov. 19  Received payment from Roger Addison of the maturity value of his dishonoured note, the protest fee, and interest on both for 40 days beyond maturity at 10%.

Dec. 23  Wrote off the Fred Calhoun account against Allowance for Doubtful Accounts.

The Doreen Granger Company had some surplus cash balances on hand and projected that excess cash would continue to be available over the next few years. Following is a series of events and other facts relevant to the temporary investment activity of the company:

**Problem 8–8**
Entries and LCM application for temporary investments
**(LO 1)**

1996

May 8  Purchased 1,000 shares of BCE at $40.40 plus $1,515 commission.

July 14  Purchased 2,000 shares of Dupont A at $32.40 plus $2,430 commission.

Sept. 29  Purchased 3,000 shares of Molson A at $19.20 plus $2,160 commission.

Dec. 31  These per share market values were known for the shares in the portfolio: BCE, $50.00; Dupont A, $29.00; Molson A, $14.40.

1997

Feb.   4    Sold 2,000 shares of Dupont A at $20.20 less $1,515 commission.

July   12    Sold 3,000 shares of Molson A, at $17.20 less $1,935 commission.

Aug.   17    Purchased 4,000 shares of Oshawa A at $13.60 plus $2,040 commission.

Dec.   15    Purchased 2,400 shares of Imperial Oil at $40.60 plus $3,654 commission.

        31    These per share market values were known for the shares in the portfolio: BCE, $60.60; Oshawa A, $8.20; Imperial Oil, $34.80.

1998

Jan.   2    Purchased 4,000 shares of Petro Canada at $7.20 plus $1,080 commission.

Feb.   2    Sold 4,000 shares of Oshawa A at $19.80 less $2,970 commission.

May   18    Sold 1,000 shares of BCE at $72.40 less $2,715 commission.

Nov.   28    Purchased 1,000 shares of The Bay at $25.60 plus $960 commission.

        30    Sold 2,400 shares of Imperial Oil at $30.40 less $2,736 commission.

Dec.   31    These per share market values were known for the shares in the portfolio: Petro Canada, $11.40; The Bay, $18.00.

**Required**

1. Prepare journal entries to record the events and any year-end adjustments needed to record the application of the lower of cost or market method of accounting for temporary investments.
2. Prepare a schedule that shows how the temporary investment portfolio would be described on the balance sheet at the end of each of the three years.
3. Prepare a schedule that shows the components of income (gains and losses, including LCM effects) from these investment activities, and their total effect, for each of the three years. Ignore dividends.

**Problem 8–9**
**Analytical essay**
**(LO 1)**

Cloron Company did not own any temporary investments prior to 1996. After purchasing some temporary investments in 1996, the company's accountant made the following December 31, 1996, adjusting entry:

| Dec. | 31 | Loss on Market Decline of Temporary Investments .... | 2,750.00 | |
|---|---|---|---|---|
| | | Allowance to Reduce Temporary Investments to Market ............................... | | 2,750.00 |
| | | *To adjust temporary investments portfolio to the LCM amount.* | | |

When Cloron's accountant reviewed the year-end adjustments with an office manager of the company, the accountant commented that the previous adjustment might have been different if the company had owned temporary investments on December 31, 1995. The office manager thought the accountant must be confused. The manager said that the December 31, 1996, adjustment was supposed to record a gain that occurred during 1996, and therefore should not be affected by any events that occurred during 1995.

**Required**

Explain why the accountant's comment is correct.

Review the facts about Hallmart Company in Problem 8–3.

**Problem 8–10**
Analytical essay
**(LO 3)**

**Required**

1.  Recall that Allowance for Doubtful Accounts is a contra asset account. Nevertheless, Hallmart's unadjusted trial balance shows that this account has a $5,250 debit balance. Explain how this contra asset account could have a debit balance.
2.  In Problem 8–3, requirement 1(c) indicates that 5% of the outstanding accounts receivable ($356,700 × 5% = $17,835) will become uncollectible. Given this conclusion, explain why the adjusting entry should not include a $17,835 credit to Accounts Receivable.

Griffen Company had no temporary investments on December 31, 1996, but had the following transactions involving temporary investments during 1997:

**Problem 8–11**
Accounting for temporary investments
**(LO 1)**

Jan.  9   Paid $60,000 to buy six-month Certificate of Deposit, $60,000 principal amount, 8%, dated January 9.

Feb.  2   Purchased 800 shares of Inco common shares at 35½ plus a $400 brokerage fee.

     15   Purchased 600 shares of Seagram common shares at 64¼ plus a $300 brokerage fee.

Mar.  2   Paid $45,000 for Canada Savings Bonds, $45,000 principal amount, 9%, dated March 2, 1997, due March 2, 2001.

     16   Purchased 1,200 shares of Nynex common shares at 55⅛ plus a $975 brokerage fee.

June  2   Received a $0.45 per share cash dividend on the Inco common shares.

     16   Sold 600 shares of Inco common shares at 37 less a $300 brokerage fee.

July  11  Received a cheque for the principal and accrued interest on the Certificate of Deposit that matured on July 9.

Aug.  13  Received a $0.55 per share cash dividend on the Seagram common shares.

Sept. 2   Received a cheque for six months' interest on the Canada Savings Bonds purchased on March 2.

      2   Received a $0.45 per share cash dividend on the remaining Inco common shares owned by Griffen Company.

Nov.  13  Received a $0.55 per share cash dividend on the Seagram common shares.

   On December 31, 1997, the market prices of the equity securities held by Griffen Company were: Inco, 38½; Seagram, 63; and Nynex, 47⅞.

**Required**

1.  Prepare general journal entries to record the above transactions.
2.  Prepare a schedule to calculate the lower of cost or market of Griffen's temporary investments in marketable equity securities.
3.  Prepare adjusting entries, if necessary, to record accrued interest on Griffen Company's investments in debt obligations and to reduce the marketable equity securities to the lower of cost or market.

**Problem 8–12**
Credit sales and credit card sales
**(LO 2, 3)**

Chilton Company allows a few customers to make sales on credit. Other customers may use either of two credit cards. The Canadex Bank makes a 3% service charge for sales on its credit card but immediately credits the chequing account of its commercial customers when credit card receipts are deposited. Chilton deposits the Canadex Bank credit card receipts at the close of each business day.

When customers use the Western Credit Card, Chilton Company accumulates the receipts for two or three days and then submits them to the Western Credit Company for payment. Western makes a 4% service charge and usually pays within one week of being billed.

Chilton Company completed the following transactions:

Apr. 4    Sold merchandise on credit to Joe Blake for $1,750. (Terms of all credit sales are 2/15, n/60.)

5    Sold merchandise for $3,250 to customers who used their Canadex Bank credit cards. Sold merchandise for $3,600 to customers who used their Western credit cards.

6    Sold merchandise for $2,400 to customers who used their Western credit cards.

8    Wrote off the account of T. Kurth against Allowance for Doubtful Accounts. The $500 balance in Kurth's account stemmed from a credit sale in August of last year.

9    The Western credit card receipts accumulated since April 4 were submitted to the credit card company for payment.

19    Received Joe Blake's cheque paying for the purchase of April 4.

20    Received the amount due from Western Credit Company.

**Required**

Prepare general journal entries to record the above transactions.

**Problem 8–13**
Estimating bad debts expense
**(LO 3)**

On December 31, 1996, Defore Corporation's unadjusted trial balance included the following items:

|  | Debit | Credit |
|---|---|---|
| Cash sales . . . . . . . . . . . . . . . . . . . . . |  | $360,000 |
| Credit sales . . . . . . . . . . . . . . . . . . . . |  | 585,000 |
| Accounts receivable . . . . . . . . . . . . . . | $210,000 |  |
| Allowance for doubtful accounts . . . . . . |  | 200 |

**Required**

1. Prepare the adjusting entry on the books of Defore Corporation to estimate bad debts under each of the following independent assumptions:

    a.   Bad debts are estimated to be 2% of total sales.

    b.   Bad debts are estimated to be 3.5% of credit sales.

    c.   An analysis suggests that 7.5% of outstanding accounts receivable on December 31, 1996, will become uncollectible.

2. Show how Accounts Receivable and Allowance for Doubtful Accounts would appear on the December 3, 1996, balance sheet given the facts in 1. b above.

3. Show how Accounts Receivable and Allowance for Doubtful Accounts would appear on the December 31, 1996, balance sheet given the facts in 1. c above.

Software Corporation had credit sales of $6.5 million in 1996. On December 31, 1996, the company's Allowance for Doubtful Accounts had a debit balance of $7,400. The accountant for Software Corporation has prepared a schedule of the December 31, 1996, accounts receivable by age, and on the basis of past experience has estimated the percentage of the receivables in each age category that will become uncollectible. This information is summarized as follows:

**Problem 8–14**
Aging accounts receivable
**(LO 3)**

| December 31, 1996, Accounts Receivable | Age of Accounts Receivable | Uncollectible Percent Expected |
|---|---|---|
| $600,000 | Not due (under 30 days) | 2 |
| 300,000 | 1 to 30 days past due | 3 |
| 70,000 | 31 to 60 days past due | 15 |
| 40,000 | 61 to 90 days past due | 40 |
| 32,000 | over 90 days past due | 80 |

**Required**

1. Calculate the amount that should appear in the December 31, 1996, balance sheet as allowance for doubtful accounts.
2. Prepare the general journal entry to record bad debts expense for 1996.
3. On May 21, 1997, Software Corporation concluded that customer's $9,600 accounts receivable was uncollectible and that the account should be written off. What effect will this action have on Software Corporation's 1997 net income? Explain your answer.

After beginning operations on January 1, 1995, Johanson Company completed a number of transactions during 1995 and 1996 that involved credit sales, accounts receivable collections, and bad debts. These transactions are summarized as follows:

**Problem 8–15**
Recording accounts
receivable transactions
and bad debt adjustments
**(LO 3)**

1995

a. Sold merchandise on credit for $157,800, terms n/30.
b. Received cash of $128,900 in payment of outstanding accounts receivable.
c. Wrote off uncollectible accounts receivable in the amount of $300.
d. In adjusting the accounts on December 31, concluded that 1.5% of the outstanding accounts receivable would become uncollectible.

1996

a. Sold merchandise on credit for $198,800, terms n/30.
b. Received cash of $165,300 in payment of outstanding accounts receivable.
c. Wrote off uncollectible accounts receivable in the amount of $700.
d. In adjusting the accounts on December 31, concluded that 1.5% of the outstanding accounts receivable would become uncollectible.

**Required**

Prepare general journal entries to record the 1995 and 1996 summarized transactions of Johanson Company and the adjusting entries to record bad debts expense at the end of each year.

Prepare entries in general journal form to record these transactions by Wheat Company:

**Problem 8–16**
Journalizing notes
receivable and bad debts
transactions
**(LO 3, 4, 5)**

Jan. 10 Accepted a $3,000, 60-day, 12% note dated this day in granting a time extension on the past-due account of David Huerta.

Mar. 14 David Huerta dishonoured his note when presented for payment.

| | | |
|---|---|---|
| Mar. | 19 | Accepted a $2,100, 90-day, 10% note dated this day in granting a time extension on the past-due account of Rose Jones. |
| | 28 | Discounted the Rose Jones note at the bank at 16%. |
| June | 20 | Since notice protesting the Rose Jones note had not been received, assumed the note had been paid. |
| | 27 | Accepted $700 in cash and a $1,300, 60-day, 12% note dated this day in granting a time extension on the past-due account of Jake Thomas. |
| July | 24 | Discounted the Jake Thomas note at the bank at 14%. |
| Aug. | 29 | Received notice protesting the Jake Thomas note. Paid the bank the maturity value of the note plus a $20 protest fee. |
| Sept. | 4 | Accepted a $1,500, 60-day, 11% note dated this day in granting a time extension on the past-due account of Ginnie Bauer. |
| Oct. | 13 | Discounted the Ginnie Bauer note at the bank at 14%. |
| Nov. | 6 | Received notice protesting the Ginnie Bauer note. Paid the bank the maturity value of the note plus a $20 protest fee. |
| Dec. | 6 | Received payment from Ginnie Bauer of the maturity value of her dishonoured note, the protest fee, and interest at 11% on both for 30 days beyond maturity. |
| | 28 | Decided the accounts of David Huerta and Jake Thomas were uncollectible and write them off against Allowance for Doubtful Accounts. |

# PROVOCATIVE PROBLEMS

**Provocative Problem 8–1**
Business communications case
**(LO 3)**

As the accountant for JWest Company, you recently attended a sales managers' meeting devoted to a discussion of the company's credit policies. At the meeting, you reported that bad debts expense for the past year was estimated to be $35,000 and accounts receivable at the end of the year amounted to $645,000 less a $21,000 allowance for doubtful accounts. Chris Albertson, one of the sales managers, expressed confusion over the fact that bad debts expense and the allowance for doubtful accounts were different amounts. To save time at the meeting, you agreed to discuss the matter with Albertson after the meeting.

Because the meeting lasted longer than expected, Albertson had to leave early to catch a plane back to his sales district. As a result, you need to write a memorandum to him explaining why a difference in bad debts expense and the allowance for doubtful accounts is not unusual. (Assume that the company estimates bad debts expense to be 2% of sales.)

**Provocative Problem 8–2**
Financial reporting problem
**(LO 3)**

Builders Depot has been in business for six years and has used the direct write-off method of accounting for bad debts. The following information is available from the accounting records for the first five years:

| | 1995 | 1994 | 1993 | 1992 | 1991 |
|---|---|---|---|---|---|
| Sales ............... | $2,243,000 | $1,170,000 | $2,600,000 | $3,400,000 | $950,000 |
| Net income ............ | 336,200 | 175,000 | 390,200 | 509,500 | 142,200 |
| Bad debts written off | | | | | |
| during year .......... | 13,940 | 18,410 | 47,960 | 11,720 | 2,100 |
| Bad debts by year of sale* . | 21,300 | 11,990 | 29,790 | 32,910 | 10,640 |

*Results from classifying bad debt losses so that the losses appear in the same years as the sales that produced them. For example, the $21,300 for 1995 includes $12,500 of bad debts that became uncollectible during 1996.

You are the manager of Builders Depot and want to change the method of accounting for bad debts from the direct write-off method to the allowance method. Kelly Skyles, the president of the company, feels this is not necessary. Prepare a five-year schedule for Skyles showing:

a. Net income if bad debts expense is defined to be bad debts by year of sale.

b. The dollar amount of difference between net income using the direct write-off method and the answer to requirement *a*.

c. The answer to requirement *b* as a percentage of the answer to requirement *a*.

d. Bad debts by year of sale as a percentage of sales.

e. Bad debts written off during the year as a percentage of sales.

Use the schedule to support your argument for using the allowance method to account for bad debts.

Refer to the financial statements and related disclosures from Geac Computer Corporation Ltd.'s 1994 annual report in Appendix I. Based on your examination of this information, answer the following:

**Provocative Problem 8–3**
Financial statement analysis case
**(LO 1, 5)**

**Geac**

1. Geac's most liquid assets include cash and short-term investments, and accounts receivable. What total amount of those assets did Geac have on April 30, 1994?

2. Express Geac's total liquid assets as of April 30, 1994, (as previously defined) as a percentage of current liabilities. Do the same for 1993. Comment on Geac's ability to satisfy current liabilities at the end of fiscal year 1994, as compared to the end of fiscal year 1993.

3. Calculate Geac's accounts receivable turnover for 1994.

## ANALYTICAL AND REVIEW PROBLEMS

Shortcash Company required a loan of $15,000 and was offered two alternatives by the Security Bank. The alternatives are:

**A & R Problem 8–1***

a. Shortcash would give the bank a one-year $15,000 note payable, dated November 1, 1996, with interest at 9%.

b. Shortcash would give the bank a one-year $16,350 noninterest-bearing note payable dated November 1, 1996. The bank would precalculate and deduct $1,350 of interest from the face amount of the note.

**Required**

1. Prepare all the necessary entries (including repayment on October 31, 1997) with regard to alternative *a*. Assume that Shortcash Company's fiscal year ends December 31.

2. Repeat the journal entries for alternative *b*.

_____

*Interest to be calculated on a monthly basis.

**A & R Problem 8–2**    The Tor-Mont Company has been in business three years and has applied for a significant bank loan. Prior to considering the applications, the bank asks you to conduct an audit for the last three years. Concerning accounts receivable, you find that the company has been charging off receivables as they finally proved uncollectible and treating them as expenses at the time of write-off.

Your investigation indicates that receivable losses have approximated (and can be expected to approximate) 2% of net sales. Until this first audit, the company's sales and direct receivable write-off experience was:

| Year of Sales | Amount of Sales | Accounts Written Off In | | |
|---|---|---|---|---|
| | | 1993 | 1994 | 1995 |
| 1993 | $450,000 | $1,500 | $6,000 | $1,800 |
| 1994 | 600,000 | — | 3,000 | 7,200 |
| 1995 | 750,000 | — | — | 4,500 |

**Required**

1. Indicate the amount by which net income was understated or overstated each year because the company used the direct write-off method rather than the generally acceptable allowance method.

2. Prepare all the entries for each of the three years that would have been made if Tor-Mont had used the allowance method from the start of the business.

3. Which of the entries in (2) are year-end adjusting entries?

# CONCEPT TESTER

Test your understanding of the concepts introduced in this chapter by completing the following crossword puzzle.

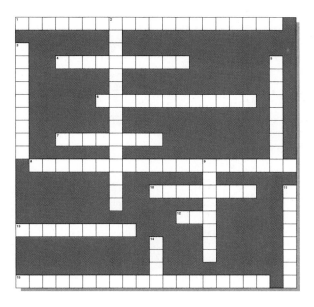

**Across Clues**

1. Securities which management intends to convert to cash in the near future (2 words).

4. The requirement that information be presented in an understandable manner (2nd of 3 words; also see 14 down, 13 across).

6. The point at which notes are due (2 words).

7. Amounts that are not collected (2 words).

8. The idea that some things may be ignored if they will not affect the decisions of those using financial statements (2 words).

10. A contra asset that estimates uncollectible amounts (3rd of 4 words; also see 3 down, 12 across, 11 down).

12. A contra asset that estimates uncollectible amounts (2nd of 4 words; also see 3 down, 10 across, 11 down).

13. The requirement that information be presented in an understandable manner (3rd of 3 words; also see 14 down, 4 across).

15. An obligation that is dependent upon the occurrence of a future event (2 words).

**Down Clues**

2. The expected proceeds from converting assets to cash (2 words).

3. A contra asset that estimates uncollectible amounts (1st of 4 words; also see 12 across, 10 across, 11 down).

5. The portion of a note which does not include interest.

9. The charge for the use of money.

11. A contra asset that estimates uncollectible amounts (4th of 4 words; also see 3 down, 12 across, 10 across).

14. The requirement that information be presented in an understandable manner (1st of 3 words; also see 4 across, 13 across).

# ANSWERS TO PROGRESS CHECKS

8–1  Temporary investments are reported at lower of cost or market; thus, they may be reported at either cost or market.

8–2  Normally once a period, at the balance sheet date.

8–3  The increase can be reversed and a recovery (gain) is recognized up to the original cost of the investments.

8–4  If cash is received as soon as copies of credit card sales receipts are deposited in the bank, the business debits Cash at the time of the sale. If the business does not receive payment until after it submits the receipts to the credit card company, it debits Accounts Receivable at the time of the sale.

8–5  The credit card expenses are recorded when the cash is received from the credit card company; however, they are incurred at the time of the related sales.

8–6  An adjusting entry must be made to satisfy the matching principle. The credit card expense must be reported in the same period as the sale.

8–7  Bad debts expense must be matched with the sales that gave rise to the accounts receivable. This requires that companies estimate bad debts before they learn which accounts are uncollectible.

8–8  Realizable value.

8–9  The estimated amount of bad debts expense cannot be credited to the Accounts Receivable account because the specific customer accounts that will prove uncollectible cannot be identified and removed from the subsidiary Accounts Receivable Ledger. If the controlling account were credited directly, its balance would not equal the sum of the subsidiary account balances.

8–10
1995
Dec. 31  Bad Debts Expense    5,702
　　　　Allow. for
　　　　　Doubtful Acc.              5,702

8–11
1996
Jan. 10  Allowance for
　　　　　Doubtful Accounts    300
　　　　Acc. Rec.—
　　　　　Felix Arthur                  300

Apr. 12  Acc. Rec.—
　　　　　Felix Arthur         300
　　　　Allow. for
　　　　　Doubtful Acc.                 300

　　12  Cash                 300
　　　　Acc. Rec.—
　　　　　Felix Arthur                  300

8–12
1995
Dec. 16  Notes Receivable     7,000
　　　　Sales                        7,000

Dec. 31  Interest Receivable      35
　　　　Interest Earned                 35
　　　　$7,000 \times 12\% \times 15/365$

8–13
1996
Mar. 16  Acc. Rec.—
　　　　　White Corp.        7,140
　　　　Interest Earned                105
　　　　Interest Rec.                   35
　　　　Notes Rec.                   7,000

8–14  Alternatives are (1) selling their accounts receivable to a factor, and (2) pledging the accounts receivable as security for a loan. The entries to record these transactions would take the following form:
(1) Cash
　　Factoring Fee Expense
　　　Accounts Receivable
(2) Cash
　　　Notes Payable

8–15  A low turnover ratio indicates that the company takes longer to convert its accounts receivables to cash. This should cause concern if the turnover ratio is much lower than the average in the industry.

# Inventories and Cost of Goods Sold

Merchandising companies buy and sell large quantities and varieties of goods. These activities lead to complex accounting problems in measuring profits. Companies use several different methods to develop information about their inventories and cost of goods sold.

aren White and Mark Smith know that there are different accounting policies that can be chosen. Their instructor indicated that the choice of one acceptable accounting approach over another can have a dramatic impact on net income. To illustrate, Moore Corporation Limited, a Canadian company that is the world's largest designer and manufacturer of business forms and related products, systems, and services, provided the following information about inventories in its 1994 annual report.

**Notes to Consolidated Financial Statements**

## 1. Summary of accounting policies (in part)

### Inventories:

Inventories of raw materials and work in process are valued at the lower of cost and replacement cost and inventories of finished goods at the lower of cost and net realizable value. The cost of the principal raw material inventories and the raw material content of finished goods inventories in the United States is determined on the last-in, first-out basis. The cost of all other inventories is determined on the first-in, first-out basis.

## 2. Inventories (in thousands)

| | 1994 | 1993 |
|---|---|---|
| Raw materials | $ 74,161 | $ 77,141 |
| Work in process | 27,280 | 26,321 |
| Finished goods | 131,883 | 141,827 |
| Other | 11,178 | 10,058 |
| | $244,502 | $255,347 |

The excess of the current cost over the last-in, first-out cost of those inventories determined on the latter basis is approximately $40,700,000 at December 31, 1994 (1993–$43,370,000).

If Moore Corporation used the current cost for its US inventories instead of the last-in, first-out basis, its 1994 net income would be increased by $40.7 million. The reason for using the last-in, first-out, method is to reduce the income tax liability for its US operations. Revenue Canada will not allow the use of the last-in, first-out method for Canadian operations.

## LEARNING OBJECTIVES

**After studying Chapter 9, you should be able to:**

1. Describe *(a)* how the matching principle relates to accounting for merchandise, *(b)* the types of items that should be included in merchandise inventory, and *(c)* the elements that make up the cost of merchandise.

2. Calculate the cost of an inventory based on *(a)* specific invoice prices, *(b)* weighted-average cost, *(c)* FIFO, and *(d)* LIFO, and explain the financial statement effects of choosing one method over the others.

3. Explain the effect of an inventory error on the income statements of the current and succeeding years.

4. Describe perpetual inventory systems and prepare entries to record merchandise transactions and maintain subsidiary inventory records under a perpetual inventory system.

5. Calculate the lower-of-cost-or-market amount of an inventory.

6. Use the retail method and the gross profit method to estimate an inventory and calculate merchandise turnover and days' stock on hand.

7. Define or explain the words and phrases listed in the chapter glossary.

The operations of merchandising businesses involve the purchase and resale of tangible goods. In Chapter 5, when we first introduced the topic of accounting for merchandisers, we left several important matters for later consideration. In this chapter, we return to the topic and examine the methods businesses use at the end of each period to assign dollar amounts to merchandise inventory and to cost of goods sold. The principles and procedures that we explain in this chapter are used in department stores, grocery stores, automobile dealerships, and any other businesses that purchase goods for resale. Since these procedures affect the reported amounts of income, assets, and equity, understanding the fundamental concepts of inventory accounting will enhance your ability to use and interpret financial statements.

The assets that a business buys and holds for resale are called *merchandise inventory*. As a rule, the items held as merchandise inventory are sold within one year or one operating cycle. Therefore, merchandise inventory is a current asset, usually the largest current asset on the balance sheet of a merchandiser.

## MATCHING MERCHANDISE COSTS WITH REVENUES

Accounting for inventories affects both the balance sheet and the income statement. However, "the method for determining cost should be one that results in the fairest matching of costs against revenues regardless of whether or not the method corresponds to the [order in which the goods leave the firm]."[1] The matching process is already a familiar topic. For inventories, it consists of deciding how much of the cost of the goods that were available for sale during a period should be deducted from the period's revenue and how much should be carried forward as inventory to be matched against a future period's revenue.

---

[1] *CICA Handbook,* section 3030, "Inventories," par. .09.

In a periodic inventory system, when the cost of goods available for sale is allocated between cost of goods sold and ending inventory, the key problem is assigning a cost to the ending inventory. Remember, however, that by assigning a cost to the ending inventory, you are also determining cost of goods sold. This is true because the ending inventory is subtracted from the cost of goods available for sale to determine cost of goods sold.

The following schedule illustrates this relationship:

**LO 1**

Describe *(a)* how the matching principle relates to accounting for merchandise; *(b)* the types of items that should be included in merchandise inventory; and *(c)* the elements that make up the cost of merchandise.

> Cost of goods sold:
>
>    Beginning inventory
> + Purchases
> = Cost of goods available for sale
> − Ending inventory
> = Cost of goods sold

## ITEMS TO INCLUDE IN MERCHANDISE INVENTORY

The merchandise inventory of a business includes all goods owned by the business and held for sale, regardless of where the goods may be located at the time inventory is counted. In applying this rule, most items present no problem. All that is required is to see that all items are counted, that nothing is omitted, and that nothing is counted more than once. However, goods in transit, goods sold but not delivered, goods on consignment, and obsolete and damaged goods require special attention.

Should merchandise be included in the inventory of a business if the goods are in transit from a supplier to a business on the date the business takes an inventory? The answer to this question depends on whether the rights and risks of ownership have passed from the supplier to the purchaser. If ownership has passed to the purchaser, they should be included in the purchaser's inventory. If the buyer is responsible for paying the freight charges, ownership usually passes as soon as the goods are loaded on the means of transportation. (As mentioned in Chapter 5, the terms would be FOB the seller's factory or warehouse.) On the other hand, if the seller is to pay the freight charges, ownership passes when the goods arrive at their destination (FOB destination).

Goods on consignment are goods shipped by their owner (known as the **consignor**) to another person or firm (called the **consignee**) who is to sell the goods for the owner. Consigned goods belong to the consignor and should appear on the consignor's inventory. For example, a company pays sports celebrities such as Silken Laumann, Wayne Gretzky and Roberto Alomar to sign memorabilia. The autographed baseballs, jerseys, photos, and so on, are then offered to the shopping networks on consignment as well as sold through catalogs and dealers.

Damaged goods and deteriorated or obsolete goods should not be counted in the inventory if they are not salable. If such goods can be sold at a reduced price, they should be included in the inventory at a conservative estimate of their **net realizable value** (sales price less the cost of making the sale). Thus, the accounting period in which the goods deteriorated, were damaged, or became obsolete suffers the resultant loss.

## ELEMENTS OF MERCHANDISE COST

As applied to merchandise, cost means the sum of the expenditures and charges directly or indirectly incurred in bringing an article to its existing condition and location.[2] Therefore, the cost of an inventory item includes the invoice price, less any discount, plus any additional or incidental costs necessary to put the item into place and condition for sale. The additional costs may include import duties, transportation-in, storage, insurance, and any other related costs such as those incurred during an aging process (for example, the aging of wine).

All of these costs should be included in the cost of merchandise. When calculating the cost of a merchandise inventory, however, some concerns do not include the incidental costs of acquiring merchandise. They price the inventory on the basis of invoice prices only. As a result, the incidental costs are allocated to cost of goods sold during the period in which they are incurred.

In theory, a share of each incidental cost should be assigned to every unit purchased. This causes a portion of each to be carried forward in the inventory to be matched against the revenue of the period in which the inventory is sold. However, the effort of computing costs on such a precise basis may outweigh the benefit from the extra accuracy. Therefore, many businesses take advantage of the *materiality principle* and charge such costs to cost of goods sold.

## TAKING AN ENDING INVENTORY

As you learned in Chapter 5, when a *periodic inventory system* is used, the dollar amount of the ending inventory is determined as follows: count the units of each product on hand, multiply the count for each product by its cost per unit, and add the costs for all products. In making the count, items are less likely to be counted twice or omitted from the count if you use prenumbered **inventory tickets** like the one in Illustration 9–1.

Before beginning the inventory count, a sufficient number of the tickets, at least one for each product on hand, is issued to the employees who make the count. Next, the employees count the quantity of each product. From the count and the price tag attached to the merchandise, the required inventory tickets are filled in and attached to the counted items. By the time the count is completed, inventory tickets should have been attached to all counted items. After checking for uncounted items, the employees remove the tickets and send them to the accounting department. To ensure that no ticket is lost or left attached to merchandise, the accounting department verifies that all the prenumbered tickets issued have been returned.

In the accounting department, the unit and cost data on the tickets are aggregated by multiplying the number of units of each product by its unit cost. This gives the dollar amount of each product in the inventory and the total for all the products is the dollar total of the inventory.

The use of computers has made physical stocktaking somewhat easier by having the computer do the extensions and additions. Scanners can facilitate the transfer of the data into the computer. However, it is still necessary to perform a check on the print-outs to ensure that the data is complete and that there are no errors.

---

[2] Ibid., par. 3030.02.

**Illustration 9-1**    Inventory Tickets Used to Tag Inventory Items as They Are Counted

INVENTORY TICKET NO. _786_    Quantity counted _____

Item _____    Sales price $ _____

Counted by _____    Cost price $ _____

Checked by _____    Purchase date _____

A common error is one where prices are entered incorrectly so that an item which costs, for example, $50 per hundred, is priced as $50 per unit. This error can significantly overvalue the inventory.

---

**Progress Check**

**(Answers to Progress Checks are provided at the end of the chapter.)**

9-1    Which accounting principle most directly governs the allocation of cost of goods available for sale between the ending inventory and cost of goods sold?

9-2    If Campbell sells goods to Thompson, FOB Campbell's factory, and the goods are still in transit from Campbell to Thompson, which company should include the goods in its inventory?

9-3    Kramer Gallery purchased an original painting for $11,400. Additional costs incurred in obtaining and offering the artwork for sale included $130 for transportation-in, $150 for import duties, $100 for insurance during shipment, $180 for advertising costs, $400 for framing, and $800 for sales salaries. In calculating the cost of inventory, what total cost should be assigned to the painting? *(a)* $11,400; *(b)* $11,530; *(c)* $11,780; *(d)* $12,180.

---

## ASSIGNING COSTS TO INVENTORY ITEMS

**LO 2**

Calculate the cost of an inventory based on *(a)* specific invoice prices, *(b)* weighted-average cost, *(c)* FIFO, and *(d)* LIFO, and explain the financial statement effects of choosing one method over the others.

One of the major issues in accounting for merchandise involves determining the unit cost amounts that will be assigned to items in the inventory. When all units are purchased at the same unit cost, this process is easy. However, when identical items are purchased at different costs, a problem arises as to which costs apply to the ending inventory and which apply to the goods sold. There are four commonly used methods of assigning costs to goods in the ending inventory and to goods sold. They are (1) specific invoice prices; (2) weighted-average cost; (3) first-in, first-out; and (4) last-in, first-out. All four methods are generally accepted.

To illustrate the four methods under the periodic inventory system, assume that a company has 12 units of Product X on hand at the end of its annual accounting period. Also, assume that the inventory at the beginning of the year and the purchases during the year were as follows:

| Jan. | 1 | Beginning inventory | .... | 10 units @ $100 = $1,000 |
| Mar. | 13 | Purchased | ........... | 15 units @ $108 = 1,620 |
| Aug. | 17 | Purchased | ........... | 20 units @ $120 = 2,400 |
| Nov. | 10 | Purchased | ........... | 10 units @ $125 = 1,250 |
| Total | | | ...................... | 55 units        $6,270 |

## Specific Invoice Prices

When each item in an inventory can be clearly related to a specific purchase and its invoice, **specific invoice inventory pricing** may be used to assign costs. For example, assume that 6 of the 12 unsold units of Product X were from the November purchase and 6 were from the August purchase. With this information, specific invoice prices can be used to assign costs to the ending inventory and to goods sold as follows:

| | | |
|---|---:|---:|
| Total cost of 55 units available for sale ................ | | $6,270 |
| Less ending inventory priced by means of specific invoices: | | |
|    6 units from the November purchase at $125 each ...... | $750 | |
|    6 units from the August purchase at $120 each ......... | 720 | |
| Ending inventory (12 units) ......................... | | 1,470 |
| Cost of goods sold ............................... | | $4,800 |

## Weighted Average

When using **weighted-average inventory pricing,** multiply the per unit costs of the beginning inventory and of each purchase by the number of units in the beginning inventory and each purchase. Then, divide the total of these amounts by the total number of units available for sale to find the weighted-average cost per unit as follows:

```
10 units @ $100 = $1,000
15 units @ $108 =  1,620
20 units @ $120 =  2,400
10 units @ $125 =  1,250
55                $6,270
$6,270/55 = $114 weighted-average cost per unit
```

After determining the weighted-average cost per unit, use this average to assign costs to the inventory and to the units sold as follows:

| | |
|---|---:|
| Total cost of 55 units available for sale ........ | $6,270 |
| Ending inventory priced on a weighted average | |
|    cost basis: 12 units at $114 each ........... | 1,368 |
| Cost of goods sold ...................... | $4,902 |

## First-In, First-Out

**First-in, first-out inventory pricing (FIFO)** assumes the items in the beginning inventory are sold first. Additional sales are assumed to come in the order in which they were purchased. Thus, the costs of the last items received are assigned to the ending inventory, and the remaining costs are assigned to goods sold. For example, when first-in, first-out is used, the costs of Product X are assigned to the inventory and goods sold as follows:

| | | |
|---|---:|---:|
| Total cost of 55 units available for sale . . . . . . . . . . . | | $6,270 |
| Less ending inventory priced on a basis of FIFO: | | |
| 10 units from the November purchase at $125 each . . | $1,250 | |
| 2 units from the August purchase at $120 each . . . . | 240 | |
| Ending inventory (12 units) . . . . . . . . . . . . . . . . . . . . | | 1,490 |
| Cost of goods sold . . . . . . . . . . . . . . . . . . . . . . . . . . | | $4,780 |

Understand that FIFO is acceptable whether or not the physical flow of goods actually follows a first-in, first-out pattern. The physical flow of products depends on the nature of the product and the way the products are stored. If a product is perishable (for example, fresh tomatoes), the business attempts to sell them in a first-in, first-out pattern. Other products, for example, bolts or screws kept in a large bin, may tend to be sold on a last-in, first-out basis. In either case, the FIFO method of allocating cost may be used.

## Last-In, First-Out

Under the **last-in, first-out inventory pricing (LIFO)** method, the costs of the last goods received are charged to cost of goods sold and matched with revenue from sales. Again, this method is acceptable even though the physical flow of goods may not be on a last-in, first-out basis.

One argument for the use of LIFO is based on the fact that a going concern must replace the inventory items it sells. When goods are sold, replacements are purchased. Thus, a sale causes the replacement of goods. From this point of view, a correct matching of costs with revenues would be to match replacement costs with the sales that made replacements necessary. Although the costs of the most recent purchases are not quite the same as replacement costs, they usually are close approximations of replacement costs. Because LIFO assigns the most recent purchase costs to the income statement, LIFO (compared to FIFO or weighted average) comes closest to matching replacement costs with revenues.

Under LIFO, costs are assigned to the 12 remaining units of Product X and to the goods sold as follows:

| | | |
|---|---:|---:|
| Total cost of 55 units available for sale . . . . . . . . . . | | $6,270 |
| Less ending inventory priced on a basis of LIFO: | | |
| 10 units in the beginning inventory at $100 each . . | $1,000 | |
| 2 units from the March purchase at $108 each . . . | 216 | |
| Ending inventory (12 units) . . . . . . . . . . . . . . . . . . . | | 1,216 |
| Cost of goods sold . . . . . . . . . . . . . . . . . . . . . . . . . | | $5,054 |

Notice that when LIFO is used to match costs and revenues, the ending inventory cost is the cost of the oldest 12 units.

## Comparison of Methods

In a stable market where prices remain unchanged, the choice of an inventory pricing method is not important. When prices are unchanged over a period of time, all methods give the same cost figures. However, in a changing market where prices are rising or falling, each method may give a different result. These differences are shown in Illustration 9–2, where we assume that Product X sales were $6,000 and operating expenses were $500.

In Illustration 9–2, note the differences that resulted from the choice of an inventory pricing method. Because purchase prices were rising throughout the period, FIFO resulted in the lowest cost of goods sold, the highest gross profit, and the highest net income. On the other hand, LIFO resulted in the highest cost of goods sold, the lowest gross profit, and the lowest net income. As you would expect, the results of using the weighted-average method fall between FIFO and LIFO. The results of using specific invoice prices depend entirely on which units were actually sold.

Each of the four pricing methods is generally accepted, and arguments can be made for using each. In one sense, one might argue that specific invoice prices exactly match costs and revenues. It is clearly the most appropriate method when each unit of product has unique features that affect the cost of that particular unit. However, this method may not be practical except for relatively high-priced items when just a few units are kept in stock and sold. Weighted-average costs tend to smooth out price fluctuations. FIFO provides an inventory valuation on the balance sheet that most closely approximates current replacement cost. LIFO causes the last costs incurred to be assigned to cost of goods sold. Therefore, it results in a better matching of current costs with revenues on the income statement.

Because the choice of an inventory pricing method often has material effects on the financial statements, the choice of a method should be disclosed in the notes to the statements. This information is important to an understanding of the statements and is required by the *full-disclosure principle*.[3]

## The Consistency Principle

Because the choice of an inventory pricing method can have a material effect on the financial statements, some companies might be inclined to make a new choice each year. Their objective would be to select whichever method would result in the most favourable financial statements. If this were allowed, however, readers of financial statements would find it extremely difficult to compare the company's financial statements from one year to the next. If income increased, the reader would have difficulty deciding whether the increase resulted from more successful operations or from the change in the accounting method. The **consistency principle** is used to avoid this problem.

---

[3]Ibid., par. 3030.10

| | Specific Invoice Prices | Weighted Average | FIFO | LIFO |
|---|---|---|---|---|
| Sales . . . . . . . . . . . . . . . . . . . . . . . . . . . . . | $6,000 | $6,000 | $6,000 | $6,000 |
| Cost of goods sold: | | | | |
| Merchandise inventory, January 1 . . . . . . . | $1,000 | $1,000 | $1,000 | $1,000 |
| Purchases . . . . . . . . . . . . . . . . . . . . . . | 5,270 | 5,270 | 5,270 | 5,270 |
| Cost of goods available for sale . . . . . . . . | $6,270 | $6,270 | $6,270 | $6,270 |
| Merchandise inventory, December 31 . . . . | 1,470 | 1,368 | 1,490 | 1,216 |
| Cost of goods sold . . . . . . . . . . . . . . . . . | $4,800 | $4,902 | $4,780 | $5,054 |
| Gross profit . . . . . . . . . . . . . . . . . . . . . . | $1,200 | $1,098 | $1,220 | $ 946 |
| Operating expenses . . . . . . . . . . . . . . . . | 500 | 500 | 500 | 500 |
| Income before taxes . . . . . . . . . . . . . . . . | $ 700 | $ 598 | $ 720 | $ 446 |

**Illustration 9–2**
The Income Statement Effects of Alternative Inventory Pricing Methods

The *consistency principle* requires that a company use the same accounting methods period after period, so that the financial statements of succeeding periods will be comparable.[4] The *consistency principle* is not limited just to inventory pricing methods. Whenever a company must choose between alternative accounting methods, consistency requires that the company continue to use the selected method period after period. As a result, a reader of a company's financial statements may assume that in keeping its records and in preparing its statements, the company used the same procedures employed in previous years. Only on the basis of this assumption can meaningful comparisons be made of the data in a company's statements year after year.

The consistency principle does not require a company to use one inventory valuation method exclusively, however; it can use different methods to value different categories of inventory. For example, **Texaco, Inc.,** includes the following note in its financial statements:

> Virtually all inventories of crude oil, petroleum products, and petrochemicals are stated at cost, determined on the last-in, first-out (LIFO) method. Other merchandise inventories are stated at cost, determined on the first-in, first-out (FIFO) method. Inventories are valued at the lower of cost or market. Materials and supplies are stated at average cost.

In achieving comparability, the *consistency principle* does not mean that a company can never change from one accounting method to another. Rather, if a company justifies a different acceptable method or procedure as an improvement in financial reporting, a change may be made. However, when such a change is made, the *full-disclosure principle* requires that the nature of the change, justification for the change, and the effect of the change on net income be disclosed in the notes to the statements.[5]

---

[4]Ibid., par. 1000.23.
[5]Ibid., par. 1506.16.

**Progress Check**

**9–4**    A company with the following beginning inventory and purchases ended the period with 30 units on hand:

|  | Units | Unit Cost |
|---|---|---|
| Beginning Inventory . . . . . | 100 | $10 |
| Purchases #1 . . . . . . . . . | 40 | 12 |
| Purchases #2 . . . . . . . . . . | 20 | 14 |

Using the data above, match the following:

|  |  |  |  | Choices |  |
|---|---|---|---|---|---|
| Ending inventory using | (1) | FIFO | _____ | (a) | $ 330 |
|  | (2) | LIFO | _____ | (b) | $ 400 |
|  | (3) | Weighted average | _____ | (c) | $ 300 |
| Cost of goods sold using | (1) | FIFO | _____ | (a) | $1430 |
|  | (2) | LIFO | _____ | (b) | $1360 |
|  | (3) | Weighted average | _____ | (c) | $1460 |

**9–5**    In a period of rising prices, which method (LIFO or FIFO) reports the higher net income?

**9–6**    In a period of rising prices, what effect will LIFO as compared to FIFO have on the balance sheet?

## INVENTORY ERRORS— PERIODIC SYSTEM

**LO 3**

Explain the effect of an inventory error on the income statements of the current and succeeding years.

Companies that use the *periodic inventory system* must be especially careful in taking the end-of-period inventory. If an error is made, it will cause misstatements in cost of goods sold, gross profit, net income, current assets, and owner's equity. Also, the ending inventory of one period is the beginning inventory of the next. Therefore, the error will carry forward and cause misstatements in the succeeding period's cost of goods sold, gross profit, and net income. Furthermore, since the amount involved in an inventory often is large, the misstatements can materially reduce the usefulness of the financial statements.

To illustrate the effects of an inventory error, assume that in each of the years 1994, 1995, and 1996, a company had $100,000 in sales. If the company maintained a $20,000 inventory throughout the period and made $60,000 in purchases in each of the years, its cost of goods sold each year was $60,000 and its annual gross profit was $40,000. However, assume the company incorrectly calculated its December 31, 1994, inventory at $16,000 rather than $20,000. Note the effects of the error in Illustration 9–3.

Observe in Illustration 9–3 that the $4,000 understatement of the December 31, 1994, inventory caused a $4,000 overstatement in 1994 cost of goods sold and a $4,000 understatement in gross profit and net income. Also, because the ending inventory of 1994 became the beginning inventory of 1995, the error caused an understatement in the 1995 cost of goods sold and a $4,000 overstatement in gross profit and net income. However, by 1996 the error had no effect.

In Illustration 9–3, the December 31, 1994, inventory is understated. Had it been overstated, it would have caused opposite results—the 1994 net income would have been overstated and the 1995 income understated.

**Illustration 9-3**   Effects of Inventory Errors—Periodic Inventory System

| | 1994 | | 1995 | | 1996 | |
|---|---|---|---|---|---|---|
| Sales ..................... | | $100,000 | | $100,000 | | $100,000 |
| Cost of goods sold: | | | | | | |
|   Beginning inventory ......... | $20,000 | | $16,000* | | $20,000 | |
|   Purchases ................ | 60,000 | | 60,000 | | 60,000 | |
|   Goods for sale ............ | $80,000 | | $76,000 | | $80,000 | |
|   Ending inventory ........... | 16,000* | | 20,000 | | 20,000 | |
|   Cost of goods sold ......... | | 64,000 | | 56,000 | | 60,000 |
| Gross profit ............... | | $ 36,000 | | $ 44,000 | | $ 40,000 |
| *Should have been $20,000. | | | | | | |

Because inventory errors correct themselves by causing offsetting errors in the next period, you might be inclined to think that they are not serious. Do not make this mistake. Management, creditors, and owners base many important decisions on fluctuations in reported net income. Therefore, inventory errors must be avoided.

---

**Progress Check**

**9-7   Falk Company maintains its inventory records on a periodic basis. In making the physical count of inventory at 1996 year-end, an error was made that overstated the 1996 ending inventory by $10,000. Will this error cause cost of goods sold to be over- or understated in 1996? In 1997? By how much?**

---

The previous discussion of inventories focused on the periodic inventory system. Under the periodic system, the Merchandise Inventory account is updated only once each accounting period, at the end of the period. Then, the Merchandise Inventory account reflects the current balance of inventory only until the first purchase or sale in the following period. Thereafter, the Merchandise Inventory account no longer reflects the current balance.

By contrast, a *perpetual inventory system* updates the Merchandise Inventory account after each purchase and after each sale. As long as all entries have been posted, the account shows the current amount of inventory on hand. The system takes its name from the fact that the Merchandise Inventory account is perpetually up to date. When a perpetual system is used, management is able to monitor the inventory on hand on a regular basis. This aids in planning future purchases.

Before the widespread use of computers in accounting, only companies that sold a limited number of products of relatively high value used perpetual inventory systems. The cost and effort of maintaining perpetual inventory records were simply too great for other types of companies. However, since computers have made the record-keeping chore much easier, an increasing number of firms are switching from periodic to perpetual systems.

## PERPETUAL INVENTORY SYSTEMS

**LO 4**

Describe perpetual inventory systems and prepare entries to record merchandise transactions and maintain subsidiary inventory records under a perpetual inventory system.

## COMPARING JOURNAL ENTRIES UNDER PERIODIC AND PERPETUAL INVENTORY SYSTEMS

By using parallel columns in Illustration 9–4, we show the typical journal entries made under periodic and perpetual inventory systems. Observe the entries for the purchase of transaction 1. The perpetual system does not use a Purchases account. Instead, the cost of the items purchased is debited directly to Merchandise Inventory. Also, in transaction 2, the perpetual system credits the cost of purchase returns directly to the Merchandise Inventory account instead of using a Purchases Returns and Allowances account.

Transaction 3 involves the sale of merchandise. Note that the perpetual system requires two entries to record the sale, one to record the revenue and another to record cost of goods sold. Thus, the perpetual system uses a Cost of Goods Sold account. In the periodic system the elements of cost of goods sold are not transferred to such an account. Instead, they are transferred to Income Summary in the process of recording the closing entries.

The closing entries under the two systems are shown as item 4 in Illustration 9–4. Under the periodic system, all of the cost elements related to inventories are transferred to Income Summary. By comparison, under the perpetual system, those cost elements were already recorded in a Cost of Goods Sold account. Thus, the closing entries simply transfer the balance in the Cost of Goods Sold account to Income Summary. Of course, Sales must be closed under both inventory systems. In Illustration 9–4, both inventory systems result in the same amounts of sales, cost of goods sold, and end-of-period merchandise inventory.

## SUBSIDIARY INVENTORY RECORDS— PERPETUAL SYSTEM

When a company sells more than one product and uses the perpetual inventory system, the Merchandise Inventory account serves as a controlling account to a subsidiary Merchandise Inventory Ledger. This ledger contains a separate record for each product in stock. This ledger may be computerized or kept on a manual basis. In either case, the record for each product shows the number of units and cost of each purchase, the number of units and cost of each sale, and the resulting balance of product on hand.

Illustration 9–5 shows an example of a subsidiary merchandise inventory record. This particular record is for Product Z, which is stored in Bin 8 of the stockroom. In this case, the record also shows the company's policy of maintaining no more than 25 or no less than 5 units of Product Z on hand.

In Illustration 9–5, note that the beginning inventory consisted of 10 units that cost $10 each. The first transaction occurred on January 5 and was a sale of five units at $17 per unit. Next, 20 units were purchased on January 8 at a cost of $10.50 per unit. Then, three units were sold on January 10 for $17 per unit. The entries to record the January 10 sale are:

| | | | | |
|---|---|---|---|---|
| Jan. | 10 | Cash (or Accounts Receivable) . . . . . . . . . . . . . . . . . | 51.00 | |
| | | Sales . . . . . . . . . . . . . . . . . . . . . . . . . . . . . . . . . . . . | | 51.00 |
| | | 3 × $17.00 = $51 | | |
| | 10 | Cost of Goods Sold . . . . . . . . . . . . . . . . . . . . . . . . . | 30.00 | |
| | | Merchandise Inventory . . . . . . . . . . . . . . . . . . . . . | | 30.00 |
| | | 3 × $10.00 = $30 | | |

In the second entry, notice that the cost per unit assigned to these three units was $10. This indicates that a first-in, first-out basis is being assumed for this product. In

**Illustration 9–4**  A Comparison of Entries under Periodic and Perpetual Inventory Systems

X Company purchases merchandise for $15 per unit and sells it for $25. The company begins the current period with five units of product on hand, which cost a total of $75.

| **Periodic** | | | **Perpetual** | | |
|---|---|---|---|---|---|

1. *Purchased on credit 10 units of merchandise for $15 per unit:*

| Periodic | | | Perpetual | | |
|---|---|---|---|---|---|
| Purchases ..................... | 150 | | Merchandise Inventory ............. | 150 | |
|     Accounts Payable ........... | | 150 |     Accounts Payable ............. | | 150 |

2. *Returned 3 units of merchandise originally purchased in (1):*

| Periodic | | | Perpetual | | |
|---|---|---|---|---|---|
| Accounts Payable ............... | 45 | | Accounts Payable ............... | 45 | |
|     Purchases Returns and ........ | | |     Merchandise Inventory ......... | | 45 |
|         Allowances .............. | | 45 | | | |

3. *Sold eight units for $200 cash:*

| Periodic | | | Perpetual | | |
|---|---|---|---|---|---|
| Cash ......................... | 200 | | Cash ......................... | 200 | |
|     Sales ..................... | | 200 |     Sales ..................... | | 200 |
| | | | Cost of Goods Sold ............... | 120 | |
| | | |     Merchandise Inventory ......... | | 120 |

4. *Closing entries:*

| Periodic | | | Perpetual | | |
|---|---|---|---|---|---|
| Merchandise Inventory (Ending) ...... | 60 | | Income Summary ................ | 120 | |
| Sales ........................ | 200 | |     Cost of Goods Sold ........... | | 120 |
| Purchases Returns and Allowances .... | 45 | | | | |
|     Income Summary ........... | | 305 | Sales ........................ | 200 | |
| | | |     Income Summary | | 200 |
| Income Summary ............... | 225 | | | | |
|     Merchandise Inventory (Beginning) | | 75 | | | |
|     Purchases ................. | | 150 | | | |

| | **Units** | **Cost** | **Merchandise Inventory** | | | |
|---|---|---|---|---|---|---|
| Beginning inventory .............. | 5 | $ 75 | Transaction No. | Dr. | Cr. | Bal. |
| Purchases .................... | 10 | 150 | Opening Balance | | | 75 |
| Purchases returns ............... | (3) | (45) | 1. | 150 | | 225 |
| Goods available ................ | 12 | $180 | 2. | | 45 | 180 |
| Goods sold ................... | (8) | (120) | 3. | | 120 | 60 |
| Ending inventory ............... | 4 | $ 60 | | | | |

addition to FIFO, perpetual inventory systems can be designed to accommodate an average cost flow assumption. Perpetual inventory systems rarely use LIFO in the subsidiary records. If a company wants its financial statements to reflect LIFO, special adjustments are made at the end of each accounting period to convert the balances from FIFO or weighted average to LIFO. The details of using weighted average and LIFO with perpetual systems are explained in a more advanced accounting course.

**Illustration 9–5    A Subsidiary Inventory Record Using FIFO**

| Item _Product Z_ | | | | Location in stock room _Bin 8_ | | | | | |
|---|---|---|---|---|---|---|---|---|---|

Maximum ___25___          Minimum ___5___

| Date | Received | | | Sold | | | Balance | | |
|---|---|---|---|---|---|---|---|---|---|
| | Units | Cost | Total | Units | Cost | Total | Units | Cost | Balance |
| Jan. 1 | | | | | | | 10 | 10.00 | 100.00 |
| Jan. 5 | | | | 5 | 10.00 | 50.00 | 5 | 10.00 | 50.00 |
| Jan. 8 | 20 | 10.50 | 210.00 | | | | 5 | 10.00 | |
| | | | | | | | 20 | 10.50 | 260.00 |
| Jan.10 | | | | 3 | 10.00 | 30.00 | 2 | 10.00 | |
| | | | | | | | 20 | 10.50 | 230.00 |
| | | | | | | | | | |

All companies should take a physical inventory at least annually, even if a perpetual inventory system is used. By taking a physical inventory, management confirms the accuracy of the perpetual inventory records. When the physical inventory shows that the perpetual records are incorrect, a special adjusting entry should be prepared to update the accounts.

Before the widespread use of computers, many companies avoided the use of a perpetual inventory system in favour of the periodic system. Computers greatly facilitate the record keeping required in a perpetual system. The use of point-of-sale scanners and other systems in grocery and department stores allows management to track the inventory from the receiving dock, to the warehouse, to the store shelf, to the customer. This technology allows better purchase planning and better service to the consumer. In addition, since inventories can be controlled, the amount of inventory and the carrying costs can be reduced.

---

**Progress Check**

**9–8**    What account is used in a perpetual inventory system but not in a periodic system?

**9–9**    In a perpetual inventory system, which of the following statements are true?
   a. The Merchandise Inventory account balance shows the amount of merchandise on hand.
   b. Subsidiary inventory records are maintained for each type of product.
   c. A sale of merchandise requires two entries, one to record the revenue and one to record the cost of goods sold.
   d. A separate Cost of Goods Sold account is used.
   e. All of the above are correct.

As we have discussed, the cost of the ending inventory is determined by using one of the four pricing methods (FIFO, LIFO, weighted average, or specific invoice prices). However, the cost of the inventory is not necessarily the amount reported on the balance sheet. Generally accepted accounting principles require that the inventory be reported at market value whenever market is lower than cost. Thus, merchandise inventory is shown on the balance sheet at the **lower of cost or market (LCM)**.

## LOWER OF COST OR MARKET

LO 5

Calculate the lower-of-cost-or-market amount of an inventory.

## Determination of Market

In applying lower of cost or market to merchandise inventories, what do accountants mean by the term *market*? For the purpose of assigning a value to merchandise inventory, market can be either *net realizable value* or *replacement cost*. Replacement cost means the price a company would pay if it bought new items to replace those in its inventory. When the cost to replace merchandise drops below original cost, the sales price of the merchandise is also likely to fall. Therefore, the merchandise is worth less to the company and should be written down to replacement cost (or market). Net realizable value means the amount the company expects to receive when it sells the merchandise less any costs of preparing the merchandise for sale, such as repairs, or selling costs, such as commissions. If the net realizable value (NRV) is less than original cost, then the merchandise should be written down to NRV (or market).

The choice of either NRV or replacement cost as the market value depends on which amount is more reliable. Most Canadian companies tend to use NRV as their definition of market value.[6]

| Product | Units on Hand | Cost | Per Unit Replacement Cost | Total Cost | Total Market | Lower of Cost or Market (by product) |
|---------|--------------|------|--------------------------|-----------|-------------|-------------------------------------|
| X | 20 | $8 | $7 | $160 | $140 | $140 |
| Y | 10 | 5 | 6 | 50 | 60 | 50 |
| Z | 5 | 9 | 7 | 45 | 35 | 35 |
| Total cost originally incurred | | | | $255 | | |
| LCM (applied to whole inventory) | | | | | $235 | |
| LCM (applied to each product) | | | | | | $225 |

Note that when LCM is applied to the whole inventory, the total is $235, which is $20 lower than the $255 cost. And when the method is applied separately to each product, the sum is only $225. In general, a company may apply LCM three different ways:

1. LCM may be applied separately to each product.
2. LCM may be applied to major categories of products.

---

[6]CICA, *Financial Reporting in Canada 1993,* (Toronto: 1993), p. 92.

3.  If the products are not too different, LCM may be applied to the inventory as a whole.

## THE CONSERVATISM PRINCIPLE

Generally accepted accounting principles require writing inventory down to market when market is less than cost. On the other hand, inventory generally cannot be written up to market when market exceeds cost. If writing inventory down to market is justified, why not also write inventory up to market? What is the reason for this apparent inconsistency?

The reason is that the gain from a market value increase is not realized until a sales transaction provides verifiable evidence of the amount of the gain. But why, then, are inventories written down when market is below cost?

Accountants often justify the lower-of-cost-or-market rule by citing the **conservatism principle.** This principle attempts to guide the accountant in uncertain situations where amounts must be estimated. In general terms, it implies that when "uncertainty exists estimates [should] ensure that assets, revenues and gains are not overstated and conversely, that liabilities, expenses and losses are not understated."[7] Because the value of inventory is uncertain, writing the inventory down when its market value falls is clearly the less optimistic estimate of the inventory's value to the company.

---

**Progress Check**

**9-10**   A company's ending inventory includes the following items:

| Product | Units on Hand | Unit Cost | Market Value per Unit |
|---------|---------------|-----------|-----------------------|
| A | 20 | $ 6 | $ 5 |
| B | 40 | 9 | 8 |
| C | 10 | 12 | 15 |

The inventory's lower of cost or market, applied separately to each product, is:
(a) $520;  (b) $540;  (c) $570;  (d) $600.

---

## METHODS OF ESTIMATING INVENTORY VALUE

**LO 6**

Use the retail method and the gross profit method to estimate an inventory and calculate merchandise turnover and days' stock on hand.

Most companies prepare financial statements on a quarterly or monthly basis. These monthly or quarterly statements are called **interim statements,** because they are prepared between the regular year-end statements. The cost of goods sold information that is necessary to prepare interim statements is readily available if a perpetual inventory system is used. However, a periodic system requires a physical inventory to determine cost of goods sold. To avoid the time-consuming and expensive process of taking a physical inventory each month or quarter, some companies use the **retail inventory method** to estimate cost of goods sold and ending inventory. Then, they take a physical inventory at the end of each year. Other companies also use the retail inventory method to prepare the year-end statements. Another method used to estimate inventories is the gross profit method. However, all companies should take a physical inventory at least once each year to correct any errors or shortages.

---

[7]*CICA Handbook,* section 1000, "Financial Statement Concepts," par. .21(d).

## The Retail Method of Estimating Inventories

When the retail method is used to estimate an inventory, the company's records must show the amount of inventory it had at the beginning of the period both at *cost* and at *retail*. You already understand the cost of an inventory. The retail amount of an inventory simply means the dollar amount of the inventory at the marked selling prices of the inventory items.

In addition to the beginning inventory, the accounting records must show the net amount of goods purchased during the period both at cost and at retail. This is the balance of the Purchases account less returns and discounts. Also, the records must show the amount of net sales at retail. With this information, you estimate the ending inventory as follows:

**Step 1:** Compute the amount of goods available for sale during the period both at cost and at retail.

**Step 2:** Divide the goods available at cost by the goods available at retail to obtain a **retail method cost ratio.**

**Step 3:** Deduct net sales (at retail) from goods available for sale (at retail) to determine the ending inventory at retail.

**Step 4:** Multiply the ending inventory at retail by the cost ratio to reduce the inventory to a cost basis.

Look at Illustration 9–6 to see these calculations.

This is the essence of Illustration 9–6: (1) The company had $100,000 of goods (at marked selling prices) for sale during the period. (2) The cost of these goods was 60% of their $100,000 marked retail sales value. (3) The company's records (its Sales account) showed that $70,000 of these goods were sold, leaving $30,000 (retail value) of unsold merchandise in the ending inventory. (4) Since cost in this store is 60% of retail, the estimated cost of this ending inventory is $18,000.

An ending inventory calculated as in Illustration 9–6 is an estimate arrived at by deducting sales (goods sold) from goods available for sale. As we said before, this method may be used for interim statements or even for year-end statements. Nevertheless, a store must take a physical count of the inventory at least once each year to correct any errors or shortages.

## Using the Retail Method to Reduce a Physical Inventory to Cost

In retail stores, items for sale normally have price tags attached that show selling prices. So, when a store takes a physical inventory, it commonly takes the inventory at the marked selling prices of the items on hand. It then reduces the dollar total of this inventory to a cost basis by applying its cost ratio. It does this because the selling prices are readily available and the application of the cost ratio eliminates the need to look up the invoice price of each item on hand.

For example, assume that the company in Illustration 9–6 estimates its inventory by the retail method and takes a physical inventory at the marked selling prices of the goods. Also assume that the total retail amount of this physical inventory is $29,600. The company can calculate the cost for this inventory simply by applying its cost ratio to the inventory total as follows:

$$\$29,600 \times 60\% = \$17,760$$

Illustration 9-6
Calculating the Ending
Inventory Cost by the
Retail Method

|  |  | At Cost | At Retail |
|---|---|---|---|
| (Step 1) | Goods available for sale: |  |  |
|  | Beginning inventory .................. | $20,500 | $ 34,500 |
|  | Net purchases ...................... | 39,500 | 65,500 |
|  | Goods available for sale ............... | $60,000 | $100,000 |
| (Step 2) | Cost ratio: ($60,000/$100,000) × 100 = 60% |  |  |
| (Step 3) | Deduct net sales at retail ................ |  | 70,000 |
|  | Ending inventory at retail ............... |  | $ 30,000 |
| (Step 4) | Ending inventory at cost ($30,000 × 60%) .... | $18,000 |  |

The $17,760 cost figure for this company's ending physical inventory is a satisfactory figure for year-end statement purposes. It is also acceptable for income tax purposes.

## Inventory Shortage

An inventory determined as in Illustration 9–6 is an estimate of the amount of goods on hand. Since it is determined by deducting sales from goods for sale, it does not reveal any shortages due to breakage, loss, or theft. However, you can estimate the amount of such shortages by comparing the inventory as calculated in Illustration 9–6 with the amount that results from taking a physical inventory.

For example, in Illustration 9–6, we estimated that the ending inventory at retail was $30,000. Then, we assumed that this same company took a physical inventory and counted only $29,600 of merchandise on hand (at retail). Therefore, the company must have had an inventory shortage at retail of $30,000 − $29,600 = $400. Stated in terms of cost, the shortage is $400 × 60% = $240.

## Gross Profit Method of Estimating Inventories

Sometimes, a business that does not use a perpetual inventory system or the retail method may need to estimate the cost of its inventory. For example, if the inventory is destroyed by fire or is stolen, the business must estimate the inventory so that it can file a claim with its insurance company. In cases such as this, the cost of the inventory can be estimated by the **gross profit method.** With this method, the historical relationship between cost of goods sold and sales is applied to sales of the current period as a way of estimating cost of goods sold during the current period. Then, cost of goods sold is subtracted from the cost of goods available for sale to get the estimated cost of the ending inventory.

To use the gross profit method, several items of accounting information must be available. This includes information about the normal gross profit margin or rate, the cost of the beginning inventory, the cost of net purchases, transportation-in, and the amount of sales and sales returns.

For example, assume that the inventory of a company was totally destroyed by a fire on March 27, 1996. The company's average gross profit rate during the past five years has been 30% of net sales. On the date of the fire, the company's accounts showed the following balances:

**Illustration 9–7**
The Gross Profit
Method of Estimating
Inventory

| Goods available for sale: | | |
|---|---|---|
| Inventory, January 1, 1996 . . . . . . . . . . . . . . . . . | | $12,000 |
| Net purchases . . . . . . . . . . . . . . . . . . . . . . . . . . | $20,000 | |
| Add transportation-in . . . . . . . . . . . . . . . . . . | 500 | 20,500 |
| Goods available for sale . . . . . . . . . . . . . . . . . . | | $32,500 |
| Less estimated cost of goods sold: | | |
| Sales . . . . . . . . . . . . . . . . . . . . . . . . . . . . . . . | $31,500 | |
| Less sales returns . . . . . . . . . . . . . . . . . . . . | (1,500) | |
| Net sales . . . . . . . . . . . . . . . . . . . . . . . . . . . . | $30,000 | |
| Estimated cost of goods sold (70% × $30,000) . . . . | | (21,000) |
| Estimated March 27 inventory and inventory loss . . . . | | $11,500 |

| | |
|---|---|
| Sales . . . . . . . . . . . . . . . . . . | $31,500 |
| Sales returns . . . . . . . . . . . . . | 1,500 |
| Inventory, January 1, 1996 . . . . | 12,000 |
| Net purchases . . . . . . . . . . . . | 20,000 |
| Transportation-in . . . . . . . . . . | 500 |

With this information, the gross profit method may be used to estimate the company's inventory loss. To apply the gross profit method, the first step is to recognize that whatever portion of each dollar of net sales was gross profit, the remaining portion was cost of goods sold. Thus, if the company's gross profit rate averages 30%, then 30% of each net sales dollar was gross profit, and 70% was cost of goods sold. In Illustration 9–7, we show how the 70% is used to estimate the inventory that was lost.

To understand Illustration 9–7, recall that an ending inventory is normally subtracted from goods available for sale to determine the cost of goods sold. Then, observe in Illustration 9–7 that the opposite subtraction is made. Estimated cost of goods sold is subtracted from goods available for sale to determine the estimated ending inventory.

As we mentioned, the gross profit method is often used to estimate the amount of an insurance claim. Accountants also use this method to see if an inventory amount determined by management's physical count of the items on hand is reasonable.

## USING THE INFORMATION— MERCHANDISE TURNOVER AND DAYS' STOCK ON HAND

In prior chapters, we explained some ratios that you can use to evaluate a company's short-term liquidity. These ratios include the current ratio, the acid-test ratio, days' sales uncollected, and accounts receivable turnover. A company's ability to pay its short-term obligations also depends on how rapidly it sells its merchandise inventory. To evaluate this, you may calculate **merchandise turnover.** The formula for this ratio is:

$$\text{Merchandise turnover} = \frac{\text{Cost of goods sold}}{\text{Average merchandise inventory}}$$

In this ratio, the average merchandise inventory is usually calculated by adding the beginning and ending inventory amounts and dividing the total by two. However, if the company's sales vary by season of the year, you may want to take an average of the inventory amounts at the end of each quarter.

Analysts use merchandise turnover in evaluating short-term liquidity. In addition, they may use it to assess whether management is doing a good job of controlling the amount of inventory kept on hand. A ratio that is high compared to the ratios of competing companies may indicate that the amount of merchandise held in inventory is too low. As a result, sales may be lost because customers are unable to find what they want. A ratio that is low compared to other companies may indicate an inefficient use of assets. In other words, the company may be holding more merchandise than is needed to support its sales volume.

Earlier in this chapter, we explained how the choice of an inventory costing method (such as FIFO, weighted average, or LIFO) affects the reported amounts of inventory and cost of goods sold. The choice of an inventory costing method also affects the calculated amount of merchandise turnover. Therefore, comparing the merchandise turnover ratios of different companies may be misleading unless they use the same costing method.

Another inventory statistic used to evaluate the liquidity of the merchandise inventory is **days' stock on hand.** This is similar to the days' sales uncollected measure described in Chapter 7. The formula for days' stock on hand is:

$$\text{Days' stock on hand} = \frac{\text{Ending inventory}}{\text{Cost of goods sold}} \times 365$$

Notice the difference in the focus of merchandise turnover and days' stock on hand. Merchandise turnover is an average that occurred during an accounting period. By comparison, the focus of days' stock on hand is on the end-of-period inventory. Days' stock on hand is an estimate of how many days it will take to convert the inventory on hand at the end of the period into accounts receivable or cash.

In **The GAP, Inc.'s** 1993 annual report, management reported that they had initiated an aggressive new strategy of selling a more creative mix of merchandise and improving inventory management. This enabled The GAP to realize a 22.6% increase in net earnings for 1993 based on sales that only increased by 11.3%. The following data from The GAP's financial statements show that GAP's days' stock on hand decreased from 68.2 days in 1992 to 56.9 days in 1993 and inventory turnover increased from 5.8 to 6.1 times.

| | 1993 | 1992 | 1991 |
|---|---|---|---|
| Cost of goods sold and occupancy expenses .. | $2,121,789 | $1,955,553 | |
| Ending merchandise inventory . . . . . . . . . . . | 331,155 | 365,692 | $313,899 |

Days' stock on hand:

$$1993: \frac{\$331,155}{\$2,121,789} \times 365 = 56.9 \text{ days}$$

$$1992: \frac{\$365,692}{\$1,955,553} \times 365 = 68.2 \text{ days}$$

**Progress Check**

9-11 The following data relates to Taylor Company's inventory during the year:

|  | Cost | Retail |
|---|---|---|
| Beginning inventory .... | $324,000 | $530,000 |
| Purchases ........... | 204,000 | 348,000 |
| Purchases returns ..... | 9,000 | 13,000 |
| Sales .............. |  | 320,000 |

Using the retail method, the estimated cost of the ending inventory is:
(a) $545,000;  (b) $324,200;  (c) $333,200;  (d) $314,000;  (e) $327,000.

9-12 Describe the method for determining the merchandise turnover figure.

**SUMMARY OF THE CHAPTER IN TERMS OF LEARNING OBJECTIVES**

**LO 1.** **Describe** *(a)* **how the matching principle relates to accounting for merchandise,** *(b)* **the types of items that should be included in merchandise inventory, and** *(c)* **the elements that make up the cost of merchandise.** The allocation of the cost of goods available for sale between cost of goods sold and ending inventory is an accounting application of the *matching principle*. Merchandise inventory should include all goods that are owned by the business and held for resale. This includes items the business has placed on consignment with other parties but excludes items that the business has taken on consignment from other parties. The cost of merchandise includes not only the invoice price less any discounts but also any additional or incidental costs incurred to put the merchandise into place and condition for sale.

**LO 2.** **Calculate the cost of an inventory based on** *(a)* **specific invoice prices,** *(b)* **weighted-average cost,** *(c)* **FIFO, and** *(d)* **LIFO, and explain the financial statement effects of choosing one method over the others.** When specific invoice prices are used to price an inventory, each item in the inventory is identified and the cost of the item is determined by referring to the item's purchase invoice. With weighted-average cost, the total cost of the beginning inventory and of purchases is divided by the total number of units available to determine the weighted-average cost per unit. Multiplying this cost by the number of units in the ending inventory yields the cost of the inventory. FIFO prices the ending inventory based on the assumption that the first units purchased are the first units sold. LIFO is based on the assumption that the last units purchased are the first units sold. All of these methods are acceptable.

**LO 3.** **Explain the effect of an inventory error on the income statements of the current and succeeding years.** When the periodic inventory system is used, an error in counting the ending inventory affects assets (inventory), net income (cost of goods sold), and owner's equity. Since the ending inventory is the beginning inventory of the next period, an error at the end of one period affects the cost of goods sold and the net income of the next period. These next period effects offset the financial statement effects in the previous period.

**LO 4.** **Describe perpetual inventory systems and prepare entries to record merchandise transactions and maintain subsidiary inventory records under a perpetual inventory system.** Under a perpetual inventory system, purchases and purchases returns are recorded in the Merchandise Inventory account. At the time sales are recorded, the cost of goods sold is credited to Merchandise Inventory. As a result, the Merchandise Inventory is kept up to date throughout the accounting period.

  LO 5.  **Calculate the lower-of-cost-or-market amount of an inventory.** When lower of cost or market is applied to merchandise inventory, market can mean net realizable value or replacement cost. Lower of cost or market may be applied separately to each product, to major categories of products, or to the merchandise inventory as a whole.

  LO 6.  **Use the retail method and the gross profit method to estimate an inventory and calculate merchandise turnover and days' stock on hand.** When the retail method is used, sales are subtracted from the retail amount of goods available for sale to determine the ending inventory at retail. This is multiplied by the cost ratio to reduce the inventory amount to cost. To calculate the cost ratio, divide the cost of goods available by the retail value of goods available (including markups but excluding markdowns).

  With the gross profit method, multiply sales by (1 − the gross profit rate) to estimate cost of goods sold. Then, subtract the answer from the cost of goods available for sale to estimate the cost of the ending inventory.

  Analysts use merchandise turnover and days' stock on hand in evaluating a company's short-term liquidity. They also use merchandise turnover to evaluate whether the amount of merchandise kept in inventory is too high or too low.

**DEMONSTRATION PROBLEM**

Tale Company uses a periodic inventory system and had the following beginning inventory and purchases during 1996:

|  | | Item X | |
|---|---|---|---|
| **Date** | | **Units** | **Unit Cost** |
| Jan. 1 | Inventory | 400 | $14 |
| Mar. 10 | Purchase | 200 | 15 |
| May 9 | Purchase | 300 | 16 |
| Sept. 22 | Purchase | 250 | 20 |
| Nov. 28 | Purchase | 100 | 21 |

At December 31, 1996, there were 550 units of X on hand.

**Required**

1. Using the preceding information, apply FIFO inventory pricing and calculate the cost of goods available for sale in 1996, the ending inventory, and the cost of goods sold.

2. In preparing the financial statements for 1996, the bookkeeper was instructed to use FIFO but failed to do so and computed the cost of goods sold according to LIFO. Determine the size of the misstatement of 1996's income from this error. Also determine the effect of the error on the 1997 income. Assume no income taxes.

- Multiply the units of each purchase and the beginning inventory by the appropriate unit costs to determine the total costs. Then, calculate the cost of goods available for sale.

- For FIFO, calculate the ending inventory by multiplying the units on hand by the unit costs of the latest purchases. Then, subtract the ending inventory from the cost of goods available for sale.

- For LIFO, calculate the ending inventory by multiplying the units on hand by the unit costs of the beginning inventory and the earliest purchases. Then, subtract the total ending inventory from the cost of goods available for sale.

- Compare the ending 1996 inventory amounts under FIFO and LIFO to determine the misstatement of 1996 income that resulted from using LIFO. The 1997 and 1996 errors are equal in amount but have opposite effects.

*Planning the Solution*

1. FIFO basis:

| | | |
|---|---|---|
| Jan. 1 inventory (400 @ $14) . . . . . . | | $ 5,600 |
| Purchases: | | |
| Mar. 10 purchase (200 @ $15) . . . | $3,000 | |
| May. 9 purchase (300 @ $16) . . . . | 4,800 | |
| Sept. 22 purchase (250 @ $20) . . . | 5,000 | |
| Nov. 28 purchase (100 @ $21) . . . | 2,100 | 14,900 |
| Cost of goods available for sale . . . . | | $20,500 |
| Ending inventory at FIFO cost: | | |
| Nov. 28 purchase (100 @ $21) . . . | $2,100 | |
| Sept. 22 purchase (250 @ $20) . . . | 5,000 | |
| May. 9 purchase (200 @ $16) . . . . | 3,200 | |
| FIFO cost of ending inventory . . . | | 10,300 |
| Cost of goods sold . . . . . . . . . . . . . | | $10,200 |

2. LIFO basis:

| | | |
|---|---|---|
| Cost of goods available for sale . . . . | | $20,500 |
| Ending inventory at LIFO cost: | | |
| Jan. 1 inventory (400 @ $14) . . . . | $5,600 | |
| Mar. 10 purchase (150 @ $15) . . . | 2,250 | |
| LIFO cost of ending inventory . . . | | 7,850 |
| Cost of goods sold . . . . . . . . . . . . . | | $12,650 |

*Solution to Demonstration Problem*

If LIFO is mistakenly used when FIFO should have been used, cost of goods sold in 1996 would be overstated by $2,450, which is the difference between the FIFO and LIFO amounts of ending inventory. Income would be understated in 1996 by $2,450. In 1997, income would be overstated by $2,450 because of the understatement of the beginning inventory.

# GLOSSARY

**Conservatism principle**  the accounting principle that guides accountants to select the less optimistic estimate when two estimates of amounts to be received or paid are about equally likely. p. 464

**Consignee**  one who receives and holds goods owned by another party for the purpose of selling the goods for the owner. p. 451

**Consignor**  an owner of goods who ships them to another party who will then sell the goods for the owner. p. 451

**Consistency principle**  the accounting requirement that a company use the same accounting methods period after period so that the financial statements of succeeding periods will be comparable. p. 456

**Days' stock on hand**  an estimate of how many days it will take to convert the inventory on hand at the end of the period into accounts receivable or cash; calculated by dividing the ending inventory by cost of goods sold and multiplying the result by 365. p. 468

**First-in, first-out (FIFO) inventory pricing**  the pricing of an inventory under the assumption that the first items received were the first items sold. p. 455

**Gross profit inventory method**  a procedure for estimating an ending inventory in which the past gross profit rate is used to estimate cost of goods sold, which is then subtracted from the cost of goods available for sale to determine the estimated ending inventory. p. 466

**Interim statements**  monthly or quarterly financial statements prepared in between the regular year-end statements. p. 464

**Inventory ticket**  a form attached to the counted items in the process of taking a physical inventory. p. 452

**Last-in, first-out (LIFO) inventory pricing**  the pricing of an inventory under the assumption that the last items received were the first items sold. p. 455

**Lower of cost or market (LCM)**  the required method of reporting merchandise inventory in the balance sheet, in which market may be defined as net realizable value or replacement cost on the date of the balance sheet. p. 463

**Merchandise turnover**  the number of times a company's average inventory was sold during an accounting period, calculated by dividing cost of goods sold by the average merchandise inventory balance. p. 467

**Net realizable value**  the expected sales price of an item less any additional costs to sell. p. 451

**Retail inventory method**  a method for estimating an ending inventory based on the ratio of the amount of goods for sale at cost to the amount of goods for sale at marked selling prices. p. 464

**Retail method cost ratio**  the ratio of goods available for sale at cost to goods available for sale at retail prices. p. 465

**Specific invoice inventory pricing**  the pricing of an inventory where the purchase invoice of each item in the ending inventory is identified and used to determine the cost assigned to the inventory. p. 454

**Weighted-average inventory pricing**  an inventory pricing system in which the unit prices of the beginning inventory and of each purchase are weighted by the number of units in the beginning inventory and each purchase. The total of these amounts is then divided by the total number of units available for sale to find the unit cost of the ending inventory and of the units that were sold. p. 454

# SYNONYMOUS TERM

**Specific invoice inventory pricing**  specific identification method.

# QUESTIONS

1. Where is merchandise inventory disclosed in the financial statements?

2. Why are incidental costs often ignored in pricing an inventory? Under what accounting principle is this permitted?

3. Give the meanings of the following when applied to inventory: *(a)* FIFO; *(b)* LIFO; *(c)* cost; and *(d)* perpetual inventory.

4. If prices are falling, will the LIFO or the FIFO method of inventory valuation result in the lower cost of goods sold?

5. May a company change its inventory pricing method each accounting period?

6. Does the accounting principle of consistency preclude any changes from one accounting method to another?

7. What effect does the full-disclosure principle have if a company changes from one acceptable accounting method to another?

8. What is meant when it is said that under a periodic inventory system, inventory errors correct themselves?

9. If inventory errors under a periodic inventory system correct themselves, why be concerned when such errors are made?

10. What guidance for accountants is provided by the principle of conservatism?

11. What accounts are used in a periodic inventory system but not in a perpetual inventory system?

12. What is the usual meaning of the word *market* as it is used in determining the lower of cost or market for merchandise inventory?

13. In deciding whether to reduce an item of merchandise to the lower of cost or market, what is the importance of the item's net realizable value?

14. Refer to Geac Computer Corporation's financial statements in Appendix I. On April 30, 1994, what percentage of Geac's current assets was represented by inventory?

---

# QUICK STUDY (Five Minute Exercises)

*a.* Explain how the matching principle applies to the accounting for inventory.

*b.* Fun Stuff Inc., a distributor of novelty items, operates out of owner Margaret Falcaro's home. At the end of the accounting period, Falcaro tells us she has 2,000 units of product in her basement, 50 of which were damaged by water leaks and cannot be sold. She also has another 400 units in her van ready to deliver to fill a customer order, terms FOB destination, and has another 100 units out on consignment to a friend who owns a stationery store. How many units should be included in the end-of-the-period inventory?

**QS 9–1**
**(LO 1)**

The Victorian Attic, an antique dealer, purchased the contents of an estate for a bulk bid price of $45,000. The terms of the purchase were FOB shipping point and the cost of trans-

**QS 9–2**
**(LO 1)**

porting the goods to Victorian Attic was $2,000. Victorian Attic insured the shipment at the cost of $200. Prior to placing the goods in the store, they cleaned and refurbished some merchandise at a cost of $600 for labour and parts. Determine the cost of the inventory acquired in the purchase of the estate contents.

**QS 9–3
(LO 2)**

A company had the following beginning inventory and purchases during a period. What is the cost of the 110 units that remain in the ending inventory, assuming *(a)* FIFO, *(b)* LIFO, and *(c)* weighted average?

|  | Units | Unit Cost |
|---|---|---|
| Beginning inventory on January 1 . . . . | 200 | $6.00 |
| Purchase on March 20 . . . . . . . . . . . . . | 50 | $6.50 |
| Purchase on July 2 . . . . . . . . . . . . . . . | 80 | $7.00 |

**QS 9–4
(LO 2)**

Identify the inventory costing method most closely related to each of the following statements assuming a period of rising costs:

*a.* Results in a balance sheet inventory closest to replacement costs.

*b.* Matches recent costs against revenue.

*c.* Provides a tax advantage.

*d.* Is best because each unit of product has unique features that affect cost.

*e.* Understates current value of inventory on a balance sheet.

**QS 9–5
(LO 3)**

Gardner Company maintains its inventory records on a periodic basis. In taking a physical inventory at the end of 1995, certain units were counted twice. Explain how this error affects the following: *(a)* cost of goods sold, *(b)* gross profit, *(c)* 1995 net income, *(d)* 1996 net income, *(e)* the combined two-year income, *(f)* income in years after 1996.

**QS 9–6
(LO 4)**

*a.* Journalize the following transactions under the periodic inventory system and under the perpetual inventory system:

Nov. 2   Purchased and received 100 cases of soda at a cost of $11 per case, FOB destination.

  5   Sold 20 cases of soda on account for $15 per case.

  17   Returned 30 cases of soda to supplier.

*b.* Under which of the two alternative inventory systems would the inventory account have a November 17 balance that represented the cost of the 50 cases of soda that remain on hand?

**QS 9–7
(LO 5)**

Media-Tec has the following products in its ending inventory:

| Product | Quantity | Cost | Market |
|---|---|---|---|
| A | 4 | $300 | $240 |
| B | 15 | 400 | 420 |
| C | 8 | 200 | 180 |

Calculate lower of cost or market *(a)* for the inventory as a whole, and *(b)* applied separately to each product.

**QS 9–8
(LO 6)**

The inventory of Abba Cadabba was destroyed by a fire on April 15. The following data were found in the accounting records:

```
Jan. 1 inventory . . . . . . . . . . . . . .      $20,000
Jan. 1–Apr. 15 purchases (net)  . . . .        38,000
Sales . . . . . . . . . . . . . . . . . . . . . .        86,000
Estimated gross profit rate  . . . . . . .          54%
```

Determine the cost of the inventory destroyed in the fire.

# EXERCISES

Serges Company began a year and purchased merchandise as follows:

| | | | | |
|---|---|---|---|---|
| Jan. | 1 | Beginning inventory  . . . . | 80 units @ $60.00 = | $ 4,800 |
| Feb. | 16 | Purchased . . . . . . . . . . . . | 400 units @ $56.00 = | 22,400 |
| Sept. | 2 | Purchased . . . . . . . . . . . | 160 units @ $50.00 = | 8,000 |
| Nov. | 26 | Purchased . . . . . . . . . . . | 320 units @ $46.00 = | 14,720 |
| Dec. | 4 | Purchased . . . . . . . . . . . | 240 units @ $40.00 = | 9,600 |
| | | Total . . . . . . . . . . . . . . | 1,200 units | $59,520 |

Exercise 9–1
Alternative cost flow
assumptions, periodic
inventory system
(LO 2)

## Required

The company uses a periodic inventory system, and the ending inventory consists of 300 units, 100 from each of the last three purchases. Determine the share of the $59,520 cost of the units for sale that should be assigned to the ending inventory and to goods sold under each of the following: *(a)* costs are assigned on the basis of specific invoice prices, *(b)* costs are assigned on a weighted-average cost basis, *(c)* costs are assigned on the basis of FIFO, and *(d)* costs are assigned on the basis of LIFO. Which method provides the highest and lowest net income?

Finest Company began a year and purchased merchandise as follows:

| | | | | |
|---|---|---|---|---|
| Jan. | 1 | Beginning inventory  . . . . | 80 units @ $40.00 = | $ 3,200 |
| Feb. | 16 | Purchased . . . . . . . . . . . . | 400 units @ $46.00 = | 18,400 |
| Sept. | 2 | Purchased . . . . . . . . . . . | 160 units @ $50.00 = | 8,000 |
| Nov. | 26 | Purchased . . . . . . . . . . . | 320 units @ $56.00 = | 17,920 |
| Dec. | 4 | Purchased . . . . . . . . . . . | 240 units @ $60.00 = | 14,400 |
| | | Total . . . . . . . . . . . . . . | 1,200 units | $61,920 |

Exercise 9–2
Alternative cost flow
assumptions, periodic
inventory system
(LO 2)

## Required

The company uses a periodic inventory system, and the ending inventory consists of 300 units, 100 from each of the last three purchases. Determine the share of the $61,920 cost of the units for sale that should be assigned to the ending inventory and to goods sold under each of the following: *(a)* costs are assigned on the basis of specific invoice prices, *(b)* costs are assigned on a weighted-average cost basis, *(c)* costs are assigned on the basis of FIFO, and *(d)* costs are assigned on the basis of LIFO. Which method provides the highest and lowest net income?

Coe Company had $435,000 of sales during each of three consecutive years, and it purchased merchandise costing $300,000 during each of the years. It also maintained a $105,000 inventory from the beginning to the end of the three-year period. However, in accounting under a periodic inventory system, it made an error at the end of 1995 that caused its ending 1995 inventory to appear on its statements at $90,000 rather than the correct $105,000.

Exercise 9–3
Analysis of inventory
errors
(LO 3)

**Required**

1. State the actual amount of the company's gross profit in each of the years.

2. Prepare a comparative income statement like Illustration 9–3 to show the effect of this error on the company's cost of goods sold and gross profit in 1995, 1996, and 1997.

**Exercise 9–4**
Perpetual inventory system—FIFO cost flow
**(LO 4)**

In its beginning inventory on January 1, 1996, Stable Company had 120 units of merchandise that cost $8 per unit. Prepare general journal entries for Stable to record the following transactions during 1996, assuming a perpetual inventory system and a first-in, first-out cost flow.

Apr.  3   Purchased on credit 300 units of merchandise at $10.00 per unit.

     9   Returned 60 defective units from the April 3 purchase to the supplier.

July 16   Purchased for cash 180 units of merchandise at $8.50 per unit.

Aug.  5   Sold 200 units of merchandise for cash at a price of $12.50 per unit.

Dec. 31   Prepare entries to close the revenue and expense accounts to the Income Summary.

**Exercise 9–5**
Lower of cost or market
**(LO 5)**

Crystal Corporation's ending inventory includes the following items:

| Product | Units on Hand | Unit Cost | NRV per Unit |
|---|---|---|---|
| W | 40 | $30 | $34 |
| X | 50 | 48 | 40 |
| Y | 60 | 26 | 24 |
| Z | 44 | 20 | 20 |

Net realizable value is determined to be the best measure of market. Calculate lower of cost or market for the inventory *(a)* as a whole, and *(b)* applied separately to each product.

**Exercise 9–6**
Estimating ending inventory—retail method
**(LO 6)**

During an accounting period, Felder Company sold $220,000 of merchandise at marked retail prices. At the period end, the following information was available from its records:

| | At Cost | At Retail |
|---|---|---|
| Beginning inventory . . . . | $ 62,180 | $102,000 |
| Net purchases . . . . . . . . . | 115,820 | 176,125 |

Use the retail method to estimate Felder's ending inventory at cost.

**Exercise 9–7**
Reducing physical inventory to cost—retail method
**(LO 6)**

Assume that in addition to estimating its ending inventory by the retail method, Felder Company of Exercise 9–6 also took a physical inventory at the marked selling prices of the inventory items. Assume further that the total of this physical inventory at marked selling prices was $50,500. Then, *(a)* determine the amount of this inventory at cost and *(b)* determine the store's inventory shrinkage from breakage, theft, or other causes at retail and at cost.

**Exercise 9–8**
Estimating ending inventory—gross profit method
**(LO 6)**

On January 1, a store had a $216,000 inventory at cost. During the first quarter of the year, it purchased $735,000 of merchandise, returned $10,500, and paid freight charges on purchased merchandise totaling $22,300. During the past several years, the store's gross profit on sales has averaged 25%. Under the assumption the company had $890,000 of sales during the first quarter of the year, use the gross profit method to estimate its inventory at the end of the first quarter.

From the following information for Jester Company, calculate merchandise turnover for 1996 and 1995 and days' stock on hand at December 31, 1996, and 1995.

**Exercise 9–9**
Merchandise turnover
and days' stock on hand
**(LO 6)**

|  | **1996** | **1995** | **1994** |
|---|---|---|---|
| Cost of goods sold . . . . . . . . | $367,900 | $243,800 | $223,600 |
| Inventory (December 31) . . . . | 77,120 | 69,400 | 73,200 |

Comment on Jester's efficiency in using its assets to support increasing sales from 1995 to 1996.

# PROBLEMS

Hart Company began a year with 3,000 units of Product A in its inventory that cost $25 each, and it made successive purchases of the product as follows:

**Problem 9–1**
Alternative cost flows—
periodic system
**(LO 2)**

| Jan. 29 . . . . | 4,500 units @ $30 each |
|---|---|
| Apr. 4 . . . . | 5,000 units @ $35 each |
| Sept. 8 . . . . | 4,800 units @ $40 each |
| Dec. 9 . . . . | 4,500 units @ $45 each |

The company uses a periodic inventory system. On December 31, a physical count disclosed that 6,000 units of Product A remained in inventory.

**Required**

1.  Prepare a calculation showing the number and total cost of the units available for sale during the year.

2.  Prepare calculations showing the amounts that should be assigned to the ending inventory and to cost of goods sold assuming *(a)* a FIFO basis, *(b)* a LIFO basis, and *(c)* a weighted-average cost basis. Round your calculation of the weighted-average cost per unit to three decimal places.

MDI Company sold 7,800 units of its product at $55 per unit during 1996. Incurring operating expenses of $8 per unit in selling the units, it began the year and made successive purchases of the product as follows:

**Problem 9–2**
Income statement
comparisons and cost
flow assumptions
**(LO 2)**

| January 1 beginning inventory . . . . | 800 units costing $30.00 per unit |
|---|---|
| Purchases: | |
| March 3 . . . . . . . . . . . . . . . . . . | 1,000 units costing $31.00 per unit |
| June 9 . . . . . . . . . . . . . . . . . | 2,000 units costing $32.00 per unit |
| October 17 . . . . . . . . . . . . . . . | 4,500 units costing $33.00 per unit |
| December 6 . . . . . . . . . . . . . . | 600 units costing $34.00 per unit |

**Required**

*Preparation component:*

1.  Prepare a comparative income statement for the company, showing in adjacent columns the net incomes earned from the sale of the product assuming the company uses a periodic inventory system and prices its ending inventory on the basis of: *(a)* FIFO, *(b)* LIFO, and *(c)* weighted-average cost. Round your calculation of the weighted-average cost per unit to three decimal places.

*Analysis component:*

2.  In comparing the results of the three alternatives, how would they change if MDI had been experiencing declining prices in the aquisition of additional inventory?

**Problem 9–3**
Analysis of inventory
errors
**(LO 3)**

Ying Company keeps its inventory records on a periodic basis. The following amounts were reported in the company's financial statements:

|  | **Financial Statements for Year Ended December 31** | | |
| --- | --- | --- | --- |
|  | **1994** | **1995** | **1996** |
| *(a)* Cost of goods sold . . . . . | $130,000 | $154,000 | $140,000 |
| *(b)* Net income . . . . . . . . . | 40,000 | 50,000 | 42,000 |
| *(c)* Total current assets . . . . | 210,000 | 230,000 | 200,000 |
| *(d)* Owner's equity . . . . . . . | 234,000 | 260,000 | 224,000 |

In making the physical counts of inventory, the following errors were made:

| | | |
| --- | --- | --- |
| Inventory on December 31, 1994 . . . . | Understated | $12,000 |
| Inventory on December 31, 1995 . . . . | Overstated | 6,000 |

**Required**

*Preparation component:*

1.  For each of the preceding financial statement items—*(a), (b), (c),* and *(d)*—prepare a schedule similar to the following and show the adjustments that would have been necessary to correct the reported amounts.

|  | **1994** | **1995** | **1996** |
| --- | --- | --- | --- |
| Cost of goods sold: | | | |
| Reported . . . . . . . . . . . . . . . . . . | _____ | _____ | _____ |
| Adjustments: Dec. 31/94 error . . . | _____ | _____ | _____ |
| Dec. 31/95 error . . . | _____ | _____ | _____ |
| Corrected . . . . . . . . . . . . . . . . . | ══════ | ══════ | ══════ |

*Analysis component:*

2.  What is the error in the aggregate net income for the three-year period that resulted from the inventory errors? Explain why this result occurs. Also explain why the understatement of inventory by $12,000 in 1994 resulted in an understatement of equity by the same figure that year.

**Problem 9–4**
Lower of cost or market
**(LO 5)**

The following information pertains to the physical inventory of Home Appliance Centre taken at December 31:

|  |  | **Per Unit** | |
| --- | --- | --- | --- |
| **Product** | **Units on Hand** | **Cost** | **NRV** |
| Kitchen: | | | |
| Refrigerators . . . . . . . | 165 | $380 | $405 |
| Stoves . . . . . . . . . . . | 120 | 203 | 181 |
| Dishwashers . . . . . . . . | 158 | 140 | 165 |
| Microwaves . . . . . . . . | 200 | 50 | 40 |
| Entertainment: | | | |
| Stereos . . . . . . . . . . . | 140 | 250 | 312 |
| Televisions . . . . . . . . | 360 | 304 | 320 |

| Cleaning/Maintenance: | | | |
|---|---|---|---|
| Washers . . . . . . . . . . | 245 | 190 | 146 |
| Dryers . . . . . . . . . . . | 280 | 188 | 162 |
| Vacuum Cleaners  . . . . | 104 | 67 | 79 |

**Required**

In each of these independent cases, calculate the lower of cost or market *(a)* for the inventory as a whole, *(b)* for the inventory by major category, and *(c)* for the inventory, applied separately to each product.

The records of The Unlimited provided the following information for the year ended December 31:

**Problem 9–5**
Retail inventory method
**(LO 6)**

|  | At Cost | At Retail |
|---|---|---|
| January 1 beginning inventory  . . . . | $ 160,450 | $ 264,900 |
| Purchases . . . . . . . . . . . . . . . . . | 1,113,140 | 1,828,200 |
| Purchases returns  . . . . . . . . . . . . | 17,600 | 34,100 |
| Sales  . . . . . . . . . . . . . . . . . . . . |  | 1,570,200 |
| Sales returns . . . . . . . . . . . . . . . . |  | 15,600 |

**Required**

1.  Prepare an estimate of the company's year-end inventory by the retail method.

2.  Under the assumption the company took a year-end physical inventory at marked selling prices that totaled $478,800, prepare a schedule showing the store's loss from theft or other cause at cost and at retail.

Cafferty Company wants to prepare interim financial statements for the first quarter of 1996. The company uses a periodic inventory system but would like to avoid making a physical count of inventory. During the last five years, the company's gross profit rate has averaged 35%. The following information for the year's first quarter is available from its records:

**Problem 9–6**
Gross profit method
**(LO 6)**

| | |
|---|---|
| January 1 beginning inventory  . . . . | $  600,520 |
| Purchases . . . . . . . . . . . . . . . . . | 1,890,400 |
| Purchases returns  . . . . . . . . . . . . | 26,100 |
| Transportation-in . . . . . . . . . . . . . | 13,800 |
| Sales  . . . . . . . . . . . . . . . . . . . . | 2,382,300 |
| Sales returns . . . . . . . . . . . . . . . . | 18,900 |

**Required**

Use the gross profit method to prepare an estimate of the company's March 31 inventory.

**Part 1.** Draton Company's inventory includes a product that cost $9 per unit. Replacement cost is $8, expected sales price is $12, and additional costs to sell are $2. Explain the reason why the inventory should or should not be written down.

**Problem 9–7**
Analytical essay
**(LO 3)**

**Part 2.** Flavour Company's inventory includes a damaged product that cost $16 per unit. Replacement cost is $15, expected sales price is $17, additional costs that must be incurred to sell the product are $3. Explain the reason why the inventory should not be reported on the balance sheet at $16. At what value should it be reported? Why?

Review the facts about Hart Company presented in Problem 9–1 and notice that Hart uses a periodic inventory system. The facts of Problem 9–1 indicate that Hart Company had 21,800 units of product available for sale, had 6,000 units on hand at the end of the period,

**Problem 9–8**
Analytical essay
**(LO 2, 5)**

and, therefore, had sales of 15,800 units during the period. Now assume that the sale occurred as follows:

| | |
|---|---|
| March 1 . . . . . . . . | 4,000 units |
| June 1 . . . . . . . . . | 5,000 units |
| November 1 . . . . . | 5,300 units |
| December 20 . . . . | 1,500 units |

**Required**

1. Explain what effect, if any, these additional facts would have on the solution to requirement 2*a* and 2*b* of Problem 9–1.

2. Given the preceding information about the timing of sales, explain whether the Problem 9–1 solution to requirement 2*a* and 2*b* would provide the same answers under a perpetual inventory system as it does under a periodic inventory system.

**Problem 9–9**
Lower of cost or market
**(LO 2)**

**Case 1:** In this case, an evaluation of the expected selling price and normal profit margin for each product shows that replacement cost is the best measure of market. The inventory includes:

| Product | Units on Hand | Cost | Replacement Cost |
|---|---|---|---|
| A . . . . | 800 | $20 | $23 |
| B . . . . | 900 | 32 | 29 |
| C . . . . | 400 | 22 | 21 |

**Case 2:** In this case, the inventories of Products D and E have been damaged. If $15 additional cost per unit is paid to repackage the Product D units, they can be sold for $50 per unit. The Product E units can be sold for $70 per unit after paying additional cleaning costs of $18 per unit. The inventory includes:

| Product | Units on Hand | Cost | Replacement Cost |
|---|---|---|---|
| D . . . . | 330 | $44 | $46 |
| E . . . . | 500 | 60 | 55 |

**Required**

In each of the above independent cases, calculate the lower of cost or market *(a)* for the inventory as a whole and *(b)* for the inventory, applied separately to each product.

**Problem 9–10**
Analysis of inventory errors
**(LO 3)**

Milicia Company keeps its inventory records on a periodic basis. The following amounts were reported in the company's financial statements:

| | | Financial Statements for Year Ended December 31 | | |
|---|---|---|---|---|
| | | **1996** | **1997** | **1998** |
| *(a)* | Cost of goods sold . . . . . . . . . | $ 67,000 | $ 75,000 | $ 65,000 |
| *(b)* | Net income . . . . . . . . . . . . . | 24,000 | 39,000 | 21,000 |
| *(c)* | Total current assets . . . . . . . . | 108,000 | 115,000 | 100,000 |
| *(d)* | Owners' equity . . . . . . . . . . . | 144,000 | 157,000 | 162,000 |

In making the physical counts of inventory, the following errors were made:

| | | |
|---|---|---|
| Inventory on December 31, 1996 . . . . . . . | Understated | $9,000 |
| Inventory on December 31, 1997 . . . . . . . | Overstated | 14,000 |

## Required

1. For each of the financial statement items listed above as *(a)*, *(b)*, *(c)*, and *(d)*, prepare a schedule similar to the following and show the adjustments that would have
   been necessary to correct the reported amounts.

|  | 1996 | 1997 | 1998 |
|---|---|---|---|
| Cost of goods sold: | | | |
| Reported ..................... | _____ | _____ | _____ |
| Adjustments: Dec. 31, 1996 error ... | _____ | _____ | _____ |
| Dec. 31, 1997 error ... | _____ | _____ | _____ |
| Corrected .................... | ══════ | ══════ | ══════ |

2. What is the error in the aggregate net income for the three-year period that resulted
   from the inventory errors?

The Turner Company sells a product called TurnUp and uses a perpetual inventory system
to account for its merchandise. The beginning balance of TurnUps and transactions during
January of this year were as follows:

**Problem 9–11**
Inventory records under
FIFO and weighted
average—perpetual
system
**(LO 4)**

Jan. 1  Balance: 25 units costing $8 each.
    3  Purchased 50 units costing $9 each.
    7  Sold 20 units.
  19  Sold 15 units.
  21  Purchased 30 units costing $11 each.
  24  Sold 15 units.
  29  Sold 32 units.

## Required

1. Under the assumption the concern keeps its records on a FIFO basis, enter the beginning balance and the transactions on a subsidiary inventory record like the one
   illustrated in this chapter.
2. Assume the 32 units sold on January 29 were sold on credit to Sally Rugby at $25
   each and prepare general journal entries to record the sale on a FIFO basis.

Calico Stores takes a year-end physical inventory at marked selling prices and uses the retail method to reduce the inventory total to a cost basis for statement purposes. It also uses
the retail method to estimate the amount of inventory it should have at the end of a year
and by comparison determines any inventory shortage due to shoplifting or other cause. At
the end of last year, its physical inventory at marked selling prices totaled $138,200, and
the following information was available from its records:

**Problem 9–12**
Retail inventory method
**(LO 5)**

|  | At Cost | At Retail |
|---|---|---|
| Beginning inventory .... | $ 52,930 | $ 80,200 |
| Purchases ............ | 267,840 | 405,000 |
| Purchases returns ...... | 5,520 | 8,400 |
| Sales .............. | | 340,000 |
| Sales returns ......... | | 4,400 |

**Required**

1. Use the retail method to estimate the store's year-end inventory at cost.
2. Use the retail method to reduce the company's year-end physical inventory to a cost basis.
3. Prepare a schedule showing the inventory shortage at cost and at retail.

**Problem 9–13**
Gross profit method
**(LO 5)**

When the Accessory Store was opened for business on the morning of March 10, it was discovered that thieves had broken in and stolen the store's entire inventory. The following information for the period January 1 through March 10 was available to establish the amount of loss:

| | |
|---|---|
| January 1 merchandise inventory at cost .... | $125,100 |
| Purchases ......................... | 370,000 |
| Purchases returns .................... | 3,225 |
| Transportation-in .................... | 15,750 |
| Sales ............................ | 720,400 |
| Sales returns ....................... | 13,200 |

**Required**

Under the assumption the store had earned an average 38% gross profit on sales during the past five years, prepare a statement showing the estimated loss.

**Problem 9–14**
Gross profit method
**(LO 5)**

Herbert Florists wants to prepare interim financial statements for the first quarter of 1996. The company uses a periodic inventory system but would like to avoid making a physical count of inventory. During the last five years, the company's gross profit rate has averaged 30%, and the following information for the year's first quarter is available from its records:

| | |
|---|---|
| January 1 beginning inventory .... | $ 70,560 |
| Purchases ................... | 115,240 |
| Purchases returns ............. | 3,900 |
| Transportation-in ............. | 9,420 |
| Sales .................... | 227,000 |
| Sales returns ................ | 5,040 |

**Required**

Use the gross profit method to prepare an estimate of the company's March 31 inventory.

# PROVOCATIVE PROBLEMS

**Provocative Problem 9–1**
Sampson's Sporting Goods
**(LO 6)**

The retail outlet of Samson's Sporting Goods suffered extensive smoke and water damage and a small amount of fire damage on October 5. The company carried adequate insurance, and the insurance company's claims adjuster appeared the same day to inspect the damage. After completing his survey, the adjuster agreed with Sam Corbin, the store's owner, that the inventory could be sold to a company specializing in fire sales for about one-third of its cost. The adjuster offered Corbin $235,400 in full settlement for the damage to the inventory. He suggested that the offer be accepted and said he had authority to deliver at once a cheque for that amount. He also pointed out that a prompt settlement would provide funds to replace the inventory in time for the store to participate in the Christmas shopping season.

Corbin felt the loss might exceed $235,400, but he recognized that a time-consuming count and inspection of each item in the inventory would be required to establish the loss more precisely. He was anxious to get back into business before the Christmas rush, the season making the largest contribution to annual net income, and was reluctant to take the time for the inventory count. Yet, he was also unwilling to take a substantial loss on the insurance settlement.

Corbin asked for and received one day in which to consider the insurance company's offer and immediately went to his records for the following information:

|  |  | At Cost | At Retail |
|---|---|---|---|
| a. | January 1 inventory | $ 387,700 | $ 640,315 |
|  | Purchases, Jan. 1 through Oct. 5 | 1,347,200 | 2,250,450 |
|  | Net sales, Jan. 1 through Oct. 5 |  | 2,261,400 |

b. On March 1, the remaining inventory of winter sportswear and equipment was marked down from $110,400 to $87,000 and placed on sale in the annual end-of-the-winter-season sale. Two-thirds of the merchandise was sold. The markdown on the remainder was canceled, thereby returning the prices to regular retail amounts. (A markdown cancellation is subtracted from a markdown, and a markup cancellation is subtracted from a markup.)

c. In May, a special line of swimwear proved popular, and 110 suits were marked up from their normal $42.00 retail price to $52.50 per suit. Seventy suits were sold at the higher price; and on August 5, the markup on the remaining 40 suits was canceled and they were returned to their regular $42.00 price.

d. Between January 1 and October 5, markdowns totaling $11,300 were taken on several odd lots of sportswear. Recommend whether or not you think Corbin should accept the insurance company's offer. Back your recommendations with figures.

**Provocative Problem 9–2 Modern Furniture Store (LO 5)**

Modern Furniture Store has been in operation for six years, during which it has earned a 32% average gross profit on sales. However, the night before last, June 2, it suffered a disastrous fire that destroyed its entire inventory, and Marie Lauzon, the store's owner, has filed a $119,040 inventory loss claim with the insurance company. When asked on what she based her claim, she replied that during the day before the fire, she had marked every item in the store down 20% in preparation for the annual summer clearance sale, and during the marking-down process, she had taken an inventory of the merchandise in the store. "Furthermore," she said, "it's a big loss, but every cloud has a silver lining, because I am giving you fellows [the insurance company] the benefit of the 20% markdown in filing this claim."

When it was explained to Madame Lauzon that she had to back her loss claim with more than her word as to the amount of the loss, she produced the following information from her presale inventory and accounting records, which fortunately were in a fireproof vault and were not destroyed in the fire.

1. The store's accounts were closed on Dec. 31 of last year.
2. After posting was completed, the accounts showed the following June 2 balances:

| Merchandise inventory, Jan 1 balance | $103,800 |
|---|---|
| Purchases | 279,400 |
| Purchases returns | 2,950 |
| Freight-in | 7,050 |
| Sales | 448,100 |
| Sales returns | 10,100 |

3.   Madame Lauzon's prefire inventory totaled $148,800 at premarkdown prices.

From the information given, present figures to show the amount of loss suffered by Madame Lauzon. Also, show how she arrived at the amount of her loss claim. Can her presale inventory figure be used to substantiate the actual amount of her loss? If so, use the presale inventory figure to substantiate the actual loss.

**Provocative Problem 9–3**
**Financial statement analysis case**
**(LO 1, 2)**

**Geac**

Refer to the financial statements and related disclosures from Geac Computer Corporation Limited's 1994 annual report in Appendix I. Based on your examination of this information, answer the following:

1.   What was the total amount of inventories held as current assets by Geac at April 30, 1994? At April 30, 1993?
2.   Inventories represented what percentage of total assets at April 30, 1994? At April 30, 1993?
3.   Comment on the relative size of inventories Geac holds compared to other types of assets.
4.   What method did Geac use to determine the inventory amounts reported on its balance sheet?
5.   Calculate merchandise turnover for fiscal year 1994 and days' stock on hand at April 30, 1994, and April 30, 1993. (Use "costs, excluding amounts shown below," for cost of goods sold.)

# ANALYTICAL AND REVIEW PROBLEMS

**A & R Problem 9–1**

The following information is taken from the records of Bradford Company for four consecutive operating periods:

|  | Periods | | | |
|---|---|---|---|---|
|  | **1** | **2** | **3** | **4** |
| Beginning inventory ..... | $29,000 | $41,000 | $31,000 | $37,000 |
| Ending inventory ....... | 41,000 | 31,000 | 37,000 | 19,000 |
| Net income .......... | 25,000 | 29,000 | 33,000 | 41,000 |

Assume that the company made the errors below:

| Period | Error in Ending Inventory | |
|---|---|---|
| 1 .... | Overstated | $9,000 |
| 2 .... | Understated | 7,000 |
| 3 .... | Overstated | 8,000 |

**Required**

1.   Compute the revised net income for each of the four periods.
2.   Assuming that the company's ending inventory for period 4 is correct, how would these errors affect the total net income for the four periods combined? Explain.

The records of Walker Company as of December 31, 1996, show the following: **A & R Problem 9–2**

| | Net Purchases | Net Income | Accounts Payable | Inventory |
|---|---|---|---|---|
| Balance per company's books $20,500 | | $235,000 | $22,100 | $29,200 |
| (a) | | | | |
| (b) | | | | |
| (c) | | | | |
| (d) | _____ | _____ | _____ | _____ |
| (e) | ====== | ====== | ====== | ====== |
| Correct balances . . . . . . . . . . . . . | | | | |

The accountant of Walker Company discovers in the first week of January 1997 that the following errors were made by his staff.

a. Goods costing $4,500 were in transit (FOB shipping point) and were not included in the ending inventory. The invoice had been received and the purchase recorded.

b. Damaged goods (cost $3,900) that were being held for return to the supplier were included in inventory. The goods had been recorded as a purchase and the entry for the return of these goods had also been made.

c. Inventory items costing $2,600 were incorrectly excluded from the final inventory. These goods had not been recorded as a purchase and had not been paid for by the company.

d. Goods that were shipped FOB destination had not yet arrived and were not included in inventory. However, the invoice had arrived on December 30, 1996, and the purchase for $2,100 was recorded.

e. Goods that cost $2,700 were segregated and not included in inventory because a customer expressed an intention to buy the goods. The sale of the goods for $4,200 had been recorded in December 1996.

**Required**

Using the format provided above, show the correct amount for net purchases, net income, accounts payable, and inventory for Walker Company as at December 31, 1996.

## CONCEPT TESTER

Test your understanding of the concepts introduced in this chapter by completing the following crossword puzzle.

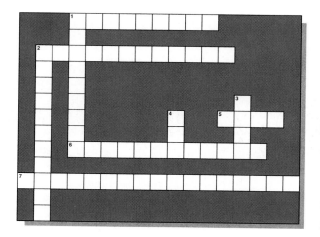

**Across Clues**

1. One who holds goods for sale that are owned by another party.
2. Principle that calls for less optimistic estimate when two estimates are equally likely.
5. Inventory pricing method that assumes units sold first come from units purchased first.
6. Inventory estimation method based on ratio of cost of goods available to selling price (2 words).
7. Financial statements prepared on a monthly or quarterly basis (2 words).

**Down Clues**

1. Owner of goods who transfers them to another party who will attempt to sell them for the owner.
2. Principle that calls for using the same accounting methods period after period.
3. Inventory pricing method that assumes units sold come from latest purchases.
4. Required method of reporting inventory at replacement cost when that is less than cost.

# ANSWERS TO PROGRESS CHECKS

9–1  The matching principle.

9–2  Thompson.

9–3  d

9–4  Ending inventory      (1) b
                           (2) c
                           (3) a
     Cost of goods sold    (1) b
                           (2) c
                           (3) a

9–5  FIFO. LIFO results in a higher cost of goods sold and therefore a lower gross profit, which carries through to a lower net income.

9–6  LIFO will result in a smaller inventory figure on the balance sheet, as compared to FIFO which will result in an inventory figure that is close to current replacement costs.

9–7  The cost of goods sold will be understated by $10,000 in 1996 and overstated by $10,000 in 1997.

9–8  An account used only in a perpetual inventory system is Cost of Goods Sold.

9–9  e

9–10  b

9–11  e

9–12  Merchandise turnover =

$$\frac{\text{Cost of goods sold}}{(\text{Opening inventory} + \text{Closing inventory})/2}$$

# CHAPTER 10

# Payroll Liabilities

*Accounting for employees' wages and salaries is one task that is shared by almost every business entity. Payroll acccounting provides the means to comply with governmental regulations and provides valuable information regarding labour costs.*

**K**aren White and Mark Smith's instructor stressed that wages, salaries and benefits form an important part of the expenses of every business. However, some businesses are more labour intensive than others. The following table compares the proportion of total expenses represented by labour costs for selected Canadian industries.

**Wages, Salaries and Benefits as Percent of Total Expenses[1]**

| Industry | Percent |
| --- | --- |
| Insurance and real estate agencies | 58.2 |
| Primary steel industries | 21.6 |
| Motor vehicle industry | 16.7 |
| Department stores | 14.2 |
| Television, radio, and stereo stores | 14.2 |
| Supermarkets | 9.3 |

[1]Source: CICA, "The Canadian Small Business Financial Performance Survey," 1994 Edition (Toronto: 1994).

## LEARNING OBJECTIVES

**After studying Chapter 10, you should be able to:**

1. **List the taxes and other items frequently withheld from employees' wages.**
2. **Make the calculations necessary to prepare a Payroll Register and prepare the entry to record payroll liabilities.**
3. **Prepare journal entries to record the payments to employees and explain the operation of a payroll bank account.**
4. **Calculate the payroll costs levied on employers and prepare the entries to record the accrual and payment of these amounts.**
5. **Calculate and record employee fringe benefit costs and show the effect of these items on the total cost of employing labour.**
6. **Define or explain the words and phrases listed in the chapter glossary.**

Wages or salaries generally amount to one of the largest expenses incurred by a business. Accounting for employees' wages and salaries is one task that is shared by almost all business entities.

Payroll accounting:

- records cash payments to employees
- provides valuable information regarding labour costs
- accounts for amounts withheld from employees' pay
- accounts for employee (fringe) benefits and payroll costs paid by the employer
- provides the means to comply with governmental regulations on employee compensation

As you study this chapter, you will learn the general processes all businesses follow to account for these items.

## ITEMS WITHHELD FROM EMPLOYEES' WAGES

**LO 1**

List the taxes and other items frequently withheld from employees' wages.

An understanding of payroll accounting and the design and use of payroll records requires some knowledge of the laws and programs that affect payrolls. Many of these require **payroll deductions,** amounts withheld from the wages of employees. Consequently, the more pertinent of these are discussed in the first portion of this chapter before the subject of payroll records is introduced.

### Withholding Employees' Income Tax

With few exceptions, employers are required to calculate, collect, and remit to the Receiver General of Canada the income taxes of their employees. Historically, when the first federal income tax law became effective in 1917, it applied to only a few individuals having high earnings. It was not until World War II that income taxes were levied on substantially all wage earners. At that time Parliament recognized that many individual wage earners could not be expected to save sufficient money with which to pay their income taxes once each year. Consequently, Parliament instituted a system of pay-as-you-go withholding of taxes at their source each payday. This pay-as-you-go withholding of employee income taxes requires an employer to act as a tax collecting agent of the federal government.

The amount of income taxes to be withheld from an employee's wages is determined by his or her wages and the amount of **personal tax credits.** Each individual is entitled, in 1995, to some or all of the following annual amounts which are subject to tax credits (as applicable):

| | | |
|---|---|---|
| 1. | Basic personal amount | $6,456 |
| 2. | Married or equivalent | 5,380 |
| | (with maximum earnings stipulated) | |

The total of each taxpayer's personal tax credits is deducted from income to determine the level of income tax deductions from the individual's gross pay. For example, an individual with a gross weekly salary of $500 and personal tax credits of $6,456 (1995 net claim code 1 on the TD1 form) would have $92.55 of income taxes withheld. Another individual with the same gross salary but with personal tax credits of $11,783 (claim code 5) would have $64.40 withheld.

Employers are responsible for determining the amount of income tax owed by each employee every payday and withholding it from his or her pay for that period. However, to do this an employer must know the credits claimed by each employee. Consequently, every employee is required to file with the employer an employee's Personal Tax Credit Return, Form TD1, on which he or she claims the applicable credit. The taxpayer must file a revised Form TD1 each time the exemptions change during a year. The TD1 form is shown in Illustration 10–1.

In determining the amounts of income taxes to be withheld from the wages of employees, employers normally use tax withholding tables provided by Revenue Canada, Taxation. The tables indicate the tax to be withheld from any amount of wages and with any number of credits. The to-be-withheld amounts include both federal and provincial income taxes except for the province of Quebec. The province of Quebec levies and collects its own income tax and its own pension plan contributions. Employers in that province remit separately, to the respective authority, federal and provincial tax deductions. In addition to determining and withholding income taxes from each employee's wages every payday, employers are required to remit the withheld taxes to the Receiver General of Canada each month.

## Canada Pension Plan (CPP)

The **Canada Pension Plan** applies, with few exceptions, to everyone who is working. Every employee and self-employed person between the ages of 18 and 70 must make contributions in required amounts to the Canada Pension Plan (CPP). Self-employed individuals are required to periodically remit appropriate amounts to the Receiver General of Canada. Employee contributions are deducted by the employer from salary, wages, or other remuneration paid to the employee. Furthermore, each employer is required to contribute an amount equal to that deducted from the employees' earnings.

Contributions are based on earnings, with the first $3,400 of each employee's annual income being exempt. On earnings above that amount and up to the 1995 ceiling of $34,900 a year, the employee contributes at a rate of 2.7%. The total contribution from both employee and employer is 5.4% on the $31,500 of annual earnings between $3,400 and $34,900. Thus, the maximum contribution to the

**Illustration 10-1  TDI Form**

 Revenue Revenu
Canada Canada

## PERSONAL TAX CREDITS RETURN

TD1(E)
Rev. 95

### Instructions

**You have to complete this return if you have a new employer or payer, and you received one or more of the following types of income:**

- salary, wages, commissions, pensions, or any other remuneration; or
- Unemployment Insurance benefits, including training allowances.

Complete a new return no later than seven days after your marital or parental status changes or when you expect a change in your personal credits for the year. It is an offence to file a false return.

If you receive non-employment income, such as a pension or Old Age Security, and you want to have extra tax deducted at source, you can complete Form TD3, *Request for Income Tax Deduction on non-employment income.*

If you have deductions such as registered retirement savings plan contributions, alimony payments, or child care expenses, the amount of tax to be withheld from your income can be reduced. You have to send a written application to your district income tax office. A tax office letter of authority is not needed when a court order states that alimony or maintenance payments have to be deducted at source from an employee's salary.

If you need help, ask your employer or payer, or call the Employer Services Division of your income tax office. The number for this office is listed in the government pages of your telephone book under Revenue Canada.

**Confidential calculation on back  -  Employee's copy**

Employer's or payer's copy

 Revenue Revenu
Canada Canada

## PERSONAL TAX CREDITS RETURN

TD1(E)
Rev. 95

**After you complete this return, give it to your employer or payer.**

| Last name (capital letters) | Usual first name and initials | Employee number |
|---|---|---|

| Address | For non-residents only - country of permanent residence | Social insurance number |
|---|---|---|

| Postal code | | Date of birth |
|---|---|---|
| | | Year    Month    Day |

### 1.  Basic personal amount

Everyone can claim **$6,456** as the basic personal amount.

- If you choose to claim this amount, enter $6,456.
- If you choose not to claim this amount (e.g., when you have more than one employer or payer and you have already claimed the basic personal amount), **enter 0 in box A** on the other side of this return and do not complete sections 2 to 8. You may with to complete sections 9 to 11.
- If you are a non-resident, and you will be including most of your annual world income (90% or more) when determining your taxable income in Canada, you can claim certain personal amounts. If you are not sure about your non-resident status, or need more information, call the Client Assistance Division of your income tax office

Credit claimed  $

### 2.  Spousal amount or equivalent-to-spouse amount.

You can claim an amount for supporting your spouse if you are **married or have a common-law spouse**. A common-law spouse is a person of the opposite sex with whom you live in a common-law relationship for any continuous period of at least 12 months, including any period of separation (due to a breakdown in the relationship) of less than 90 days, or with whom you live in a common-law relationship and who is the natural or adoptive parent of your child.

You can claim an equivalent-to-spouse amount if you are **single, divorced, separated, or widowed**, and you support a relative who is:
- residing in Canada (if the relative is your child, the child does not have to reside in Canada);
- living with you in a home you maintain;
- related to you by blood, marriage, or adoption; and
- under 18 years old, except for a relative who has a mental or physical infirmity.

**Calculating the amount**
If you marry during the year, your spouse's net income includes the income earned before and during the marriage.
If the net income of your spouse or relative for the year will be:
- over $5,918, **enter 0**
- $538 or less, **enter $5,380**; or
- more than $538, complete calculation no. 2 on the back of this return and enter the result as credit claimed.

**Any person you claim here cannot be claimed again in section 3.**

Credit claimed  $

### 3.  Amount for disabled dependent relatives

With the introduction of the child tax benefit, there is no amount for dependent children who are under the age of 18 at the end of the year. However, you can claim an amount for each disabled dependant who is:
- your or your spouse's child or grandchild, 18 years old or older, and who has a physical or mental infirmity; or
- your or your spouse's parent, grandparent, brother, sister, aunt, uncle, niece, or nephew, who is 18 years old or older, and who has a physical or mental infirmity and is resident in Canada.

**Calculating the amount for a disabled dependent relative:**
If your dependant's net income for the year will be:
- $2,690 or less, **enter $1,583** in section 3 of this return; or
- more than $2,690, complete calculation no. 3 on the back of this return and enter the result as credit claimed.

**You can claim an amount for each disabled dependent relative you have.**

Credit claimed  $

### 4.  Amount for eligible pension

An eligible pension income includes pension payments received from a pension plan or fund as a life annuity, and foreign pension payments. It does not include payments form the Canada or Quebec Pension Plan, Old Age Security, guaranteed supplements, or lump-sum withdrawals from a pension fund.

If you receive an eligible pension income, you can claim your eligible pension income or $1,000, whichever amount is less.

Credit claimed  $

### 5.  Age amount

If your estimated net income from all sources for the year will be:
- $25,921 or less, **enter $3,482**;
- over $25,921, but not over $49,134.33, complete calculation no. 5 on the back of this return and **enter** the result as credit claimed; or
- over $49,134.33, enter $0.

Credit claimed  $

Ce formulaire existe aussi en français.

**Illustration 10-1** *(concluded)*

| | | |
|---|---|---|
| **Calculation no. 2 •** more than $538, calculate: | | **$ 5,918** |
| | Minus: net income of spouse or relative | _____ |
| | **Total calculated:** | ══════ |
| | Report total in section 2 as credit claimed | ══════ |
| **Calculation no. 3 •** more than $2,690, calculate: | | **$ 4,273** |
| | Minus: dependant's net income | _____ |
| | **Total calculated:** | ══════ |
| | Report total in section 3 as credit claimed | ══════ |

**Calculation no. 5:**
• over $25,921, but not over $49,134.33, calculate:
Basic age amount: . . . . . . . . . . . . . . . . . . . . . . . . . . .   **$ 3,482 A.**
Reduced by:
1. Annual estimated net income. $ _____
2. Less base amount . . . . . . . – $   25,921
3. Line 1 minus line 2 . . . . . . . = $ _____
4. Line 3 by 15% . . . . . . . . . . . . . . . . . . . . . . . . . . . . . .   **B.**
                                              $ = _____
**Subtract A from B.** If negative, enter 0
Report total in section 5 as credit claimed

| Claim Codes | |
|---|---|
| **Total claim amount** | **Claim codes** |
| No claim amount | 0 |
| Minimum   $ 6,456 | 1 |
| $ 6,456.01 -   8,037 | 2 |
| 8,037.01 -   9,619 | 3 |
| 9,619.01 - 11,202 | 4 |
| 11,202.01 - 12,783 | 5 |
| 12,783.01 - 14,364 | 6 |
| 14,364.01 - 15,946 | 7 |
| 15,946.01 - 17,527 | 8 |
| 17,527.01 - 19,109 | 9 |
| 19,109.01 - 20,693 | 10 |
| $ 20,693.01 -  and over Manual calculation required by employer | X |
| No tax withholding required | E |

**6. Tuition fees and education amount**

**Enter** your tuition fees, for courses you will take in the year, to attend a university, college, or an institution that the Minister of Human Resources Development has certified · · · · · · · · · · · · · · · · · · · · · · _____

**Add** $80 for each month in the year that you will be enrolled full-time in a qualifying educational program at a university, college, or a school offering job retraining courses or correspondence courses, as indicated on Form T2202 or T2202A · · · · · · · · · · · · · · · · · · _____

**Subtract** any scholarships, fellowships, or bursaries you will receive in the year (do not report the first $500) . . . . . . . . . . . . . . . . . _____

**Enter** the total amount claimed. If you arrive at a negative amount, **enter 0** . . . . . . . . . . . . . . . . . . . . . . . **Credit claimed**  $ _____

**7. Disability amount**

**You can claim $4,233** for a person who is severely impaired, mentally or physically, and for whom you will claim the disability amount by using Form T2201, *Disability Tax Credit Certificate.*
Such an impairment has to markedly restrict the person in his or her daily living activities. The impairment has to last, or be expected to last, for a continuous period of at least 12 months.
**Enter** the total amount claimed: . . . . . . . . . . . . . . . . . . . . . . . . . . . . **Credit claimed**  $ _____

**8. Amounts transferred from your spouse, relatives, or dependants**

You can transfer any of the following amounts that your spouse, relative, or dependants do not need to reduce their federal income tax to zero.

**Age amount** - If, this year, your spouse will be 65 or older, you can claim any unused balance of the age amount to a maximum of **$3,482** . . . . . . . . . . . . . . . . . . . . . . . . . . . . . . . . . . . . . . . . . . . . . . . . _____

**Pension income amount** - If your spouse receives eligible pension income, you can claim any unused balance of the eligible pension income amount to a maximum of **$1,000** . . . . . . . . . . . . . . . . . . . . _____

**Disability amount** - If your spouse, relatives, or dependants are disabled, you can claim their unused balance of the disability amount to a maximum of **$4,233** for each person . . . . . . . . . . . . . . . . . . . . . . . . . . . _____

**Tuition fees and education amount** - If you are supporting a spouse, relative, or dependants who are attending a university, college, or a certified educational institution, you can claim their unused balance of tuition fees and education amount to a maximum of **$4,000** for each person . . . . . . . . . . . . . . . . . . . . . . . . . . . . . . . . . . . . . _____

**Enter** the total amount calculated . . . . . . . . . . . . . . . . . . . . . . . . . . . . . . . . **Credit claimed**  $ _____

**Total all your personal tax credit amounts from sections 1 to 8** . . . . . . . . . . . . . . . . . . .   $ _____

**Total of credits**

At the top of this form, see the claim codes to determine the claim code that applies to you, and enter this code in box **A** . If the total of your tax credits is greater than your employment income for the year, your claim code is "E."  [ ___ ] **A**

## Additional information

**9. Additional tax to be deducted**

if you receive additional income you may find it convenient to have additional tax deducted from each payment. This will help you avoid having to pay tax when you file your income tax return. If so, state the amount of additional tax you want to have deducted from each payment. If you want to change this extra deduction later, you have to complete a new TD1 return.   $ _____

**10. Deduction for living in a designated area (e.g., Yukon Territory, or Northwest Territories)**

If you live in the Yukon Territory, Northwest Territories, or another designated area for more than six months in a row, beginning or ending this year, you can claim:

• $7.50 for each day that you live in the designated area; or
• $15 for each day that you live in the designated area, if during that time you live in a dwelling that you maintain, and you are the only person living in that dwelling who is claiming this deduction.
   For more information, including a list and categories of designated areas, see the income tax guide called *Northern Residents Deduction,* available at any income tax office.   $ _____

**11.** If you reside in **Ontario, Manitoba, Saskatchewan** or **British Columbia,** enter the number of your dependants under 18 years old at the end of the year.

For **Ontario, Manitoba** and **Saskatchewan** residents, only the spouse with the higher net income can indicate an amount.
**If you reside in Ontario, Manitoba** or **British Columbia,** the number of children indicated should not include a child claimed for purposes of the equivalent-to-spouse amount   [ ___ ]

I certify that, to the Best of my knowledge, the information given on this form is correct and complete.

Signature _____     Date _____

Canada Pension Plan is $850.50 each from the employee and the employer. The $3,400 exemption is adjusted for weekly or monthly pay periods by dividing by the appropriate number; that is, 52, 12, and so on.

Employers are responsible for making the proper deductions from their employees' earnings. They remit these deductions each month, together with their own contributions, to the Receiver General of Canada.

Self-employed individuals pay the combined rate for employees and employers, or 5.4% on annual earnings between $3,400 and the exempt ceiling of $34,900.

## Unemployment Insurance (UI)

To alleviate hardships caused by interruptions in earnings through unemployment, the federal government, with the concurrence of all provincial governments, implemented an employee/employer-financed unemployment insurance plan. Under the Unemployment Insurance Act, 1971, compulsory **unemployment insurance** coverage was extended to all Canadian workers who are not self-employed. As of January 1, 1995, over 12 million employees, including teachers, hospital workers, and top-level executives, were covered by the insurance plan.

The purpose of an unemployment insurance program is usually twofold:

1. To pay unemployment compensation for limited periods to unemployed individuals eligible for benefits.
2. To establish and operate employment facilities that assist unemployed individuals in finding suitable employment and assist employers in finding employees.

The unemployment insurance fund from which benefits are paid is jointly financed by employees and their employers. Under the current act, in 1995 employers are required to deduct from their employees' wages 3% of insured earnings, to add a contribution of 1.4 times the amount deducted from employees' wages, and to remit both amounts to the Receiver General of Canada. Insured earnings refer to average weekly gross pay in the range of $163 to $815. Employees paid in whole or in part on a time-worked or fixed-salary basis must be employed at least 15 hours in a weekly pay period or earn 20% of the maximum weekly insurable earnings ($815 in 1995) in order to be insurable. The maximum amount deductible per year is $1,271.40 (in 1995). This amount is adjusted for weekly or monthly pay periods by dividing by the appropriate number; that is, 52, 12, and so on.

The Unemployment Insurance Act, in addition to setting rates, requires that an employer

1. Withhold from the wages of each employee each payday an amount of unemployment insurance tax calculated at the current rate.
2. Pay an unemployment insurance tax equal to 1.4 times the amount withheld from the wages of all employees.
3. Periodically remit both the amounts withheld from employees' wages and the employer's tax to the Receiver General of Canada. (Remittance is discussed later in this chapter.)
4. Complete a "Record of Employment" form for employees who experience an "interruption of earnings" because of termination of employment, illness, injury, or pregnancy.

5. Keep a record for each employee that shows among other things wages subject to unemployment insurance and taxes withheld. (The law does not specify the exact form of the record, but most employers keep individual employees earnings records similar to the one shown later in this chapter.)

## Weekly Unemployment Benefits

The amount of weekly benefits received by an unemployed individual who qualifies is based on his or her average insurable weekly earnings. The federal government has varied the benefit period from region to region on the basis of percentage and duration of unemployment in the region.

## Use of Withholding Tables

Most employers use **wage bracket withholding tables** similar to the one for 1995 shown in Illustration 10–2 in determining Canada Pension Plan and unemployment insurance to be withheld from employees' gross earnings. The illustrated table is for a weekly pay period; different tables are provided for different pay periods. Somewhat similar tables are available for determining income tax withholdings. These tables are also available on computer discs from Revenue Canada for computer applications.

Determining the amount of withholdings from an employee's gross wages is quite easy when withholding tables are used. First, the employee's wage bracket is located in the first two columns. Then the amounts to be withheld for Canada Pension Plan and unemployment insurance are found on the line of the wage bracket in the appropriate columns.

## The T-4 Form

Employers are required to report wages and deductions both to each employee and to the local office of Revenue Canada. On or before the last day of February, the employer must give each employee a T-4 summary, a statement that tells the employee

a. Total wages for the preceding year.
b. Taxable benefits received from the employer.
c. Income taxes withheld.
d. Deductions for registered pension plan.
e. Canada Pension Plan contributions.
f. Unemployment insurance deductions.

On or before the last day of February, the employer must forward to the district taxation office copies of the employee's T-4 statements plus a T-4 that summarizes the information contained on the employee's T-4 statements. The T-4 form is shown in Illustration 10–3.

## Wages, Hours, and Union Contracts

All provinces have laws establishing maximum hours of work and minimum pay rates. And while the details vary with each province, generally employers are required to pay an employee for hours worked in excess of 40 in any one week at the employee's regular pay rate plus an overtime premium of at least one-half of

**Illustration 10-2**   1995 Wage Bracket Withholding Tables—UIC and CPP

| UNEMPLOYMENT INSURANCE PREMIUMS | COTISATIONS À L'ASSURANCE-CHÔMAGE |
|---|---|
| For minimum and maximum insurable earnings amounts for various pay periods see Schedule II. For the maximum premium deduction for various pay periods see bottom of this page. | Les montants minimum et maximum des gains assurables pour diverses périodes de paie figurent en annexe II. La déduction maximale de primes pour diverses périodes de paie figure au bas de la présente page. |

| Remuneration Rémunération From-de | To-à | U.I. Premium Cotisation d'a.-c. | Remuneration Rémunération From-de | To-à | U.I. Premium Cotisation d'a.-c. | Remuneration Rémunération From-de | To-à | U.I. Premium Cotisation d'a.-c. | Remuneration Rémunération From-de | To-à | U.I. Premium Cotisation d'a.-c. |
|---|---|---|---|---|---|---|---|---|---|---|---|
| 192.17 | 192.49 | 5.77 | 216.17 | 216.49 | 6.49 | 240.17 | 240.49 | 7.21 | 264.17 | 264.49 | 7.93 |
| 192.50 | 192.83 | 5.78 | 216.50 | 216.83 | 6.50 | 240.50 | 240.83 | 7.22 | 264.50 | 264.83 | 7.94 |
| 192.84 | 193.16 | 5.79 | 216.84 | 217.16 | 6.51 | 240.84 | 241.16 | 7.23 | 264.84 | 265.16 | 7.95 |
| 193.17 | 193.49 | 5.80 | 217.17 | 217.49 | 6.52 | 241.17 | 241.49 | 7.24 | 265.17 | 265.49 | 7.96 |
| 193.50 | 193.83 | 5.81 | 217.50 | 217.83 | 6.53 | 241.50 | 241.83 | 7.25 | 265.50 | 265.83 |  |
| 193.84 | 194.16 | 5.82 | 217.84 | 218.16 | 6.54 | 241.84 | 242.16 | 7.26 | 265.84 | 266.16 |  |
| 194.17 | 194.49 | 5.83 | 218.17 | 218.49 | 6.55 | 242.17 | 242.49 | 7.27 | 266.17 |  |  |
| 194.50 | 194.83 | 5.84 | 218.50 | 218.83 | 6.56 | 242.50 | 242.83 | 7.28 |  |  |  |
| 194.84 | 195.16 | 5.85 | 218.84 | 219.16 | 6.57 | 242.84 | 243.16 | 7.29 |  |  |  |
| 195.17 | 195.49 | 5.86 | 219.17 | 219.49 | 6.58 | 243.17 |  |  |  |  |  |
| 195.50 | 195.83 | 5.87 | 219.50 | 219.83 | 6.59 | 243.50 |  |  |  |  |  |
| 195.84 | 196.16 | 5.88 | 219.84 | 220.16 | 6.60 |  |  |  |  |  |  |
| 196.17 | 196.49 | 5.89 | 220.17 | 220.49 |  |  |  |  |  |  |  |
| 196.50 | 196.83 | 5.90 | 220.50 | 220.83 |  |  |  |  |  |  |  |
| 196.84 | 197.16 | 5.91 | 220.84 |  |  |  |  |  |  |  |  |
| 197.17 | 197.49 | 5.92 |  |  |  |  |  |  |  |  |  |
| 197.50 | 197.83 | 5.93 |  |  |  |  |  |  |  |  |  |
| 197.84 | 198.16 |  |  |  |  |  |  |  |  |  |  |
| 198.17 | 198.49 |  |  |  |  |  |  |  |  |  |  |
| 198.50 | 198.83 |  |  |  |  |  |  |  |  |  |  |
| 198.84 | 199.16 |  |  |  |  |  |  |  |  |  |  |
| 199.17 | 199.49 |  |  |  |  |  |  |  |  |  |  |
| 199.50 | 199.83 |  |  |  |  |  |  |  |  |  |  |
| 199.84 | 200.16 |  |  |  |  |  |  |  |  |  |  |

CANADA PENSION PLAN CONTRIBUTIONS / COTISATIONS AU RÉGIME DE PENSIONS DU CANADA

WEEKLY PAY PERIOD — PÉRIODE HEBDOMADAIRE DE PAIE

181.33—301.32

| Remuneration Rémunération From-de | To-à | C.P.P. R.P.C | Remuneration Rémunération From-de | To-à | C.P.P. R.P.C | Remuneration Rémunération From-de | To-à | C.P.P. R.P.C | Remuneration Rémunération From-de | To-à | C.P.P. R.P.C |
|---|---|---|---|---|---|---|---|---|---|---|---|
| 181.33 | 182.15 | 2.98 | 211.33 | 212.15 | 3.60 | 241.33 | 242.15 | 4.32 | 271.33 | 271.73 | 5.04 |
| 181.74 | 182.98 | 2.89 | 211.74 | 212.57 | 3.61 | 241.74 | 242.57 | 4.33 | 271.74 | 272.15 | 5.05 |
| 182.16 | 182.98 | 2.90 | 212.16 | 212.98 | 3.62 | 242.16 | 242.98 | 4.34 | 272.16 | 272.57 | 5.06 |
| 182.58 | 183.40 | 2.91 | 212.58 | 213.40 | 3.63 | 242.58 | 243.40 | 4.35 | 272.58 | 272.98 | 5.07 |
| 182.99 | 183.82 | 2.92 | 212.99 | 213.82 | 3.64 | 242.99 | 243.40 | 4.36 | 272.99 | 273.40 | 5.08 |
| 183.41 | 184.65 | 2.93 | 213.41 | 214.23 | 3.65 | 243.41 | 244.15 | 4.37 | 273.41 | 273.82 | 5.09 |
| 183.83 | 184.65 | 2.94 | 213.83 | 214.65 | 3.66 | 243.83 | 244.65 | 4.38 | 273.83 | 274.65 | 5.11 |
| 184.24 | 185.07 | 2.95 | 214.24 | 215.07 | 3.67 | 244.24 | 245.07 | 4.39 | 274.24 | 275.07 | 5.12 |
| 184.66 | 185.48 | 2.96 | 214.66 | 215.48 | 3.68 | 244.66 | 245.48 | 4.40 | 274.66 | 275.07 | 5.13 |
| 185.08 | 185.48 | 2.97 | 215.08 | 215.90 | 3.69 | 245.08 | 245.90 | 4.42 | 275.08 | 275.90 | 5.15 |
| 185.49 | 185.90 | 2.98 | 215.49 | 216.32 | 3.71 | 245.49 | 246.32 | 4.43 | 275.49 | 275.92 | 5.16 |
| 185.91 | 186.73 | 2.99 | 215.91 | 216.73* | 3.72 | 245.91 | 246.73 | 4.44 | 275.91 | 276.73 | 5.17 |
| 186.33 | 187.15 | 3.00 | 216.33 | 217.15 | 3.73 | 246.33 | 247.15 | 4.45 | 276.33 | 277.15 | 5.18 |
| 186.74 | 187.57 | 3.01 | 216.74 | 217.57 | 3.74 | 246.74 | 247.57 | 4.46 | 276.74 | 277.57 | 5.19 |
| 187.16 | 187.98 | 3.02 | 217.16 | 217.98 | 3.76 | 247.16 | 247.98 | 4.47 | 277.16 | 277.98 | 5.20 |
| 187.58 | 188.40 | 3.03 | 217.58 | 218.40 | 3.77 | 247.58 | 248.40 | 4.48 | 277.58 | 278.40 | 5.21 |
| 187.99 | 188.82 | 3.04 | 217.99 | 218.82 |  | 247.99 | 248.82 |  | 277.99 | 278.82 | 5.22 |
| 188.41 |  | 3.05 | 218.41 |  |  | 248.41 |  | 4.50 | 278.41 |  | 5.23 |
| 188.83 | 189.23 | 3.06 | 218.83 | 219.23 | 3.78 | 248.83 | 249.23 | 4.51 | 278.63 | 279.23 | 5.24 |
| 189.24 | 189.65 | 3.07 | 219.24 | 219.65 | 3.80 | 249.24 | 249.65 | 4.52 | 279.24 | 279.65 | 5.25 |
| 189.66 | 190.07 | 3.08 | 219.66 | 220.07 | 3.81 | 249.66 | 250.07 | 4.53 | 279.65 | 280.07 | 5.26 |
| 190.08 | 190.48 | 3.09 | 220.08 | 220.90 | 3.82 | 250.08 | 250.90 | 4.54 | 280.08 | 280.48 | 5.27 |
| 190.49 | 190.90 | 3.10 | 220.91 | 221.73 | 3.84 | 250.91 | 251.32 | 4.55 | 280.49 | 281.32 | 5.28 |
| 190.91 | 191.32 | 3.11 | 221.33 | 221.73 | 3.85 | 251.33 | 252.15 | 4.56 | 281.33 | 282.15 | 5.29 |
| 191.33 | 191.73 | 3.12 | 221.74 | 222.57 | 3.86 | 251.74 | 252.15 |  | 281.74 | 282.57 | 5.30 |
| 191.74 | 192.15 | 3.13 | 222.16 |  |  | 252.16 |  | 4.58 | 282.16 |  | 5.31 |
| 192.16 | 192.57 | 3.14 | 222.58 | 222.98 | 3.87 | 252.53 | 252.98 | 4.59 | 282.58 | 282.98 | 5.32 |
| 192.58 | 192.98 | 3.15 | 222.99 | 223.40 | 3.88 | 252.99 | 253.40 | 4.60 | 282.99 | 283.40 | 5.33 |
| 192.99 | 193.40 | 3.16 | 223.41 | 223.82 | 3.89 | 253.41 | 253.42 | 4.61 | 283.41 | 283.82 |  |
| 193.41 | 193.82 | 3.17 | 223.83 |  | 3.90 | 253.43 |  | 4.62 | 283.83 | 284.23 |  |
| 193.83 | 194.23 | 3.19 |  |  | 3.91 |  |  |  | 284.24 |  |  |

his or her regular rate. This gives an employee an overtime rate of at least 1½ times his or her regular hourly rate for hours in excess of 40 in any one week. In addition, employers commonly operate under contracts with their employees' union that provide even better terms. For example, union contracts often provide for time-and-a-half for work on Saturdays, and double time for Sundays and holidays. When an employer is under a union contract in which the terms are better than those provided for by law, the contract terms take precedence over the law.

In addition to specifying working hours and wage rates, union contracts often provide for the collection of employees' union dues by the employer. Such a requirement commonly provides that the employer shall deduct dues from the wages of each employee and remit the amounts deducted to the union. The employer is usually required to remit once each month reporting each employee's name and the amount deducted from his or her pay.

**Illustration 10-3    T-4 Form**

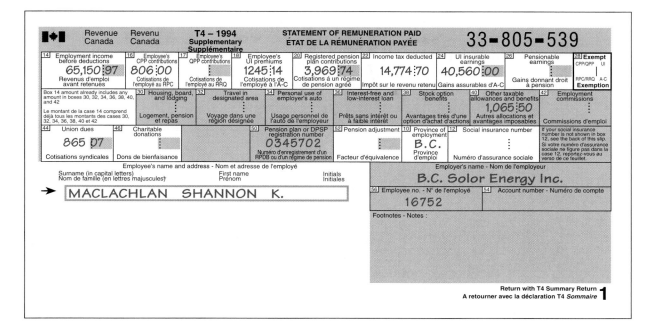

## Other Payroll Deductions

In addition to the payroll deductions discussed thus far, employees may individually authorize additional deductions. Some examples of these might be

1. Deductions to accumulate funds for the purchase of Canada Savings Bonds.
2. Deductions to pay health, accident, hospital, or life insurance premiums.
3. Deductions to repay loans from the employer or the employees' credit union.
4. Deductions to pay for merchandise purchased from the company.
5. Deductions for donations to charitable organizations such as the United Way.

## Timekeeping

Compiling a record of the time worked by each employee is called **timekeeping.** The method used to compile such a record depends on the nature of the company's business and the number of its employees. In a very small business, timekeeping may consist of no more than notations of each employee's working time made in a memorandum book by the manager or owner. In many companies, however, time clocks are used to record on clock cards each employee's time of arrival and departure. The time clocks are usually placed near entrances to the office, store, or factory. At the beginning of each payroll period, a **clock card** for each employee (see Illustration 10–4) is placed in a rack for use by the employee. Upon arriving at work, each employee takes his or her card from the rack and places it in a slot in the time clock. This actuates the clock to stamp the date and arrival time on the card. The employee then returns the card to the rack. Upon leaving the plant, store, or office for lunch or at the end of the day, the procedure is repeated. The em-

**Illustration 10–4    An Employee's Clock Card**

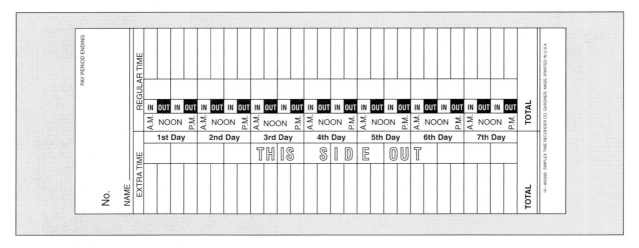

ployee takes the card from the rack, places it in the clock, and the time of departure is automatically stamped. At a result, at the end of each period, the card shows the hours the employee was at work.

---

**Progress Check**

**10–1    What is the purpose of the federal Unemployment Insurance scheme?**

**10–2    When must T-4 statements be given to employees?**

**10–3    What are other typical nonmandatory payroll deductions?**

---

## THE PAYROLL REGISTER

**LO 2**

Make the calculations necessary to prepare a Payroll Register and prepare the entry to record payroll liabilities.

Each pay period the total hours worked as compiled on clock cards or by other means is summarized in a Payroll Register, an example of which is shown in Illustration 10–5. The illustrated register is for a weekly pay period and shows the payroll data for each employee on a separate line.

In Illustration 10–5, the columns under the heading Daily Time show the hours worked each day by each employee. The total of each employee's hours is entered in the column headed Total Hours. If hours worked include overtime hours, these are entered in the column headed O.T. Hours.

The Regular Pay Rate column shows the hourly pay rate of each employee. Total hours worked multiplied by the regular pay rate equals regular pay. Overtime hours multiplied by the overtime premium rate (50% in this case) equals overtime premium pay. And regular pay plus overtime premium pay is the **employee's gross pay.**

The amounts withheld from each employee's gross pay are recorded in the Deductions columns of the payroll register. For example, you determine the income tax deductions by matching the gross pay of each employee to the tax deduction tables and then enter the results in the tax deduction column. Income tax deductions are based on the gross pay less the amounts deducted for unemployment insurance and Canada Pension Plan. The tax tables allow for these adjustments and separate books are available for each province. However, for simplicity, assume that income tax deductions are 20% of the employee's gross pay.

**Illustration 10–5** Payroll Register

| | | | | | | | | | | | | | Payroll Week Ended | |
|---|---|---|---|---|---|---|---|---|---|---|---|---|---|---|

| | | | | | | | | | | | Earnings | | | |
|---|---|---|---|---|---|---|---|---|---|---|---|---|---|---|
| Employees | Clock Card No. | Daily Time | | | | | | | Total Hours | O.T. Hours | Reg. Pay Rate | Regular Pay | O.T. Premium Pay | Gross Pay | |
| | | M | T | W | T | F | S | S | | | | | | | |
| Auer, John | 118 | 8 | 8 | 8 | 8 | 8 | | | 40 | | 10.00 | 400.00 | | 400.00 | 1 |
| Cheung, Joan | 109 | 0 | 8 | 8 | 8 | 8 | 8 | | 40 | | 12.00 | 480.00 | | 480.00 | 2 |
| Daljit, Moe | 121 | 8 | 8 | 8 | 8 | 8 | 8 | 4 | 52 | 12 | 15.00 | 780.00 | 90.00 | 870.00 | 3 |
| Lee, Shannon | 104 | 8 | 8 | | 8 | 8 | 8 | 4 | 44 | 4 | 14.00 | 616.00 | 28.00 | 644.00 | 4 |
| Prasad, Sunil | 108 | | 8 | 8 | 8 | 8 | 4 | 8 | 44 | 4 | 15.00 | 660.00 | 30.00 | 690.00 | 5 |
| Rupert, Allan | 105 | 8 | 8 | 8 | 8 | 8 | | | 40 | | 12.00 | 480.00 | | 480.00 | 6 |
| Totals | | | | | | | | | | | | 3,416.00 | 148.00 | 3,564.00 | |

**Register June 11, 1995**

| | Deductions | | | | | Payment | | Distribution | |
|---|---|---|---|---|---|---|---|---|---|
| | U.I. Premium | Income Taxes | Hosp. Ins. | C.P.P. | Total Deductions | Net Pay | Cheque No. | Sales Salaries | Office Salaries |
| 1 | 12.00 | 80.00 | 18.00 | 9.03 | 119.03 | 280.97 | 754 | 400.00 | |
| 2 | 14.40 | 96.00 | 18.00 | 11.19 | 139.59 | 340.41 | 755 | 480.00 | |
| 3 | 26.10 | 174.00 | 24.00 | 21.63 | 245.73 | 624.27 | 756 | | 870.00 |
| 4 | 19.32 | 128.80 | 18.00 | 15.62 | 181.74 | 462.26 | 757 | | 644.00 |
| 5 | 20.71 | 138.00 | 24.00 | 16.77 | 199.48 | 490.52 | 758 | 690.00 | |
| 6 | 14.40 | 96.00 | 18.00 | 11.19 | 139.59 | 340.41 | 759 | 480.00 | |
| | 106.93 | 712.80 | 120.00 | 85.43 | 1,025.16 | 2,538.84 | | 2,050.00 | 1,514.00 |

As previously stated, the income tax withheld depends on each employee's gross pay and personal tax credits. You can determine these amounts by first referring to the personal tax credits and then to the appropriate wage bracket withholding tables. You then enter them in the column headed Income Taxes.

The column headed Hosp. Ins. shows the amounts withheld to pay for hospital insurance for the employees and their families. The total withheld from all employees is a current liability of the employer until paid to the insurance company. Likewise, the total withheld for employees' union dues is a current liability until paid to the union.

Additional columns may be added to the Payroll register for any other deductions that occur sufficiently often to warrant special columns. For example, a company that regularly deducts amounts from its employees' pay for Canada Savings bonds may add a special column for this deduction.

An employee's gross pay less total deductions is the **employee's net pay** and is entered in the Net Pay column. The total of this column is the amount the employees are to be paid. The numbers of the cheques used to pay the employees are entered in the column headed Cheque No.

The Distribution columns are used to classify the various salaries in terms of different kinds of expense. Here you enter each employee's gross salary in the proper column according to the type of work performed. The column totals then indicate the amounts to be debited to the salary expense accounts.

## Recording the Payroll

Generally, a Payroll Register such as the one shown is a supplementary memo-randum record. As such, you do not post its information directly to the accounts. Instead, you must first record the payroll with a General Journal entry, which is then posted to the accounts. The entry to record the payroll shown in Illustration 10–5 is:

| June | 11 | Sales Salaries Expense ....................... | 2,050.00 | |
|------|----|-----------------------------------------------|----------|-----------|
| | | Office Salaries Expense ..................... | 1,514.00 | |
| | |     Unemployment Insurance Payable ............ | | 106.93 |
| | |     Employees' Income Taxes Payable ............ | | 712.80 |
| | |     Employees' Hospital Insurance Payable ........ | | 120.00 |
| | |     Canada Pension Plan Payable ............... | | 85.43 |
| | |     Payroll Payable ......................... | | 2,538.84 |
| | | *To record the June 11 payroll.* | | |

The debits of the entry were taken from the Payroll Register's distribution col-umn totals. They charge the employees' gross earnings to the proper salary expense accounts. The credits to UI Payable, Employees' Income Taxes Payable, Employ-ees' Hospital Insurance Payable, and CPP Payable record these amounts as current liabilities. The credit to Payroll Payable (also called Salaries Payable, Wages Payable, or Accrued Salaries Payable, etc.) records as a liability the net amount to be paid to the employees.

---

### Progress Check

**10–4    What constitutes the employee's gross pay?**

**10–5    What is the employee's net pay?**

---

## PAYING THE EMPLOYEES

### LO 3

Prepare journal entries to record the payments to employees and explain the operation of a payroll bank account.

Almost every business pays its employees by cheques. In a company that has few employees, these cheques often are drawn on the regular bank account and entered in a Cash Disbursements Journal (or Cheque Register) like the one described in Chapter 6. Since each cheque is debited to the Payroll Payable account, posting labour can be saved by adding a Salaries Payable column in the journal. If such a column is added, entries to pay the employees shown in the Illustration 10–5 pay-roll will appear as in Illustration 10–6.

Most employers furnish each employee an earnings statement each payday. The statement gives the employee a record of hours worked, gross pay, deductions, and net pay. The statement often takes the form of a detachable paycheque portion that is removed before the cheque is cashed. A paycheque with a detachable earnings statement is reproduced in Illustration 10–7.

## Payroll Bank Account

A business with many employees will often use a special **payroll bank account** to pay its employees. When such an account is used, one cheque for the total pay-roll is drawn on the regular bank account and deposited in the special payroll bank

**Illustration 10-6**   Cash Disbursements Journal

| Cash Disbursements Journal | | | | | | | | | |
|---|---|---|---|---|---|---|---|---|---|
| Date | Cheque No. | Payee | Account Debited | PR | Other Accts. Debit | Accts. Pay. Debit | Payroll Pay. Debit | Pur. Dis. Credit | Cash Credit |
| June 11 | 754 | John Auer | Payroll Pay. | | | | 280.97 | | 280.97 |
| June 11 | 755 | Joan Cheung | " | | | | 340.41 | | 340.41 |
| June 11 | 756 | Moe Daljit | " | | | | 624.27 | | 624.27 |
| June 11 | 757 | Shannon Lee | " | | | | 462.26 | | 462.26 |
| June 11 | 758 | Sunil Prasad | " | | | | 490.52 | | 490.52 |
| June 11 | 759 | Allan Rupert | " | | | | 340.41 | | 340.41 |

**Illustration 10-7**   A Payroll Cheque

| Employee | Total Hours | O.T. Hours | Reg. Pay Rate | Regular Pay | O.T. Prem. Pay | Gross Pay | U.I. Premium | Income Taxes | C.P. Plan | Hosp. Ins. | Total Deductions | Net Pay |
|---|---|---|---|---|---|---|---|---|---|---|---|---|
| John Auer | 40 | | 10.00 | 400.00 | | 400.00 | 12.00 | 80.00 | 9.03 | 18.00 | 119.03 | 280.97 |

STATEMENT OF EARNINGS AND DEDUCTIONS FOR EMPLOYEE'S RECORDS—DETACH BEFORE CASHING CHEQUE

**VALLEY SALES COMPANY**
2590 Dixon Road • Cambridge, Ontario   **No. 893**

PAY TO THE ORDER OF ___ John Auer ___   Date _June 11, 1995_   $ _280.97_

_Two hundred eighty dollars and ninety-seven cents_ - - - - - - - - - - - - - - -

Merchants National Bank
Cambridge, Ontario

VALLEY SALES COMPANY
_Jane R. Morris_

account. Then individual payroll cheques are drawn on this special account. Because only one cheque for the payroll total is drawn on the regular bank account each payday, use of a special payroll bank account simplifies internal control, especially the reconciliation of the regular bank account. It may be reconciled without considering the payroll cheques outstanding, and there may be many of these. Many financial institutions offer a payroll service whereby the employees' net pay is transferred electronically into their accounts. The employer simply transfers the net amount of the payroll to the institution along with the employees' names and the accounts to be credited.

When a company uses a special payroll bank account, it must complete the following steps to pay the employees:

1. Record the information shown on the Payroll Register in the usual manner with a General Journal entry similar to the one previously illustrated. This entry causes the sum of the employees' net pay to be credited to the liability account (Salaries Payable).

2. Have a single cheque written that is payable to Payroll Bank account for the total amount of the payroll and enter the payment in the Cheque Register. This requires a debit to Salaries Payable and a credit to Cash.

3. Have the cheque deposited in the payroll bank account. This transfers an amount of money equal to the payroll total from the regular bank account to the special payroll bank account.

4. Have individual payroll cheques drawn on the special payroll bank account and delivered to the employees. As soon as all employees cash their cheques, the funds in the special account will be exhausted. Typically, companies will arrange for the bank to charge all service costs to the regular bank account.

A special Payroll Cheque Register may be used in connection with a payroll bank account. However, most companies do not use such a register. Instead, the payroll cheque numbers are entered in the Payroll Register so that it serves as a Cheque Register.

## Employee's Individual Earnings Record

An **Employee's Individual Earnings Record,** as shown in Illustration 10–8, provides for each employee in one record a full year's summary of the employee's working time, gross earnings, deductions, and net pay. In addition, it accumulates information that

1. Serves as a basis for the employer's payroll tax returns.
2. Indicates when an employee's earnings have reached the maximum amounts for CPP and UI deductions.
3. Supplies data for the T4 slip, which must be given to the employee at the end of the year.

The payroll information on an Employee's Individual Earnings Record is taken from the Payroll Register. The information as to earnings, deductions, and net pay is first recorded on a single line in the Payroll Register. Then, each pay period, the information is posted from the Payroll Register to the earnings record. Note the last column of the record. It shows an employee's cumulative earnings and is used to determine when the earnings reach the maximum amounts taxed and are no longer subject to the various payroll taxes.

**Progress Check**

**10–6    Why would a company use a special payroll bank account?**

**10–7    What is the purpose of the employee's earnings record?**

**Illustration 10–8**  Employee's Individual Earnings Record

| | | | | | | | | | | | | | | | | | | |
|---|---|---|---|---|---|---|---|---|---|---|---|---|---|---|---|---|---|---|

Employee's Name _____John Auer_____  SIN. No. _____123-456-789_____  Employee No. _____114_____

Home Address _____111 South Greenwood_____  Notify in Case of Emergency _____Margaret Auer_____  Phone No. _____964-9834_____

Employed _____May 15, 1993_____  Date of Termination _____  Reason _____

Date of Birth _____June 6, 1972_____  Date Becomes 65 _____June 6, 2037_____  Male (X)  Female ( )  Married ( )  Single (X)  Number of Exemptions __0__  Pay Rate __$10.00__

Occupation _____Clerk_____  Place _____Warehouse_____

| Date | | Time Lost | | Time Worked | | | | | | | | | | | | | |
|---|---|---|---|---|---|---|---|---|---|---|---|---|---|---|---|---|---|
| Per. Ends | Paid | Hrs. | Rea-son | Total | O.T. Hours | Reg. Pay | O.T. Prem. Pay | Gross Pay | U.I. Prem. | Income Taxes | Hosp. Ins. | CPP | Total Deduc-tions | Net Pay | Cheque No. | Cumu-lative Pay |
| Ja 6 | Ja 6 | | | 40 | | 400.00 | | 400.00 | 12.00 | 80.00 | 18.00 | 9.03 | 119.03 | 280.97 | 673 | 280.97 |
| Ja 13 | Ja 13 | | | 40 | | 400.00 | | 400.00 | 12.00 | 80.00 | 18.00 | 9.03 | 119.03 | 280.97 | 701 | 561.94 |
| Ja 20 | Ja 20 | | | 40 | | 400.00 | | 400.00 | 12.00 | 80.00 | 18.00 | 9.03 | 119.03 | 280.97 | 743 | 842.91 |
| Ja 27 | Ja 27 | 4 | Sick | 36 | | 360.00 | | 360.00 | 10.80 | 72.00 | 18.00 | 7.95 | 108.75 | 251.25 | 795 | 1,094.16 |
| Fe 3 | Fe 3 | | | 40 | | 400.00 | | 400.00 | 12.00 | 80.00 | 18.00 | 9.03 | 119.03 | 280.97 | 839 | 1,375.13 |
| Fe 10 | Fe 10 | | | 40 | | 400.00 | | 400.00 | 12.00 | 80.00 | 18.00 | 9.03 | 119.03 | 280.97 | 854 | 1,656.10 |
| Fe 17 | Fe 17 | | | 40 | | 400.00 | | 400.00 | 12.00 | 80.00 | 18.00 | 9.03 | 119.03 | 280.97 | 893 | 1,937.07 |
| Fe 24 | Fe 24 | | | 40 | | 400.00 | | 400.00 | 12.00 | 80.00 | 18.00 | 9.03 | 119.03 | 280.97 | 932 | 2,218.04 |
| Ju 11 | Ju 11 | | | 40 | | 400.00 | | 400.00 | 12.00 | 80.00 | 18.00 | 9.03 | 119.03 | 280.97 | 1517 | 6,432.59 |

## PAYROLL DEDUCTIONS REQUIRED OF THE EMPLOYER

**LO 4**

Calculate the payroll costs levied on employers and prepare the entries to record the accrual and payment of these amounts.

Under the previous discussion of the Canada Pension Plan, it was pointed out that pension deductions are required in like amounts on both employed workers and their employers. A covered employer is required by law to deduct from the employees' pay the amounts of their Canada Pension Plan, but in addition, the employer must pay an amount equal to the sum of the employees' Canada pension. Commonly, the amount deducted by the employer is recorded at the same time the payroll to which it relates is recorded. Also, since both the employees' and employer's shares are reported on the same form and are paid in one amount, the liability for both is normally recorded in the same liability account, the Canada Pension Plan Payable account.

In addition to the Canada Pension Plan, an employer is required to pay unemployment insurance that is 1.4 times the sum of the employees' unemployment insurance deductions. Most employers record both of these payroll deductions with a General Journal entry that is made at the time the payroll to which they relate is recorded. For example, the entry to record the employer's amounts on the payroll of Illustration 10–5 is:

| June | 11 | Benefits Expense ........................... | 235.13 | |
| | | Unemployment Insurance Payable ............ | | 149.70 |
| | | Canada Pension Plan Payable ................ | | 85.43 |
| | | *To record the employer's payroll taxes.* | | |

The debit of the entry records as an expense the payroll taxes levied on the employer, and the credits record the liabilities for the taxes. The $149.70 credit to Unemployment Insurance Payable is 1.4 times the sum of the amounts deducted from the pay of the employees whose wages are recorded in the Payroll Register of Illustration 10–5, and the credit to Canada Pension Plan Payable is equal to the total of the employees' pension plan deductions.

## PAYING THE PAYROLL DEDUCTIONS

Income tax, Unemployment Insurance, and Canada Pension Plan amounts withheld each payday from the employees' pay plus the employer's portion of unemployment insurance and Canada Pension Plan are current liabilities until paid to the Receiver General of Canada. The normal method of payment is to pay the amounts due at any chartered bank or remit directly to the Receiver General of Canada. Payment of these amounts is usually required to be made before the 15th of the month following the month that deductions were made from the earnings of the employees. Large employers are required to remit on the 10th and 25th of each month. Payment of these liabilities is recorded in the same manner as payment of any other liabilities.

## ACCRUING PAYROLL DEDUCTIONS ON WAGES

Mandatory payroll deductions are levied on wages actually paid. In other words, accrued wages are not subject to payroll deductions until they are paid. Nevertheless, if the requirements of the matching principle are to be met, both accrued wages and the accrued deductions on the wages should be recorded at the end of an accounting period. However, since the amounts of such deductions vary little from one accounting period to the next and often are small in amount, many employers apply the materiality principle and do not accrue payroll deductions.

---

**Progress Check**

10-8   **If Marita Company deducted $1,750 for Unemployment Insurance and $1,275 for CPP from its employees in April, what would the benefits expense be for the month?**

10-9   **When are the payments for employee deductions due to the Receiver General?**

---

## EMPLOYEE (FRINGE) BENEFIT COSTS

In addition to the wages earned by employees and the related payroll amounts paid by the employer, many companies provide their employees a variety of benefits. Since the costs of these benefits are paid by the employer and the benefits are in addition to the amount of wages earned, they are often called **employee fringe benefits.** For example, an employer may pay for part (or all) of the employees' medical insurance, life insurance, and disability insurance. Another typical employee benefit involves employer contributions to a retirement income plan. Workers' compensation is required to be paid by employers according to the legislation in each province. Perhaps the most typical employee benefit is vacation pay.

LO 5

Calculate and record employee fringe benefit costs and show the effect of these items on the total cost of employing labour.

## Workers' Compensation

Legislation is in effect in all provinces for payments to employees for an injury or disability arising out of or in the course of their employment. Under the provincial workers' compensation acts, employers are, in effect, required to insure their employees against injury or disability that may arise as a result of employment. Premiums are normally based on (1) accident experience of the industrial classification to which each business is assigned and (2) the total payroll.

Procedures for payment are as follows:

1.  At the beginning of each year, every covered employer is required to submit to the Workers' Compensation Board an estimate of his or her expected payroll for the ensuing year.

2.  Provisional premiums are then established by the board by relating estimated requirements for disability payments to estimated payroll. Provisional premium notices are then sent to all employers.

3.  Provisional premiums are normally payable in from three to six installments during the year.

4.  At the end of each year, actual payrolls are submitted to the board, and final assessments are made based on actual payrolls and actual payments. Premiums are normally between 1% and 3% of gross payroll and are borne by the employer.

## Employer Contributions to Employee Insurance and Retirement Plans

The entries to record employee benefit costs depend on the nature of the benefit. Some employee retirement plans are quite complicated and involve accounting procedures that are too complex for discussion in this introductory course. In other cases, however, the employer simply makes periodic cash contributions to a retirement fund for each employee and records the amounts contributed as expense. Other employee benefits that require periodic cash payments by the employer include employer payments of insurance premiums for employees.

In the case of employee benefits that simply require the employer to make periodic cash payments, the entries to record the employer's obligations are similar to those used for payroll deductions.[1] For example, assume an employer with five employees has agreed to pay medical insurance premiums of $40 per month for each employee. The employer also will contribute 10% of each employee's salary to a retirement program. If each employee earns $2,500 per month, the entry to record these employee benefits for the month of March is

---

[1]Some payments of employee benefits must be added to the gross salary of the employee for the purpose of calculating income tax, CPP, and UI payroll deductions. However, in this chapter and in the problems at the end of the chapter, the possible effect of employee benefit costs on payroll taxes is ignored to avoid undue complexity in the introductory course.

| Mar. | 31 | Benefits Expense .......................... | 1,450.00 | |
|------|----|----|----|----|
| | | Employees' Medical Insurance Payable ........ | | 200.00 |
| | | Employees' Retirement Program Payable | | |
| | | [($2,500 × 5) × 10%] ................... | | 1,250.00 |

## Vacation Pay

Employers are required to allow their employees paid vacation time (at a minimum rate of 4% of gross earnings) as a benefit of employment. For example, many employees receive 2 weeks' vacation in return for working 50 weeks each year. The effect of a 2-week vacation is to increase the employer's payroll expenses by 4% (2/50 = .04). After five years of service most employees are entitled to a 3-week vacation (i.e., 6%). However, new employees often do not begin to accrue vacation time until after they've worked for a period of time, perhaps as much as a year. The employment contract may say that no vacation is granted until the employee works one year, but if the first year is completed, the employee receives the full 2 weeks. Contracts between the employer and employees may allow for vacation pay in excess of the 4% minimum.

To account for vacation pay, an employer should estimate and record the additional expense during the weeks the employees are working and earning the vacation time. For example, assume that a company with a weekly payroll of $20,000 grants two weeks' vacation after one year's employment. The entry to record the estimated vacation pay is

| Date | | Benefits Expense .......................... | 800.00 | |
|------|----|----|----|----|
| | | Estimated Vacation Pay Liability | | |
| | | ($20,000 × .04) ........................ | | 800.00 |

As employees take their vacations and receive their vacation pay, the entries to record the vacation payroll take the following general form:

| Date | | Estimated Vacation Pay Liability .............. | xxx | |
|------|----|----|----|----|
| | | Employees' UI and CPP Payable ............ | | xxx |
| | | Employees' Income Taxes Payable ........... | | xxx |
| | | Other withholding liability accounts such | | |
| | | as Employees' Hospital Insurance Payable .... | | xxx |
| | | Payroll Payable ........................ | | xxx |

Mandatory payroll deductions and employee benefits costs are often a major category of expense incurred by a company. They may amount to well over 25% of the salaries earned by employees.

---

**Progress Check**

10-10   **How is the cost of Workers' Compensation determined?**

10-11   **Assume a company with an annual payroll of $160,000 grants three weeks' vacation to its employees. Record the estimated vacation pay for the year.**

---

Manually prepared records like the ones described in this chapter are used in many small companies. However, an increasing number of companies use computers to process their payroll. The computer programs are designed to take advantage of the fact that the same calculations are performed each pay period. Also, much of the same information must be entered for each employee in the Payroll Register, on the employee's earnings record, and on the employee's paycheque. The computers simultaneously store or print the information in all three places.

## COMPUTERIZED PAYROLL SYSTEMS

## SUMMARY OF THE CHAPTER IN TERMS OF LEARNING OBJECTIVES

**LO 1.  List the taxes and other items frequently withheld from employees' wages.** Amounts withheld from employees' wages include federal income taxes, unemployment insurance, and Canada Pension Plan. Payroll costs levied on employers include unemployment insurance, Canada Pension, and workers' compensation.

An employee's gross pay may be the employee's specified wage rate multiplied by the total hours worked plus an overtime premium rate multiplied by the number of overtime hours worked. Alternatively, it may be the given periodic salary of the employee. Taxes withheld and other deductions for items such as union dues, insurance premiums, and charitable contributions are subtracted from gross pay to determine the net pay.

**LO 2.  Make the calculations necessary to prepare a Payroll Register and prepare the entry to record payroll liabilities.** A Payroll Register is used to summarize all employees' hours worked, regular and overtime pay, payroll deductions, net pay, and distribution of gross pay to expense accounts during each pay period. It provides the necessary information for journal entries to record the accrued payroll and to pay the employees.

**LO 3.  Prepare journal entries to record the payments to employees and explain the operation of a payroll bank account.** A payroll bank account is a separate account that is used solely for the purpose of paying employees. Each pay period, an amount equal to the total net pay of all employees is transferred from the regular bank account to the payroll bank account. Then cheques are drawn against the payroll bank account for the net pay of the employees.

**LO 4.  Calculate the payroll costs levied on employers and prepare the entries to record the accrual and payment of these amounts.** When a payroll is accrued at the end of each pay period, payroll deductions and levies also should be accrued with a debit to Benefits Expense and credits to appropriate liability accounts.

**LO 5. Calculate and record employee fringe benefit costs and show the effect of these items on the total cost of employing labour.** Fringe benefit costs that involve simple cash payments by the employee should be accrued with an entry similar to the one used to accrue payroll levies. To account for the expense associated with vacation pay, you should estimate the expense and allocate the estimated amount to the pay periods during the year. These allocations are recorded with a debit to Employees' Benefits Expense and a credit to Estimated Vacation Pay Liability. Then payments to employees on vacation are charged to the estimated liability.

## DEMONSTRATION PROBLEM

Presented below are various items of information about three employees of the Deluth Company for the week ending November 25, 1995.

| | Billings | Dephir | Singe |
|---|---|---|---|
| Wage rate (per hour) | $   15 | $   30 | $   18 |
| Overtime premium | 50% | 50% | 50% |
| Annual vacation | 2 weeks | 4 weeks | 3 weeks |
| Cumulative wages as of November 18, 1995 | $28,500 | $52,600 | $14,800 |
| For the week (pay period) ended November 25, 1995: | | | |
| Hours worked | 40 | 44 | 48 |
| Medical insurance: | | | |
| Deluth's contribution | $   25 | $   25 | $   25 |
| Withheld from employee | 18 | 18 | 18 |
| Union dues withheld | 50 | 70 | 50 |
| Income tax withheld | 120 | 276 | 187 |
| Unemployment insurance withheld | 18 | 24 | 24 |
| Canada Pension withheld | 16 | — | 25 |

Payroll deduction rates:
Income taxes                     assume 20% of gross wages
Unemployment insurance           3.0% to a maximum of $24 per week
Canada Pension Plan              2.7% less annual exemption of
                                 $3,400; maximum per year is $850.50

### Required

In solving the following requirements, round all amounts to the nearest whole dollar. Prepare schedules that determine, for each employee and for all employees combined, the following information:

1.  Wages earned for the regular 40-hour week, total overtime pay, and gross wages.
2.  Vacation pay accrued for the week.
3.  Deductions withheld from the employees' wages.
4.  Costs imposed on the employer.
5.  Employees' net pay for the week.
6.  Employer's total payroll-related cost (wages, mandatory deductions, and fringe benefits).

Present journal entries to record the following:

7.  Payroll expense.
8.  Payroll deductions and employees' benefits expense.

- Calculate the gross pay for each employee.
- Compute the amounts deducted for each employee and their net pay.
- Compute the employer's share of payroll deductions.
- Prepare the necessary journal entries.

*Planning the Solution*

*Solution to Demonstration Problem*

1. The gross wages (including overtime) for the week:

|  | **Billings** | **Dephir** | **Singe** | **Total** |
|---|---|---|---|---|
| Regular wage rate | $ 15 | $ 30 | $ 18 | |
| Regular hours | × 40 | × 44 | × 48 | |
| Regular pay | $600 | $1,320 | $864 | $2,784 |
| Overtime premium | $ 7.5 | $ 15 | $ 9 | |
| Overtime hours | 0 | × 4 | × 8 | |
| Total overtime pay | $ 0 | $ 60 | $ 72 | $ 132 |
| Gross wages | $600 | $1,380 | $936 | $2,916 |

2. The vacation pay accrued for the week:

|  | **Billings** | **Dephir** | **Singe** | **Total** |
|---|---|---|---|---|
| Annual vacation | 2 weeks | 4 weeks | 3 weeks | |
| Weeks worked in year | 50 weeks | 48 weeks | 49 weeks | |
| Vacation pay as a percentage of regular pay | 4.00% | 8.33% | 6.12% | |
| Regular pay this week | × $600 | × $1,320 | × $864 | |
| Vacation pay this week | $24 | $110 | $53 | $187 |

The information in the following table is needed for parts 3 and 4:

| | | | **Earnings Subject to** | |
|---|---|---|---|---|
| **Employees** | **Earnings through November 25** | **Earnings This Week** | **CPP** | **Unemploy-ment Ins.** |
| Billings | $28,500 | $ 600 | $ 535 | $ 600 |
| Dephir | 52,600 | 1,380 | — | 815 |
| Singe | 14,800 | 936 | 871 | 815 |
| Totals | | $2,916 | $1,406 | $2,230 |

3. Amounts withheld from the employees:

|  | **Billings** | **Dephir** | **Singe** | **Total** |
|---|---|---|---|---|
| Income tax withheld | $120 | $276 | $187 | $583 |
| CPP withheld | 14 | — | 24 | 38 |
| UI withheld | 18 | 24 | 24 | 66 |
| Totals | $152 | $300 | $235 | $687 |

4. The costs imposed on the employer:

|  | **Billings** | **Dephir** | **Singe** | **Total** |
|---|---|---|---|---|
| CPP (1.0) | $14 | — | $24 | $ 38 |
| Unemployment Insurance (1.4) | 25 | $34 | 34 | 93 |
| Totals | $39 | $34 | $58 | $131 |

5. The net amount paid to the employees:

|  | Billings | Dephir | Singe | Total |
|---|---|---|---|---|
| Regular pay | $600 | $1,320 | $864 | $2,784 |
| Overtime pay | 0 | 60 | 72 | 132 |
| Gross pay | $600 | $1,380 | $936 | $2,916 |
| Withholdings: | | | | |
| Income tax withholding | $120 | $ 276 | $187 | $ 583 |
| CPP withholding | 14 | — | 24 | 38 |
| UI withholding | 18 | 24 | 24 | 66 |
| Medical insurance | 18 | 18 | 18 | 54 |
| Union dues | 50 | 70 | 50 | 170 |
| Total withholdings | $220 | $ 388 | $303 | $ 911 |
| Net pay to employees | $380 | $ 992 | $633 | $2,005 |

6. The total payroll-related cost to the employer:

|  | Billings | Dephir | Singe | Total |
|---|---|---|---|---|
| Regular pay | $600 | $1,320 | $ 864 | $2,784 |
| Overtime pay | 0 | 60 | 72 | 132 |
| Gross pay | $600 | $1,380 | $ 936 | $2,916 |
| Deductions and fringe benefits: | | | | |
| CPP | $ 14 | $ — | $ 24 | $ 38 |
| UI | 25 | 34 | 34 | 93 |
| Vacation Pay | 24 | 110 | 53 | 187 |
| Medical insurance | 25 | 25 | 25 | 75 |
| Total deductions and fringe benefits | $ 88 | $ 169 | $ 136 | $ 393 |
| Total payroll-related cost | $688 | $1,549 | $1,072 | $3,309 |

7. Journal entry for salary expense:

| 1995 | | | |
|---|---|---|---|
| Nov. 25 | Salary Expense .................................. | 2,916.00 | |
| | Employees' Income Taxes Payable .............. | | 583.00 |
| | Employees' CPP Payable .................... | | 38.00 |
| | Employees' UI Payable ...................... | | 66.00 |
| | Employees' Medical Insurance Payable .......... | | 54.00 |
| | Employees' Union Dues Payable .............. | | 170.00 |
| | Payroll Payable ............................ | | 2,005.00 |
| | *To record payroll expense.* | | |

# GLOSSARY

**Canada Pension Plan**  a national contributory retirement pension scheme. p. 491

**Clock card**  a card issued to each employee that the employee inserts in a time clock to record the time of arrival and departure to and from work. p. 497

**Employee fringe benefits**  payments by an employer, in addition to wages and salaries, that are made to acquire employee benefits such as insurance coverage and retirement income. p. 504

**Employee's gross pay**  the amount an employee earns before any deductions for taxes or other items such as union dues or insurance premiums. p. 498

**Employee's Individual Earnings Record**  a record of an employee's hours worked, gross pay, deductions, net pay, and certain personal information about the employee. p. 502

**Employee's net pay** the amount an employee is paid, determined by subtracting from gross pay all deductions for taxes and other items that are withheld from the employee's earnings. p. 499

**Payroll bank account** a special bank account a company uses solely for the purpose of paying employees by depositing in the account each pay period an amount equal to the total employees' net pay and drawing the employees' payroll cheques on that account. p. 500

**Payroll deduction** an amount deducted from an employee's pay, usually based on the amount of an employee's gross pay. p. 490

**Personal tax credits** amounts that may be deducted from an individual's income taxes and that determine the amount of income taxes to be withheld. p. 491

**Timekeeping** the process of recording the time worked by each employee. p. 497

**Unemployment insurance** an employee/employer-financed unemployment insurance plan. p. 494

**Wage bracket withholding table** a table showing the amounts to be withheld from employees' wages at various levels of earnings. p. 495

## QUESTIONS

1. Who pays the contributions to the Canada Pension Plan?
2. Who pays premiums under the workers' compensation laws?
3. What benefits are paid to unemployed workers for funds raised by the Federal Unemployment Insurance Act?
4. Who pays federal unemployment insurance? What is the rate?
5. What are the objectives of unemployment insurance laws?
6. To whom and when are payroll deductions remitted?
7. What determines the amount that must be deducted from an employee's wages for income taxes?
8. What is a tax withholding table?
9. What is the Canada Pension Plan deduction rate for self-employed individuals?
10. How is a clock card used in recording the time an employee is on the job?
11. How is a special payroll bank account used in paying the wages of employees?
12. At the end of an accounting period a firm's special payroll bank account has a $562.35 balance because the payroll cheques of two employees have not cleared the bank. Should this $562.35 appear on the firm's balance sheet? If so, where?
13. What information is accumulated on an employee's individual earnings record? Why must this information be accumulated? For what purposes is the information used?
14. What payroll charges are levied on the employer? What amounts are deducted from the wages of an employee?
15. What are employee fringe benefits? Name some examples.

## QUICK STUDY (Five-Minute Exercises)

A company deducts $260 in unemployment insurance and $205 in Canada pension from the weekly payroll of its employees. How much is the company's expense for these items for the week?

**QS 10–1 (LO 1)**

Tracon Co. has six employees, each of whom earns $3,000 per month. Income taxes are 20% of gross pay and the company deducts UI and CPP. Prepare the March 31 journal entry to record the payroll for the month.

**QS 10–2 (LO 2)**

**QS 10–3**
**(LO 3)**

Use the information in QS 10–2 to record the payment of the wages to the employees for March assuming that Tracon uses a payroll bank account.

**QS 10–4**
**(LO 3)**

Racon Co. has eight employees, each of whom earns $3,500 per month. Income taxes are 20% of gross pay and the company deducts UI and CPP. Prepare the April 30 journal entry to record Racon's payroll expenses for the month.

**QS 10–5**
**(LO 3)**

Racon Co. (see QS 10–4) contributes 8% of an employee's salary to a retirement program, medical insurance premiums of $60 per employee, and vacation allowance equivalent to 5% of the employee's salary. Prepare a journal entry to record the fringe benefit costs for April.

# EXERCISES

**Exercise 10–1**
Calculating gross
and net pay
**(LO 1)**

Julie Leung, an employee of the Import Company Limited, worked 48 hours during the week ended January 5. Her pay rate is $20 per hour, and her wages are subject to no deductions other than income taxes, unemployment insurance, and Canada Pension Plan. The overtime premium is 50% and is applicable to any time greater than 40 hours per week. Calculate her regular pay, overtime premium pay, gross pay, UI, CPP, income tax deductions (assume a tax deduction rate of 20%), total deductions, and net pay.

**Exercise 10–2**
Journalizing payroll
information
**(LO 3)**

On January 5, at the end of its first weekly pay period in the year, Nasah Company's payroll record showed that its sales employees had earned $3,720 and its office employees had earned $2,300. The employees were to have $210 of UI and $150 of CPP withheld plus $1,030 of income taxes, $180 of union dues, and $570 of hospital insurance premiums. Give the General Journal entry to record the payroll.

**Exercise 10–3**
Calculating payroll
deductions and recording
the payroll
**(LO 1)**

The following information as to earnings and deductions for the pay period ended May 17 was taken from a company's payroll records:

| Employees' Names | Weekly Gross Pay | Earnings to End of Previous Week | Income Taxes | Health Insurance Deductions |
|---|---|---|---|---|
| Hellena Chea | $ 720 | $12,510 | $144.00 | $ 24.00 |
| Joseph Lim | 610 | 10,320 | 91.00 | 24.00 |
| Dino Patelli | 830 | 15,500 | 142.00 | 36.00 |
| Shari Quinata | 1,700 | 29,500 | 395.00 | 24.00 |
| | $3,860 | | $772.00 | $108.00 |

Calculate the employees' UI and CPP withholdings, the amounts paid to each employee, and prepare a General Journal entry to record the payroll. Assume all employees work in the office.

**Exercise 10–4**
Calculating and recording
payroll deductions
**(LO 4)**

Use the information provided in Exercise 10–3 to complete the following requirements:

1. Prepare a General Journal entry to record the employer's payroll costs resulting from the payroll.

2. Prepare a General Journal entry to record the following employee benefits incurred by the company: (a) health insurance costs equal to the amounts contributed by each employee and (b) contributions equal to 10% of gross pay for each employee's retirement income program.

Manchuran Company's employees earn a gross pay of $20 per hour and work 40 hours each week. Manchuran Company contributes 8% of gross pay to a retirement program for employees and pays medical insurance premiums of $50 per week per employee. What is Manchuran Company's total cost of employing a person for one hour? (Assume that individual wages are less than the $34,900 Canada Pension Plan limit.)

**Exercise 10–5**
Analyzing total labour costs
**(LO 5)**

Bellward Corporation grants vacation time of two weeks to those employees who have worked for the company one complete year. After 10 years of service, employees receive four weeks of vacation. The monthly payroll for January totals $320,000 of which 70% is payable to employees with 10 or more years of service. On January 31, record the January expense arising from the vacation policy of the company.

**Exercise 10–6**
Calculating fringe benefit costs
**(LO 5)**

O'Riley Company's payroll costs and fringe benefit expenses include the normal CPP and UI contributions, retirement fund contributions of 10% of total earnings, and health insurance premiums of $120 per employee per month. Given the following list of employee annual salaries, payroll costs and fringe benefits constitute what percentage of salaries?

**Exercise 10–7**
Analyzing the cost of payroll deductions and fringe benefits
**(LO 4, 5)**

| | |
|---|---|
| Doherty | $36,000 |
| Fane | 61,000 |
| Kahan | 59,000 |
| Martin | 37,000 |
| Poon | 48,000 |

Sharon Von Hatton is single and earns a weekly salary of $940. In response to a citywide effort to obtain charitable contributions to the local United Way programs, Von Hatton has requested that her employer withhold 2% of her salary (net of CPP, UI, and income taxes—assume a tax deduction rate of 20%). Under this program, what will be Von Hatton's annual contribution to the United Way?

**Exercise 10–8**
Other payroll deductions
**(LO 1)**

# PROBLEMS

On January 6, at the end of the first weekly pay period of the year, a company's Payroll Register showed that its employees had earned $19,570 of sales salaries and $6,230 of office salaries. Withholdings from the employees' salaries were to include $740 of UI, $660 of CPP, $5,310 of income taxes, $930 of hospital insurance, and $420 of union dues.

**Problem 10–1**
The Payroll Register and the payroll bank account
**(LO 1, 3)**

**Required**

1. Prepare the General Journal entry to record the January 6 payroll.
2. Prepare a General Journal entry to record the employer's payroll expenses resulting from the January 6 payroll.
3. Under the assumption the company uses a payroll bank account and special payroll cheques in paying its employees, give the Cheque Register entry (Cheque No. 542) to transfer funds equal to the payroll from the regular bank account to the payroll bank account.
4. Answer this question: After the Cheque Register entry is made and posted, are additional debit and credit entries required to record the payroll cheques and pay the employees?

**Problem 10–2**
The Payroll Register, the payroll bank account, and payroll deductions
**(LO 1, 3, 4)**

The payroll records of Brownlee Corporation provided the following information for the weekly pay period ended December 21:

| Employees | Clock Card No. | Daily Time | | | | | | | Pay Rate | Hospital Insurance | Union Dues | Earnings to End of Previous Week |
|---|---|---|---|---|---|---|---|---|---|---|---|---|
| | | M | T | W | T | F | S | S | | | | |
| Ray Loran | 11 | 8 | 8 | 8 | 8 | 8 | 4 | 0 | 20.00 | 40.00 | 16.00 | 42,000 |
| Kathy Sousa | 12 | 7 | 8 | 6 | 7 | 8 | 4 | 0 | 18.00 | 40.00 | 15.00 | 46,000 |
| Gary Smith | 13 | 8 | 8 | 0 | 8 | 8 | 4 | 4 | 16.00 | 40.00 | 14.00 | 21,000 |
| Nicole Parton | 14 | 8 | 8 | 8 | 8 | 8 | 0 | 0 | 20.00 | 40.00 | 16.00 | 32,000 |
| Diana Wood | 15 | 0 | 6 | 6 | 6 | 6 | 8 | 8 | 18.00 | 40.00 | 15.00 | 36,000 |
| | | | | | | | | | | 200.00 | 76.00 | |

### Required

1. Enter the relevant information in the proper columns of a Payroll Register and complete the register for CPP and UI deductions. Charge the wages of Kathy Sousa to Office Salaries Expense and the wages of the remaining employees to Service Wages Expense. Calculate income tax deductions at 20% of gross pay.
2. Prepare a General Journal entry to record the Payroll Register information.
3. Make the Cheque Register entry (Cheque No. 399) to transfer funds equal to the payroll from the regular bank account to the payroll bank account under the assumption the company uses special payroll cheques and a payroll bank account in paying its employees. Assume the first payroll cheque is numbered 530 and enter the payroll cheque numbers in the Payroll Register.
4. Prepare a General Journal entry to record the employer's payroll costs resulting from the payroll.

**Problem 10–3**
The Payroll Register, payroll taxes, and employee fringe benefits
**(LO 1, 4, 5)**

A company accumulated the following information for the weekly pay period ended December 22:

| Employees | Clock Card No. | Daily Time | | | | | | | Pay Rate | Medical Insurance | Union Dues | Earnings to End of Previous Week |
|---|---|---|---|---|---|---|---|---|---|---|---|---|
| | | M | T | W | T | F | S | S | | | | |
| Shannon Fong | 21 | 8 | 8 | 8 | 8 | 8 | 4 | 0 | 18.00 | 30.00 | 20.00 | 41,000 |
| Karen Horta | 22 | 7 | 8 | 6 | 7 | 8 | 4 | 0 | 16.00 | 28.00 | 18.00 | 44,000 |
| Garth Koran | 23 | 8 | 8 | 0 | 8 | 8 | 4 | 4 | 14.00 | 25.00 | 16.00 | 19,000 |
| Nicha Daljit | 24 | 8 | 8 | 8 | 8 | 8 | 0 | 0 | 18.00 | 30.00 | 20.00 | 34,000 |
| | | | | | | | | | | 113.00 | 74.00 | |

### Required

1. Enter the relevant information in the proper columns of a Payroll Register and complete the register for CPP and UI deductions. Assume the first employee is a salesperson, the second two work in the shop, and the last one works in the office. Calculate income tax deductions at 20% of gross pay.

2. Prepare a General Journal entry to record the Payroll Register information.

3. Make the Cheque Register entry to transfer funds equal to the payroll from the regular bank account to the payroll bank account (Cheque No. 522) under the assumption the company uses special payroll cheques and a payroll bank account in paying its employees. Assume the first payroll cheque is numbered 230 and enter the payroll cheque numbers in the Payroll Register.

4. Prepare a General Journal entry to record the employer's payroll deductions resulting from the payroll.

5. Prepare General Journal entries to accrue employee fringe benefit costs for the week. Assume the company matches the employees' payments for medical insurance and contributes an amount equal to 8% of each employees' gross pay to a retirement program. Also, each employee accrues vacation pay at the rate of 6% of the wages and salaries earned. The company estimates that all employees eventually will be paid their vacation pay.

A company has three employees, each of whom has been employed since January 1, earns $2,600 per month, and is paid on the last day of each month. On March 1, the following accounts and balances appeared in its ledger:

**Problem 10–4**
General Journal entries for payroll transactions **(LO 3)**

a. Employees Income Taxes Payable, $1,480 (liability for February only).
b. Unemployment Insurance Payable, $475 (liability for February).
c. Canada Pension Plan Payable, $390 (liability for February).
d. Employees' Medical Insurance Payable, $980 (liability for January and February).

During March and April, the company completed the following transactions related to payroll:

Mar. 11  Issued Cheque No. 320 payable to Receiver General of Canada. The cheque was in payment of the February employee income taxes, UI, and CPP amounts due.

31  Prepared a General Journal entry to record the March Payroll Record which had the following column totals:

| Income Taxes | UI | CPP | Medical Insurance | Total Deductions | Net Pay | Office Salaries | Shop Wages |
|---|---|---|---|---|---|---|---|
| $1,460 | $230 | $190 | $260 | $2,280 | $5,660 | $2,600 | $5,200 |

31  Recorded the employer's $260 liability for its 50% contribution to the medical insurance plan of employees and 4% vacation pay accrued to the employees.

31  Issued Cheque No. 351 payable to Payroll Bank Account in payment of the March payroll. Endorsed the cheque, deposited it in the payroll bank account, and issued payroll cheques to the employees.

31  Prepared a General Journal entry to record the employer's payroll costs resulting from the March payroll.

Apr. 15  Issued Cheque No. 375 payable to the Receiver General in payment of the March mandatory deductions.

15  Issued Cheque No. 376 payable to All Canadian Insurance Company in payment of the employee medical insurance premiums for the first quarter.

**Required**

Prepare the necessary Cheque Register and General Journal entries to record the transactions.

**Problem 10–5**

The Payroll Register and the payroll bank account
**(LO 1, 3)**

Chechoff Company's first weekly pay period of the year ended on January 8. On that date the column totals of the company's Payroll Register indicated its sales employees had earned $32,500, its office employees had earned $12,800, and its delivery employees had earned $4,800. Withholdings from the employees' salaries included $1,200 of UI, $960 of CPP, $9,700 federal income taxes, $1,620 medical insurance deductions, and $540 of union dues.

**Required**

1. Prepare the General Journal entry to record the January 8 payroll.
2. Prepare a General Journal entry to record the employer's payroll deductions resulting from the January 8 payroll.
3. Under the assumption the company uses special payroll cheques and a payroll bank account in paying its employees, give the Cheque Register entry (Cheque No. 378) to transfer funds equal to the payroll from the regular bank account to the payroll bank account.
4. Answer this question: After the Cheque Register entry is made and posted, are additional debit and credit entries required to record the payroll cheques and pay the employees?

**Problem 10–6**

The Payroll Register, the payroll bank account, and payroll deductions
**(LO 1, 3, 4)**

The following information was taken from the payroll records of Radical Software Company for the weekly pay period ending December 20:

| Employees | Clock Card No. | Daily Time | | | | | | | Pay Rate | Hospital Insurance | Union Dues | Earnings to End of Previous Week |
|---|---|---|---|---|---|---|---|---|---|---|---|---|
| | | M | T | W | T | F | S | S | | | | |
| Pam Loella | 41 | 0 | 8 | 8 | 8 | 8 | 4 | 4 | 18.00 | 40.00 | 20.00 | 40,000 |
| Martan Mann | 42 | 6 | 7 | 8 | 7 | 8 | 4 | 0 | 16.00 | 30.00 | 18.00 | 31,000 |
| George Singe | 43 | 8 | 4 | 0 | 8 | 8 | 4 | 4 | 18.00 | 40.00 | 20.00 | 26,000 |
| Nathan Tang | 44 | 8 | 8 | 8 | 8 | 8 | 0 | 4 | 16.00 | 30.00 | 18.00 | 35,000 |
| Terry Vaughan | 45 | 0 | 6 | 6 | 6 | 0 | 0 | 4 | 14.00 | 20.00 | 10.00 | 18,000 |
| | | | | | | | | | | 160.00 | 86.00 | |

**Required**

1. Enter the relevant information in the proper columns of a Payroll Register and complete the register for CPP and UI deductions. The company pays time-and-a-half for hours in excess of 40 each week. Also, work on Saturdays is paid at time-and-a-half whether the total for the week is over 40 or not. Charge the wages of George Singe to Office Salaries Expense and the wages of the remaining employees to Plant Salaries Expense. Calculate income tax deductions at 20% of gross pay.
2. Prepare a General Journal entry to record the Payroll Register information.
3. Assume the company uses special payroll cheques drawn on a payroll bank account in paying its employees and make the Cheque Register entry (Cheque No. 484) to transfer funds equal to the payroll from the regular bank account to the payroll bank account. Also, assume the first payroll cheque is No. 632 and enter the payroll cheque numbers in the Payroll Register.
4. Prepare a General Journal entry to record the employer's payroll deductions resulting from the payroll.

The following information for the weekly pay period ended December 10 was taken from the records of a company:

Problem 10–7
The Payroll Register,
payroll taxes, and
employee fringe benefits
(LO 1, 3, 5)

| Employees | Clock Card No. | Daily Time | | | | | | | Pay Rate | Medical Insurance | Union Dues | Earnings to End of Previous Week |
|---|---|---|---|---|---|---|---|---|---|---|---|---|
| | | M | T | W | T | F | S | S | | | | |
| Ralph Abdoul | 61 | 8 | 8 | 8 | 8 | 8 | 4 | 0 | 25.00 | 60.00 | 22.00 | 52,000 |
| Ali Johnston | 62 | 7 | 8 | 6 | 7 | 8 | 4 | 0 | 20.00 | 60.00 | 20.00 | 56,000 |
| Sarah Bigalow | 63 | 8 | 8 | 0 | 8 | 8 | 4 | 4 | 18.00 | 60.00 | 18.00 | 23,000 |
| Leslie Worbetts | 64 | 8 | 8 | 8 | 8 | 8 | 0 | 0 | 25.00 | 60.00 | 22.00 | 35,000 |
| Ainsley Vangough | 65 | 0 | 6 | 6 | 6 | 6 | 8 | 8 | 20.00 | 60.00 | 20.00 | 41,000 |
| | | | | | | | | | | 300.00 | 102.00 | |

**Required**

1. Enter the relevant information in the proper columns of a Payroll Register and complete the register for CPP and UI deductions. Assume that the first employee works in the office, the second is a salesperson, and the last two work in the shop. Calculate tax deductions at 20% of gross pay.
2. Prepare a General Journal entry to record the Payroll Register information.
3. Make the Cheque Register entry (Cheque No. 389) to transfer funds equal to the payroll from the regular bank account to the payroll bank account. Assume the first payroll cheque is numbered 632 and enter the payroll cheque numbers in the Payroll Register.
4. Prepare a General Journal entry to record the employer's payroll deductions resulting from the payroll.
5. Prepare a General Journal entry to accrue employee fringe benefit costs for the week. Assume the company matches the employees' payments for medical insurance and contributes an amount equal to 8% of each employees' gross pay to a retirement program. Also, each employee accrues vacation pay at the rate of 6% of the wages and salaries earned. The company estimates that all employees eventually will be paid their vacation pay.

A company has five employees, each of whom has been employed since January 1, earns $1,900 per month, and is paid on the last day of each month. On June 1 the following accounts and balances appeared on its ledger:

Problem 10–8
General Journal entries
for payroll transactions
(LO 3)

a. Employees' Income Taxes Payable, $1,670. (The balance of this account represents the liability for the May 31 payroll only.)
b. Unemployment Insurance Payable, $820 (liability for May only).
c. Canada Pension Payable, $575 (liability for May).
d. Employees' Medical Insurance Payable, $1,420 (liability for April and May).

During June and July, the company completed the following payroll-related transactions:

June 10   Issued Cheque No. 726 payable to the Receiver General for Canada. The cheque was in payment of the May employee income taxes, CPP, and UI amounts due.

30   Prepared a General Journal entry to record the June Payroll Record which had the following column totals:

| Income Taxes | UI | CPP | Medical Insur- ance | Total Deduc- tions | Net Pay | Office Salaries | Shop Wages |
|---|---|---|---|---|---|---|---|
| $1,960 | $285 | $240 | $620 | $3,105 | $6,395 | $5,700 | $3,800 |

30   Recorded the employer's $620 liability for its 50% contribution to the medical insurance plan of employees and 4% vacation pay accrued to the employees.

30   Issued Cheque No. 766 payable to Payroll Bank Account in payment of the June payroll. Endorsed the check, deposited it in the payroll bank account, and issued payroll cheques to the employees.

30   Prepared a General Journal entry to record the employer's payroll costs resulting from the June payroll.

July 15   Issued Cheque No. 790 payable to Receiver General in payment of the June mandatory deductions.

15   Issued Cheque No. 791 payable to Blacke Insurance Company. The cheque was in payment of the April, May, and June employee health insurance premiums.

### Required

Prepare the necessary Cheque Register and General Journal entries to record the transactions.

## PROVOCATIVE PROBLEMS

**Provocative Problem 10–1**
Sharpe Limited
**(LO 1, 4)**

Sharpe Limited, which has 90 regular employees, has recently received an order for a line of archery equipment from a chain of department stores. The order should be very profitable and will probably be repeated each year. In filling the order, Sharpe can manufacture the various bows and other supplies with present machines and employees. However, it will have to add 30 persons to its work force for 40 hours per week for 20 weeks to finish the crossbows and pack them for shipment.

The company can hire these workers and add them to its own payroll, or it can secure the services of 30 people through Personnel, Inc. Sharpe will pay Personnel, Inc., $15.00 per hour for each hour worked by each person supplied. The people will be employees of Personnel, Inc., and it will pay their wages and all taxes on the wages. On the other hand, if Sharpe Limited employs the workers and places them on its payroll, it will pay them $12 per hour and will also pay the following payroll costs on their wages: Canada Pension Plan and unemployment insurance. The company will also have to pay medical insurance costs of $15 per employee per week.

Should Sharpe Limited place the temporary help on its own payroll, or should it secure their services through Personnel, Inc.? Justify your answer.

VideoConference Company employs a systems specialist at an annual salary of $75,000. The company pays the usual portion of mandatory unemployment insurance and Canada Pension. VideoConference also pays $120 per month for the employee's medical insurance. Effective June 1, the company agreed to contribute 10% of the specialist's gross pay to a retirement program.

**Provocative Problem 10–2**
VideoConference Company
**(LO 4, 5)**

What was the total monthly cost of employing the specialist in January, March, July, and December? Assuming the employee works 200 hours each month, what is the cost per hour in January? If the annual gross salary is increased by $5,000, what will be the increase in the total annual costs of employing the specialist?

## ANALYTICAL AND REVIEW PROBLEMS

Using current year's withholding tables for Canada Pension Plan, unemployment insurance, and income tax, update the Payroll Register of Illustration 10–5. In computing income tax withholdings, state your assumption as to each employee's personal deductions. Assume that hospital insurance deductions continue at the same amounts as in Illustration 10–5.

**A & R Problem 10–1**

The following data were taken from the Payroll Register of Eastcoastal Company:

**A & R Problem 10–2**

| | |
|---|---|
| Gross salary . . . . . . . . . . . . . . . . . . . . | xxx |
| Employees' income tax deductions . . . . | xxx |
| UI deductions . . . . . . . . . . . . . . . . . . | xxx |
| CPP deductions . . . . . . . . . . . . . . . . . | xxx |
| Hospital insurance deductions . . . . . . . . | xxx |
| Union dues deductions . . . . . . . . . . . . . | xxx |

Eastcoastal contributes an equal amount to the hospital insurance plan, in addition to the statutory payroll taxes, and 6% of the gross salaries to a pension program.

### Required

Record in General Journal form the payroll, payment of the employees, and remittance to the appropriate authority amounts owing in connection with the payroll. (Note: All amounts are to be indicated as xxx.)

# CONCEPT TESTER

Test your understanding of the concepts introduced in this chapter by completing the following crossword puzzle.

**Across Clues**

1. An item used by employees to record arrival and departure times (2 words).
5. A national retirement scheme (3rd of 3 words; also see 1 down, 5 down).
6. Special bank account used for paying employees (2nd of 3 words; also see 10 across, 2 down).
9. Payment by employers to enhance the employees' wages (2nd of 3 words).
10. Special bank account used for paying employees (1st of 3 words; see also 6 across, 2 down).
11. The amount an employee earns before any deductions (2 words).
12. Payments by employers to enhance the employees' wages (1st of 3 words; also see 9 across, 7 down).
13. A government program to assist those who are out of work (1st of 2 words; also see 8 down).

**Down Clues**

1. A national retirement scheme (1st of 3 words; also see 5 down, 5 across).
2. Special bank account used for paying employees (3rd of 3 words; also see 10 across, 6 across).
3. An amount subtracted from the employee's pay (2 words).
4. Process of recording when an employee is on the job.
5. A national retirement scheme (2nd of 3 words; also see 1 down, 5 across).
7. Payments by employers to enhance the employees' wages (3rd of 3 words; also see 12 across, 9 across).
8. A government program to assist those who are out of work (2nd of 2 words; also see 13 across).

# ANSWERS TO PROGRESS CHECKS

10–1  Unemployment insurance is designed to alleviate hardships caused by interruptions in earnings through unemployment.

10–2  On or before the last day in February.

10–3  Deductions for Canada Savings Bonds, health or life insurance premiums, loan repayments, and donations to charitable organizations.

10–4  Regular pay plus overtime pay.

10–5  Gross pay less all the deductions.

10–6  A payroll bank account simplifies the payments to the employees and the internal control.

10–7  An employee's earnings record serves as a basis for the employer's tax returns, indicates when the maximum CPP and UI deductions have been reached and supplies the data for the employees' T-4 slips.

10–8  $3,725 = ($1,750 \times 1.4) + $1,275$

10–9  Normally by the 15th of the following month; large employers must remit on the 10th and 25th of each month.

10–10  Premiums are based on the accident experience in the specific industry and on the size of the employer's payroll.

10–11  $9,600 = ($160,000 \times .06)$

# Present and Future Values: An Expansion

**After studying Appendix F, you should be able to:**

1. Explain what is meant by the present value of a single amount and the present value of an annuity and be able to use tables to solve present value problems.
2. Explain what is meant by the future value of a single amount and the future value of an annuity and be able to use tables to solve future value problems.

LEARNING OBJECTIVES

The concept of present value is introduced and applied to accounting problems in Chapters 13 and 18 (Volume II). This appendix supplements those presentations with additional discussion, more complete tables, and additional homework exercises. In studying this appendix, you also learn about the concept of future value.

The present value of a single amount to be received or paid at some future date may be expressed as:

$$p = \frac{f}{(1 + i)^n}$$

where

**PRESENT VALUE OF A SINGLE AMOUNT**

LO 1
Explain what is meant by the present value of a single amount and the present value of an annuity, and be able to use tables to solve present value problems.

$p$ = Present value
$f$ = Future value
$i$ = Rate of interest per period
$n$ = Number of periods

For example, assume that $2.20 is to be received one period from now. It would be useful to know how much must be invested now, for one period, at an interest rate of 10% to provide $2.20. We can calculate that amount with this formula:

$$p = \frac{f}{(1 + i)^n} = \frac{\$2.20}{(1 + .10)^1} = \$2.00$$

Alternatively, we can use the formula to find how much must be invested for two periods at 10% to provide $2.42:

$$p = \frac{f}{(1 + i)^n} = \frac{\$2.42}{(1 + .10)^2} = \$2.00$$

Note that the number of periods ($n$) does not have to be expressed in years. Any period of time such as a day, a month, a quarter, or a year may be used. However, whatever period is used, the interest rate ($i$) must be compounded for the same period. Thus, if a problem expresses $n$ in months, and $i$ equals 12% per year, then 1% of the amount invested at the beginning of each month is earned during that month and added to the investment. Thus, the interest is compounded monthly.

A present value table shows present values for a variety of interest rates ($i$) and a variety of numbers of periods ($n$). Each present value is based on the assumption that the future value ($f$) is 1. The following formula is used to construct a table of present values of a single future amount:

$$p = \frac{1}{(1 + i)^n}$$

Table F–1 on page AP–8 is a table of present values of a single future amount and often is called a *present value of 1* table.

---

**Progress Check**

F–1  **Lamar Company is considering an investment that will yield $70,000 after six years. If Lamar requires an 8% return, how much should it be willing to pay for the investment?**

---

## FUTURE VALUE OF A SINGLE AMOUNT

**LO 2**

Explain what is meant by the future value of a single amount and the future value of an annuity, and be able to use tables to solve future value problems.

The following formula for the present value of a single amount can be modified to become the formula for the future value of a single amount with a simple step:

$$p = \frac{f}{(1 + i)^n}$$

By multiplying both sides of the equation by $(1 + i)^n$, the result is:

$$f = p \times (1 + i)^n$$

For example, we can use this formula to determine that $2.00 invested for one period at an interest rate of 10% will increase to a future value of $2.20:

$$f = p \times (1 + i)^n$$
$$= \$2.00 \times (1 + .10)^1$$
$$= \$2.20$$

Alternatively, assume that $2.00 will remain invested for three periods at 10%. The $2.662 amount that will be received after three periods is calculated with the formula as follows:

$$f = p \times (1 + i)^n$$
$$= \$2.00 \times (1 + .10)^3$$
$$= \$2.662$$

A future value table shows future values for a variety of interest rates ($i$) and a variety of numbers of periods ($n$). Each future value is based on the assumption that the present value ($p$) is 1. Thus, the formula used to construct a table of future values of a single amount is:

$$f = (1 + i)^n$$

Table F–2 on page AP–9 is a table of future values of a single amount and often is called a *future value of 1* table.

In Table F–2, look at the row where $n = 0$ and observe that the future value is 1 for all interest rates because no interest is earned.

Observe that a table showing the present values of 1 and a table showing the future values of 1 contain exactly the same information because both tables are based on the same equation:

$$p = \frac{f}{(1 + i)^n}$$

This equation is nothing more than a reformulation of:

$$f = p \times (1 + i)^n$$

Both tables reflect the same four variables, $p$, $f$, $i$, and $n$. Therefore, any problem that can be solved with one of the two tables can also be solved with the other table.

For example, suppose that a person invests $100 for five years and expects to earn 12% per year. How much should the person receive after five years? To solve the problem using Table F–2, find the future value of 1, five periods from now, compounded at 12%. In the table, $f = 1.7623$. Thus, the amount to be accumulated over five years is $176.23 ($100 $\times$ 1.7623).

Table F–1 shows that the present value of 1, discounted five periods at 12% is 0.5674. Recall that the relationship between present value and future value may be expressed as:

$$p = \frac{f}{(1 + i)^n}$$

This formula can be restated as:

$$p = f \times \frac{1}{(1 + i)^n}$$

In turn, it can be restated as:

$$f = \frac{p}{\dfrac{1}{(1 + i)^n}}$$

Because we know from Table F–1 that $1/(1 + i)^n$ equals 0.5674, the future value of $100 invested for five periods at 12% is:

$$f = \frac{\$100}{0.5674} = \$176.24$$

In summary, the future value can be found two ways. First, we can multiply the amount invested by the future value found in Table F–2. Second, we can divide the amount invested by the present value found in Table F–1. As you can see in this problem, immaterial differences can occur between these two methods through rounding.

---

**Progress Check**

F-2   On May 9, Cindy Huber was notified that she had won $150,000 in a sweepstakes. She decided to deposit the money in a savings account that yields an 8% annual rate of interest and plans on quitting her job when the account equals $299,850. How many years will it be before Cindy is able to quit working? *(a)* 2; *(b)* 8; *(c)* 9.

---

# PRESENT VALUE OF AN ANNUITY

**LO 3**

Explain what is meant by the present value of a single amount and the present value of an annuity, and be able to use tables to solve present value problems.

An annuity is a series of equal payments occurring at equal intervals, such as three annual payments of $100 each. The present value of an annuity is defined as the present value of the payments one period prior to the first payment. Graphically, this annuity and its present value ($p$) may be represented as follows:

One way to calculate the present value of this annuity finds the present value of each payment with the formula and adds them together. For this example, assuming an interest rate of 15%, the calculation is:

$$p = \frac{\$100}{(1 + .15)^1} + \frac{\$100}{(1 + .15)^2} + \frac{\$100}{(1 + .15)^3} = \$228.32$$

Another way calculates the present value of the annuity by using Table F–1 to compute the present value of each payment then taking their sum:

| | |
|---|---|
| First payment: | $p = \$100 \times 0.8696 = \$\ 86.96$ |
| Second payment: | $p = \$100 \times 0.7561 = \ \ \ 75.61$ |
| Third payment: | $p = \$100 \times 0.6575 = \ \ \ 65.75$ |
| Total: | $p = \underline{\underline{\$228.32}}$ |

We can also use Table F–1 to solve the problem by first adding the table values for the three payments and then multiplying this sum by the $100 amount of each payment:

| From Table F–1: | $i = 15\%, n = 1, p =$ | 0.8696 |
|---|---|---|
| | $i = 15\%, n = 2, p =$ | 0.7561 |
| | $i = 15\%, n = 3, p =$ | 0.6575 |
| | | 2.2832 |

$$2.2832 \times \$100 = \underline{\underline{\$228.32}}$$

An easier way to solve the problem uses a different table that shows the present values of annuities like Table F–3 on page AP–10, which often is called a *present value of an annuity of 1* table. Look in Table F–3 on the row where $n = 3$ and $i = 15\%$ and observe that the present value is 2.2832. Thus, the present value of an annuity of 1 for three periods, discounted at 15%, is 2.2832.

Although a formula is used to construct a table showing the present values of an annuity, you can construct one by adding the amounts in a present value of 1 table.[1] Examine Table F–1 and Table F–3 to confirm that the following numbers were drawn from those tables:

|  | **From Table F–1** | **From Table F–3** |  |
|---|---|---|---|
| $i = 8\%, n = 1$ .... | 0.9259 |  |  |
| $i = 8\%, n = 2$ .... | 0.8573 |  |  |
| $i = 8\%, n = 3$ .... | 0.7938 |  |  |
| $i = 8\%, n = 4$ .... | 0.7350 |  |  |
| Total ......... | 3.3120 | $i = 8\%, n = 4$ ...... | 3.3121 |

The minor difference in the results occurs only because the numbers in the tables have been rounded.

In addition to the preceding methods, you can use preprogrammed business calculators and spreadsheet computer programs to find the present value of annuities.

**Progress Check**

**F–3** Smith & Company is considering an investment that would pay $10,000 every six months for three years. The first payment would be received in six months. If Smith & Company requires an annual return of 8%, they should be willing to invest no more than: *(a)* $25,771; *(b)* $46,229; *(c)* $52,421.

## FUTURE VALUE OF AN ANNUITY

Just as an annuity has a present value, it also has a future value. The future value of an annuity is the accumulated value of the annuity payments and interest as of the date of the final payment. Consider the earlier annuity of three annual payments of $100. These are the points in time at which the present value ($p$) and the future value ($f$) occur:

Note that the first payment is made two periods prior to the point at which the future value is determined. Therefore, for the first payment, $n = 2$. For the second payment, $n = 1$. Since the third payment occurs on the future value date, $n = 0$.

One way to calculate the future value of this annuity uses the formula to find the future value of each payment and adds them together. Assuming an interest rate of 15%, the calculation is:

$$f = \$100 \times (1 + .15)^2 + \$100 \times (1 + .15)^1 + \$100 \times (1 + .15)^0 = \$347.25$$

---

[1]The formula for the present value of an annuity of 1 is:

$$p = \frac{1 - \frac{1}{(1 + i)^n}}{i}$$

Another way calculates the future value of the annuity by using Table F–2 to find the sum of the future values of each payment:

First payment:      $f = \$100 \times 1.3225 = \$132.25$
Second payment:   $f = \$100 \times 1.1500 = \phantom{0}115.00$
Third payment:     $f = \$100 \times 1.0000 = \phantom{0}\underline{100.00}$
Total:                                    $f = \underline{\underline{\$347.25}}$

A third approach adds the future values of three payments of 1 and multiplies the sum by $100:

From Table F–1:   $i = 15\%, n = 2, f = \phantom{0}1.3225$
                        $i = 15\%, n = 1, f = \phantom{0}1.1500$
                        $i = 15\%, n = 0, f = \phantom{0}\underline{1.0000}$
                                    $\text{Sum} = \phantom{0}\underline{3.4725}$
Future value $= 3.4725 \times \$100 = \underline{\underline{\$347.25}}$

A fourth and easier way to solve the problem uses a table that shows the future values of annuities, often called a *future value of an annuity of 1* table. Table F–4 on page AP–11 is such a table. Note in Table F–4 that when $n = 1$, the future values are equal to 1 ($f = 1$) for all rates of interest because the annuity consists of only one payment and the future value is determined on the date of the payment. Thus, the future value equals the payment.

Although a formula is used to construct a table showing the future values of an annuity of 1, you can construct one by adding together the amount in a future value of 1 table like Table F–2.[2] Examine Table F–2 and Table F–4 to confirm that the following numbers were drawn from those tables:

| From Table F–2 | | From Table F–4 | |
|---|---|---|---|
| $i = 8\%, n = 0$ .... | 1.0000 | | |
| $i = 8\%, n = 1$ .... | 1.0800 | | |
| $i = 8\%, n = 2$ .... | 1.1664 | | |
| $i = 8\%, n = 3$ .... | 1.2597 | | |
| Total  ......... | 4.5061 | $i = 8\%, n = 4$ ...... | 4.5061 |

Minor differences may occur because the numbers in the tables have been rounded.

You can also use business calculators and spreadsheet computer programs to find the future values of annuities.

Observe that the future value in Table F–2 is 1.0000 when $n = 0$ but the future value in Table F–4 is 1.0000 when $n = 1$. Why does this apparent contradiction arise? When $n = 0$ in Table F–2, the future value is determined on the date that the single payment occurs. Thus, no interest is earned and the future value equals the payment. However, Table F–4 describes annuities with equal payments occurring

_____

[2]The formula for the future value of an annuity of 1 is:

$$f = \frac{(1 + i)^n - 1}{i}$$

each period. When $n = 1$, the annuity has only one payment, and its future value also equals 1 on the date of its final and only payment.

---

**Progress Check**

**F–4**    **Syntel Company invests $45,000 per year for five years at 12%. Calculate the value of the investment at the end of five years.**

---

**LO 1. Explain what is meant by the present value of a single amount and the present value of an annuity, and be able to use tables to solve present value problems.** The present value of a single amount to be received at a future date is the amount that could be invested now at the specified interest rate to yield that future value. The present value of an annuity is the amount that could be invested now at the specified interest rate to yield that series of equal periodic payments. Present value tables and business calculators simplify calculating present values.

**LO 2. Explain what is meant by the future value of a single amount and the future value of an annuity, and be able to use tables to solve future value problems.** The future value of a single amount invested at a specified rate of interest is the amount that would accumulate at a future date. The future value of an annuity to be invested at a specified rate of interest is the amount that would accumulate at the date of the final equal periodic payment. Future value tables and business calculators simplify calculating future values.

**SUMMARY OF THE APPENDIX IN TERMS OF LEARNING OBJECTIVES**

**Table F-1**  Present Value of 1 Due in *n* Periods

| Periods | Rate | | | | | | | | | | | |
|---|---|---|---|---|---|---|---|---|---|---|---|---|
| | 1% | 2% | 3% | 4% | 5% | 6% | 7% | 8% | 9% | 10% | 12% | 15% |
| 1 | 0.9901 | 0.9804 | 0.9709 | 0.9615 | 0.9524 | 0.9434 | 0.9346 | 0.9259 | 0.9174 | 0.9091 | 0.8929 | 0.8696 |
| 2 | 0.9803 | 0.9612 | 0.9426 | 0.9246 | 0.9070 | 0.8900 | 0.8734 | 0.8573 | 0.8417 | 0.8264 | 0.7972 | 0.7561 |
| 3 | 0.9706 | 0.9423 | 0.9151 | 0.8890 | 0.8638 | 0.8396 | 0.8163 | 0.7938 | 0.7722 | 0.7513 | 0.7118 | 0.6575 |
| 4 | 0.9610 | 0.9238 | 0.8885 | 0.8548 | 0.8227 | 0.7921 | 0.7629 | 0.7350 | 0.7084 | 0.6830 | 0.6355 | 0.5718 |
| 5 | 0.9515 | 0.9057 | 0.8626 | 0.8219 | 0.7835 | 0.7473 | 0.7130 | 0.6806 | 0.6499 | 0.6209 | 0.5674 | 0.4972 |
| 6 | 0.9420 | 0.8880 | 0.8375 | 0.7903 | 0.7462 | 0.7050 | 0.6663 | 0.6302 | 0.5963 | 0.5645 | 0.5066 | 0.4323 |
| 7 | 0.9327 | 0.8706 | 0.8131 | 0.7599 | 0.7107 | 0.6651 | 0.6227 | 0.5835 | 0.5470 | 0.5132 | 0.4523 | 0.3759 |
| 8 | 0.9235 | 0.8535 | 0.7894 | 0.7307 | 0.6768 | 0.6274 | 0.5820 | 0.5403 | 0.5019 | 0.4665 | 0.4039 | 0.3269 |
| 9 | 0.9143 | 0.8368 | 0.7664 | 0.7026 | 0.6446 | 0.5919 | 0.5439 | 0.5002 | 0.4604 | 0.4241 | 0.3606 | 0.2843 |
| 10 | 0.9053 | 0.8203 | 0.7441 | 0.6756 | 0.6139 | 0.5584 | 0.5083 | 0.4632 | 0.4224 | 0.3855 | 0.3220 | 0.2472 |
| 11 | 0.8963 | 0.8043 | 0.7224 | 0.6496 | 0.5847 | 0.5268 | 0.4751 | 0.4289 | 0.3875 | 0.3505 | 0.2875 | 0.2149 |
| 12 | 0.8874 | 0.7885 | 0.7014 | 0.6246 | 0.5568 | 0.4970 | 0.4440 | 0.3971 | 0.3555 | 0.3186 | 0.2567 | 0.1869 |
| 13 | 0.8787 | 0.7730 | 0.6810 | 0.6006 | 0.5303 | 0.4688 | 0.4150 | 0.3677 | 0.3262 | 0.2897 | 0.2292 | 0.1625 |
| 14 | 0.8700 | 0.7579 | 0.6611 | 0.5775 | 0.5051 | 0.4423 | 0.3878 | 0.3405 | 0.2992 | 0.2633 | 0.2046 | 0.1413 |
| 15 | 0.8613 | 0.7430 | 0.6419 | 0.5553 | 0.4810 | 0.4173 | 0.3624 | 0.3152 | 0.2745 | 0.2394 | 0.1827 | 0.1229 |
| 16 | 0.8528 | 0.7284 | 0.6232 | 0.5339 | 0.4581 | 0.3936 | 0.3387 | 0.2919 | 0.2519 | 0.2176 | 0.1631 | 0.1069 |
| 17 | 0.8444 | 0.7142 | 0.6050 | 0.5134 | 0.4363 | 0.3714 | 0.3166 | 0.2703 | 0.2311 | 0.1978 | 0.1456 | 0.0929 |
| 18 | 0.8360 | 0.7002 | 0.5874 | 0.4936 | 0.4155 | 0.3505 | 0.2959 | 0.2502 | 0.2120 | 0.1799 | 0.1300 | 0.0808 |
| 19 | 0.8277 | 0.6864 | 0.5703 | 0.4746 | 0.3957 | 0.3305 | 0.2765 | 0.2317 | 0.1945 | 0.1635 | 0.1161 | 0.0703 |
| 20 | 0.8195 | 0.6730 | 0.5537 | 0.4564 | 0.3769 | 0.3118 | 0.2584 | 0.2145 | 0.1784 | 0.1486 | 0.1037 | 0.0611 |
| 25 | 0.7798 | 0.6095 | 0.4776 | 0.3751 | 0.2953 | 0.2330 | 0.1842 | 0.1460 | 0.1160 | 0.0923 | 0.0588 | 0.0304 |
| 30 | 0.7419 | 0.5521 | 0.4120 | 0.3083 | 0.2314 | 0.1741 | 0.1314 | 0.0994 | 0.0754 | 0.0573 | 0.0334 | 0.0151 |
| 35 | 0.7059 | 0.5000 | 0.3554 | 0.2534 | 0.1813 | 0.1301 | 0.0937 | 0.0676 | 0.0490 | 0.0356 | 0.0189 | 0.0075 |
| 40 | 0.6717 | 0.4529 | 0.3066 | 0.2083 | 0.1420 | 0.0972 | 0.0668 | 0.0460 | 0.0318 | 0.0221 | 0.0107 | 0.0037 |

**Table F-2** Future Value of 1 Due in *n* Periods

| Periods | 1% | 2% | 3% | 4% | 5% | 6% | 7% | 8% | 9% | 10% | 12% | 15% |
|---------|-----|-----|-----|-----|-----|-----|-----|-----|-----|------|------|------|
| 0 | 1.0000 | 1.0000 | 1.0000 | 1.0000 | 1.0000 | 1.0000 | 1.0000 | 1.0000 | 1.0000 | 1.0000 | 1.0000 | 1.0000 |
| 1 | 1.0100 | 1.0200 | 1.0300 | 1.0400 | 1.0500 | 1.0600 | 1.0700 | 1.0800 | 1.0900 | 1.1000 | 1.1200 | 1.1500 |
| 2 | 1.0201 | 1.0404 | 1.0609 | 1.0816 | 1.1025 | 1.1236 | 1.1449 | 1.1664 | 1.1881 | 1.2100 | 1.2544 | 1.3225 |
| 3 | 1.0303 | 1.0612 | 1.0927 | 1.1249 | 1.1576 | 1.1910 | 1.2250 | 1.2597 | 1.2950 | 1.3310 | 1.4049 | 1.5209 |
| 4 | 1.0406 | 1.0824 | 1.1255 | 1.1699 | 1.2155 | 1.2625 | 1.3108 | 1.3605 | 1.4116 | 1.4641 | 1.5735 | 1.7490 |
| 5 | 1.0510 | 1.1041 | 1.1593 | 1.2167 | 1.2763 | 1.3382 | 1.4026 | 1.4693 | 1.5386 | 1.6105 | 1.7623 | 2.0114 |
| 6 | 1.0615 | 1.1262 | 1.1941 | 1.2653 | 1.3401 | 1.4185 | 1.5007 | 1.5869 | 1.6771 | 1.7716 | 1.9738 | 2.3131 |
| 7 | 1.0721 | 1.1487 | 1.2299 | 1.3159 | 1.4071 | 1.5036 | 1.6058 | 1.7138 | 1.8280 | 1.9487 | 2.2107 | 2.6600 |
| 8 | 1.0829 | 1.1717 | 1.2668 | 1.3686 | 1.4775 | 1.5938 | 1.7182 | 1.8509 | 1.9926 | 2.1436 | 2.4760 | 3.0590 |
| 9 | 1.0937 | 1.1951 | 1.3048 | 1.4233 | 1.5513 | 1.6895 | 1.8385 | 1.9990 | 2.1719 | 2.3579 | 2.7731 | 3.5179 |
| 10 | 1.1046 | 1.2190 | 1.3439 | 1.4802 | 1.6289 | 1.7908 | 1.9672 | 2.1589 | 2.3674 | 2.5937 | 3.1058 | 4.0456 |
| 11 | 1.1157 | 1.2434 | 1.3842 | 1.5395 | 1.7103 | 1.8983 | 2.1049 | 2.3316 | 2.5804 | 2.8531 | 3.4785 | 4.6524 |
| 12 | 1.1268 | 1.2682 | 1.4258 | 1.6010 | 1.7959 | 2.0122 | 2.2522 | 2.5182 | 2.8127 | 3.1384 | 3.8960 | 5.3503 |
| 13 | 1.1381 | 1.2936 | 1.4685 | 1.6651 | 1.8856 | 2.1329 | 2.4098 | 2.7196 | 3.0658 | 3.4523 | 4.3635 | 6.1528 |
| 14 | 1.1495 | 1.3195 | 1.5126 | 1.7317 | 1.9799 | 2.2609 | 2.5785 | 2.9372 | 3.3417 | 3.7975 | 4.8871 | 7.0757 |
| 15 | 1.1610 | 1.3459 | 1.5580 | 1.8009 | 2.0789 | 2.3966 | 2.7590 | 3.1722 | 3.6425 | 4.1772 | 5.4736 | 8.1371 |
| 16 | 1.1726 | 1.3728 | 1.6047 | 1.8730 | 2.1829 | 2.5404 | 2.9522 | 3.4259 | 3.9703 | 4.5950 | 6.1304 | 9.3576 |
| 17 | 1.1843 | 1.4002 | 1.6528 | 1.9479 | 2.2920 | 2.6928 | 3.1588 | 3.7000 | 4.3276 | 5.0545 | 6.8660 | 10.7613 |
| 18 | 1.1961 | 1.4282 | 1.7024 | 2.0258 | 2.4066 | 2.8543 | 3.3799 | 3.9960 | 4.7171 | 5.5599 | 7.6900 | 12.3755 |
| 19 | 1.2081 | 1.4568 | 1.7535 | 2.1068 | 2.5270 | 3.0256 | 3.6165 | 4.3157 | 5.1417 | 6.1159 | 8.6128 | 14.2318 |
| 20 | 1.2202 | 1.4859 | 1.8061 | 2.1911 | 2.6533 | 3.2071 | 3.8697 | 4.6610 | 5.6044 | 6.7275 | 9.6463 | 16.3665 |
| 25 | 1.2824 | 1.6406 | 2.0938 | 2.6658 | 3.3864 | 4.2919 | 5.4274 | 6.8485 | 8.6231 | 10.8347 | 17.0001 | 32.9190 |
| 30 | 1.3478 | 1.8114 | 2.4273 | 3.2434 | 4.3219 | 5.7435 | 7.6123 | 10.0627 | 13.2677 | 17.4494 | 29.9599 | 66.2118 |
| 35 | 1.4166 | 1.9999 | 2.8139 | 3.9461 | 5.5160 | 7.6861 | 10.6766 | 14.7853 | 20.4140 | 28.1024 | 52.7996 | 133.176 |
| 40 | 1.4889 | 2.2080 | 3.2620 | 4.8010 | 7.0400 | 10.2857 | 14.9745 | 21.7245 | 31.4094 | 45.2593 | 93.0510 | 267.864 |

Rate

**Table F-3** Present Value of an Annuity of 1 per Period

| | | | | | | | Rate | | | | | | |
|---|---|---|---|---|---|---|---|---|---|---|---|---|---|
| **Periods** | **1%** | **2%** | **3%** | **4%** | **5%** | **6%** | **7%** | **8%** | **9%** | **10%** | **12%** | **15%** |
| 1 | 0.9901 | 0.9804 | 0.9709 | 0.9615 | 0.9524 | 0.9434 | 0.9346 | 0.9259 | 0.9174 | 0.9091 | 0.8929 | 0.8696 |
| 2 | 1.9704 | 1.9416 | 1.9135 | 1.8861 | 1.8594 | 1.8334 | 1.8080 | 1.7833 | 1.7591 | 1.7355 | 1.6901 | 1.6257 |
| 3 | 2.9410 | 2.8839 | 2.8286 | 2.7751 | 2.7232 | 2.6730 | 2.6243 | 2.5771 | 2.5313 | 2.4869 | 2.4018 | 2.2832 |
| 4 | 3.9020 | 3.8077 | 3.7171 | 3.6299 | 3.5460 | 3.4651 | 3.3872 | 3.3121 | 3.2397 | 3.1699 | 3.0373 | 2.8550 |
| 5 | 4.8534 | 4.7135 | 4.5797 | 4.4518 | 4.3295 | 4.2124 | 4.1002 | 3.9927 | 3.8897 | 3.7908 | 3.6048 | 3.3522 |
| 6 | 5.7955 | 5.6014 | 5.4172 | 5.2421 | 5.0757 | 4.9173 | 4.7665 | 4.6229 | 4.4859 | 4.3553 | 4.1114 | 3.7845 |
| 7 | 6.7282 | 6.4720 | 6.2303 | 6.0021 | 5.7864 | 5.5824 | 5.3893 | 5.2064 | 5.0330 | 4.8684 | 4.5638 | 4.1604 |
| 8 | 7.6517 | 7.3255 | 7.0197 | 6.7327 | 6.4632 | 6.2098 | 5.9713 | 5.7466 | 5.5348 | 5.3349 | 4.9676 | 4.4873 |
| 9 | 8.5660 | 8.1622 | 7.7861 | 7.4353 | 7.1078 | 6.8017 | 6.5152 | 6.2469 | 5.9952 | 5.7590 | 5.3282 | 4.7716 |
| 10 | 9.4713 | 8.9826 | 8.5302 | 8.1109 | 7.7217 | 7.3601 | 7.0236 | 6.7101 | 6.4177 | 6.1446 | 5.6502 | 5.0188 |
| 11 | 10.3676 | 9.7868 | 9.2526 | 8.7605 | 8.3064 | 7.8869 | 7.4987 | 7.1390 | 6.8052 | 6.4951 | 5.9377 | 5.2337 |
| 12 | 11.2551 | 10.5753 | 9.9540 | 9.3851 | 8.8633 | 8.3838 | 7.9427 | 7.5361 | 7.1607 | 6.8137 | 6.1944 | 5.4206 |
| 13 | 12.1337 | 11.3484 | 10.6350 | 9.9856 | 9.3936 | 8.8527 | 8.3577 | 7.9038 | 7.4869 | 7.1034 | 6.4235 | 5.5831 |
| 14 | 13.0037 | 12.1062 | 11.2961 | 10.5631 | 9.8986 | 9.2950 | 8.7455 | 8.2442 | 7.7862 | 7.3667 | 6.6282 | 5.7245 |
| 15 | 13.8651 | 12.8493 | 11.9379 | 11.1184 | 10.3797 | 9.7122 | 9.1079 | 8.5595 | 8.0607 | 7.6061 | 6.8109 | 5.8474 |
| 16 | 14.7179 | 13.5777 | 12.5611 | 11.6523 | 10.8378 | 10.1059 | 9.4466 | 8.8514 | 8.3126 | 7.8237 | 6.9740 | 5.9542 |
| 17 | 15.5623 | 14.2919 | 13.1661 | 12.1657 | 11.2741 | 10.4773 | 9.7632 | 9.1216 | 8.5436 | 8.0216 | 7.1196 | 6.0472 |
| 18 | 16.3983 | 14.9920 | 13.7535 | 12.6593 | 11.6896 | 10.8276 | 10.0591 | 9.3719 | 8.7556 | 8.2014 | 7.2497 | 6.1280 |
| 19 | 17.2260 | 15.6785 | 14.3238 | 13.1339 | 12.0853 | 11.1581 | 10.3356 | 9.6036 | 8.9501 | 8.3649 | 7.3658 | 6.1982 |
| 20 | 18.0456 | 16.3514 | 14.8775 | 13.5903 | 12.4622 | 11.4699 | 10.5940 | 9.8181 | 9.1285 | 8.5136 | 7.4694 | 6.2593 |
| 25 | 22.0232 | 19.5235 | 17.4131 | 15.6221 | 14.0939 | 12.7834 | 11.6536 | 10.6748 | 9.8226 | 9.0770 | 7.8431 | 6.4641 |
| 30 | 25.8077 | 22.3965 | 19.6004 | 17.2920 | 15.3725 | 13.7648 | 12.4090 | 11.2578 | 10.2737 | 9.4269 | 8.0552 | 6.5660 |
| 35 | 29.4086 | 24.9986 | 21.4872 | 18.6646 | 16.3742 | 14.4982 | 12.9477 | 11.6546 | 10.5668 | 9.6442 | 8.1755 | 6.6166 |
| 40 | 32.8437 | 27.3555 | 23.1148 | 19.7928 | 17.1591 | 15.0463 | 13.3317 | 11.9246 | 10.7574 | 9.7791 | 8.2438 | 6.6418 |

**Table F-4** Future Value of an Annuity of 1 per Period

| Periods | 1% | 2% | 3% | 4% | 5% | 6% | 7% | 8% | 9% | 10% | 12% | 15% |
|---|---|---|---|---|---|---|---|---|---|---|---|---|
| | | | | | | Rate | | | | | | |
| 1 | 1.0000 | 1.0000 | 1.0000 | 1.0000 | 1.0000 | 1.0000 | 1.0000 | 1.0000 | 1.0000 | 1.0000 | 1.0000 | 1.0000 |
| 2 | 2.0100 | 2.0200 | 2.0300 | 2.0400 | 2.0500 | 2.0600 | 2.0700 | 2.0800 | 2.0900 | 2.1000 | 2.1200 | 2.1500 |
| 3 | 3.0301 | 3.0604 | 3.0909 | 3.1216 | 3.1525 | 3.1836 | 3.2149 | 3.2464 | 3.2781 | 3.3100 | 3.3744 | 3.4725 |
| 4 | 4.0604 | 4.1216 | 4.1836 | 4.2465 | 4.3101 | 4.3746 | 4.4399 | 4.5061 | 4.5731 | 4.6410 | 4.7793 | 4.9934 |
| 5 | 5.1010 | 5.2040 | 5.3091 | 5.4163 | 5.5256 | 5.6371 | 5.7507 | 5.8666 | 5.9847 | 6.1051 | 6.3528 | 6.7424 |
| 6 | 6.1520 | 6.3081 | 6.4684 | 6.6330 | 6.8019 | 6.9753 | 7.1533 | 7.3359 | 7.5233 | 7.7156 | 8.1152 | 8.7537 |
| 7 | 7.2135 | 7.4343 | 7.6625 | 7.8983 | 8.1420 | 8.3938 | 8.6540 | 8.9228 | 9.2004 | 9.4872 | 10.0890 | 11.0668 |
| 8 | 8.2857 | 8.5830 | 8.8923 | 9.2142 | 9.5491 | 9.8975 | 10.2598 | 10.6366 | 11.0285 | 11.4359 | 12.2997 | 13.7268 |
| 9 | 9.3685 | 9.7546 | 10.1591 | 10.5828 | 11.0266 | 11.4913 | 11.9780 | 12.4876 | 13.0210 | 13.5795 | 14.7757 | 16.7858 |
| 10 | 10.4622 | 10.9497 | 11.4639 | 12.0061 | 12.5779 | 13.1808 | 13.8164 | 14.4866 | 15.1929 | 15.9374 | 17.5487 | 20.3037 |
| 11 | 11.5668 | 12.1687 | 12.8078 | 13.4864 | 14.2068 | 14.9716 | 15.7836 | 16.6455 | 17.5603 | 18.5312 | 20.6546 | 24.3493 |
| 12 | 12.6825 | 13.4121 | 14.1920 | 15.0258 | 15.9171 | 16.8699 | 17.8885 | 18.9771 | 20.1407 | 21.3843 | 24.1331 | 29.0017 |
| 13 | 13.8093 | 14.6803 | 15.6178 | 16.6268 | 17.7130 | 18.8821 | 20.1406 | 21.4953 | 22.9534 | 24.5227 | 28.0291 | 34.3519 |
| 14 | 14.9474 | 15.9739 | 17.0863 | 18.2919 | 19.5986 | 21.0151 | 22.5505 | 24.2149 | 26.0192 | 27.9750 | 32.3926 | 40.5047 |
| 15 | 16.0969 | 17.2934 | 18.5989 | 20.0236 | 21.5786 | 23.2760 | 25.1290 | 27.1521 | 29.3609 | 31.7725 | 37.2797 | 47.5804 |
| 16 | 17.2579 | 18.6393 | 20.1569 | 21.8245 | 23.6575 | 25.6725 | 27.8881 | 30.3243 | 33.0034 | 35.9497 | 42.7533 | 55.7175 |
| 17 | 18.4304 | 20.0121 | 21.7616 | 23.6975 | 25.8404 | 28.2129 | 30.8402 | 33.7502 | 36.9737 | 40.5447 | 48.8837 | 65.0751 |
| 18 | 19.6147 | 21.4123 | 23.4144 | 25.6454 | 28.1324 | 30.9057 | 33.9990 | 37.4502 | 41.3013 | 45.5992 | 55.7497 | 75.8364 |
| 19 | 20.8109 | 22.8406 | 25.1169 | 27.6712 | 30.5390 | 33.7600 | 37.3790 | 41.4463 | 46.0185 | 51.1591 | 63.4397 | 88.2118 |
| 20 | 22.0190 | 24.2974 | 26.8704 | 29.7781 | 33.0660 | 36.7856 | 40.9955 | 45.7620 | 51.1601 | 57.2750 | 72.0524 | 102.444 |
| 25 | 28.2432 | 32.0303 | 36.4593 | 41.6459 | 47.7271 | 54.8645 | 63.2490 | 73.1059 | 84.7009 | 98.3471 | 133.334 | 212.793 |
| 30 | 34.7849 | 40.5681 | 47.5754 | 56.0849 | 66.4388 | 79.0582 | 94.4608 | 113.283 | 136.308 | 164.494 | 241.333 | 434.745 |
| 35 | 41.6603 | 49.9945 | 60.4621 | 73.6522 | 90.3203 | 111.435 | 138.237 | 172.317 | 215.711 | 271.024 | 431.663 | 881.170 |
| 40 | 48.8864 | 60.4020 | 75.4013 | 95.0255 | 120.800 | 154.762 | 199.635 | 259.057 | 337.882 | 442.593 | 767.091 | 1,779.09 |

# EXERCISES

**Exercise F–1**
Present value of an
amount
**(LO 1)**

Jasper Company is considering an investment which, if paid for immediately, is expected to return $172,500 five years hence. If Jasper demands a 9% return, how much will it be willing to pay for this investment?

**Exercise F–2**
Future value of an
amount
**(LO 2)**

LCV Company invested $529,000 in a project expected to earn a 12% annual rate of return. The earnings will be reinvested in the project each year until the entire investment is liquidated 10 years hence. What will the cash proceeds be when the project is liquidated?

**Exercise F–3**
Present value of an
annuity
**(LO 1)**

Cornblue Distributing is considering a contract that will return $200,400 annually at the end of each year for six years. If Cornblue demands an annual return of 7% and pays for the investment immediately, how much should it be willing to pay?

**Exercise F–4**
Future value of an
annuity
**(LO 2)**

Sarah Oliver is planning to begin an individual retirement program in which she will invest $1,200 annually at the end of each year. Oliver plans to retire after making 30 annual investments in a program that earns a return of 10%. What will be the value of the program on the date of the last investment?

**Exercise F–5**
Interest rate on an
investment
**(LO 1)**

Kevin Smith has been offered the possibility of investing $0.3152 for 15 years, after which he will be paid $1. What annual rate of interest will Smith earn? (Use Table F–1 to find the answer.)

**Exercise F–6**
Number of periods of an
investment
**(LO 1)**

Laura Veralli has been offered the possibility of investing $0.5268. The investment will earn 6% per year and will return Veralli $1 at the end of the investment. How many years must Veralli wait to receive the $1? (Use Table F–1 to find the answer.)

**Exercise F–7**
Number of periods of an
investment
**(LO 2)**

Tom Albertson expects to invest $1 at 15% and, at the end of the investment, receive $66.2118. How many years will elapse before Albertson receives the payment? (Use Table F–2 to find the answer.)

**Exercise F–8**
Interest rate on an
investment
**(LO 2)**

Ed Teller expects to invest $1 for 35 years, after which he will receive $20.4140. What rate of interest will Teller earn? (Use Table F–2 to find the answer.)

**Exercise F–9**
Interest rate on an
investment
**(LO 1)**

Helen Fanshawe expects an immediate investment of $9.3936 to return $1 annually for 13 years, with the first payment to be received in one year. What rate of interest will Fanshawe earn? (Use Table F–3 to find the answer.)

**Exercise F–10**
Number of periods of an
investment
**(LO 1)**

Ken Priggin expects an investment of $7.6061 to return $1 annually for several years. If Priggin is to earn a return of 10%, how many annual payments must he receive? (Use Table F–3 to find the answer.)

Steve Church expects to invest $1 annually for 40 years and have an accumulated value of $95.0255 on the date of the last investment. If this occurs, what rate of interest will Church earn? (Use Table F–4 to find the answer.)

**Exercise F–11**
Interest rate on an investment
**(LO 2)**

Bitsy Brennon expects to invest $1 annually in a fund that will earn 8%. How many annual investments must Brennon make to accumulate $45.7620 on the date of the last investment? (Use Table F–4 to find the answer.)

**Exercise F–12**
Number of periods of an investment
**(LO 2)**

Bill Lenehan financed a new automobile by paying $3,100 cash and agreeing to make 20 monthly payments of $450 each, the first payment to be made one month after the purchase. The loan was said to bear interest at an annual rate of 12%. What was the cost of the automobile?

**Exercise F–13**
Present value of an annuity
**(LO 1)**

Stephanie Powell deposited $4,900 in a savings account that earns interest at an annual rate of 8%, compounded quarterly. The $4,900 plus earned interest must remain in the account 10 years before it can be withdrawn. How much money will be in the account at the end of the 10 years?

**Exercise F–14**
Future value of an amount
**(LO 2)**

Sally Sayer plans to have $90 withheld from her monthly paycheque and deposited in a savings account that earns 12% annually, compounded monthly. If Sayer continues with her plan for 2½ years, how much will be accumulated in the account on the date of the last deposit?

**Exercise F–15**
Future value of an annuity
**(LO 2)**

Stellar Company plans to issue 12%, 15-year, $500,000 par value bonds payable that pay interest semiannually on June 30 and December 31. The bonds are dated December 31, 1996, and are to be issued on that date. If the market rate of interest for the bonds is 10% on the date of issue, what will be the cash proceeds from the bond issue?

**Exercise F–16**
Present value of bonds
**(LO 1)**

Travis Company has decided to establish a fund that will be used 10 years hence to replace an aging productive facility. The company makes an initial contribution of $150,000 to the fund and plans to make quarterly contributions of $60,000 beginning in three months. The fund is expected to earn 12%, compounded quarterly. What will be the value of the fund 10 years hence?

**Exercise F–17**
Future value of an amount plus an annuity
**(LO 2)**

McCoy Company expects to earn 10% per year on an investment that will pay $756,400 six years hence. Use Table F–2 to calculate the present value of the investment.

**Exercise F–18**
Present value of an amount
**(LO 1)**

Comet Company invests $216,000 at 7% per year for nine years. Use Table F–1 to calculate the future value of the investment nine years hence.

**Exercise F–19**
Future value of an amount
**(LO 2)**

## ANSWERS TO PROGRESS CHECKS

F–1    $70,000 × 0.6302 = $44,114

F–2    *c*    $299,850/$150,000 = 1.9990
       Table F–2 shows this value for nine years at 8%.

F–3    *c*    $10,000 × 5.2421 = $52,421

F–4    $45,000 × 6.3528 = $285,876

# Accounting Principles and Conceptual Framework

**After studying Appendix G, you should be able to:**

1. Explain the difference between descriptive concepts and prescriptive concepts.
2. Explain the difference between bottom-up and top-down approaches to the development of accounting concepts.
3. Describe the major components in the Accounting Standards Board's "Financial Statement Concepts."

LEARNING
OBJECTIVES

Accounting principles or concepts are not laws of nature. They are broad ideas developed as a way of *describing* current accounting practices and *prescribing* new and improved practices. In studying Appendix G, you will learn about some new accounting concepts that the Accounting Standards Board (AcSB) developed in an effort to guide future changes and improvements in accounting.

## ACCOUNTING PRINCIPLES AND CONCEPTUAL FRAMEWORK

To fully understand the importance of financial accounting concepts or principles, you must realize that they serve two purposes. First, they provide general descriptions of existing accounting practices. In doing this, concepts and principles serve as guidelines that help you learn about accounting. Thus, after learning how the concepts or principles are applied in a few situations, you develop the ability to apply them in different situations. This is easier and more effective than memorizing a very long list of specific practices.

Second, these concepts or principles help accountants analyze unfamiliar situations and develop procedures to account for those situations. This purpose is especially important for the Accounting Standards Board, which is charged with developing uniform practices for financial reporting in Canada and with improving the quality of such reporting.

In prior chapters, we defined and illustrated several important accounting principles. These principles, listed together here for convenience, describe in general terms the practices currently used by accountants.

**DESCRIPTIVE
AND
PRESCRIPTIVE
ACCOUNTING
CONCEPTS**

LO 1
Explain the difference between descriptive concepts and prescriptive concepts.

---

**Generally Accepted Principles**

| | | |
|---|---|---|
| Business entity principle | Going-concern principle | Revenue recognition |
| Conservatism principle | Matching principle | principle |
| Consistency principle | Materiality principle | Time-period principle |
| Cost principle | Objectivity principle | Unit of measure |
| Full-disclosure principle | | assumption |

---

The listed principles (defined on pages 20–23) are useful for teaching and learning about accounting practice and are helpful for dealing with some unfamiliar transactions. As business practices have evolved in recent years, however, these principles have become less useful as guides for accountants to follow in dealing with new and different types of transactions. This problem has occurred because the principles are intended to provide general descriptions of current accounting practices. In other words, they describe what accountants currently do; they do not necessarily describe what accountants should do. Also, since these principles do not identify weaknesses in accounting practices, they do not lead to major changes or improvements in accounting practices.

In order to improve accounting practices, principles or concepts should not merely *describe* what was being done, they should *prescribe* what ought to be done to make things better.

Before we examine the concepts enunciated in the conceptual framework, we need to look more closely at the differences between descriptive and prescriptive uses of accounting concepts.

## THE PROCESSES OF DEVELOPING DESCRIPTIVE AND PRESCRIPTIVE ACCOUNTING CONCEPTS

**LO 2**

Explain the difference between bottom-up and top-down approaches to the development of accounting concepts.

Sets of concepts differ in how they are developed and used. In general, when concepts are intended to describe current practice, they are developed by looking at accepted specific practices and then making some general rules to encompass them. This bottom-up approach is diagrammed in Illustration G–1 which shows the arrows going from the practices to the concepts. The outcome of the process is a set of general rules that summarize practice and that can be used for education and for solving some new problems. For example, this approach leads to the concept that asset purchases are recorded at cost. However, these kinds of concepts often fail to show how new problems should be solved. To continue the example, the concept that assets are recorded at cost does not provide much direct guidance for situations in which assets have no cost because they are donated to a company by a local government. Further, because these concepts are based on the presumption that current practices are adequate, they do not lead to the development of new and improved accounting methods. To continue the example, the concept that assets are initially recorded at cost does not encourage asking the question of whether they should always be carried at that amount.

In contrast, if concepts are intended to *prescribe* improvements in accounting practices, they are likely to be designed by a top-down approach (Illustration G–2). Note that the top-down approach starts with broad accounting objectives. The process then generates broad concepts about the types of information that should be reported. Finally, these concepts should lead to specific practices that ought to be used. The advantage of this approach is that the concepts are good for solving

**Illustration G–1**   A Bottom-Up Process of Developing Descriptive Accounting Concepts

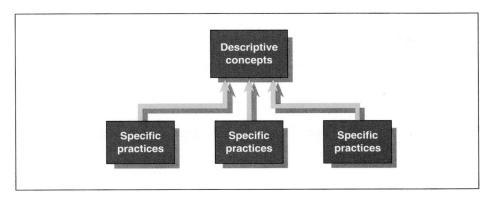

**Illustration G–2**   A Top-Down Process of Developing Prescriptive Accounting Concepts

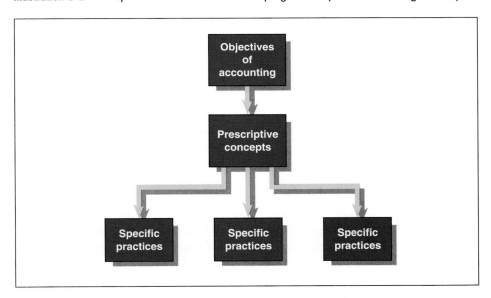

new problems and evaluating old answers; its disadvantage is that the concepts may not be very descriptive of current practice. In fact, the suggested practices may not be in current use.

Since the AcSB uses accounting concepts to prescribe accounting practices, the Board used a top-down approach to develop its conceptual framework. The Board's concepts are not necessarily more correct than the previously developed concepts. However, the new concepts are intended to provide better guidelines for developing new and improved accounting practices. The Board has stated that it will use them as a basis for its future actions and already has used them to justify important changes in financial reporting.

---

**Progress Check**

G–1  **The AcSB's conceptual framework is intended to:**
  *a.*  **provide a historical analysis of accounting practice.**
  *b.*  **describe current accounting practice.**
  *c.*  **provide concepts that are prescriptive of what should be done in accounting practice.**

G–2  **What is the starting point in a top-down approach to developing accounting concepts?**

G–3  **What is the starting point in a bottom-up approach to developing accounting concepts?**

---

## THE CONCEPTUAL FRAMEWORK

**LO 3**

Describe the major components in the Accounting Standards Board's "Financial Statement Concepts."

During the 1970s the accounting profession in both Canada and the United States turned its attention to the apparent need for improvement in financial reporting. In 1980 *Corporate Reporting: Its Future Evolution,* a research study, was published by the Canadian Institute of Chartered Accountants, and in 1989 "Financial Statement Concepts," section 1000 of the *CICA Handbook,* was approved. In the United States the Financial Accounting Standards Board (FASB) published, in the 1978–85 period, six statements regarded as the most comprehensive pronouncement of the conceptual framework of accounting. FASB *(SFAC 1)* and Accounting Standards Board *(CICA Handbook,* section 1000) identified the broad objectives of financial reporting.

### The Objectives of Financial Reporting

"Financial Statement Concepts" identified the broad objectives of financial reporting. The most general objective stated in the *CICA Handbook,* par. 1000.12, is to "communicate information that is useful to investors, creditors, and other users in making resource allocation decisions and/or assessing management stewardship." From this beginning point the Accounting Standards Board (AcSB) expressed other, more specific objectives. These objectives recognize that (1) financial reporting should help users predict future cash flow and (2) in making such predictions, information about a company's resources and obligations is useful if it possesses certain qualities. All of the concepts in the "Financial Statement Concepts" are intended to be consistent with these general objectives. Of course, present accounting practice already provides information about a company's resources and obligations. Thus, although the conceptual framework is intended to be prescriptive of new and improved practices, the concepts in the framework are also descriptive of many current practices.

### The Qualities of Useful Information

The AcSB discussed the fact that information can be useful only if it is understandable to users. However, the users are assumed to have the training, experience, and motivation to analyze financial reports. With this decision, the Board indicated that financial reporting should not try to meet the needs of unsophisticated or other casual report users.

The AcSB said that information is useful if it is (1) relevant, (2) reliable, and (3) comparable. Information is *relevant* if it can make a difference in a decision.

## As a Matter of Opinion

*Ms. Gordon received a B.A. in economics and commerce and both an M.A. and a Ph.D. in economics at Simon Fraser University, where she has been a member of the faculty of business administration since 1981. Ms. Gordon teaches financial accounting and is engaged in research in the areas of positive accounting theory, the accounting-economics interface, social responsibility accounting, and issues in accounting education. She has been a member of CGA-Canada Research Committee since 1984 and was president of the Canadian Academic Accounting Association for 1988–1989.*

**While my university degrees all carry economics in the title, my Ph.D. courses, thesis, and subsequent research have heavily emphasized accounting issues ranging from pensions to internal control to accounting theory.**

**Accounting research is fundamentally interdisciplinary in character. It is this breadth of character that initially sparked my interest and has held it over time. Additionally, in a world where accounting standard setters' decisions are made which have an effect on differing cultures, societies, economic systems, and individuals, this interdisciplinary emphasis is vital. The link between the research of individual accounting academics and standard setting is both important and a "two-way street." Without continuing accounting research, the standard setting process might lack the background or new ways to view our rapidly changing world. As well this linkage gives a purpose to much of the ongoing accounting research.**

Irene M. Gordon, CGA

Information has this quality when it helps users predict the future or evaluate the past, and when it is received in time to affect their decisions.

Information is *reliable* if users can depend on it to be free from bias and error. Reliable information is verifiable and faithfully represents what is supposed to be described. In addition, users can depend on information only if it is neutral. This means that the rules used to produce information should not be designed to lead users to accept or reject any specific decision alternative.

Information is *comparable* if users can use it to identify differences and similarities between companies. Comparability is possible only if companies follow uniform practices. However, even if all companies uniformly follow the same practices, comparable reports do not result if the practices are not appropriate. For example, comparable information would not be provided if all companies were to ignore the useful lives of their assets and amortize all assets over two years.

Comparability also requires consistency, which means that a company should not change its accounting practices unless the change is justified as a reporting improvement. Another important concept discussed is materiality.

## Elements of Financial Statements

Another important step in developing the conceptual framework was to determine the elements of financial statements. This involved defining the categories of information that should be contained in financial reports. The AcSB's discussion of financial statement elements includes definitions of important elements such as assets, liabilities, equity, revenues, expenses, gains, and losses. In earlier chapters, we referred to many of these definitions when we explained various accounting procedures.

## Recognition and Measurement

The AcSB, in paragraphs 36-47 of section 1000, established concepts for deciding (1) when items should be presented (or recognized) in the financial statements, and (2) how to assign numbers to (or measure) those items. In general, the Board concluded that items should be recognized in the financial statements if they meet the following criteria:

- Definitions. The item meets the definition of an element of financial statements.
- Measurability. It has a relevant attribute measurable with sufficient reliability.
- Relevance. The information about it is capable of making a difference in user decisions.
- Reliability. The information is representationally faithful, verifiable, and neutral.

The question of how items should be measured raises the fundamental question of whether financial statements should be based on cost or on value. Since this question is quite controversial, the AcSB's discussion of this issue is more descriptive of current practice than it is prescriptive of new measurement methods. However, before we consider alternative accounting valuation systems, let us review and expand upon the accounting concepts or principles.

## ACCOUNTING PRINCIPLES

An understanding of accounting principles begins with the recognition of the broad concepts as to the nature of the economic setting in which accounting operates.

### The Business Entity Principle

Every business unit or enterprise is treated in accounting as a separate entity, with the affairs of the business and those of the owner or owners being kept entirely separate.

### The Going-Concern Principle

Unless there is strong evidence to the contrary, it is assumed that a business will continue to operate as a going concern, earning a reasonable profit for a period longer than the life expectancy of any of its assets.

### The Time-Period Principle

The environment in which accounting operates—the business community and the government—requires that the life of a business be divided into relatively short periods and that changes be measured over these short periods. Yet, it is generally agreed that earnings cannot be measured precisely over a short period and that it is impossible to learn the exact earnings of a business until it has completed its last transaction and converted all its assets to cash.

### Cost Principle

The cost principle specifies that cash-equivalent cost is the most useful basis for the initial accounting of the elements that are recorded in the accounts and reported on the financial statements. It is important to note that the cost principle applies to the initial recording of transactions and events.

The cost principle is supported by the fact that at the time of a completed arm's-length business transaction, the market value of the resources given up in the transaction provides reliable evidence of the valuation of the item acquired in the transaction.

When a noncash consideration is involved, cost is measured as the market value of the resources given or the market value of the item received, whichever is more reliably determinable. For example, an asset may be acquired with a debt given as settlement. Cost in this instance is the present value of the amount of cash to be paid in the future, as specified by the terms of the debt. The cost principle applies to all of the elements of financial statements, including liabilities.

The cost principle provides guidance at the original recognition date. However, the original cost of some items acquired is subject to depreciation, depletion, amortization, and write-down in conformity with the matching principle and the conservatism constraint (discussed in the sections that follow).

## Revenue Recognition Principle

The revenue recognition principle specifies when revenue should be recognized in the accounts and reported in the financial statements. Revenue is measured as the market value of the resources received or the product or service given, whichever is the more reliably determinable.

Under the revenue recognition principle, revenue from the sale of goods is recognized according to the sales method (i.e., at the time of sale) because the earning process usually is complete at the time of sale. At that time, the relevant information about the asset inflows to the seller would be known with reliability.

Under revenue recognition principle, revenue from the sale of services is recognized on the basis of performance because performance determines the extent to which the earning process is complete.

The revenue recognition principle requires accrual basis accounting rather than cash basis accounting for revenues. For example, completed transactions for the sale of goods or services on credit usually are recognized as revenue in the period in which the sale or service occurred rather than in the period in which the cash is eventually collected.

## Matching Principle

A major objective of accounting is the determination of periodic net income by matching appropriate costs against revenues. The principle recognizes that streams of revenues continually flow into a business, and it requires (1) that there be a precise cutoff in these streams at the end of an accounting period, (2) that the inflows of the period be measured, (3) that the costs incurred in securing the inflows be determined, and (4) that the sum of the costs be deducted from the sum of the inflows to determine the period's net income.

## The Objectivity Principle

The objectivity principle holds that changes in account balances should be supported to the fullest extent possible by objective evidence.

Bargained transactions supported by verifiable business documents originating outside the business are the best objective evidence obtainable, and whenever possible, accounting data should be supported by such documents.

## Full-Disclosure Principle

The full-disclosure principle requires that the financial statements of a business clearly report all of the relevant information about the economic affairs of the enterprise. This principle rests upon the primary characteristic of relevance. Full disclosure requires (a) reporting of all information that can make a difference in a decision and (b) that the accounting information reported must be understandable (i.e., not susceptible to misleading inferences). Full disclosure also requires that the major accounting policies and any special accounting policies used by the company be explained in the notes to the financial statements.

## The Consistency Principle

In many cases two or more methods or procedures have been derived in accounting practice to accomplish a particular accounting objective. While recognizing the validity of different methods under varying circumstances, it is still necessary, in order to ensure a high degree of comparability in any concern's accounting data, to insist on a consistent application in the company of any given accounting method, period after period. It is also necessary to insist that any departures from this doctrine of consistency be fully disclosed in the financial statements and the effects thereof on the statements be fully described.

## The Principle of Conservatism

The principle of conservatism holds that the accountant should be conservative in his or her estimates and opinions and in the selection of procedures, choosing those that neither unduly understate nor overstate the situation.

## The Principle of Materiality

A strict adherence to accounting principles is not required for items of little significance. Consequently, the accountant must always weigh the costs of complying with an accounting principle against the extra accuracy gained thereby, and in those situations where the cost is relatively great and the lack of compliance will have no material effect on the financial statements, compliance is not necessary.

There is no clear-cut distinction between material and immaterial items. Each situation must be individually judged, and an item is material or immaterial as it relates to other items. As a guide, the amount of an item is material if its omission, in the light of the surrounding circumstances, makes it probable that the judgment of a reasonable person would have been changed or influenced.

## Implementation Constraints

Two of the principles listed, materiality and conservatism, are different from the other principles. In fact, some regard these as constraints which exert a modifying influence on financial accounting and reporting. The two other constraints are cost-benefit and industry peculiarities.

The cost of preparing and reporting accounting information should not exceed the value or usefulness of such information. Accounting focuses on usefulness and substance over form. Thus, pecularities and practices of an industry may warrant selective exceptions to accounting principles and practices. These exceptions are permitted for specific items where there is a clear precedent in the industry based on uniqueness and usefulness.

Departure from the strict application of accounting principles and concepts must be fully disclosed whether it be on the basis of (*a*) materiality, (*b*) conservatism, (*c*) cost-benefit, or (*d*) industry peculiarity.

## Unit-of-Measure Assumption

The unit-of-measure assumption specifies that accounting should measure and report the results of the entity's economic activities in terms of a monetary unit such as the Canadian dollar. The assumption recognizes that the monetary unit of measure is an effective means of communicating financial information. Thus, money is the common denominator—the yardstick used in accounting. Using money allows dissimilar things to be aggregated.

Unfortunately, use of a monetary unit for measurement purposes poses a dilemma. Unlike a yardstick which is always the same length, the dollar changes in value. Therefore, during times of inflation or deflation, dollars of different size are entered in the accounts and intermingled as if they possessed equal purchasing power. Because of the practice of ignoring changes in the purchasing power of a dollar, accounting implicitly assumes that the magnitude of change in the value of the monetary unit is not material. This is incorrect. However, this problem and the efforts of the accounting profession to develop alternative valuation systems that report the effects of changes in prices is beyond the scope of this textbook.

---

**Progress Check**

G-4    That a business should be consistent from year to year in its accounting practices most directly relates to the AcSB's concept that information reported in financial statements should be: *(a)* relevant; *(b)* material; *(c)* reliable; *(d)* comparable.

G-5    What are the characteristics of accounting information that make it reliable?

G-6    What is the meaning of the phrase *elements of financial statements?*

---

**LO 1.** Some accounting concepts provide general descriptions of current accounting practices. Other concepts prescribe the practices accountants should follow. These prescriptive concepts are most useful in developing accounting procedures for new types of transactions and making improvements in accounting practice.

**LO 2.** A bottom-up approach to developing concepts examines current practices and then develops concepts to provide general descriptions of those practices. In contrast, a top-down approach begins by stating accounting objectives and from there, develops concepts that prescribe the types of accounting practices accountants should follow.

**SUMMARY OF APPENDIX G IN TERMS OF LEARNING OBJECTIVES**

LO 3. The AcSB's financial statement concepts identify the broad objectives of financial reporting and the qualitative characteristics accounting information should possess. The elements contained in financial reports are defined and the recognition and measurement criteria to be used are identified.

# QUESTIONS

1. Why are concepts developed with a bottom-up approach less useful in leading to accounting improvements than those developed with a top-down approach?

2. What is the starting point in a top-down approach to developing accounting concepts?

3. What is the starting point in a bottom-up approach to developing accounting concepts?

4. What are the basic objectives of external financial reporting according to "Financial Statement Concepts"?

5. What is implied by saying that financial information should have the qualitative characteristic of relevance?

6. What are the characteristics of accounting information that make it reliable?

# PROBLEM

**Problem G–1**
Analytical essay
**(LO 1, 2, 3)**

Write a brief essay that explains why a top-down approach to developing descriptive accounting concepts is not likely to be effective. Also explain why a bottom-up approach is more likely to be effective. Finally, explain why the conceptual framework reflects a top-down approach to developing concepts.

# ANSWERS TO PROGRESS CHECKS

G–1  c

G–2  A top-down approach to developing accounting concepts begins by identifying appropriate objectives of accounting reports.

G–3  A bottom-up approach to developing accounting starts by examining existing accounting practices and determining the general features that characterize those procedures.

G–4  d

G–5  To have the qualitative characteristic of being reliable, accounting information should be free from bias and error, should be verifiable, should faithfully represent what is supposed to be described, and should be neutral.

G–6  The elements of financial statements are the objects and events that financial statements should describe, for example, assets, liabilities, revenues, and expenses.

# Accounting for Corporate Income Taxes

**After studying Appendix H, you should be able to:**

1. **Explain why income taxes for accounting purposes may be different from income taxes for tax purposes.**

2. **Prepare an income tax schedule and journal entries for a company where timing differences exist between accounting and taxable income.**

Financial statements for a business should be prepared in accordance with generally accepted accounting principles. Income tax returns, on the other hand, must be prepared in accordance with income tax laws. As a result, a corporation's *income before taxes* measured in accordance with generally accepted accounting principles is almost never the same as *taxable income* calculated on income tax returns.

You have already learned how to determine net income under GAAP for a profit-oriented entity. However, the determination of taxable income for a corporation, while starting with the accounting net income, is done using the Canadian Income Tax Act. Almost always, this results in taxable income being different from the GAAP accounting income.

A major difference between accounting income and taxable income results from what are known as timing differences. These arise because some items are included as revenue or expense in one period under GAAP, whereas they are included in a different period under the income tax rules. For example:

1. The application of accounting principles for installment sales requires that gross profit on these sales is recognized in accounting income before it is recognized in taxable income under the income tax rules.

2. Accounting principles require an estimate of future costs, such as costs of making good on guarantees; they also require a deduction of such costs from revenue in the year the guaranteed goods are sold. However, tax rules do not permit the deduction of such costs until they are actually incurred.

3. Reported net income also differs from taxable income because the taxpayer uses a method or procedure believed to fairly reflect periodic net income for accounting purposes, but is required to use a different method of procedure for tax purposes. For example, the last-in, first-out inventory method of cost allocation may be used for accounting purposes, but is not permitted for tax purposes. Likewise, many companies use straight-line amortization of capital assets for accounting purposes but are required to use a different procedure, called *capital cost allowances,* for tax purposes.

## ACCOUNTING AND TAXABLE INCOME

**LO 1**

Explain why income taxes for accounting purposes may be different from income taxes for tax purposes.

# CAPITAL COST ALLOWANCES

Depreciation (amortization) accounting has been greatly influenced by income tax laws. The 1948 Income Tax Act replaced the complex body of rules that had developed for the purpose of limiting the amount of amortization allowed for tax purposes. The act defined and set a limit on amounts which could be deducted, for tax purposes, in respect to the cost of amortizable assets. These amounts are known as *capital cost allowances* (CCA).

The capital cost allowances are identical in nature and purpose with the accountants' concept of amortization and are based on the declining-balance method, discussed in Chapter 11. For tax purposes, the taxpayer may claim the maximum allowed or any part thereof in any year regardless of the amortization method and the amounts used in the accounting records.

Although capital cost allowances are based on the declining-balance method, certain procedures have been set out by the Regulations of the Act. The more important of these are as follows:

1. All amortizable assets are grouped into a comparatively small number of classes and a maximum rate allowed is prescribed for each group. The assets most commonly in use are set out below according to the class to which they belong, with the maximum rate of allowance for each such class (as at the time of writing).

   Class 1 (4%): Buildings or other structures.
   Class 7 (15%): Ships, scows, canoes, and rowboats.
   Class 8 (20%): Machinery, equipment, and furniture.
   Class 10 (30%): Automobiles, trucks, tractors, and computer hardware.

2. The assets of a designated class are considered to form a separate pool of costs. The costs of asset additions are added to their respective pools of unamortized capital cost. When assets are disposed of, the proceeds (up to the original cost) received from disposal are deducted from the proper pool. The balance of each pool of costs is also diminished by the accumulated capital cost allowance claimed. A capital cost allowance is claimed on the balance, referred to as the *unamortized capital cost* (UCC), in the pool at the end of the fiscal year. However, when there are net additions to the pool, only one half of the amount added is used in the calculation of CCA in the year of the net additions. The effect is that the assets are assumed to have been acquired halfway through the fiscal year.

3. "Losses" and "gains" on disposal of individual assets disappear into the pool of unamortized capital costs except when an asset is sold for more than its capital cost. In this case, proceeds of disposal in excess of the capital cost of the asset are normally treated as a capital gain. Where the proceeds of disposal (excluding the capital gain, if any) exceed the unamortized capital cost of the class immediately before the sale, the amount of the excess is treated as a "recapture" of capital cost allowances previously taken. Such a recapture is considered as ordinary income. When all of the assets in a class are disposed of and the proceeds are less than the unamortized capital cost of the class immediately before the sale, the proceeds less the unamortized capital cost may be deducted in determining the year's taxable income.

Companies must, with few exceptions, use capital cost allowances for tax purposes, but commonly use straight-line amortization in their accounting records. A problem arising from this practice is discussed in the next section.

## TAXES AND THE DISTORTION OF NET INCOME

**LO 2**

Prepare an income tax schedule and journal entries when timing differences exist.

When one accounting procedure is required for tax purposes and a different procedure is used in the accounting records, a problem arises as to how much income tax expense should be deducted each year on the income statement. If the tax actually incurred in such situations is deducted, reported net income often varies from year to year due to the postponement and later payment of taxes. Consequently, in such cases, since shareholders may be misled by these variations, many accountants are of the opinion that income taxes should be allocated in such a way that any distortion resulting from postponing taxes is removed from the income statement.

To appreciate the problem involved here, assume that a corporation has installed a $100,000 machine, the product of which will produce a half-million dollars of revenue in each of the succeeding four years and $80,000 of income before amortization and taxes. Assume further that the company must pay income taxes at a 40% rate (round number assumed for easy calculation) and that it plans to use straight-line amortization in its records but the capital cost allowance for tax purposes. If the machine has a four-year life and a $10,000 salvage value and if the maximum permitted capital cost allowance rate on this particular machine is 50%, annual amortization calculated by each method will be as follows:

| Year | Straight-Line | Capital Cost Allowance |
|---|---|---|
| 1996 . . . . . . . | $22,500 | $25,000 |
| 1997 . . . . . . . | 22,500 | 37,500 |
| 1998 . . . . . . . | 22,500 | 18,750 |
| 1999 . . . . . . . | 22,500 | 8,750* |
| Totals . . . . | $90,000 | $90,000 |

*Use $8,750 in order to match salvage value.
CCA allowed is $9,375.

In the year of acquisition, only one-half of the CCA otherwise allowed may be claimed. In subsequent years, CCA may be claimed up to the maximum amounts allowed.

Since the company uses capital cost allowance for tax purposes, it will be liable for $22,000 of income tax on the first year's income, $17,000 on the second, $24,500 on the third, and $28,500 on the fourth. The calculation of these taxes is shown in Illustration H–1.

Furthermore, if the company were to deduct its actual tax payable each year in arriving at income to be reported to its shareholders, it would report the amounts shown in Illustration H–2.

Observe in Illustrations H–1 and H–2 that total amortization, $90,000, is the same whether calculated by the straight-line or the declining-balance method. Also

**Illustration H–1**
Calculation of Income Taxes

| Annual Income Taxes | 1996 | 1997 | 1998 | 1999 | Total |
|---|---|---|---|---|---|
| Income before amortization and income taxes | $80,000 | $80,000 | $80,000 | $80,000 | $320,000 |
| Amortization for tax purposes (declining-balance)/CCA | 25,000 | 37,500 | 18,750 | 8,750 | 90,000 |
| Taxable income | $55,000 | $42,500 | $61,250 | $71,250 | $230,000 |
| Annual income taxes (40% of taxable income) | $22,000 | $17,000 | $24,500 | $28,500 | $ 92,000 |

**Illustration H–2**   Calculation of Remaining Income

| Income after Deducting Actual Tax Liabilities | 1996 | 1997 | 1998 | 1999 | Total |
|---|---|---|---|---|---|
| Income before amortization and income taxes | $80,000 | $80,000 | $80,000 | $80,000 | $320,000 |
| Amortization per books (straight-line) | 22,500 | 22,500 | 22,500 | 22,500 | 90,000 |
| Income before taxes | 57,500 | 57,500 | 57,500 | 57,500 | 230,000 |
| Income taxes (actual liability of each year) | 22,000 | 17,000 | 24,500 | 28,500 | 92,000 |
| Remaining income | $35,500 | $40,500 | $33,000 | $29,000 | $138,000 |

note that the total tax paid over the four years, $92,000, is the same in each case. Then note the distortion of the final income figures in Illustration H–2 due to the postponement of taxes.

If this company should report successive annual income figures of $35,500, $40,500, $33,000, and then $29,000, some of its shareholders might be misled as to the company's earnings trend. Consequently, in cases such as this, many accountants think income taxes should be allocated so that the distortion caused by the postponement of taxes is removed from the income statement. These accountants advocate that

> when one accounting procedure is used in the accounting records and a different procedure is used for tax purposes, the tax expense deducted on the income statement should not be the actual tax liability but the amount that would be payable if the procedure used in the records were also used in calculating the tax.

If the foregoing is applied in this case, the corporation will report to its shareholders in each of the four years the amounts of income shown in Illustration H–3.

In examining Illustration H–2, recall that the company's taxes payable are actually $22,000 in the first year, $17,000 in the second, $24,500 in the third, and $28,500 in the fourth, a total of $92,000. Then observe that when this $92,000 liability is allocated evenly over the four years, the distortion of the annual net incomes due to the postponement of taxes is removed from the published income statements.

**Illustration H-3**  Tax Expense Based on Accounting Income

| Net Income That Should Be Reported to Shareholders | 1996 | 1997 | 1998 | 1999 | Total |
|---|---|---|---|---|---|
| Income before amortization and income taxes. . . . . . . . . . . . | $80,000 | $80,000 | $80,000 | $80,000 | $320,000 |
| Amortization per books (straight-line) . . . | 22,500 | 22,500 | 22,500 | 22,500 | 90,000 |
| Income before taxes . . . . . . . . . . | 57,500 | 57,500 | 57,500 | 57,500 | 230,000 |
| Income taxes (amounts based on straight-line amortization). . . . . . . | 23,000 | 23,000 | 23,000 | 23,000 | 92,000 |
| Net income. . . . . . . . . . . . . . | $34,500 | $34,500 | $34,500 | $34,500 | $138,000 |

**ENTRIES FOR THE ALLOCATION OF TAXES**

When income taxes are allocated as in Illustration H–3, the tax payable for each year and the deferred income tax are recorded with an adjusting entry. The adjusting entries for the four years of Illustration H–2 and the entries in General Journal form for the payment of the taxes (without explanations) are as follows:

| | | | |
|---|---|---|---|
| 1996 | Income Tax Expense . . . . . . . . . . . . . . . . . . . . . . . . . . . . | 23,000 | |
| | Income Taxes Payable . . . . . . . . . . . . . . . . . . . . . . . | | 22,000 |
| | Deferred Income Tax . . . . . . . . . . . . . . . . . . . . . . . | | 1,000 |
| | | | |
| | Income Taxes Payable . . . . . . . . . . . . . . . . . . . . . . . | 22,000 | |
| | Cash . . . . . . . . . . . . . . . . . . . . . . . . . . . . . . . | | 22,000 |
| | | | |
| 1997 | Income Tax Expense . . . . . . . . . . . . . . . . . . . . . . . . . . . . | 23,000 | |
| | Income Taxes Payable . . . . . . . . . . . . . . . . . . . . . . . | | 17,000 |
| | Deferred Income Tax . . . . . . . . . . . . . . . . . . . . . . . | | 6,000 |
| | | | |
| | Income Taxes Payable . . . . . . . . . . . . . . . . . . . . . . . | 17,000 | |
| | Cash . . . . . . . . . . . . . . . . . . . . . . . . . . . . . . . | | 17,000 |
| | | | |
| 1998 | Income Tax Expense . . . . . . . . . . . . . . . . . . . . . . . . . . . . | 23,000 | |
| | Deferred Income Tax . . . . . . . . . . . . . . . . . . . . . . . . . . . | 1,500 | |
| | Income Taxes Payable . . . . . . . . . . . . . . . . . . . . . . . | | 24,500 |
| | | | |
| | Income Taxes Payable . . . . . . . . . . . . . . . . . . . . . . . | 24,500 | |
| | Cash . . . . . . . . . . . . . . . . . . . . . . . . . . . . . . . | | 24,500 |
| | | | |
| 1999 | Income Tax Expense . . . . . . . . . . . . . . . . . . . . . . . . . . . . | 23,000 | |
| | Deferred Income Tax . . . . . . . . . . . . . . . . . . . . . . . . . . . | 5,500 | |
| | Income Taxes Payable . . . . . . . . . . . . . . . . . . . . . . . | | 28,500 |
| | | | |
| | Income Taxes Payable . . . . . . . . . . . . . . . . . . . . . . . | 28,500 | |
| | Cash . . . . . . . . . . . . . . . . . . . . . . . . . . . . . . . | | 28,500 |

Note: To simplify the illustration, it is assumed that the entire year's tax liability is paid at one time. However, corporations are usually required to pay estimated taxes on a monthly basis.

In the entries the $23,000 debited to Income Tax Expense each year is the amount that is deducted on the income statement in reporting annual net income. Also, the amount credited to Income Taxes Payable each year is the actual tax liability of that year.

Observe in the entries that since the actual tax payable in each of the first two years is less than the amount debited to Income Tax Expense, the difference is credited to *Deferred Income Tax*. Then note that in the last two years, because the actual liability each year is greater than the debit to Income Tax Expense, the difference is debited to Deferred Income Tax. Now observe in the following illustration of the company's Deferred Income Tax account that the debits and credits exactly balance each other out over the four-year period:

**Deferred Income Tax**

| Year | Explanation | Debit | Credit | Balance |
|------|-------------|-------|--------|---------|
| 1996 | | | 1,000 | 1,000 |
| 1997 | | | 6,000 | 7,000 |
| 1998 | | 1,500 | | 5,500 |
| 1999 | | 5,500 | | –0– |

In passing, it should be observed that many accountants believe the interests of government, business, and the public would be better served if there were more uniformity between taxable income and reported net income. However, since the federal income tax is designed to serve other purposes in addition to raising revenue, it is apt to be some time before this is achieved.

Before concluding this appendix on income taxes, we should mention some additional features of the rules that govern accounting for income taxes.

1. In the example above, we assumed an income tax rate of 40% in each year. However, if the income tax rate changes, we use the rate in effect for that year. When the timing difference reverses, the average rate over the accumulation period should be used to avoid throwing the deferred tax amount into a debit balance (this point is covered more thoroughly in later courses).

2. In the example, 1996 income before taxes was *more than* taxable income because of a timing difference that was expected to reverse in 1998 or 1999. As a result, we recognized a deferred tax balance on the December 31, 1996, balance sheet. In other situations, just the opposite kind of timing difference may occur. In other words, a timing difference that will reverse in the future may cause income before taxes to be *less than* taxable income. These latter situations may, under certain conditions, result in the recognition of a deferred tax debit.

3. The Deferred Income Tax account balance may be reported as a long-term liability or as a current liability, depending on how far in the future the amount will reverse.

4. Federal tax laws generally require corporations to estimate their current year's tax liability and make advance payments of the estimated amount before the final tax return is filed. As a result, the end-of-year entries to record income taxes, such as those shown above, often have to be altered to take

into consideration any previously recorded prepayments.

5.  The income tax rate varies depending on the type of organization, small or large, and manufacturing or nonmanufacturing.

**LO 1   Explain why income taxes for accounting purposes may be different from income taxes for tax purposes.** Accounting income and taxable income will differ when revenues and/or expenses may be included in one period for accounting purposes and in a different period for tax purposes.

**LO 2   Prepare an income tax schedule and journal entries for a company where timing differences exist between accounting and taxable income.** Reconcile accounting and taxable income by adding or subtracting the items which constitute timing differences. Income tax expense is based on accounting income, income tax payable on taxable income, and the debit or credit to deferred taxes on the net timing differences.

**SUMMARY OF APPENDIX H IN TERMS OF LEARNING OBJECTIVES**

---

## EXERCISES

Indicate which of the following items might cause timing differences for a corporation:

*a.*   Sales on account.
*b.*   Capital cost allowances.
*c.*   Wages paid to employees.
*d.*   Property taxes.
*e.*   Installment sales.
*f.*   Cost of goods sold.
*g.*   Warranty expenses.
*h.*   Rents received in advance.
*i.*   Cash sales.

**Exercise H–1**
Timing differences
**(LO 1)**

*a.*   Explain why accounting income is usually different from taxable income.
*b.*   What reasons can you give for the two sets of rules?

**Exercise H–2**
Taxable vs. accounting income
**(LO 1)**

Vacon Inc. began operations on January 1, 1996. During 1996, Vacon's operations resulted in a current tax payable of $350,000. In addition, Vacon sold land for $210,000 that had cost $70,000. The sale qualified as an installment sale for tax purposes, so the gain was subject to tax as cash was received. The purchaser agreed to pay for the land on June 1, 1997. Present the December 31, 1996, entry to record Vacon Inc.'s income taxes. Assume a tax rate of 45% and that the profit on the land is fully taxable.

**Exercise H–3**
Recording corporate income tax expense
**(LO 2)**

Buster Corporation would have had identical accounting and taxable income for the three years 1996–1998 were it not for the fact that for tax purposes an operational asset that cost $24,000 was amortized $\frac{3}{6}$, $\frac{2}{6}$, $\frac{1}{6}$ (assumed for problem purposes to be acceptable), whereas for accounting purposes, the straight-line method was used. The asset has a three-year op-

**Exercise H–4**
Recording corporate income tax expense
**(LO 2)**

erational life and no residual value. Income before amortization and income taxes for the years concerned follow:

|                                              | 1996     | 1997     | 1998     |
|----------------------------------------------|----------|----------|----------|
| Pretax accounting income (before amortization) | $40,000  | $45,000  | $50,000  |

Assume an income tax rate of 40% for each year.

### Required

1. Calculate the accounting and taxable income for each year.
2. Prepare journal entries to record the income tax expense for each year.

**Exercise H–5**
Analyze timing differences; entries
**(LO 2)**

Castor Corporation reports the following information for the year ended December 31, 1996:

| Revenue | $525,000 |
|---------|----------|
| Expenses | 390,000 |
| Net income before tax | $135,000 |

Additional information:

a. Revenues (above) do not include $30,000 of rent which is taxable in 1996 but was earned at the end of 1996.

b. Capital cost allowances for 1996 are $32,000 greater than the amortization expense included above.

c. Expenses (above) include $12,000 of estimated warranty expenses which are not deductible for tax purposes in 1996.

d. Assume an income tax rate of 40%.

Prepare a journal entry to record income taxes for Castor Corporation on December 31, 1996.

**Exercise H–6**
Timing differences; entries
**(LO 2)**

Income tax returns on Vastly Corporation reflected the following:

|                        | Year Ended Dec. 31 |          |          |
|------------------------|----------|----------|----------|
|                        | 1996     | 1997     | 1998     |
| Royalty income         | $180,000 |          |          |
| Investment income      | 30,000   | $20,000  | $40,000  |
| Rent income            | 10,000   | 10,000   | 10,000   |
|                        | $220,000 | $30,000  | $50,000  |
| Deductible expenses    | 30,000   | 20,000   | 20,000   |
| Taxable income         | $190,000 | $10,000  | $30,000  |

Assume the average income tax rate for each year was 40%.

The only differences between taxable income on the tax returns and the pretax accounting income relate to royalty income. For accounting purposes, royalty income was recognized ratably (equally) over the three-year period.

### Required

Give journal entries such as would appear at the end of each year to reflect income tax and allocation.

(CGA adapted)

# Geac

**ANNUAL REPORT
1994**

# FINANCIAL HIGHLIGHTS

## 5 YEAR FINANCIAL INFORMATION

| (millions of dollars, except per share amounts) | 1994 | 1993 | Years Ended April 30 1992 | 1991 | 1990 |
|---|---|---|---|---|---|
| Revenues | **152.2** | 105.1 | 85.3 | 82.2 | 73.5 |
| Income from operations before unusual items & taxes | **26.9** | 17.9 | 12.7 | 5.0 | 5.2 |
| Unusual items | **-** | (10.7) | - | (9.8) | 4.7 |
| Income (loss) before income taxes | **26.9** | 7.2 | 12.7 | (4.8) | 9.9 |
| Net income (loss) | **22.9** | 4.5 | 11.1 | (5.5) | 8.2 |
| Cash | **53.3** | 40.9 | 32.0 | 24.4 | 13.5 |
| Earnings (loss) per share | $ **0.81** | $ 0.17 | $ 0.50 | $ (0.25) | $ 0.38 |

## SALES BY REGION
for the years ended April 30, 1994 (1993)

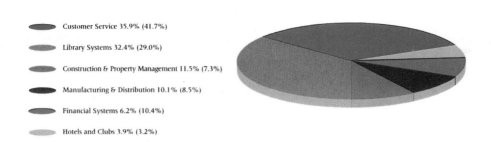

- Canada 13.7% (18.0%)
- USA 44.2% (38.4%)
- Europe 24.9% (33.8%)
- Australasia 17.2% (9.8%)

## SALES BY DIVISION
for the years ended April 30, 1994 (1993)

- Customer Service 35.9% (41.7%)
- Library Systems 32.4% (29.0%)
- Construction & Property Management 11.5% (7.3%)
- Manufacturing & Distribution 10.1% (8.5%)
- Financial Systems 6.2% (10.4%)
- Hotels and Clubs 3.9% (3.2%)

# FINANCIAL REVIEW

## MANAGEMENT DISCUSSION AND ANALYSIS OF FINANCIAL CONDITION AND RESULTS OF OPERATIONS

### Acquisitions

During fiscal 1994, Geac acquired a number of new businesses:

Assets of New Tech Hospitality Systems Pty Ltd., an Australian developer and marketer of hotel and resort software, effective June 30, 1993. Geac initially entered the hotel software market as part of the Jonas and Erickson acquisition in fiscal 1991.

Claymore Systems Group, a Canadian developer of asset valuation software for the real estate industry, effective June 30, 1993. This complements Geac's property management software.

ECI Computer, Inc., a USA based developer of hotel management software with a worldwide customer base, effective August 4, 1993. ECI's advanced Informix based product is targeted at major chains and larger full service hotels.

Datamark International Limited, a New Zealand developer and marketer of manufacturing and distribution software, its Australian subsidiary, Dmark International Pty Limited, both effective September 30, 1993, and the assets of Convergent Solutions Pty Ltd., Datamark's main Australian distributor, effective November 1, 1993. Together with previous strategic acquisitions, these make Geac the largest provider of hardware, software, consulting and support solutions to manufacturers in the fast growing Australasian region.

Assets of Hotel Systems Pty Limited in Australia and Hotel Computer Systems Limited in New Zealand, effective January 31, 1994. Together with New Tech and the Australasian customers of ECI, this makes Geac the largest supplier of hotel and resort management solutions in the region.

These eight acquisitions were made for a total cash consideration of $5.7 million. After their respective dates of acquisition, they contributed about $11 million to fiscal 1994 sales and achieved approximately breakeven operating income. Because of the restructuring and integration of the acquired businesses with Geac's existing business, sales and profitability of the acquired businesses prior to their respective dates of acquisition are not meaningful.

As a result of these acquisitions, Geac included on its balance sheet as other assets $2.2 million of acquired software development and $5.6 million of goodwill. The nature of the assets acquired requires that they be capitalized in accordance with generally accepted accounting principles in Canada.

### Results of Operations

Geac reported a net income of $22.9 million for fiscal 1994 compared to a net income of $4.5 million in fiscal 1993. During fiscal 1993, the Company expensed as an unusual item $10.7 million of purchased software research. Income from operations before the unusual item and income taxes increased to $26.9 million (17.9% of sales) from $17.9 million (17.4% of sales) in 1993.

Sales revenue was $150.3 million in fiscal 1994 compared to $102.7 million in fiscal 1993. Service revenue, primarily contracted support of customers' hardware and licensed software, increased to $73.0 million compared to $55.1 million in the prior year. Service revenue represented 49% of sales compared to 54% in fiscal 1993, as new product sales increased more rapidly in a stronger economy. Computer hardware represents about 20% of sales. Higher margin software licences and consulting sold to new and existing customers account for over 30% of sales.

Interest income decreased to $1.8 million from $2.4 million in the prior year due to generally declining average interest rates worldwide.

Provision for income taxes was $4.0 million compared to $2.8 million in fiscal 1993. Geac operates through wholly owned subsidiaries in several countries. The tax consequences of these operations vary significantly based on the results of each legal entity and the tax laws of each country. Future effective tax rates on operating income are likely to be substantially lower than the combined basic Canadian federal and provincial rate of 44% because most countries in which Geac operates have lower effective tax rates and the subsidiaries have a total of $26 million of tax losses and $4 million of favourable timing differences to apply against future income. The utilization of tax losses and timing differences depends on the financial results of individual subsidiaries and, because individual subsidiary future earnings are not certain, some tax losses may expire before they can be used.

**Liquidity and Capital Resources**

Cash balances of $53.3 million at April 30, 1994 increased by $12.4 million during the year. The Company has no bank borrowings and no long-term debt. Current cash balances and future operating cash flows are more than sufficient to cover foreseeable cash requirements. Commitments at April 30, 1994 consist primarily of lease obligations for office space. No significant fixed asset expenditures are anticipated. In the 1995 fiscal year, cash potentially may be used for the repurchase of the Company's outstanding common shares under a Normal Course Issuer Bid and for the acquisition of new businesses.

Cash is invested in short-term, low risk financial instruments, such as treasury bills and bankers' acceptances. Cash is held in various countries and currencies according to anticipated future needs. Foreign exchange gains included in operations were $0.8 million in fiscal 1994 and $0.1 million in fiscal 1993. Substantially all cash is freely remittable to Canada.

**Outlook**

Geac's historical and ongoing emphasis is to provide a total solution consisting of hardware, software, service and support to customers in selected vertical markets. Vertical markets are specific groups of current and potential customers where the Company provides complete integrated application software solutions to meet critical system requirements. Vertical markets in which Geac participates include academic and public libraries, leasing and asset finance, consumer banking institutions including credit unions, savings banks and savings and loans, manufacturing and distribution, construction, property management, hotels and clubs.

Geac generally enjoys long-term relationships with its customers, providing hardware and software service, support, maintenance and upgrades as well as consulting in the years following the initial sale. On average, subsequent revenues exceed the initial hardware and software sale. As a result, more than 50% of Geac's annual revenue has been relatively stable. Geac's well established worldwide service network and strong financial position give new and existing customers confidence that Geac support will continue over the life of their systems.

Since 1990, Geac has offered its products on a broad range of industry standard hardware platforms which support a Unix-based Open Systems environment. Geac is now a large worldwide vendor of Unix vertical market application software. Customers benefit from Open Systems solutions because the market for RISC/Unix hardware and peripherals is highly competitive and prices continue to decline rapidly as technology advances. As a result, Geac's revenue from selling equivalent computer processing power has continued to decline. Since the highly competitive hardware market limits hardware revenue and margins, there is a trend towards software and services forming an increasing portion of Geac's sales mix. The primary market trend affecting the Company is the continuing decline in hardware prices. Management continues to focus on operating efficiencies by controlling direct operating expenses and overheads.

## MANAGEMENT'S REPORT

The consolidated financial statements and other financial information in this annual report were prepared by management of Geac Computer Corporation Limited, reviewed by the Audit Committee and approved by the Board of Directors.

Management is responsible for the consolidated financial statements and believes that they fairly present the Company's financial condition and results of operations in conformity with generally accepted accounting principles. Management has included in the Company's consolidated financial statements amounts based on estimates and judgements that it believes are reasonable under the circumstances.

To discharge its responsibilities for financial reporting and safeguarding of assets, management believes that it has established appropriate systems of internal accounting control which provide reasonable assurance that the financial records are reliable and form a proper basis for the timely and accurate preparation of financial statements. Consistent with the concept of reasonable assurance, the Company recognizes that the relative cost of maintaining these controls should not exceed their expected benefits. Management further assures the quality of the financial records through careful selection and training of personnel, and through the adoption and communication of financial and other relevant policies.

The shareholders have appointed Deloitte & Touche to audit the consolidated financial statements. Their report outlines the scope of their examination and their opinion.

**Stephen J. Sadler**
**President and**
**Chief Executive Officer**

**David G.B. Scott**
**Vice President,**
**Finance and Administration**

## AUDITORS' REPORT

**To the Shareholders of Geac Computer Corporation Limited:**

We have audited the consolidated balance sheets of Geac Computer Corporation Limited as at April 30, 1994 and 1993 and the consolidated statements of operations, retained earnings and changes in financial position for the years then ended. These financial statements are the responsibility of the Company's management. Our responsibility is to express an opinion on these financial statements based on our audits.

We conducted our audits in accordance with generally accepted auditing standards. Those standards require that we plan and perform an audit to obtain reasonable assurance whether the financial statements are free of material misstatement. An audit includes examining, on a test basis, evidence supporting the amounts and disclosures in the financial statements. An audit also includes assessing the accounting principles used and significant estimates made by management, as well as evaluating the overall financial statement presentation.

In our opinion, these consolidated financial statements present fairly, in all material respects, the financial position of the Company as at April 30, 1994 and 1993 and the results of its operations and the changes in its financial position for the years then ended in accordance with generally accepted accounting principles.

**Chartered Accountants**
**Markham, Canada**
**June 17, 1994**

## CONSOLIDATED BALANCE SHEETS

| (thousands of dollars) | April 30 1994 | 1993 |
|---|---|---|
| **Assets** | | |
| Current assets: | | |
| Cash and short-term investments | $ 53,327 | $ 40,943 |
| Accounts receivable | 29,389 | 21,277 |
| Unbilled receivables | 7,437 | 7,591 |
| Inventory (note 2) | 16,269 | 16,166 |
| Prepaid expenses | 1,878 | 2,534 |
| | 108,300 | 88,511 |
| Fixed assets (note 3) | 16,083 | 15,196 |
| Other assets (note 4) | 24,645 | 14,165 |
| | $ 149,028 | $ 117,872 |
| **Liabilities** | | |
| Current liabilities: | | |
| Accounts payable and accrued liabilities | $ 24,327 | $ 21,830 |
| Income taxes payable (note 9) | 1,761 | 218 |
| Deferred sales revenue | 25,996 | 25,146 |
| | 52,084 | 47,194 |
| **Shareholders' Equity** | | |
| Share capital (note 5): | | |
| Common shares | 63,611 | 61,366 |
| Convertible preference shares | - | 269 |
| Retained earnings | 32,041 | 9,277 |
| Cumulative foreign exchange translation adjustment (note 6) | 1,292 | (234) |
| | 96,944 | 70,678 |
| | $ 149,028 | $ 117,872 |

Approved by the Board of Directors:

**Donald C. Webster**
**Chairman of the Board**

**Stephen J. Sadler**
**President and Chief Executive Officer,**
**Director**

## CONSOLIDATED STATEMENTS OF OPERATIONS

| (thousands of dollars, except per share amounts) | Years ended April 30 | |
| --- | --- | --- |
| | 1994 | 1993 |
| Revenues: | | |
| Sales (note 8) | $ 150,335 | $ 102,718 |
| Interest income | 1,821 | 2,356 |
| | 152,156 | 105,074 |
| Expenses: | | |
| Costs, excluding amounts shown below | 113,137 | 77,152 |
| Research and development expenses | 8,469 | 8,233 |
| Research and development grants and investment tax credits (note 9) | (2,093) | (2,012) |
| Depreciation and amortization | 5,632 | 3,695 |
| Interest expense | 79 | 129 |
| | 125,224 | 87,197 |
| Income from operations before unusual item and income taxes | 26,932 | 17,877 |
| Unusual item: | | |
| Purchased software research (note 11) | - | (10,674) |
| Income before income taxes | 26,932 | 7,203 |
| Provision for income taxes (note 9) | 4,000 | 2,750 |
| Net income for the year | $ 22,932 | $ 4,453 |
| Earnings per share: | | |
| Basic | $ 0.81 | $ 0.17 |
| Fully diluted | $ 0.80 | $ 0.17 |

## CONSOLIDATED STATEMENTS OF RETAINED EARNINGS

| (thousands of dollars) | Years ended April 30 | |
| --- | --- | --- |
| | 1994 | 1993 |
| Retained earnings at the beginning of the year | $ 9,277 | $ 4,824 |
| Premium on redemption of Series 2 preference shares (note 5) | (168) | - |
| Net income for the year | 22,932 | 4,453 |
| Retained earnings at the end of the year | $ 32,041 | $ 9,277 |

## CONSOLIDATED STATEMENTS OF CHANGES
## IN FINANCIAL POSITION

| | Years ended April 30 | |
|---|---|---|
| *(thousands of dollars)* | *1994* | *1993* |
| **Operating activities** | | |
| Net income for the year | $ 22,932 | $ 4,453 |
| Adjusted for amounts not affecting cash: | | |
| Depreciation of fixed assets | 5,352 | 3,662 |
| Amortization of other assets | 2,763 | 624 |
| Purchased software research (note 11) | - | 10,674 |
| | 31,047 | 19,413 |
| Changes in non-cash working capital components | (5,605) | (1,064) |
| Cash provided by operating activities | 25,442 | 18,349 |
| **Investing activities** | | |
| Additions to fixed assets, net | (5,435) | (3,341) |
| Additions to capitalized software development | (5,385) | (1,403) |
| Acquisitions less cash acquired (note 11) | (5,572) | (21,231) |
| Foreign exchange translation adjustment | 1,526 | (267) |
| Cash used in investing activities | (14,866) | (26,242) |
| **Financing activities** | | |
| Issue of common shares | 2,245 | 16,938 |
| Issue of preference shares | - | 93 |
| Conversion of preference shares | (74) | (222) |
| Redemption of Series 2 preference shares | (363) | - |
| Cash provided by financing activities | 1,808 | 16,809 |
| **Cash and short-term investments** | | |
| Net cash increase during the year | 12,384 | 8,916 |
| Cash position at the beginning of the year | 40,943 | 32,027 |
| Cash position at the end of the year | $ 53,327 | $ 40,943 |

# NOTES TO CONSOLIDATED FINANCIAL STATEMENTS

## 1. ACCOUNTING POLICIES

**Accounting principles**

These consolidated financial statements are prepared in conformity with accounting principles generally accepted in Canada.

**Basis of consolidation**

These consolidated financial statements comprise the financial statements of Geac Computer Corporation Limited and its subsidiary companies.

**Inventory**

Finished goods inventory is stated at the lower of cost on a first-in first-out basis and net realizable value. Maintenance and service parts are recorded net of a provision for obsolescence which amortizes their cost over an estimated useful life of four to six years.

**Fixed assets**

Fixed assets are recorded at cost and are depreciated as follows:
- Computers, processing and office equipment - declining balance at rates ranging between 18.5% and 20%.
- Leasehold improvements - straight-line over the lease term.

**Goodwill**

Goodwill represents the excess of purchase consideration over fair market value of net identifiable assets acquired, and is amortized on a straight-line basis over forty years.

**Revenue recognition**

The Company's activities are the design, manufacture, sale, service and rental of computer systems and software. System sales revenues are recognized at the time of shipment or upon customer acceptance. The timing of revenue recognition often differs from contract payment schedules, resulting in revenues that have been earned but not billed. These amounts are included in unbilled receivables. Service and rental revenues are recognized rateably over applicable contractual periods or as services are performed. Amounts billed but not yet earned are recorded as deferred revenue.

**Research and development costs**

Research and development costs relate principally to computer software intended for licensing to end-user customers. All costs up to the date on which the software is considered technically and commercially viable, as well as software maintenance and documentation, are expensed as incurred, net of government grants and other amounts recoverable. Software development, after technical and commercial viability is established, is deferred and amortized on a straight-line basis over its expected useful life, not exceeding four years. The amortization is included in research and development expenses in the statement of operations.

**Foreign exchange**

All of the Company's foreign subsidiaries are considered self-sustaining. Assets and liabilities of these subsidiaries are translated into Canadian dollars at exchange rates in effect at the balance sheet dates. Income and expense items are translated at average exchange rates for the periods. Accumulated net translation adjustments are included as a separate component of shareholders' equity.

The monetary assets and liabilities of the Corporation which are denominated in foreign currencies are translated at the year-end exchange rates. Revenues and expenses are translated at rates of exchange prevailing on the transaction dates. All exchange gains or losses are recognized currently in earnings.

## 2. INVENTORY

| (thousands of dollars) | April 30 1994 | 1993 |
|---|---|---|
| Finished goods | $ 4,914 | $ 4,960 |
| Maintenance and service parts | 11,355 | 11,206 |
| | $ 16,269 | $ 16,166 |

### 3.  FIXED ASSETS

| (thousands of dollars) | | | April 30 1994 | 1993 |
|---|---|---|---|---|
| | Cost | Accumulated Depreciation | Net | Net |
| Computers and processing equipment | $  39,413 | $  29,184 | $  10,229 | $  9,986 |
| Office equipment | 9,104 | 5,620 | 3,484 | 3,499 |
| Leasehold improvements | 4,596 | 2,226 | 2,370 | 1,711 |
| | $  53,113 | $  37,030 | $  16,083 | $  15,196 |

### 4.  OTHER ASSETS

| (thousands of dollars) | April 30 1994 | 1993 |
|---|---|---|
| Acquired capitalized software development (note 11) | $  7,736 | $  5,510 |
| Capitalized software development | 6,788 | 1,403 |
| Less: Accumulated amortization | (3,074) | (591) |
| Net capitalized software development | 11,450 | 6,322 |
| Goodwill (note 11) | 13,508 | 7,876 |
| Less: Accumulated amortization | (313) | (33) |
| Net goodwill | 13,195 | 7,843 |
| | $  24,645 | $  14,165 |

### 5.  SHARE CAPITAL

The Company is authorized to issue an unlimited number of common shares and preference shares, issuable in series, each without par value.

As final settlement under the Definitive Proposals accepted by the creditors in 1988, an additional 4,037 Series 2 preference shares were issued during the 1993 fiscal year. Between May 1 and June 15, 1993, 6,108 Series 2 preference shares were converted into 54,972 common shares. The remaining 12,097 Series 2 preference shares were redeemed for $362,910. The premium on this transaction of approximately $168,000 was charged to retained earnings in fiscal 1994.

On May 10, 1994, the Company filed notice of its intention to make a Normal Course Issuer Bid for its common shares through the facilities of The Toronto Stock Exchange. The Company may purchase up to a maximum of 1,436,996 common shares, being 5% of the 28,739,921 common shares outstanding at April 29, 1994. The price at which the Company may purchase such shares will be the market price at the time of any particular transaction. The bid commenced on May 13, 1994 and will terminate on May 12, 1995, unless the maximum number of common shares purchasable thereunder has been acquired before that time. There have been no repurchases as of June 17, 1994.

An analysis of the capital stock account is as follows:

| | Number of shares | | Thousands of dollars | |
|---|---|---|---|---|
| | 1994 | 1993 | 1994 | 1993 |
| **Common Shares** | | | | |
| Balance at the beginning of the year | 27,948,409 | 22,472,157 | $  61,366 | $  44,428 |
| Issued for cash | 741,831 | 5,311,741 | 2,171 | 16,716 |
| Converted from Series 2 preference shares | 54,972 | 164,511 | 74 | 222 |
| Balance at the end of the year | 28,745,212 | 27,948,409 | $  63,611 | $  61,366 |
| **Series 2 Convertible Preference Shares** | | | | |
| Balance at the beginning of the year | 18,205 | 32,447 | $  269 | $  398 |
| Converted to common shares | (6,108) | (18,279) | (74) | (222) |
| Issued under Definitive Proposals | - | 4,037 | - | 93 |
| Redeemed for cash | (12,097) | - | (195) | - |
| Balance at the end of the year | - | 18,205 | $  - | $  269 |

**Stock Ownership Plan**

An Employee Stock Ownership Plan under which employees may make quarterly purchases of shares in the Company at a 10% discount from the prevailing market price has been in existence since 1984. During 1994, 20,981 shares were issued to employees under this plan (1993 - 25,741) and 120,000 shares were cancelled. The aggregate number of shares still available to be issued under this plan is 115,580 (1993 - 256,561).

**Stock Options**

Options have been granted to management personnel to purchase common shares at or above the prevailing market price at the time of the grant under the Employee Stock Option Plan. These options are vested or vest at various times over the next 3 years and expire 5 years after vesting.

An analysis of the stock options is as follows:

| (thousands of shares) | 1994 | 1993 |
|---|---|---|
| Balance at the beginning of the year | 1,334 | 1,821 |
| Options granted | 767 | 171 |
| Options exercised at option prices from $1.10 to $9.25 | (720) | (606) |
| Options cancelled or expired | (68) | (52) |
| Balance at the end of the year | 1,313 | 1,334 |

The outstanding options as at April 30, 1994 were granted at prices from $1.10 to $14.50 (1993 - $1.10 to $11.75) per common share.

In addition, other options to senior management personnel to purchase 80,000 common shares at $1.60 per share were outstanding at the beginning of the year and remain outstanding at the end of the year.

**6.   CUMULATIVE FOREIGN EXCHANGE TRANSLATION ADJUSTMENT**

| (thousands of dollars) | April 30 | | | |
|---|---|---|---|---|
| | | 1994 | | 1993 |
| Cumulative unrealized gain (loss) at the beginning of the year | $ | (234) | $ | 33 |
| Unrealized gain (loss) for the year on translation of net assets | | 2,190 | | (495) |
| Realized (gain) loss on dividends and return of capital paid by foreign operations | | (664) | | 228 |
| | $ | 1,292 | $ | (234) |

**7.   COMMITMENTS AND CONTINGENCIES**

The Company has operating leases on rental equipment for varying terms up to a maximum of four years and has entered into leases for rental of premises for varying terms up to a maximum of thirteen years. Aggregate lease payments in each of the five years ending April 30, 1999 and subsequent are as follows:

| (thousands of dollars) | | |
|---|---|---|
| 1995 | $ | 4,965 |
| 1996 | | 4,041 |
| 1997 | | 3,359 |
| 1998 | | 2,440 |
| 1999 | | 1,797 |
| 2000 and subsequent | | 5,169 |
| | $ | 21,771 |

As at April 30, 1994, letters of credit are outstanding for approximately $378,000. The Company is potentially liable for approximately $16 million of performance bonds which are routinely issued on its behalf by insurance companies and other third parties in connection with outstanding contracts with various public sector customers. There has never been a claim under any of the Company's performance bonds and any estimated outstanding contract obligations are provided for in the accounts.

There are certain legal actions pending against the Company which management believes are without merit and will not result in any material liability. No benefit has been recorded for certain pending legal actions by the Company against others, the outcome of which cannot be reasonably determined.

## 8.  SEGMENTED INFORMATION

The business of the Company is carried on in one industry segment: the design, manufacture, sale, service and rental of computer systems and software products.

Revenues are derived from system sales and from service and rental agreements, as follows:

| (thousands of dollars) | Years ended April 30 1994 | 1993 |
|---|---|---|
| System sales | $ 77,291 | $ 47,657 |
| Service and rental | 73,044 | 55,061 |
| Total sales revenues | $ 150,335 | $ 102,718 |

The Company operates in four geographic segments as follows:

**Year ended April 30, 1994**

| (thousands of dollars) | Canada | USA | Europe | Australasia | Eliminations | Total |
|---|---|---|---|---|---|---|
| Segment revenue: | | | | | | |
| Sales revenues | $ 20,629 | $ 66,451 | $ 37,425 | $ 25,830 | $ - | $ 150,335 |
| Transfers between segments | 2,065 | - | - | - | (2,065) | - |
| | $ 22,694 | $ 66,451 | $ 37,425 | $ 25,830 | $ (2,065) | $ 150,335 |
| Segment operating income | $ 8,483 | $ 12,121 | $ 6,783 | $ 1,982 | $ - | $ 29,369 |
| Expenses (income): | | | | | | |
| Corporate expenses | | | | | | 4,179 |
| Interest, net | | | | | | (1,742) |
| Provision for income taxes | | | | | | 4,000 |
| Net income for the year | | | | | | $ 22,932 |
| Total identifiable assets | $ 44,056 | $ 52,605 | $ 36,388 | $ 15,979 | $ - | $ 149,028 |

**Year ended April 30, 1993**

| (thousands of dollars) | Canada | USA | Europe | Australasia | Eliminations | Total |
|---|---|---|---|---|---|---|
| Segment revenue: | | | | | | |
| Sales revenues | $ 18,485 | $ 39,409 | $ 34,678 | $ 10,146 | $ - | $ 102,718 |
| Transfers between segments | 4,313 | 15 | - | 100 | (4,428) | - |
| | $ 22,798 | $ 39,424 | $ 34,678 | $ 10,246 | $ (4,428) | $ 102,718 |
| Segment operating income (loss) | $ 9,519 | $ 4,546 | $ 5,985 | $ (785) | $ - | $ 19,265 |
| Expenses (income): | | | | | | |
| Corporate expenses | | | | | | 3,615 |
| Interest, net | | | | | | (2,227) |
| Unusual item | | | | | | 10,674 |
| Provision for income taxes | | | | | | 2,750 |
| Net income for the year | | | | | | $ 4,453 |
| Total identifiable assets | $ 32,721 | $ 37,442 | $ 39,889 | $ 7,820 | $ - | $ 117,872 |

## 9.  INCOME TAXES

Substantially all of the Company's activities are carried out through operating subsidiaries in a number of countries. The income tax effect of operations depends on the tax legislation in each country and the operating results of each subsidiary and the parent Company.

In fiscal 1994, the Company recognized the benefit of $1,800,000 (1993 - $1,800,000) of previously unrealized investment tax credits as their realization became reasonably assured due to the earnings history of the relevant subsidiary. The benefit is included in the statement of operations as a reduction of expense under the caption "Research and development grants and investment tax credits". The Company has remaining unrealized investment tax credits of approximately $4,000,000 (1993 - $5,000,000) which are available to reduce income taxes payable in future years and expire as shown in the table below. The benefit of unrealized investment tax credits will be included in the statement of operations as a reduction in research and development expense when realization is reasonably assured.

The Company has non-capital losses of approximately $26,000,000 (1993 - $30,000,000) which are available for carryforward against taxable income in future years, which expire as shown in the table below and will be recognized when realized by a reduction in the provision for income taxes.

The Company has net favourable timing differences of approximately $4,000,000 (1993 - $4,000,000) which may be applied against taxable income of future years. The timing differences relate primarily to contract revenues, accrued expenses, deferred revenue and depreciation and amortization of assets which are recognized in the financial statements in periods other than those in which they are included in taxable income in accordance with the tax laws of the countries in which the Company and its subsidiaries operate. Timing differences do not expire. When realized, they will be recognized by a reduction in the provision for income taxes.

| (thousands of dollars) | Non-capital losses | Investment tax credits |
|---|---|---|
| 1995 | $      - | $      300 |
| 1996 | 800 | 1,000 |
| 1997 | 3,800 | 600 |
| 1998 | 1,000 | 600 |
| 1999 - 2009 | 5,000 | 1,000 |
| Losses without expiry date | 15,400 | 500 |
| | $   26,000 | $    4,000 |

The provision for income taxes reflects an effective tax rate which differs from the corporate tax rate for the following reasons:

| (thousands of dollars) | 1994 | 1993 |
|---|---|---|
| Combined basic Canadian federal and provincial income tax rate | 44% | 44% |
| Provision for income taxes based on above rate | $   11,850 | $    3,170 |
| Increase (decrease) resulting from: | | |
| Permanent differences - | | |
| Purchased software research expensed | - | 4,600 |
| Other | 1,000 | 200 |
| Lower rate on earnings of foreign subsidiaries | (80) | (140) |
| Losses of subsidiaries not tax effected | 700 | 500 |
| Benefit of previously unrecognized losses and timing differences realized in the year | (9,000) | (4,900) |
| Other | (470) | (680) |
| Provision for income taxes per statement of operations | $    4,000 | $    2,750 |

## 10.  RELATED PARTY TRANSACTIONS

During the year the Company paid $225,000 (1993 - $310,000) for management services including investigation of potential acquisitions to Helix Investments (Canada) Inc. (formerly Helix Investments Limited), a significant shareholder.

## 11.  ACQUISITIONS

**Year ended April 30, 1994**

During the year ended April 30, 1994, the Company acquired for cash the businesses shown in the table below. New Tech, Convergent, and Hotel Systems were asset purchases. In each of the other acquisitions, the Company acquired all of the issued and outstanding shares of the companies. Acquisitions are accounted for by the purchase method with the results of operations of each business included in the financial statements from the respective dates of acquisition.

The total purchase price was $5,673,000. The acquired businesses included, at fair value, $101,000 of cash, $2,798,000 of other current assets, $2,226,000 of software development which met the Company's criteria for capitalization (note 4), $804,000 of fixed assets, and $5,888,000 of current liabilities.

The difference between the total purchase price and the net fair value of all identifiable assets and liabilities acquired was $5,632,000 and is accounted for as goodwill.

| Acquisition | Effective Date |
| --- | --- |
| Assets of New Tech Hospitality Systems Pty Ltd. | June 30, 1993 |
| 957024 Ontario Inc. (operating as Claymore Systems Group) | June 30, 1993 |
| ECI Computer, Inc. | August 4, 1993 |
| Datamark International Limited | September 30, 1993 |
| Dmark International Pty Limited | September 30, 1993 |
| Assets of Convergent Solutions Pty Ltd. | November 1, 1993 |
| Assets of Hotel Systems Pty Limited | January 31, 1994 |
| Assets of Hotel Computer Systems Limited | January 31, 1994 |

**Year ended April 30, 1993**

During the year ended April 30, 1993, the Company acquired for cash the businesses shown in the table below. Albion and McDonnell Douglas Information Systems were asset purchases. In each of the other acquisitions, the Company acquired all of the issued and outstanding shares of the companies. Acquisitions are accounted for by the purchase method with the results of operations of each business included in the financial statements from the respective dates of acquisition.

The total purchase price was $22,421,000. The acquired businesses included, at fair value, $1,190,000 of cash, $25,305,000 of other current assets, $5,510,000 of software development which met the Company's criteria for capitalization (note 4), $5,419,000 of fixed assets and $33,553,000 of current liabilities.

In the CLSI acquisition, $10,674,000 of the purchase price was allocated to purchased software research related to new products which had not achieved technical and commercial viability.

The difference between the total purchase price and the net fair value of all identifiable assets and liabilities acquired, including the purchased software research, was $7,876,000 and is accounted for as goodwill.

| Acquisition | Effective Date |
| --- | --- |
| Assets of Albion Computing Australia Pty Limited | June 1, 1992 |
| Assets of McDonnell Douglas Information Systems Canada, Inc. | November 30, 1992 |
| CLSI, Inc. and its UK, France, Netherlands and Canadian affiliates | November 30, 1992 |
| Mentat Computer Systems Pty Ltd. | February 26, 1993 |
| Concord Management Systems, Inc. | February 28, 1993 |
| Computer Library Services International Pty Limited and its subsidiary Aldis Pty Limited | March 31, 1993 |
| NBI Canada, Inc., subsequently renamed Geac (Canada) Services Limited | April 30, 1993 |
| MAI United Kingdom Limited | April 30, 1993 |
| Tekserv Computer Services Limited | April 30, 1993 |

## 12.  COMPARATIVE FIGURES

Certain of the prior year's figures have been reclassified to conform with the current year's presentation.

# Comprehensive List of Accounts Used in Exercises and Problems

## Current Assets

| | |
|---|---|
| 101 | Cash |
| 102 | Petty cash |
| 103 | Cash equivalents |
| 104 | Temporary investments |
| 105 | Allowance to reduce temporary investments to market |
| 106 | Accounts receivable |
| 107 | Allowance for doubtful accounts |
| 108 | Legal fees receivable |
| 109 | Interest receivable |
| 110 | Rent receivable |
| 111 | Notes receivable |
| 115 | Subscriptions receivable, common shares |
| 116 | Subscriptions receivable, preferred shares |
| 119 | Merchandise inventory |
| 120 | _____ inventory |
| 121 | _____ inventory |
| 124 | Office supplies |
| 125 | Store supplies |
| 126 | _____ supplies |
| 128 | Prepaid insurance |
| 129 | Prepaid interest |
| 130 | Prepaid property taxes |
| 131 | Prepaid rent |
| 132 | Raw materials inventory |
| 133 | Goods in process inventory, _____ |
| 134 | Goods in process inventory, _____ |
| 135 | Finished goods inventory |

## Long-Term Investments

| | |
|---|---|
| 141 | Investment in _____ shares |
| 142 | Investment in _____ bonds |
| 144 | Investment in _____ |
| 145 | Bond sinking fund |

## Capital Assets

| | |
|---|---|
| 151 | Automobiles |
| 152 | Accumulated amortization, automobiles |
| 153 | Trucks |
| 154 | Accumulated amortization, trucks |
| 155 | Boats |
| 156 | Accumulated amortization, boats |
| 157 | Professional library |
| 158 | Accumulated amortization, professional library |
| 159 | Law library |
| 160 | Accumulated amortization, law library |
| 163 | Office equipment |
| 164 | Accumulated amortization, office equipment |
| 165 | Store equipment |
| 166 | Accumulated amortization, store equipment |
| 167 | _____ equipment |
| 168 | Accumulated amortization, _____ equipment |
| 169 | Machinery |
| 170 | Accumulated amortization, machinery |
| 173 | Building _____ |
| 174 | Accumulated amortization, building _____ |
| 175 | Building _____ |
| 176 | Accumulated amortization, building _____ |
| 179 | Land improvements _____ |
| 180 | Accumulated amortization, land improvements _____ |
| 181 | Land improvements _____ |
| 182 | Accumulated amortization, land improvements _____ |
| 183 | Land |

## Natural Resources

185    Mineral deposit
186    Accumulated depletion, mineral deposit

## Intangible Assets

191    Patents
192    Leasehold
193    Franchise
194    Copyrights
195    Leasehold improvements
196    Organization costs
197    Deferred income tax debits

## Current Liabilities

201    Accounts payable
202    Insurance payable
203    Interest payable
204    Legal fees payable
205    Short-term notes payable
206    Discount on short-term payable
207    Office salaries payable
208    Rent payable
209    Salaries payable
210    Wages payable
211    Accrued payroll payable
214    Estimated warranty liability
215    Income taxes payable
216    Common dividend payable
217    Preferred dividend payable
218    UI payable
219    CPP payable
221    Employees' medical insurance payable
222    Employees' retirement program payable
223    Employees' union dues payable
224    PST payable
225    GST payable
226    Estimated vacation pay liability

### Unearned Revenues

230    Unearned consulting fees
231    Unearned legal fees
232    Unearned property management fees
233    Unearned _____ fees
234    Unearned _____
235    Unearned janitorial revenue
236    Unearned _____ revenue
238    Unearned rent _____

## Long-Term Liabilities

251    Long-term notes payable
252    Discount on notes payable

253    Long-term lease liability
254    Discount on lease liability
255    Bonds payable
256    Discount on bonds payable
257    Premium on bonds payable
258    Deferred income tax credit

## Owners' Equity

301    _____, capital
302    _____, withdrawals
303    _____, capital
304    _____, withdrawals
305    _____, capital
306    _____, withdrawals

### Corporate Contributed Capital

307    Common shares
309    Common shares subscribed
310    Common stock dividend distributable
313    Contributed capital from the retirement of common shares
315    Preferred shares
317    Preferred shares subscribed

### Retained Earnings

318    Retained earnings
319    Cash dividends declared
320    Stock dividends declared

## Revenues

401    _____ fees earned
402    _____ fees earned
403    _____ services revenue
404    _____ services revenue
405    Commissions earned
406    Rent earned
407    Dividends earned
408    Earnings from investment in _____
409    Interest earned
410    Sinking fund earnings
413    Sales
414    Sales returns and allowances
415    Sales discounts

## Cost of Goods Sold Items

501    Amortization of patents
502    Cost of goods sold
503    Depletion of mine deposit
505    Purchases
506    Purchases returns and allowances
507    Purchases discounts
508    Transportation-in

## Manufacturing Accounts

| | |
|---|---|
| 520 | Raw materials purchases |
| 521 | Freight-in on raw materials |
| 530 | Factory payroll |
| 531 | Direct labour |
| 540 | Factory overhead |
| 541 | Indirect materials |
| 542 | Indirect labour |
| 543 | Factory insurance expired |
| 544 | Factory supervision |
| 545 | Factory supplies used |
| 546 | Factory utilities |
| 547 | Miscellaneous production costs |
| 548 | Property taxes on factory building |
| 550 | Rent on factory building |
| 551 | Repairs, factory equipment |
| 552 | Small tools written off |
| 560 | Amortization of factory equipment |
| 561 | Amortization of factory building |

## Standard Cost Variance Accounts

| | |
|---|---|
| 580 | Direct material quantity variance |
| 581 | Direct material price variance |
| 582 | Direct labour quantity variance |
| 583 | Direct labour price variance |
| 584 | Factory overhead volume variance |
| 585 | Factory overhead controllable variance |

# Expenses

## Amortization (Depreciation and Depletion Expenses)

| | |
|---|---|
| 601 | Amortization expense, _____ |
| 602 | Amortization expense, copyrights |
| 603 | Depletion expense, _____ |
| 604 | Amortization expense, boats |
| 605 | Amortization expense, automobiles |
| 606 | Amortization expense, building _____ |
| 607 | Amortization expense, building _____ |
| 608 | Amortization expense, land improvements _____ |
| 609 | Amortization expense, land improvements _____ |
| 610 | Amortization expense, law library |
| 611 | Amortization expense, trucks |
| 612 | Amortization expense, _____ equipment |
| 613 | Amortization expense, _____ equipment |
| 614 | Amortization expense, _____ |
| 615 | Amortization expense, _____ |

## Employee Related Expenses

| | |
|---|---|
| 620 | Office salaries expense |
| 621 | Sales salaries expense |
| 622 | Salaries expense |
| 623 | _____ wages expense |
| 624 | Employees' benefits expense |
| 625 | Payroll taxes expense |

## Financial Expenses

| | |
|---|---|
| 630 | Cash over and short |
| 631 | Discounts lost |
| 633 | Interest expense |

## Insurance Expenses

| | |
|---|---|
| 635 | Insurance expense, delivery equipment |
| 636 | Insurance expense, office equipment |
| 637 | Insurance expense, _____ |

## Rental Expenses

| | |
|---|---|
| 640 | Rent expense |
| 641 | Rent expense, office space |
| 642 | Rent expense, selling space |
| 643 | Press rental expense |
| 644 | Truck rental expense |
| 645 | _____ rental expense |

## Supplies Expense

| | |
|---|---|
| 650 | Office supplies expense |
| 651 | Store supplies expense |
| 652 | _____ supplies expense |
| 653 | _____ supplies expense |

## Miscellaneous Expenses

| | |
|---|---|
| 655 | Advertising expense |
| 656 | Bad debts expense |
| 657 | Blueprinting expense |
| 658 | Boat expense |
| 659 | Collection expense |
| 661 | Concessions expense |
| 662 | Credit card expense |
| 663 | Delivery expense |
| 664 | Dumping expense |
| 667 | Equipment expense |
| 668 | Food and drinks expense |
| 669 | Gas, oil, and repairs expense |
| 671 | Gas and oil expense |
| 672 | General and administrative expense |
| 673 | Janitorial expense |
| 674 | Legal fees expense |
| 676 | Mileage expense |
| 677 | Miscellaneous expenses |
| 678 | Mower and tools expense |
| 679 | Operating expenses |
| 681 | Permits expense |
| 682 | Postage expense |
| 683 | Property taxes expense |
| 684 | Repairs expense, _____ |
| 685 | Repairs expense, _____ |
| 687 | Selling expenses |

| | |
|---|---|
| 688 | Telephone expense |
| 689 | Travel and entertainment expense |
| 690 | Utilities expense |
| 691 | Warranty expense |
| 695 | Income taxes expense |

## Gains and Losses

| | |
|---|---|
| 701 | Gain on retirement of bonds |
| 702 | Gain on sale of machinery |
| 703 | Gain on sale of temporary investments |
| 704 | Gain on sale of trucks |
| 705 | Gain on _____ |
| 801 | Loss on disposal of machinery |
| 802 | Loss on exchange of equipment |
| 803 | Loss on exchange of _____ |

| | |
|---|---|
| 804 | Loss on market decline of temporary investments |
| 805 | Loss on retirement of bonds |
| 806 | Loss on sale of investments |
| 807 | Loss on sale of machinery |
| 808 | Loss on sale of _____ |
| 809 | Loss on _____ |
| 810 | Loss or gain from liquidation |

## Clearing Accounts

| | |
|---|---|
| 901 | Income summary |
| 902 | Manufacturing summary |

The Gap, Inc., 468
**General accounting,** 11, **18**
**General and administrative expenses,** 253, **267**
**General journal,** 89, **104**
    entries to, 317
    recording transactions in, 89–91
**General Ledger,** 301, 319, 405, **431**
**Going-concern principle,** 29–30, **49,** AP20
Goods and service tax (GST), 312–315
    remittance of, 315–317
**Government accountants,** 8–9, **18**
Greyhound Lines Inc., 238
**Gross method of recording purchases,** 372, **377**
**Gross profit,** 239, **267**
**Gross profit inventory method,** 466–467, **472**
GST (Goods and Services Tax), 320

Hardware/software, 294
Hard-wired hookups, 300
Human resources, 3

**IASC (International Accounting Standards Committee),** 48, **49**
Imperial Oil Limited, 99, 151, 259, 304, 318
Implementation constraints, AP22–23
**Income statement,** 22–24, 39, **49**
    for estimating bad debts, 411–412
**Income Summary,** 190, **211**
Income Tax Act (1948), AP26
**Input device,** 293–294, **320**
**Installment accounts receivable,** 417, **431**
Institutes of Chartered Accountants, 9
**Intangible assets,** 148, **159**
**Interest,** 368, 418, **431**
    calculating, 418–419, 421–422
    collection of, 421
Interest income, 139–140
**Interim financial reports,** 129, **159**
**Interim statements,** 464, **472**
Internal accounting standards, 47–48, 73
**Internal auditing,** 12, **18**
Internal controls, 4
**Internal control system,** 346–347, **377**
    for cash, 349–351
    computers and, 348–349
    gross method of recording purchases, 372
    net method of recording purchases, 373
**Internal transactions,** 104
International Business Machines Corporation (IBM), 296
Inventory shortage, 466
Inventory shrinkage, 252–253
**Inventory tickets,** 452, **472**
Inventory valuation
    gross profit method, 466–467
    retail method, 465

Investments, 147
    temporary, 398–400
**Invoice,** 356, **378**
**Invoice approval form,** 356–359, **378**

**Journal,** 88–89, **104**
    computerized, 91

King, Lorrie L., 298

Land, 77
**Last-in, first-out inventory pricing (LIFO),** 455, **472**
**Ledger,** 79–81, **104**
    testing accuracy of, 311–312
**Liabilities,** 25, **49**
    recording to accounts, 77–78
**Liquid asset,** 344, **378**
**Liquidity,** 344, **378**
**List price,** 247, **267**
Local area networks (LANS), 300
Long-term commitments under contracts, 425–426
Long-term liabilities, 148, 159
**Lower of cost or market (LCM),** 400, **472**
    determination of market, 463

Magna International, Inc., 36
**Maker of a note,** 418, **431**
Management, executive, 4
**Management advisory services,** 12, **18**
Managerial accounting, 9–11
Marketing, 4
MasterCard, 403
**Matching principle,** 130, **159,** 404, AP21
**Materiality principle,** 417, **431,** AP22
**Maturity date of a note,** 418, **431**
**Maturity value of a note,** 424, **431**
**Merchandise,** 238, **267**
    elements of cost, 452
    matching costs revenue, 450–451
**Merchandise inventory,** 239, **267**
    adjusting entries for changes in, 265–266
    assigning costs to, 453
    closing entries for changes, 266
    FIFO pricing method, 455
    LIFO pricing method, 455
    measuring and recording, 246
    taking ending, 452–453
    using specific costs of, 454
    weighted-average pricing of, 454
**Merchandise turnover,** 467–469, **472**
Merchandising companies, 238–239
    closing entries for, 255–258
    work sheet for, 259
Modems, 300
Month-end postings, 307
**Multiple-step income statement,** 253, **267**

**Natural business year,** 129, **159**
**Net assets,** 25, **49**
**Net income,** 23, **49**
    corporate income taxes and, AP27–29
**Net loss,** 23, **49**
**Net method of recording purchases,** 373, **378**
**Net realizable value,** 451, **472**
**Nominal accounts,** 193, **211**
Notes payable, 77
Notes receivable, 75
    discounting, 423–425
    dishonoured, 420–421
    end-of-period adjusting, 421
    recording receipt of, 419–420

**Objectivity principle,** 28, **49,** AP21–22
Office supplies, 76
**On-line processing,** 299, **320**
Operating cycle of business, 146, **159**
Organizations
    accounting function in, 2
    finance within, 2–3
    human resources in, 3
    management in, 4
    marketing in, 4
    production in, 3–4
    research and development, 3
**Output devices,** 295–296, **320**
**Outstanding cheques,** 367, **378**
Owner's accounts, 78–79
Owners' equity, 25–26, 39

**Paid-in capital,** 31, **50**
Parent, Lee, 23
**Partnerships,** 30, **50**
    accounting for, 207
**Payee of a note,** 418, **431**
Paying employees, 500–502
    recording payroll, 500
**Payroll bank account,** 500–502, **511**
**Payroll deduction,** 490, **511**
Payroll register, 500
Payroll withholdings
    accruing deductions, 504
    Canadian Pension Plan, 491, 495
    fringe benefits, 504–505
    income taxes, 490–491
    miscellaneous deductions, 497
    paying the deductions, 504
    required deductions, 503–504
    unemployment insurance, 494–495
**Periodic inventory system,** 243–244, **268,** 452
    errors in, 458–459
    journal entries for, 460
**Permanent accounts,** 193, **211**
**Perpetual inventory system,** 243, **268,** 459
    journal entries for, 460
    subsidiary records for, 460–462
**Personal tax credits,** 491, **511**
Petro-Canada, 194

# NOTES

# NOTES

# NOTES

# NOTES

# NOTES

# NOTES

# NOTES

# NOTES